The Select Series: Microsoft® Access 2002 Volume I

Pamela R. Toliver

Prentice Hall

Upper Saddle River, New Jersey

LIBRARY OF CONGRESS CATALOGING-IN-PUBLICATION DATA

Toliver, Pamela R.
The select series. Microsoft Access 2002 / Pamela R. Toliver.
p. cm.
Includes index.
ISBN 0-13-060150-0
1. Database management. 2. Microsoft Access. I. Title: Microsoft Access 2002. II. Title

QA76.9.D3 T635 2001
005.75'65—dc21 2001036724

Publisher and Vice President: Natalie E. Anderson
Executive Acquisitions Editor: Jodi McPherson
Managing Editor: Monica Stipanov
Assistant Editor: Jennifer Cappello
Editorial Assistant: Dayna Hilinsky
Developmental Editor: Christy Parrish and Samantha Penrod
Media Project Manager: Cathleen Profitko
Marketing Manager: Emily Williams Knight
Production Manager: Gail Steier De Acevedo
Project Manager: Tim Tate
Associate Director, Manufacturing: Vincent Scelta
Manufacturing Buyer: Natacha St. Hill Moore
Design Manager: Pat Smythe
Interior Design: Lorraine Castellano and Proof Positive/Farrowlyne Associates, Inc.
Cover Design: Lorraine Castellano
Full-Service Composition: Proof Positive/Farrowlyne Associates, Inc.
Printer/Binder: Banta Book Group, Menasha

Credits and acknowledgments borrowed from other sources and reproduced, with permission, in this textbook appear on the appropriate page within the text or at the end of the respective project.

Prentice Hall

10 9 8 7 6 5 4 3 2 1
ISBN 0-13-060150-0

THE SELECT SERIES:
MICROSOFT® OFFICE XP

Series Authors

Pamela R. Toliver and Yvonne Johnson

Volume I

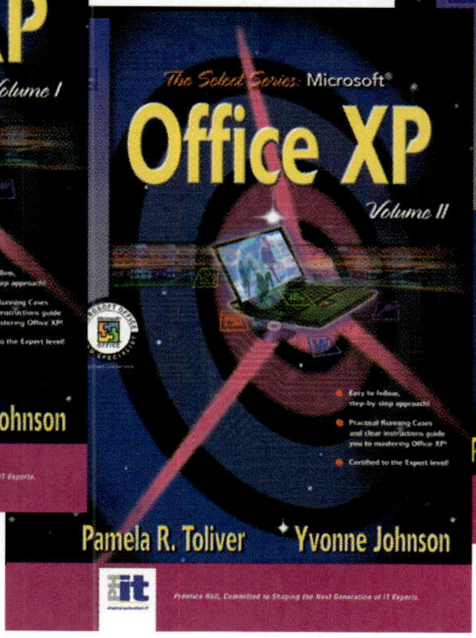

Volume II

Brief

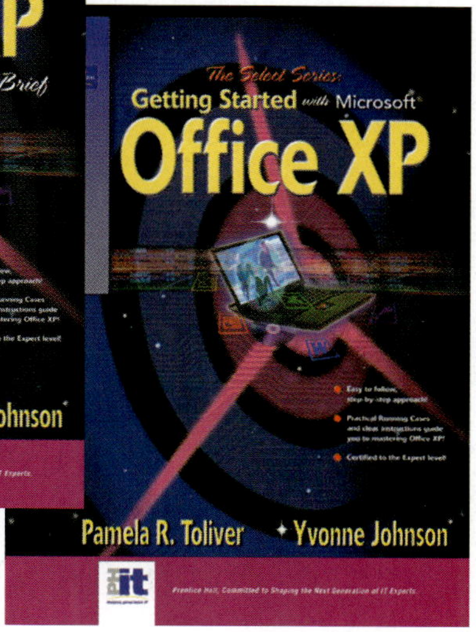

Getting Started

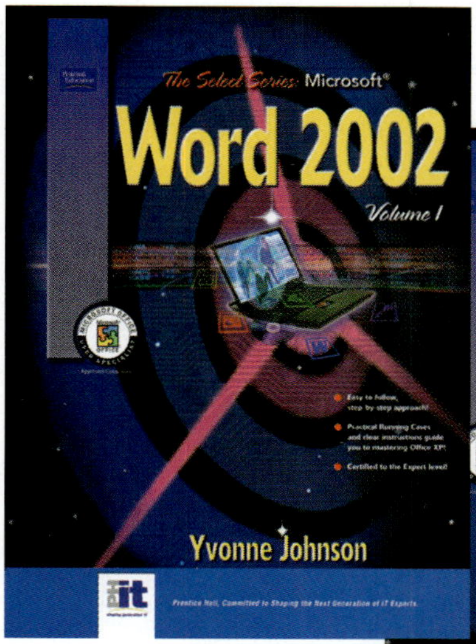

Volume I

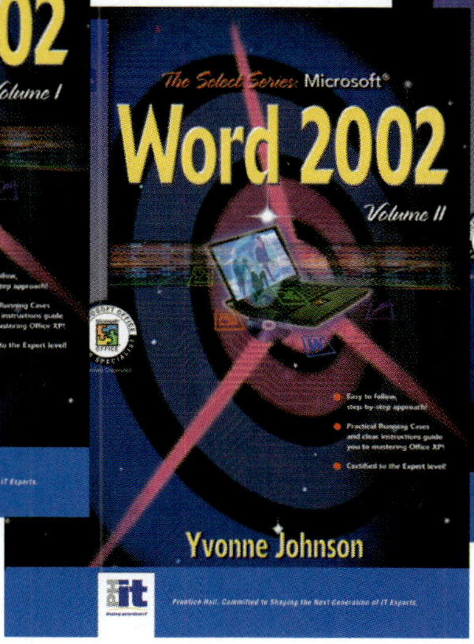

Volume II

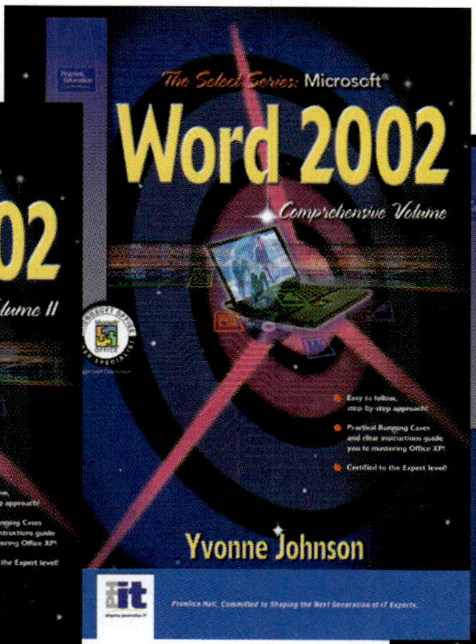

Comprehensive

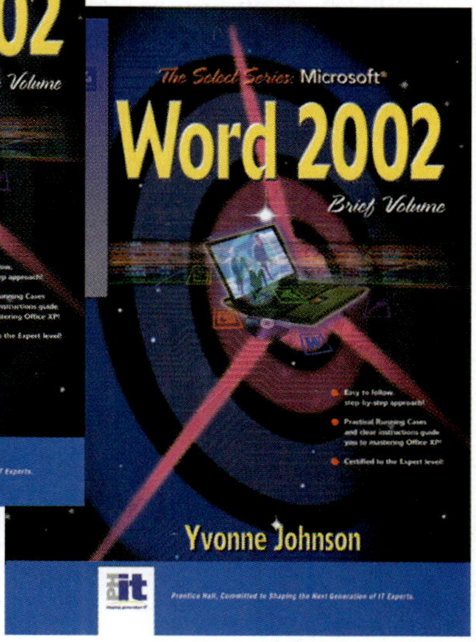

Brief

Dedication

This book is dedicated to my husband, John, who spent so much time during the writing of this work visiting me evenings and weekends in my office. Without his love and support, this work would not have been possible.

Acknowledgments

Completing a work of this magnitude is like a snowball rolling downhill, gathering speed and picking up so much help along the way. Without the support and growth, this work would not have been completed:

To the development staff, I say thank you for keeping us on track.

To the technical reviewers, thanks for trying to keep us accurate.

To the copy editors, thanks for keeping us consistent.

To production and design, thanks for laying it all out, expanding and compressing to make it fit so beautifully within the boundaries.

But most of all, thanks to those with whom we were in almost daily contact, who kept us motivated and moving toward our accomplished goal:

To Monica—the best managing editor I have ever had—it couldn't always have been easy, but it's been great.

To Christy—the most organized and focused and easy-to-work-with project manager I have ever known—thanks for sticking with us to the end.

To Jennifer—who kept plugging for the supplemental material—thanks for pulling it together so well.

To Martha—a friend and compatriot who tested the steps and looked at the pictures so many times—someday, perhaps we can make our program installations match more completely.

And to Jodi—who came to the project later—you've done great, and guided this work in a better direction. Thanks for finessing this work to completion.

And most of all, thanks to my co-author for listening, collaborating, and picking up the pieces with me. Cheers!

Pam

Preface

About this Series

The Select Series uses a class-tested, highly visual, project-based approach that teaches students through tasks using step-by-step instructions. You will find extensive full-color figures and screen captures that guide learners through the basic skills and procedures necessary to demonstrate proficiency in their use of each software application.

The Select Series introduces an all-new design for Microsoft Office XP. The easy-to-follow design now has larger screen shots with steps listed on the left side of the accompanying screen. This unique design program, along with the use of bold color, helps reduce distraction and keeps students focused and interested as they work. In addition, selectively placed Tip boxes and Other Ways boxes enhance student learning by explaining various ways to complete a task.

Our approach to learning is designed to provide the necessary visual guidance in a project-oriented setting. Each project concludes with a review section that includes a Summary, Key Terms & Skills, Study Questions, Guided Exercises, and On Your Own Exercises. This extensive end-of-project section provides students with the opportunity to practice and gain further experience with the tasks covered in each project.

What's New in the Select Series for Office XP

The entire Select Series has been revised to include the new features found in the Office XP suite, which contains Word 2002, Excel 2002, Access 2002, PowerPoint 2002, Publisher 2002, FrontPage 2002, and Outlook 2002.

The Select Series provides students with clear, concise instruction supported by its new design, which includes bigger screen captures. Steps are now located in the margin for ease of use and readability. This instruction is further enhanced by graded exercises in the end-of-project material.

Another exciting update is that every project begins with a Running Case from Selections, Inc., a department store that has opened shop online as e-Selections.com. Students are put in an e-commerce–based business environment so that they can relate what they are learning in Office XP to a real world situation. Everything is within a scenario that puts them in the department store where they perform tasks that relate to a particular division of the store or Web site.

About the Book

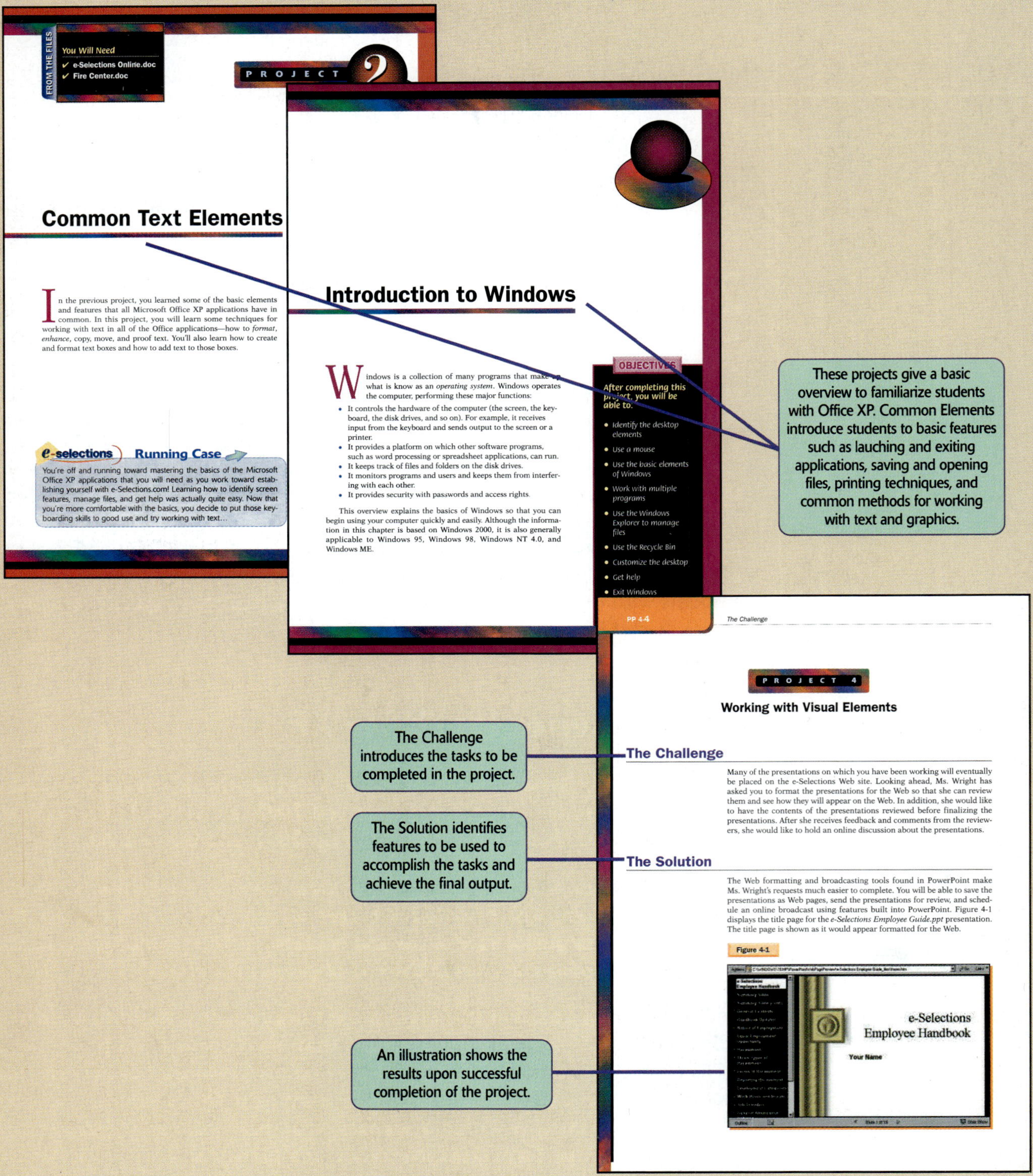

These projects give a basic overview to familiarize students with Office XP. Common Elements introduce students to basic features such as lauching and exiting applications, saving and opening files, printing techniques, and common methods for working with text and graphics.

The Challenge introduces the tasks to be completed in the project.

The Solution identifies features to be used to accomplish the tasks and achieve the final output.

An illustration shows the results upon successful completion of the project.

Steps have been moved into the margin next to corresponding screen captures for ease of use and readability.

New, full-color, full-size screen captures move the emphasis toward visual-based instruction.

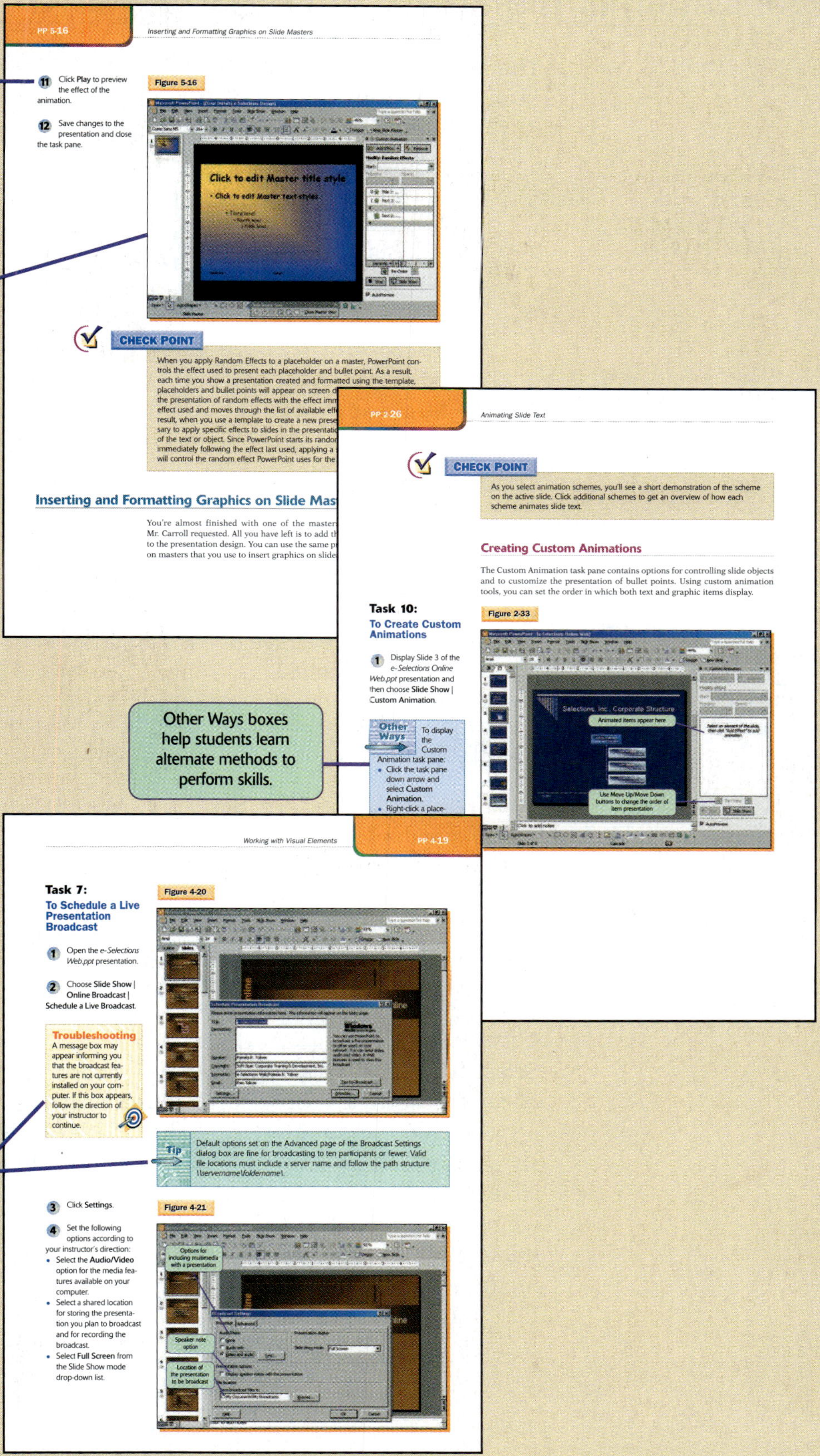

Other Ways boxes help students learn alternate methods to perform skills.

Troubleshooting and Tip boxes appear at appropriate places throughout each project to highlight important, helpful information pertinent to the topic being discussed.

Organization of the Select Series for Office XP

The new Select Series for Office XP includes four combined Office XP texts from which to choose:

- **Microsoft Office XP Volume I** is MOUS certified in each of the major applications in the Office suite (Word, Excel, Access, and PowerPoint). Four additional supplementary modules (Introduction to Internet Explorer, Introduction to Windows, Introduction to Outlook, and Common Elements) are also included. In addition, three integrated projects are included which integrate files and data among Word, Excel, Access, and PowerPoint.
- **Microsoft Office XP Volume II** picks up where Volume I leaves off, covering advanced topics for the individual applications.
- **Microsoft Office XP Brief** provides less coverage of the individual applications than Volume I (a total of four projects as opposed to six). The supplementary modules are also included.
- A new volume, **Getting Started with Microsoft Office XP,** contains the Introduction and first chapter from each application (Word, Excel, Access, and PowerPoint) plus the four supplementary modules.

Individual texts for Word 2002, Excel 2002, Access 2002, and PowerPoint 2002 provide complete coverage of each application and are MOUS certified. They are available in Volume I and Volume II texts and also as Comprehensive texts.

This series of books has been approved by Microsoft to be used in preparation for Microsoft Office User Specialist exams.

MICROSOFT OFFICE USER SPECIALIST
APPROVED COURSEWARE

The Microsoft Office User Specialist (MOUS) program is globally recognized as the standard for demonstrating desktop skills with the Microsoft Office suite of business productivity applications (Microsoft Word, Microsoft Excel, Microsoft PowerPoint, Microsoft Access, and Microsoft Outlook). With MOUS certification, thousands of people have demonstrated increased productivity and have proved their ability to utilize the advanced functionality of these Microsoft applications.

Customize the Select Series with Prentice Hall's Custom Binding program. The Select Series is part of the Custom Binding Program, enabling instructors to create their own texts by selecting projects from Office XP to suit the needs of a specific course. An instructor could, for example, create a custom text consisting of the specific projects that he or she would like to cover from the entire suite of products. The Select Series is part of PHit's Value Pack program in which multiple books can be shrink-wrapped together at substantial savings to the student. A value pack is ideal in courses that require complete coverage of multiple applications.

Instructor and Student Resources

Instructor's Resource CD-ROM

The **Instructor's Resource CD-ROM** that is available with the Select Office XP Series contains:

- Student data files
- Solutions to all exercises and problems
- PowerPoint lectures
- Instructor's manuals in Word format that enable the instructor to annotate portions of the instructor manual for distribution to the class
- A Windows-based test manager and the associated test bank in Word format

MyPHLIP www.prenhall.com/select

This text is accompanied by a companion Web site at ***www.prenhall.com/select*** that is supported by MyPHLIP. PHLIP stands for Prentice Hall's Learning on the Internet Partnership. This enhancement brings you and your students a richer, more interactive Web experience.

Features of this new site include the ability for you to customize your homepage with real-time news headlines, current events, exercises, an interactive study guide, student data files, and downloadable supplements. This site is designed to take learning Microsoft Office XP with the Select Series to the next level.

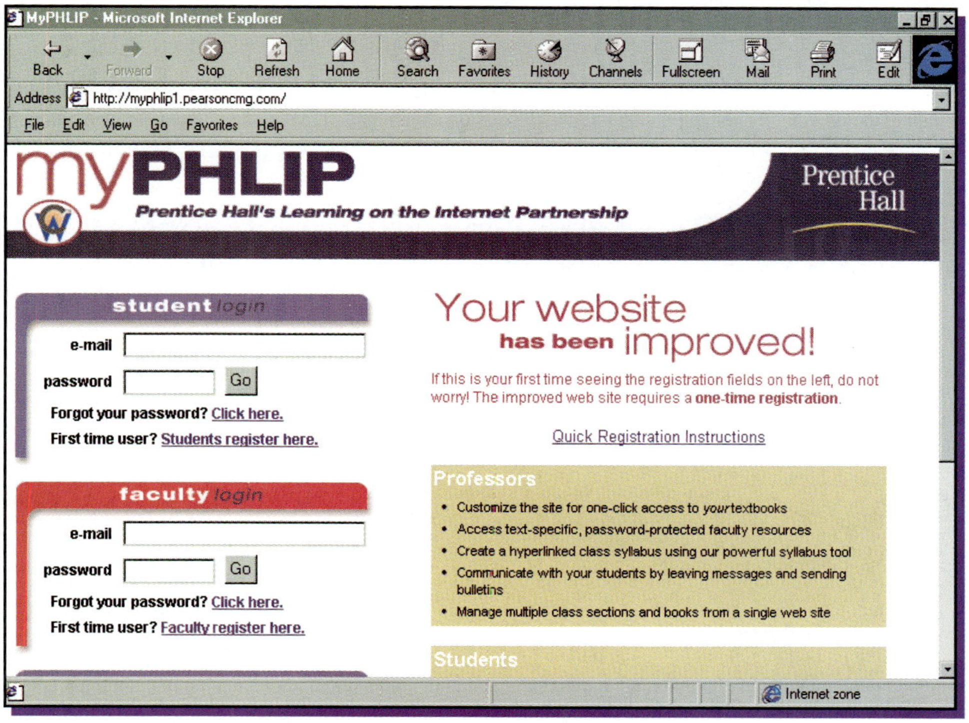

Now you have the freedom to personalize your own online course materials! Prentice Hall provides the content and support you need to create and manage your own online course in WebCT, Blackboard, or Prentice Hall's own Course Compass. Choose "Standard" content to enhance the material from this text or "Premium" content, which provides you with even more lecture material, interactive exercises, and projects.

Training and Assessment www.prenhall.com/phit

Prentice Hall offers Performance Based Training and Assessment in one product, Train&Assess IT. The Training component offers computer-based training that a student can use to preview, learn, and review Microsoft Office application skills. Web- or CD-ROM delivered, Train IT offers interactive, multimedia, computer-based training to augment classroom learning. Built-in prescriptive testing suggests a study path based not only on student test results but also on the specific textbook chosen for the course.

The Assessment component offers computer-based testing that shares the same user interface as Train IT and is used to evaluate a student's knowledge about specific topics in Word, Excel, Access, PowerPoint, Windows, Outlook, and the Internet. It does this in a task-oriented environment to demonstrate proficiency as well as comprehension of the topics by the students. More extensive than the testing in Train IT, Assess IT offers more administrative features for the instructor and additional questions for the student.

Assess IT also allows professors to test students out of a course, place students in appropriate courses, and evaluate skill sets.

CourseCompass www.coursecompass.com

CourseCompass is a dynamic, interactive online course-management tool powered exclusively for Pearson Education by Blackboard. This exciting product allows you to teach market-leading Pearson Education content in an easy-to-use, customizable format.

BlackBoard www.prenhall.com/blackboard

Prentice Hall's abundant online content, combined with Blackboard's popular tools and interface, result in robust Web-based courses that are easy to implement, manage, and use—taking your courses to new heights in student interaction and learning.

WebCT www.prenhall.com/webct

Course-management tools within WebCT include page tracking, progress tracking, class and student management, gradebook, communication, calendar, reporting tools, and more. GOLD LEVEL CUSTOMER SUPPORT, available exclusively to adopters of Prentice Hall courses, is provided free-of-charge upon adoption and provides you with priority assistance, training discounts, and dedicated technical support.

Brief Table of Contents

Table of Contents

FROM THE FILES

You Will Need

- ✔ e-Selections.doc
- ✔ Sample Northeast Colleges.xls

PROJECT 1

Basic Common Elements

One of the greatest advantages of using the ever-popular Microsoft Office suite is the number of features common to all programs that make up the Office suite. Microsoft Office XP takes full advantage of many common elements. The large number of common elements means that techniques you learn in one Office XP application can be used to accomplish the same task in other Office XP applications. This section introduces you to many of the features common to Office XP applications and describes some of the unique twists you'll find with these common features as you move from application to application in Microsoft Office XP.

e-selections Running Case

You have recently been hired as a part-time office clerk for e-Selections.com, the online branch of Selections, Inc. Your goals are to advance in the company as you advance in your college studies and to position yourself for an upper-level position after you graduate. Because you are new to the office and unfamiliar with the software applications that are used, you decide to begin by exploring the software installed on your computer. e-Selections.com uses the most recent release of Microsoft Office.

OBJECTIVES

After completing this project, you will be able to:

- *Launch applications*
- *Work with screen elements*
- *Perform basic file management tasks*
- *Use Help*
- *Preview and print files*
- *Exit applications*

PROJECT 1

Basic Common Elements

The Challenge

Microsoft Office applications contain numerous features that are common to the four primary Office applications. You have been asked to identify basic elements that are common to Word, Excel, Access, and PowerPoint and to develop the skills necessary for performing tasks associated with these common features.

The Solution

Because the features you have been asked to identify are common to the four primary Office applications, it's a great idea to learn the basics that apply to all applications in one centralized location. Then, when you start using each of the Microsoft Office applications, you can focus on their unique features.

Overview of Office XP Applications

Microsoft Office XP contains a number of different applications. Each application is designed to make the process of creating electronic files that contain different types of data and information more efficient. The Microsoft Office XP applications addressed in this text are listed and described in Table 1-1.

Table 1-1 Microsoft Office XP Applications and Their Uses

Application	Description
Microsoft Word 2002	The word processing program used to create, format, and save letters, manuscripts, newsletters, and other documents.
Microsoft Excel 2002	The spreadsheet program used to create, format, and save columnar data and display it graphically.
Microsoft Access 2002	The database program used to create, format, and save volumes of information (data) related to specific subjects or purposes.
Microsoft PowerPoint 2002	The presentation program used to create visual slides that present summaries of data used to enhance oral presentations.
Microsoft Outlook 2002	The e-mail, calendar, and address program used to create and store e-mail messages, list appointment and meeting dates and times, and record the names and addresses of associates.

Launching Applications

Office XP offers a variety of techniques for launching applications. The procedure you use will depend on how Office XP is installed on your computer and your personal preferences.

To *launch* Office XP applications, use one of the following procedures:

- Choose **Start | Programs,** and then select the Office XP application you want to launch.

Figure 1-1

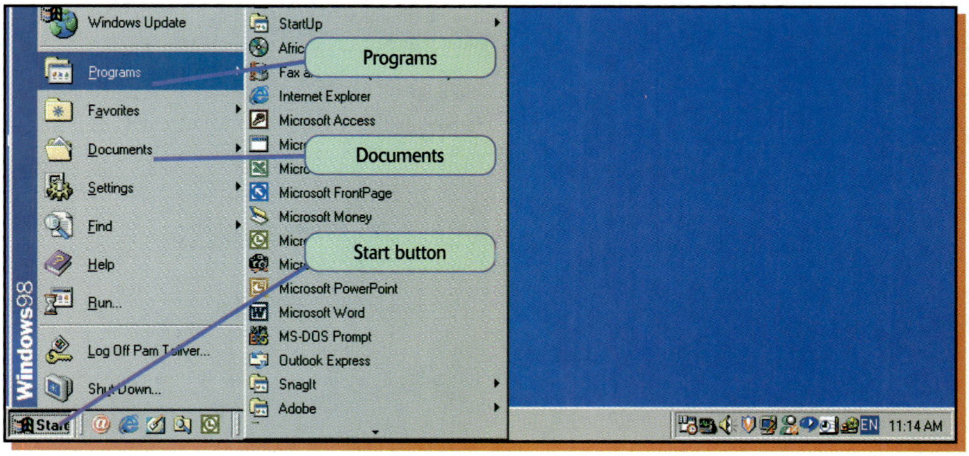

Troubleshooting
If shortcuts to the Office XP applications do not appear on your Programs list, click the arrow button at the bottom of the Programs list and scroll until the applications appear.

- Choose **Start | New Office Document,** and then double-click the **Blank** file type for the application you want to launch—the application required to create that type of file launches.

Figure 1-2

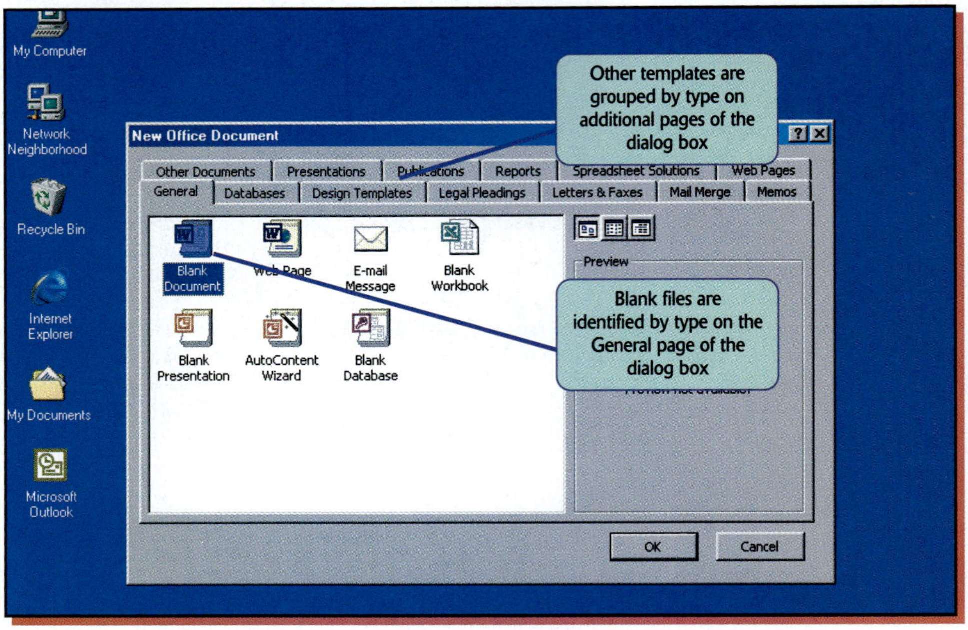

CHECK POINT

Office XP offers a series of professionally designed file formats called templates that you can choose to create a variety of different files. Click the tab for the type of file you want to create (e.g., Memos), click a template name, and view the template preview in the lower right corner of the dialog box. The templates listed depend on those installed on your computer. As a result, your templates may appear different from those listed here.

- Double-click the application shortcut icon on the desktop.
- Click the application icon on the Microsoft Office bar, if it is installed on your computer. When it is installed, the Microsoft Office bar usually appears on the right side of the computer screen. The arrangement of buttons on the bar may be different due to customizations.

Tip Items shown on the desktop in Figure 1-3 represent program icons that generally appear when Microsoft Office XP is installed on a computer running Windows 95 or Windows 98 that has no additional program shortcuts placed on the desktop. Program icons and other features found on your desktop will be different from those shown here because of system customizations.

Figure 1-3

Tip The Documents list shows files from all applications—not just Microsoft Office files. The icon beside each file identifies the application used to create or edit the files.

- Choose **Start | Documents** and select a recently used file to open. The application used to create the file launches. The Documents list holds the last 15 documents accessed. It may contain few items when you first start using the computer, but the list grows as you complete activities.
- Open **My Computer** or **Windows Explorer**, open the folder containing the file you want to open, and double-click the file. The application used to create the file launches.

Depending on the application you launch, the initial screen will differ:

- Word, Excel, and PowerPoint display new files: Word displays a new blank document, Excel displays a new blank workbook, and PowerPoint creates a new blank presentation.
- Access displays an empty screen and the New File task pane with a palette of tools for creating a new file or opening an existing file.

Because accessing and using most of the common elements covered in this section is easiest in Word, it will be used to introduce many common features. The procedures for launching Word 2002 described here should be accessible from all computers on which Office XP is installed.

Identifying Screen Elements

Screen elements common to all Microsoft Office XP applications are identified in Figure 1-4 and described in Table 1-2.

Task 1: Launching Microsoft Word 2002

1. Choose **Start | Programs.**
2. Scroll to the bottom of the Programs list, if necessary.
3. Select Microsoft Word to launch Word.

Figure 1-4

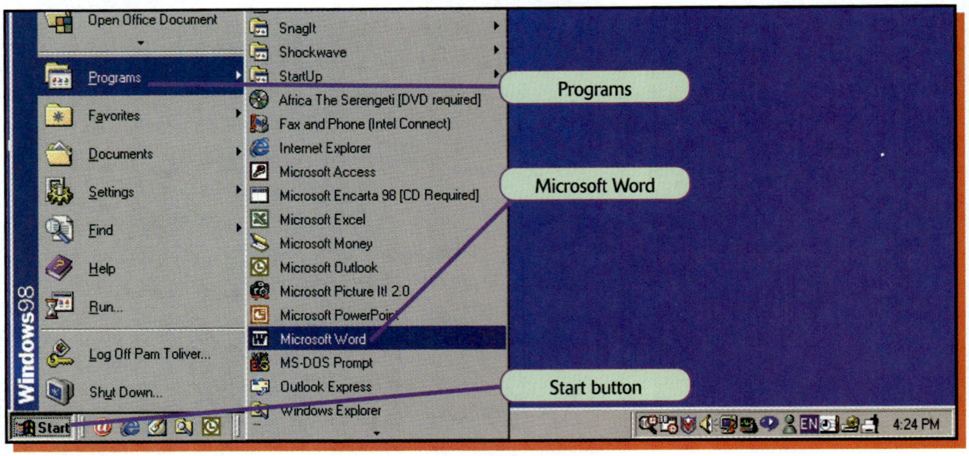

Troubleshooting The icons that appear at the right end of the task bar on your computer may be different from those shown in Figure 1-4. They represent programs that are running in the background on the active computer.

4. Review screen elements identified in Figure 1-5.

Tip Because installations and setups vary from computer to computer and set up changes from user to user, screen elements may vary from those shown here.

Figure 1-5

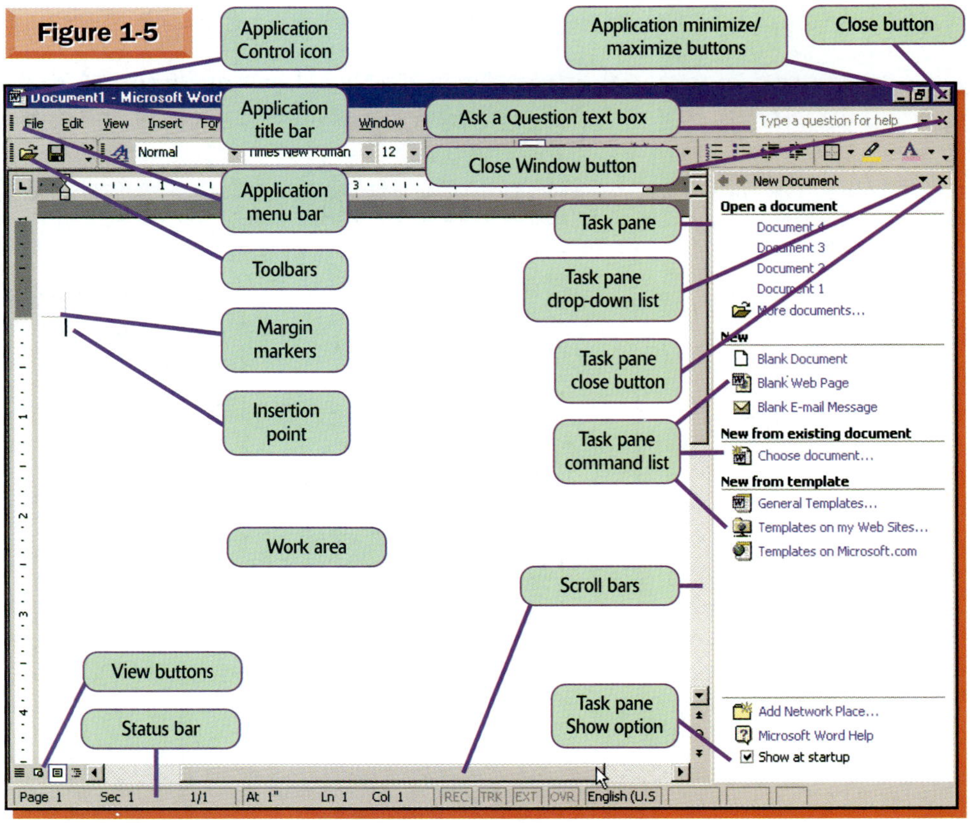

Table 1-2 Word Screen Features

Feature	Description
Application title bar	Identifies the program and file that is open.
Application menu bar	Groups task commands by type.
Application Control icon	Displays options for maximizing, minimizing, resizing, and closing the application window.
Toolbars	Provide single-click access to frequently performed tasks.
Work area	Provides room to type text.
Status bar	Identifies active application features and the insertion point position.
Insertion point	Identifies the typing position.
Application minimize/ maximize buttons	Control window size.
Close button	Exits the application.
Close Window button	Closes the active file and leaves the application running.
Scroll bars	Display different areas of the file on screen.
Task pane	Displays tools for creating and opening files and tools for performing special tasks.
Task pane Close button	Closes the task pane.
Ask a question text box	Accesses help about the topic entered.
Margin markers	Identify margin positions on screen.
Task pane command list	Displays a grouped list from which you can access the Office Clipboard and the program search feature, select a command, create a new document, open a recently edited document, or create a formatted document.
View buttons	Change the appearance of the document on screen.
Task pane drop-down list	Presents a list of different elements and features that can be displayed on the Task Pane.
Task pane Show option	Controls whether the task pane appears each time you start Word.

Working with Screen Elements

Many of the screen elements seen in Microsoft Word are common to other Office XP applications. As a result, once you learn how to navigate the screen elements in one Office application, you can apply the techniques to comparable features in other Office XP applications.

Using the Task Pane

The *task pane* is a new feature in Microsoft Office. It provides access to some of the most basic file management tools you will need as you progress through each application. You can close the task pane to increase the work area in a program and then redisplay it as needed.

The task pane is divided into distinct sections identified by the tasks to be performed. Options for performing tasks appear in blue text below each section heading. Options followed by ellipses are options that open dialog boxes; options that have no ellipses carry out a command. Task pane tools are also found on menus and *toolbars*.

Task 2:
To Close and Open the Task Pane

1. Click the task pane **Close** X button. The task pane closes.

2. Choose **View | Task Pane**. The task pane opens.

Figure 1-6

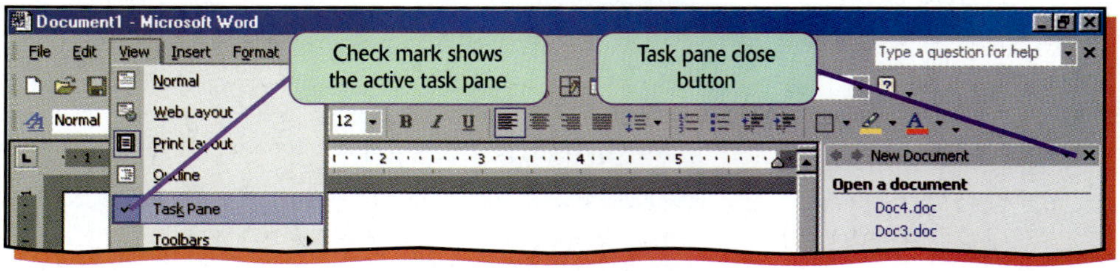

Other Ways

You can also display the task pane by pointing to a toolbar, right-clicking, and selecting **Task Pane** or by choosing **View | Toolbars | Task Pane**. To prevent the task pane from opening each time you launch Word, clear the **Show at startup** option at the bottom of the task pane.

Hiding and Displaying Toolbars

A variety of different toolbars can be displayed in Office XP applications, each designed to assist with specific tasks. In each application, the Standard and Formatting toolbars contain buttons for performing the most frequently completed tasks. Other toolbars appear automatically as you perform specific tasks. There will be times as you work in the different applications when you will want to display additional toolbars.

Tip

To identify the name of a toolbar button, position the mouse pointer on the button and pause. A Screen Tip will tell you what the name of the button is.

Task 3:
To Display and Hide Toolbars

1. Choose **View | Toolbars** to display a list of available toolbars.

2. Select **Formatting.** The Formatting toolbar is hidden.

Figure 1-7

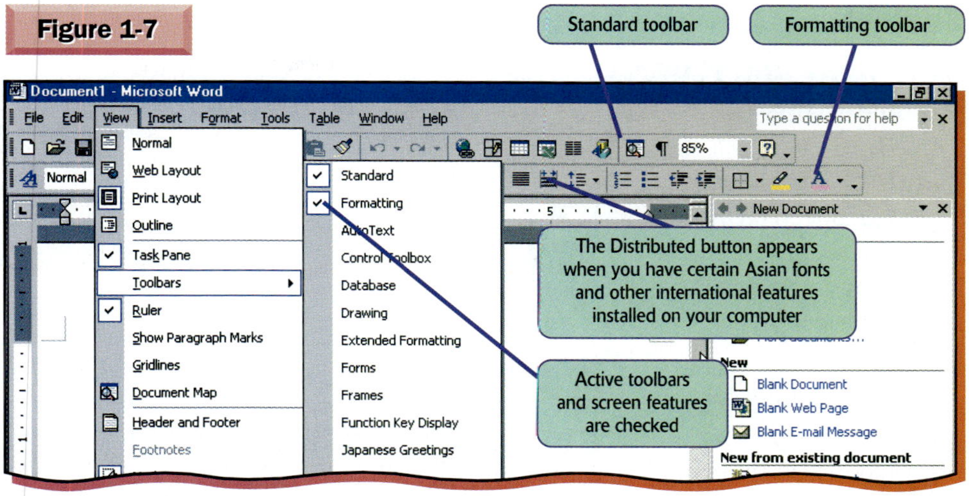

3. Point to the Standard toolbar and right-click. A list of available toolbars appears.

4. Select **Formatting.** The Formatting toolbar appears on screen in its original position.

Figure 1-8

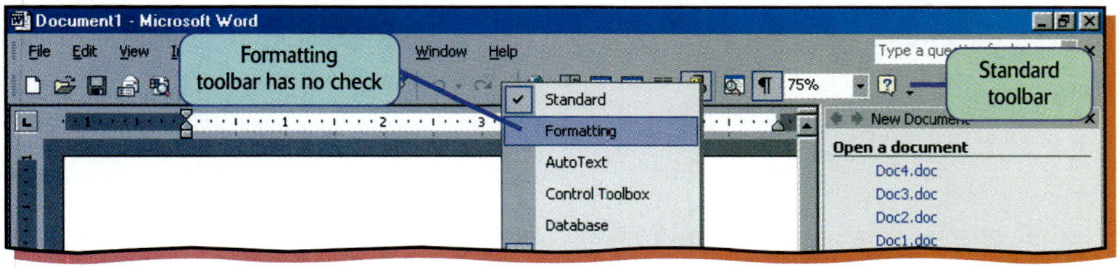

CHECK POINT

Selections, Inc., in an effort to accommodate clients worldwide through its e-Selections Online Division, has a number of International fonts, such as Asian, Japanese, and so forth, installed on some of the computers at its corporate offices. As a result, additional features are available to those who use the international workstations. You will notice additional buttons on toolbars, added menu commands, and other extra features as you work with Office XP. These features are designed to help those who develop materials for the international market to access the tools more efficiently.

Displaying and Hiding the Language Bar

The *Language bar*, when it is installed and displayed, appears as a floating toolbar in all Office XP applications. It contains tools related to the language features that are built in to Office XP. When the Language bar is closed, it appears as an icon on the taskbar tray so that it is easy to call up when you need it.

Task 4:
To Display and Hide the Language Bar

1. Click the **Language** EN button on the Windows taskbar tray and select **Show Language Bar** to open the toolbar.

2. Click the Language bar **Minimize** button. A message box displays information about how to redisplay the Language bar.

3. Click **OK**. The Language button appears on the tray of the Windows taskbar.

Troubleshooting

If the Language bar is closed, open it by choosing **Start | Settings | Control Panel | Text Services** to open the Text Services dialog box. Then click the Language Bar button and select the Show the Language bar on the desktop option. Then click OK twice and close the Control Panel dialog box.

Tip Depending on the setup on your computer, the menus and toolbars may already display on two lines.

Figure 1-9

Figure 1-10

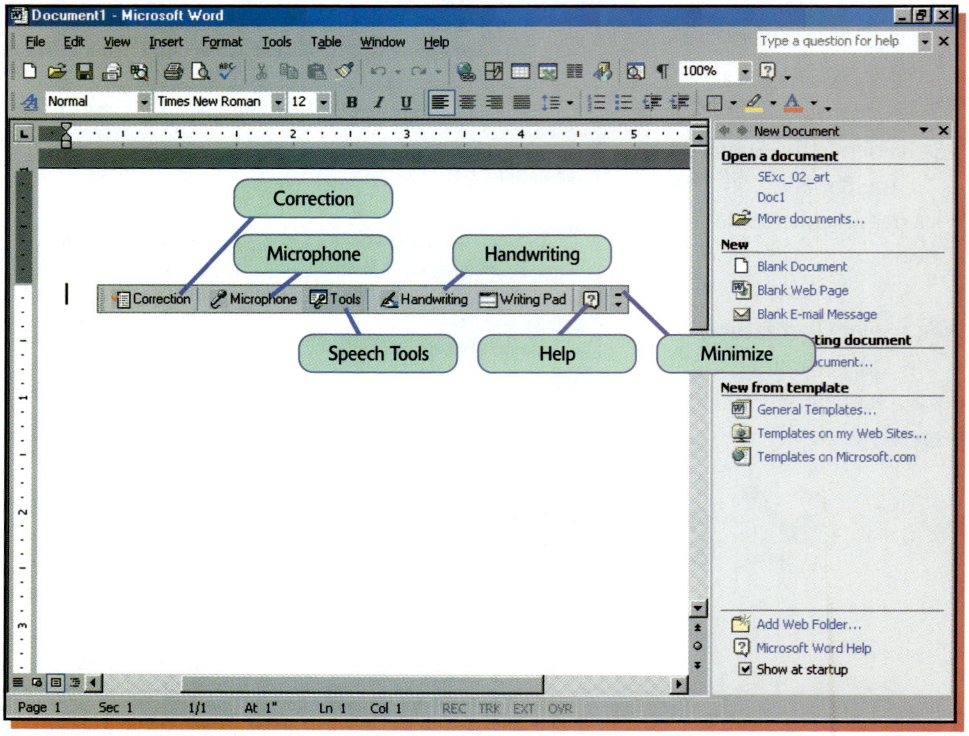

Resetting Menus and Toolbars

Menus and toolbars in Office XP are set to auto-customize as you work. Here's how they work:

- When menus in Office XP applications are displayed, only the most frequently used commands appear on the initial menu. After the menu is displayed for a few seconds, the extended menu shows additional menu commands.
- When you select a menu command from the extended menu, the command is placed on the initial menu in its standard position so that it is more readily available the next time you need it.
- The Standard and Formatting toolbars are initially displayed on one line to increase the work area on screen. Buttons for additional commands appear on a Toolbar Options drop-down list at the right end of displayed toolbars.

- When you select a button from the Toolbar Options drop-down palette, the button is placed at its standard location on the appropriate toolbar.

So that the steps presented in this book are accurate for each class working on lab computers, it is necessary to turn off this auto-customization feature.

Task 5:
To Turn Off Auto-Customization Features

1 Choose **Tools | Customize**. The Customize dialog box opens.

Other Ways

To display the Customize dialog box:
- Right-click a toolbar that is already displayed and select Customize from the shortcut menu.

Figure 1-11

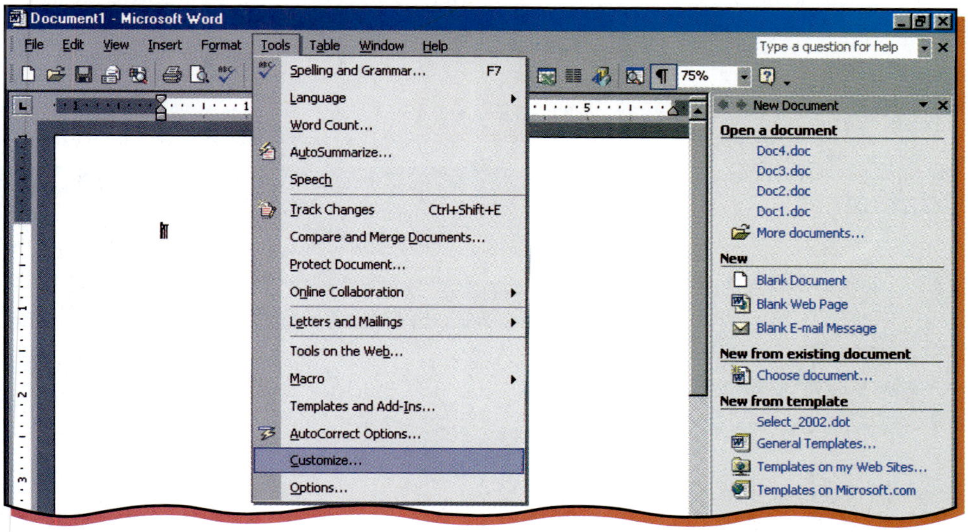

2 Click the **Options** tab, if necessary.

3 Select the **Show Standard and Formatting toolbars on two rows** option to display the full Standard and Formatting toolbars on separate rows.

4 Select the **Always show full menus** option, if necessary.

5 Click **Close**.

Figure 1-12

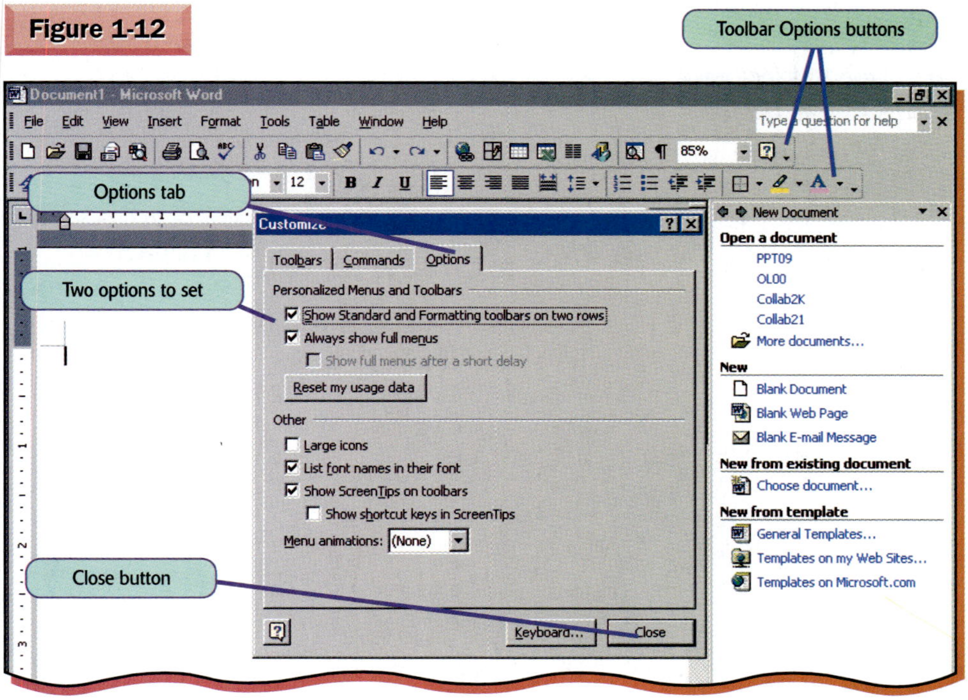

Tip

To toggle toolbars between one- and two-line displays, click the Toolbar Options button that appears as a down arrow at the end of each toolbar and select **Show Buttons on Two (or One) Row(s)**.

Changing Zoom Settings

The *Zoom* setting controls the portion of a file that appears on screen and can be used to make file text easier to read. After the auto-customization feature is turned off and the Standard and Formatting toolbars appear on separate rows, the Zoom control tool appears on the Standard toolbar.

Troubleshooting The list of Zoom values changes depending on the application and current view.

Task 6: To Set Zoom Control

1. Click the **Zoom** down arrow on the Standard toolbar. A list of available sizing options appears.
2. Select **50%**. The document shifts on screen.
3. Click in the **Zoom** box on the Standard menu.
4. Type 100 and press Enter. The document size is restored.

Figure 1-13

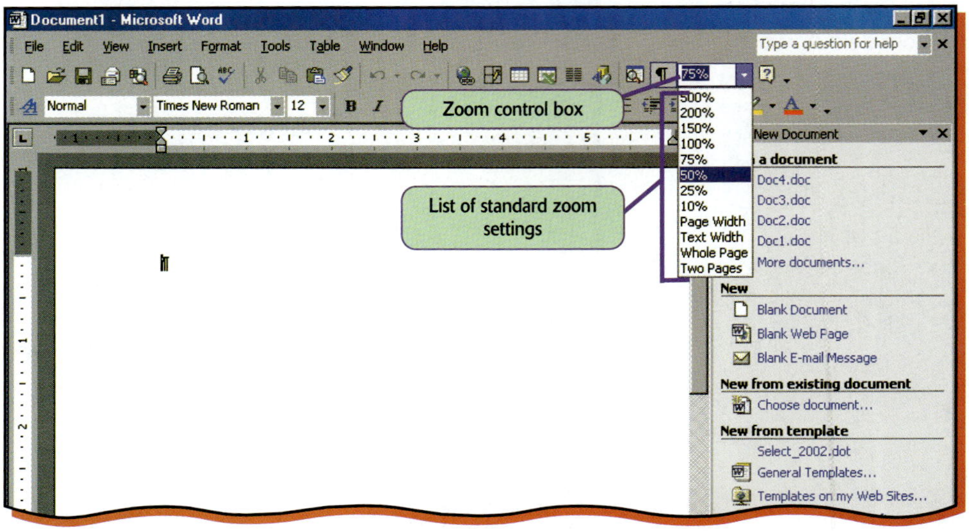

Performing Basic File Management Tasks

Basic file management tasks include opening files, creating new files, saving files, and editing file properties. The procedures for accomplishing these tasks are similar in all Office XP applications.

Opening Files

Office XP provides a number of different procedures that you can use to open an existing document, workbook, presentation, or database. The Open dialog box has been redesigned in Office XP and presents a Web-like look that even contains links to Web servers. To open a file, do one of the following:

- Choose **File | Open.**
- Click the **Open** button on the Standard toolbar.
- Press Ctrl + O.
- Choose **Start | Open Office Document.**
- Click **More Documents** in the **Open a document** area of the task pane.

Regardless of which procedure you use to open a file, an Open dialog box similar to the one shown in Figure1-14 appears. Features of the Open dialog box are described in Table 1-3.

Tip A folder in Windows can contain files or additional folders.

Figure 1-14

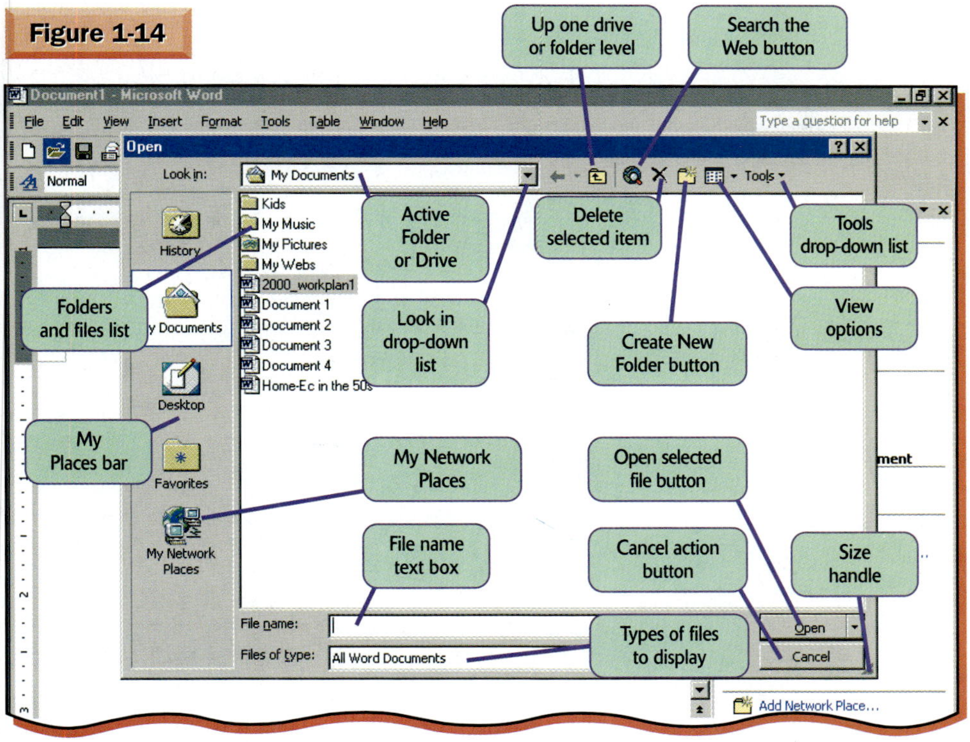

Table 1-3 Open dialog box elements

Feature	Description
Look in drop-down list	Identifies the current drive and/or folder.
Up One Level button	Accesses the "parent" folder when a folder is active; My Computer when a drive is active; and Desktop when the My Documents folder is open.
Search the Web button	Launches Internet Explorer 5.5, or your default Web browser, to the Microsoft Homepage so that you can perform a search for the document to open.
Delete button	Removes the selected document or folder.
Create New Folder button	Creates a new folder within the active drive or folder.
View drop-down list	Displays a list of options that change the way files and folders are displayed in the dialog box.
Tools drop-down list	Contains commands that enable you to find and delete files and folders, print files, and identify properties of files and folders.
My Places bar	Contains links to folders and file storage locations so that you can open them quickly, and it can be customized to hold the folders you use most frequently.
My Network Places	Displays links to Web sites and other Network Places that you have designated on networked computers to which you have access.
Dialog box size handle	Can be dragged to change the size and shape of the dialog box.
File name text box	Enables you to type the name of the document to open.
Files of type text box	Identifies the types of files displayed. You can display other types of files by altering the file type selected.
Folders and Files list	Shows all folders and files in the active folder or on the active drive for the active application.
Open button	Opens the selected (highlighted) file or folder. It contains a drop-down list that enables you to open a copy of the file, open the file in Read-Only mode, Open and Repair, or open a Web document in a browser.
Cancel button	Closes the dialog box without opening a file or folder.

CHECK POINT

By default, the last four files opened in that application on your computer appear at the bottom of the File menu. In addition, the last fifteen files accessed appear on the Documents list displayed from the Start menu. As a result, two alternative procedures can be used to open files.

- Select the file from the bottom of the File menu.
- Choose **Start | Documents** and select the recently edited file to open.

You can change the number of files that appear at the bottom of the File menu for any application using the **Tools | Options** command and then setting the Recently used file list on the **General** page of the Options dialog box.

Task 7:

To Open a Copy of a Document

1 Launch Word, if necessary, close the task pane, and choose **File** | **Open**. The Open dialog box opens.

Figure 1-15

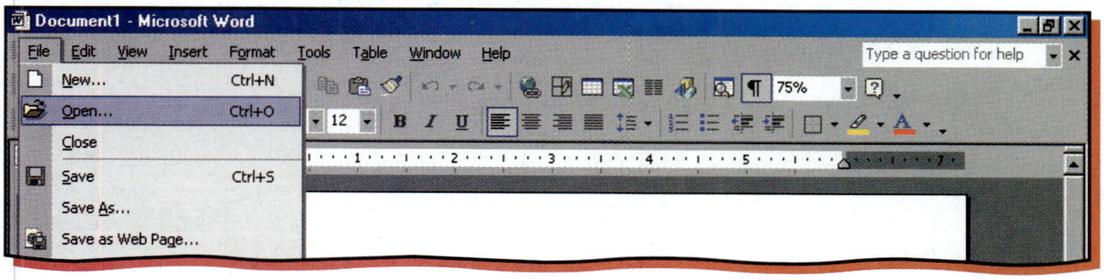

2 Click the **Look in** down arrow and open the disk drive and/or folder containing the *e-Selections.doc* file. The disk drive and/or folder name appears in the Look in text box.

3 Select the *e-Selections.doc* file. The file name appears highlighted.

4 Click the drop-down list arrow on the **Open** button and select **Open as Copy**.

Figure 1-16

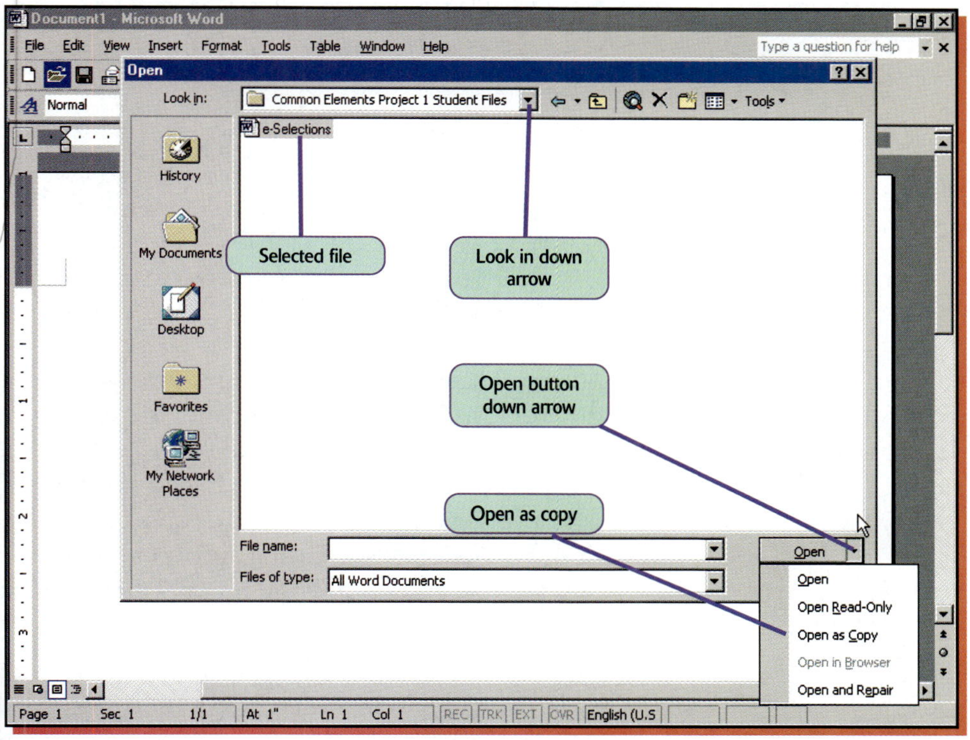

Tip You can also open a read-only copy of a document to preserve the original file. When you open a read-only copy of a document, make changes to the file, and want to save the changes, you must save the file using a new file name.

Troubleshooting The current settings on your computer control the appearance of the document on your screen. As a result, your screen may be different from the screen pictured in Figure 1-17.

5 Review the document.

Tip Opening a copy of an existing document leaves the original intact so that you can use it later, if necessary.

Figure 1-17

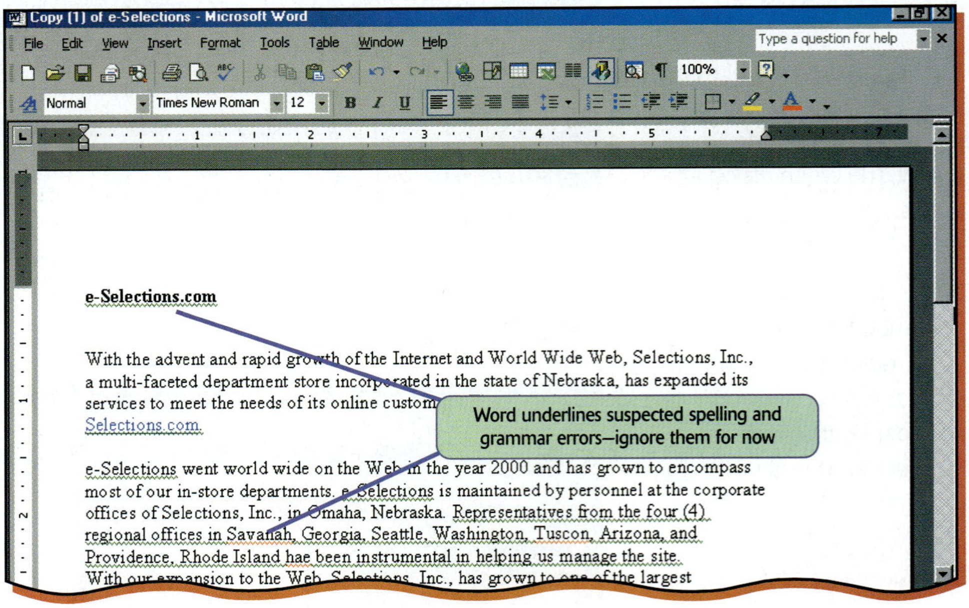

Creating New Files

As you discovered with opening files, Microsoft Office XP offers a variety of different techniques for performing tasks. Take creating new files for example; a new document appears when you launch Word, a new blank workbook is created each time you launch Excel, and a new blank presentation is created when you start PowerPoint. As you explore all Office XP applications, you'll find that options for creating and opening files are presented when you launch Access. To create a new file in any Office XP application after it is launched, you can use one of the following procedures:

- Click the **New** button on the Standard toolbar of any Office XP application. A new blank file appears if you are working in Word, Excel, and PowerPoint. In Access, clicking the New button displays the New File task pane so that you can create a blank database or a database using a template.
- Press Ctrl + N. A new blank file appears in Word, Excel, or PowerPoint. In Access, the New File task pane opens so that you can select the type of database you want to create.
- Choose **File | New**. The New dialog box opens and displays a list of templates—professionally designed, preformatted file formats specific to the application you're using—that you can use to create a specific type of file.
- Click the option for a new file from the task pane:
  - **New Blank Document** to create a new blank file;
  - **New from existing *file* | Choose *File*** to open the New from Existing File dialog box;
  - **New from template** to display the same list of templates shown using the **File | New** command.

Task 8:
To Create New Files

1 Launch Word, if necessary, and click the **New** button on the Standard toolbar to create a new blank document.

2 Display the task pane and click **Blank Document** on the task pane. Document3 appears and another document button appears on the taskbar.

3 Point to the bottom of the screen, if necessary, to display the taskbar.

Tip In addition to buttons representing different document files that are open, you may see taskbar buttons for other programs—such as e-mail programs—that are running on your computer.

Figure 1-18

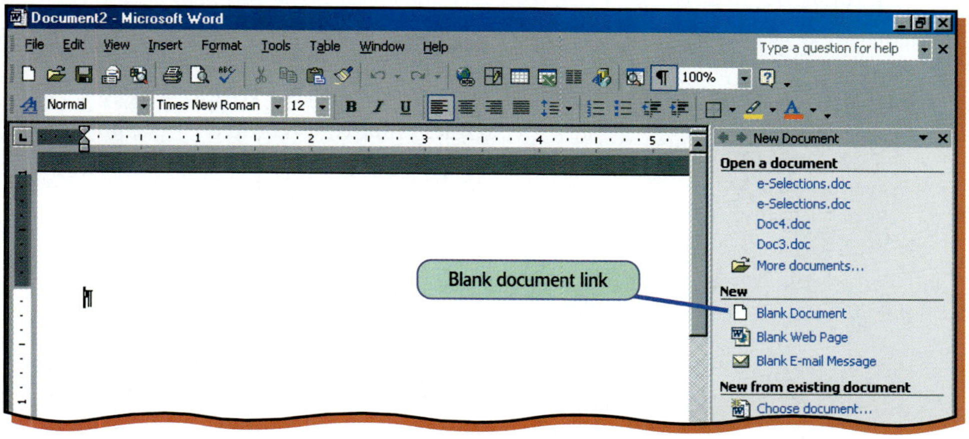

Figure 1-19

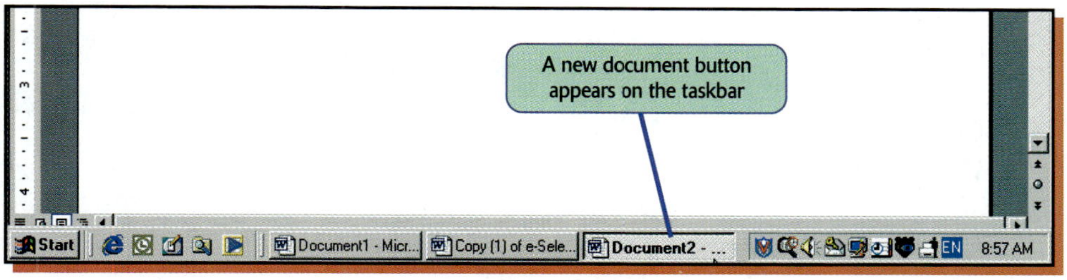

Tip When you use multiple applications in Office, more than one program may be open, but only one is active. Similarly, if you have multiple documents, workbooks, or presentations open, only one of them is actually active at any given time.

Switching Among Open Files

Word, Excel, and PowerPoint enable you to open or create multiple files without closing files that are already open. These three applications place a file button on the Windows taskbar for each file you have open. To switch from one open file to another, you can:

- Click the **Windows taskbar** button for the open file you want to access.
- Press Ctrl + F6 to browse open files for the active application.
- Press Ctrl + Shift + F6 to move backward among open files for the active application.
- Click the file name in the task pane.
- Press Alt + Tab to switch among programs and files from all open applications.
- Choose the **Window** menu and then select the file you want to access from the bottom of the menu.

Closing Files

Office XP applications provide a variety of techniques for closing files. To close the active file:

- Click the file **Close** Window X button at the right end of the menu bar.
- Right-click the Windows taskbar button for the file you want to close and select **Close**.
- Choose **File | Close**.
- Press Ctrl + F4.

Troubleshooting When only one file is open in Word, Excel, or Powerpoint, a Close button also appears at the right end of the title bar. This button enables you to exit the application, so be sure you click the correct Close button.

Task 9:
To Close a File

1. Switch to Document3, if necessary.
2. Click the **Close Window** X button.
3. Display Document2, if necessary.
4. Choose **File | Close**. The Copy of *e-Selections* appears on screen. Leave it open for the next task.

Figure 1-20

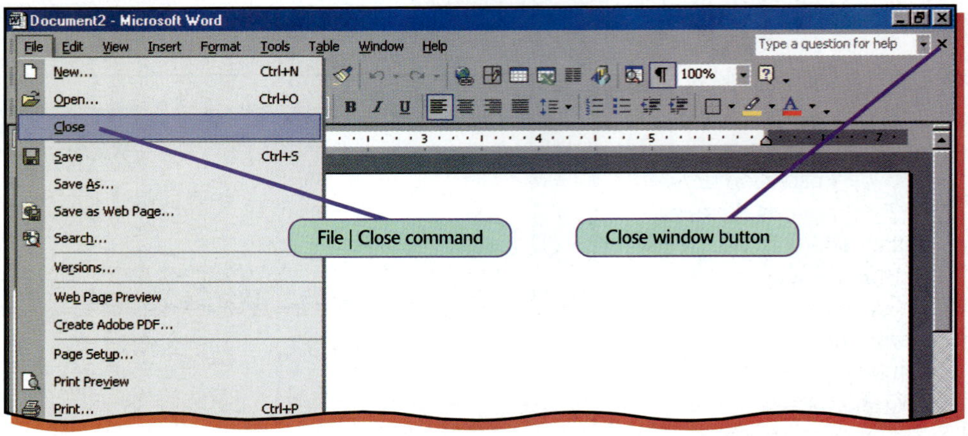

Saving Files

Each new document you create, each copy of an existing document you open, and each document you edit needs to be saved. You'll find a number of different Save commands listed on the File menu of Office XP applications. Knowing the difference between the Save commands is important. Here's how they work:

Tip The **File | Save** commands in other applications may contain different options. Be sure to review the File menu to determine different save options.

Table 1-4 Save Commands

Command	Description
Save	Automatically overwrites previously saved files that you open and edit. Opens the Save As dialog box the first time a document is saved so that you can name and select a storage location for new files. The dialog box contains text boxes where you can type a file name and select a save format. Saves copies of existing files that you open using the Open as Copy command in the same folder of the same disk using the filename *Copy (#) of xx.doc*. In Access, Save enables you to save a database object.
Save As	In Word, Excel, and PowerPoint, this command opens the Save As dialog box, which you can use to save an existing file using a different file name, save the active file in a different drive or folder, or save a file as a different file type. In Access, Save As enables you to export a selected database object to create another specific database object only.
Save as Web Page	Opens the Save As dialog box, automatically activates **Web Page** as the Save as type, and adds a page title using the first line of text in the file.

Tip Folders you create in other applications such as Windows Explorer are available for storing files from Microsoft Office XP applications.

To initiate the Save command, you can use one of the following techniques:

- Click the **Save** button on the Standard toolbar.
- Press Ctrl + S.
- Choose **File | Save**.
- Choose **File | Save As**.

Creating Folders. Because file management is so important, Office applications streamline the process by enabling you to create new folders "on the fly" from the Open and Save As dialog boxes. In addition, you can embed fonts as you save documents to ensure that the document will look the way you intended when it is opened on a different computer.

Task 10: To Save a Copy of a File with Embedded Fonts in a New Folder

1. Click the title bar of the *Copy (1) of e-Selections.doc* file to make it active, if necessary. Active windows usually have a darker title bar than inactive windows.

2. Choose **File | Save As** to open the Save As dialog box.

Figure 1-21

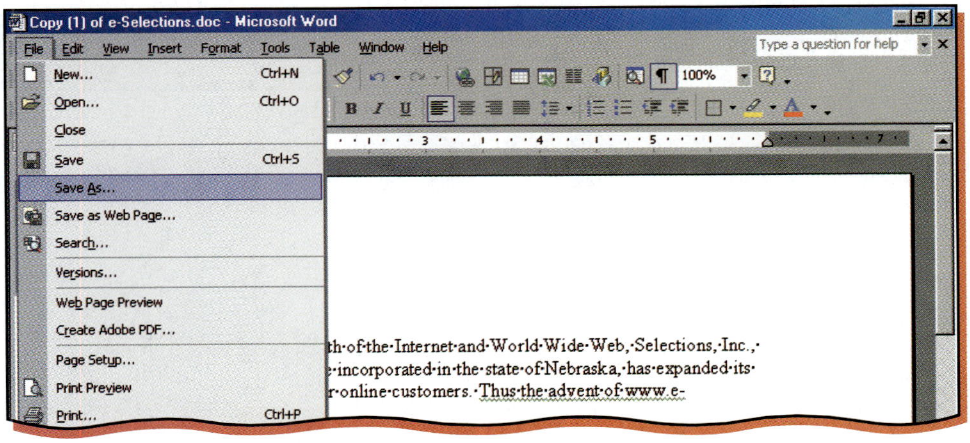

3 Click the **Save in** down arrow, select the disk drive on which you want to create a new folder, and click the **Create New Folder** button.

Figure 1-22

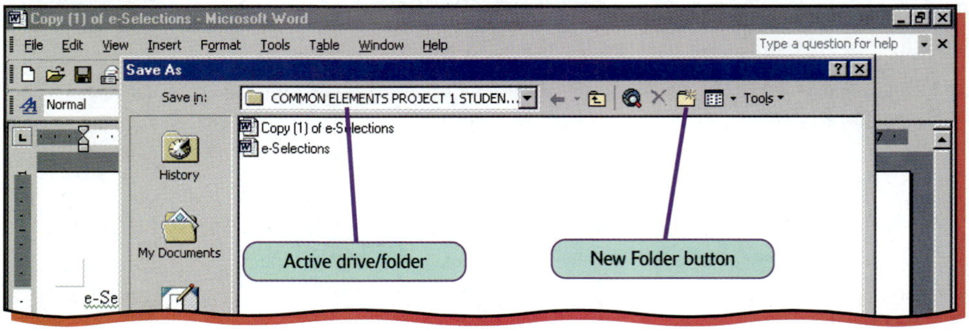

4 Type ***Your Initials*** followed by ***Your Class Name*** in the **Name** text box and click **OK**. The new folder opens and appears in the Save in text box at the top of the Save As dialog box.

Figure 1-23

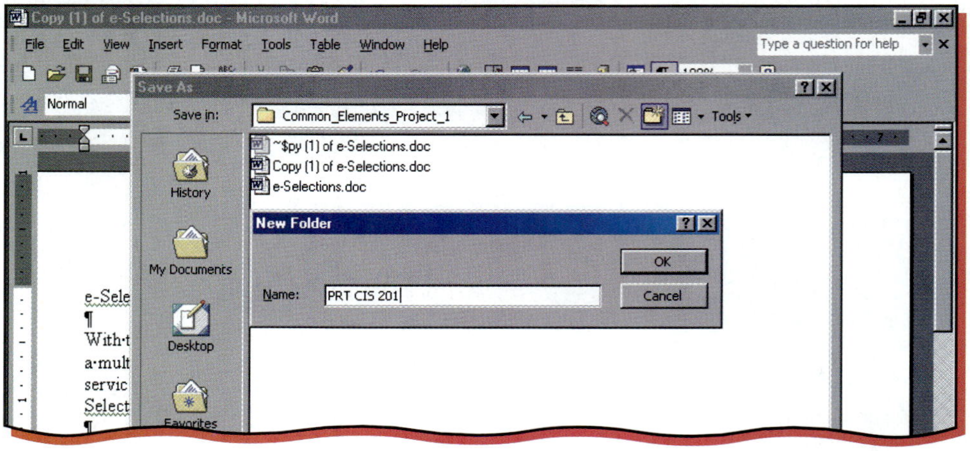

Troubleshooting If you want to create a subfolder, you must open the folder in which you want to place the subfolder.

5 Click the **Tools** down arrow and select **Save Options** to open the Save dialog box that contains save options.

Figure 1-24

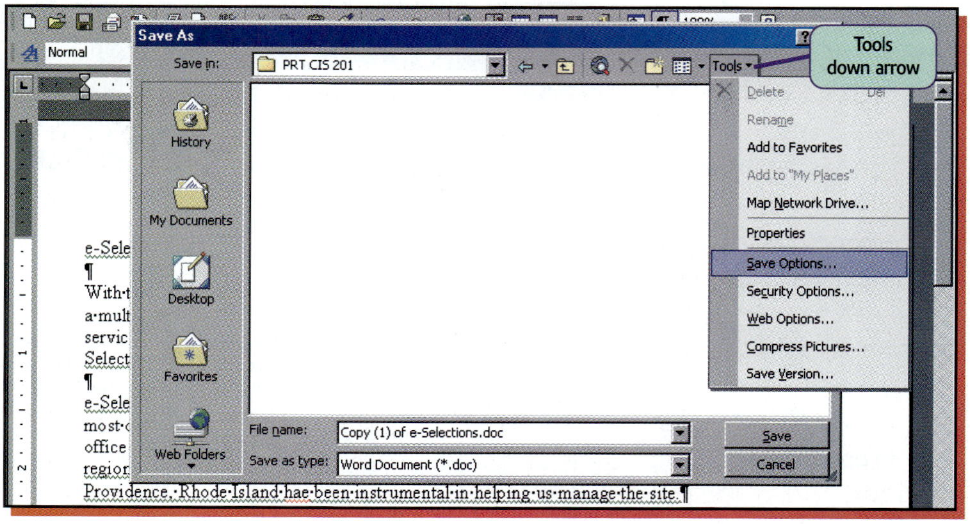

6 Select the **Embed TrueType fonts** and the **Do not embed common system fonts** options.

7 Click **OK**.

8 Click **Save**. The new file named *Copy (1) of e-Selections.doc* appears in the new folder, and the file name also appears in the title bar of the document.

Tip Be sure to review options that appear in the Save dialog box. Knowing what options are available may come in handy sometime in the future.

Figure 1-25

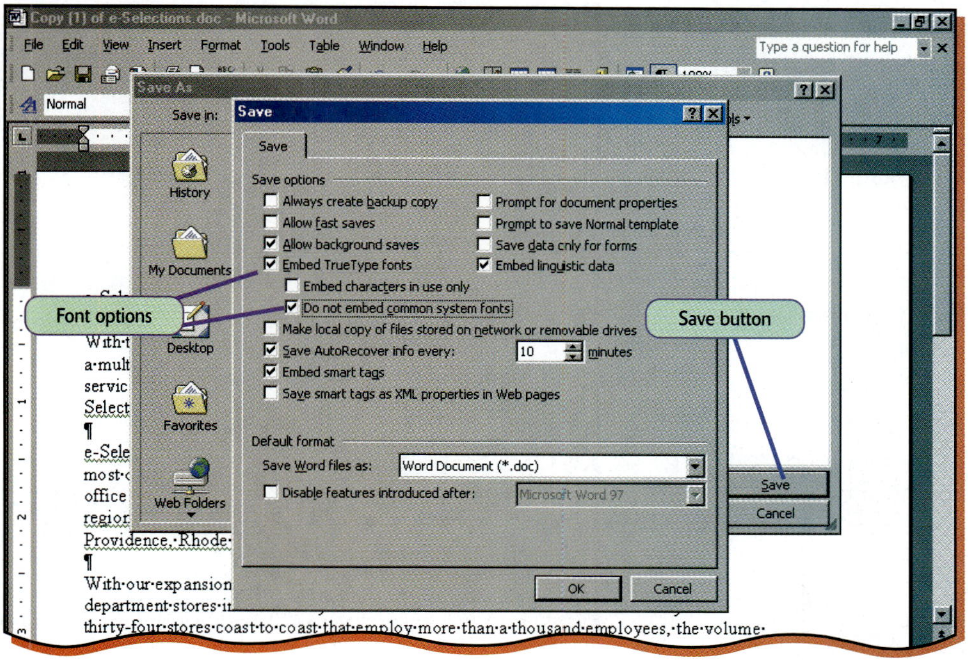

WEB TIP

You can save a Web page using the same basic save techniques used to save files in Office XP applications. Simply display the Web page in the browser and choose **File | Save As**, open the folder in which to store the file, type a file name for the file, and click **OK**.

Customizing the My Places Bar and Sizing Dialog Boxes

The *My Places bar* contains a default set of folders, Web sites, and files for the user to access—the default places on the bar may or may not be locations that you would want to access. As a result, the My Places bar can be customized to hold the folders and sites you visit most. Now that you have created a folder to hold your work, you can add the folder to My Places bar to make it more accessible.

Task 11:

To Add a Folder to the My Places Bar and Size a Dialog Box

1. Launch Word, if necessary, close the task pane, and click the **Open** button on the Standard toolbar. The Open dialog box opens.

2. Locate the personal folder you created in Task 10 and select it (but don't open it).

3. Click the **Tools** drop-down list on the dialog box toolbar and select **Add to "My Places"**.

4. Click the down arrow at the bottom of the Places bar. The new folder appears.

5. Drag the dialog box size handle to increase the size of the dialog box so that all the folders are visible. The down-arrow button disappears.

6. Click **Cancel** to close the dialog box.

Tip Adding a folder or site to the My Places bar of one dialog box adds it to all dialog boxes in all Office XP applications.

Figure 1-26

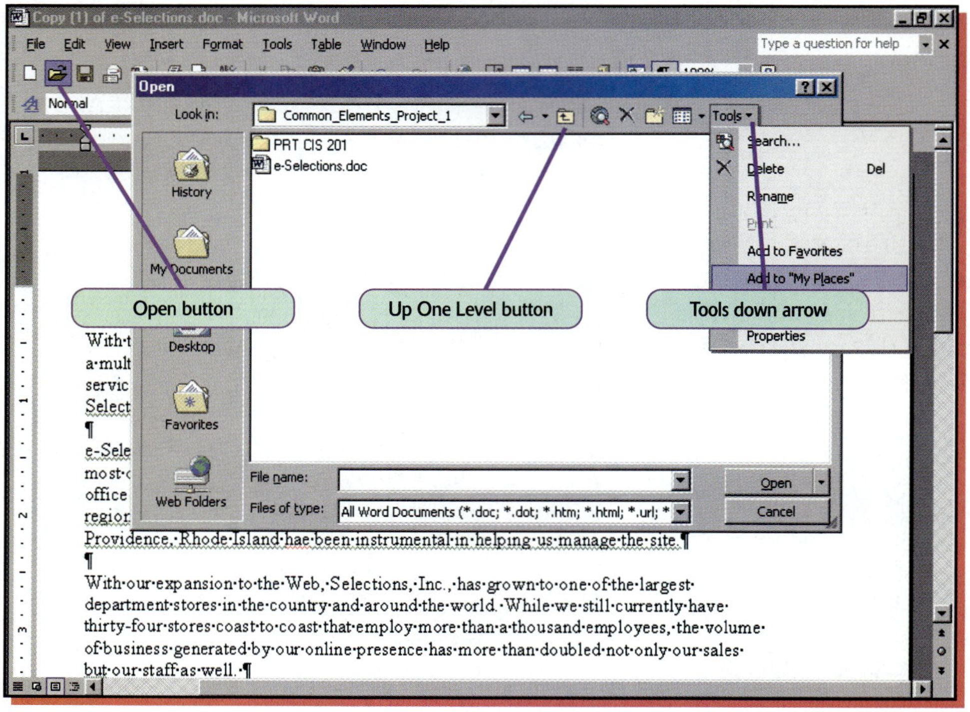

Figure 1-27

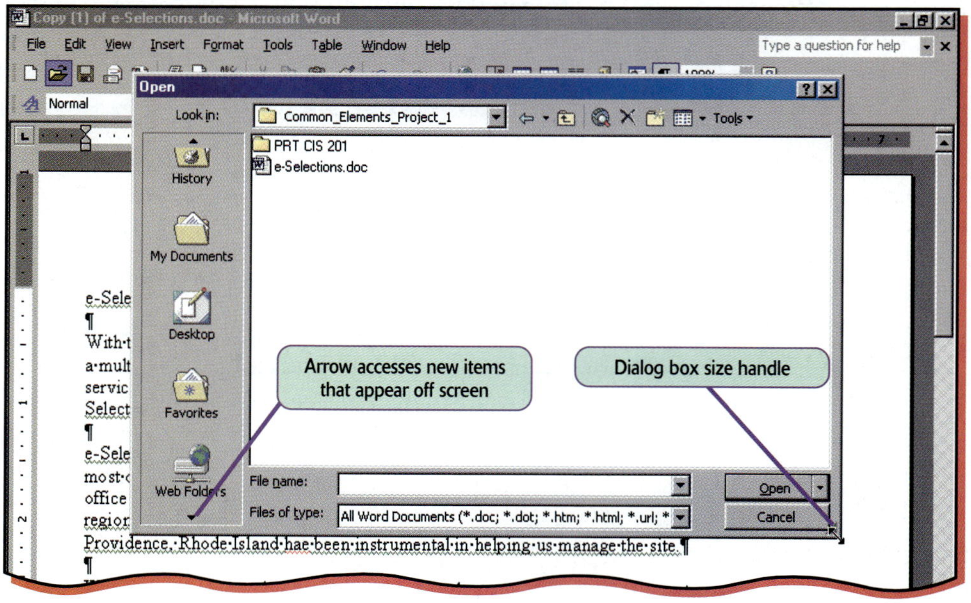

Troubleshooting Because your personal folder was the last folder you used, it may appear in the **Look in** box at the top of the dialog box and the folder will be open. Click the **Up One Level** button on the dialog box toolbar to close the folder and then select it.

Saving and Previewing Web Pages

Each Office XP application can be used to save files as Web pages and to view those files as they would appear in a Web browser. Whereas the specific steps required to save files as Web pages vary from application to application within Office XP, the basic steps for initiating the process and for viewing the files is the same for all applications.

Task 12:

To Save a File as a Web Page and View the Web File

1. Open your *Copy (1) of e-Selections.doc*, if necessary.
2. Choose **File | Save as Web Page**.
3. Click your folder in the Places bar to open the folder, if necessary.
4. Click the **Change Title** button. The Set Page Title dialog box opens.

Troubleshooting
Changing the page title has no impact on the file name or document text. The Page Title appears in the title bar of the browser when you display the document in the browser window.

5. Type *Your Initials* **First Web Page** in the **Page title** text box and then click **OK**.

Figure 1-28

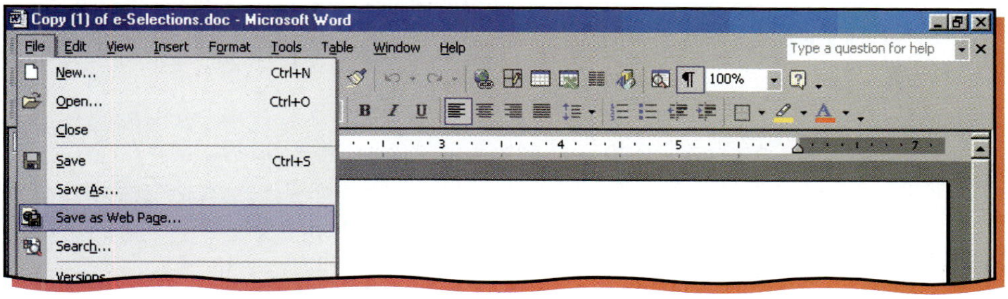

Figure 1-29

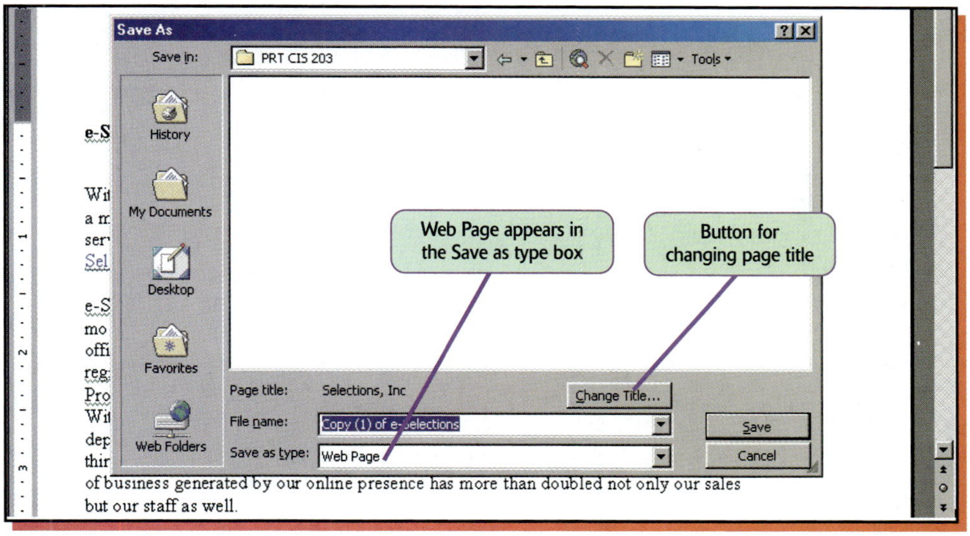

Figure 1-30

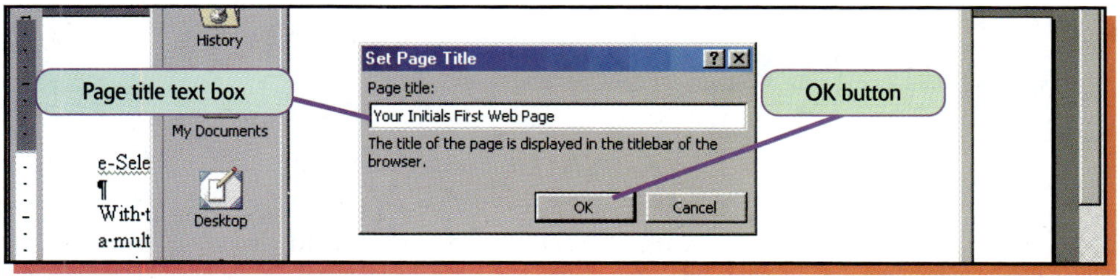

6 Type ***Your Initials* First Web Page** in the **File name** text box.

7 Click **Save**. The file is saved as a Web page and the Web Layout View becomes active.

Figure 1-31

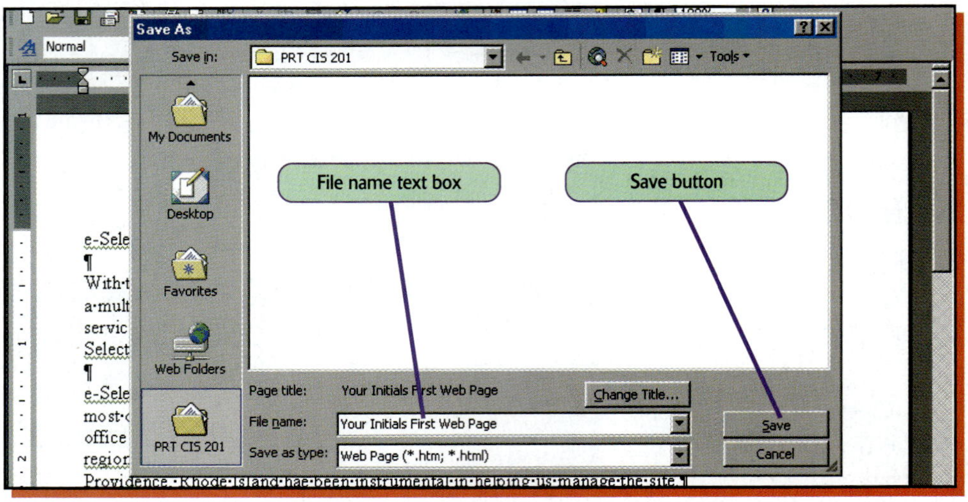

8 Choose **File | Web Page Preview**. Your Web browser application will open and enable you to view the document as a Web page.

Troubleshooting
The settings on your browser may be different from those shown here because of programs and other features installed on your computer.

9 Click the browser application **Close** ✕ button.

Figure 1-32

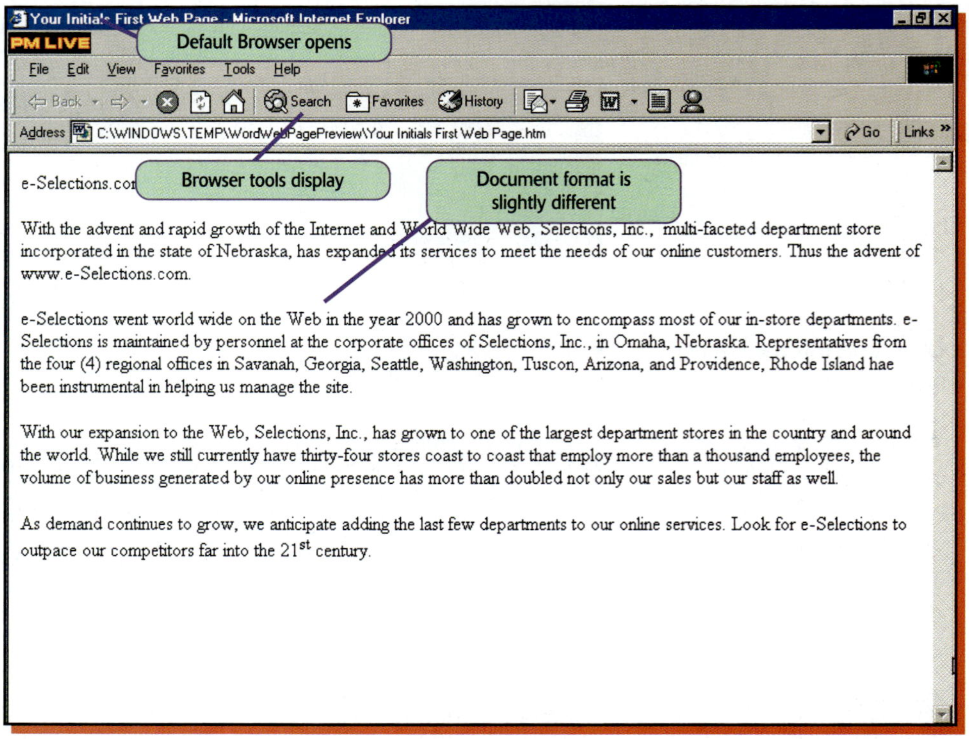

Changing File Properties

Properties, the term used to describe important information about a file, are automatically stored with each Office XP file you save. Properties are grouped into different categories and provide detailed information about the file, such as the date on which the file was created, the date on which it was last edited, the author's name, the author's company, the file size, and other application-specific information (e.g., the number of words in a Word document). In addition, the Office XP application used to create the file assigns a title for the file based on the file name assigned to the file. You can edit and check existing file information or add additional bits of information about the file.

Task 13: To Edit File Properties

1 Choose **File | Properties** to open the Properties dialog box.

Tip In Access, the name of this command on the File menu is Database Properties.

2 Select the word *first* in the Title text box.

3 Type **e-Selections** to replace *first*. The title now appears as *Your Initials e-Selections Web Page*.

4 Click **OK and close the file.**

Figure 1-33

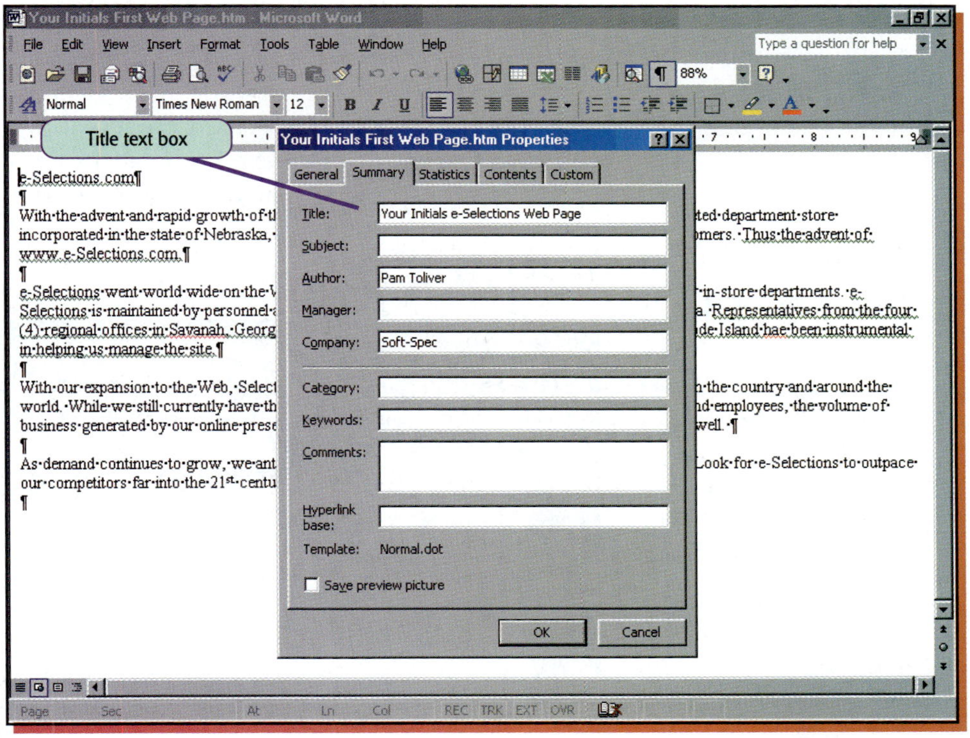

CHECK POINT

Because of the need for privacy in transmitting documents electronically, Office XP has implemented a procedure for removing personal information from a file on save. To set this option so that personal information is not transmitted with your files, follow these quick steps:

1. Choose **Tools | Options | Security.**
2. Select the **Remove personal information from this file on save** option.
3. Click **OK.**

Setting this option and then saving files prevents your name and other personal information from appearing in the Properties dialog box. It does NOT, however, prevent information about the document, such as creation date, edit date, and your company name, from appearing in the Properties dialog box.

Getting Help

In the Windows section, you learned how to use Windows Help and how to locate information about specific topics. Each Office XP application comes equipped with a variety of help features that will have you getting help from all over the world—right on your computer as you work!

Asking Questions

A new *Ask a Question* tool has been added to the right end of the menu bar. Using the Ask a Question text box, you can simply enter a question and receive a list of possible topics related to answering the question.

Task 14: To Ask a Question

1. Create a new blank document, click the **Ask a Question** text box on the menu bar to position the insertion point in the box.
2. Type **How do I display the Office Assistant?** and press Enter.
3. Click **Display tips and messages through the Office Assistant**.
4. Click the **Show** button on the Help window toolbar to display other help associated with the topic.
5. Click the Help window **Close** button. The Help window closes and Word resizes to screen size.

Troubleshooting

Because the help files are updated frequently, the list you see when you search for help may be different from the lists shown in Tasks 14 and 15.

Figure 1-34

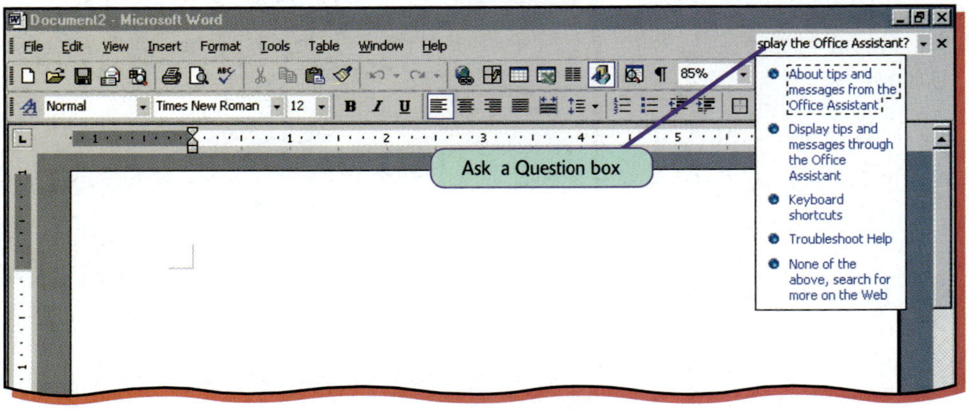

Figure 1-35

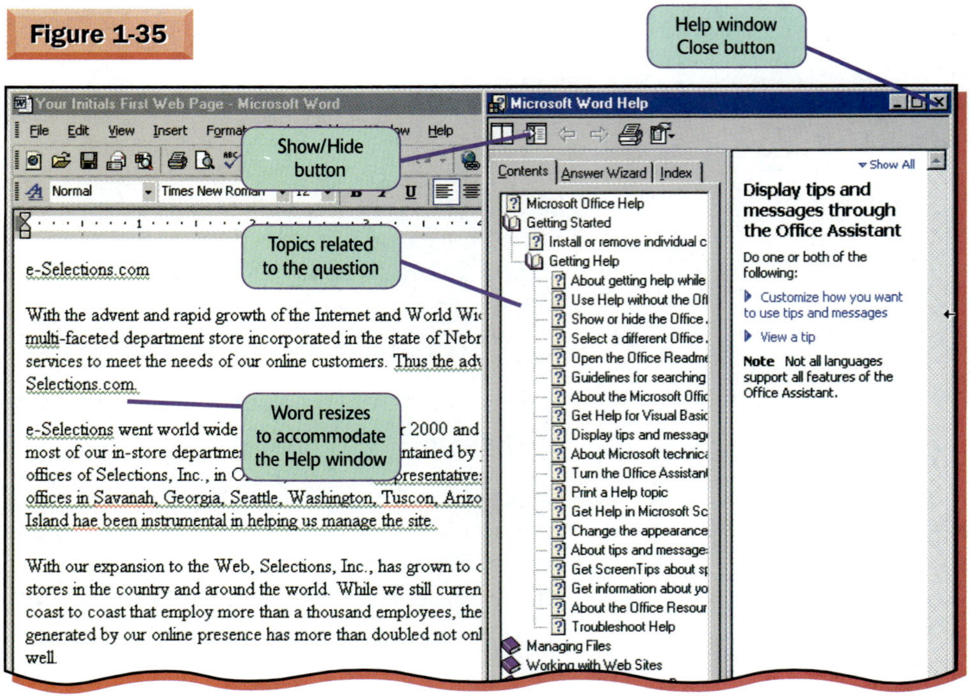

Using the Office Assistant

> **Tip** While Clippit is the default Office Assistant, Microsoft Office applications come with a gallery of different Office Assistant shapes you can select. Search the Help files to learn how to change the Office Assistant.

The *Office Assistant* is a help feature that is growing in popularity. The Office Assistant is easy to use, is personably animated, and provides a focused list of help topics related to questions you "ask."

If the Assistant was displayed the last time one of the Office applications was used, it will appear on screen when you launch an application. When closed, the Assistant waits on the Standard toolbar and appears when you call it to look up information about topics for which you need help. After you start the Office Assistant in one application, it remains on screen until you close it—even when you open another Office application. The information it provides when you ask it a question relates to the application that is active at the time you ask a question—regardless of what application was active when you started the Office Assistant.

Task 15:
To Use the Office Assistant

1. Launch Excel using the same techniques you used to launch Word.

2. Choose **Help | Show the Office Assistant**.

Figure 1-36

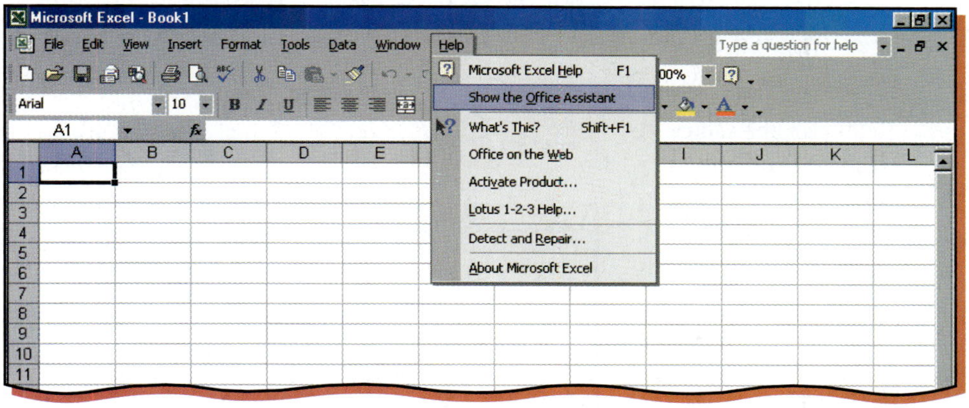

3. Click the **Office Assistant**.

Figure 1-37

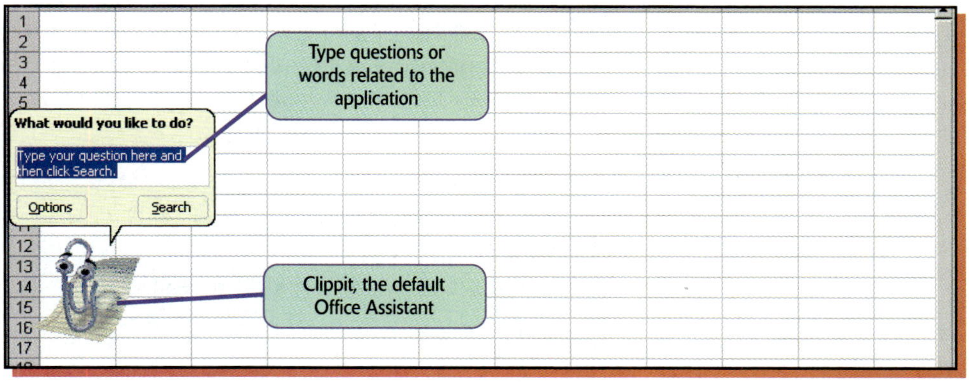

> **Tip** The Office Assistant dialog box opens in different shapes and sizes, depending on how it was last used.

4 Type **How do I print a worksheet?** The Office Assistant takes notes as you type.

5 Click **Search** to locate associated help topics and then select **About printing**. Information and topics containing information about printing worksheets appears.

6 Close the **Help** window. The Excel window resizes to its original size.

Figure 1-38

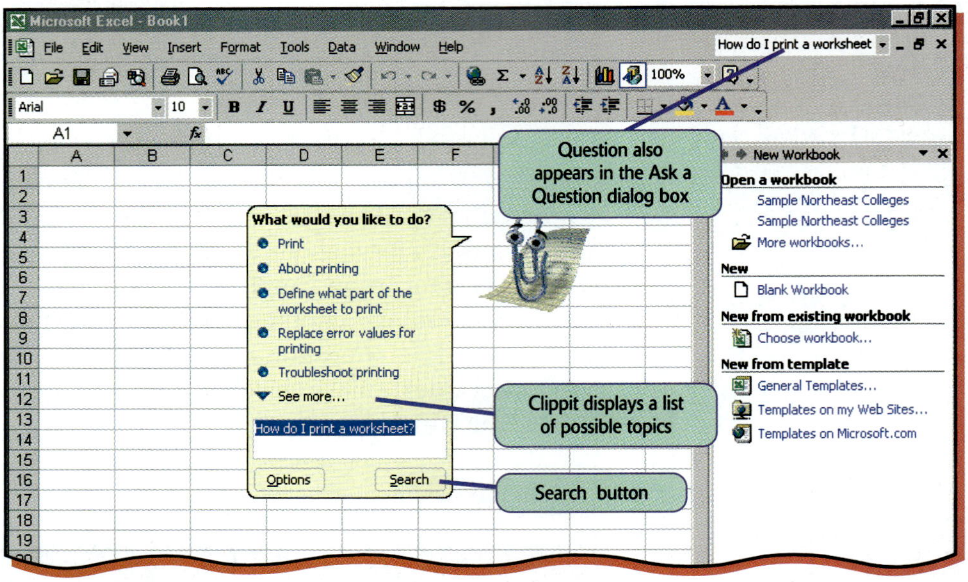

7 Right-click the **Office Assistant** and select **Hide**. The Office Assistant disappears and waits to be called again.

Figure 1-39

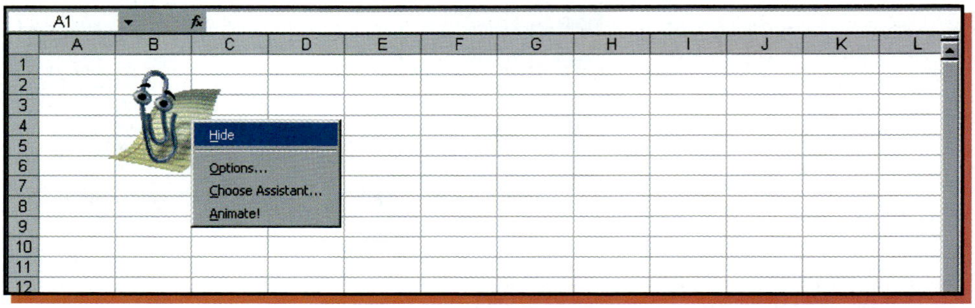

Troubleshooting After you select Hide several times, a dialog box will appear asking if you want to deactivate the Office Assistant. Read the options carefully and select the option that best represents how you want to use the Office Assistant.

Tip As you work with Help, you'll discover that the format of information displayed after you select a topic varies. In some cases, a list of step-by-step instructions appears in the Help window, and at other times, a list of further topics related to the subject you selected appears.

CHECK POINT

A number of features are available in Office XP to help you recover files. Each of these features is described in Table 1-5.

Table 1-5 Recovery Features

Feature	Description
Save on Crash	Word, Excel, and PowerPoint files that are open when a crash occurs are automatically saved so that they can be recovered after the system is restored.
Timed recovery save (AutoRecover)	An option set in Word, Excel, and PowerPoint to automatically save open files at regular intervals so that they can be recovered in case of power outages and Save on Crash failure.
Document Recovery task pane	An application pane that opens on the left side of an application window after a crash or improper shutdown, if recovery files are available. Users can choose to view both the recovery file and the original file to determine which file to use.
Hang Manager	A feature designed to "break" into a nonresponding application so that a Save on Crash action can be performed. You'll find this feature by choosing **Start | Programs | Microsoft Office Tools | Microsoft Office Application Recovery**.
Corrupt document recovery	An explicit corrupt document tool for recovering or repairing Word and Excel files. Simply select **Open and Repair** from the Open drop-down list as you open the file.
Office Safe Mode	Office-specific tools designed to fix and troubleshoot failed application startups. When an Office application fails to launch, a prompt should appear explaining the error and presenting start alternatives.

WEB TIP

If you're connected to the Internet, you can access one of several Web sites maintained by Microsoft to provide up-to-the-minute help online. The Web provides information directly from Microsoft support team members as well as information and helpful hints from other Office users. To access the Microsoft Web site directly from an Office XP application, choose **Help | Office on the Web**. Your default Web browser launches and displays the Office XP Update page.

Previewing and Printing

While each Office XP application has printing features that are specific to the application, printing basics are the same for all applications. In addition, each application has features that enable you to preview your files before printing them.

Previewing Pages

Even though most applications display files in WYSIWYG (*what you see is what you get*) format, sometimes what you see on paper is not quite what you expected. It is always a good idea to preview pages before sending them to the printer so that you can prevent some of these surprises. Each Office XP application has some type of Print Preview feature that enables you to see what the file will look like when it's printed.

- For all applications, you can display the preview by choosing **File | Print Preview,** or by clicking the **Print Preview** button on the Standard toolbar.
- In PowerPoint, you can display each slide on screen by choosing **View | Slide Show**, by pressing F5, by choosing **Slide Show | View Show**, or by clicking the **Slide Show** button at the bottom of the presentation window.

Task 16:
To Preview a File

1. Launch Word, if necessary, and open your *Copy (1) of e-Selections* file.
2. Click the **Print Preview** button on the Standard toolbar.

Figure 1-40

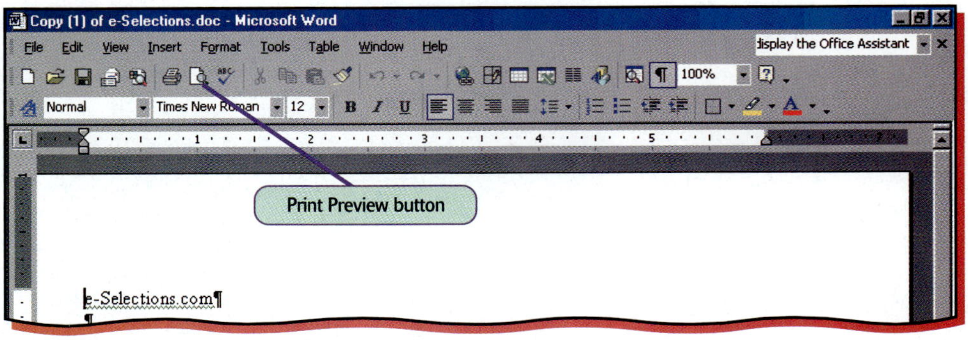

3. Click the **Close** button on the Preview toolbar.

Figure 1-41

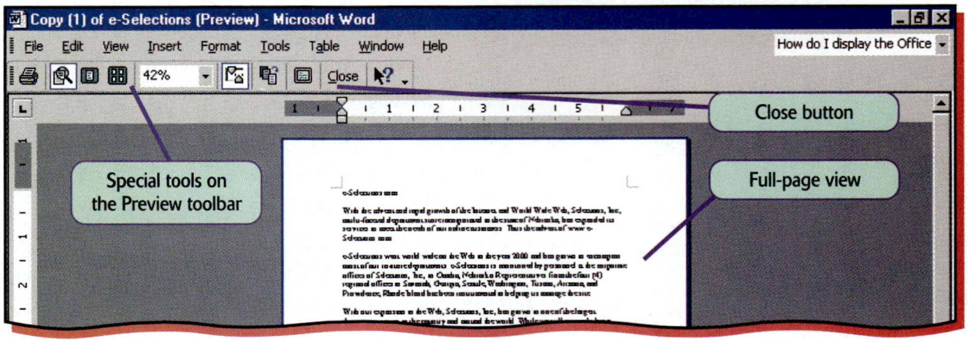

Setting Print Options and Printing

There are three basic methods for printing documents:

- Choose **File | Print** to display the Print dialog box and set print options.
- Click the **Print** button on the Standard toolbar to print the active file using default settings.
- Press Ctrl + P to display the Print dialog box and set print options.

The options displayed in the Print dialog box vary among Office applications. There are a number of options, however, that are common to the Print dialog boxes of all the applications.

Troubleshooting If the printer you want to use is not installed on your computer, check with your instructor or the lab assistant to obtain the necessary information and disks to install the printer.

Task 17:
To Set Print Options and Print a File

1. Choose **File** | **Print**.
2. Review print options and then click **OK**.

Tip You can print comments added to documents and other file materials by selecting items from the Print what drop-down list.

Figure 1-42

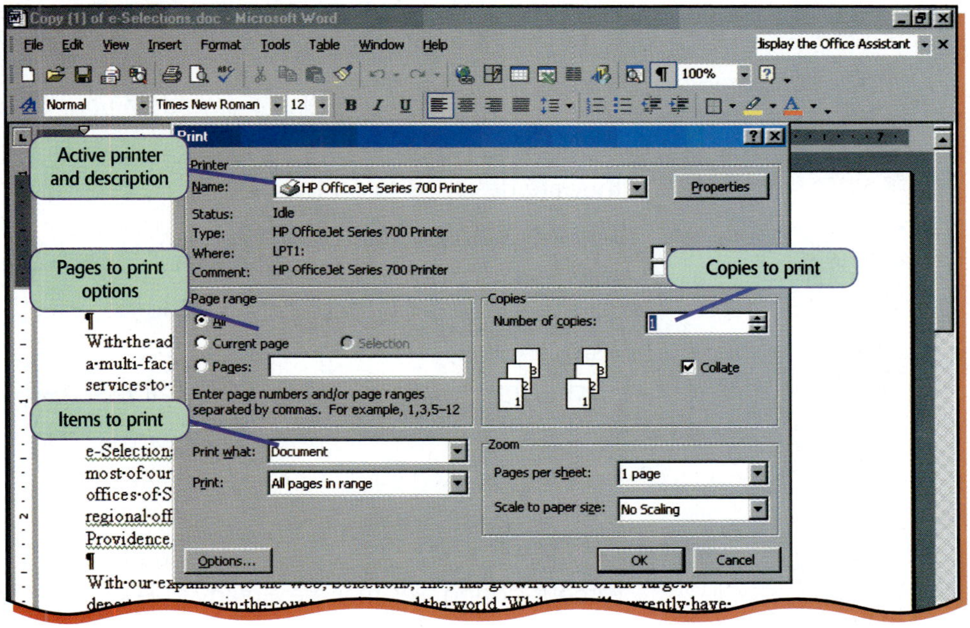

Exiting Applications

Before you exit Office XP applications, you should save work that you want to keep and close the files you have open. If you exit an application without saving changes to open files, the Office XP application prompts you to save changes to the file. Be sure to read these prompts carefully to ensure that you take the action you intend and avoid unnecessary loss of data.

To exit Office XP applications, use one of the following procedures:

- Click the application **Close** ☒ button.
- Choose **File | Exit**. If multiple files are open in the application, all files close as you exit the application.
- Click the **Application Control** icon at the left end of the title bar, and select **Close**.
- Press Alt + F4.
- Right-click the **application** button on the Windows taskbar and select **Close**.

SUMMARY AND EXERCISES

SUMMARY

- The many common elements of Office XP enable you to use techniques learned in one application to accomplish the same task in other applications.
- Applications can be launched in a variety of ways, based on your preferences and how Office XP is installed on your computer.
- Screen elements appear each time you open an Office XP application; they are designed to control the way files appear in the application window, to aid in file management tasks, and to provide easy access to commonly performed tasks.
- File management tasks include opening files, creating new files, saving files, and editing file properties.
- Documents can be opened as a copy or as a read-only file to ensure that your original remains intact.
- New documents can be created as blank files or by using a predesigned template.
- Word, Excel, and PowerPoint enable you to open or create multiple files without closing files that are already open.
- When you elect to close a file that has been edited, regardless of which procedure you use, the application will prompt you to save the file.
- Files from all applications can be saved in a format recognized by the Web.
- Files saved as Web pages can be previewed from Office XP applications.
- The My Places bar, which appears in the Open and Save As dialog boxes, can be customized to hold folders and files you access frequently.
- The Open and Save As dialog boxes can be sized to display more information.
- File properties are automatically stored with each file you save unless you set options to prevent personal information from being saved with the file.
- Numerous help features are available. The Office Assistant and the Ask a Question features enable you to ask questions about the active application.
- Printing basics, such as previewing and setting print options, are basically the same for all Office XP applications.

KEY TERMS & SKILLS

KEY TERMS

corrupt document (p. 1-29)
embedded fonts (p. 1-19)
Hang Manager (p. 1-29)
Language bar (p. 1-9)
launch (p. 1-3)
My Places bar (p. 1-14)
Office Assistant (p. 1-27)
Office Safe mode (p. 1-29)
properties (p. 1-24)
Status bar (p. 1-7)
task pane (p. 1-7)
templates (p. 1-4)
toolbar (p. 1-7)
View buttons (p. 1-7)
Zoom (p. 1-12)

SKILLS

Add a folder to the My Places bar (p. 1-22)
Close a file (p. 1-18)
Close and open the task pane (p. 1-8)
Create new files (p. 1-16)
Create new folders (p. 1-19)
Display and hide toolbars (p. 1-9)
Edit file properties (p. 1-25)
Exit applications (p. 1-31)
Hide and display the Language bar (p. 1-9)
Launch applications (p. 1-3)
Launch Microsoft Word (p. 1-6)
Obtain help online (p. 1-29)
Open a copy of a document (p. 1-15)
Open a file (p. 1-13)
Preview pages (p. 1-30)
Print (p. 1-31)
Recover files (p. 1-29)
Remove personal information from a file on save (p. 1-25)
Save a copy of a file (p. 1-19)
Save a file (p. 1-18)
Save a file as a Web page (p. 1-21)
Set print options (p. 1-30)
Set Zoom control (p. 1-12)
Size a dialog box (p. 1-21)
Switch among open files (p. 1-17)
Turn off auto-customization features for menus and toolbars (p. 1-11)
Use Ask a Question (p. 1-26)
Use the Office Assistant (p. 1-27)
View the Web file (p. 1-23)

STUDY QUESTIONS

MULTIPLE CHOICE

1. Which procedures for accomplishing tasks are basically the same in all Office XP applications?
   a. presentation design
   b. file management
   c. data management
   d. toolbar options
2. Which are three options for initiating commands in Office XP?
   a. toolbar buttons, keystrokes, and mouse options
   b. taskbar buttons, menu commands, and keystrokes
   c. menu commands, keystrokes, and toolbar buttons
   d. both b and c
3. Which of the following procedures is *not* an option to open an existing document, workbook, presentation, or database?
   a. choose **Start | Open Office Document**
   b. choose **File | Open**
   c. press Ctrl + P
   d. click the **Open** button
4. The programs that display new files when you launch them are
   a. Access, PowerPoint, and Word.
   b. Excel, Access, and PowerPoint.
   c. Access and Excel.
   d. Word, Excel, and PowerPoint.
5. To change the portion of the file that appears on screen, adjust the
   a. task pane.
   b. Zoom control.
   c. toolbars.
   d. status bar.
6. Save commands include all the following *except*
   a. Save.
   b. Save As.
   c. Save as HTML.
   d. Save as Web Page.
7. To create a new file after an application is launched,
   a. press Ctrl + N.
   b. click the **New** button on the Standard toolbar.
   c. choose **File | New**.
   d. all of the above
8. The Ask a Question text box appears on the
   a. title bar.
   b. menu bar.
   c. toolbar.
   d. task pane.
9. Techniques for recovering files in Office XP include
   a. AutoRecover.
   b. recovering corrupt files.
   c. saving on crash.
   d. all of the above

SHORT ANSWER

1. List three different ways you can launch an application.
2. Identify several different ways to exit an application.
3. How do you open and close the task pane?
4. Regardless of the procedure you are using, what features will help prevent unwanted loss of data, and when will this option be presented to you?
5. How can you turn off the Office Assistant?
6. What is the difference between Save and Save As and when would you use each command?
7. What is Office Safe mode and when will it be used?
8. When would you remove personal information from files?
9. What are embedded fonts?
10. How do you resize a dialog box?

FILL IN THE BLANK

1. When you want to leave the original file intact but also want to use the file as a basis for a new file, you can open a(n) ____________ of the original file and save it as a new file.
2. The ____________ appears down the left side of the Open and Save As dialog boxes.
3. ____________ is the default Office Assistant.
4. Click the ____________ button to switch to a different open file.
5. ____________ enables you to see what your printout will look like before you print it.
6. Display a list of toolbars by choosing the ____________ command on the ____________menu.
7. The ____________ setting controls the portion of a file that appears on screen.
8. Files saved for Web use are saved with a(n) ____________ extension.
9. The ____________ toolbar appears to float on screen when it is active in an Office XP application.
10. Options for turning off the auto-customization feature appear in the ____________ dialog box.

FOR DISCUSSION

1. Briefly discuss when, how, and why you would use the Office Assistant.
2. Discuss the different ways to save a document and explain when and why you might choose each particular option.
3. The Word screen on one computer in the lab looks different from the Word screen on another computer in the lab. Explain the possible reasons why.
4. How do you add a folder to the My Places bar and why would you want to?

GUIDED EXERCISES

1 LAUNCHING APPLICATIONS

A good way to test the capacity of your computer system is to launch multiple applications and see if the performance speed keeps pace. You already have Word and Excel running. To test your system, you will launch various applications using a variety of different techniques.

1. Choose **Start** | **Programs** | **Accessories** | **Windows Explorer**.
2. Choose **Start** | **Programs** | **Accessories** | **Calculator**.
3. Choose **Start** | **Programs** | **Internet Explorer**.

2 SWITCHING AND EXITING APPLICATIONS

Now that you have examined the capacity of your computer, you can close all the open applications except Word.

1. Switch to Calculator and click the **Close** button.
2. Switch to Windows Explorer and choose **File** | **Close**.
3. Switch to Internet Explorer and press Alt + F4.
4. Right-click the **Excel** button on the taskbar and select **Close**.

3 PRINTING AND SAVING FILES

The e-Selections file that you opened and saved can be printed and then saved using a different file name.

1. Switch to the *Copy of e-Selections.doc* file, if necessary.
2. Choose **File** | **Print**, review print options and close the Print dialog box.
3. Click the **Print** button to print the file using default settings.
4. Choose **File** | **Save As** and open your personal folder on the My Places bar.
5. Type *Your Initials* **e-Selections** in the **File name** text box and press Enter.

4 CREATING A NEW FILE

The main purpose for creating new documents is to type text in the document work area. It's time to create your first document and type some text.

1. Switch to Word, if necessary.
2. Create a new document using the procedure you prefer.
3. Type the text shown here at the top of the document—it's okay if you make mistakes—and don't worry if your lines break at different spots from those shown here in this text.

   An apple or two for lunch on Monday is an excellent antidote to a weekend of overeating. Besides all this, the apple comes in its own packaging, travels well, and keeps indefinitely. What could be simpler?

4. Save your document in your personal folder, naming the file *An Apple on Monday*.
5. Follow your instructor's direction for placing your name on the document. Then print a copy of the document.

ON YOUR OWN

The difficulty of these case studies varies:

are the least difficult; *are more difficult; and* *are the most difficult.*

1 LAUNCHING APPLICATIONS AND WORKING WITH TOOLBARS

Launch Microsoft Excel 2002 and display the Picture toolbar. Record the names of each of the tools contained on the toolbar and identify when you would use the toolbar. Hide the toolbar.

2 CHANGING THE ZOOM SETTING

Change the Zoom setting for the blank Excel workbook to Selection using the Zoom dialog box. Record how the workbook appears. Then change the Zoom setting to 50% using the Zoom drop-down list on the Standard toolbar and record how the workbook appears on screen. Change the Zoom settings back to 100% using the preferred procedure.

3 OPENING AND SAVING AN EXCEL FILE

Open the *Sample Northeast Colleges.xls* file that you downloaded from the Prentice Hall Web site. Type Your Name in the active location. Then save your file as a new file in your personal folder. Name the file *Your Initials Sample Colleges*.

4 PREVIEWING AND PRINTING EXCEL FILES

Preview your *Sample Colleges* Excel file to see how it will print. Print a copy of the file.

5 SAVING, PREVIEWING, AND PRINTING AN EXCEL FILE AS A WEB PAGE

Save your *Sample Colleges* worksheet as a Web page, storing it in your personal folder. Preview the file in your default Web browser. Print a copy of the file from the Web browser.

FROM THE FILES

You Will Need

- ✔ e-Selections Online.doc
- ✔ Fire Center.doc

PROJECT 2

Common Text Elements

In the previous project, you learned some of the basic elements and features that all Microsoft Office XP applications have in common. In this project, you will learn some techniques for working with text in all of the Office applications—how to *format*, *enhance*, copy, move, and proof text. You'll also learn how to create and format text boxes and how to add text to those boxes.

OBJECTIVES

After completing this project, you will be able to:

- *Navigate documents*
- *Select text*
- *Insert, delete, and replace text*
- *Enhance, format, and align text*
- *Move and copy text and text format*
- *Use the Office Clipboard*
- *Undo and redo changes*
- *Use Office proofing tools*
- *Use AutoCorrect*
- *Use text boxes*

e-selections Running Case

You're off and running toward mastering the basics of the Microsoft Office XP applications that you will need as you work toward establishing yourself with e-Selections.com! Learning how to identify screen features, manage files, and get help was actually quite easy. Now that you're more comfortable with the basics, you decide to put those keyboarding skills to good use and try working with text…

PROJECT 2

Common Text Elements

The Setup

In Common Elements Project 1, you learned a number of screen features and other tools that control the way documents appear on screen. As you worked with these screen features, the figures in the text changed to reflect screen changes. Before starting Common Elements Projects 2 and 3, it is important that you check some of those screen settings to ensure that your screen matches the figures in the projects. The settings shown in Table 2-1 will be used in both Projects 2 and 3.

Table 2-1 Common Elements Projects 2 and 3 Screen Settings

Feature	Setting
Office Assistant	Hide the Office Assistant.
Toolbars and Menus	Set the toolbars to appear on two lines and set the Always show full menus option. Hide all toolbars except Standard and Formatting.
Task pane	Close the task pane.

Troubleshooting Because screen settings and installation options vary, you may see differences between your screens and those shown in this text.

The Challenge

Typing and formatting text is a skill required for working in all Office XP applications. The *e-Selections Online* document needs to be dressed up a bit. Formatting and text enhancements can be applied to create the document shown in Figure 2-1.

Figure 2-1

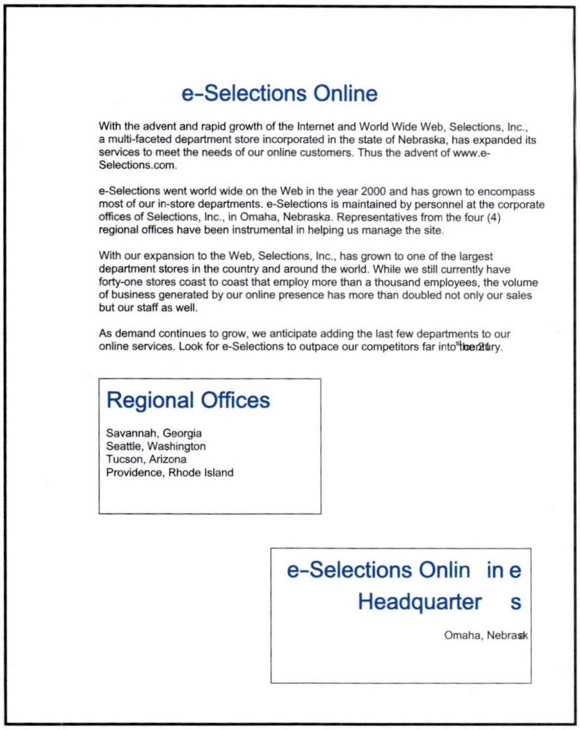

e-Selections Online

With the advent and rapid growth of the Internet and World Wide Web, Selections, Inc., a multi-faceted department store incorporated in the state of Nebraska, has expanded its services to meet the needs of our online customers. Thus the advent of www.e-Selections.com.

e-Selections went world wide on the Web in the year 2000 and has grown to encompass most of our in-store departments. e-Selections is maintained by personnel at the corporate offices of Selections, Inc., in Omaha, Nebraska. Representatives from the four (4) regional offices have been instrumental in helping us manage the site.

With our expansion to the Web, Selections, Inc., has grown to one of the largest department stores in the country and around the world. While we still currently have forty-one stores coast to coast that employ more than a thousand employees, the volume of business generated by our online presence has more than doubled not only our sales but our staff as well.

As demand continues to grow, we anticipate adding the last few departments to our online services. Look for e-Selections to outpace our competitors far into the 21st century.

Regional Offices

Savannah, Georgia
Seattle, Washington
Tucson, Arizona
Providence, Rhode Island

e-Selections Onlin in e
Headquarter s

Omaha, Nebrask

The Solution

Using Word, you will apply text formatting features that are common to all Office XP applications—exceptions will be noted.

Working with Text

Whether you're typing a letter in Word, entering values in an Excel worksheet, adding data to an Access table, or creating slides in PowerPoint, you'll type and edit text. Learning how to navigate, edit, enhance, format, *align*, move, and copy text now will make working with text in each application easier.

Navigating Text

Navigating text simply means moving from character to character, paragraph to paragraph, screen to screen, or page to page in a file. You can use both the keyboard and the mouse to move the insertion point within a file. Mouse techniques that are common to all Office applications include using scroll bars to display different parts of a file and clicking to position the insertion point in the paragraph, cell, or field you want to edit. Table 2-2 identifies navigation keystrokes common to Word, Excel, PowerPoint, and Access.

Table 2-2 Navigation Keystrokes

Press	To Move
←	Left one character or column
→	Right one character or column
↓	Down one line or row
↑	Up one line or row
Page Up	Up one screen
PageDown	Down one screen
Home	To the beginning of a line or row
End	To the end of a line or row
Ctrl + End	To the end of a file
Ctrl + Home	To the beginning of a file

As you work with each application, you'll discover additional keystrokes specific to that application. For example: in Excel, you'll learn to move from worksheet to worksheet in a workbook; in PowerPoint, you'll learn to display presentation slides; and in Access, you'll learn to move among records in forms using the navigation controls.

Inserting, Deleting, and Typing Over Text

All Office XP applications are set with *Insert mode* active so that you simply position the insertion point where you want to insert text and start typing. Existing text moves over to make room for the new text. To *replace* existing text with new text, you can select text that you want to replace (see Table 2-3) and type the new text in its place.

Tip In Word, you can also switch to *Overtype mode* by pressing Insert on the keyboard or by double-clicking the OVR area of the status bar.

The technique used to *delete* text depends on the position of the insertion point:

- Position the insertion point immediately before the text you want to delete and press Delete once for each character and space you want to delete.
- Position the insertion point immediately after the text you want to delete and press Bksp once for each character and space you want to delete.

You can also use text selection techniques to select text and replace it with other text. Techniques for selecting text vary somewhat from application to application, but some basics are common to all applications. Table 2-3 summarizes common text selection techniques.

Table 2-3 Common Text Selection Techniques

Action	To Select
Double-click a word	The word
Triple-click a word	The paragraph or table cell
Press Shift + arrow keys	Characters, lines, or rows from the insertion point

Text appears highlighted—white text on a black background—when it is selected. Text you type and keyboard keys you press while text is selected replace selected text.

Tip The task pane also contains formatting features that are explored more thoroughly in the Microsoft Word 2002 book and the Word section of the Microsoft Office XP book.

Enhancing and Formatting Text

Word, Excel, PowerPoint, and Access datasheets share common methods for changing the appearance of text. Special features enable you to enhance and format text by changing the text *font*—the shape and size of text characters—as well as changing text *attributes*—how text characters appear. Changes you make to text that has already been typed affect the selected text only. However, you can "turn on" an enhancement or change font characteristics before typing text and it will remain active until you turn the enhancement "off" or change the font again when you are finished. Tools on the Formatting toolbar, menu commands on the Format menu, and dialog boxes can all be used to format text.

Task 1: To Navigate, Select, Enhance, and Format Text

1. Open the document *e-Selections Online.doc.*
2. Select the title *e-Selections Online.* The text appears highlighted.
3. Click the **Bold** button on the Formatting toolbar to make the text appear in bold letters.

Figure 2-2

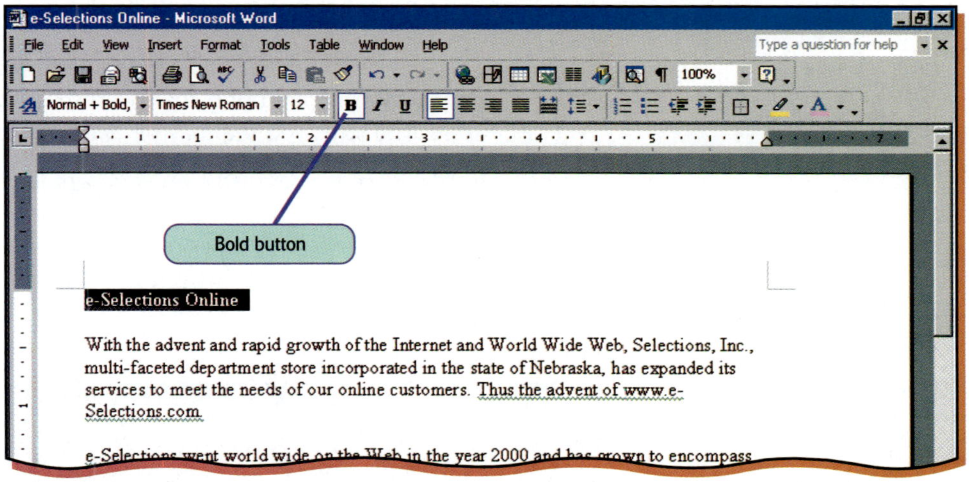

4. Click the **Font** down arrow.

5. Select **Arial Black**. The selected text reformats with the new font.

Figure 2-3

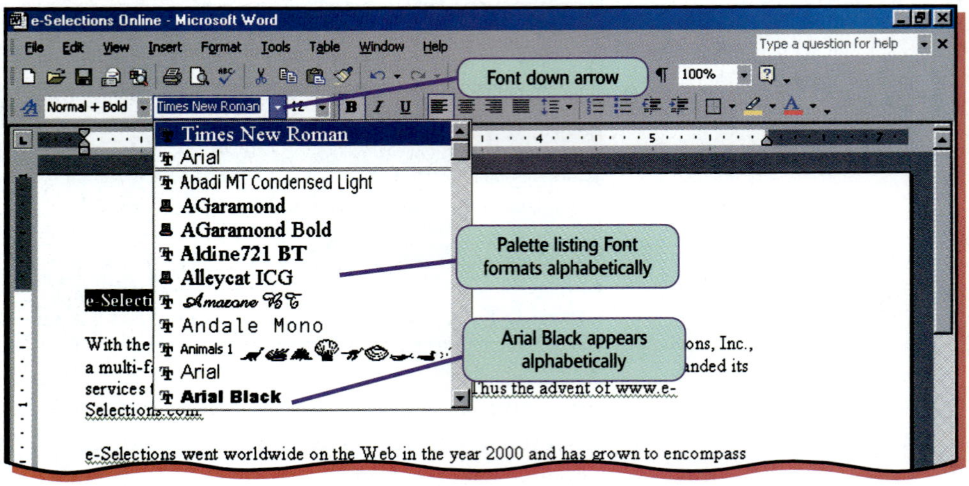

6. Click the **Font Size** down arrow. A list of numbers appears on a palette, with the current font size highlighted.

7. Select **24**. The title appears much larger.

8. Click the **Italic** *I* button on the Formatting toolbar. The title appears slanted and the Italic button is white.

Figure 2-4

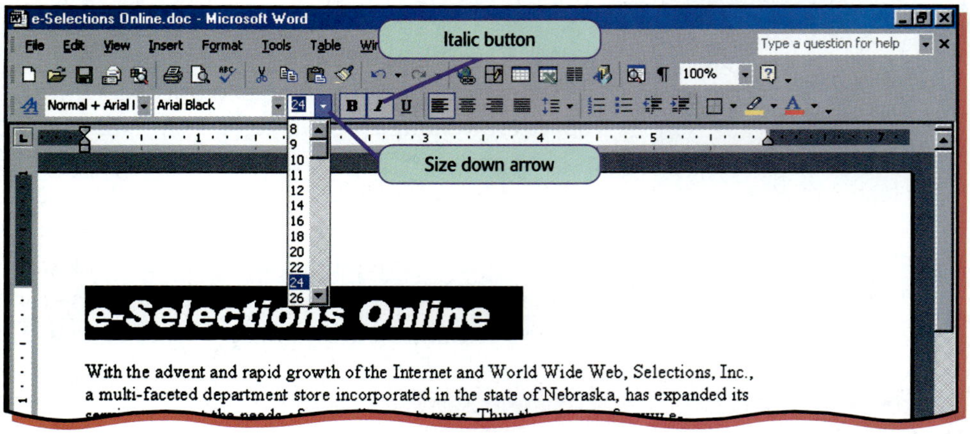

Troubleshooting The fonts installed on your computer and the printer that you are using control, to some extent, the fonts that you see listed. The fonts you see may be different from those shown here.

If Arial Black is unavailable on your font list, select a similar font or follow the direction of your instructor.

9. Choose **Format | Font** to open the Font dialog box.

Figure 2-5

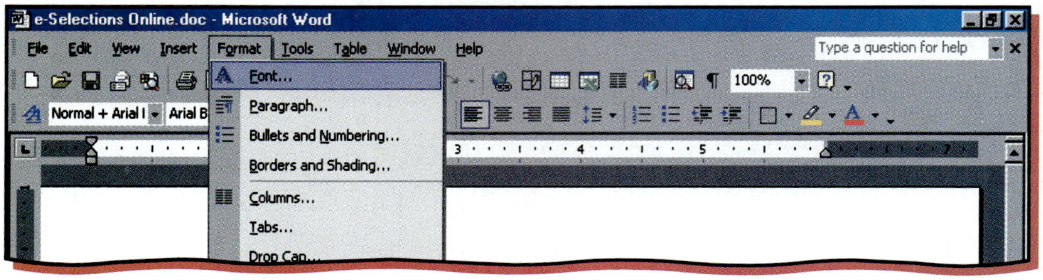

10 Click the **Font color** down arrow. A palette of colors appears.

11 Click **Blue** and click **OK**. The title text is reformatted in blue print.

> **Tip** Notice the special effects listed in the Font dialog box. As you become more comfortable applying standard enhancements to text, you may want to try applying some of these special effects and explore options contained on other pages of this dialog box.

Figure 2-6

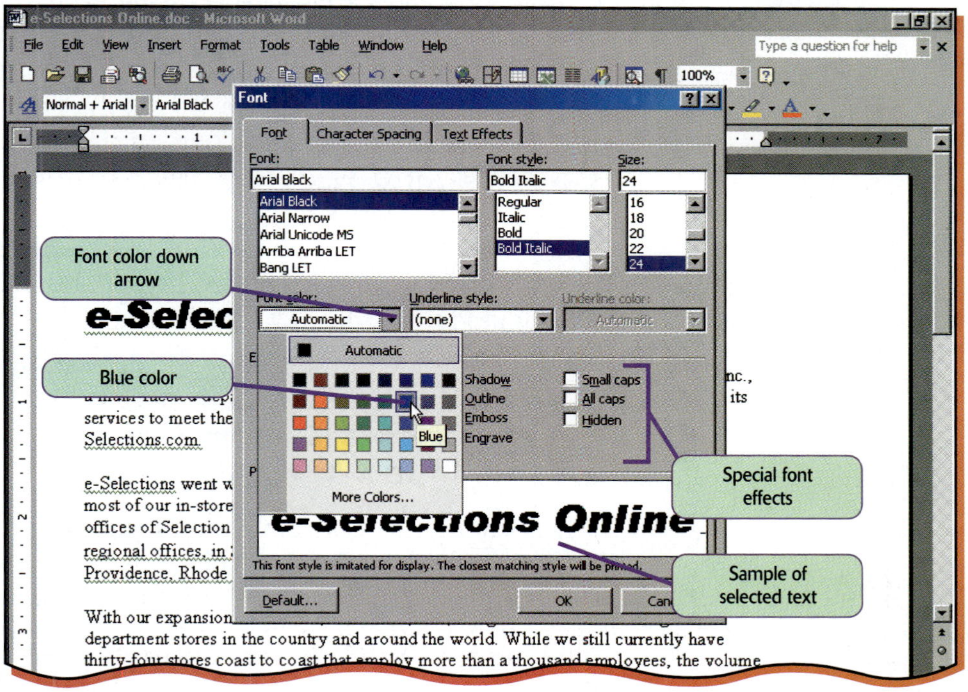

12 Press Ctrl + End to position the insertion point at the bottom of the document.

13 Choose **File | Save As** and save the file using the file name *Your Initials e-Selections Online*.

> **Other Ways** To apply font color:
>
> - Click the Font Color down arrow on the Formatting toolbar.

Figure 2-7

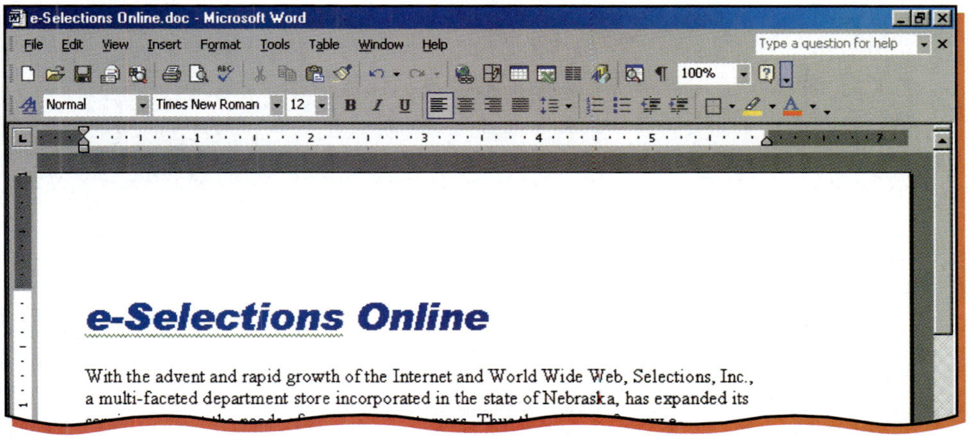

WEB TIP

Additional fonts are available online from a variety of different companies. Search the Internet for fonts to see what's available.

Copying and Moving Text

The *Cut* command is used to remove text from its current position. The *Copy* command leaves text at its current position. Office XP offers three different techniques for moving and copying text:

- Click the **Cut**, **Copy**, or **Paste** buttons on the Standard toolbar.
- Choose **Edit | Cut/Copy/Paste**.
- Press Ctrl + X to Cut; Ctrl + C to Copy; or Ctrl + V to Paste.

When you use the Cut command to move text or the Copy command to copy text, Office XP applications place the selected text or information on the Clipboard, where it stays until you *paste* it where you want it.

Although other Windows applications store only one snippet of information on the Clipboard, Office XP contains a special feature that enables you to store multiple snippets of information (up to 24) from all types of Office applications on a special Office Clipboard. You can then choose the snippet or snippets to place when you paste. The Office Clipboard appears in the task pane when it is active.

Task 2:
To Display the Office Clipboard

1 Choose **Edit | Office Clipboard**. The task pane opens and displays the Office Clipboard.

Tip To display the Office Clipboard when the task pane is already open, click the task pane down arrow and select **Clipboard**.

Figure 2-8

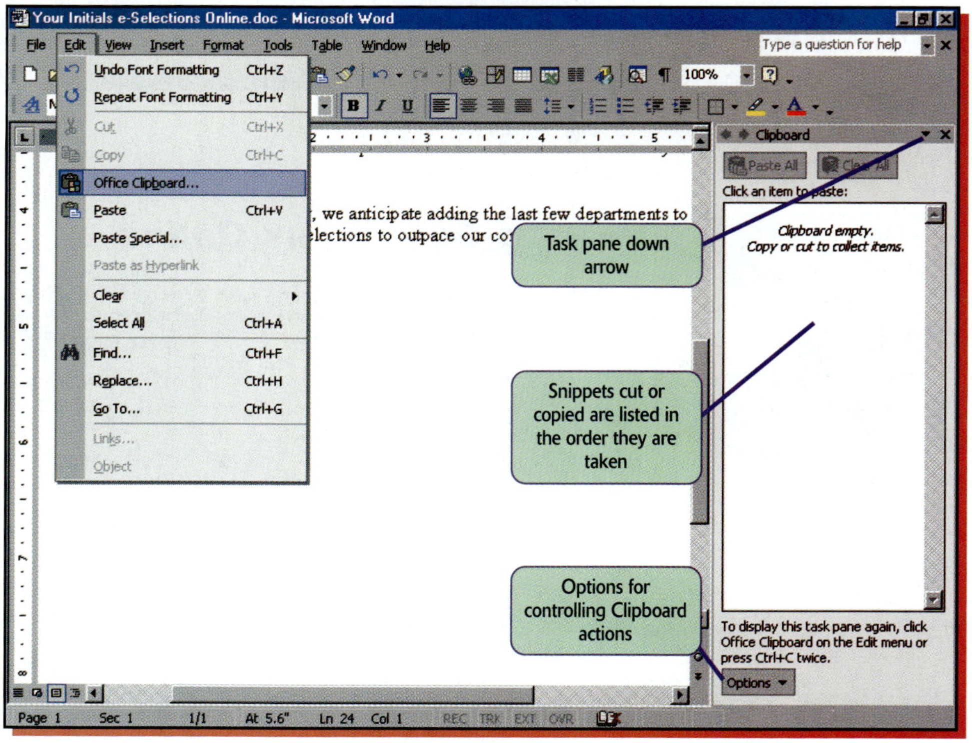

CHECK POINT

The Office Clipboard may appear automatically as you work when you cut or copy multiple snippets of information in one or more Office XP applications. Normally, items are added to the Office Clipboard only when it is active. Options that control the way the Office Clipboard acts are found on the Options drop-down list that appears at the bottom of the Clipboard task pane. These options are described in Table 2-4.

Table 2-4 Options for Controlling the Office Clipboard

Select the Option	To
Show Office Clipboard Automatically	Activate the Office Clipboard when you cut or copy the second snippet.
Collect Without Showing Office Clipboard	Places items on the Office Clipboard even when it is not open.
Show Office Clipboard Icon on Taskbar	Places an Office Clipboard icon on the tray of the Taskbar so that you can access the Office Clipboard more easily.
Show Status Near Taskbar When Copying	Displays a screen tip above the tray on the Taskbar each time you copy something to the Clipboard. The tip lets you know how many items are currently on the Office Clipboard.

In addition, you can display the Office Clipboard by pressing Ctrl + C twice. The icons that appear beside snippets on the Office Clipboard identify the application from which the snippet was taken. You can paste all snippets at the current cursor location by clicking the Paste All button. You can also click an individual snippet to insert it at the insertion point.

Task 3:
To Copy and Move Text

1. Position the insertion point at the bottom of the document, if necessary.

2. Click the **Bold** **B** button and type Regional Offices.

3. Click the **Bold** **B** button to turn bold off and then press Enter twice.

Figure 2-9

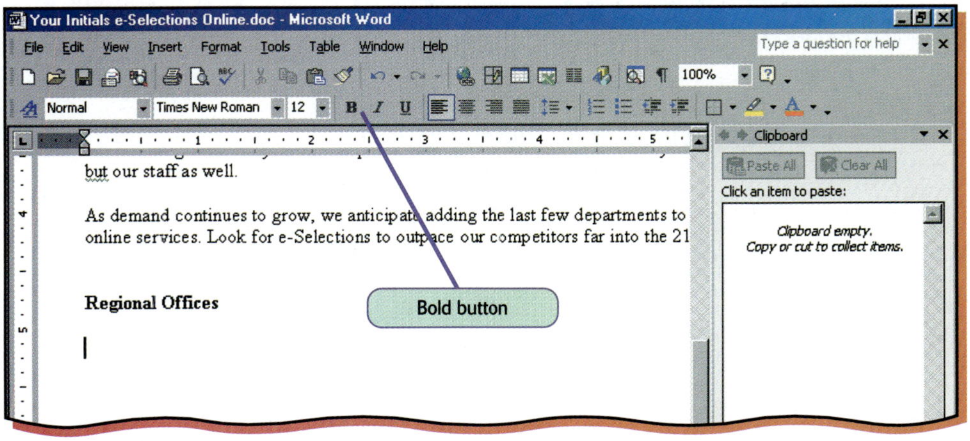

4 Select the text *Savanah, Georgia* in the second paragraph and click the **Cut** button to remove selected text from its current position and place it on the clipboard.

Figure 2-10

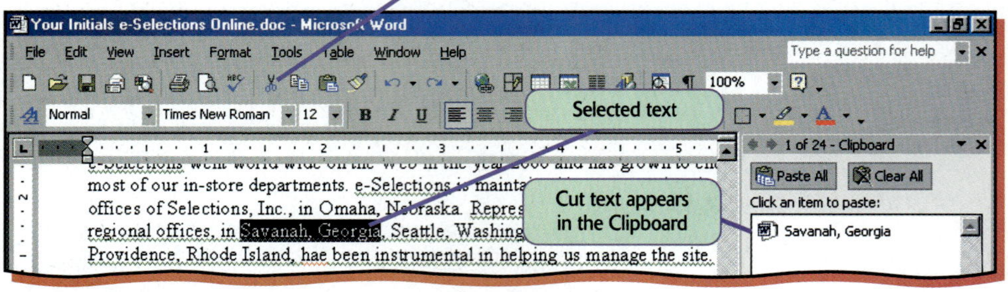

5 Move to the end of the document and click the **Paste** button to place text from the clipboard at the end of the document.

Figure 2-11

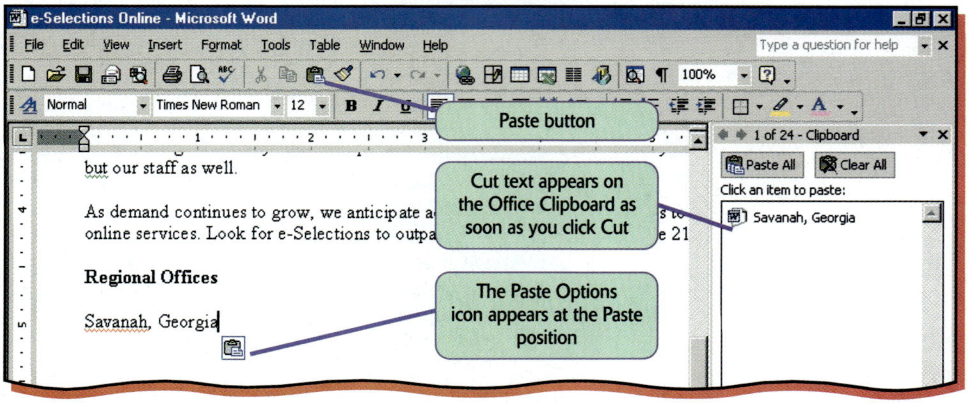

6 Click the **Paste Options** icon next to the pasted text and review the options that appear.

7 Select **Keep Source Formatting** to close the option list and then press Enter.

Figure 2-12

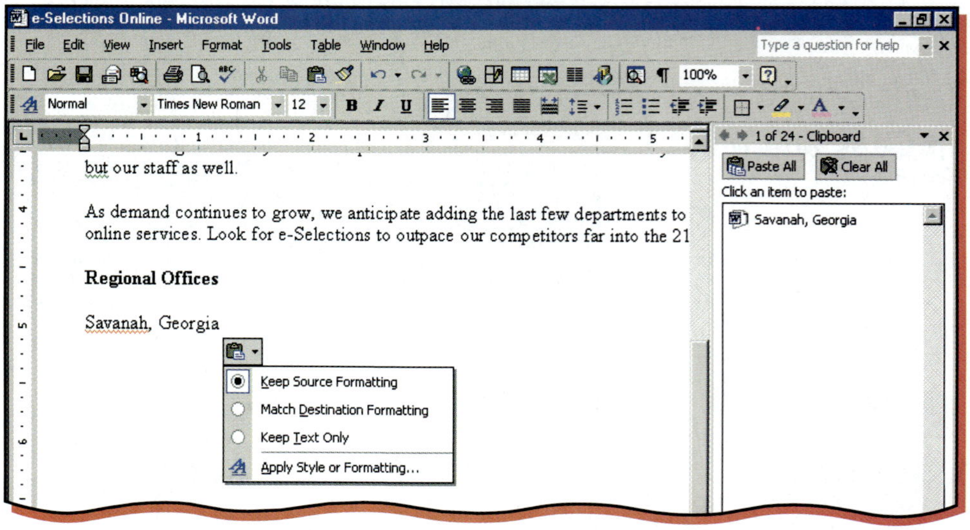

Tip

Selecting the Keep Source Formatting option tells Word to include any enhancements and special formatting that were originally applied to the text when you paste the text in the new location. To drop special formatting from the original text so that text is formatted to follow font characteristics of the paragraph in which you paste the text, you would select Match Destination Formatting from the Past Options list.

8 Repeat the procedures in Steps 4–6 to move the cities and states for the other three regional offices so that they appear as shown in Figure 2-13.

9 Select the text, *in,,, and,* that is highlighted in Figure 2-13 and delete it.

10 Save changes to the document.

Tip Snippets of information are collected on the Clipboard task pane in the order in which you cut or copy them. The most recently cut or copied snippet appears at the top of the task pane for easy access.

Figure 2-13

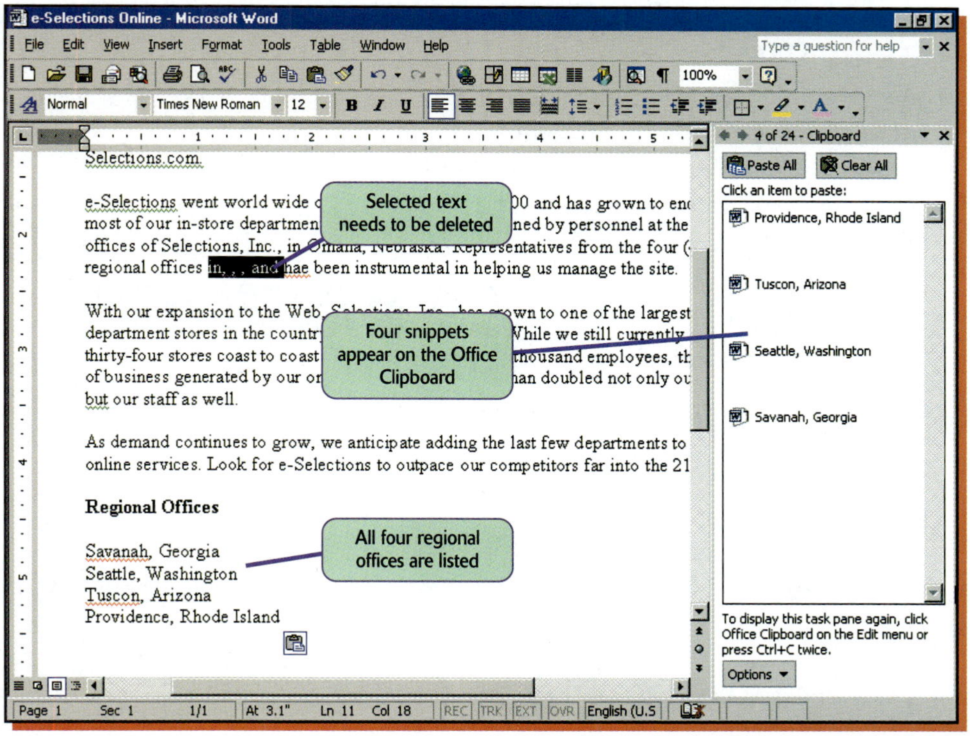

Copying Text Formats

Formatting text by applying enhancements, color, and font styles can be tedious—especially when you want to format text in several different locations and maintain consistency of format. You're in luck! Office XP applications are equipped with a *Format Painter* that's designed to help you copy text format and apply the format to other text. Using the Format Painter to copy format is basically a three-step process:

1. Select the text with the format that you want to copy.
2. Click the **Format Painter** button.
3. "Paint" the format onto the text you want to format.

Tip Double-click the Format Painter button to copy format to multiple locations. When you're finished painting all the text with the copied format, click the Format Painter button again to turn it off.

Task 4:

To Copy Text Formats Using the Format Painter

1. Close the Office Clipboard and then select the formatted title text, *e-Selections Online*.

2. Click the **Format Painter** button on the Standard toolbar to copy the format of the selected text.

3. Scroll to the bottom of the document page until the *Regional Offices* text appears on the screen.

4. Click and drag the paintbrush across the text *Regional Offices* to paint the copied format onto the text.

5. Click anywhere in the document to deselect the text.

Tip Double-click the Format Painter to apply the format to text in multiple places in a file or to text in other files.

Figure 2-14

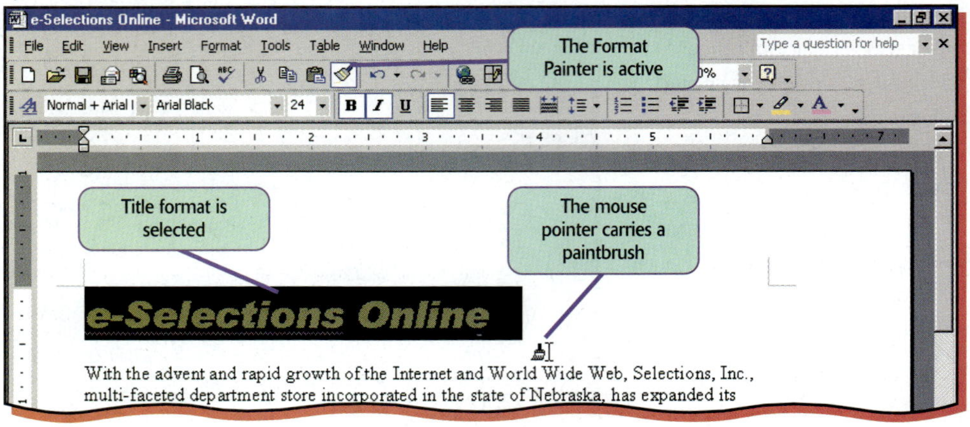

Figure 2-15

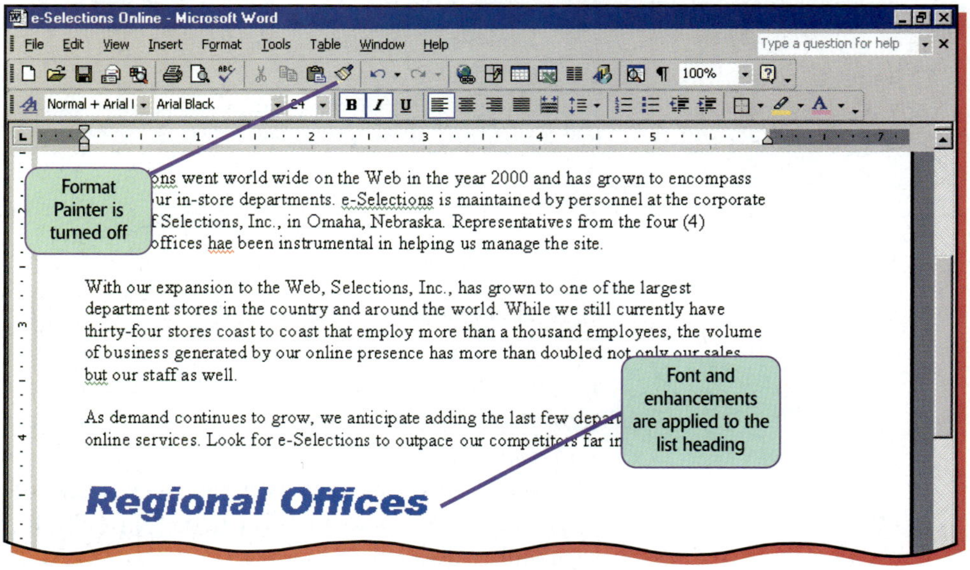

Troubleshooting Positioning the insertion point in a word is usually sufficient to copy the text format, but when multiple fonts and character settings are contained in a paragraph or in a word select the character that contains the format you want to copy.

Using Undo and Redo

The *Undo* feature in all Office XP applications reverses actions; the *Redo* feature restores actions that were reversed. Using Undo and Redo is quite simple. Office XP applications offer keyboard, mouse, and menu procedures for these two features, as shown in Table 2-5.

Table 2-5 Undo/Redo Procedures

Command	Mouse	Keyboard	Menu
Undo	Click the **Undo** button on the Standard toolbar.	Press Ctrl + Z	Choose **Edit** | **Undo**
Redo	Click the **Redo** button on the Standard toolbar.	Press Ctrl + Y	Choose **Edit** | **Redo**

Each of these actions reverses the last action, but Office XP applications enable you to reverse numerous actions in succession. In addition, you can click the down arrow beside the Undo or Redo buttons and select the action you want to reverse. All actions down to and including the action you select can be reversed.

Aligning Text

Among the buttons you'll find on the Formatting toolbars in Word, Excel, PowerPoint, and on Access Forms are buttons that control text alignment. You can use these alignment buttons to adjust the position of text in document paragraphs, table or worksheet cells, database forms, and presentation slides. You can also access alignment commands using the keyboard. The menu commands for setting alignment vary among the applications. Table 2-6 identifies common procedures for aligning text in Word, Excel, PowerPoint, and on Access Forms.

Table 2-6 Alignment Commands

Command	Mouse	Keyboard
Align Left	Click the **Align Left** button on the Formatting toolbar.	Press Ctrl + L
Center	Click the **Center** button on the Formatting toolbar.	Press Ctrl + E
Align Right	Click the **Align Right** button on the Formatting toolbar.	Press Ctrl + R
Justify	Click the **Justify** button on the Formatting toolbar.	Press Ctrl + J

Task 5:

To Align Text and Use Undo and Redo

1. Position the insertion point in the title of your *e-Selections Online.doc* document.
2. Click the **Align Right** button on the Formatting toolbar.
3. Undo the action to reposition the text at the left margin.
4. Center the title.
5. Save changes to the document.

Figure 2-16

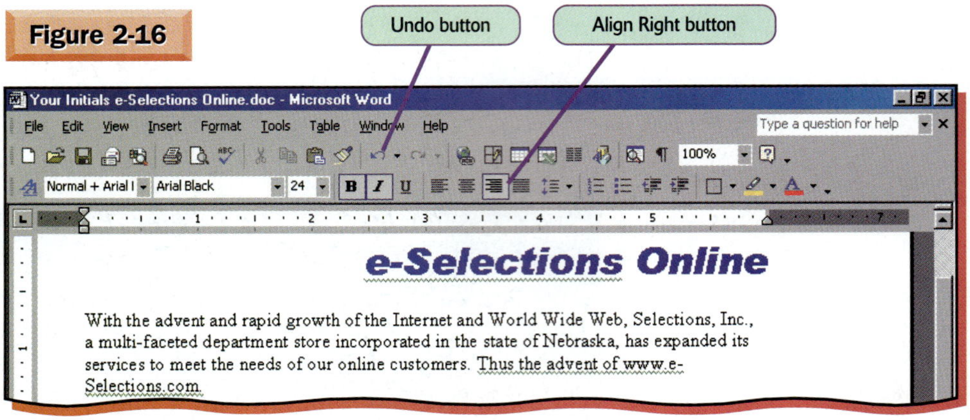

Figure 2-17

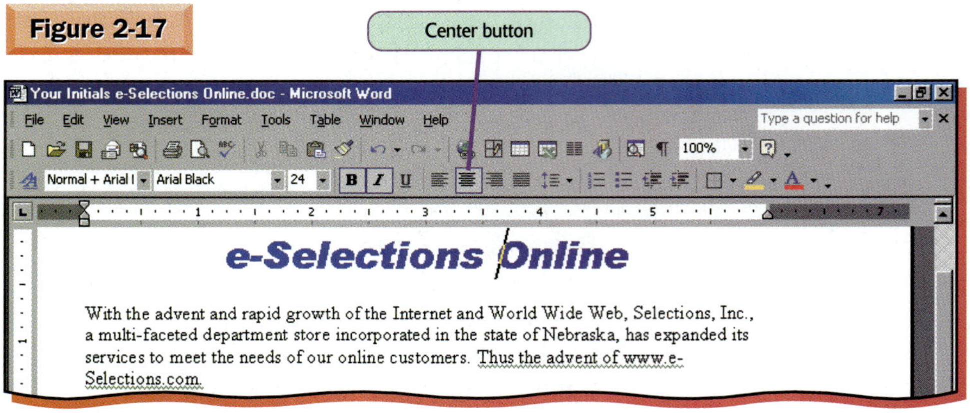

Tip If special fonts required to develop documents in different languages such as Japanese have been installed on your computer, you may see a special Distributed alignment button on the Formatting toolbar. Try aligning text using the Distributed alignment and view the results.

Using Proofing Tools

Proofing tools built into Office XP applications make it easy to locate text, replace text, and check the spelling in your files. There is also a tool that is shared by Word, Excel, Access, and PowerPoint that enables you to enter frequently mistyped text and have the Office application automatically correct your error! The procedures for using these tools are consistent among all Office XP applications.

Running the Spelling Checker

When you first opened *e-Selections Online.doc*, you saw red, wavy underlines below misspelled words in the document. Unless the spell-as-you-go feature is turned off, the *spelling checker* feature runs continuously as you work in Office XP applications. The spelling checker feature locates words that don't appear in the Office XP dictionary and highlights them for you so that you can determine whether they are correct or need to be changed.

Tip

Words that are underlined as you work can be corrected quite easily. Simply point to the misspelled word and right-click. A list of suggested spellings for the word that is not recognized appears at the top of the shortcut menu. Select the correct spelling of the word, click **Ignore All**, or click **Add** to add the word to the dictionary.

Task 6:

To Use Spelling Checker on a File

1. Press Ctrl + Home to move to the beginning of the document and then click the **Spelling** button on the Standard toolbar.

2. Click **Ignore Rule**—this text appears as you want it to appear. Word locates the next possible error and highlights it.

Figure 2-18

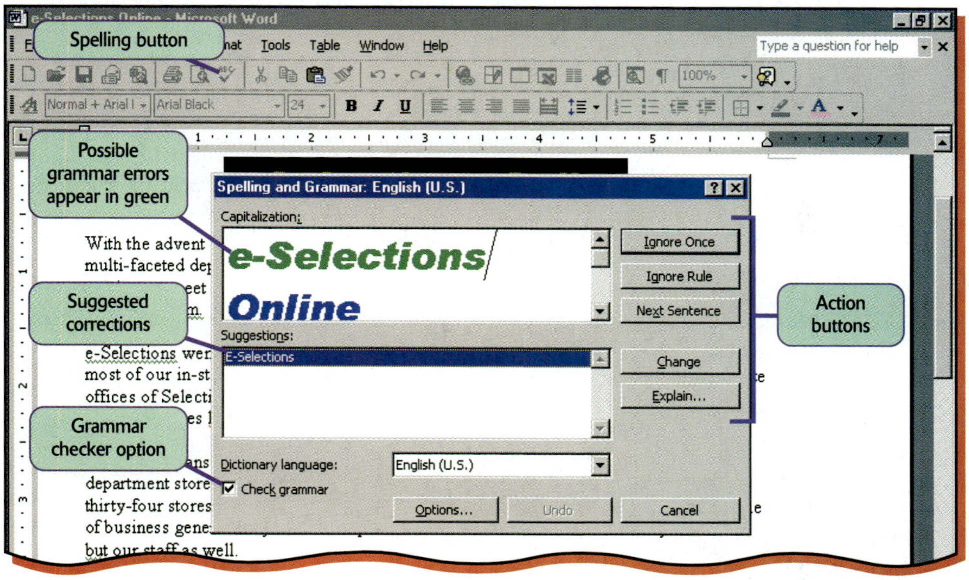

3. Click **Ignore Once**. The next possible error is highlighted.

4. Click **Ignore Rule** to ignore this rule, too.

Figure 2-19

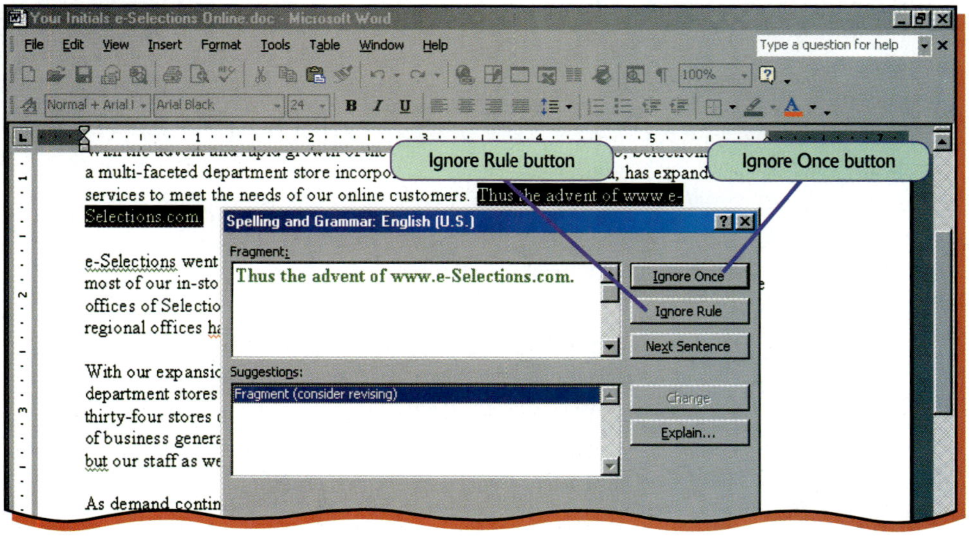

Troubleshooting

If you start the spelling checker in the middle of a document, a different message window may appear that asks if you want to continue proofing the document from the beginning. Click **Yes** and continue until the spelling checker is complete.

5 Select *have* from the **Suggestions** list and click **Change**. Word highlights the next possible error.

6 Continue checking the file, correcting errors that appear, until Word tells you the spelling and grammar check is complete.

Figure 2-20

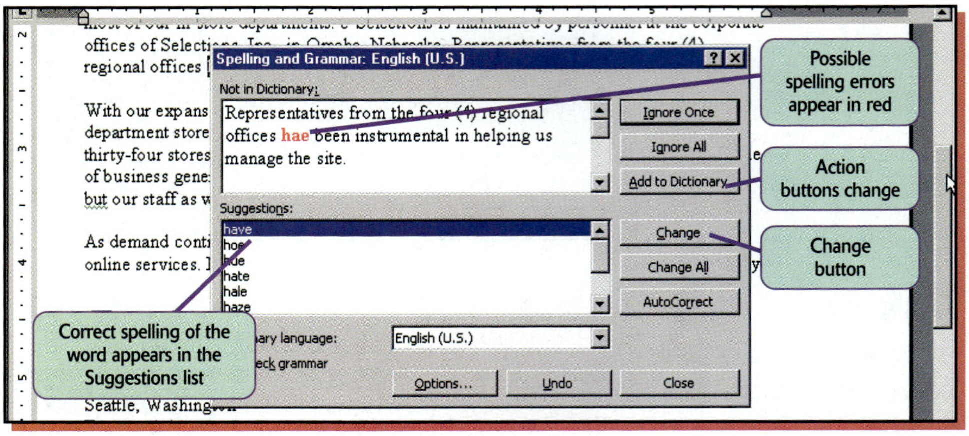

Tip If Word fails to present the correct spelling in the list of suggested words, you can correct the spelling of the word in the Not in Document area of the Spelling and Grammar dialog box and then click Change.

7 Click **OK** and save changes to the file.

Tip It is often tempting to click the Replace All button to replace all occurrences of a misspelled in a document with another spelling of the word. Carefully consider whether replacing all occurrences of a word with the selected replacement is the correct action—Word follows your directive explicitly—sometimes with unexpected results!

Figure 2-21

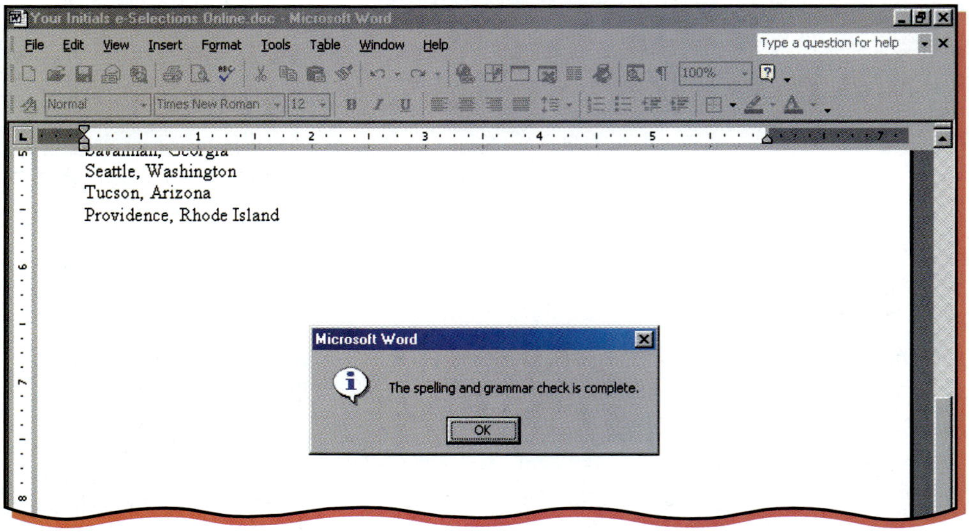

Finding and Replacing Text

The Find and Replace features enable you to locate text if it appears in a file and replace text with substitute text. These features are powerful tools for navigating and editing large files.

Task 7:

To Find and Replace Text

1 Press Ctrl + Home to position the insertion point at the top of the document and then choose **Edit | Find**. The Find and Replace dialog box opens.

2 Type thirty-four in the **Find what** text box and click **Find Next**.

Troubleshooting Word searches the document for the phrase beginning at the insertion point. As a result, you may find a different occurrence of the phrase.

Figure 2-22

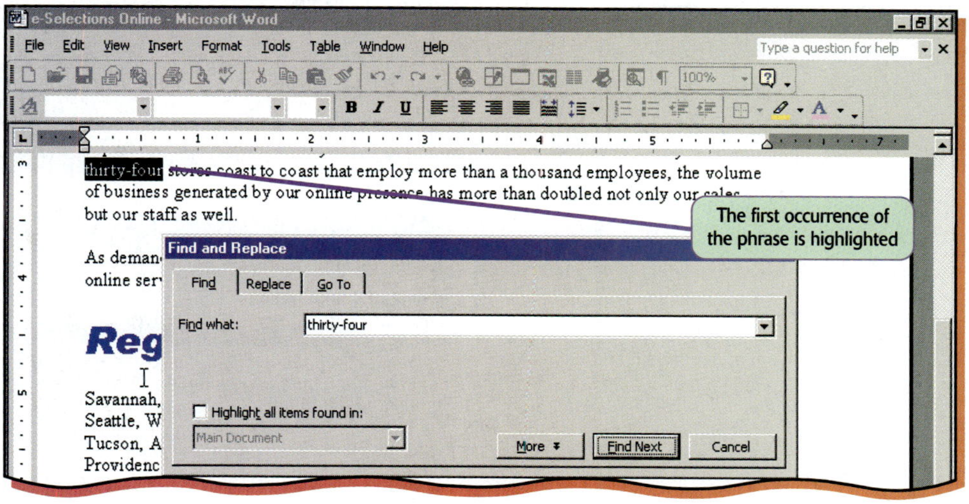

Troubleshooting In Access, the Find command is available only when an object is open. Find does not appear on the Edit menu when the database window is active.

3 Click the **Replace** tab.

4 Type forty-one in the **Replace with** text box and click **Replace All**. Word replaces all occurrences of the number thirty-four with the number forty-one. A message window tells you how many replacements were made.

Figure 2-23

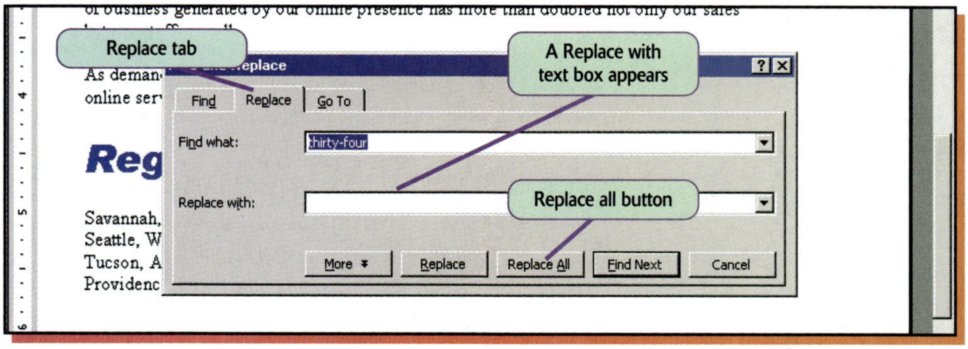

5 Click **OK**, close the dialog box, and save your changes to the document.

Figure 2-24

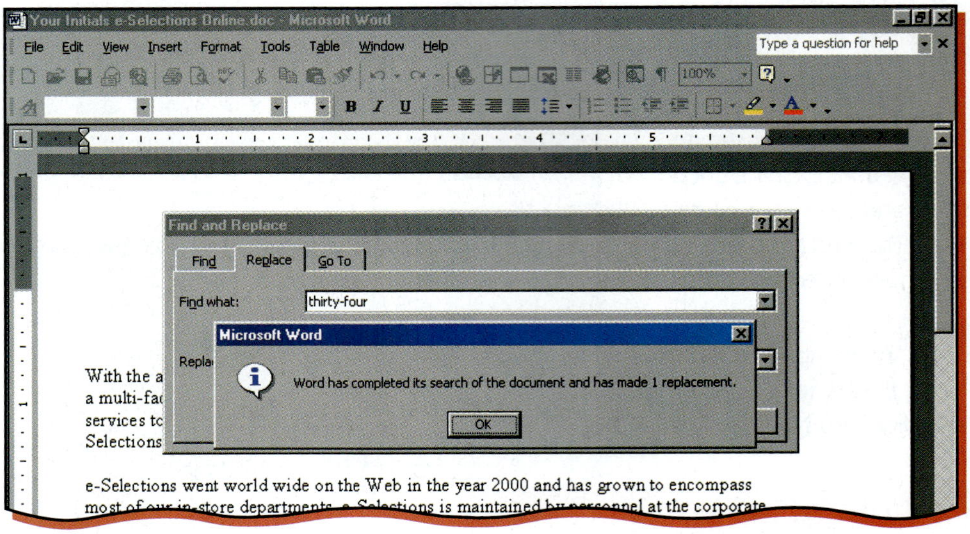

CHECK POINT

The Find command is a useful tool for locating text in the active document. But what about those times when you want to locate information contained in another file or in an e-mail message?

The **Search** command is a feature new to Office XP applications. It makes it possible to locate text contained in files stored on your computer (including all disk drives), on a network, or in an e-mail message. When you become more comfortable with the basic Find and Replace functions, you'll want to explore this new Search feature using the Microsoft documentation and online Help features.

Creating and Using AutoCorrect Entries

Each of the Office XP applications comes equipped with an *AutoCorrect* feature that is designed to automatically correct the most frequently misspelled or mistyped words. When you type *t-e-h* or *a-h-v-e,* for example, the Office application automatically changes the words to *t-h-e* and *h-a-v-e* to correct the spelling. Office comes with a built-in set of commonly mistyped words that can be edited. You can also add the words *you* most frequently mistype to the AutoCorrect list and use AutoCorrect to create entries that will substitute frequently used phrases for abbreviations. Mistyped or abbreviated text is replaced after you press the spacebar, an end-of-sentence punctuation mark, or Enter.

Task 8:
To Create AutoCorrect Entries

1. Open *e-Selections Online.doc*, if necessary.
2. Select the word *e-Selections*.
3. Choose **Tools | AutoCorrect Options** to open the AutoCorrect dialog box.

Troubleshooting
The AutoCorrect entries you see may be different from those shown here.

4. Type **esel** in the **Replace** text box.
5. Click **Add**. The entry *esel* appears alphabetically on the AutoCorrect list.
6. Click **OK**. The dialog box closes.

Tip Other options that appear on the AutoCorrect page of the AutoCorrect dialog box control how Word corrects typing errors as your work. For example, you can ensure that Word automatically capitalizes the days of the week when you forget to capitalize them, have Word correct two initial capital letters at the beginning of a word, or capitalize the first letter of each sentence when you fail to do so.

Figure 2-25

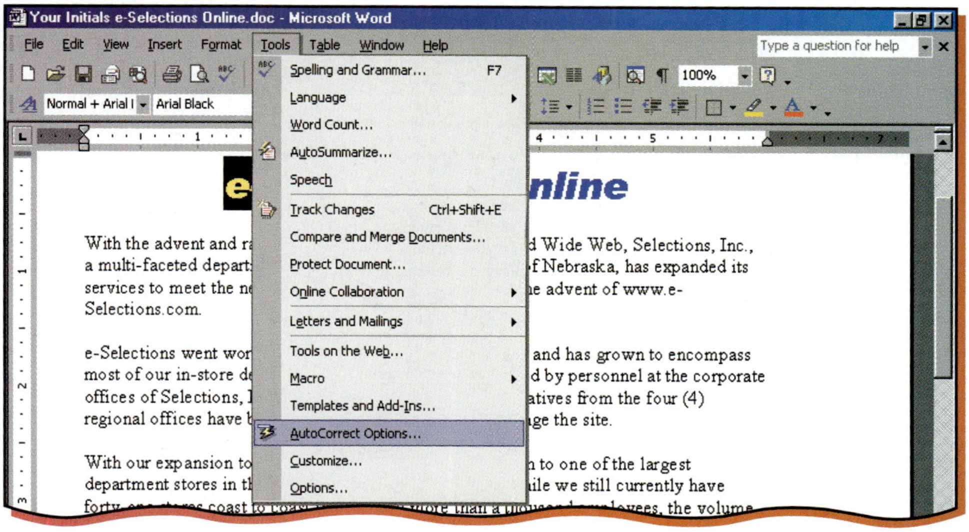

Figure 2-26

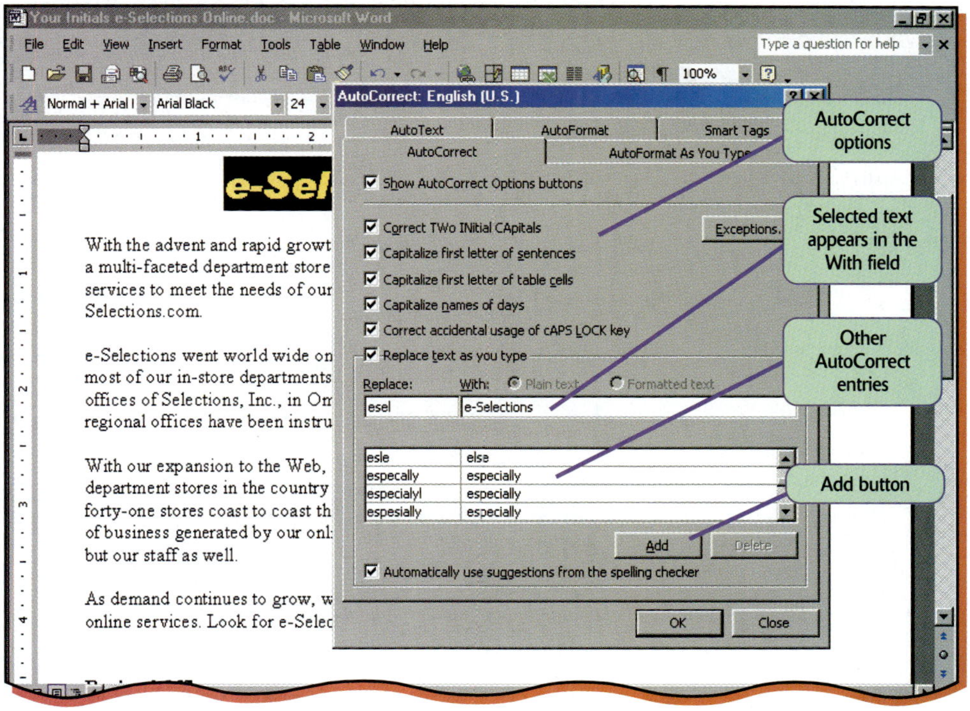

7 Move to the end of the document, press Enter twice, type **esel**, and press Spacebar. AutoCorrect expands the text and substitutes e-Selections for the abbreviation.

8 Point to the replacement text. A small blue rectangle appears below the first character of the replacement text.

9 Point to the blue rectangle.

Figure 2-27

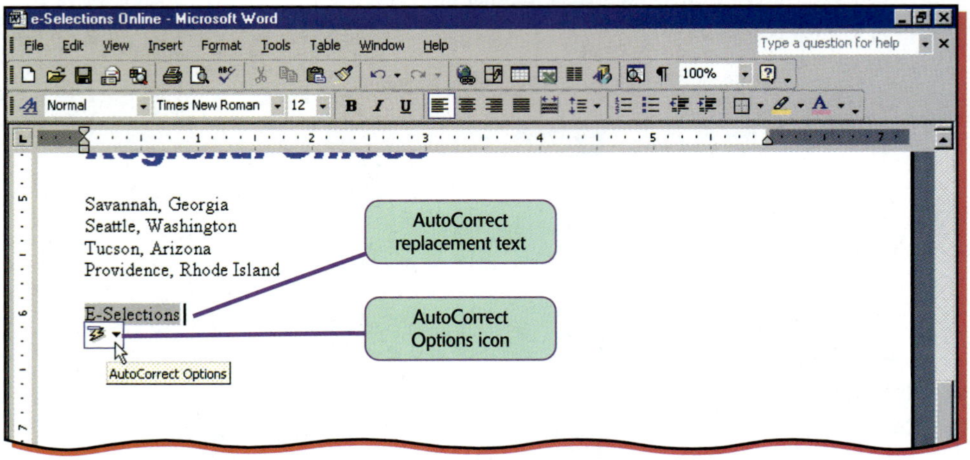

Troubleshooting The AutoCorrect Options button appears only when you point to the blue rectangle.

10 Click the **AutoCorrect Options** icon.

11 Press Esc to close the AutoCorrect Options list.

12 Delete the line added using AutoCorrect and then save the changes to the file.

Figure 2-28

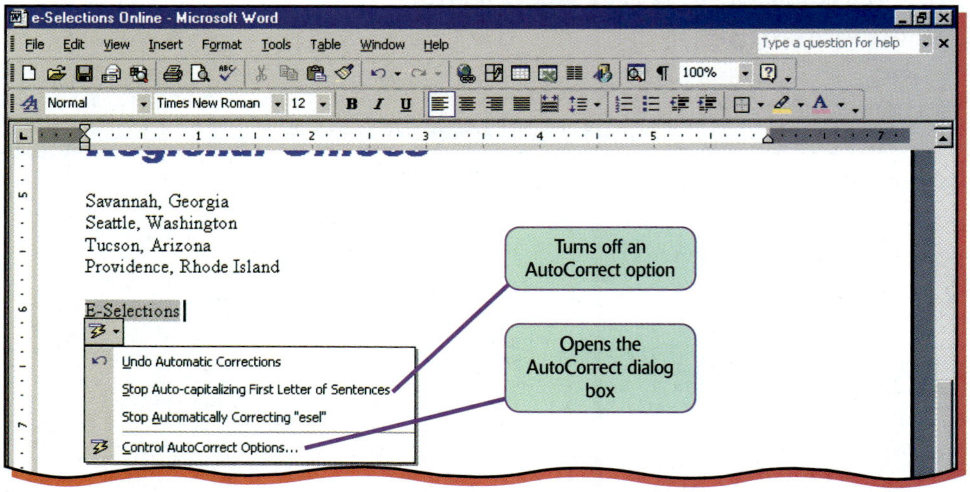

Tip Options displayed on the AutoCorrect Options list enable you to undo an AutoCorrect action, turn off the AutoCorrect entry you just typed, or set AutoCorrect Options. Additional options appear on the AutoCorrect Options list when Word takes an AutoCorrect action such as capitalizing the first word of a sentence or correcting two initial capital letters in a word.

Creating Text Boxes

Most text added to Office XP files appears within the basic file structure; between margins of documents, within cells of spreadsheets, within placeholders of presentation slides, and within database objects. Text boxes enable you to add text outside the parameters of the file structure. Text boxes are drawn on screen and text is typed within the text box. Text boxes can be repositioned within the file as needed.

Task 9:
To Create a Text Box

1 Open *e-Selections Online.doc,* if necessary, and position the insertion point at the end of the document.

2 Click the **Drawing** button on the Standard toolbar to open the Drawing toolbar at the bottom of the window.

3 Select the *Regional Offices* title and list text at the bottom of the document.

4 Click the **Text Box** tool on the Drawing toolbar. The mouse pointer changes to a crosshair pointer that looks like a plus (+) sign.

Tip The crosshair pointer is used to draw text boxes and other shapes identified in Common Elements Project 3. The center of the crosshair pointer marks the position of the box or object start point.

Figure 2-29

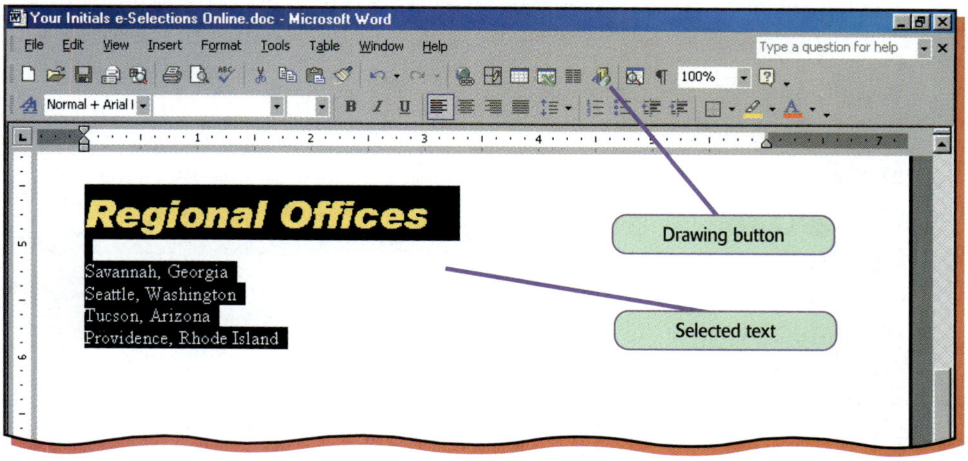

Figure 2-30

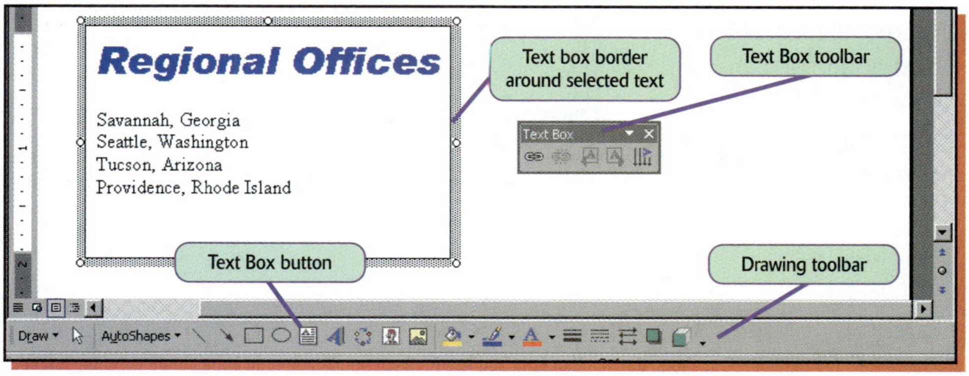

Troubleshooting In Word, a Drawing Canvas appears if you click the Text Box tool before selecting text. You can draw the text box anywhere on the document, either inside or outside the Drawing Canvas, or press Esc to close the Drawing Canvas.

Adding Text to Text Boxes and Repositioning the Text Box

You can also create a new text box and type text directly into the text box. Then change the shape and format of the text box and reposition the text box wherever you want it in the document. Document text will automatically adjust to appear around the text box.

Task 10: To Add Text to Text Boxes

1. Scroll to the bottom of the document and position the insertion point to the right of the existing text box.

2. Click the **Text Box** tool and then press Esc to close the Drawing Canvas, if necessary.

3. Position the mouse pointer on the document page where the upper left corner of the text box should be and drag the mouse diagonally to draw a second text box beside the existing text box.

Figure 2-31

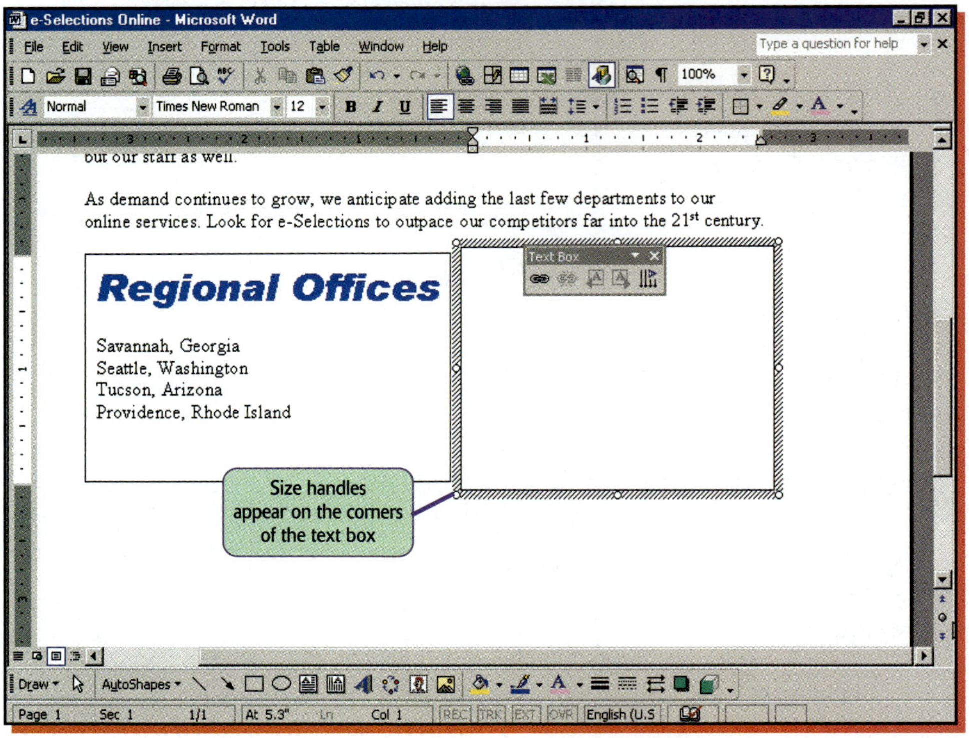

4 Type the text shown in Figure 2-32 in the new text box.

Tip Typing text in text boxes requires basically the same skills used to type text in the document outside the text boxes. Text wraps within the confines of the text box. Press Enter to start new lines when necessary.

Figure 2-32

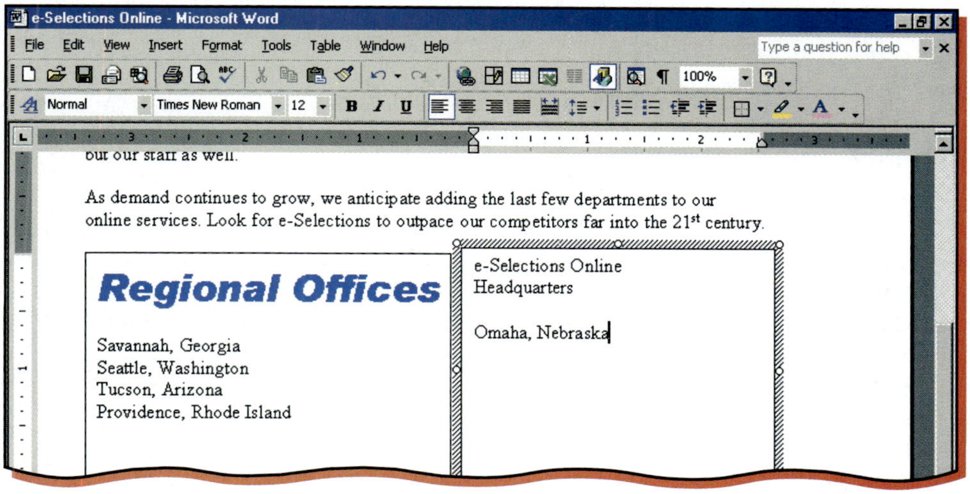

5 Copy the format from the *Regional Offices* title to the *e-Selections Online Headquarters* title using the Format Painter.

Troubleshooting If you paint the format onto the city and state shown in the text box, undo the action and try again.

Figure 2-33

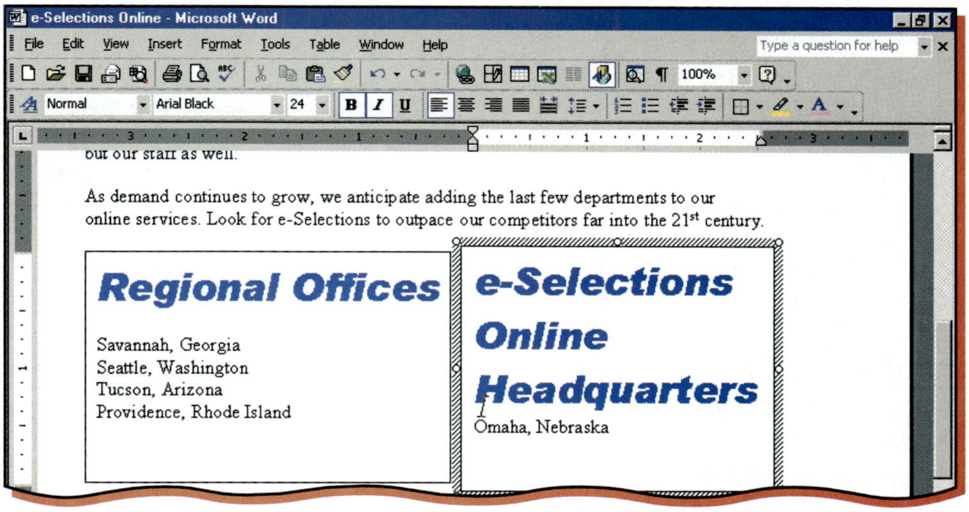

6 Select the new text box, position the mouse pointer on the lower right corner size handle, and then click and drag the handle to resize the text box as shown in Figure 2-34.

Troubleshooting
If you accidentally drag the side of the text box off the page, you can undo the action and try again. It often takes several tries to get the hang of box sizing.

Figure 2-34

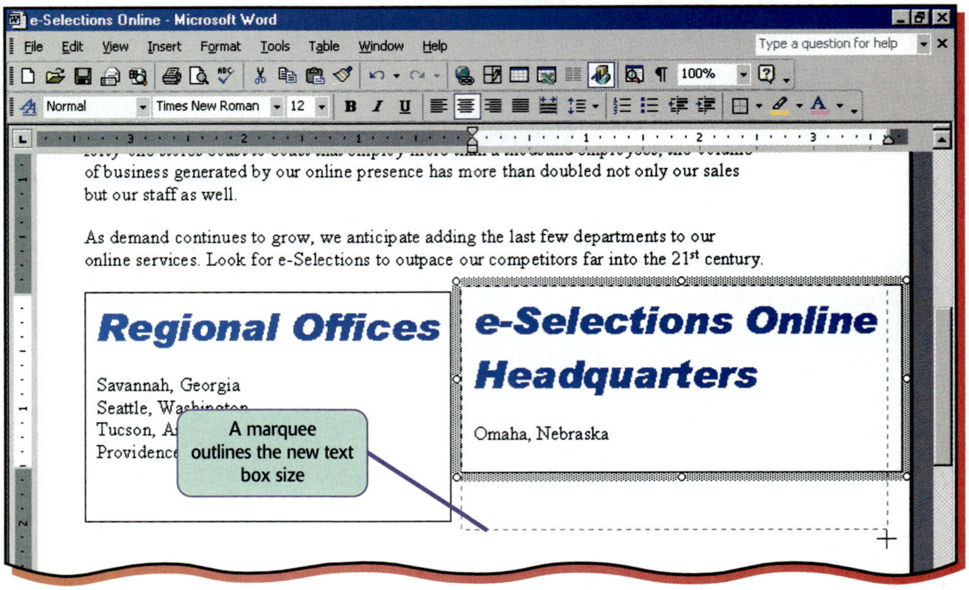

7 Press Shift and click the text box, position the insertion point on a border of the text box until you see a four-headed mouse pointer, and then click and drag the new text box to position it as shown in Figure 2-35.

Tip
Pressing Shift while clicking drawn objects selects the whole object rather than positioning the insertion point in the text within the text box.

8 Right align text in the new text box and then save changes and close the file.

Figure 2-35

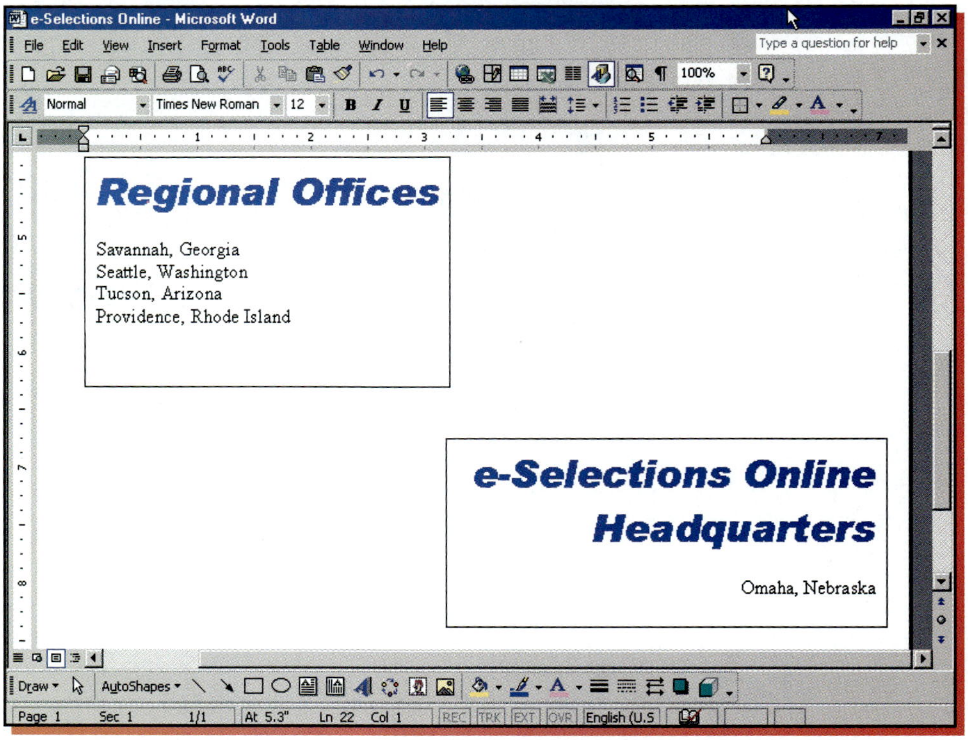

SUMMARY AND EXERCISES

SUMMARY

- Navigating text enables you to move from character to character, paragraph to paragraph, screen to screen, or page to page.
- By selecting text, you can apply enhancements to text, change fonts, or move and copy text.
- Inserting and deleting text is the same in all Office XP applications. Word enables you to switch to Overtype mode to replace text as you type.
- Enhancing and formatting text is made easy using the buttons on the Formatting toolbar.
- Text can be cut, copied, and moved within or among all Office XP applications.
- The Office Clipboard can hold up to 24 snippets of information and can be displayed at any time an Office application is open.
- Office XP makes it easy to maintain text format consistency by using Format Painter.
- Using the Undo feature enables you to reverse the last action, and using the Redo feature enables you to restore actions that were reversed using the Undo feature. In Office XP you can also reverse multiple actions.
- Text can be aligned left or right, centered, or justified on the left or right.
- Proofing tools are used to locate text, replace text, and check the spelling of text in files.
- The AutoCorrect feature corrects commonly misspelled words and enables you to enter your own words to be automatically corrected.
- Text boxes can be drawn on screen and can be used to hold text and position the text more precisely in a file.

KEY TERMS & SKILLS

KEY TERMS

align (p. 2-3)
attributes (p. 2-5)
delete (p. 2-4)
enhance (p. 2-1)
font (p. 2-5)
format (p. 2-1)
Insert mode (p. 2-4)
justify (p. 2-13)
Overtype mode (p. 2-4)
paste (p. 2-8)
Redo (p. 2-13)
replace (p. 2-4)
spelling checker (p. 2-14)
Undo (p. 2-13)

SKILLS

Add text to text boxes (p. 2-22)
Align text (p. 2-13)
Copy and move text (p. 2-9)
Copy text format (p. 2-11)
Create and use AutoCorrect (p. 2-18)
Create text boxes (p. 2-21)
Display and use the Office Clipboard (p. 2-8)
Enhance and format text (p. 2-5)
Find and replace text (p. 2-16)
Insert, delete, and replace text (p. 2-4)
Navigate text (p. 2-3)
Spelling checker used in files (p. 2-15)
Use Undo and Redo (p. 2-13)

STUDY QUESTIONS

MULTIPLE CHOICE

1. Moving from character to character, paragraph to paragraph, screen to screen, or page to page is called
a. scrolling.
b. skipping.
c. navigating.
d. keystroking.

2. You can change the appearance of text by changing the font, size, and
a. art.
b. attributes.
c. paragraph.
d. selection.

3. To move up one screen, the key that is used in all applications is
a. PrtScr.
b. ↑.
c. Ctrl + Home.
d. Page Up.

4. To move to the end of a file, press
a. End.
b. Ctrl + End.
c. PageDown.
d. none of the above

5. Which application contains numerous objects but enables text formatting in only one type of object?
   a. Word
   b. Excel
   c. Access
   d. PowerPoint
6. All of the following are text attributes, *except*
   a. font face.
   b. superscript.
   c. emboss.
   d. hidden.
7. To remove text to the left of the insertion point, press
   a. Del.
   b. Bksp.
   c. Shift + ←.
   d. Insert.
8. The feature that holds multiple snippets of information in Office XP is
   a. the Clipboard.
   b. AutoCorrect.
   c. the Office Clipboard.
   d. the shortcut menu.
9. To remove selected text from its current location, click
   a. Cut.
   b. Copy.
   c. Paste.
   d. Italic.
10. To reverse the last action, click
    a. Cut.
    b. Undo.
    c. Redo.
    d. Format Painter.

SHORT ANSWER

1. What must you do before you can apply, enhance, or change the text font of existing text?
2. List three ways to delete text.
3. Which buttons can you use to reverse the last action or selected actions?
4. List the four basic alignments that can be applied to text in Office XP applications.
5. Identify the three-step process required to copy text formats using the Format Painter.
6. What are the keyboard shortcuts for Cut, Copy, and Paste?
7. Describe the difference between right alignment and justified alignment.
8. How do you turn off the grammar checker after starting the spelling checker?
9. How does formatting text contained in text boxes differ from formatting text contained in files?
10. What menu do you access to create an AutoCorrect entry from selected text?

FILL IN THE BLANK

1. You can use the keyboard or the ______________ to move within a file.
2. ______________ mode enables you to replace existing text as you type new text in Word.
3. Double-click the ______________ button to copy a text format to multiple places.

4. Misspelled words are located and corrected using ____________.
5. After clicking the Format Painter button, the mouse pointer appears to carry a ____________.
6. The ____________ ____________ is automatically activated when you start the spelling checker.
7. ____________ can be used to store frequently used, long phrases so that you can type an abbreviation and automatically enter the expanded text.
8. The ____________ feature helps you move swiftly to a particular word or phrase in an Office XP file.
9. To be able to move text to specific positions in files, place the text in a ____________ ____________.
10. The Office Clipboard can hold ____________ pieces of information.

DISCUSSION

1. Discuss several different ways of enhancing and formatting text.
2. Discuss the advantages of placing text in text boxes rather than within document margins, within spreadsheet cells, or in other locations.
3. Identify the different ways that the Office Clipboard can be used and how the Office Clipboard is accessed.

GUIDED EXERCISES

1 FORMATTING TEXT AND CREATING TEXT BOXES

Figure 2-36 contains two text boxes that appear side by side on the document page.

Figure 2-36

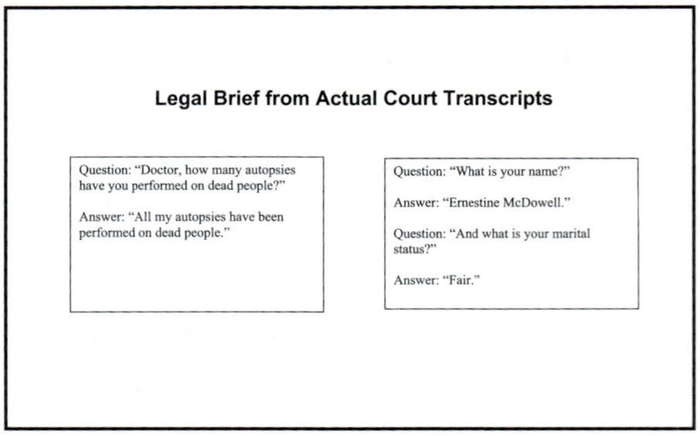
Legal Brief from Actual Court Transcripts

Question: "Doctor, how many autopsies have you performed on dead people?"

Answer: "All my autopsies have been performed on dead people."

Question: "What is your name?"

Answer: "Ernestine McDowell."

Question: "And what is your marital status?"

Answer: "Fair."

To ensure that the text boxes are the same size, you can create the first text box and then copy it before adding text to the text boxes. To create the text boxes, follow these steps.

1. Launch Word, if necessary, and create a new blank document.
2. Change the Zoom setting to **Page Width**.

3 Create the title:

- Type the title text **Legal Brief from Actual Court Transcripts.**
- Center the title.
- Format the title text using an Arial 18-point type.

4 Display the Drawing toolbar and create a new text box on the left side of the document, ensuring that the text box does not extend beyond the approximate center point on the page.

5 Press Shift and click the text box border to select it.

6 Copy the first text box:

- Click the **Copy** button.
- Click the white area on screen to clear the existing text box.

Troubleshooting If the text box remains selected, the new text box will appear within the existing text box when you paste.

- Click the **Paste** button to paste a second text box on the screen.
- Drag the copy of the text box so that it appears to the right of the first text box and align the text boxes as precisely as possible.

7 Click inside the text box on the left and type the following text:

Question: "Doctor, how many autopsies have you performed on dead people?"

Answer: "All my autopsies have been performed on dead people."

8 Click inside the text box on the right and type the following text:

Question: "What is your name?"
Answer: "Ernestine McDowell."

Question: "And what is your marital status?"
Answer: "Fair."

9 Save the document using the file name *Legal Briefs*, print a copy of the document, and then close the file.

2 CREATING AN AUTOCORRECT ENTRY

One of the most effective uses of AutoCorrect is to expand your name by simply typing your initials. Follow these instructions to create an AutoCorrect entry that enters your name.

1. Launch Word, if necessary, and create a new blank document.
2. Type *Your Name* at the top of the document and then select *Your Name*.
3. Choose **Tools** | **AutoCorrect Options** and type *Your Initials* in the **Replace** field; click OK.
4. Press Enter and then type *Your Initials* followed by the Spacebar to test your AutoCorrect entry.
5. Close the file without saving it.

WEB TIP

Government Web addresses generally have a .gov extension. Search for Government Web sites to locate the official site for the Interagency Fire Center.

ON YOUR OWN

The difficulty of these case studies varies:

are the least difficult; *are more difficult; and* *are the most difficult.*

1 FORMATTING TEXT

Open the file Fire Center. Format text contained in the file as follows:

- Title: 18 point Arial, Small Caps, centered
- Bulleted list: 14 point Arial

Replace the text Your Name at the bottom of the file by typing ***Your Name*** and then right align the text. Check the spelling in the file. Save the file using the file name Your Initials Fire Center.

2 ADDING A TEXT BOX TO AN EXISTING FILE

Open the file *Fire Center* (Substitute *Your Initials Fire Center* if you completed On Your Own Exercise 1) and add the following text to a new text box below the bulleted list:

Visit the National Interagency Fire Center Online.

Center the text, change the font size to 17 points, and format the text using Arial font. Then print a copy of the file and save changes to the file using the file name *Your Initials Fire Center*.

3 CREATING A FUN NOTICE

Create the notice shown in Figure 2-37 using a font and font size similar to the font shown in the figure. Save the file using the file name *Phantom Ghost*, print a copy of the document, and then close the document.

Figure 2-37

Good . . . Evening!

If you do not wish a curse on this house,
you must make two treats
and deliver them to two houses
in the neighborhood.
You have only two days.
Post the picture of the Phantom Ghost on
your door 'til Halloween.
This will ward off any other phantoms
that may visit!

Copy this letter and the Phantom Ghost
twice and give it with treats
to two homes that do not have
a Phantom Ghost posted.

Share the Spirit!
Have a Happy Halloween!

FROM THE FILES

You Will Need

- ✔ e-Selections Online Graphics.doc
- ✔ e-Selections Logo.jpg
- ✔ Stars.wmf
- ✔ Phantom Ghosties.doc

PROJECT 3

Common Graphics Elements

Adding art to Office XP files dresses them up and makes them more inviting. Each Office XP application offers such a wide variety of methods for adding art to your files that it's sometimes difficult to decide which feature to use. You can add *clip art* images, *scanned images*, picture files, *WordArt*, and manual drawings to files in all Office XP applications. Each art type has a complete set of tools for editing and manipulating the art object. As a result, this project is designed to get you started on your artistic journey—you can explore the features that you will need to use the most on your own.

OBJECTIVES

After completing this project, you will be able to:

- *Insert and edit clip art*
- *Display the Clip Organizer*
- *Insert graphic images*
- *Create and format WordArt*
- *Create and manipulate drawings*

e-selections Running Case

With the advent of e-Selections.com, managers plan to start publishing information from different Office applications on the Web site. The graphics design specialist assigned to e-Selections.com has asked you to explore some of the graphics capabilities available in Office XP applications so that these capabilities can be reported to those who are in charge of the different e-Selections.com divisions. You will begin your explorations using Word.

PROJECT 3

Common Graphics Elements

The Challenge

As you explore the Internet and specific Web pages, you will notice that graphics have been used extensively to create Web page designs. As you begin working with Office XP applications, you will be expected to know how to add graphics and drawings to the files you create using the different applications.

The Solution

Office XP applications share many of the same graphics and art elements. As a result, introducing the basic concepts of adding art images and drawing provides a base on which to build additional skills as you move through the different applications. Because you are already more familiar with Word than any of the other Office XP applications, you will continue to use Word as you develop your artistic talents.

Troubleshooting Be sure to review the setup section of Common Elements Project 2 for screen features and other settings that affect this project.

Working with Clip Art

All Office XP applications share a common *Clip Organizer* that contains a variety of different images that you can add to files. The first time you access the Clip Organizer, the Office XP application takes a few moments to build the gallery and then presents *thumbnails*—very small copies—of the images.

Inserting Clip Art Images

Clip art images appear at the insertion point when you add them to most Office XP files. After you get the image in the file, you can position and size the image so that it appears in the file where you want it.

Task 1:
To Insert Clip Art Images

1. Launch Word, if necessary, and create a new blank document.

2. Choose **Insert | Picture | Clip Art** to open the Insert Clip Art task pane.

Figure 3-1

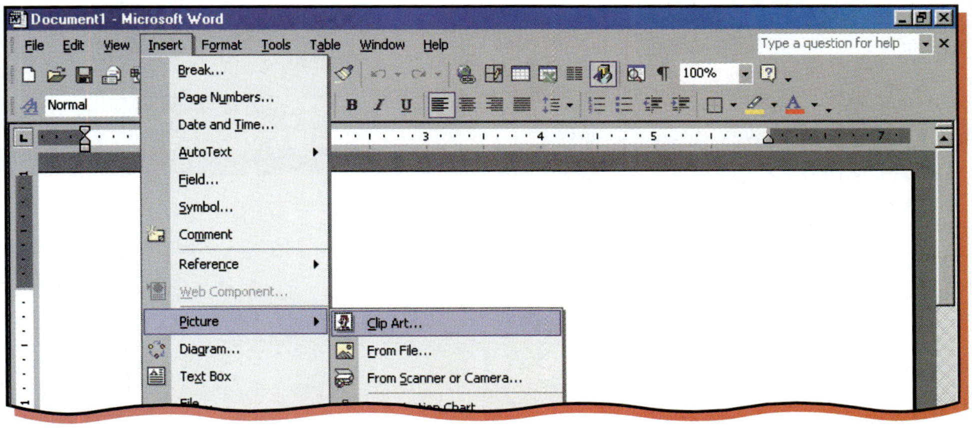

3. Type **People** in the **Search text** box and click **Search**.

Figure 3-2

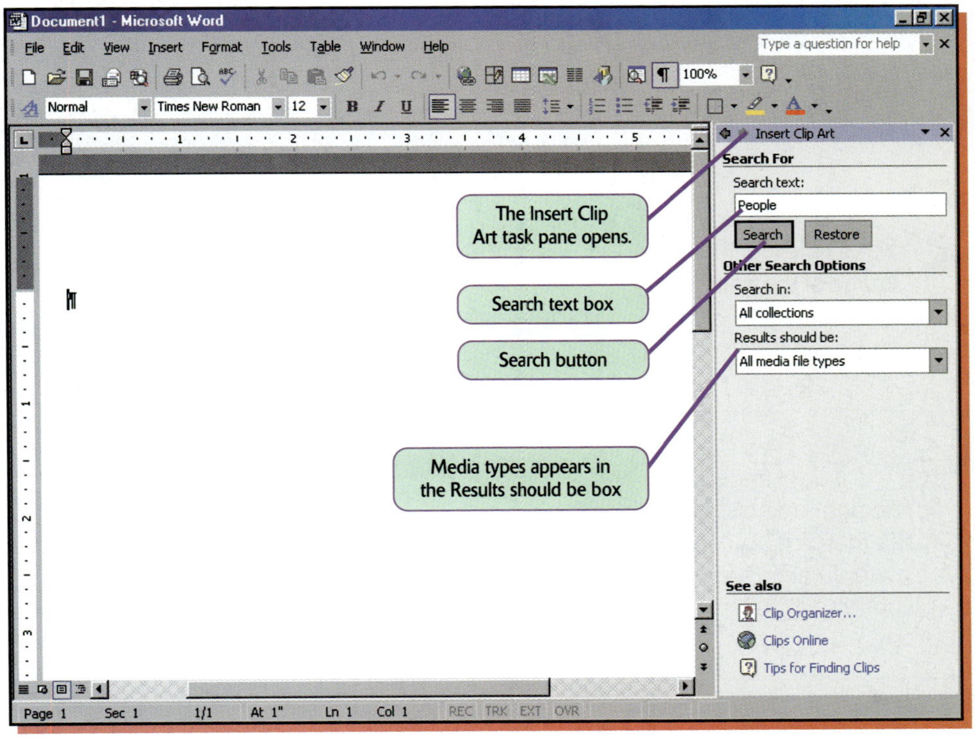

Troubleshooting

Depending on the clip art that is installed on your computer, the graphics you see may be different from those displayed here.

Tip

If Office XP has been installed more than one time on your computer, it is possible that you will see two sets of the same clip art images. If a previous version of Microsoft Office has been upgraded to Office XP, some image duplication may occur.

4 Point to one of the thumbnail images.

Troubleshooting

Screen tips may require several seconds to appear when you point to an image. Be careful to hold the mouse pointer still to see the screen tip.

Figure 3-3

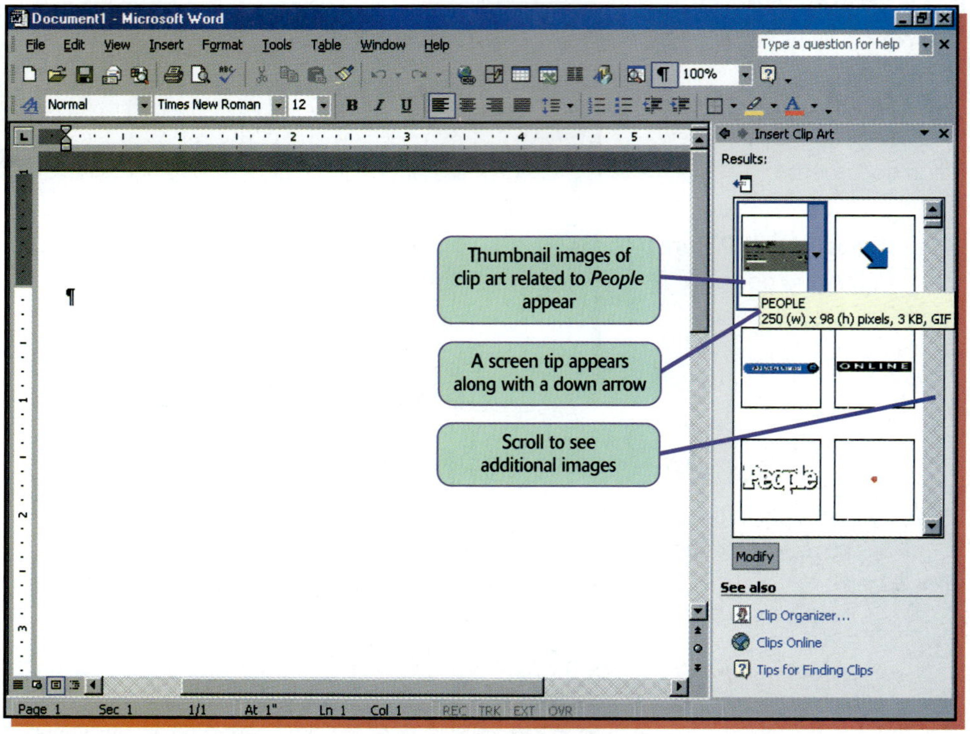

5 Scroll to locate the image of the golfer similar to the image shown in Figure 3-4.

Tip

The down arrow appears on the right side of the image to which you are pointing. Other images will not display a down arrow.

Figure 3-4

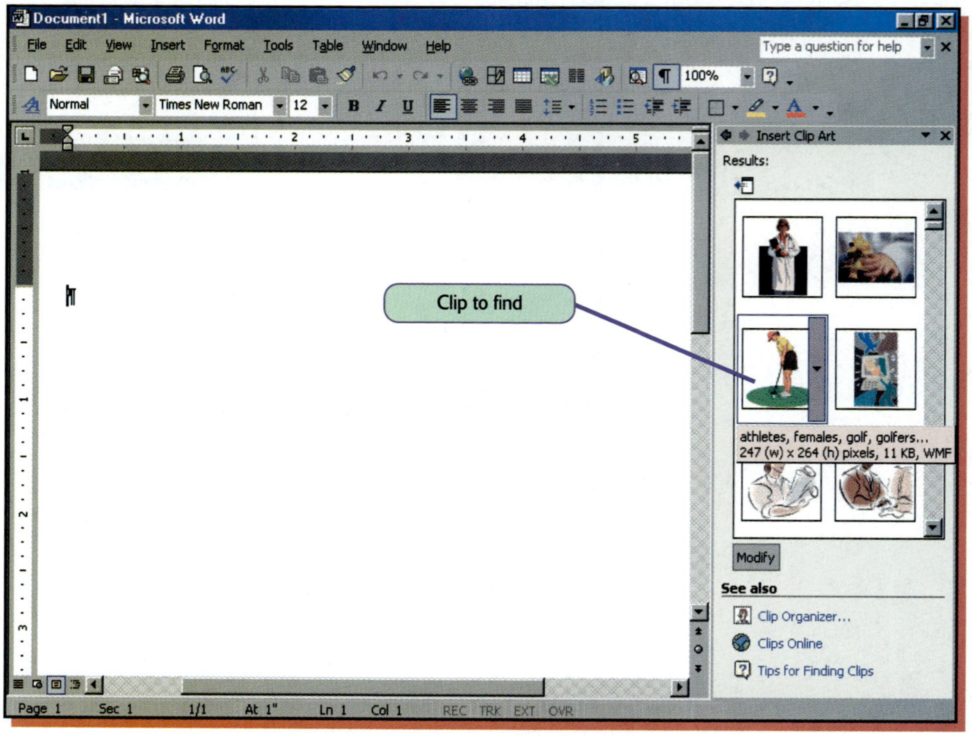

6 Click the thumbnail image in the task pane and save your file using the name *Your Initials Golfing.*

7 Close the task pane.

Tip When you close the task pane, the image will appear slightly larger.

Troubleshooting
Clip art image size and position may appear distorted in Normal view. To view the images in better format, choose **View | Print Layout.**

Figure 3-5

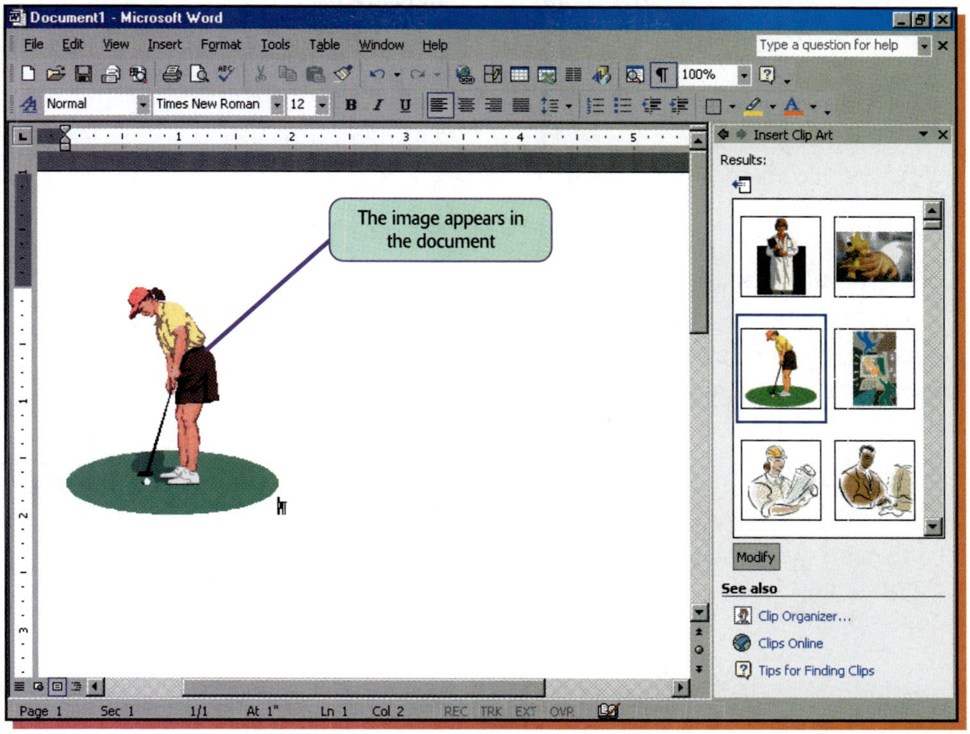

WEB TIP

The Internet is a great source for locating clip art to add to your files. You can search for sites containing clip art and download clips. In addition, Microsoft has set up a special site from which users can download new clips. Access the Microsoft Design Gallery Live from the task pane by clicking the Clips Online link or display the Clip Organizer and click the Clips Online toolbar button.

Tip Before you can move or size a clip art image that appears on a document, you must select it. The easiest way to select an image is to click it.

Moving and Sizing Clip Art Images

After you insert a clip art image into a file, you can size the image so that it fits the space you want it to occupy and move the image to position it more precisely. However, before you can move most clip art images, you have to change the image layout settings.

Task 2:
To Move and Size Clip Art Images

1. Launch Word and open the *Your Initials Golfing.doc* document, if necessary.

2. Click the golfer image and then position the insertion point on the black square in the lower right corner of the image.

Troubleshooting
If the rulers are hidden, choose **View | Ruler** to display them.

Figure 3-6

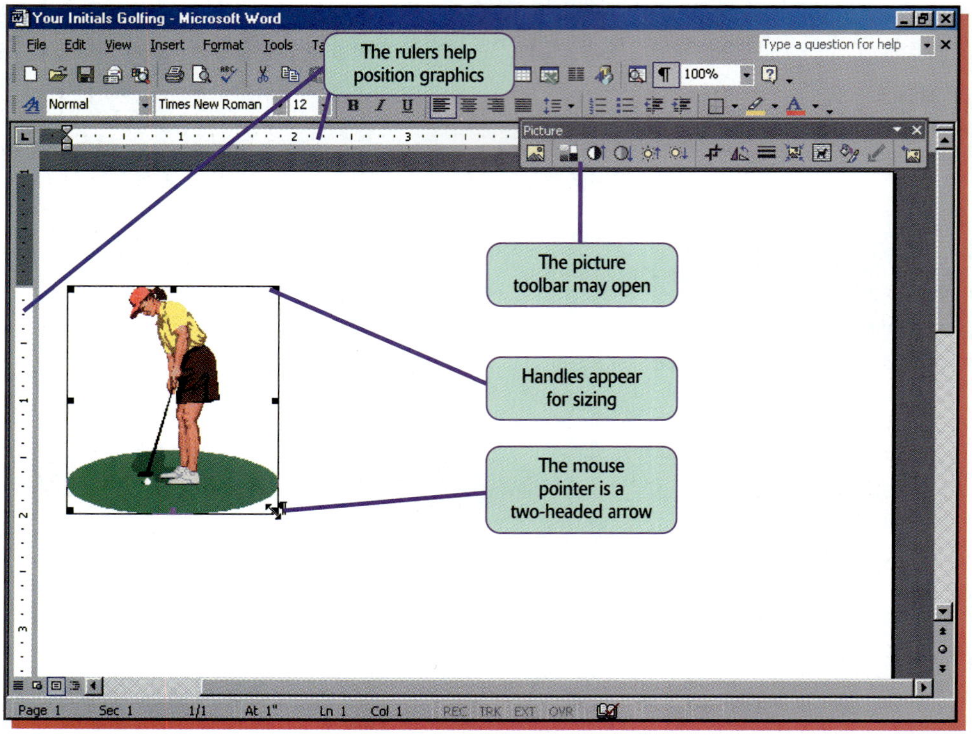

3. Drag the corner handle until the right edge of the graphic appears at about the 4" mark on the horizontal ruler and to about the 4 1/2" mark on the vertical ruler.

4. Point to the center of the selected image and right-click. The shortcut menu appears.

5. Select **Format Picture**. The Format Object dialog box appears.

Figure 3-7

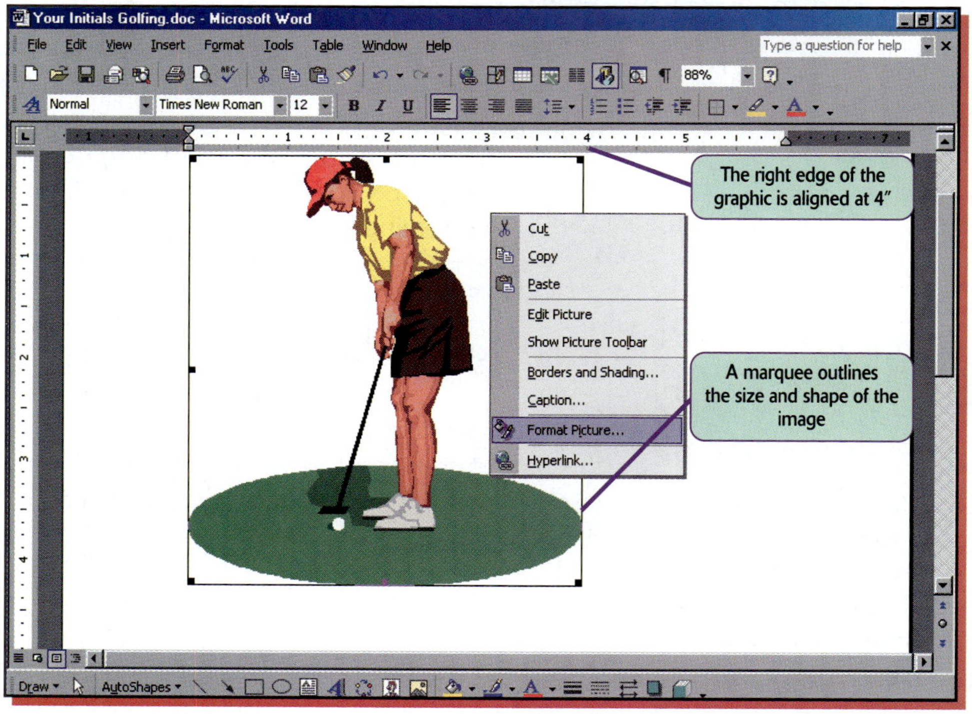

Tip Options available in the Format Object dialog box vary depending on the type of object that is active. In addition, the page of the dialog box that appears is controlled, to some extent, by the type of object selected.

6 Click the **Layout** tab.

7 Select **Square** and then click **Advanced** to display the Advanced Layout dialog box.

Tip The default layout places clip art images and other pictures in line with text. In this case, it lines up the image at the left margin because text in the document is left-aligned by default.

Figure 3-8

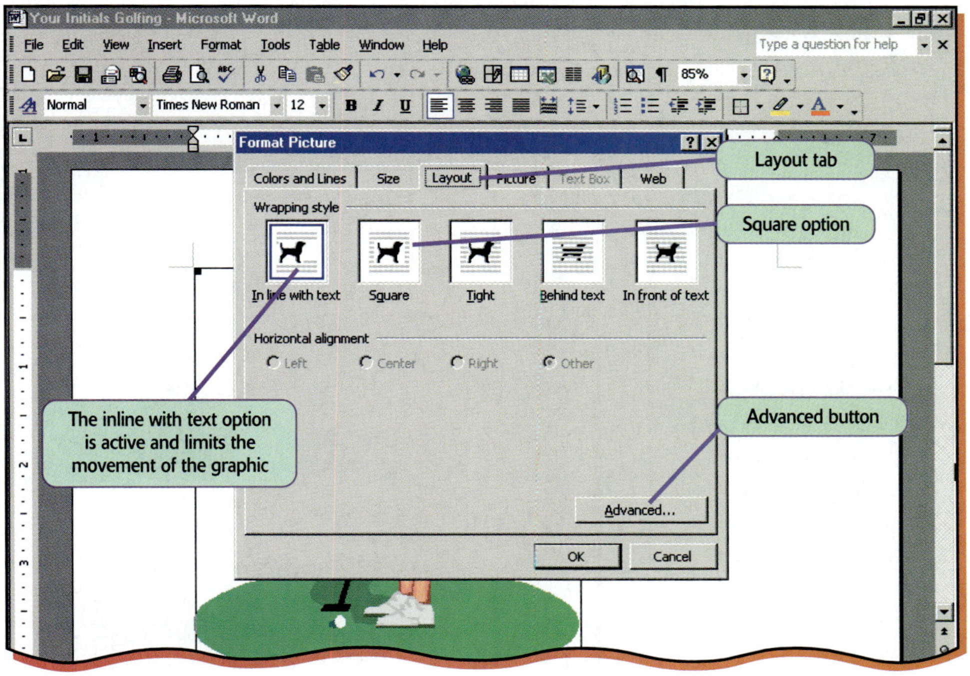

8 Clear the **Move object with text** option and click **OK** twice.

Tip Word normally attaches clip art you add to files to the text in the paragraph closest to the image. In this document, the picture is attached to the empty paragraph marker that appears on each new blank document you create. Because the paragraph is left-aligned, the clip art image appears left-aligned. Clearing the Move object with text option removes the invisible connection between the clip art image and the paragraph so that you can position the image anywhere on the page.

Figure 3-9

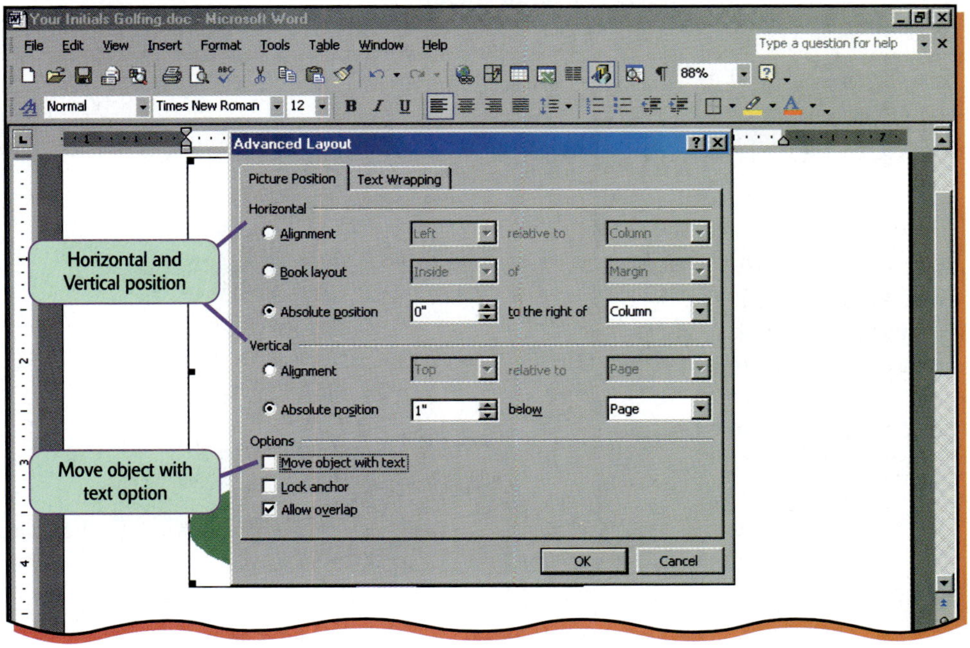

9 Point to the center of the image and click.

Tip Most clip art images can be rotated freely to position them at just the angle you want to display. To rotate an image, position the mouse pointer on the green circle that appears above the image. When you see a circular black arrow as the mouse pointer, drag the green circle to rotate the image.

Figure 3-10

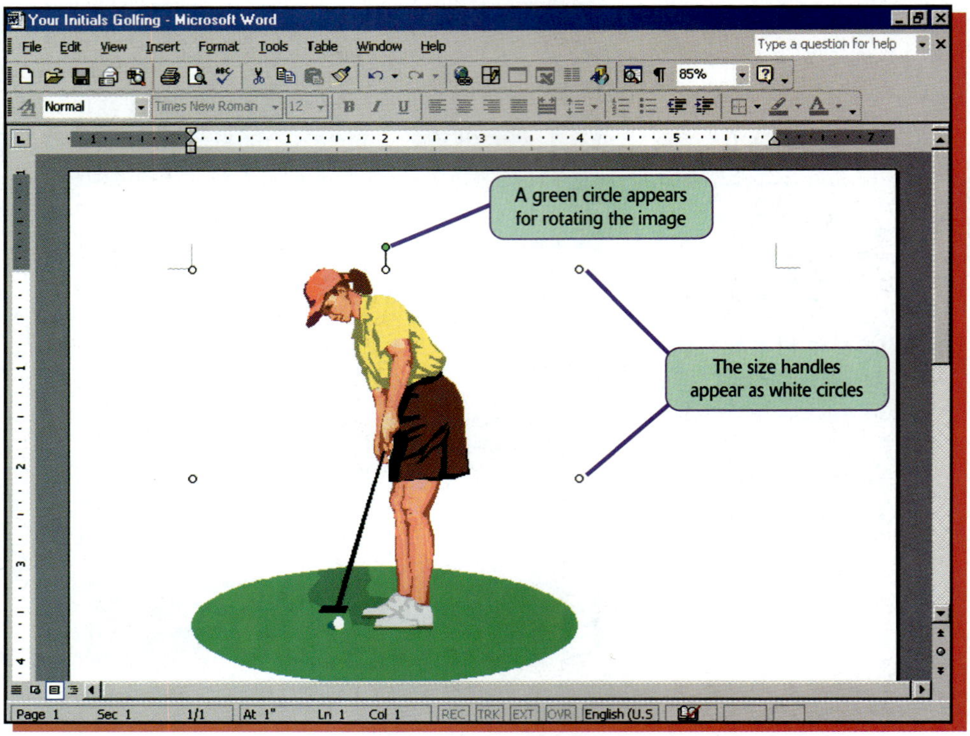

10 Drag the picture to a different location on the page.

11 Save changes to the file.

Troubleshooting Be sure to position the mouse pointer in the middle of the figure you want to move rather than on a sizing handle. Dragging a size handle changes the figure size but leaves the left edge of the figure in its original position.

Figure 3-11

Manipulating Clip Art Images

The white handles that appear on clip art images can be used to size the image, just as the black squares were used to adjust the image layout. After the image layout is adjusted so that you can move the graphic, the Rotate tool enables you to change the angle of the graphic. Clip art images can also be ungrouped so that different parts of the image can be edited, regrouped, flipped, and rotated.

Task 3:
To Ungroup Clip Art Images

1 Launch Word and open the *Your Initials Golfing.doc* document, if necessary.

2 Select the clip art image and click the **Drawing** button on the Standard toolbar.

> **Tip** The Drawing button on the Standard toolbar opens the Drawing toolbar. The Drawing toolbar appears anchored at the bottom of the Word window by default. However, you can float or reposition the toolbar just as you can other toolbars.

3 Click the **Draw** button on the Drawing toolbar to display the Draw menu.

4 Click **Ungroup** to break the image into individual pieces.

Figure 3-12

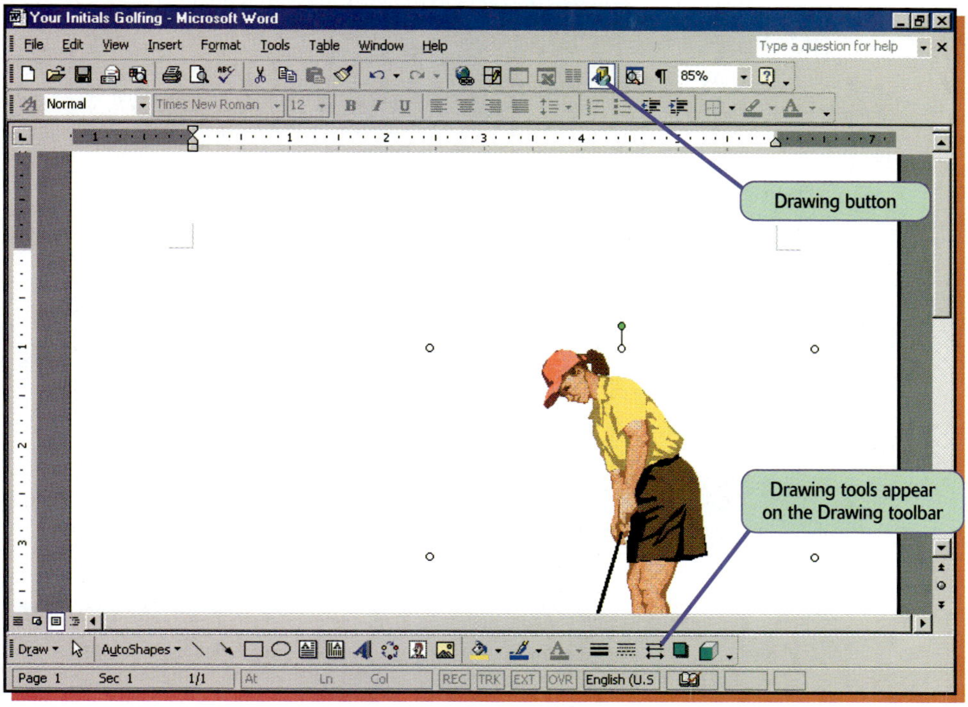

Figure 3-13

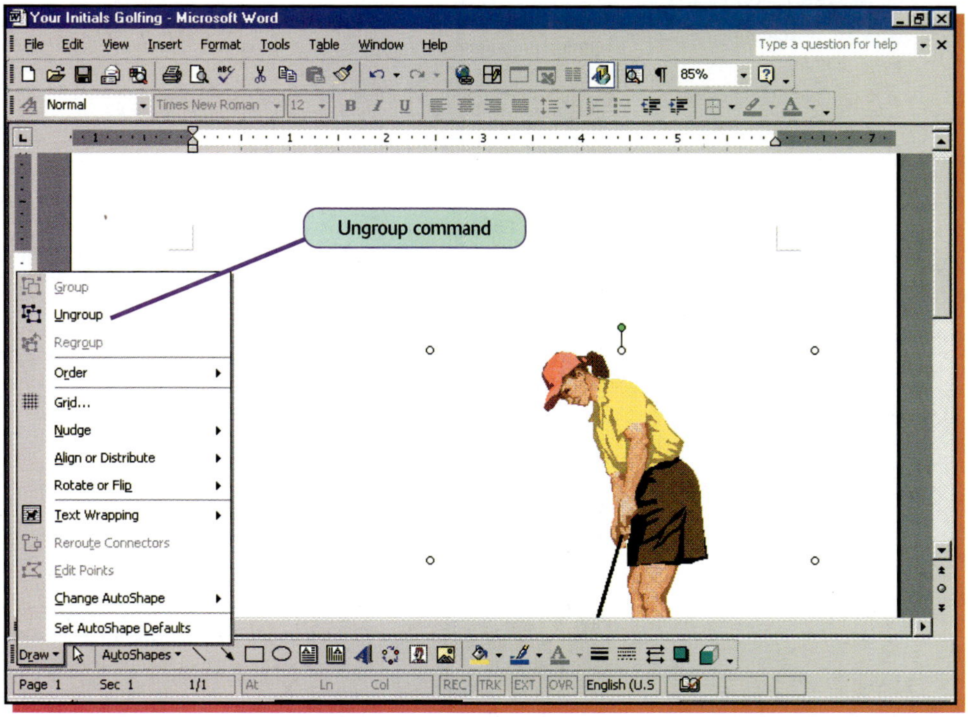

Tip Each clip art image is compiled of numerous lines and shapes grouped together so that you can move and size the whole image. To change the color of a piece of the image, you must first ungroup it. When you ungroup a clip art image, handles appear on all the individual pieces that make up the image. In some cases, an image is made up of smaller groups images that can also be ungrouped.

5 Click **Yes** to convert the image to an Office object.

Figure 3-14

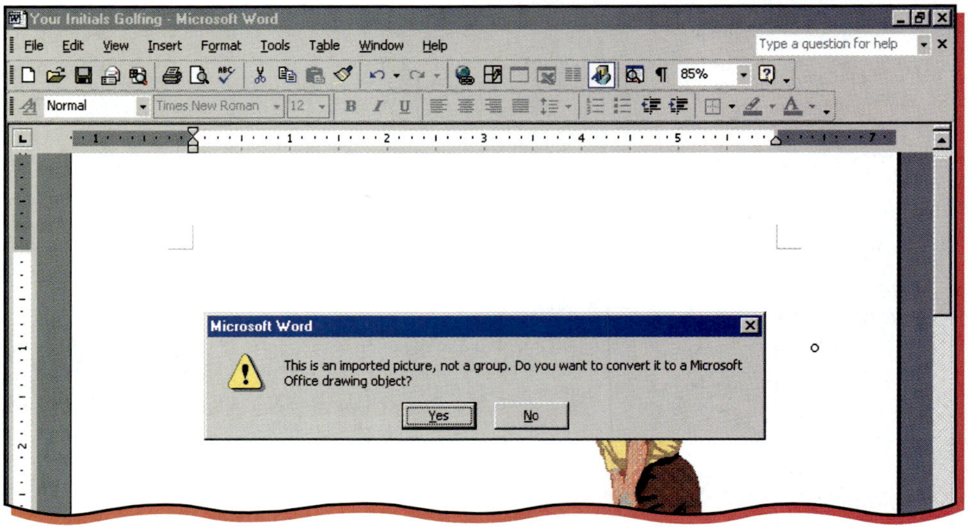

Tip Right-click on the Canvas edge and select **Show Drawing Canvas Toolbar**, if necessary, to display the *Drawing Canvas* toolbar.

6 Save changes to your work.

Figure 3-15

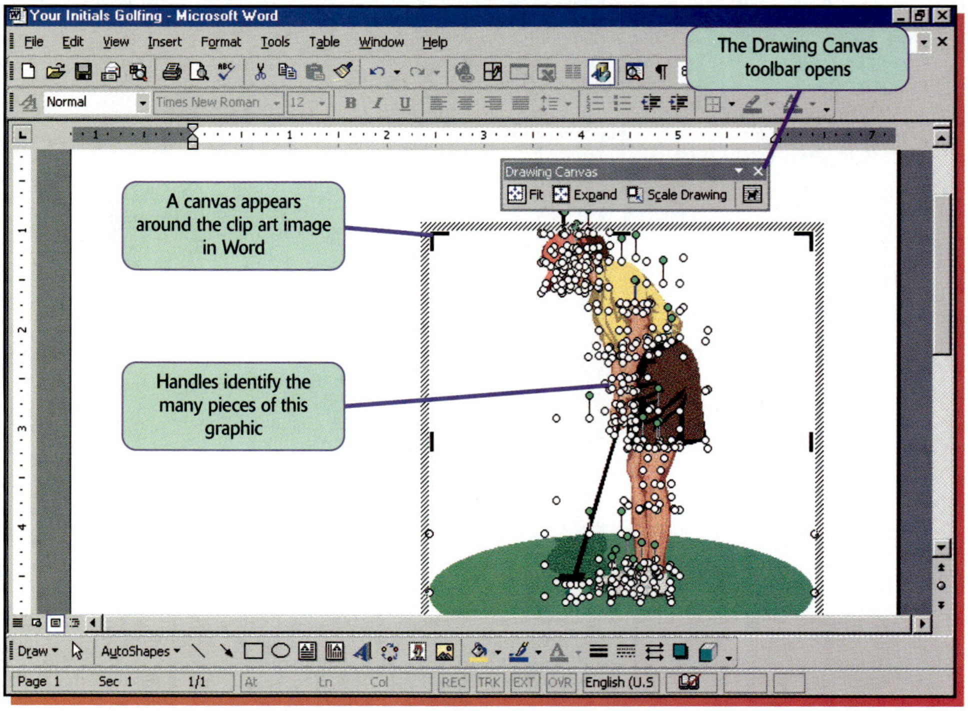

Task 4:
To Edit Clip Art Images

1 Click a white area away from the selected pieces, but inside the canvas border. All selection handles disappear.

2 Click the golfer's shorts to select the individual piece of the graphic.

3 Click the **Fill Color** down arrow on the Drawing toolbar and select the **Red** fill color. The shorts change color.

4 Click the **Expand** button on the Drawing Canvas toolbar two or three times to move the canvas border away from all parts of the graphic.

5 Position the mouse pointer below and to the right of the putting green, and then drag a marquee around all pieces of the clip art image.

6 Choose **Draw | Group** on the Drawing toolbar. The clip art image is reformed to a single object.

Figure 3-16

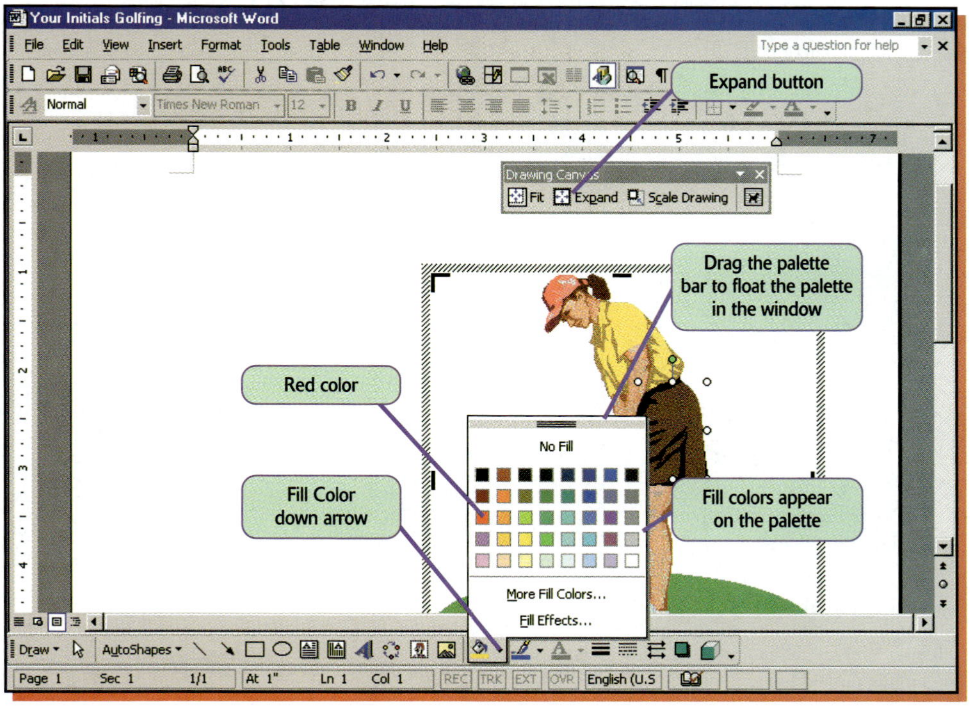

Figure 3-17

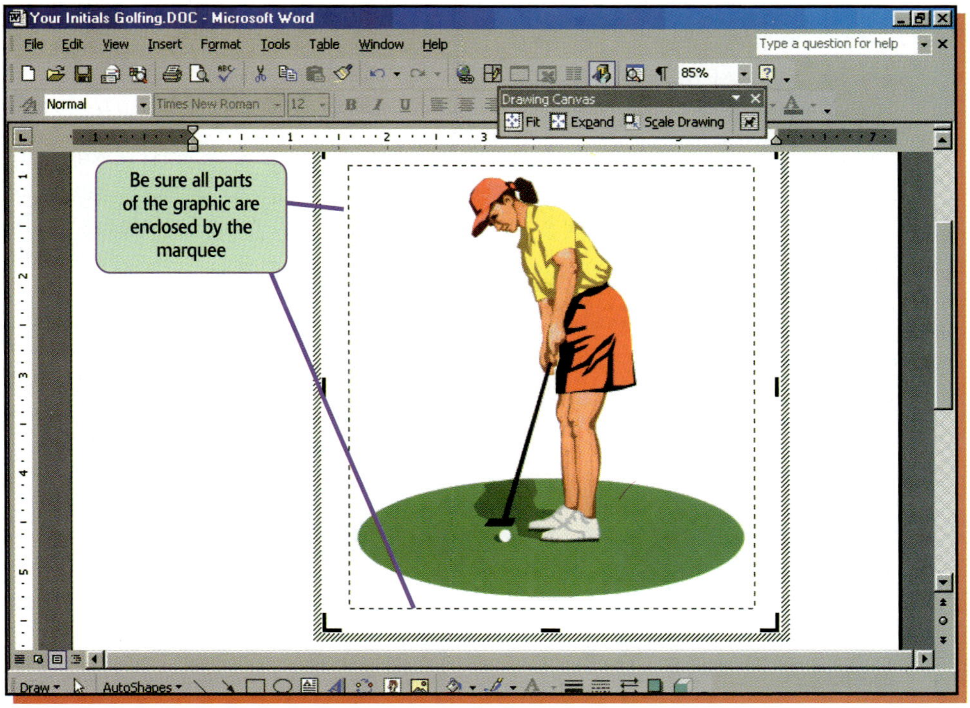

Troubleshooting The Drawing Canvas is a feature unique to Word. As you work with clip art in other applications, you will not see the Drawing Canvas.

7 Choose **Draw | Rotate or Flip | Flip Horizontal**. The golfer faces the opposite direction.

8 Save changes to your work and close the file.

Tip Design specialists often recommend that clip art and pictures added to documents be positioned so that they face toward the middle of the page. Flipping a clip art image is a great way to make the image conform to good design recommendations.

Figure 3-18

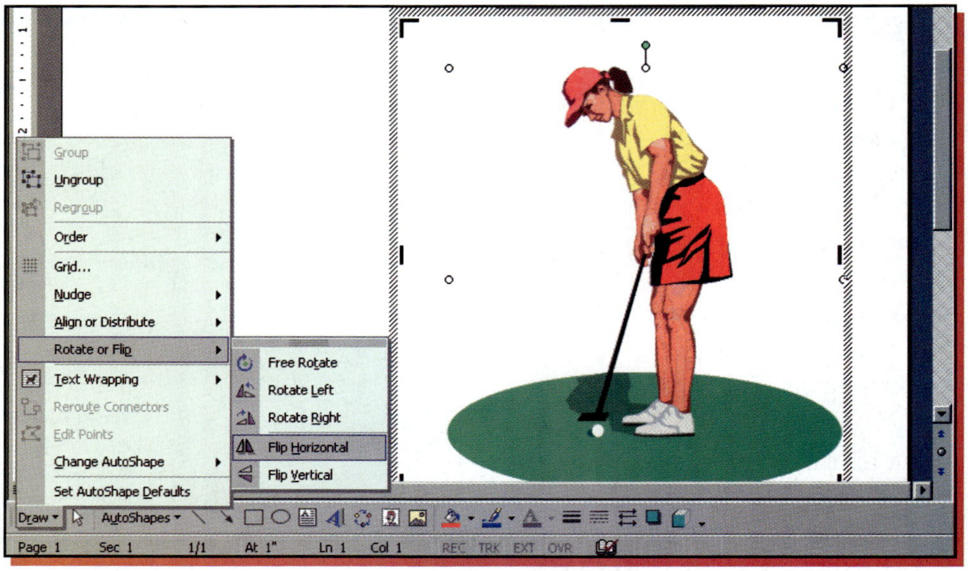

Displaying the Clip Organizer

In the previous tasks, you have worked with clip art that you inserted from the task pane. The Clip Organizer displays a list of folders containing the clip art that is available on your computer as well as other media clips, such as movies, sounds, and so forth. Images are grouped by type and placed in appropriate folders. Opening the folder related to the topic you are addressing displays thumbnails of the clip art that is available in the folder. Until you add images to the Favorites folder and download graphics from other sources, many of the folders are empty. The images displayed when you searched for banner clips are part of a set of standard clip art images that come with Office XP. These images are grouped by type into numerous folders in the Office Collection.

CHECK POINT

Do you recall how you displayed clips in the task pane that relate to a specific topic? You typed the topic in the search box and then clicked Search.

Task 5:

To Display and Use the Clip Organizer

1 Launch Word, if necessary, and create a new blank document.

2 Choose **Insert | Picture | Clip Art**. The task pane opens.

3 Click the **Clip Organizer** link at the bottom of the task pane.

Troubleshooting

If this is the first time the Clip Organizer has been started on your machine, a Microsoft Clip Organizer message may appear. Check the **Don't show this message again** option and click **OK**. The system will build the Clip Organizer for you.

4 Click the **Expansion** button beside the **Office Collections** folder to display collection subfolders.

Figure 3-19

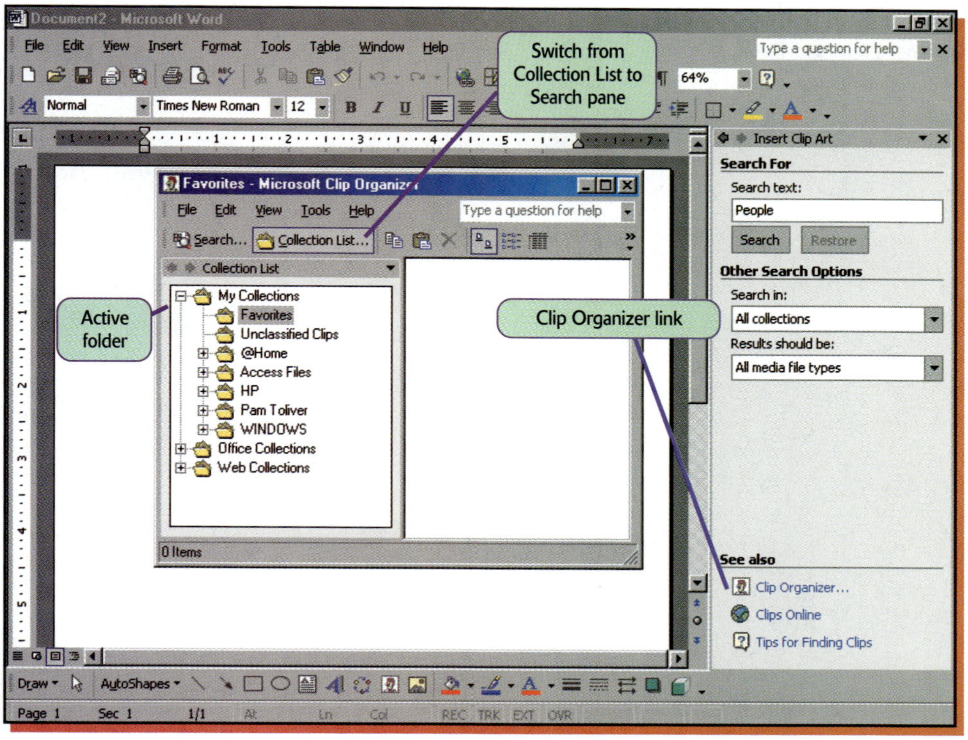

Figure 3-20

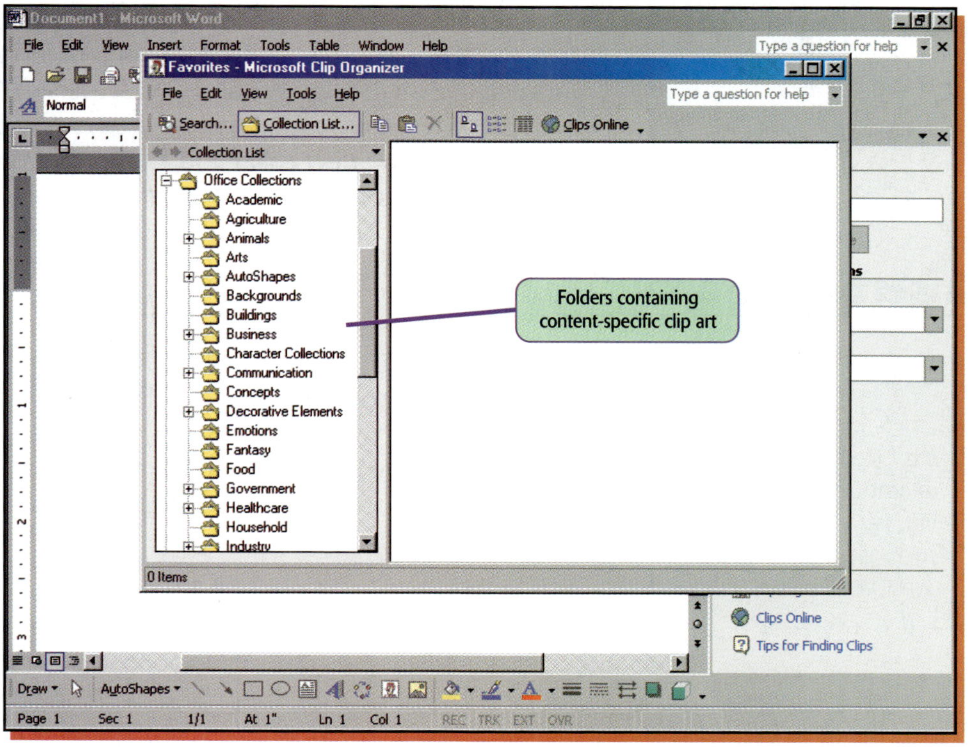

5 Select **Buildings** to open the folder and display thumbnail images contained in the folder.

6 Close the Clip Organizer and close the task pane.

Figure 3-21

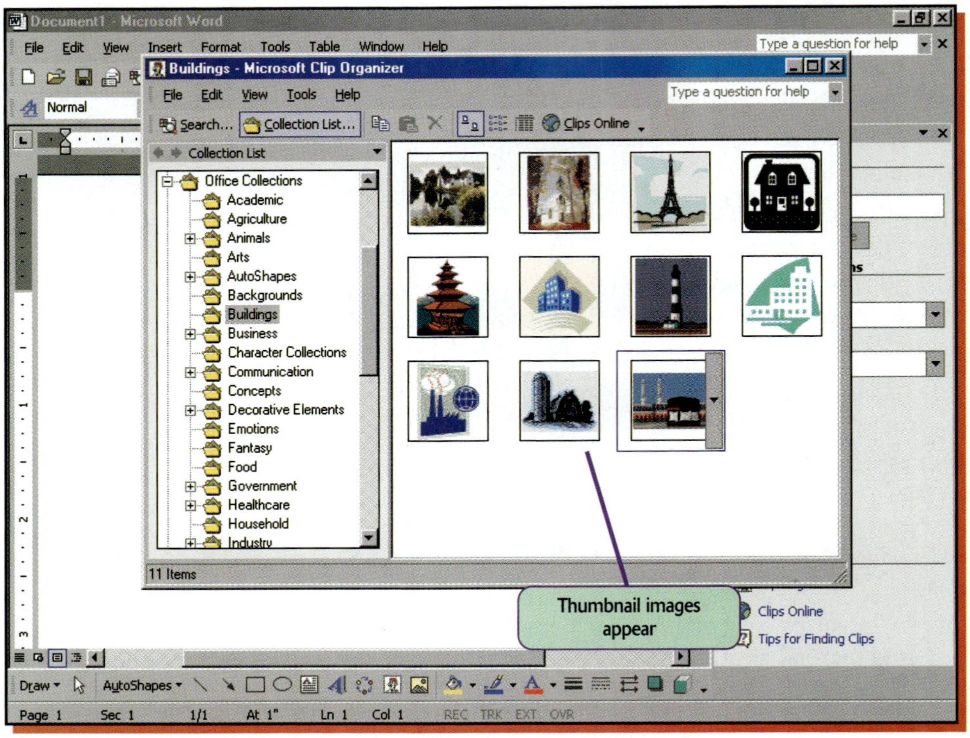

WEB TIP

As you locate clips on the Internet, you can download the clips and store them in the My Collections folders found in the Clip Organizer. You can also create new collection folders in My Collections. Simply select the My Collections folder, choose **File | New Collection,** type the name of the new collection folder, and click OK.

Inserting Graphic Images

Tip Graphic images are easy to identify by their extensions. Look for files with extensions such as .jpg, .bmp, .tif, .wmf, and .pcx.

As you continue to work with Office XP applications, you will begin to acquire images from a variety of sources—from the Internet, from scanned images from friends and relatives, and from graphics collections that you purchase. As you accumulate these images, you will often want to insert them into Office XP files. The procedure for inserting graphic images basically uses the same techniques you used to insert clip art images.

Task 6:

To Insert Graphic Files

1. Open the *e-Selections Online Graphics.doc* file.
2. Position the insertion point at the top of the document and choose **Insert | Picture | From File** to open the Insert Picture dialog box.
3. Open the disk and folder containing the *e-Selections Logo.jpg*
4. Select **e-Selections Logo** and then click **Insert** to place the figure in the document.

Figure 3-22

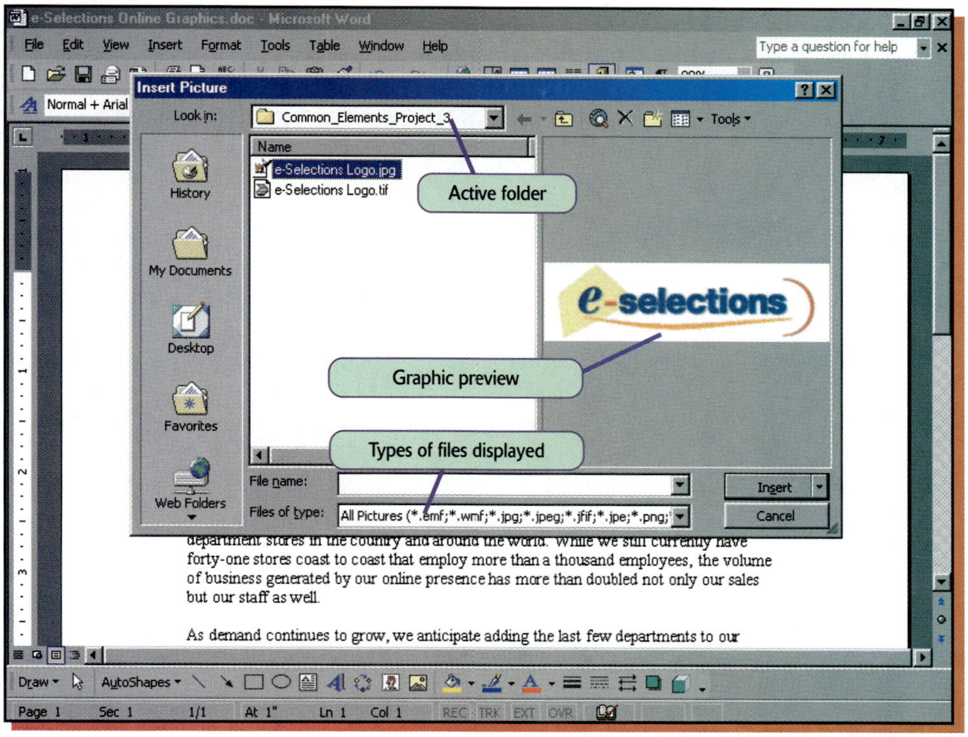

5. Change the layout of the graphic so that you can reposition it freely on screen and then size and position the graphic so that it appears in the upper left corner outside the margin area, as shown in Figure 3-23.
6. Save changes to the file and print a copy of the document.

Figure 3-23

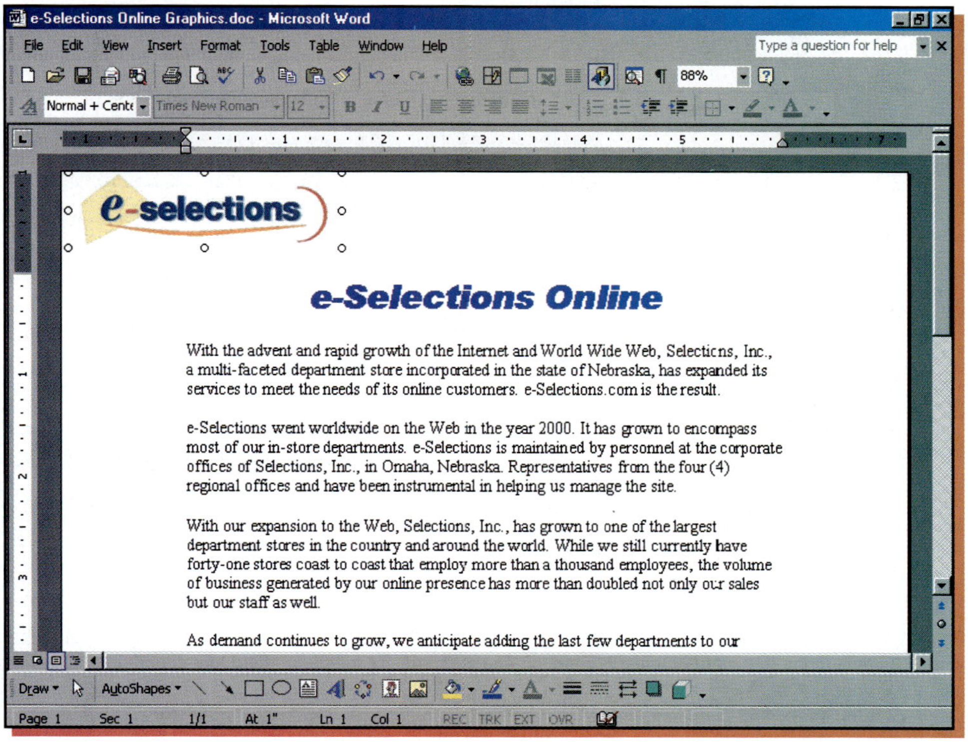

Tip While most clip art images can be ungrouped and edited, pictures you insert into files usually require a graphics editing program to edit.

CHECK POINT

Have you received pictures of your relatives attached to an e-mail message? Have you been impressed by photos that appear in newsletters? Perhaps you've even seen family photos on personal Web pages. If you have, you may have wondered how your family and friends converted their pictures to electronic files that can be sent with messages and posted on the Web.

Microsoft Office contains features that enable you to scan photographs and save them as graphics. Then it's simply a matter of inserting the files in e-mail messages or positioning the file in newsletter documents. You will, of course, need a scanner or a *digital camera* and you will also need to know the basics of how to use this equipment. Once you've got the equipment under control, you can get graphics directly from a scanner or camera using Microsoft Office XP applications. From any Microsoft Office Application, choose **Insert | Picture | From Scanner or Camera** and follow the screen prompts to capture the picture. Then use the skills you've learned in this project to manipulate the graphic.

Creating and Formatting WordArt

WordArt is a feature that enables you to dress up your files by creating graphic text—shaping text on curves and flows. WordArt is easy to create and can be positioned in a file to fit the size and shape you need. You can use WordArt to create a letterhead for your e-Selections stationery.

Task 7:
To Create WordArt

1. Launch Word, if necessary, display the Drawing toolbar, if necessary, and open a copy of *e-Selections Online Graphics.doc*.
2. Delete the logo graphics, select the title text, and then click the **Cut** button to place the text on the clipboard.
3. Click the **Bold** and **Italic** buttons to turn them off, if necessary.
4. Click the **Insert WordArt** button on the Drawing toolbar to open the WordArt Gallery.
5. Double-click the WordArt style identified in Figure 3-24.

Figure 3-24

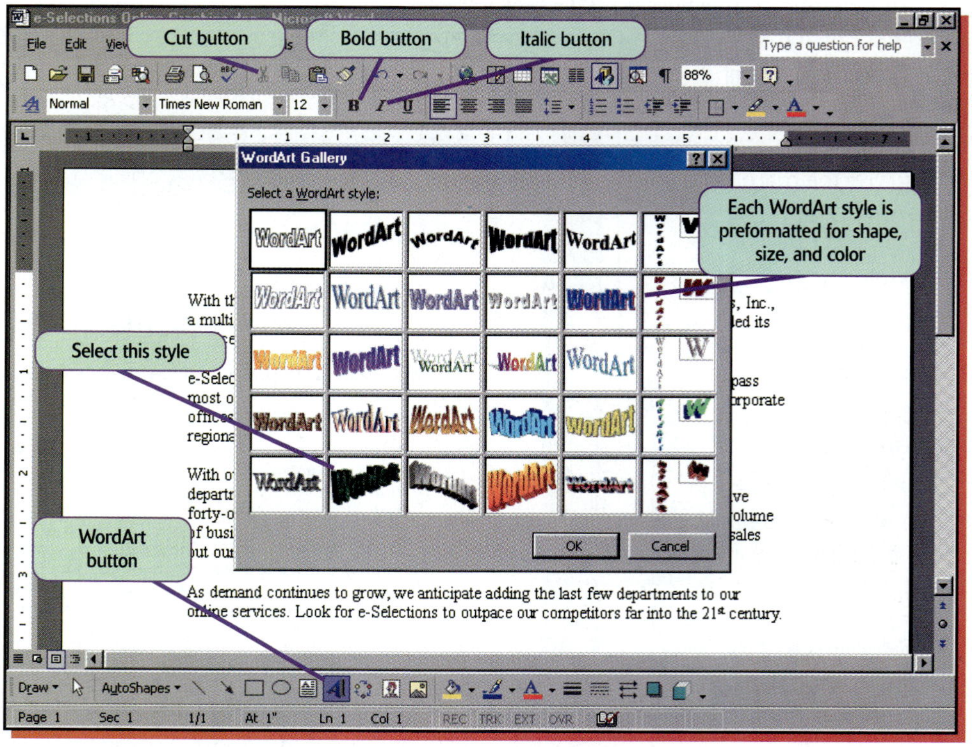

6 Press Ctrl + V to insert the title text and then click **OK**.

Tip When the Drawing toolbar is hidden, you can choose **Insert | Picture | WordArt** to create WordArt.

Figure 3-25

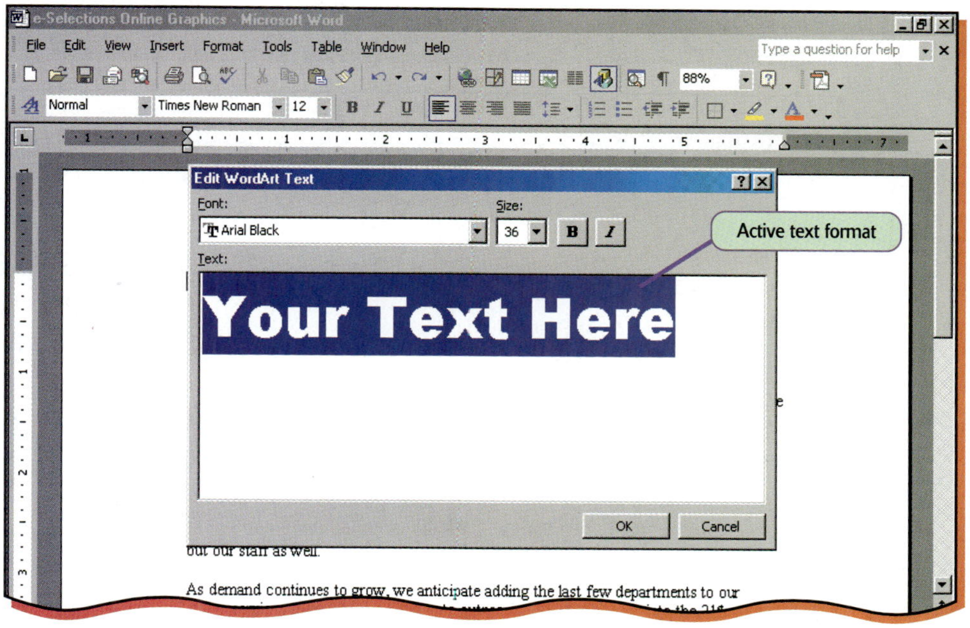

7 Save the document using the file name *Your Initials WordArt* and then close all open files.

WEB TIP

If you've purchased a book, a CD, a movie, or a video game lately, you know how quickly costs associated with these purchases can add up. Search the Web for online companies that act as resellers of these popular media items. You'll find that you can save more than half the cost by buying previously owned items!

Figure 3-26

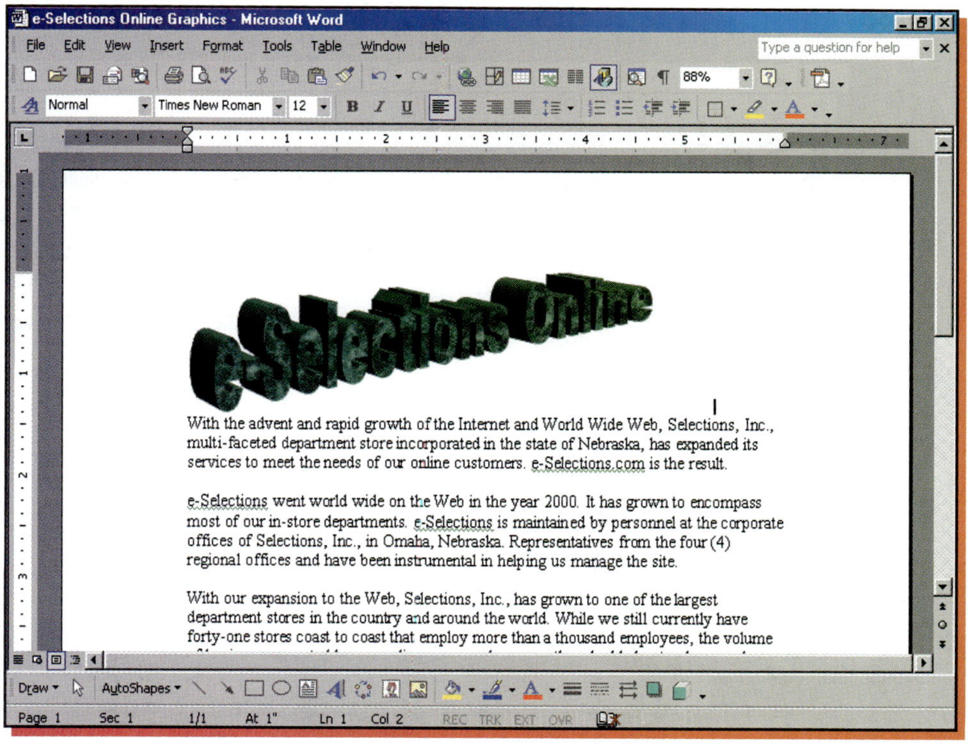

Creating and Manipulating Drawings

When you want to add shapes, lines, text boxes, and arrows to your Office XP files, you will find a sophisticated set of drawing tools that enable you to enhance files with original freehand creations. Even if you're no artist, you'll find the tools on the Drawing toolbar easy to use. Drawing is basically a three-step process:

1. Select the tool that represents the shape you want to draw.
2. Position the pointer where you want to start the drawing.
3. Click and drag the pointer to the shape ending point.

Then, while the shape is still selected, you can move, size, and edit the shape as needed.

Creating Basic Shapes and AutoShapes

Buttons for the shapes that are drawn most frequently appear on the Drawing toolbar. Other shapes are found grouped by type on the *AutoShapes* menu found on the Drawing toolbar.

Task 8:
To Create Shapes

1. Launch Word, if necessary, and create a new blank document.

2. Display the Drawing toolbar, if necessary, and click the **Rectangle** button.

Figure 3-27

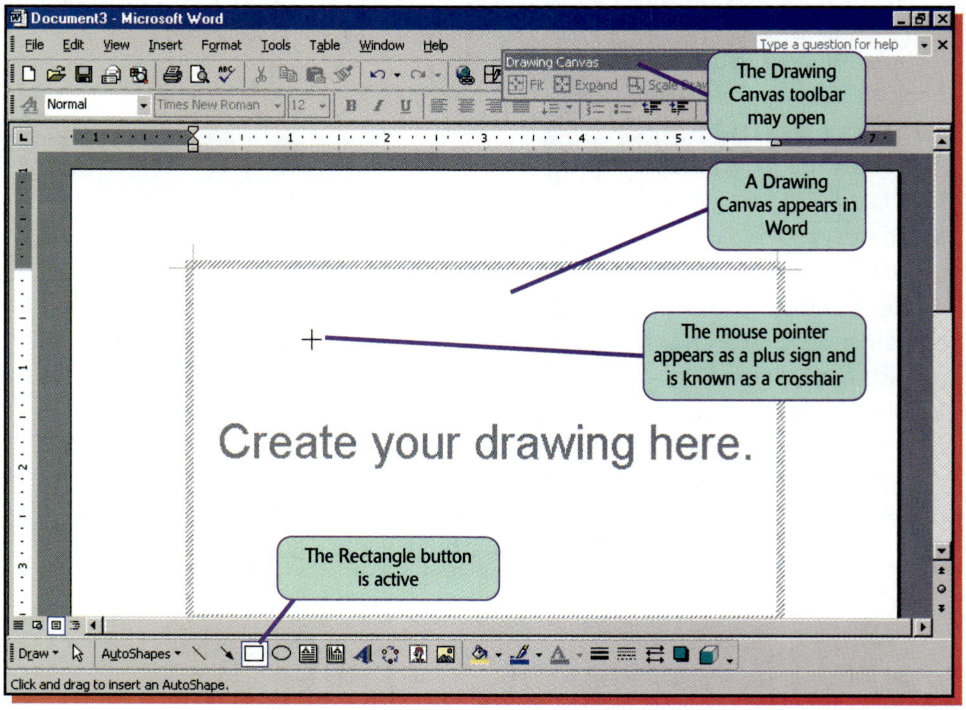

3 Position the *crosshair* mouse pointer on the left side of the Drawing Canvas and then click and drag the crosshair diagonally to form a rectangle.

Tip You can set different colors for shape fills and border. In addition, you can change the line size to add weight to shape borders. Experiment with drawing tools to create different types of custom effects.

Figure 3-28

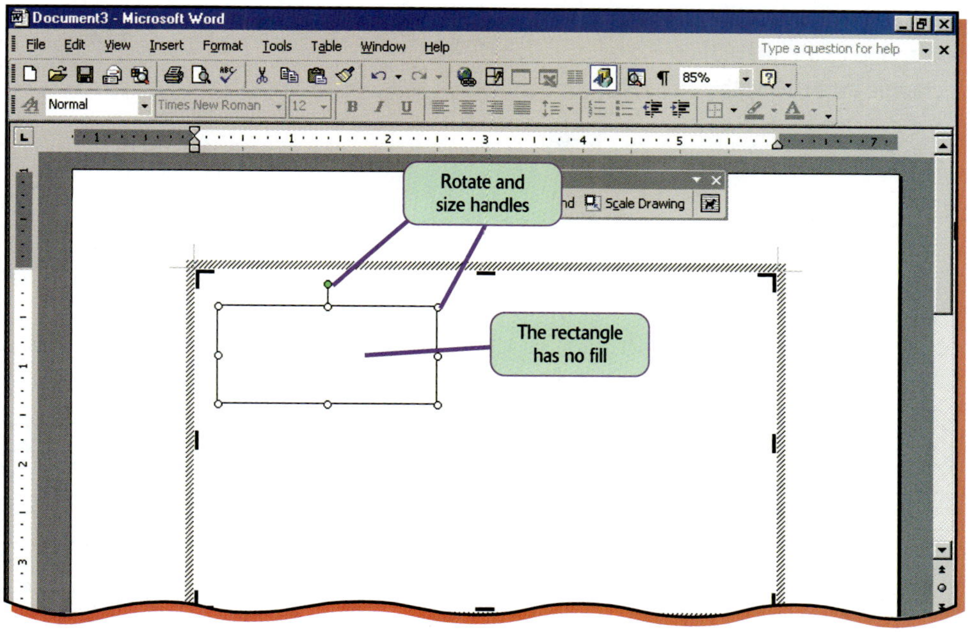

4 Click the **Fill Color** button to fill the rectangle with the default fill color.

5 Click the **AutoShapes** menu on the Drawing toolbar.

6 Select **Basic Shapes** to open the Basic Shapes palette and select the **Lightning Bolt** shape.

Tip Point to each shape on the Basic Shapes palette to identify the different shapes available. Screen tips help locate specific shapes.

Figure 3-29

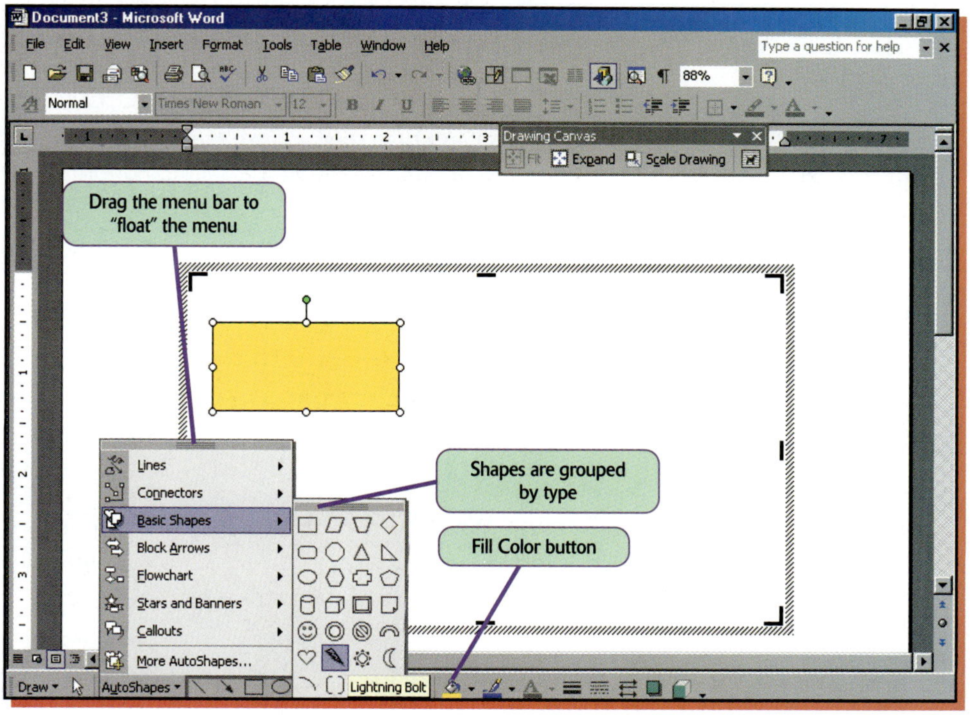

7 Repeat the procedures outlined in Steps 3 and 4 to create a lightning bolt shape to the right of the rectangle and fill it with color.

Figure 3-30

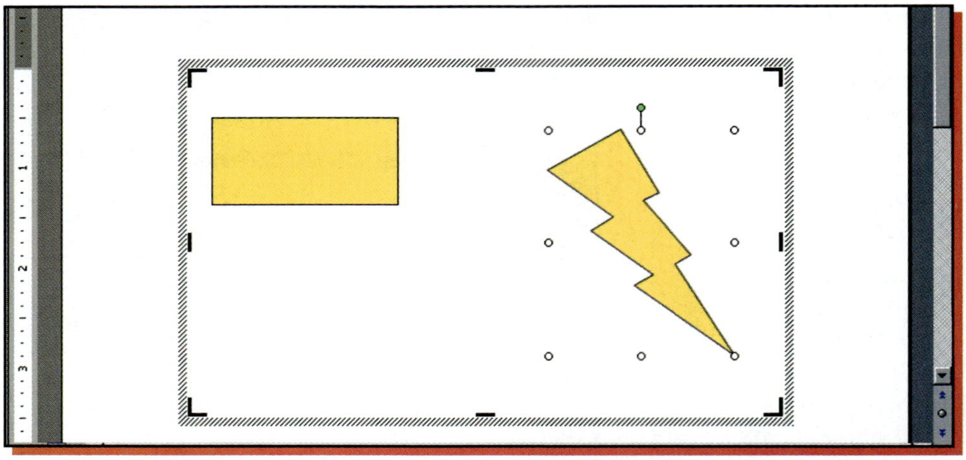

CHECK POINT

As you become more comfortable with the drawing tools available in Microsoft Office Applications, you'll find yourself wanting to be more precise in drawing shapes. Here are some tips to get you started and help you position and size both clip art and drawn objects:

- Press and hold the Ctrl key as you size objects to size the object from the center point out.
- Press and hold the Shift key while you draw lines to make them straight and while you draw shapes to make them symmetrical—rectangles become squares, ovals become circles, and triangles are equilateral.
- Press and hold the Alt key to release the "snap to" feature so that you can move a boundary or size a shape more precisely.

Formatting Shapes

You can use many of the same techniques that you used to format clip art to format drawn objects. You can size, flip, rotate, and change the color of drawn objects just as you can edit and manipulate clip art.

Setting Wrap Text Options. Text can be added to most drawn objects. After adding text, you will often need to change the text wrap option so that text appears properly on the drawn object.

Task 9:
To Set Text Wrap Options

1 Right-click the **lightning bolt** and select **Add Text**. The insertion point appears within the lightning bolt.

Figure 3-31

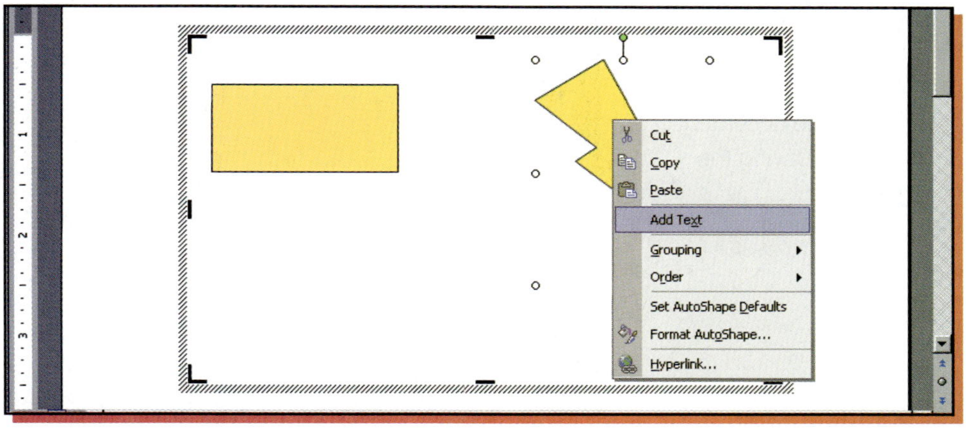

2 Type **Lightning Strikes Again!**

Troubleshooting
Text may be hidden as you type. Don't worry—we're about to fix it.

Figure 3-32

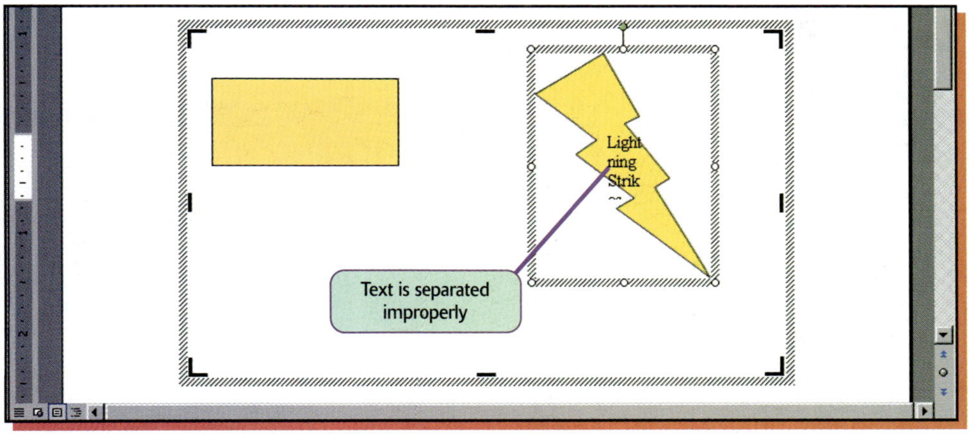

3 Right-click a blank area of the lightning bolt and select **Format AutoShape** to open the Format AutoShape dialog box.

4 Click the **Text Box** tab, select the **Resize AutoShape to fit text** option, and then click **OK**. The lightning bolt changes size to accommodate the text.

Figure 3-33

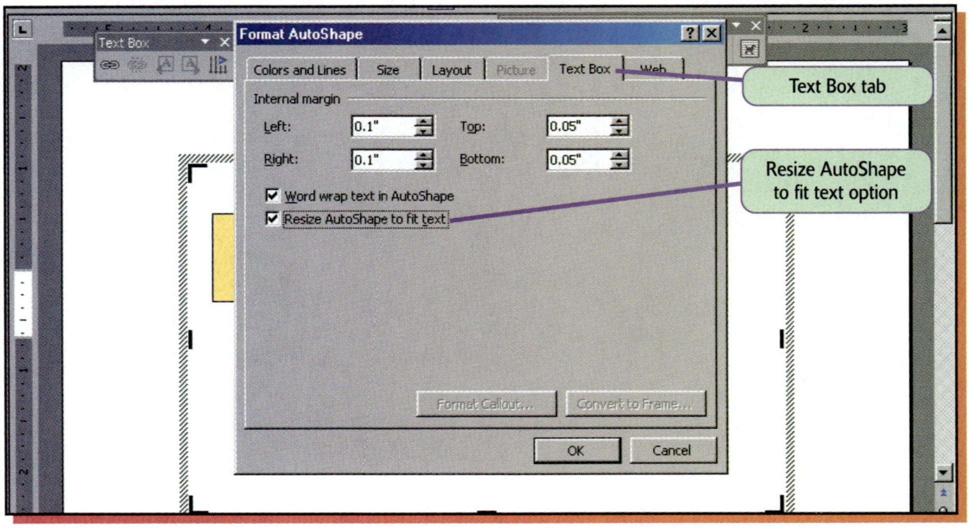

5 Manually drag handles to size the lightning bolt so that the text is within the bolt boundaries.

6 Close the document without saving the changes.

Figure 3-34

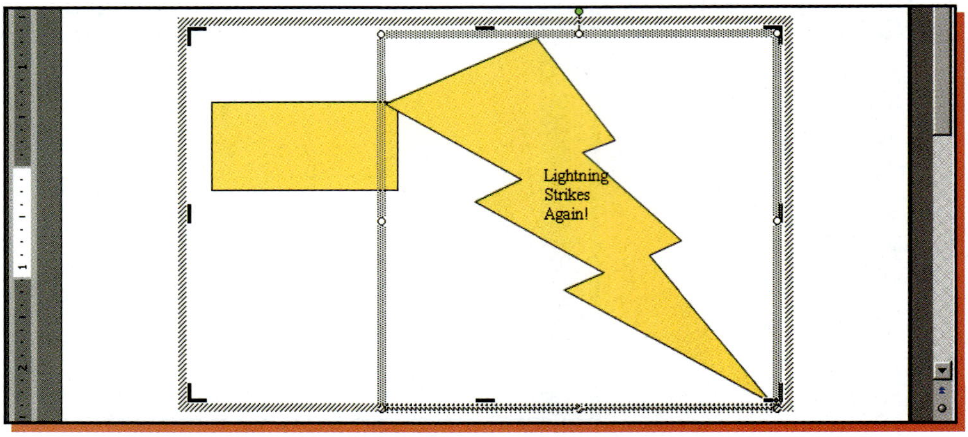

Changing the Fill and Line Color. Fill and line color can be changed to format drawn objects. In addition, special fill effects can be used to create special visual effects.

Task 10:
To Create Special Effects Using Fill and Line Color

1 Create a new blank document in Word.

2 Double-click the **Oval** button on the Drawing toolbar and create the drawing shown in Figure 3-35.

Tip Double-clicking a drawing button enables you to draw multiple shapes using the same drawing tool without having to continually click the shape.

Figure 3-35

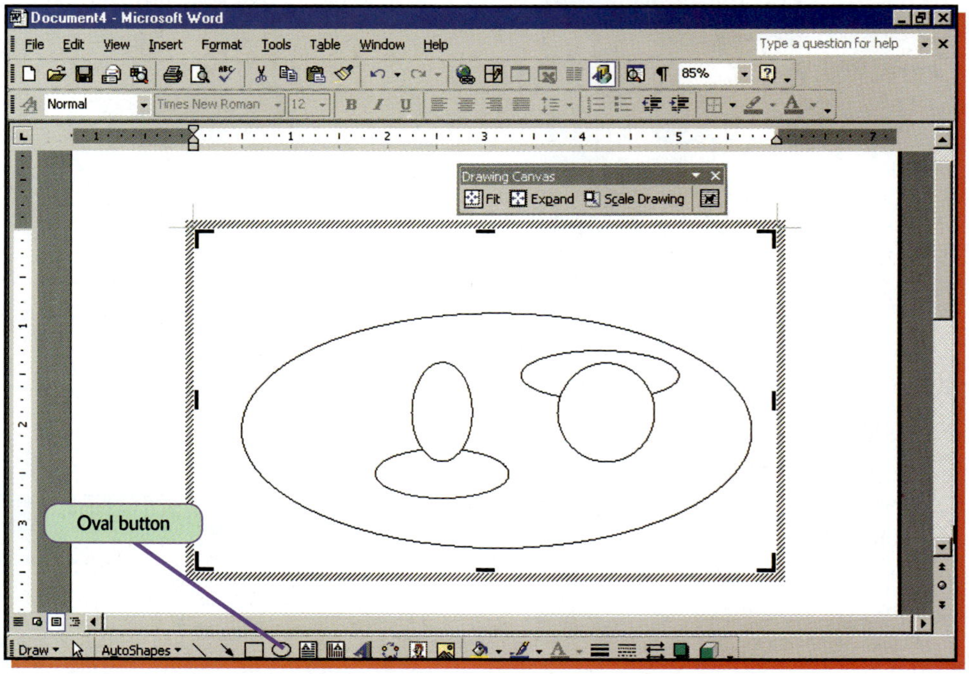

3 Press [Esc], select the largest oval in the Drawing Canvas, click the **Fill Color** down arrow, and select **Fill Effects** to open the Fill Effects dialog box.

Tip The Fill Effects dialog box contains tabbed pages that display a number of different fill effect options. Explore these effects as time permits.

Figure 3-36

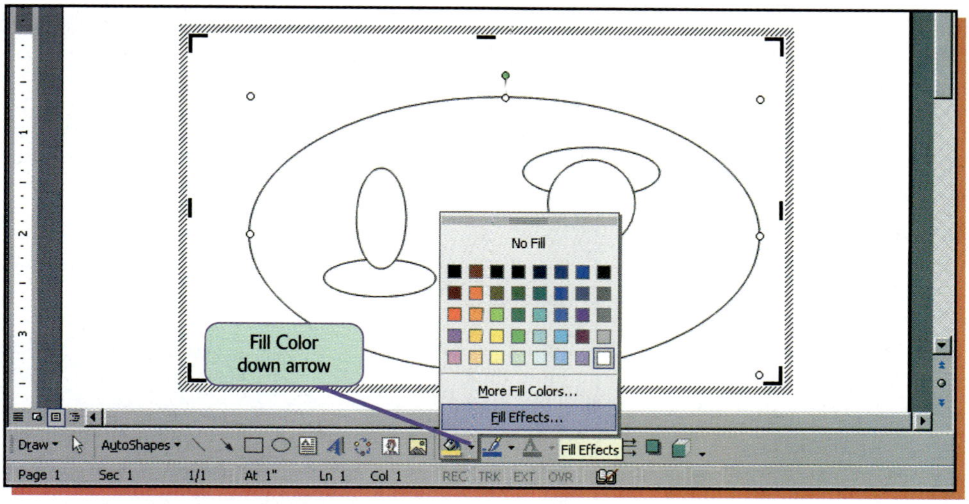

4 Click the **Gradient** tab and set the following options:

- Two colors
- Color 1: Light Blue
- Color 2: Dark Blue
- Shading Styles: Diagonal up

Troubleshooting After you select a shading style, the Variants palette displays different shading angles. The active variant appears with a darker border that is sometimes easy to miss.

Figure 3-37

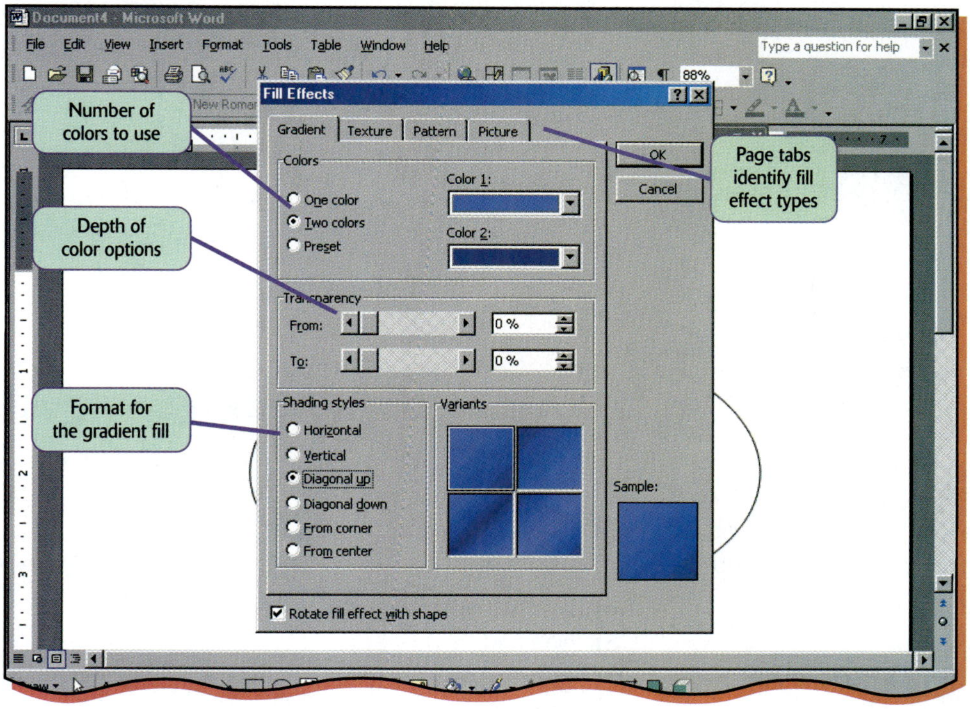

5 Click **OK** and then select the vertical oval on the left.

6 Display the **Fill Effects** dialog box and set the options listed in Step 4, changing the Shading Styles to **Diagonal Down**; then click **OK**.

7 Click the **Line Color** drop-down list arrow and select **No Line**.

8 Save the file using the file name *Your Initials Floating Circles*.

Figure 3-38

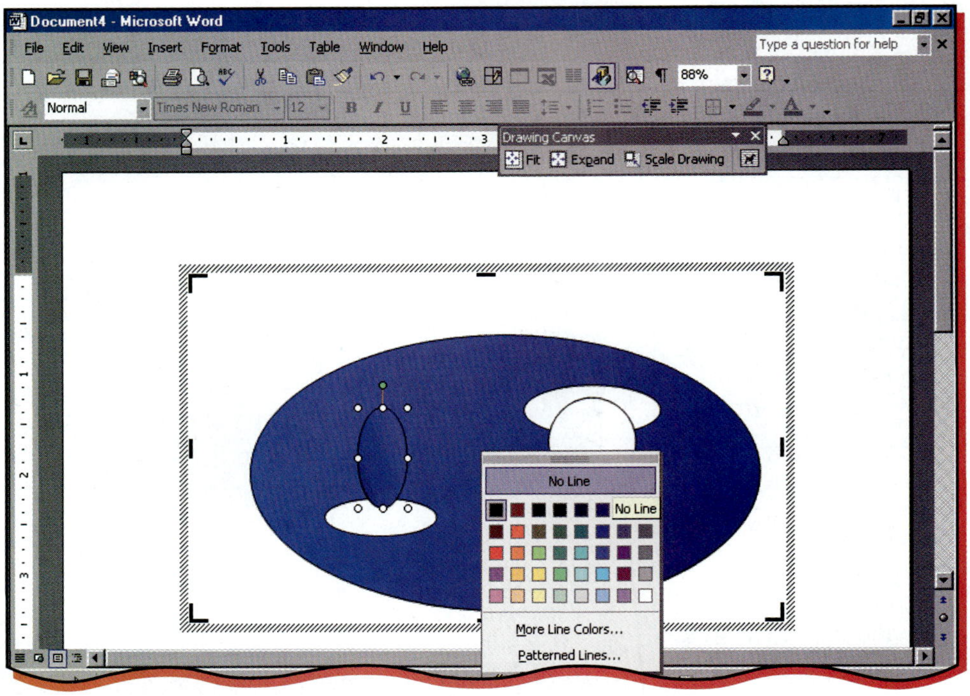

Tip Removing the line from drawn objects makes them appear to blend in with other drawn objects or with file background colors.

Changing Shapes

After a shape is created and formatted, you can change the shape just as you change the line and fill colors. The format you apply to drawn shapes can create special effects.

Task 11: To Change a Drawn Shape

1 Launch Word and open the *Your Initials Floating Circles.doc* document, if necessary.

2 Select the oval on the right to select it.

Figure 3-39

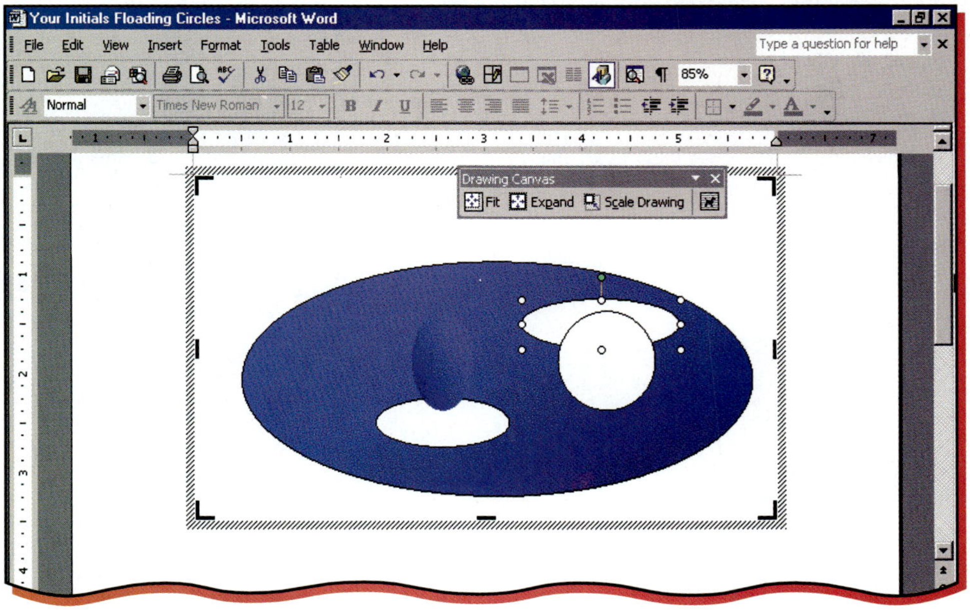

3 Choose **Draw | Change AutoShape | Basic Shapes**.

4 Select the **Change Shape to Rectangle** shape on the Basic Shapes palette.

Tip
Notice that the screen tip that appears when you point to different shapes on the palette includes the "Change Shape to" text to let you know that you are changing an existing shape to a different shape. When no drawn shape is selected, the screen tip simply identifies the shape.

Figure 3-40

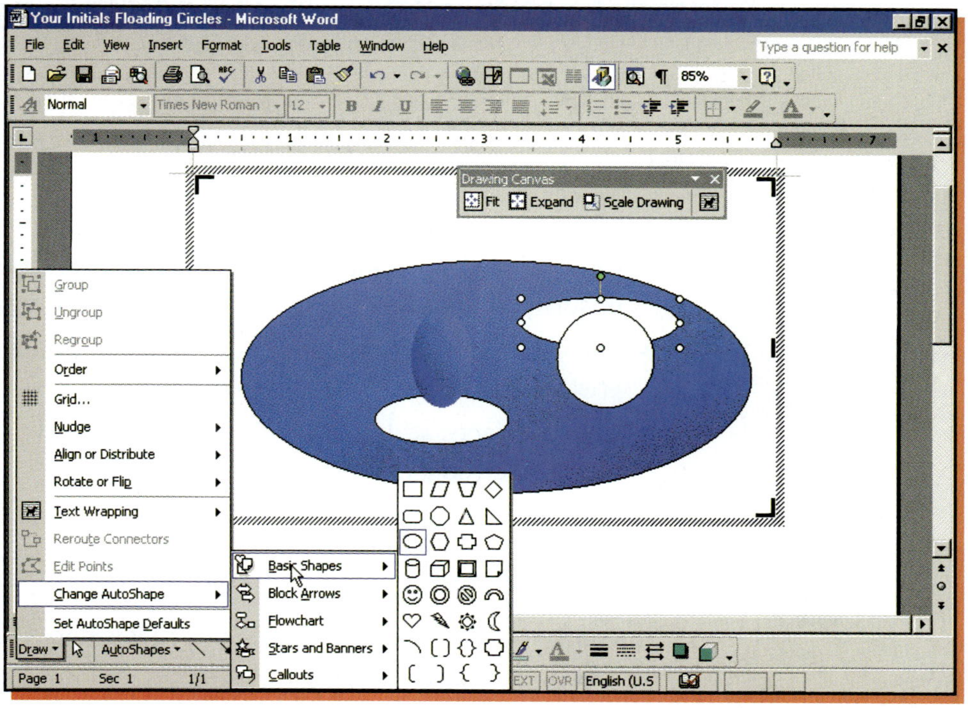

5 Save and close the document and exit Word.

Troubleshooting
You will work with this diagram in the exercises at the end of Project 3, so be sure to save it.

Figure 3-41

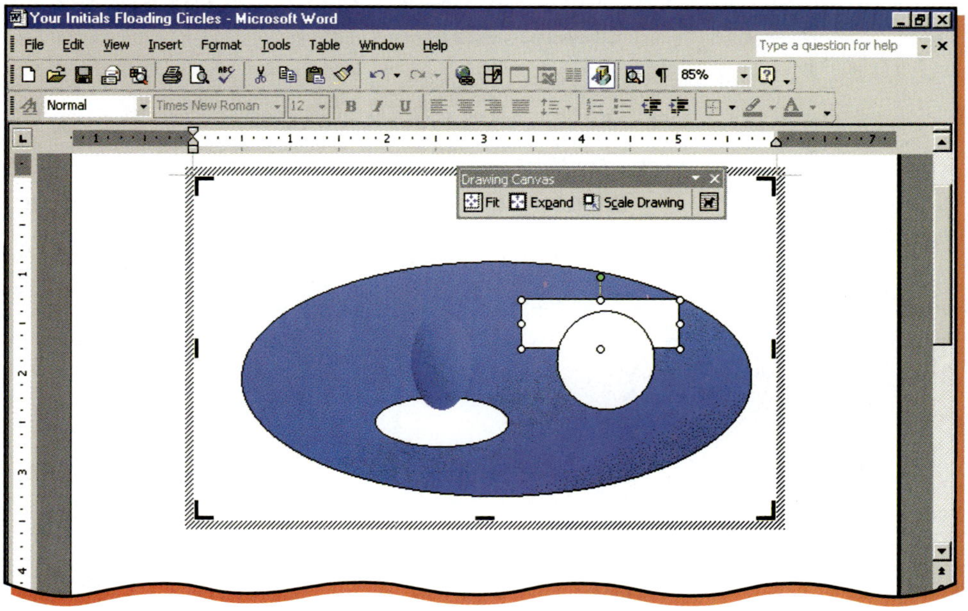

SUMMARY AND EXERCISES

SUMMARY

- Clip art images, scanned images, WordArt, and manual drawings enable you to dress up files in all Office XP applications.
- The Clip Organizer contains graphics on a number of topics and enables you to search by topic for related images.
- Clip art images added to Office XP files can be flipped, rotated, ungrouped, edited, and regrouped.
- Graphics scanned into computers or input from digital cameras as well as files of graphics received from other sources or downloaded from the Internet can be inserted in Office XP files.
- WordArt enables you to graphically format text to enhance Office XP files.
- The sophisticated set of drawing tools on the Drawing toolbar enables you to create original freehand art.
- When a shape or object is inserted, you can move, size, and edit the selected item.
- AutoShapes are grouped by type on the AutoShapes menu of the Drawing toolbar.
- Text can be added to most drawn shapes as well as to clip art and graphic items inserted into files.
- The shape chosen for a particular drawing can be changed to different shapes without deleting the original shape and redrawing it.
- Fill and line color can be changed for drawn shapes as well as for pieces of ungrouped clip art objects.

KEY TERMS & SKILLS

KEY TERMS

AutoShapes (p. 3-18)
clip art (p. 3-1)
Clip Organizer (p. 3-2)
crosshair (p. 3-19)
digital camera (p. 3-16)
Drawing Canvas (p. 3-10)
fill (p. 3-11)
gradient (p. 3-23)
scanned images (p. 3-1)
thumbnails (p. 3-2)
WordArt (p. 3-1)

SKILLS

- Change a drawn shape (p. 3-24)
- Create special effects using fill and line color (p. 3-22)
- Create WordArt (p. 3-16)
- Display and use the Clip Organizer (p. 3-13)
- Draw shapes (p. 3-18)
- Edit clip art images (p. 3-11)
- Insert clip art images (p. 3-2)
- Insert graphics from scanners and digital cameras (p. 3-14)
- Move and size clip art images (p. 3-5)
- Set text wrap options (p. 3-21)
- Ungroup clip art images (p. 3-9)

STUDY QUESTIONS

MULTIPLE CHOICE

1. The dialog box that displays clip art images is the
   a. Format Object.
   b. Clip Organizer.
   c. Drawing Palette.
   d. Edit Picture.

2. When you search for clip art images that are related to a particular topic, possible images that meet your needs appear in the
   a. task pane.
   b. active file.
   c. status bar.
   d. toolbars.

3. All of the following are different types of graphic images *except*
   a. .tif.
   b. .pcx.
   c. .jpg.
   d. .xfx.

4. The button on the Standard toolbar that displays the Drawing toolbar is
   a. Tables and Borders.
   b. Insert Hyperlink.
   c. Drawing.
   d. Insert Chart.

5. Before you can move most clip art images, you must change which settings?
   a. Picture Layout
   b. Graphic Format
   c. Image Size
   d. Object Format

6. To create a letterhead that arches over the top of a page, you would choose which feature?
   a. Headers
   b. Clip Art
   c. TextFont
   d. WordArt

7. Clearing which option restores free placement of a graphic?
   a. enable overlapping
   b. lock anchor
   c. move object with text
   d. none of the above

8. The toolbar that contains tools for drawing free shapes is the
   a. Standard toolbar.
   b. Picture toolbar.
   c. Drawing toolbar.
   d. Web toolbar.

9. The Change AutoShape command is found on what menu?
   a. Format
   b. Insert
   c. AutoShapes
   d. Draw

10. To view all text added to drawn shapes, it is sometimes necessary to set the
   a. wrap text options.
   b. shape format.
   c. fill color.
   d. line color.

SHORT ANSWER

1. What are the first three steps of adding a clip art picture to a file?
2. What commands do you use to fill a drawn object with two different colors and where are the commands located?
3. Which feature would you use to draw lines, arrows, and boxes?
4. What steps would you follow to insert a graphic from the Internet?
5. Where is the AutoShapes menu located?
6. How are shapes organized on the AutoShapes menu?
7. What are the very small copies of images in the Clip Gallery called?
8. How do you add text to drawn objects?
9. What is the difference between flipping an object and rotating it?
10. What are some additional sources for graphics that you can add to files?

FILL IN THE BLANK

1. ____________ is a feature that enables you to dress up files by creating graphic text.
2. Office XP applications share a common ____________ that contains a variety of different images you can add to your files.
3. ____________ appear on selected images, which enable you to resize or drag the object.
4. Clip art images are stored in collection ____________ that sort images by type.
5. Before you can change the color of a piece of a clip art image, you must first ____________ it.
6. The Drawing Canvas for drawing shapes appears only in the ____________ application.
7. Color added to the center of drawn objects is called ____________.
8. Small copies of clip art images are called ____________.
9. Commands for adding graphics to Office XP files appear on the ____________ menu.
10. Graphics can be captured as electronic files from printed pictures using a ____________.

DISCUSSION

1. Describe the steps you would follow to move and resize a clip art image.
2. How do the procedures for adding clip art differ from the procedures for adding other graphics to Office XP files?
3. When would you use the Clip Organizer instead of the task pane for adding items to Office XP files?
4. Explain the procedures you would follow to put a clip art image back together.

GUIDED EXERCISES

1 FLOATING OBJECTS

The ovals and rectangles you added to the *Your Initials Floating Circles.doc* document are not yet complete. The finished graphic is pictured in Figure 3-42.

Figure 3-42

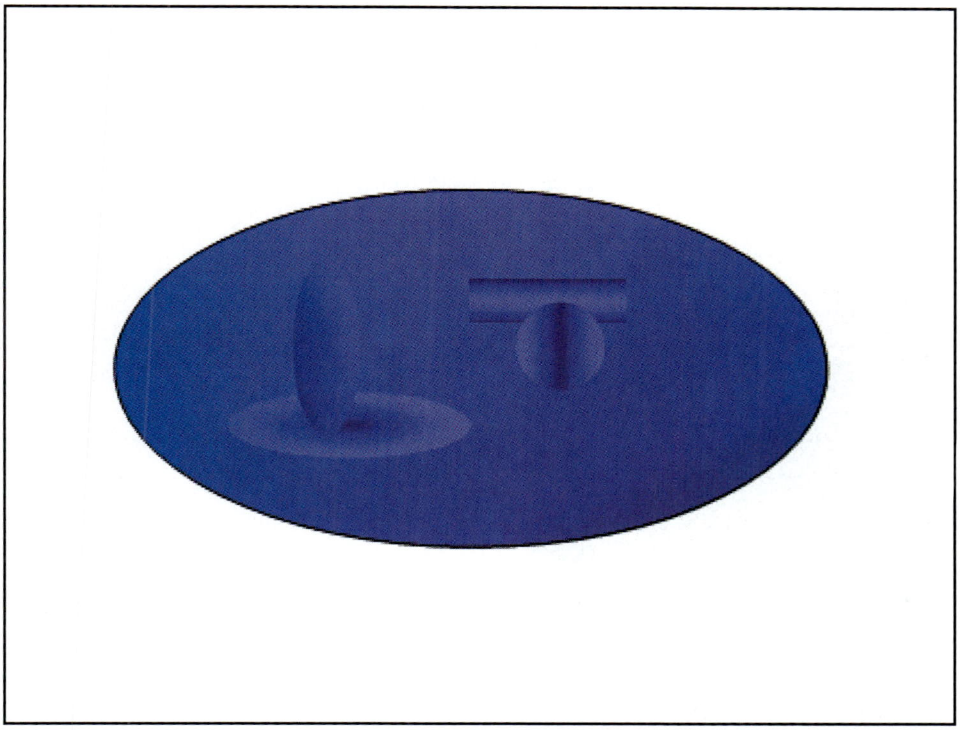

You can complete this task before moving on to other tasks. Follow these instructions:

1. Launch Word and open *Your Initials Floating Circles.doc*, if necessary.
2. Display the Drawing toolbar, if necessary.
3. Select one of the unfilled ovals.
4. Click the **Fill Color** button on the Drawing toolbar and select **Fill Effects**.
5. Set the following options on the Gradient page of the Fill Effects dialog box:
   - Colors: Two colors
   - Color 1 Light Blue
   - Color 2 Dark Blue

- Shading styles A different style from other shapes
- Variants A different variant from other shapes

6. Remove the border line from the shape.
7. Repeat the procedures outlined in Steps 3–6 for all other shapes.
8. Save changes to the file and print a copy of the drawing.

2 CREATING A GRAPHIC FLYER

Store hours for Selections, Inc., are changing in the fall. You have been asked to create the flyer pictured in Figure 3-43 so that it can be distributed to customers and placed in local newspapers to inform the public of the new hours.

Figure 3-43

Follow these steps to complete the flyer:

1. Create a new blank document.
2. Insert the picture file **Stars.wmf** and size it appropriately on the page.

Right-click the graphic and select **Format Picture**. Click the **Layout** tab and select the **Behind text** wrapping style and the **Right** Horizontal alignment option; then click OK.

4. Change the font for the flyer to Lucida Handwriting or a similar script or writing font and change the size to 36 points.

5. Click the **Align Right** button on the Formatting toolbar.

6. Type the text as shown and make adjustments as necessary to reposition the graphic or text on the page.

7. Save the document using the file name *New Store Hours Flyer* and print a copy of the flyer.

8. Close the document.

3 CREATING BUILDING BLOCKS

e-Selections personnel have decided to promote healthy eating habits. The flyer they want to distribute is shown in Figure 3-44.

Figure 3-44

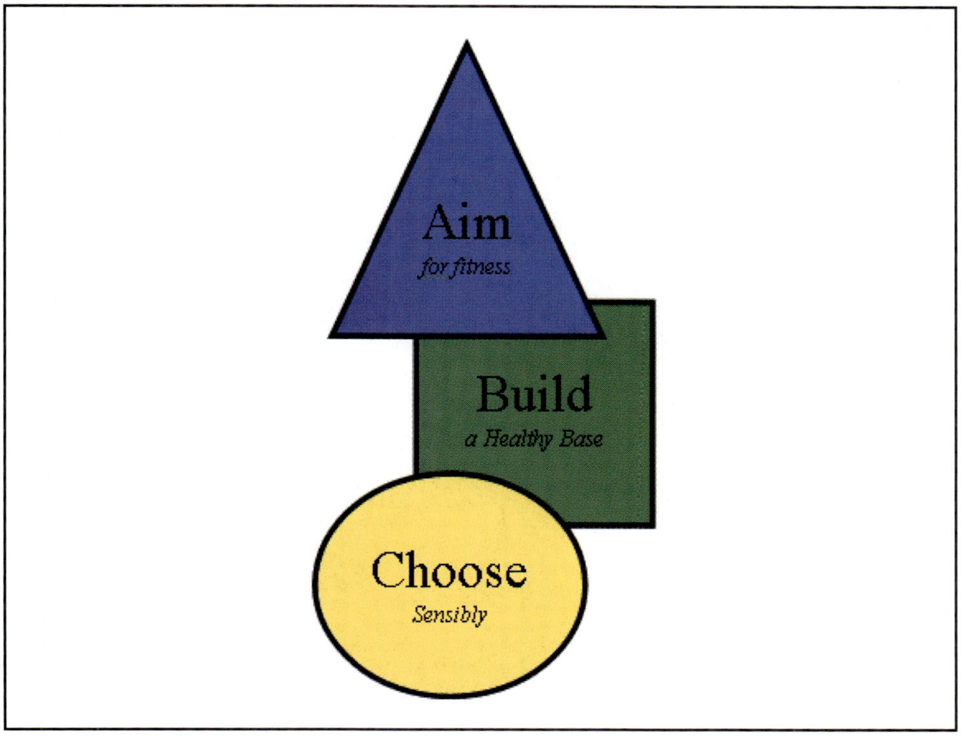

Create the graphic for the flyer by following these steps:

1. Launch Word, if necessary, and create a new blank document.
2. Create the square in the center of the building blocks and set the following options:
   - Change the fill color to green.
   - Click the **Line Style** button on the Drawing toolbar and select **3 pt**.
3. Choose **AutoShapes | Basic Shapes | Isosceles Triangle**, draw and position the triangle as shown in Figure 38, and set the following format:
   - Change the fill color to blue.
   - Change the line style to 3 pt.
4. Draw the ellipse, position it as shown, and set the following format:
   - Change the fill color to yellow.
   - Change the line style to 3 pt.
5. Right-click each of the drawn objects separately, type the text shown, and format the text as follows:
   - Center the text in all shapes.
   - Change the size of text in the first line to 28 pts.
   - Italicize text on the second line.
6. Adjust the size of the objects to accommodate the text.
7. Save your file using the file name *Your Initials Building Blocks* and print a copy of the file.

ON YOUR OWN

The difficulty of these case studies varies:

are the least difficult; *are more difficult; and* *are the most difficult.*

1 ADDING A TEXT BOX

Open the file *Phantom Ghosties.doc*. Insert a text box below the existing text on the second page and type **Phantom Ghost** in the text box. Center the text box and arrange the text so that it appears on one line. Size and format the text in the text box using the same font and size as text in the document but change the text color to black and fill the text box with orange background. Save changes to the file and print a copy of the document.

2 LOCATING LICENSE AGREEMENTS FOR CLIP ART USAGE

Search the Internet for clip art. Visit numerous sites and locate at least two different license agreements for downloading the clip art collections that you find. Print copies of the license agreements.

3 CREATING A FUN NOTICE GRAPHIC

Open the file *Phantom Ghosties.doc*. Access Clips Online to locate a clip of a ghost. Insert the clip art of a ghost below the text box. Format the graphic so that it is centered on the page and size the graphic so that it covers a large portion of the page. Save changes to the file and print a copy of the file.

FINDING CLIP ART ONLINE, INSERTING CLIP ART, AND ADDING TEXT

Search the Microsoft Design Gallery Live site for clip art graphics of apples. Download the apple you like best. Then create a new blank document in Word and add the clip art image of the apple to the document. Size the graphic so that it encompasses most of the page and position the apple in the center of the page. Then add the following text to a text box in the center of the apple:

An apple or two for lunch on Monday is an excellent antidote to a weekend of overeating. Apples travel well, come in their own packaging, and keep for a long time. What could be simpler?

Center the text in the text box and size and format the text as desired. Then change the fill color of the text box to the color of the apple. Save your file using the file name *Your Initials An Apple a Day* and print a copy of the file.

5 CREATING STATIONERY USING WORDART

Create personal stationery that contains each of the following features:

- WordArt containing your name.
- A text box containing your address and phone number—formatted using a unique font.
- A graphic that represents your personality.

Size and arrange the features attractively on the page in such a way that there is room to type letters on the stationery. Save the document using the file name *Your Initials Personal Stationery*.

6 CREATING FAMILIAR LOGOS

Many logos are quite popular and easily recognized by the general population. However, how easy are these logos to duplicate? Locate at least three logos that appear relatively simple in their construction and try to recreate these logos altogether on the same page of a document. Then download a copy of the logo from the Internet and insert the graphic logo beside your reconstructed logo. Save the file using the file name *Your Initials Logos* and print a copy of the file.

Introducing Access 2002

If you've ever needed to manage information for your business or personal use, track customer information for a business, or manage your CD collection at home, you'll want to learn about Microsoft Access. These examples represent collections of data that can be managed using a database. Access is a database management tool that enables you to create, organize, view, and print the information stored in a database just the way you need it.

e-selections Running Case

Welcome to the Administration Department of e-Selections! You have been assigned to work with Travis Traylor. Mr. Traylor has several assignments for you. The first is to create a simple database to track phone, mail, and e-mail contacts.

OBJECTIVES

After completing this project, you will be able to:

- *Define database terminology*
- *Identify Access database objects*
- *Plan and design a database*
- *Launch Microsoft Access and create a new database using the Database Wizard*
- *Identify Microsoft Access screen elements*
- *Close a database and exit Access*

Introducing Access 2002

The Challenge

Mr. Traylor wants a database that any manager can use to track customers, company associates, or others.

The Solution

You will use Microsoft Access's Database Wizard to create a contact management database. Microsoft Access comes with many of these Database Wizards that will create a fully functional database.

The Setup

Because Access is a unique and very different application, options set in other Office XP applications rarely affect the way Access appears when you launch it. As a result, the features displayed in the Access window vary, depending on the setup in the lab, computer classroom, or office you are using. Figures shown in this book are based on the default settings that appear with a typical Access 2002 installation. Table 0-1 identifies the settings that are used to get you started in Access. As you move through the different Access projects, you will customize settings and folders along the way.

Table 0-1 Access Default Settings

Default Feature	Setting
Office Assistant	Hide the Office Assistant.
Application window	Maximize the window.
Toolbars	Only the Database toolbar is active when you launch Access.
Task pane	The task pane opens when you launch Access.

Defining Database Terminology

Because Access is a different type of application from those you have used, a basic overview of the terminology associated with Access and databases in general will help get you started. Table 0-2 identifies some of the most basic terms associated with using database programs.

Table 0-2 Database Terminology

Term	Definition	Examples
Field	Each piece of information about a person, place, or thing.	A person's first name or last name, date of birth, company name, etc.
Record	All the information related to one person, place, or thing.	All the information in a personal address book about one person.
Database	A collection of all records related to a particular subject or purpose.	All the records contained in a personal address book.

Figure 0-1 displays the e-Selections employee address information with 15 records. Each record contains seven fields.

Figure 0-1

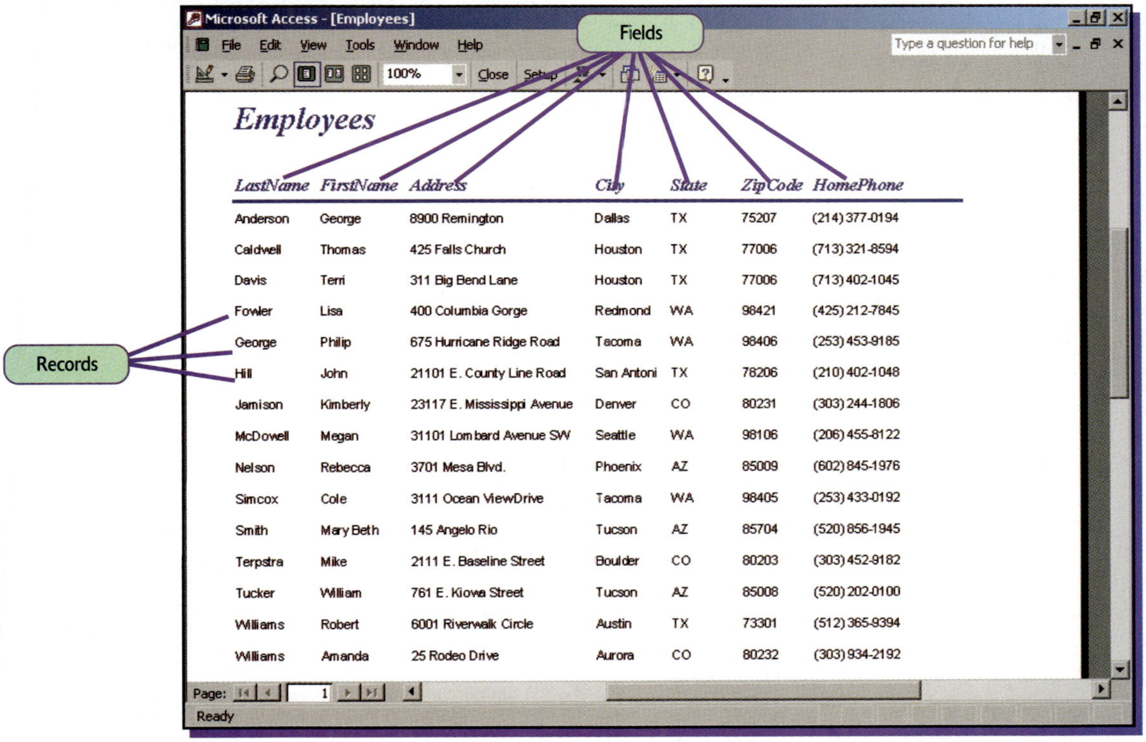

Identifying Database Objects

Access is a sophisticated database application that is often referred to as an *object-oriented database*. Object-oriented databases use different tools, called *objects*, to store and display database records and other information. Because each object stores data that is in some way related to data contained in other objects, Access is often referred to as a *relational database management system*

(*RDBMS*). In Microsoft Access, all of the database objects you create are stored in a single file with an .mdb file name extension. Microsoft Access uses seven different database objects. Each of these objects is described in Table 0-3.

Table 0-3 Seven Types of Access Database Objects

Object	Description
Table	Tables provide the basic unit and primary object for building databases because they contain the data that is organized in records (rows) and fields (columns). Each database must contain at least one table before you create any other object.
Query	Queries provide a tool for selecting data from database tables based on criteria you set, so that only the records that meet the criteria are shown and other records are filtered out. A query is always based upon and built from data contained in one or more tables.
Form	Forms are special layout designs that display data in a separate window one record at a time and that can be used to enter or view data. Forms are based on and built from tables or queries.
Report	Reports are special layouts designed to present data in a printed document format. Reports are based on and built from tables or queries.
Page	Data access pages provide a layout design for publishing database data on the Web.
Macro	Macros are used to automate tasks such as opening forms or printing reports.
Module	Modules contain Visual Basic for Applications programming code that can extend the functionality of your database.

Figure 0-2 illustrates how the address book information shown in Figure 0-1 would appear in an Access table.

Figure 0-2

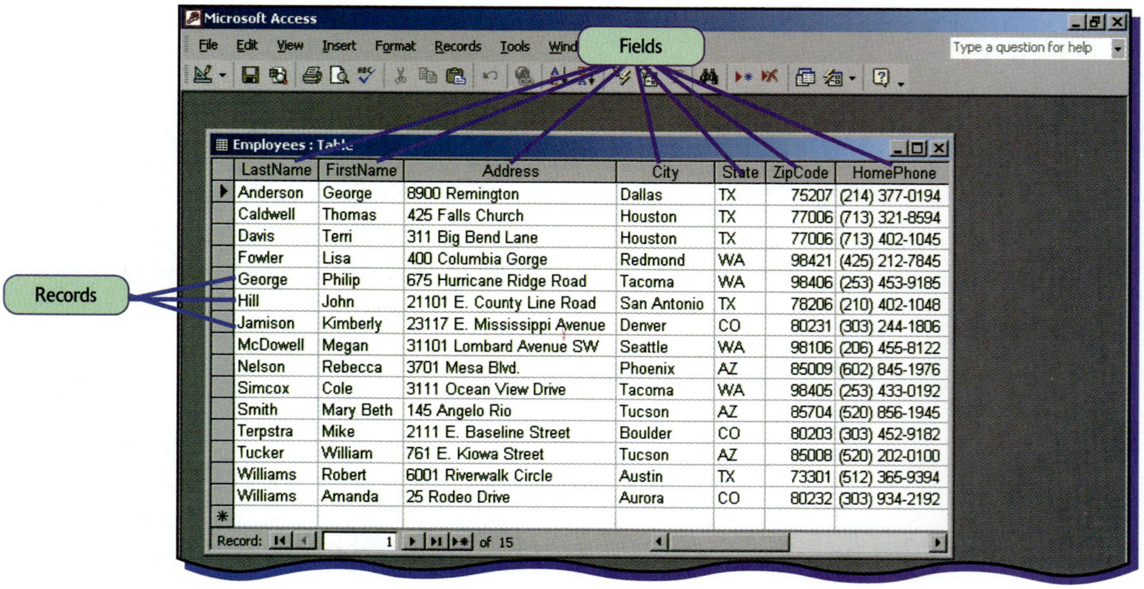

LastName	FirstName	Address	City	State	ZipCode	HomePhone
Anderson	George	8900 Remington	Dallas	TX	75207	(214) 377-0194
Caldwell	Thomas	425 Falls Church	Houston	TX	77006	(713) 321-8594
Davis	Terri	311 Big Bend Lane	Houston	TX	77006	(713) 402-1045
Fowler	Lisa	400 Columbia Gorge	Redmond	WA	98421	(425) 212-7845
George	Philip	675 Hurricane Ridge Road	Tacoma	WA	98406	(253) 453-9185
Hill	John	21101 E. County Line Road	San Antonio	TX	78206	(210) 402-1048
Jamison	Kimberly	23117 E. Mississippi Avenue	Denver	CO	80231	(303) 244-1806
McDowell	Megan	31101 Lombard Avenue SW	Seattle	WA	98106	(206) 455-8122
Nelson	Rebecca	3701 Mesa Blvd.	Phoenix	AZ	85009	(602) 845-1976
Simcox	Cole	3111 Ocean View Drive	Tacoma	WA	98405	(253) 433-0192
Smith	Mary Beth	145 Angelo Rio	Tucson	AZ	85704	(520) 856-1945
Terpstra	Mike	2111 E. Baseline Street	Boulder	CO	80203	(303) 452-9182
Tucker	William	761 E. Kiowa Street	Tucson	AZ	85008	(520) 202-0100
Williams	Robert	6001 Riverwalk Circle	Austin	TX	73301	(512) 365-9394
Williams	Amanda	25 Rodeo Drive	Aurora	CO	80232	(303) 934-2192

CHECK POINT

What other Microsoft Office applications use a table-like layout to display data?

Basic tables in word processing programs such as Microsoft Word resemble Access tables. In addition, if you are familiar with a spreadsheet program such as Microsoft Excel, you will notice that a table is similar to a worksheet. Records would be the rows in Excel and fields would be the columns. For simple databases, a spreadsheet program would give you some database functionality, but Access is a much more powerful database program.

As you become more familiar with some of the advanced features of Access, you'll learn how to create *relationships* between Access tables so that you can pull data from multiple tables to create other database objects.

WEB TIP

Want to take a tour of Access? Microsoft will give you a tour when you visit its Web site. You will also find other helpful information on the Web site to help you use Microsoft Access more effectively.

Planning a Database

Planning is essential for any databases, from a database to manage your recipes to a database to manage your multimillion-dollar business. Planning and laying out database objects ensures that no important detail is overlooked and reduces the amount of time spent editing object structures after the database is complete. The following five steps will help you plan and design an effective database:

1. Define the purpose of your database.

   Knowing what type of information you want for output helps you to determine what data needs to be used as input. It also helps to determine what specific tasks your database needs to handle.

2. Plan tables and fields.

   Specifying the fields for each table helps you identify how data in each table is related to data in other tables and helps reduce redundancy.

3. Plan queries to reorganize data.

   Identifying fields contained in database tables that might need to be displayed on screen or used in a report will help you locate specific information in the database. Planning queries also enables you to identify fields required to perform calculations.

4. Plan forms, pages, and reports.

   Displaying and printing meaningful information from databases is the ultimate goal of using databases to store data. Carefully planning forms, pages, and report layouts is essential and ensures that required information is included in tables, queries, and other objects from which forms, pages, and reports get their data.

5. Create the database objects.

   Building a database involves creating database tables, adding records and organizing them, and using table data to create other database objects.

Launching Access and Creating a New Database Using the Database Wizard

Tip Depending on your computer's setup, some of these procedures may be unavailable.

As with other Microsoft Office applications, there are several ways to launch Access:

- Double-click the Microsoft Access shortcut icon on the desktop.
- Click the Launch Microsoft Access icon on the Quick Launch toolbar.
- Choose **Start | Programs | Microsoft Access**.

Task 1: To Launch Microsoft Access and Create a New Database Using the Database Wizard

1. Choose **Start | Programs**.
2. Select **Microsoft Access**.

Figure 0-3

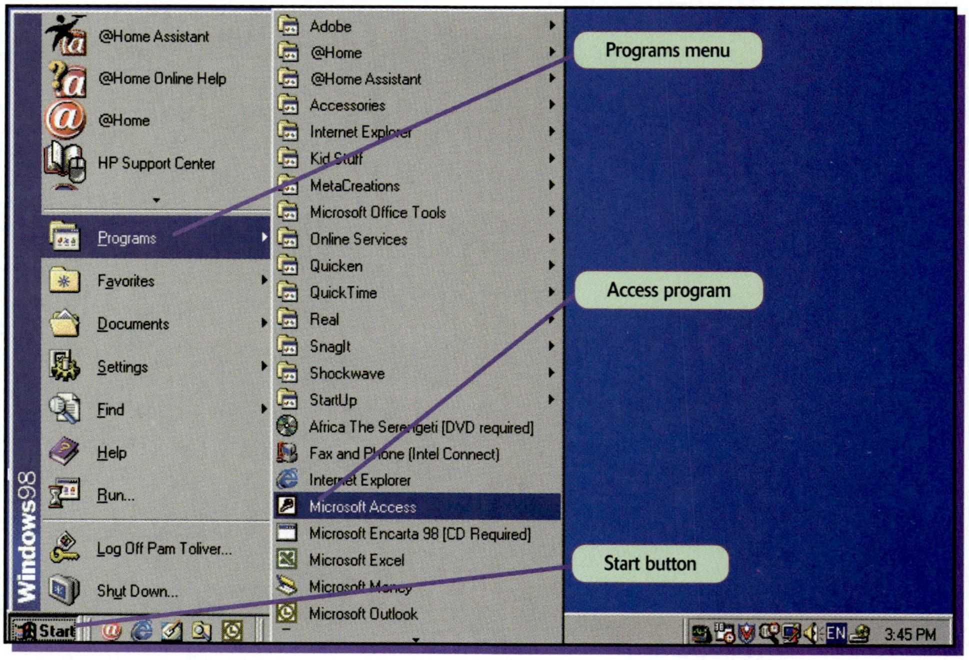

3 Click the **General Templates** link in the **New from template** list.

Figure 0-4

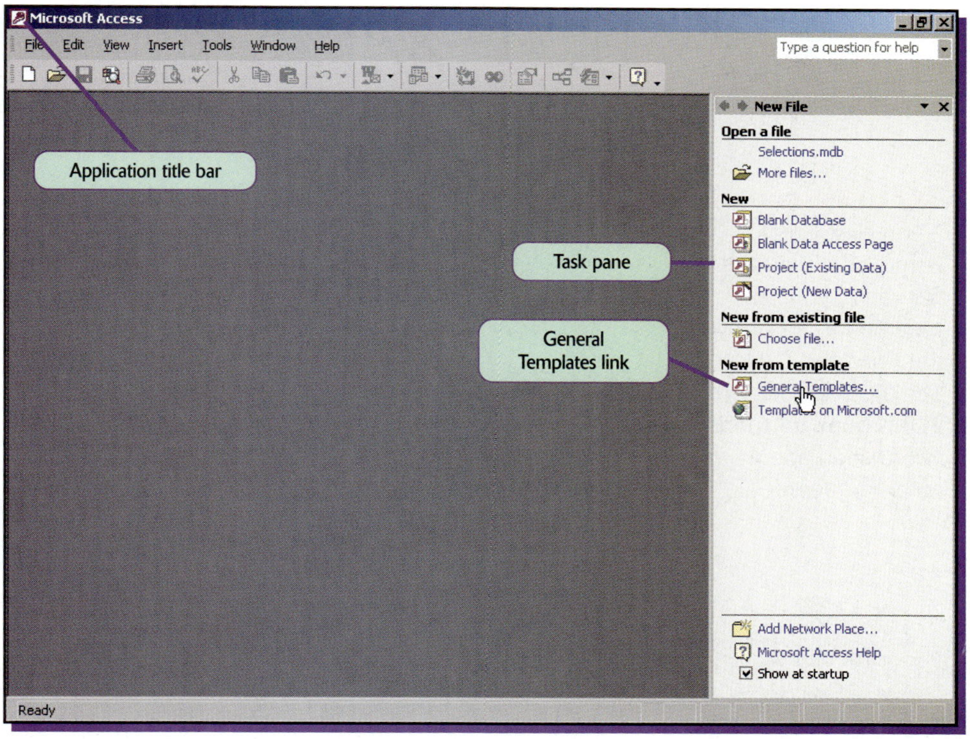

4 Click the **Databases** tab and select the **Contact Management** template.

5 Click **OK**, click the down arrow next to the **Save in** box, and select the location in which you want to save your database file.

Tip Access identifies the type of template in the template name. The wand that appears at the top of each icon identifies templates that use Wizards to walk you through the database creation process.

Figure 0-5

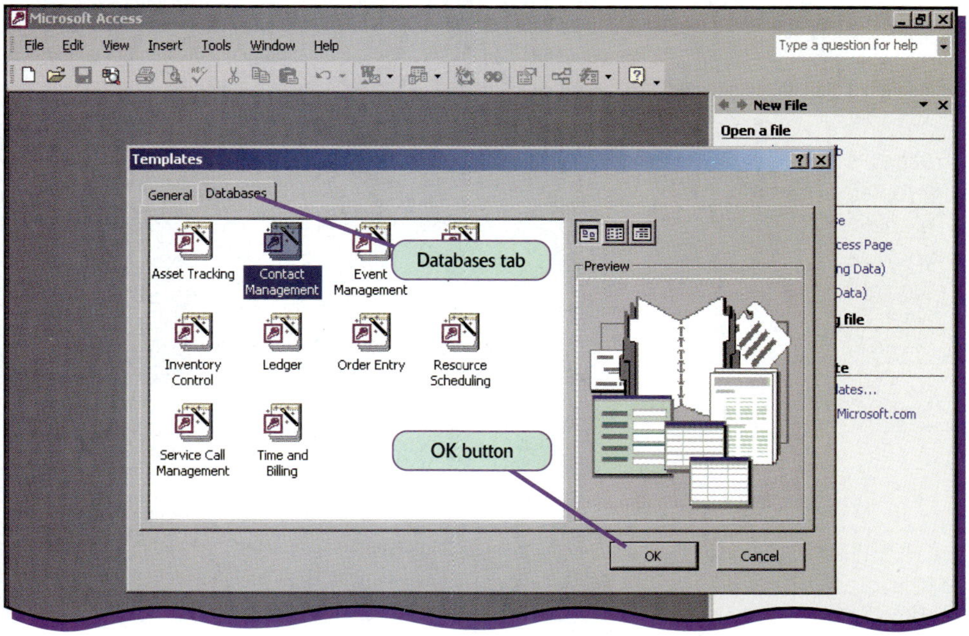

6 Triple-click the text in the **File name** text box, and type **My Contacts.**

7 Click **Create.**

Troubleshooting
If you click Create before changing the file name, you can rename the file using the Windows Explorer. See the Windows project in this book for more information about renaming files.

Figure 0-6

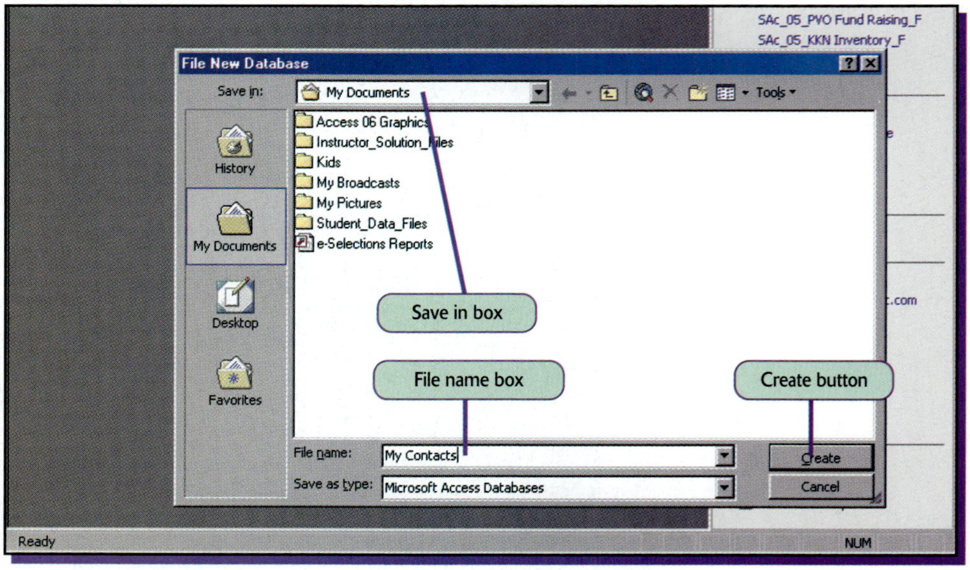

8 Click **Next.**

Tip
Each different type of template presents different pages of options you can select to format the database. The wizard that creates the contact management database presents seven different pages of options. Other templates present many of the same options you'll see as you create the contact management database.

Figure 0-7

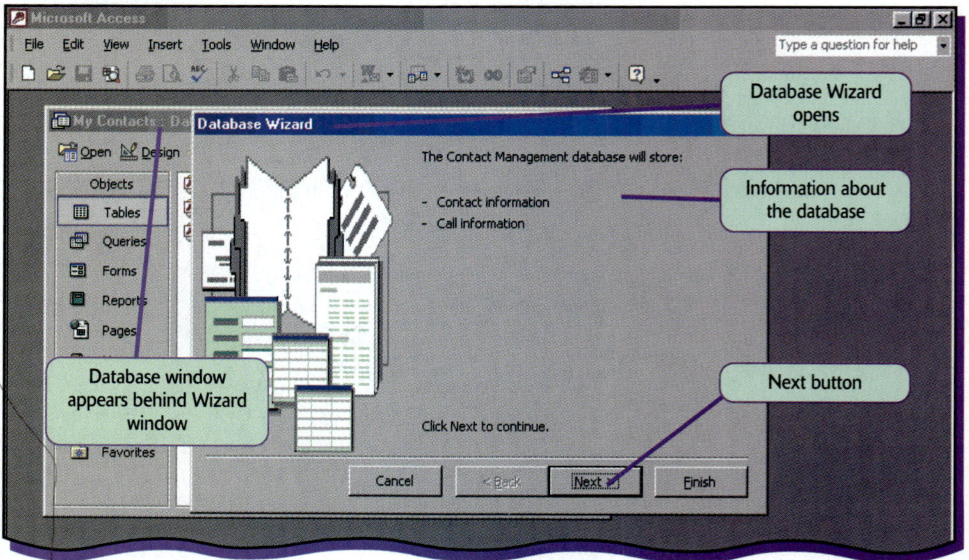

9 Click **Next** to accept the default table and field names.

Tip As you become more familiar with creating and working with databases, you will be able to identify the fields you want to include in each database.

Figure 0-8

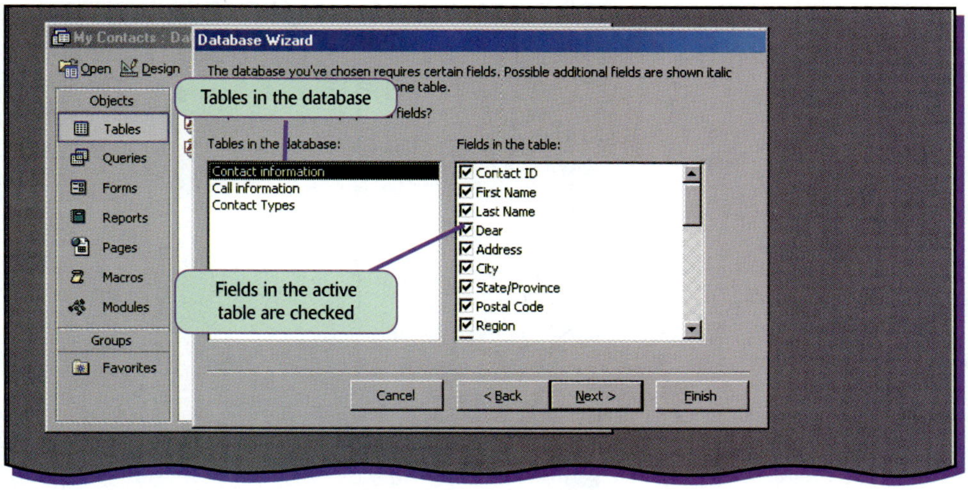

10 Select **Expedition** as the screen display style and click Next.

Tip If time permits, select other display styles from the list and review the format.

Figure 0-9

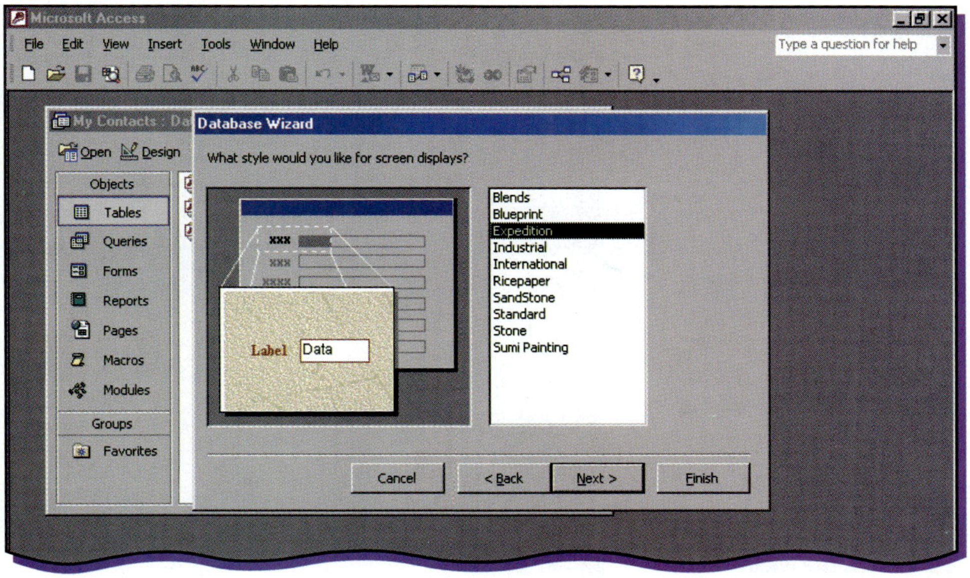

11 Select **Bold** as the style for printed reports and click Next.

Figure 0-10

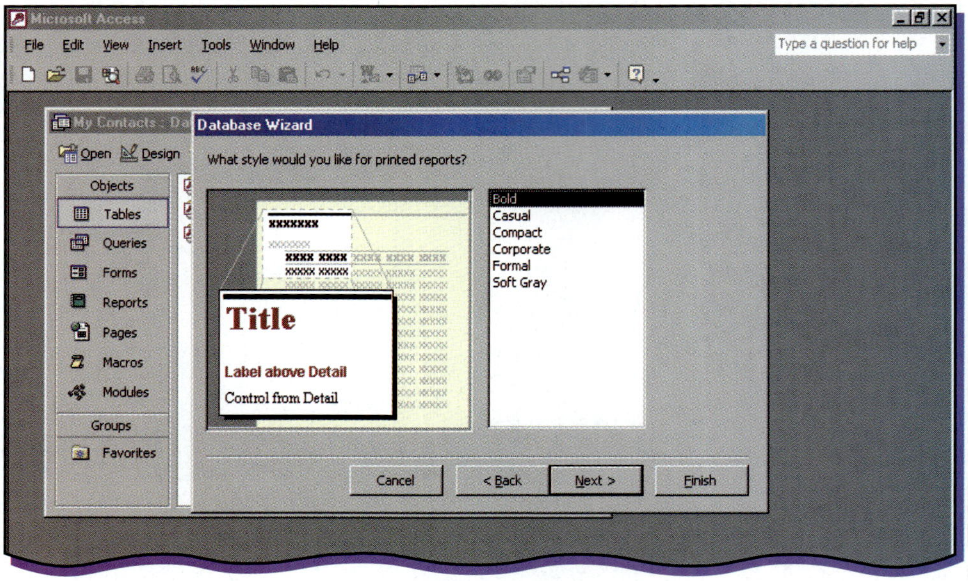

12 Review the database title options, click Next to accept the defaults, and then click **Finish**.

> **Tip** Access has to create a number of different objects based on selections you made in wizard pages. As a result, it may take a few minutes to save the database.

13 Click the Main Switchboard Close ☒ button.

14 Click the Database window Restore 🗗 button.

Figure 0-11

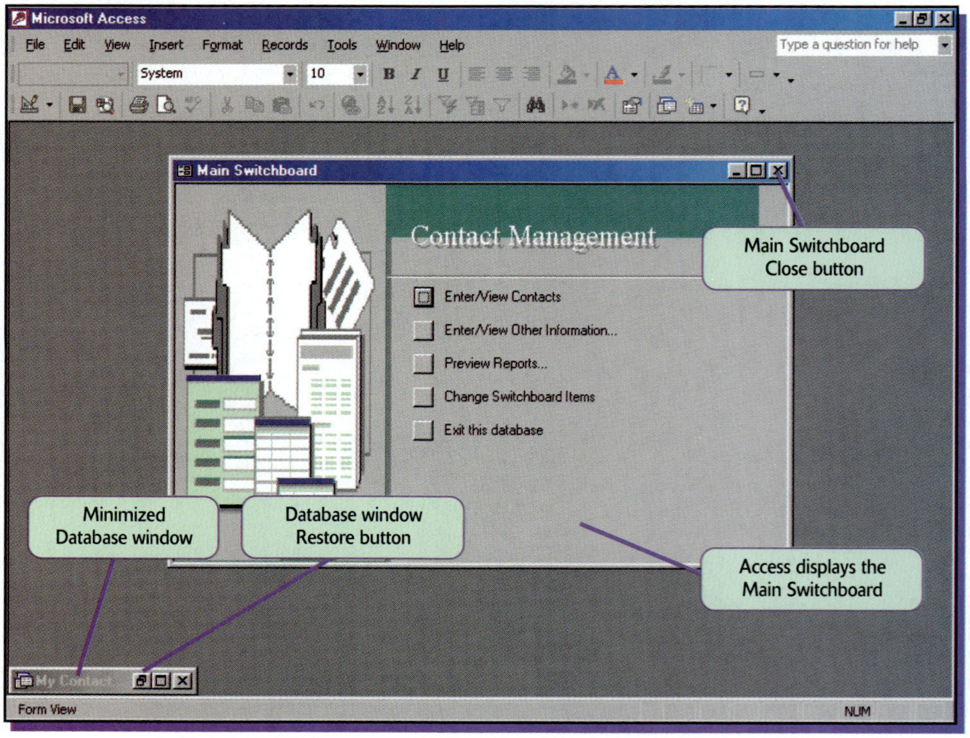

WEB TIP

The Microsoft Web site contains a wealth of additional templates for creating Access databases. To find them, launch Access and choose **File | New** to bring up the task pane. Then click the **Templates on Microsoft.com** link to open the Microsoft Template Gallery on the World Wide Web.

Identifying Microsoft Access Screen Elements

The *Database window* displays all database objects and provides a navigation bar for accessing different objects. Table 0-4 identifies the purpose of each screen element.

Table 0-4 Access Screen Elements

Screen element	Purpose
Access menu bar	Provides access to commands used to perform tasks.
Database toolbar	Contains tool buttons for accessing the most commonly used database commands.
Database window	Holds all objects added to the database and displays the Objects bar.
Objects bar	Contains buttons for accessing the seven types of database objects.
Groups bar	Displays buttons to access grouped database objects and other items.
Create object shortcuts	Provide access to wizards and other procedures for creating new database objects.
Database objects	List database objects already created and available.

Task 2:
To Display Database Objects

1. Click the Tables button in the database Objects bar.

2. Click each button in the Objects bar to view the database objects that the wizard created.

Figure 0-12

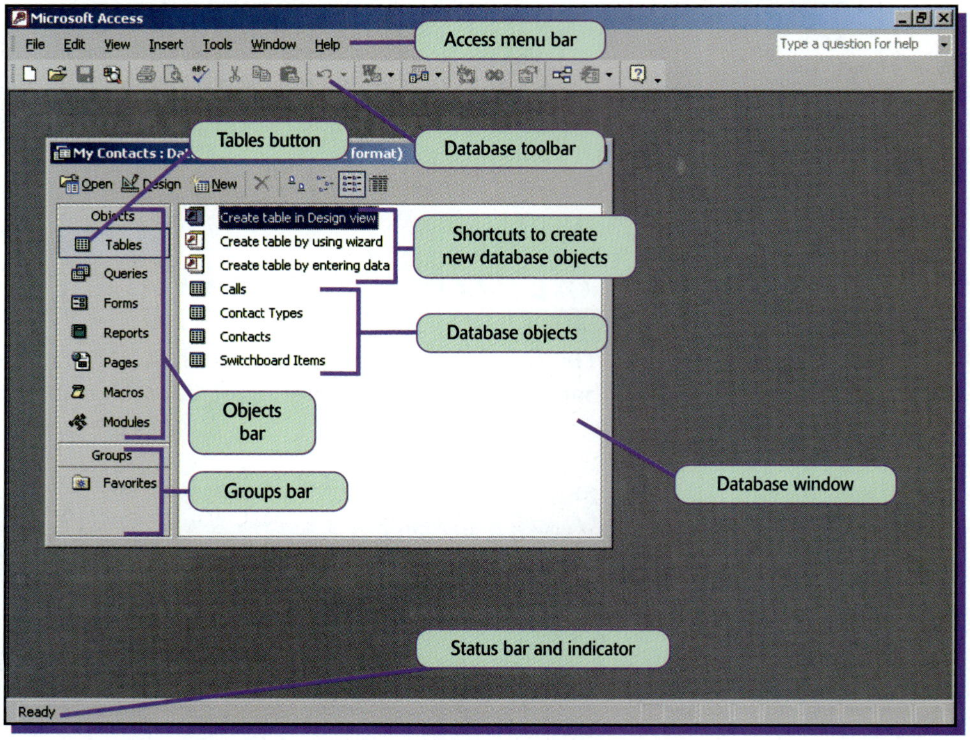

Closing a Database File and Exiting Access

As you move forward in your study of Access, you will learn that the procedures for saving databases, objects, and records are different from saving files in other Windows-based applications. Some of these differences include the following:

- Each object you add to an Access database is saved as you create it.
- Each record you add to a database table is saved as you complete the record.
- Only one Access database file can be open at a time.
- When you open a different database or create a new database, Access closes the active database.
- The Save As command is used to copy a database object to create another object within the database.
- To make a backup copy of a complete database and all database objects, you must use the Windows Explorer.

Closing the database file manually helps you prevent unwanted loss of data and reduces the risk of database file corruption. It's always a good idea to close open databases before exiting Access. Access provides the same basic options for exiting the application that you have found in other applications:

- Click the application window Close button.
- Press Alt + F4.
- Choose **File | Exit**.
- Click the application control menu and select **Close**.

Task 3:
To Close a Database File and Exit Access

1. Click the Close button on the Database window to close the open database file.

2. Choose **File** | **Exit** to exit Microsoft Access.

SUMMARY AND EXERCISES

SUMMARY

- Microsoft Access is a relational database management system (RDBMS).
- A database is a collection of information related a particular subject or purpose.
- A table contains records and fields for a particular subject.
- An Access database file can contain multiple database objects, such as tables, queries, forms, reports, pages, macros, and modules.
- Planning is the most important step to creating effective databases.
- One way to create a database is to use a Database Wizard.
- The Database window displays all of the database objects.
- Only one Access database file can be open at a time.
- Access provides the same basic options for exiting the application that you have found in other applications.

KEY TERMS & SKILLS

KEY TERMS

database (p. 3)
Database window (p. 11)
field (p. 3)
form (p. 4)
macro (p. 4)
module (p. 4)
objects (p. 3)
object-oriented database (p. 3)
page (p. 4)
query (p. 4)
record (p. 3)
report (p. 4)
relational database management system (RDBMS) (p. 3)
relationships (p. 5)
table (p. 4)

SKILLS

Create a database using the Database Wizard (p. 6)
Close an Access database file (p. 12)
Design and plan a database (p. 5)
Display database objects in the Database window (p. 12)
Exit Microsoft Access (p. 12)
Launch Microsoft Access (p. 6)

STUDY QUESTIONS

MULTIPLE CHOICE

1. Which Access object holds the data in your database?
   a. table
   b. query
   c. form
   d. report
2. In an address book database, a city is an example of what?
   a. record
   b. table
   c. field
   d. query
3. The first step in planning a database is to
   a. plan tables and fields.
   b. define the purpose of the database.
   c. plan queries to organize your data.
   d. plan reports.
4. An easy way to create a functioning Access database is to
   a. use the Database window to create the objects.
   b. create a new blank database.
   c. use the Database Wizard.
   d. create a new database project.
5. Which screen element is used to create or open database objects?
   a. Database toolbar
   b. Access Menu bar
   c. Objects bar
   d. Database window
6. Which Access object allows users to enter, edit, and view data in an easy-to-use format?
   a. table
   b. query
   c. form
   d. report
7. The purpose of the data access page is to
   a. automate your database.
   b. provide an interactive HTML page you can view on the Web.
   c. allow you to select records according to specific criteria.
   d. hold the data in your database.
8. After you have planned your database, the database object that must be created first is a
   a. table.
   b. query.
   c. form.
   d. report.
9. Database objects that you create, such as tables, forms, and reports, are easily accessible using the
   a. Database Wizard.
   b. Relationships window.
   c. Database toolbar.
   d. Database window.
10. If you needed a report of customers who live in Oregon, you would need to base the report on which database object?
    a. table
    b. form
    c. query
    d. data access page

SHORT ANSWER

1. What is the Database window?
2. What are the five steps in planning a database?
3. Which database object is used to create interactive Web pages?
4. Which database object holds the data in your database?
5. What are the rows of a table called?
6. Give an example of when you would need a query.
7. Forms are based on what database objects?
8. When would you use a Database Wizard?

FILL IN THE BLANK

1. ____________ allow information stored in separate tables to be shared in the database.
2. ____________ allow you to format and print information from your database.
3. The ____________ ____________ allows you to create and view database objects.
4. The ____________ ____________ creates functional Access databases.
5. Tables contain data that is organized in ____________ and ____________.
6. You create a ____________ to reorganize and select out specific information.
7. Forms are based on ____________ or ____________.
8. ____________ are used to automate specific database tasks.
9. To view the forms in your database, you would click the Forms button in the ____________ of the Database window.

DISCUSSION

1. Why is planning your database important?
2. What are the advantages and disadvantages of creating a database using the Database Wizard?
3. How do fields and records differ?
4. Explain how the Database window allows you to easily create or open database objects.

GUIDED EXERCISES

1 GETTING THE WIZARD TO HELP CREATE AN EXPENSE TRACKING DATABASE

The wizard feature contains other formats for creating databases designed to hold specific kinds of data. You can use one of these wizards to create a new database for tracking expenses. Follow these steps to create the database:

1. Launch Access, if necessary, and choose **File** | **New** to display the task pane, if necessary.
2. Click **General Templates** in the task pane, click the **Databases** tab, and double-click the **Expenses** template.
3. Save the database using the file name *Employee Expenses*.
4. Follow the direction and prompts presented by the Database Wizard to complete the database layout and design.
5. Click the Minimize button on the Switchboard window, click the Restore button on the Database window, and explore the objects that the wizard created.

2 OPEN AND EXPLORE THE NORTHWIND SAMPLE DATABASE

The Northwind Sample Database is a database that Microsoft created to help you learn about database design and development. It contains sample data that you can explore to learn more about database objects and to experience the full functionality of the database. Follow these steps to open and explore the database:

1. Launch Access, if necessary.
2. Choose **Help** | **Sample Database** | **Northwind Sample Database**.

Troubleshooting If the Northwind Sample Database feature is not installed, you will be asked to install it. Follow the direction of your instructor before proceeding.

3. Click **OK** to close the Northwind Database Splash screen.
4. Explore each of the database objects in the Main Switchboard, opening several objects and using the dates between 7/10/96 and 5/6/98 to preview the reports if necessary.
5. Click **Display Database Window** on the Main Switchboard and open and explore the database objects by double-clicking the database objects you want to view.

Tip To open the Main Switchboard again, click the Forms button, and then double-click **Main Switchboard**.

FROM THE FILES

You Will Need

✔ Employees.xls

PROJECT 1

Creating Basic Access Objects

To begin creating effective databases, you must start with designing and implementing tables. You can then create other database objects, such as forms and reports, using table data. In this project, you will learn several ways to create tables as well as how to use table fields and data quickly and efficiently to create forms and reports.

e-selections **Running Case**

E-Selections has hired you as a divisional database designer to create a database for storing employee and payroll information. As a database designer your job will be to create a design that will minimize redundant data but will allow the Accounting Department to create the reports they need.

OBJECTIVES

After completing this project, you will be able to:

- *Create a new Access database*
- *Plan tables*
- *Name fields and determine their data types*
- *Create a table using Design view*
- *Create a table using the Table Wizard*
- *Create a table by importing data from Excel*
- *Add records to a table using Datasheet view*
- *Create an AutoForm based on a table*
- *Create a AutoReport based on a table*
- *Preview and print database tables, forms, and reports*

Usability — Developing a User Friendly Database

A database is only as accurate as its data, and its data is only accurate and complete if the database is easy to use and understand. To use the industry catch phrase, a good database has to have a high usability rating.

Usability addresses the fact that most database users are not experts, and they aren't usually given the luxury of extensive training. A usable database is one that anticipates its users' needs and then provides the needed information in a way that they can understand, eliminating confusion.

Usability Is Critical to Success

Most people will agree that a database can be efficient and accurate when it comes to storing large amounts of data. However, for some databases, the need to be easy to use and understand is a matter of life and death—such as those used for emergency resource management.

The database used by the National Interagency Fire Center (NIFC) in Boise, Idaho, is a good example. When large wildfires occur throughout the country, local agencies contact the NIFC for both equipment and logistical support.

The NIFC database has to maintain accurate records for all of its equipment (enough to support 10,000 firefighters) and personnel resources. The database is also used to coordinate the deployment of firefighters, aircraft, and support staff at a moment's notice.

This database, like many others, is often manned by database novices who have to be able to act quickly when a situation arises. They have to be able to access the availability of resources spread throughout the country. Time lost because of errors in reading the material or in record maintenance is unacceptable.

Creating a Usable Database

Although the usability of your database is probably not a matter of life and death, it is critical to the success of your database. Because of this fact, you need to create a database that the user can understand quickly and use efficiently if you want the database used accurately.

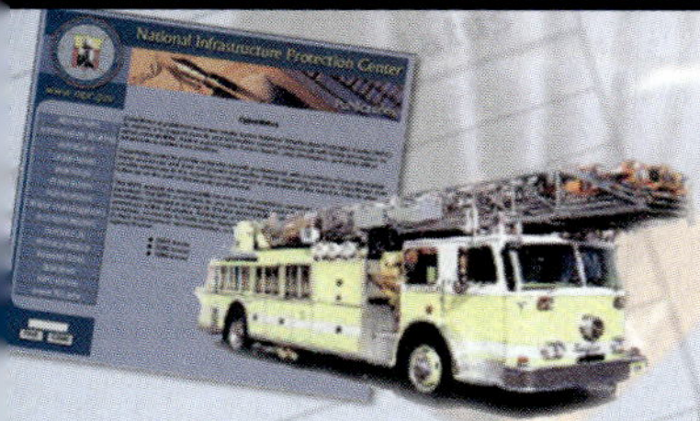

Ease of use

Simplicity

These rules will help you get started:

- Spend time with the people who will enter the data. Ask them what format would be easiest for them.
- Get copies of the forms users are familiar with. It is usually easier for the user if you create an entry form that is similar to the paper form.
- Eliminate confusion. Use only fields that the user needs to complete at that time.

When you think you created the perfect form for your users, conduct a usability test. Enlist a couple of volunteers and see if they can perform the necessary tasks, such as creating two or three new records, retrieving records, and updating them.

Watch for the following things:

- Do the users make many mistakes trying to find features?
- Does it take the users a long time to figure out how to perform the task?
- Do they master the process quickly?
- Does any feature seem to confuse them?

By employing these usability rules in the creation of your database, you can shorten the training time required, improve the accuracy of your data, and create a database that people want to use.

Just think how much time, energy, and taxpayer money could have been saved if Florida's Board of Elections had taken the time to perform a usability test for the ballots in the 2000 Presidential Election!

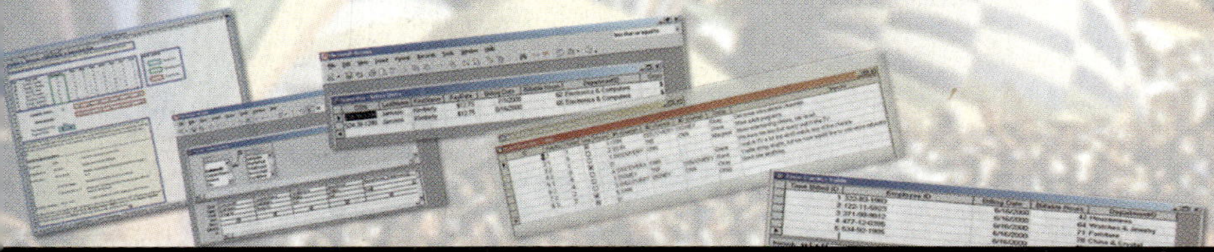

PROJECT 1

Creating Basic Access Objects

The Challenge

Mr. Travis Traylor is the head of the Finance and Accounting Department for e-Selections. He wants you to design a database for tracking employee payroll information. Specifically, he wants to be able to print payroll information for any employee in the company, by department and employee. The database must list payroll information for any pay period and list the payroll history for each employee.

The Solution

To create the database that meets Mr. Traylor's requirements, you will create several tables that will store the data. By entering the departments in one table, the payroll data for each payroll period in a second table, and the employees in a third table, you will be able to generate the reports that he has requested. Careful planning will help you design a database that enables you to enter data only once and minimize data entry errors. Figure 1-1 illustrates how data in multiple tables can be combined to create the report that Mr. Traylor wants.

Figure 1-1

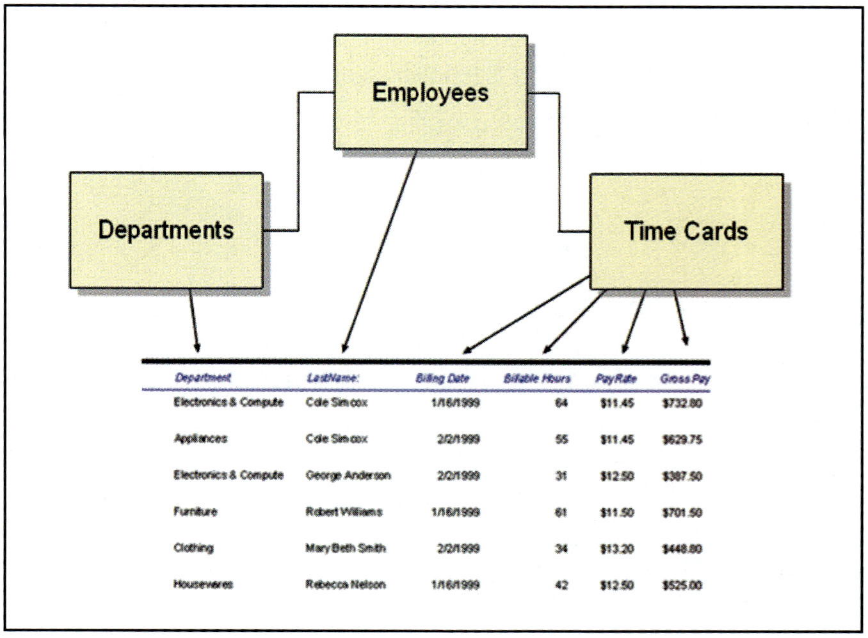

The structures of the tables are shown in Figure 1-2. Each field will be explained as you create the tables. By the end of this project your tables with the data will look like those shown in Figure 1-3.

Figure 1-2

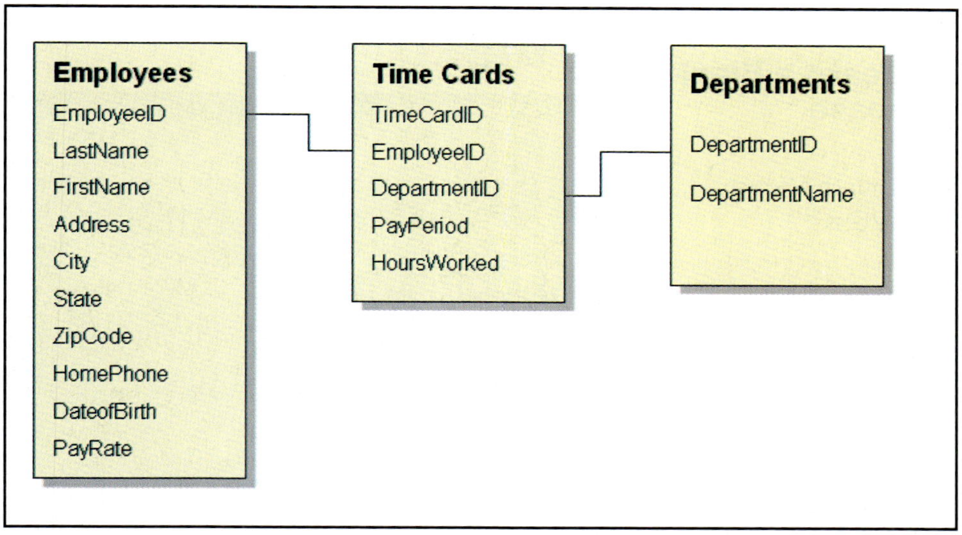

Tip Each database object that is open has its own title bar and window borders. As a result, you can drag the title bar of an object to position it in the Access window and drag an object border to change the size of the window. Windows that are maximized cannot be sized or moved within the Access window.

Figure 1-3

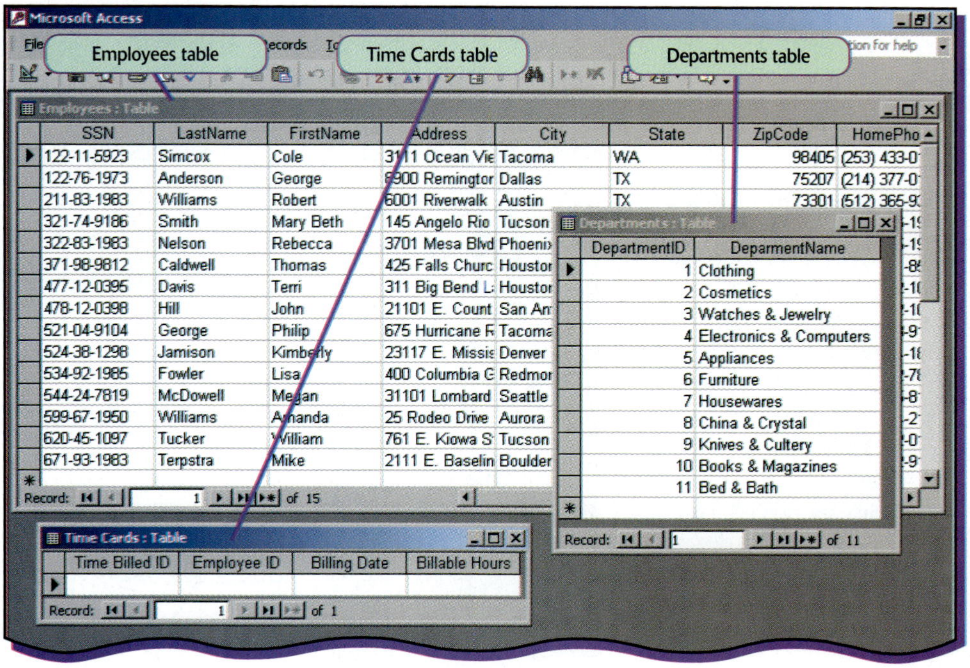

Creating a New Access Database

In Introducing Access 2002, you used a Database Wizard to create a database with accompanying tables. This time you will create a blank database file and add your own tables.

Task 1:
To Create a Blank Database

1. Launch Microsoft Access.
2. Click the New button on the Database toolbar, if necessary, to display the **New File** task pane.
3. Click **Blank Database** on the **New File** task pane.

Figure 1-4

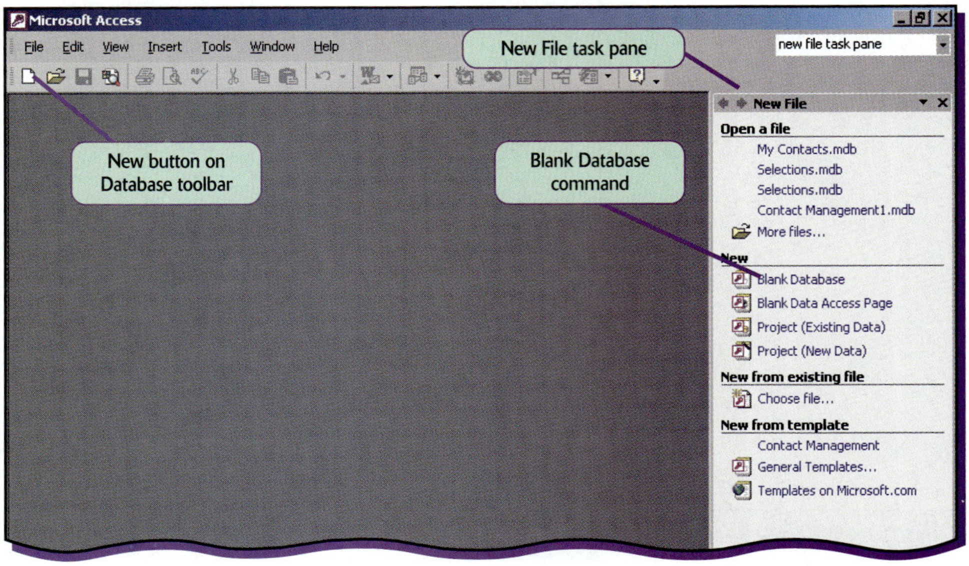

4. Type **E-Selections** in the **File name** text box.

Tip Because different labs and classes have different procedures for saving files, follow the direction of your instructor as to where you should save your work.
Access saves database files with an .mdb extension.

Figure 1-5

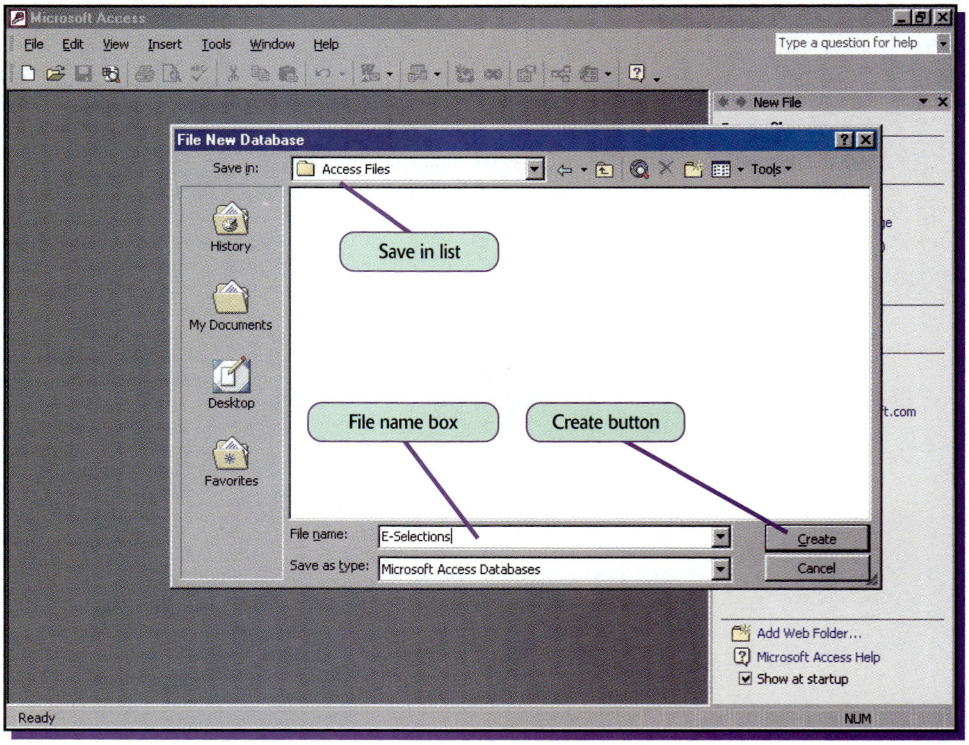

5 Click **Create** to create the database and to display the database file in the Database window.

Tip Access creates the database file in Access 2000 file format. If you prefer, you can convert the file to an Access 2002 file format by choosing **Tools | Database Utilities | Convert Database | To Access 2002 File Format**. Access 2002 files can be opened only on computers that have Access 2002 installed.

Figure 1-6

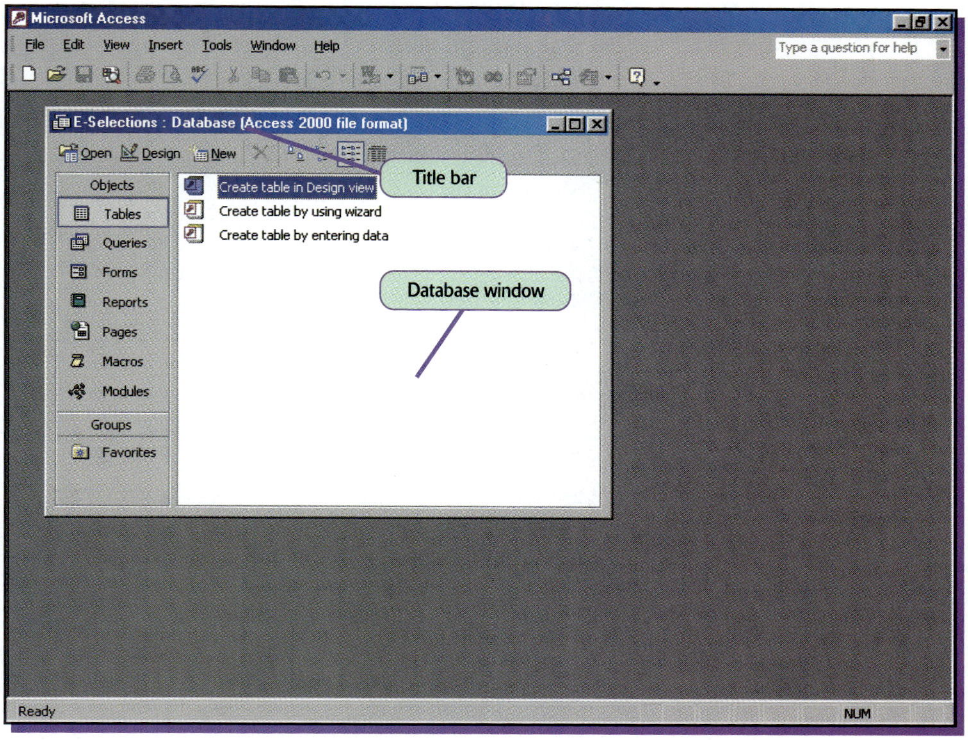

Planning Tables

Now that you have created the database file, you can add tables. Each table will contain fields grouped in such a way that the content of each table focuses on specific information, such as employees, departments, or time cards. Consider the following items as you plan and build your tables:

- Each table should have a *primary key* field that contains unique information for each record in the table. Social Security numbers make great key fields because no two people have the same number. Each record in a table must contain a value in the key field—they cannot be empty.
- Planning database tables to share data before you create them will reduce the amount of time spent editing and restructuring the database tables later. Structuring the tables so that they contain common fields (sometimes referred to as *foreign keys*) will enable you to create relationships between the tables, even though other information contained in each table is different. You will need a foreign key field in the Time Cards table to relate to a field in the Employees table.

Table 1-1 displays the structure for each of the tables you will create in this project. The primary key field for each table is shown in bold print and foreign keys appear in italics.

Table 1-1 Database Structure for the E-Selections Database

Departments table	Employees table	Time Cards table
DepartmentID	**EmployeeID**	**TimeCardID**
DepartmentName	LastName	*EmployeeID*
	FirstName	*DepartmentID*
	Address	PayPeriod
	City	HoursWorked
	State	
	ZipCode	
	HomePhone	
	DateofBirth	
	PayRate	

CHECK POINT

How do you create Access tables? You can create tables using the *Table Design view,* the *Table Wizard,* and by importing data from another data source. Regardless of the method you choose to create the table, you can always modify the structure at a later time to accommodate updated database requirements.

Tip Knowing what reports or output you want to extract from the database sometimes helps you determine the required fields.

Naming Fields and Determining Data Types

As you identify the fields to be contained in each database table, you should also identify field names and determine what type of data each field will hold. Access places few restrictions on naming the fields in a table and offers 10 different data types to identify the data a field contains. Rules and field-planning tips that apply to fields include the following items:

- A field name can be up to 64 characters in length.
- Fields may include any combination of letters, numbers, spaces, and special characters.
- Invalid characters include a period (.), an exclamation point (!), a grave accent (`), and brackets ([ ]).

- Each field is assigned a specific *data type* that defines the type of data the field contains and helps Access validate the data entered. For example, if you assign a numeric data type to a field and then try to enter alphabetic characters in the field, Access will notify you that the data is an invalid data type.
- Data types of primary and foreign key fields that will be used to create table relationships must match. For example, if the primary key is a number type, then the foreign key in the related table *must* also be a number type.

Tip As a general rule (particularly if you plan to include Visual Basic for Applications code or other complex expressions), it is best to not have any spaces in a field name.

Table 1-2 summarizes the 10 data types you may use for table data.

Table 1-2 Access Data Types for Fields

Data Type	Description
Text	Any combination of alphabetic and numeric characters, such as names, addresses, and phone numbers, that will not be used to perform calculations. The text data type holds a maximum 255 characters. This is the default data type.
Memo	Text entries that require between 256 and 65,536 characters.
Number	Numeric data to be used in mathematical calculations.
Date/Time	Fields that hold date and time values.
Currency	Numeric values representing dollar and cent values or fields in which you want to prevent rounding off during calculations.
AutoNumber	A field for which Access assigns a unique, sequential, or random number as records are added to a table. AutoNumber data cannot be modified or deleted.
Yes/No	Single-character data in a Yes/No (Boolean) format. Used for data that can be only one of two possible values, such as True/False, Yes/No, or On/Off.
OLE object	Embedded or linked objects such as a Microsoft Excel spreadsheet, a Microsoft Word document, graphics, or sounds. Stores up to 1 gigabyte.
Hyperlink	Links to Web pages or other documents accessed by clicking the link.
Lookup Wizard	A field that allows you to choose a specified value from another table or from a list of values based on criteria you set.

WEB TIP

Lots of information stored on the Web is stored in databases for quick and easy retrieval. Search the Web for statistics about your favorite sports figure and see what you can find.

Creating a Table Using Table Design View

A common method for creating tables in Access is by using Table Design view. Table Design view consists of the following two panes:

- The upper pane is used to specify field names, data types, and descriptions.
- The lower pane enables you to specify the properties for each field.

Tip A *field property* allows you to modify the characteristics (such as field size) and functionality (such as being able to look up data from a list or another table) of a field.

Task 2:

To Create the Department Table Using Table Design View

1 Click the Tables button on the Objects bar, if necessary.

2 Double-click the **Create Table in Design view** shortcut in the Database window.

Figure 1-7

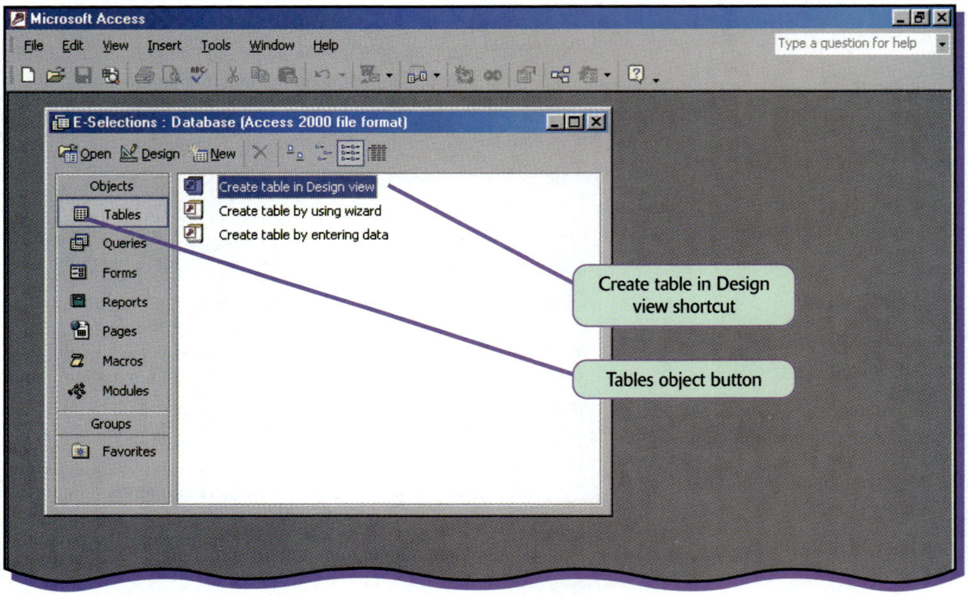

3 Type **DepartmentID** in the first row of the **Field Name** column in the upper pane and press the Tab key to move the insertion point into the **Data Type** column.

Figure 1-8

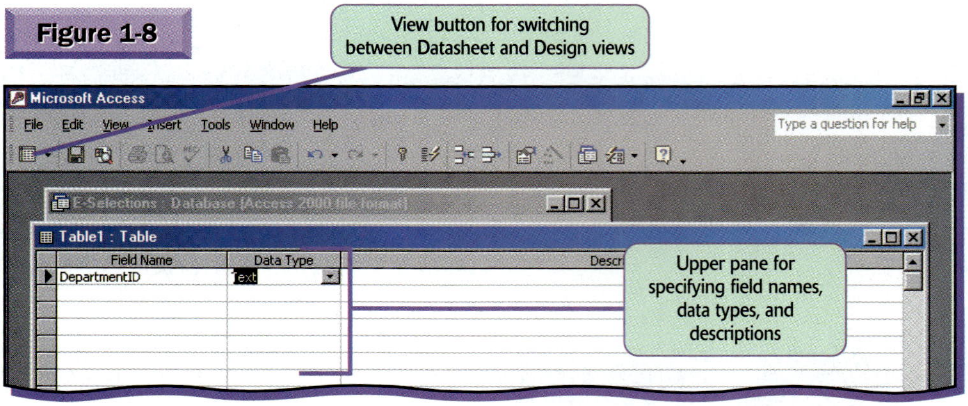

4 Click the **Data Type** down arrow, select **AutoNumber**, and press Tab to move the insertion point into the **Description** column.

Figure 1-9

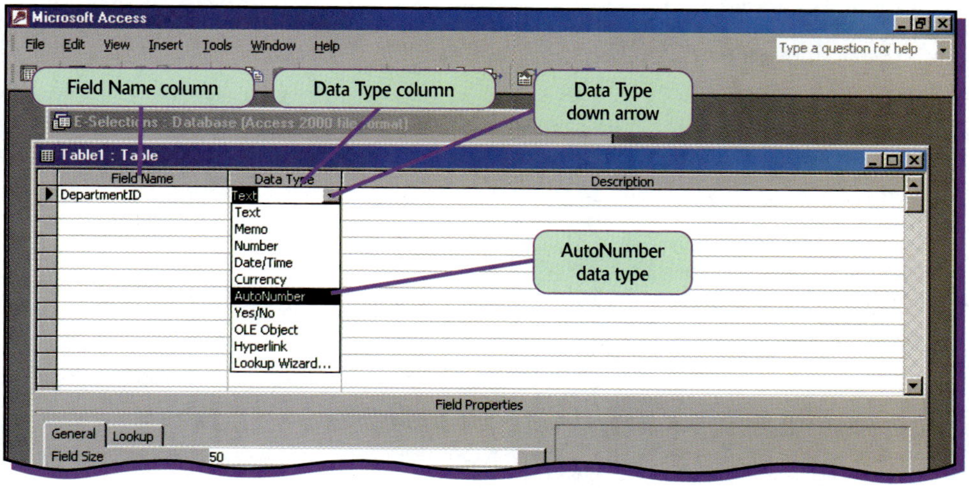

Other Ways

To change the data type:

- Type the first letter of the data type you want to set and then press Enter when the data type appears in the column.

Tip

The AutoNumber data type is often used for the primary key field since it always contains a unique, non-null value.

5 Type Primary Key.

6 Click the Primary Key button on the Database toolbar to designate this field as the primary key and press Tab to move the insertion point into the **Field Name** column for the second row.

Figure 1-10

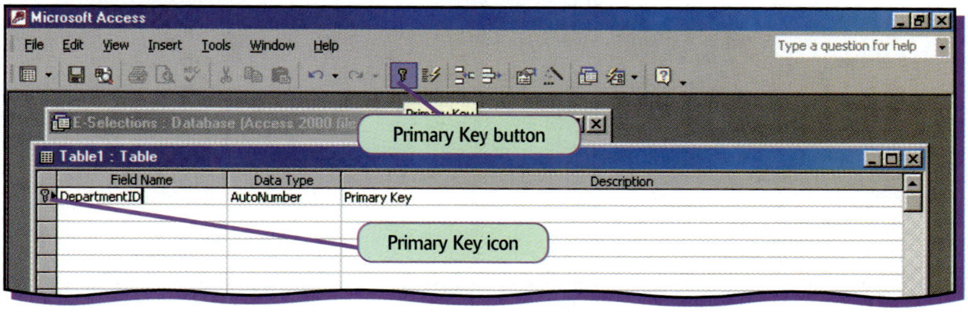

Other Ways

To assign a primary key:

- Right-click the field name you want to assign as the primary key and select **Primary Key** from the shortcut menu.

Tip

Although Access does not require anything in the Description column, it is often helpful to identify what each field represents. This is one way to *document* your database for future reference. (In this case, *document* is used as a verb.)

7 Type **DepartmentName** as the field name and press [Tab] to move the insertion point to the **Data Type** column.

8 Press the [F6] key to move the insertion point to the lower pane and type **35** in the **Field Size** box to set the size of the field.

Figure 1-11

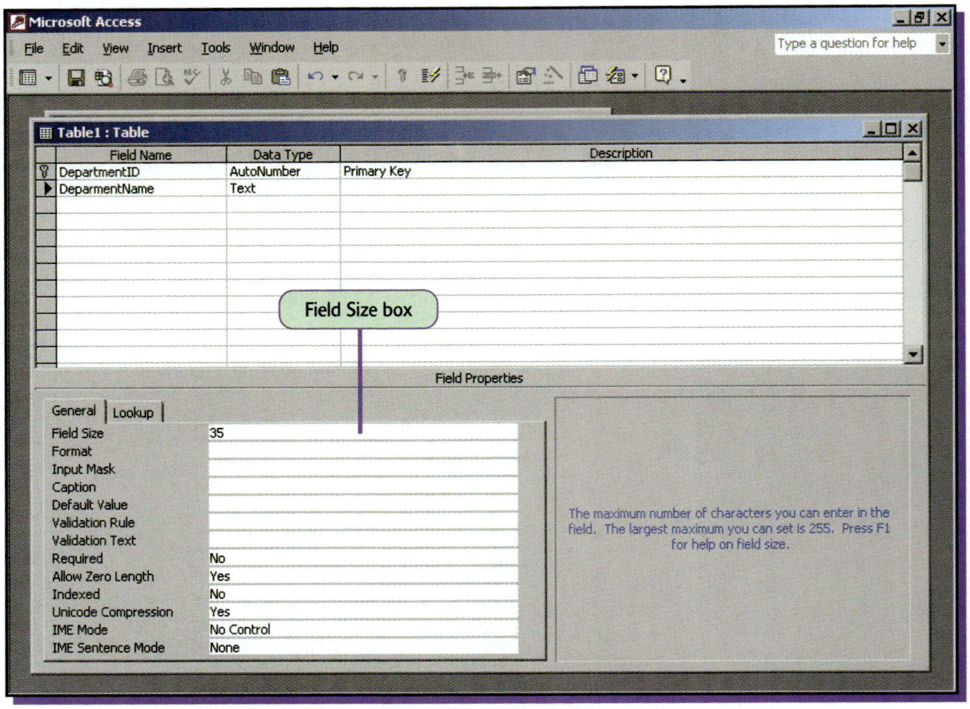

9 Click the Save button on the toolbar to open the **Save As** dialog box and type **Departments** in the **Table Name** box.

Other Ways

To open the Save As dialog box to save a database object:

- Choose **File | Save.**
- Press [Ctrl] + [S].

Figure 1-12

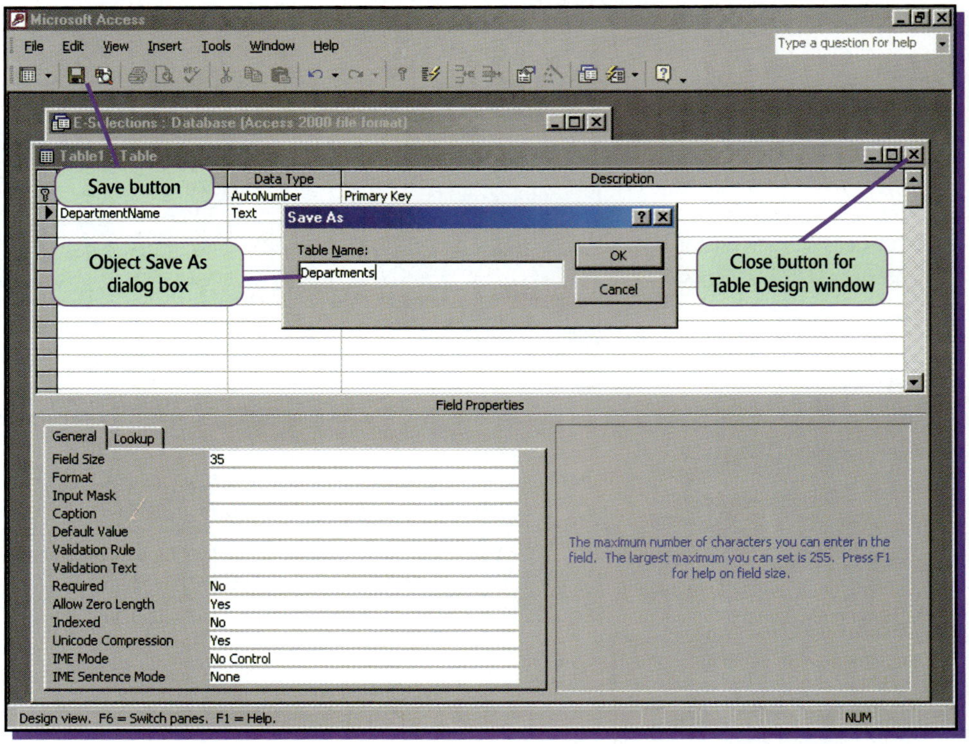

10 Click **OK** to save the database and click the Table Design Close **X** button to close the table.

Other Ways

To close a database object:

- Press Ctrl + F4.
- Choose **File | Close.**

Figure 1-13

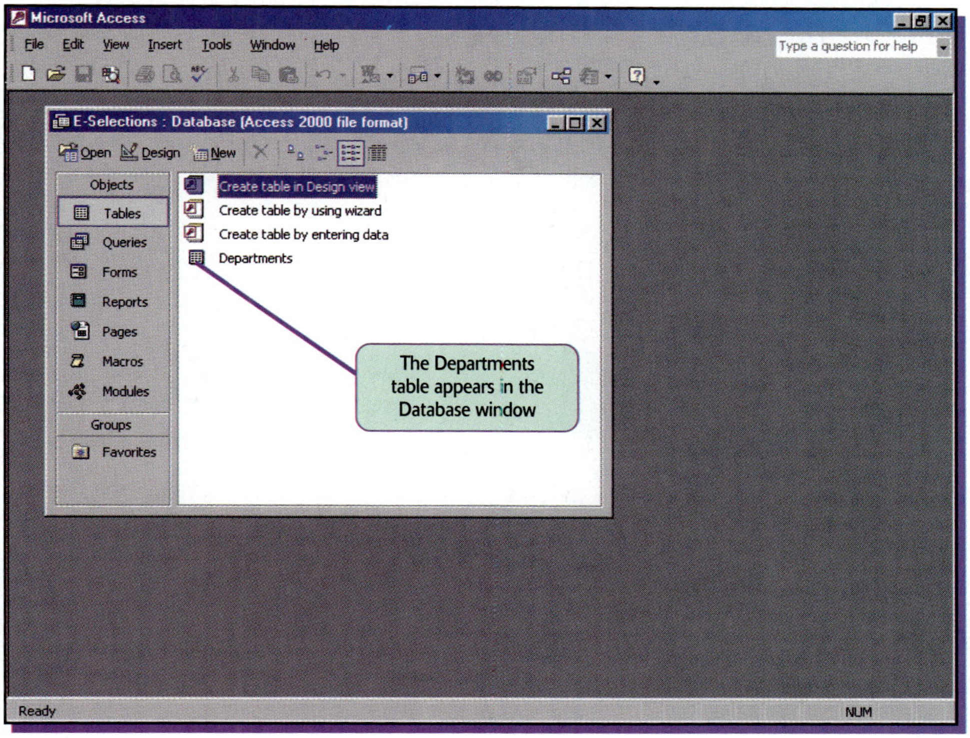

Creating a Table Using the Table Wizard

Now that you have successfully created a table using Table Design view, you can explore some of the different table types Access offers and create a table using standard field types. The Table Wizard will guide you through the process of creating the Time Cards table.

Task 3:

To Create the Time Cards Table Using Table Wizard

1 Double-click the **Create table by using wizard** shortcut in the Database window to open the Table Wizard.

2 Select **Time Billed** from the **Sample Tables** list to display the fields from that table in the **Sample Fields** list.

3 Highlight the **TimeBilledID** field, if necessary, and click the Add [>] button to move the **TimeBilledID** field from the **Sample Fields** list to the **Fields in my new table** list.

4 Add the **EmployeeID**, **BillingDate**, and **BillableHours** fields to the **Fields in my new table** list.

Figure 1-14

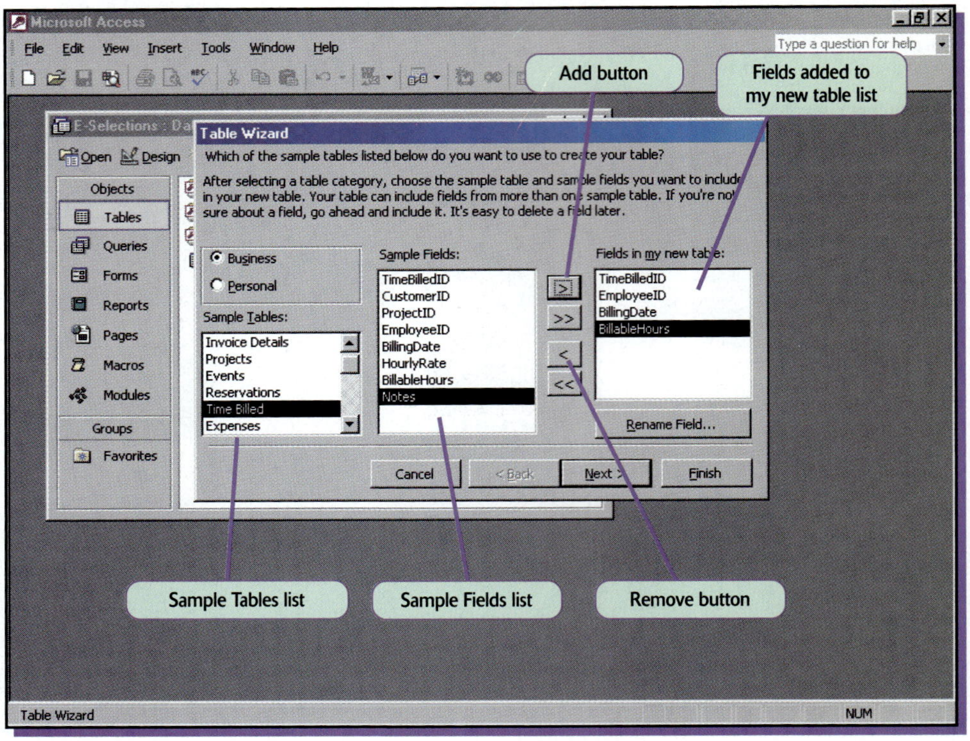

Troubleshooting If you add a field to the Fields in my new table list and want to remove it, select the field to remove and click the Remove button.

CHECK POINT

You may recall that the Time Cards table will be contain multiple records for each employee. However, because each employee's address and other personal information is stored in the Employees table, those fields can be omitted from this table.

5 Click **Next**, type Time Cards in the **What do you want to name your table** box, and select the **Yes, set a primary key for me** option and click Next.

Tip When you select the option to allow Access to set the primary key field for you, Access adds an extra field to the table and formats the field using the AutoNumber data type.

Figure 1-15

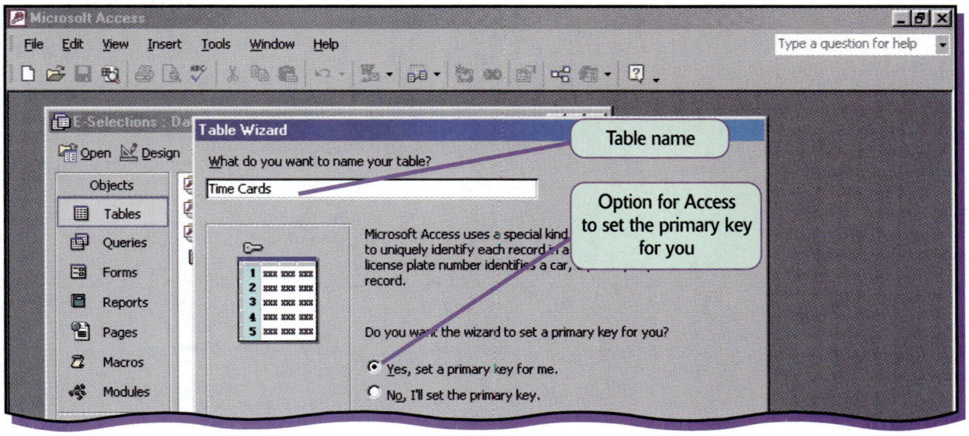

6 Click **Next** to accept the default relationship selection.

Figure 1-16

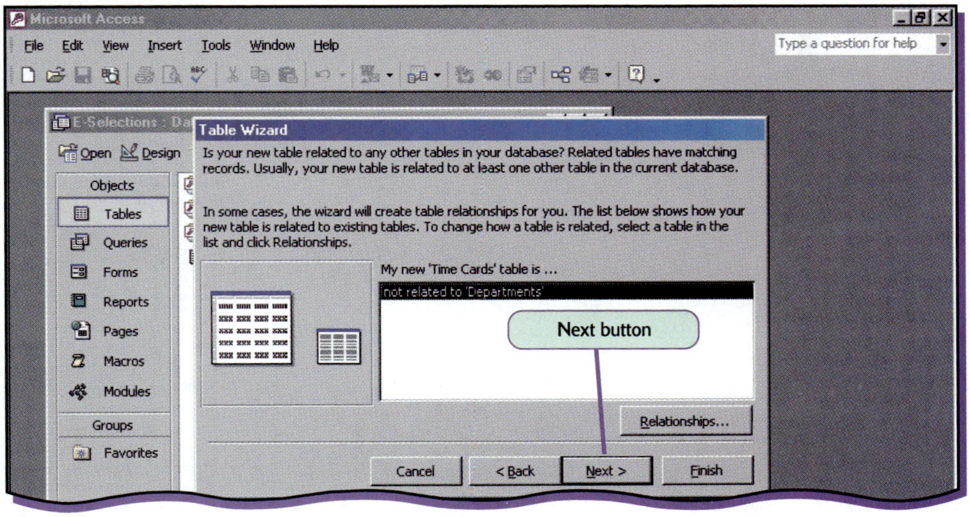

7 Select the **Modify the table design** option and click **Finish**.

Figure 1-17

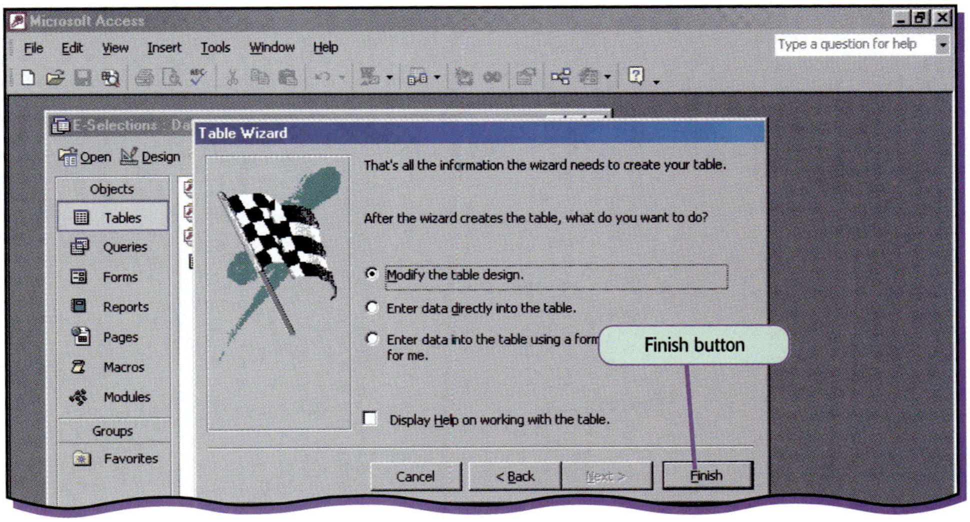

8 Click the **EmployeeID** field **Data Type** column, click the down arrow, and select **Text** as the data type.

Figure 1-18

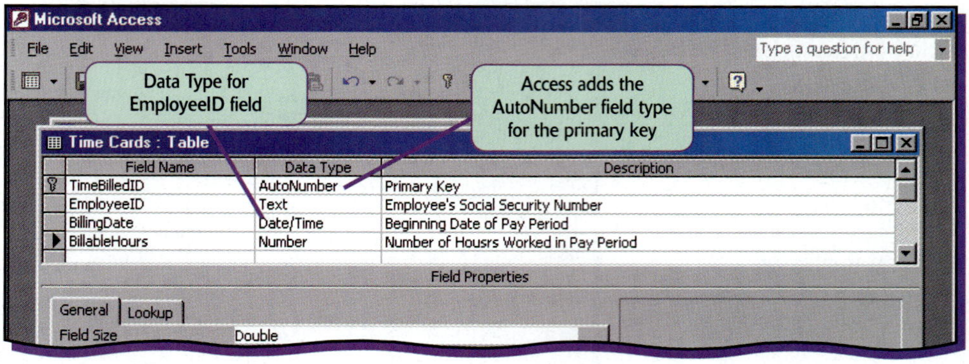

9 Select the **BillingDate** field name and type PayPeriod, select the **BillableHours** field name and type HoursWorked, and type the descriptions shown in Figure 1-19 for each field.

10 Select the **EmployeeID** field, press F6 to move to the lower pane, and type 11 as the **Field Size** value.

11 Click the Save button to save the modifications of your table design and close the Table Design window.

Figure 1-19

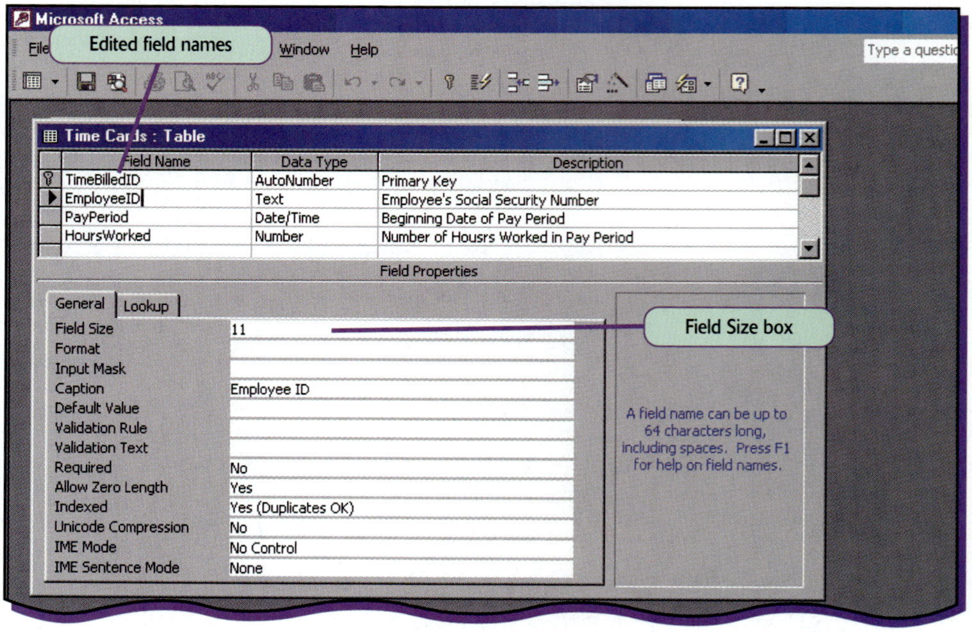

Creating a Table by Importing Data from Excel

In many circumstances, the data you want to incorporate in a database may already exist in another file. Access enables you to *import* data from a variety of formats, including the popular spreadsheet program Excel.

Task 4:
To Create a Table by Importing a Microsoft Worksheet

1 Choose **File | Get External Data | Import**.

Figure 1-20

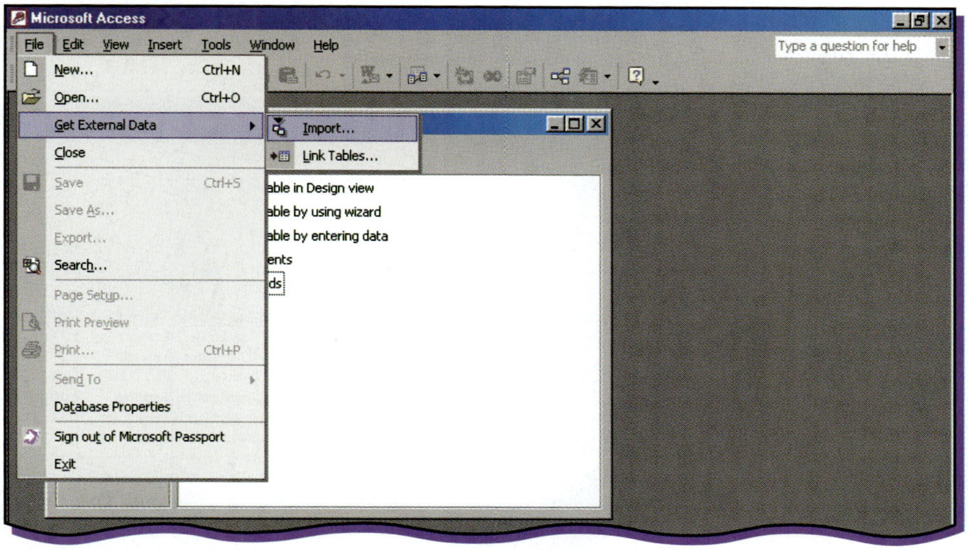

2 Select **Microsoft Excel** from the **Files of type** list, open the drive and folder containing your student files, and select the *Employees.xls* file.

Figure 1-21

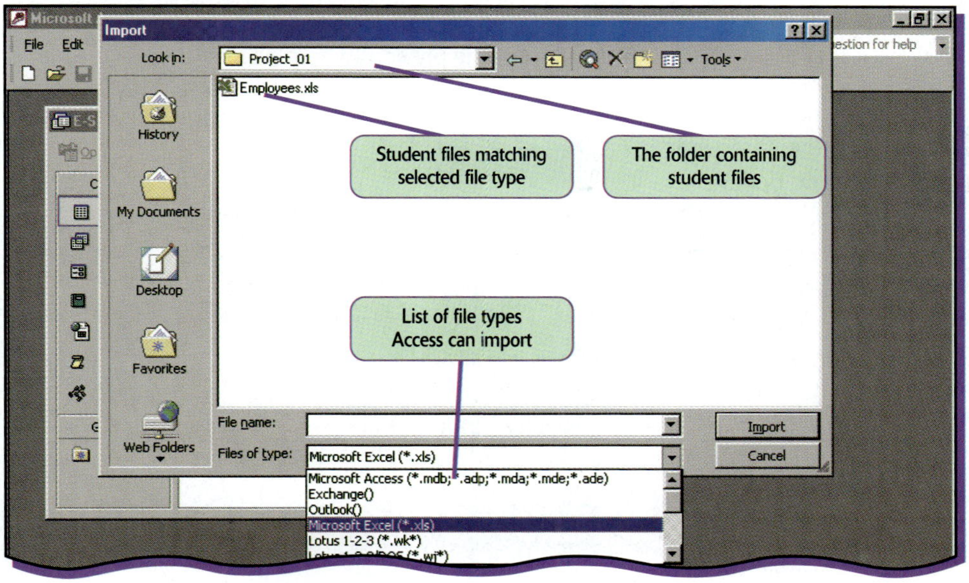

Tip The Link Tables option on the Get External Data list enables you to add a table to the active database that is currently stored in another database. When you use this technique to add tables to the database, changes you make to the table in one database are reflected in the linked table in the other database.

3 Click **Import** to open the Import Spreadsheet Wizard and select the **First Row Contains Column Headings** check box, if necessary.

Figure 1-22

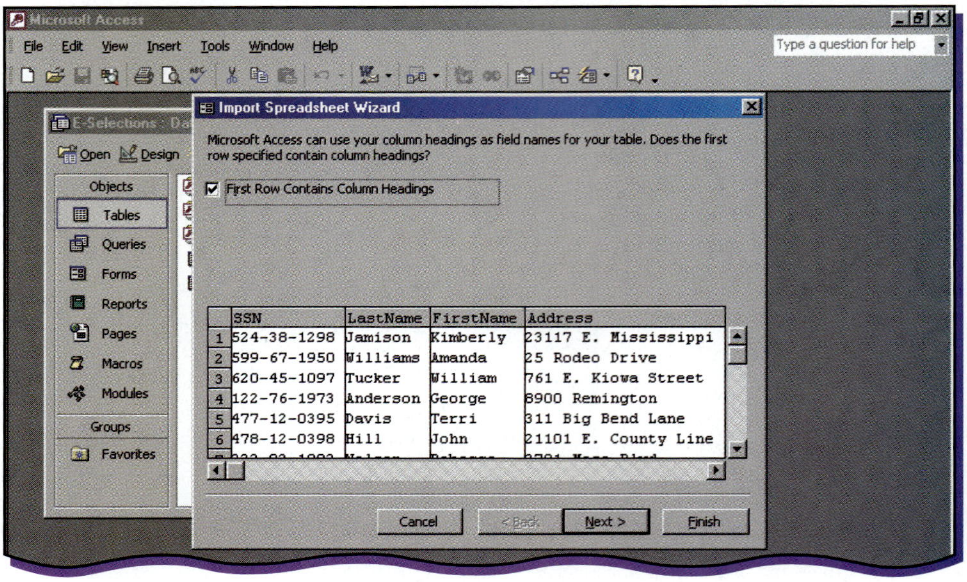

Troubleshooting Access places generic field names for tables you import when the first row does not contain column headings. If you click Next without selecting the option on this wizard page, click Back to return to the previous wizard page and select the option. Then click Next to continue.

4 Click **Next** three times, reviewing options in each wizard page and accepting the default options to store the data in a new table and the default values for field information.

5 Select the **Choose my own primary key** option and select the **SSN** field from the option list.

6 Click **Next** and then click **Finish** to accept *Employees* as the name of the table.

7 Click **OK** to return to the Database window.

Figure 1-23

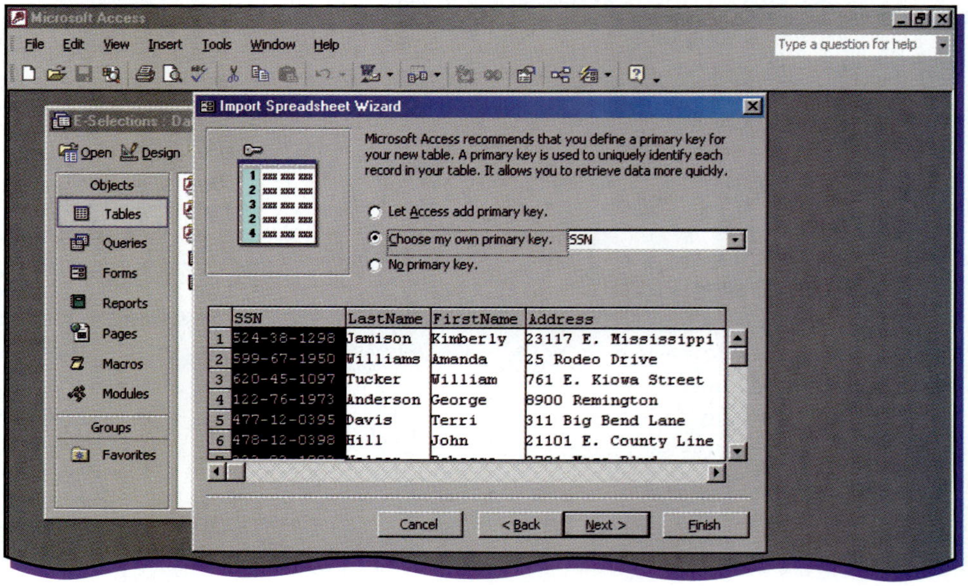

Adding Records to the Department Table

Whether you create a table using the Table Design window or the Table Wizard, the table comprises a structure to hold records. When tables contain only three or four fields, you can easily add records using *Datasheet view*, which is a two-dimensional grid similar to Word tables and Excel spreadsheets for entering and editing the data. The Departments table contains only two fields so it is easy to add records to the table using the Datasheet view.

Task 5:
Adding Records to the Departments Table Using Datasheet View

1 Click the Tables button in the Objects bar to display the table objects, if necessary.

2 Select the **Departments** table and then click the Open button to open the table.

3 Press Tab to move the insertion point to the **DepartmentName** field for the first record and type Clothing.

Figure 1-24

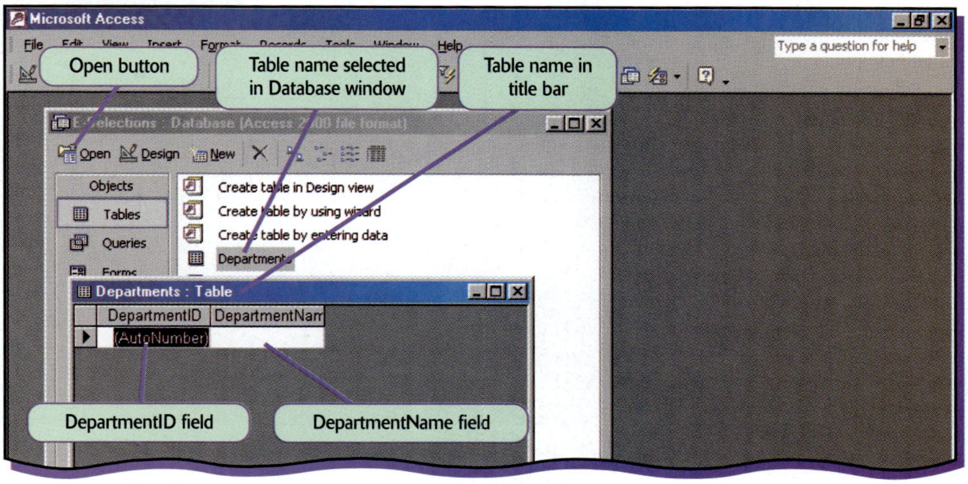

Troubleshooting When text you enter is longer than the field size, part of the text will be hidden. That's okay—you'll fix it later.

4 Press [Tab] twice to move the insertion point to the **DepartmentName** field for the next record and type Cosmetics.

5 Type the following department names using the procedures identified in Steps 3 and 4 to complete the table data shown in Figure 1-25.

6 Double-click the **DepartmentName** field right border to force the AutoFit feature to determine the optimum field width.

7 Close the table and save the changes to the table layout.

Figure 1-25

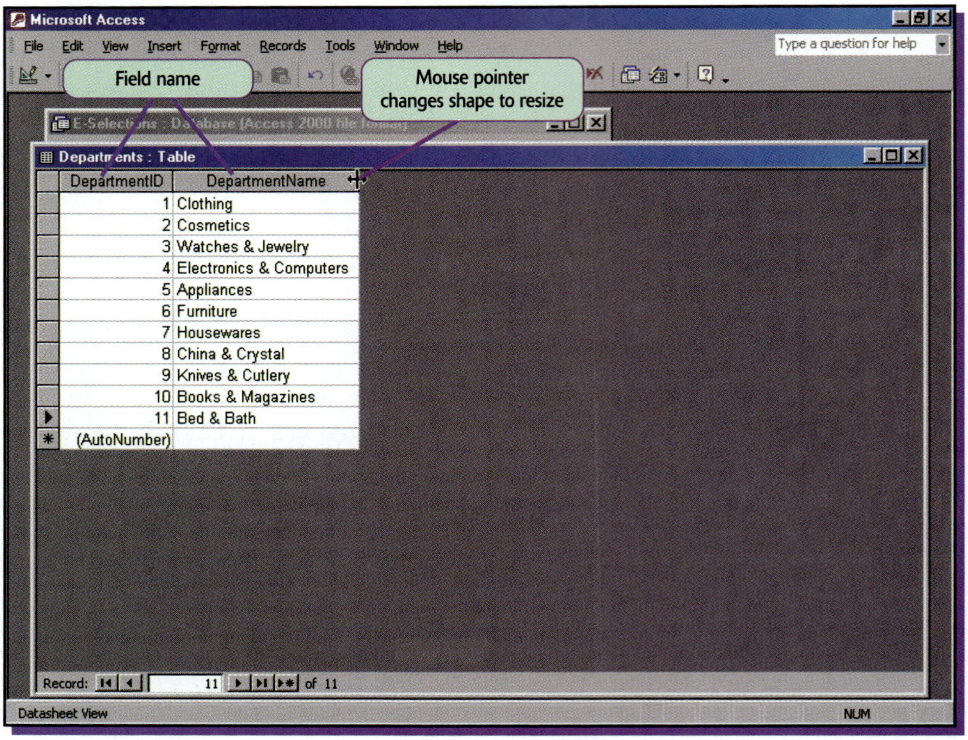

Tip Access saves each record automatically when you move to another record.

Creating an AutoForm to Display Records in the Employees Table

Entering data into Table Datasheet view is easy when you have relatively few fields in a table. When a table has many fields, or when you are designing databases that others will use, you can create forms that display each record individually on screen and present blank "pages" for entering records individually. Presenting record data individually in a page-like layout is more aesthetically pleasing to most users. While there are several methods available for creating forms, using the *AutoForm* command is the most efficient. This procedure enables you to automatically create a form based on the table you have selected.

Task 6:

To Create an AutoForm Based Upon the Employees Table

Figure 1-26

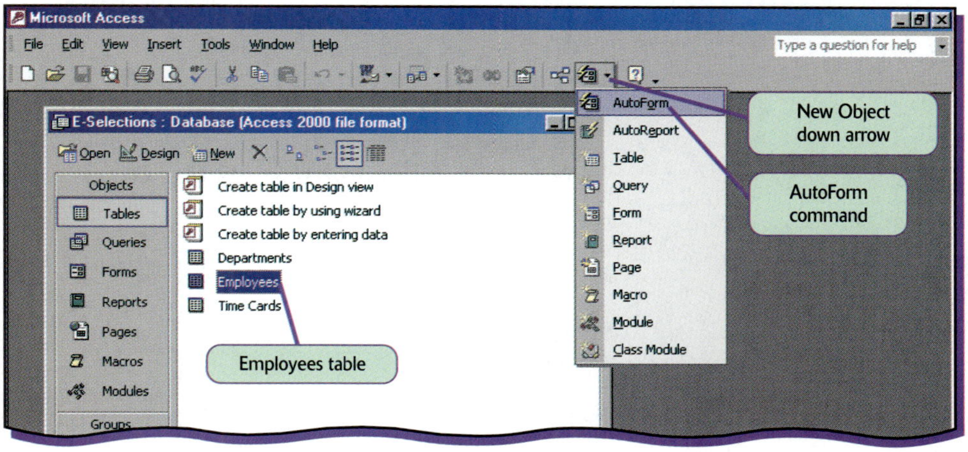

1. Open the *e-Selections.-mdb* database, if necessary, and click the **Employees** table in the Database window to select it.

2. Click the New Object down arrow button on the Database toolbar.

3. Select the AutoForm button.

4. Click the Save button, name the form *Employees*, and click OK.

5. Click the New Record button at the bottom of the form, and enter your personal information and school address into form fields, pressing Tab to move from field to field.

6. Close the form.

Figure 1-27

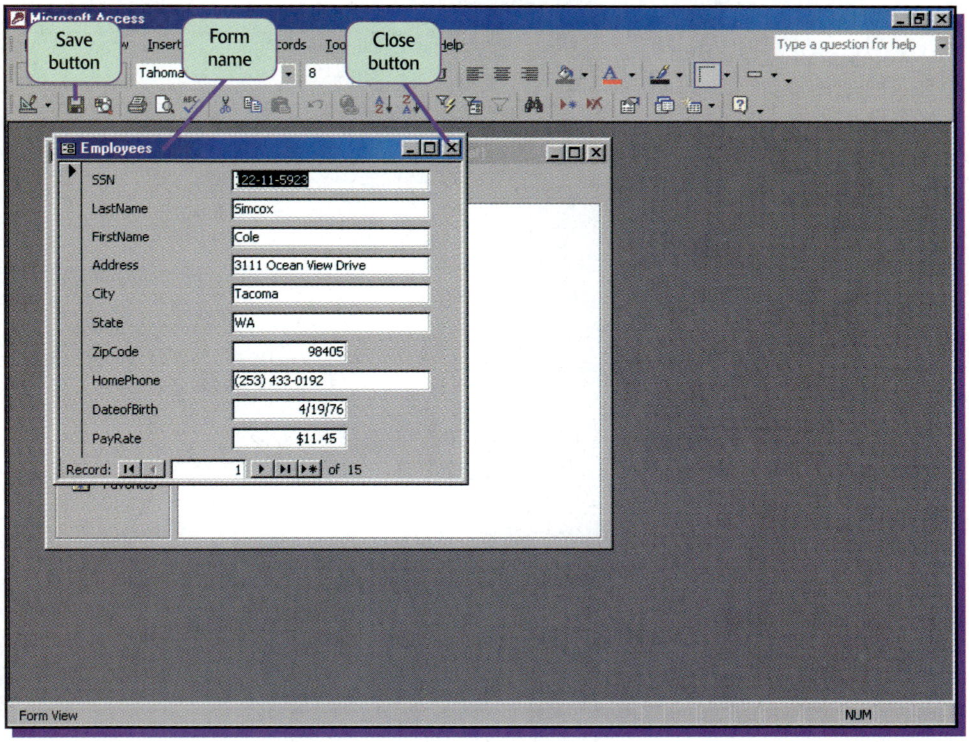

Tip To enter your date of birth, be sure to type either a hyphen (-) or a slash (/) between the month/day/year. Access will replace hyphens with slashes.

Creating an AutoReport to Display Records in the Employees Table

A form is used to enter new records, modify existing records, or display records on screen. Even though you can print datasheets and forms, creating a report provides a document that lists multiple records in an easy-to-read document. You can use the *AutoReport* feature to create a report for the Employees tables to create the report Mr. Traylor requested.

WEB TIP

Many Web sites contain forms that display data from databases. Review features of some of your favorite sites and see how many of them appear to contain data forms.

Task 7:

To Create an AutoReport Based Upon the Employees Table

1. Click the Reports button on the Objects bar and then click the New button to create a new report.

2. Select **AutoReport: Tabular** from the list of report types, click the **Choose the table or query where the object's data comes from** down arrow, and select the **Employees** table.

3. Click **OK** to create the report.

Figure 1-28

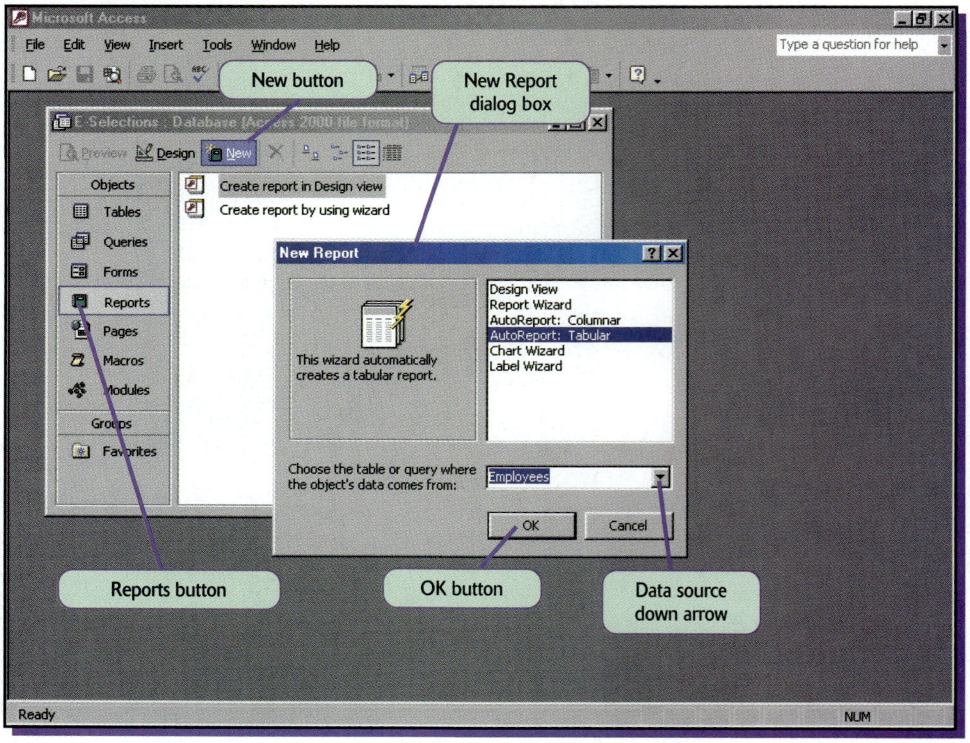

> **Tip** You can use your mouse pointer to change your view of the report. When you move the pointer over the page, it changes to a magnifying glass icon. Click the page to zoom in for a closer view of the report; click again to zoom out.

4 Close the window, click **Yes** if prompted to save the report, and type **Employees List** in the **Report Name** field.

Figure 1-29

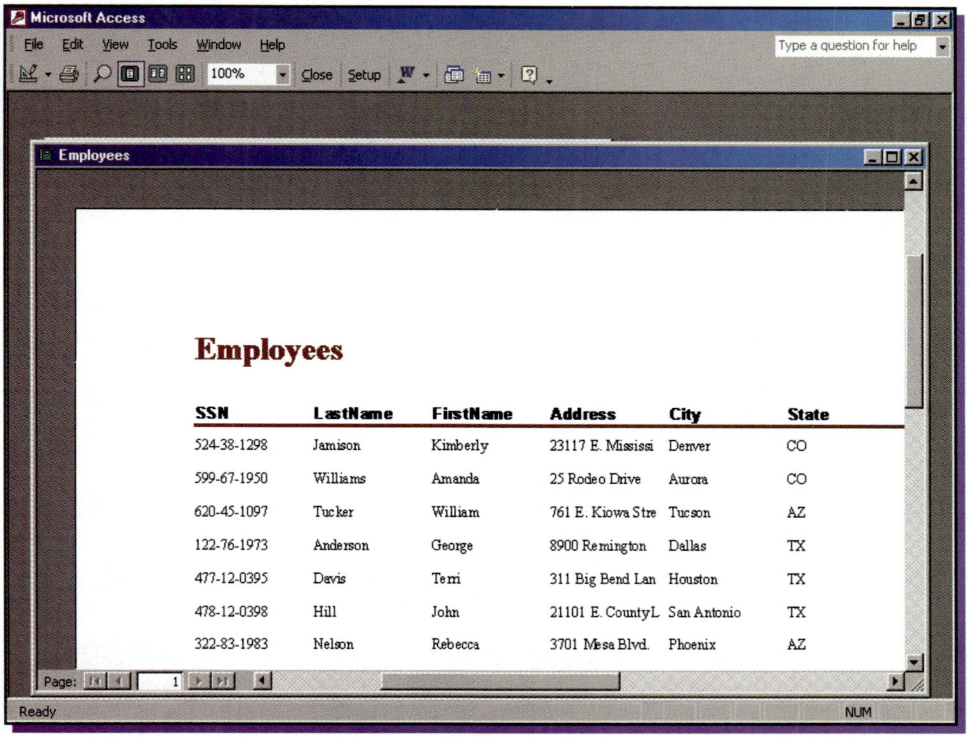

Previewing and Printing Database Objects

Each object in a database contains layout features that are different from the features found in other objects. As a result, the layout and formats of printed objects vary, depending on the objects that are open or selected in the Database window. However, the basic procedures used to preview and print different database objects are the same and are similar to the procedures used to print files in other applications.

Task 8:
To Preview and Print Basic Database Objects

1 Display the **Reports** list in the Database window and select the **Employees List** report.

2 Click **Preview**.

Figure 1-30

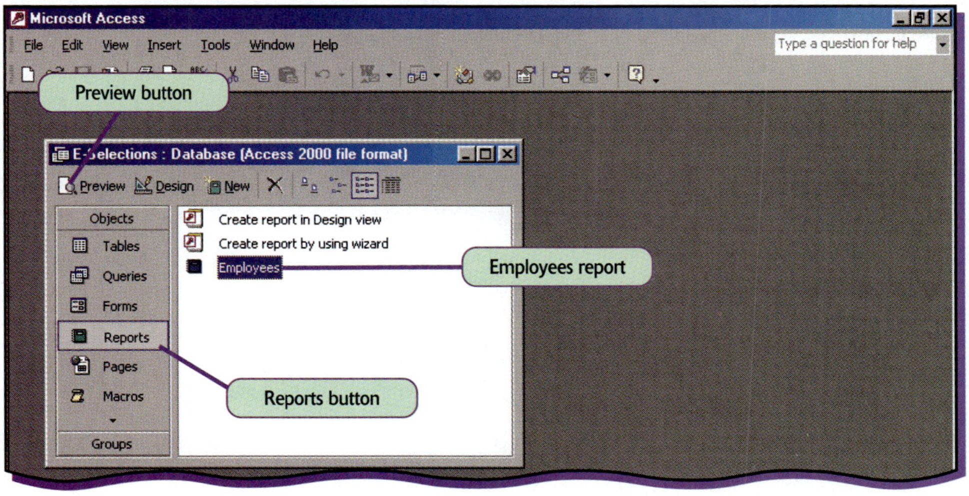

3 Point to each button on the toolbar and review the screen tip.

4 Click Close on the Preview toolbar to close the preview window.

> **Tip** Access automatically formats report layout as either Portrait or Landscape depending on the number of fields the table or query contains.

Figure 1-31

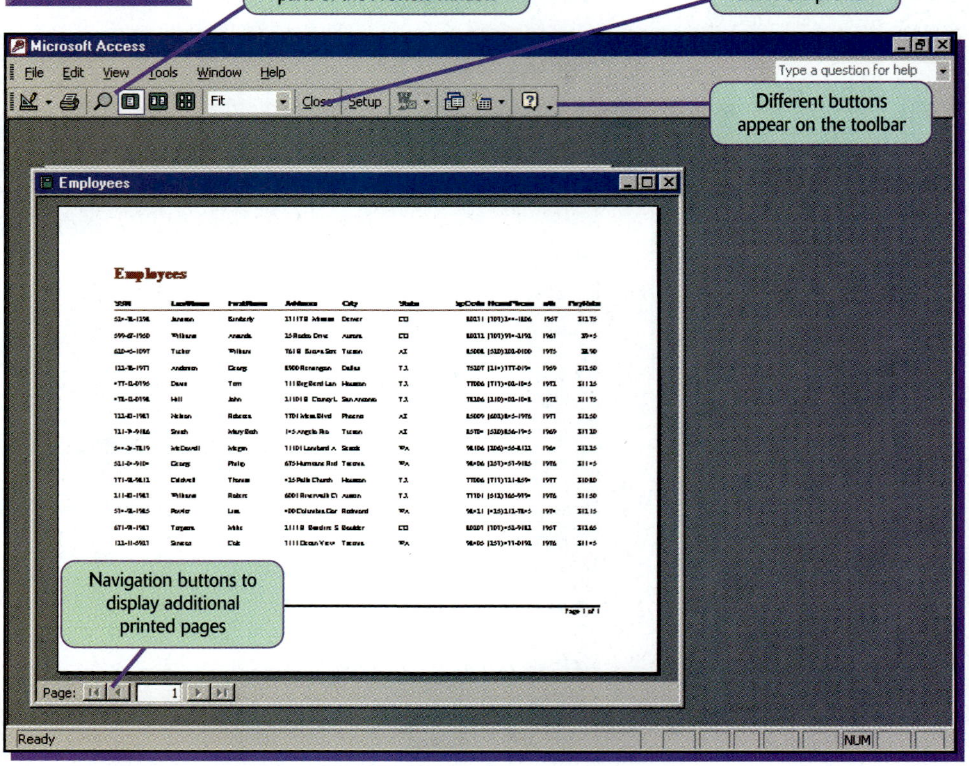

5 Display the **Tables** in the Database window, select the **Employees** table, and choose **File | Print**.

Figure 1-32

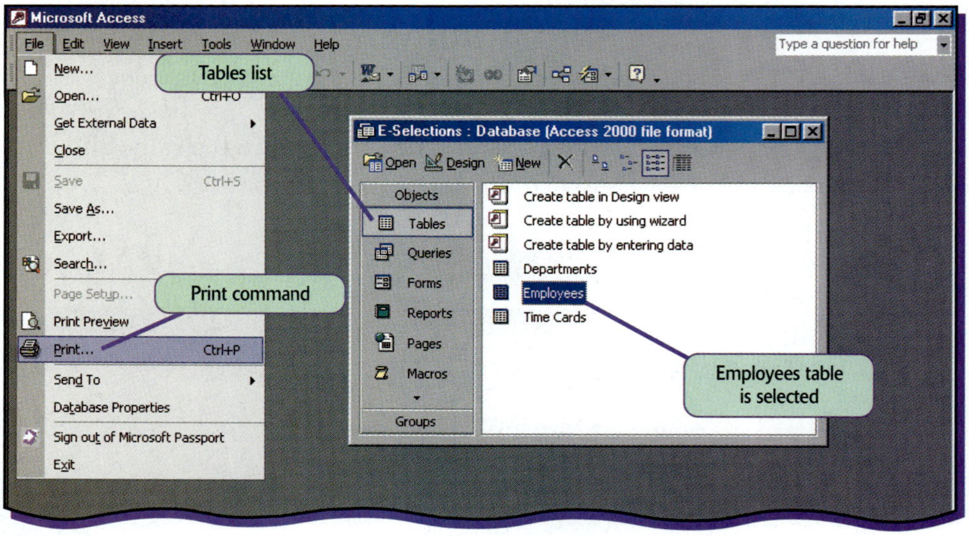

6 Click **Cancel**, close the Database window, and exit Access.

Figure 1-33

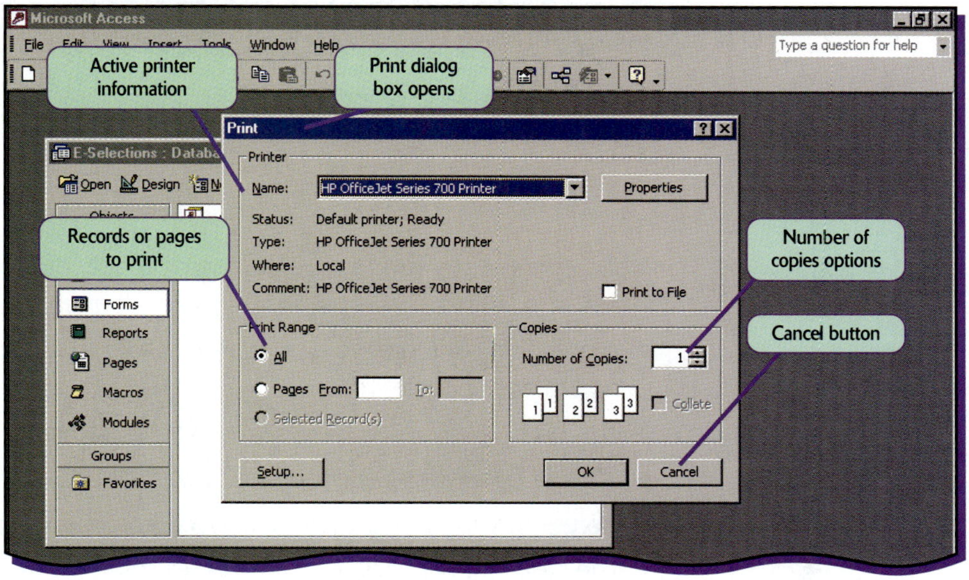

Troubleshooting Access resets print options when you click Cancel. As a result, you will need to select appropriate options the next time you access the Print dialog box.

SUMMARY AND EXERCISES

SUMMARY

- Access requires you to save and name a new database before you create any database objects, such as tables, forms, and reports.
- Every table should have a primary key field that is unique for each record in that table.
- The foreign key field enables you to relate tables and link records.
- A field's data type specifies how Access should store the data for that field.
- Access has 10 different data types you can choose from.
- The Table Design view enables you to create fields customized to the purpose of the database.
- Each field must have a name and data type assigned. Descriptions are helpful for the database developer but are optional.
- Field properties enable you to modify characteristics and functionality of a field.
- The Table Wizard will guide you through the process of creating a table.
- You can create a table by importing data from another type of data source, such as Excel.
- You can enter data into your table by using the Datasheet view or by creating a form.
- Forms enable you to enter or modify data stored in a table.
- Reports are used to print the data in an easy-to-read format.
- The layout and formats of printed objects vary, depending on the objects that are open or selected in the Database window.
- The basic procedures used to preview and print different database objects are the same and are similar to the procedures used to print files in other applications.

KEY TERMS & SKILLS

KEY TERMS

AutoForm (p. 1-20)
AutoNumber (p. 1-9)
AutoReport (p. 1-22)
currency (p. 1-9)
data type (p. 1-9)
Datasheet view (p. 1-19)
date/time (p. 1-9)
document (p. 1-11)
field property (p. 1-10)
foreign keys (p. 1-7)
hyperlink (p. 1-9)
import (p. 1-16)
Lookup Wizard (p. 1-9)
memo (p. 1-9)
number (p. 1-9)
OLE object (p. 1-9)
primary key (p. 1-7)
Table Design view (p. 1-8)
Table Wizard (p. 1-8)
text (p. 1-9)
yes/no (p. 1-9)

SKILLS

Add records to a datasheet in Datasheet view (p. 1-19)
Create a blank database (p. 1-6)
Create a table by importing data (p. 1-16)
Create a table using Table Design view (p. 1-10)
Create a table using the Table Wizard (p. 1-13)
Create an AutoForm based on a specific table (p. 1-21)
Create an AutoReport based on a specific table (p. 1-22)
Design tables with appropriate primary and foreign keys (p. 1-7)
Preview and print database tables, forms, and reports (p. 1-23)
Resize field columns in Datasheet view (p. 1-8)
Specify field data types (p. 1-8)
Specify field names (p. 1-8)
Specify field properties (p. 1-10)

STUDY QUESTIONS

MULTIPLE CHOICE

1. A primary key field is
   a. always an AutoNumber.
   b. unique for each record in the table.
   c. can contain a null value.
   d. not usually necessary in a multi-table database.

2. What data type is used to store graphics?
   a. text
   b. number
   c. memo
   d. OLE object

3. The AutoNumber data type is a good choice for
   a. a primary key field.
   b. a field that will store Social Security numbers.
   c. a foreign key field.
   d. a field that will store phone numbers.

4. Which database object would you create to allow easy data entry?
   a. table
   b. query
   c. form
   d. report

5. Which of the following fields would be the best choice for a primary key?
   a. last name
   b. address
   c. zip code
   d. Social Security number

6. What view allows you to create the table structure?
   a. Datasheet view
   b. Design view
   c. Print Preview view
   d. none of the above
7. What field type is used for mathematical calculations?
   a. text
   b. number
   c. AutoNumber
   d. OLE Object
8. The upper pane in the Table Design window is used to enter
   a. field names.
   b. field data types.
   c. field properties.
   d. a and b
9. The Table Wizard allows you to create a table by
   a. typing field names.
   b. choosing fields from sample tables.
   c. importing data from an Excel workbook.
   d. entering the field names into the datasheet.
10. To create an AutoForm or AutoReport you must specify
   a. which fields to display.
   b. what template to use.
   c. what table or query is used as the data source.
   d. what view you want to work in.

SHORT ANSWER

1. How does a database differ from a table?
2. How does a record differ from a field?
3. Where do you modify field properties?
4. What is a primary key?
5. What is a foreign key?
6. Name three methods for creating tables.
7. How do you add a new record to a table using Datasheet view?
8. How does Datasheet view differ from Table Design view?
9. What view allows you to visually inspect a report before you print it?
10. How do you display form objects in the Database window?

FILL IN THE BLANK

1. Every table should have a ____________ field that is unique for each record in that table.
2. The foreign key field allows you to ____________ the tables.
3. ____________ view allows you to define a table structure.

4. A _____________ is the database object that is best used for data entry.
5. When you define a field you must specify a _____________ and _____________.
6. The best data type for a graphic is _____________.
7. To change field characteristics you need to modify field _____________.
8. You can enter data directly into a table by using the _____________view.
9. The best way to enter data is to enter it into a _____________.
10. The object that is best for printing data is a _____________.

FOR DISCUSSION

1. What is the purpose of a primary key?
2. When would it be best to use Table Design view to create a table rather than the Table Wizard?
3. What addition fields could you include in the Employees table?
4. How can you minimize redundant data in a relational database?
5. Why is a form a better database object for data entry and display?

GUIDED EXERCISES

1 CREATING THE E-SELECTIONS HOME THEATER WARRANTY REPAIR DATABASE

Database Description: E-Selections has just released a new Home Theater System (HTS). The Warranty Repair Department wants a database they can use to track customer and repair information.

Database Purpose: The purpose of the e-Selections HTS Warranty Repair database is to maintain the data e-Selections needs to support warranty repairs on the new Home Theater System.

Database Tasks: The HTS Warranty Repair database needs to track:

- customer information
- repair information
- the technicians who performed each repair
- the parts used in each repair

Follow these directions to create the database and add tables to the new database.

1. Create a new blank database and name it **HTS Warranty Repair**.
2. Create the Customers table using the structure shown in Table 1-3. Type the name **Customers** for this table.

Table 1-3 Customers Table

Field Name	Data Type	Field Size	Primary Key	Description
CustomerID	AutoNumber		Yes	Customer ID number (Primary Key)
LastName	text	35		Customer's Last name
FirstName	text	35		Customer's first name
Address	text	50		Customer's address
City	text	25		Customer's city
State	text	2		Customer's state
ZipCode	text	11		Customer's zip code
Telephone	text	14		Customer's telephone number
Email	text	35		Customer's email address

3. Enter the data shown in Table 1-4 to the Customers table.

Table 1-4 Data for Customers Table

LastName	FirstName	Address	City	State	Zip
Jones	John	3111 Ocean Drive	Tacoma	WA	98405
Anderson	Paul	8900 Remington	Dallas	TX	75207
Smith	Robert	6001 Dog Circle	Austin	TX	73301
Williams	Mary Beth	145 Angelo Rio	Tucson	AZ	85704
Black	Rebecca	3701 Mesa Blvd.	Phoenix	AZ	85009
Green	Thomas	425 Falls Church	Houston	TX	77006
Clinton	Terri	311 Big Lane	Houston	TX	77006
Crist	John	21101 E. County Line Road	San Antonio	TX	78206
George	Philip	675 Hurricane Ridge Road	Tacoma	WA	98406

4 Create the Technicians table using the structure shown in Table 1-5.

Table 1-5 Technicians Table

Field Name	Data Type	Field Size	Primary Key	Description
TechnicianID	AutoNumber		Yes	Technician's ID (Primary Key)
LastName	text	35		Technician's Last Name
FirstName	text	35		Technician's FirstName
PayRate	currency			Technicians pay rate per hour

5 Enter the data shown in Table 1-6 to the Technicians table.

Table 1-6 Technicians Table

LastName	FirstName	PayRate
Smith	Mary	$20.00
Wan	Ben	$30.00
Hernandez	Jose	$25.00
Kwan	Betty	$40.00
Petrocci	Mike	$25.00

6 Create the Repairs table using the structure shown in Table 1-7. Type **Repairs** in the Table Name field.

Table 1-7 Repairs Table

Field Name	Data Type	Field Size	Primary Key	Description
RepairID	AutoNumber		Yes	ID code for Repair
RepairDate	Date/Time			Date of repair
SystemPart repair	Text	30		Part of system that needed
SerialNumber	Text	25		Serial number of system
CustomerID	number			Customer's ID number (Foreign Key)
TechnicianID	number			Technician's ID number (Foreign Key)
RepairTime	number			Time in hours of repair

7 Create an AutoForm using the Customers table as your data source. Type **Customer Entry Form** in the Form Name field.

8 Create an AutoReport: Tabular using the Technicians table as your data source. Name the report *Technicians List*.

9 Print the report.

10 Close the database.

2 CREATING THE E-SELECTIONS MAKE A PROFIT DATABASE

Database Description: E-Selections has just launched a new program aimed at assisting schools and other nonprofit organizations with an easy-to-use fund-raising project. Different departments of e-Selections will provide specially priced merchandise with a custom logo for each organization. As part of this initiative, they want to give each organization an Access database file that will allow them to easily keep track of inventory and to assist them in ordering items from e-Selections.

The database contains three tables:

- The Items table contains information about each item the organization can sell.
- The Departments table contains information about each e-Selections department they will order from.
- The Orders table contains information about each order that is placed with e-Selections.

Database Purpose: The purpose of the e-Selections Make a Profit database is to track inventory and order information.

Database Tasks:

- maintain item information
- maintain inventory information
- automate ordering with e-Selections

Follow these steps to complete the tasks:

1. Create a new blank database and name it *Make a Profit*.
2. Create the Items table using the structure shown in Table 1-8 and call the table **Items**.

Table 1-8

Field Name	Data Type	Field Size	Primary Key	Description
ItemID	Text	4	Yes	Item ID number (primary key)
Description	Text	25		Description of item
InStock	Number	Long integer		Number of units on hand
Cost	Currency			Cost of item
SellingPrice	Currency			Selling price of item
DepartmentCode	Text	2		e-Selections department code (foreign key)

3. Enter the data shown in Table 1-9 into the Items table.

Table 1-9

ItemID	Description	InStock Cost	Cost	Selling Price
IC15	T-Shirt (L)	25	$8.00	$9.75
IC16	T-Shirt (M)	25	$8.00	$9.75
IC17	T-Shirt (S)	25	$8.00	$9.75
FP10	Baseball Cap	50	$5.50	$6.75
HP23	Coffee Mug	35	$3.25	$4.25
IC20	Polo Shirt (S)	25	$15.50	$19.95
IC21	Polo Shirt (M)	25	$15.50	$19.95
IC22	Polo Shirt (L)	25	$15.50	$19.95

4. Create the Departments table using the structure shown in Table 1-10.

Table 1-10

Field Name	Data Type	Field Size	Primary Key	Description
DepartmentCode	Text	2	Yes	Code of e-Selections department (primary key)
DepartmentName	Text	25		Name of department
Telephone	Text	14		Phone number to order items

5. Enter the data shown in Table 1-11 into the Departments table.

Table 1-11

DepartmentCode	DepartmentName	Telephone
FP	Fields of Play	
IC	Image Control	
HP	Home Page	

6. Create the Orders table using the structure shown in Table 1-12.

Table 1-12

Field Name	Data Type	Field Size	Primary Key	Description
OrderID	AutoNumber		Yes	Primary key
OrderDate	Date			Date of order
ItemsOrdered	Number			Number of items ordered
ItemID	Text	4		ItemID of item ordered (foreign key)

7. Create an AutoForm named *Items Entry Form* using the Items table as your data source.

8. Create an AutoReport: Tabular named *Inventory Report* using the Items table as your data source. Print the report.

9. Close the database.

3 CREATING BRENT'S TOOLS CUSTOMER ORDERS DATABASE

Database Description: Brent's Tools, started by Brent Toolman in 1998, sells wholesale tools to hardware stores around the country. His company has had steady growth in sales but profits have lagged behind. Brent realizes that he needs to strengthen the company's collection methods to improve profit. He asks you to create a database in Access that will enable the company to quickly see which customers are paid in full and which have outstanding balances. The database contains two tables. The Customers table contains customer information and the Orders table will contain information concerning customer orders.

Database Purpose: The purpose of the Brent's Tools Customer Orders database is to maintain customer orders and payment information.

Database Tasks: Brent's Tools Customer Orders database needs to:

- maintain order information
- maintain customer information
- create invoice reports

Follow these steps to complete the tasks:

1. Create a new blank database named *Brent's Tools Customer Orders.*
2. Create the Customers table using the structure shown in Table 1-13.

Table 1-13

Field Name	Data Type	Field Size	Primary Key	Description
CustomerID	AutoNumber		Yes	Customer ID (primary key)
CompanyName	Text	35		Customer name
Address	Text	30		Customer address
City	Text	20		Customer city
State	Text	2		Customer state
ZipCode	Text	10		Customer zip code
Phone	Text	14		Contact phone number
FirstContact	Date/time			First date of contact

3. Enter the data shown in Table 1-14 into the Customers table.

Table 1-14

CustomerID	Company Name	Address	City	State	Zip Code	Phone	First Contact
AutoNumber	Evergreen Hardware	876 Lincoln	Evergreen	CO	80439		5/03/99
AutoNumber	Tom's Tool Shack	8765 Main St.	Fallbrook	CA	92028		7/15/99
AutoNumber	The Hardware Store	8765 White St.	Eugene	OR	89876		8/26/00
AutoNumber	Acer Hardware	876 Pine Dr.	Ogden	UT	87678		9/15/00
AutoNumber	Pine Center Lumber	876 Beaver Circle	Spanaway	WA	98776		9/25/00

4. Create the Orders table using the structure shown in Table 1-15.

Table 1-15

Field Name	Data Type	Field Size	Primary Key	Description
OrderID	AutoNumber		Yes	Order ID number (primary key)
CustomerID	Number			Customer ID (Foreign key)
SalesDate	Date/Time			Date of sales
ShipMethod	Text	10		Shipping Method (value list)
TotalInvoice	Currency			Total of invoice
AmountPaid	Currency			Amount that customer paid on invoice
PayMethod	Text	5		Method of payment

5. Create an AutoForm named *Customers* using the Customers table as the data source.

6. Create an AutoReport: Tabular named *Customers Report* using the Customers table as the data source.

7. Close the database.

ON YOUR OWN

The difficulty of these case studies varies:

are the least difficult; *are more difficult; and* *are the most difficult.*

1 SCHOOL ASSIGNMENTS DATABASE

Your classmates have asked you to create a database that will enable them to keep track of class assignments. They would like to have printouts of all assignments that are due for a specific month or week as well as printouts of all tests, quizzes, readings, or papers for a specific time period. They also want you to include the instructor's name, phone number, and e-mail address on some of the reports so that they can easily contact them for help.

Create a database that contains two tables, Classes and Assignments. Include a primary key field in each table and a foreign key field in the Assignments table so that the tables can be related. Enter your computer class information into the Classes table. Create an AutoForm based on the Classes table. Print a copy of each table even though no data has been added.

2 NANCY'S KNICK-KNACK NOOK

Your friend Nancy just opened her new Web business, Nancy's Knick-Knack Nook, which specializes in fruit and nut baskets. She would like you to create an Access database to track her inventory and suppliers. A report of her current inventory is shown in Table 1-16.

Design and create a database to track her inventory. Then create the tables and enter data into the Suppliers table. Create an AutoReport of the Suppliers table.

Table 1-16

ItemID	Description	Units on Hand	Cost	Selling Price	Code	Supplier Name	Supplier Telephone
101	Large Fruit and Gourmet Basket	100	75.95	89.95	FN	Fruits and Nuts Unlimited	800-555-4444
102	The Ambassador Gift Basket	250	40.95	59.95	AW	Acme Wholesale Gifts	888-666-6547
105	Chocolate Lovers Basket	75	30.95	39.95	XC	X-tream Candies	800-873-5476
108	Holiday Celebration Basket	100	33.95	49.95	AW	Acme Wholesale Gifts	888-666-6547
109	Annie Get Your Gun Basket	125	30.95	39.95	XC	X-tream Candies	800-873-5476
200	Never Leave Home Without It Basket	75	19.95	29.95	FN	Fruits and Nuts Unlimited	800-555-4444
205	Snack Attack Basket	100	21.95	39.95	XC	X-tream Candies	800-873-5476
300	Let's Go Nuts Basket	50	19.95	29.95	FN	Fruits and Nuts Unlimited	800-555-4444
350	Just for Her Basket	100	25.95	39.95	AW	Acme Wholesale Gifts	888-666-6547
400	Bazooka Basket	125	12.95	19.95	AW	Acme Wholesale Gifts	888-666-6547

3 PINE VALLEY OUTREACH CONTRIBUTIONS DATABASE

Organization Description: Pine Valley Outreach (PVO) is located in the small mountain town of Pine Valley, Colorado. PVO is a charitable organization that helps needy families with food, clothing, heating expenses, and other basic needs. Since PVO is a charity, they must track contributions, send out an annual statement to contributors for tax purposes, and create other reports for their Board of Trustees.

Database Purpose: The purpose of the PVO database is to maintain the data PVO needs to support the services they provide to families.

Database Tasks: The PVO database needs to:

- maintain contributor information
- record all monetary contributions
- create contribution statements to send to contributors
- provide mailing labels
- create contribution reports for the Board of Trustees
- provide on screen forms for volunteers to enter and view information

Design and create a database to meet PVO's needs. Create the necessary tables, enter some sample contributor data, and print the Contributors table to show to the PVO's director.

4 BEAVER BROOK INN AND CONFERENCE CENTER FACILITY SCHEDULING DATABASE

You have just started your first day of work at the Beaver Brook Inn and Conference Center. Your first assignment is to create an Access database that will allow BBICC to maintain the information necessary to schedule its conference facilities to organizations around the country. BBICC has five rooms available for conference use. Each room is booked on an hourly basis. Your supervisor needs the following reports: (a) a schedule for each room including the beginning and ending times each group is using the room for each day and (b) room confirmation statements that can be sent to the group before their conference begins. The statements must include all room schedule information as well as costs for each room and the total cost for the conference.

Design and create a database that will help the BBICC track contact information for each group, room information and costs, and room scheduling. Create the necessary Groups and Rooms tables and enter information into the appropriate table. Create an AutoForm and AutoReport based on the Groups table and print copies of both objects.

5 GET IN SHAPE FITNESS CLUB

The Get in Shape Fitness Club has just moved in next to your college. They are offering various fitness classes and want you to create an Access database to help track registration and payments of members and nonmembers. As a promotional incentive, nonmembers will be charged the members' price for each hour they participate in the class. The fitness club director would like the following reports: (a) a class roster with names and phone numbers and (b) statements that can be mailed to each member. The statements should list which classes the member has registered for and how much each class costs according to how many hours the member has requested. It should also list the amount the student owes.

Design and create the database to meet the GIS Fitness Club's needs. Create the tables and enter sample data. Create a simple form and report based on the Members table and print copies of each.

Photospread credits pages 1-2 & 1-3

©2000 Robert Madigan from Cartoonbank.com, all rights reserved ed; ©Pearson Education; ©Lorraine Castellano

FROM THE FILES

You Will Need

- ✔ Brent's Customers & Orders.mdb
- ✔ e-Selections@Work.mdb
- ✔ Shaping Up.mdb
- ✔ Home Theater Warranty Repair.mdb
- ✔ Profit-Making.mdb
- ✔ Nancy's Nook.mdb
- ✔ Pine Valley Fund Raising.mdb
- ✔ Collegiate Work.mdb

PROJECT 2

Manipulating Table Data

As you add records to database tables and your database grows, moving among records in the database becomes more complex. Access contains the same basic tools—Find and Replace, Spelling, etc.—that are available in other applications. You can use these features to locate records and check the spelling of data entered into tables. In addition, Access provides tools and features designed specifically for working with database objects. In this project, you'll learn different ways to find, filter, and sort records to organize data in tables and datasheets. You will also learn how to publish your data to an interactive Web page that can be placed on an intranet or the Internet.

e-selections Running Case

As a database specialist in the e-Selections division of Selections, Inc., you have been developing a payroll information database for the company. Careful planning has made the database easy to develop and you're anxious to see how well it works. Using and exploring the database will test its design.

OBJECTIVES

After completing this project, you will be able to:

- *Format and modify the layout of a datasheet for printing and viewing*
- *Navigate among records using Datasheet view*
- *Expand subdatasheets*
- *Locate and edit records*
- *Update multiple records in a table using the Replace feature*
- *Sort records in a table*
- *View table properties*
- *Filter records*
- *Export data to an Excel workbook*
- *Create a data access page*
- *View a data access page in a Web browser*
- *Compact and repair your database*

Database Detectives

Every great detective is looking for one thing—the facts; consequently, every investigation uncovers a multitude of facts. Some of them are related and some are not. Finding the patterns and connections in the facts is often the key to solving the crime. Consequently, it is no wonder that police organizations around the world are finding out that databases can help them analyze their data quickly and efficiently, saving valuable time and energy.

One advantage of using a database, which has no manual equivalent, is that of comparing a given piece of information to data stored from prior investigations, both locally and on a national scale. Laws are now in effect in many states requiring the maintenance of these databases. Some public-threat databases track specific types of criminals, such as sex offenders, and some track specific types of offenses, such as domestic violence.

Databases also use this kind of shared information to help detectives discover the identity of victims and suspects. Anyone who has ever seen or read a crime drama knows that detectives can run a set of fingerprints "through the system." The system they are referring to is a national database of fingerprints that have been collected over the years. In recent years, investigative organizations have also been adding to a database that contains DNA samples from people who have been investigated or convicted of crimes.

As computer and database technology improves, police and investigative organizations are taking advantage of these advancements to use smarter and more efficient techniques. The Special Investigative Unit Support System (SIUSS) is an example of one of these advanced systems.

Investigators enter all the information that they obtain during an investigation—such as surveillance reports, property records, arrest records, vehicle ownership, complaints, tips, and so on—into the SUISS database. While detectives continue to follow leads, the database analyzes the data, looking for similarities and patterns in the data. Because the SUISS system is continually comparing new

Comparing a given piece of information to data stored from prior investigations!

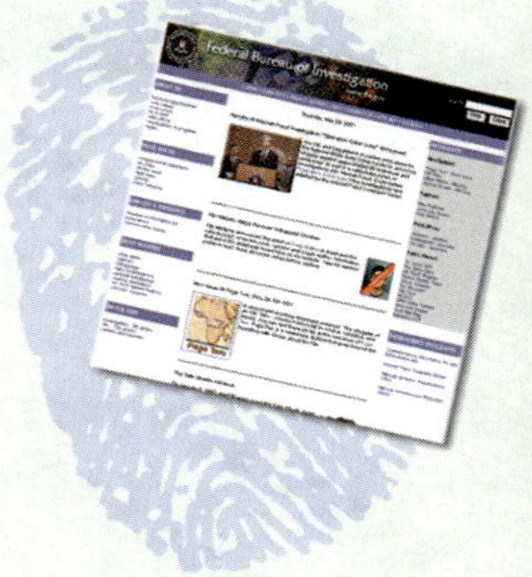

data against every piece of existing data, it is often able to identify the patterns that might otherwise have been missed.

Another technology, once seen only in big-budget spy movies, is making its way into our modern reality. At the 2001 Super Bowl, officials tested the first widespread use of facial recognition surveillance.

As visitors entered the turnstiles, video surveillance cameras captured their images. However, instead of simply storing those images to be viewed later if a crime is committed, the video feed was sent to a computer. This computer scanned the image, identified facial features and measurements, and compared it to a sample database of 1,700 known criminals and terrorists. Those images that did not match any of the records in the database were purged.

Steven Rehfeldt, Super Bowl project manager for Graphico Technologies, Inc., creator of the software system noted that images were compared to the database within seconds and confirmed that they did find 19 matches. At future events, Graphico hopes to compare scanned images to a much larger database, potentially containing tens of thousands of images.

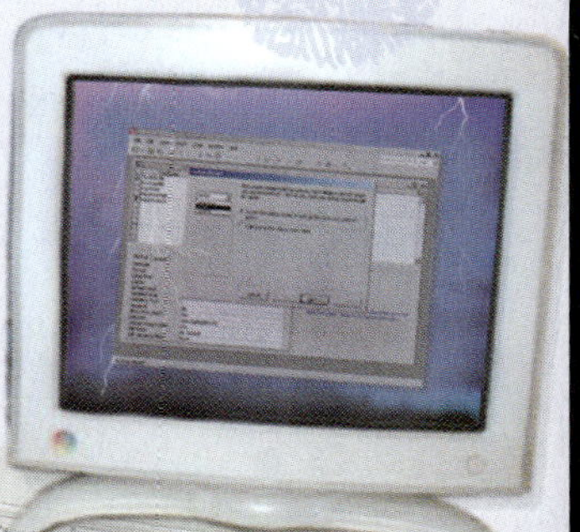

According to Rehfeldt, this technology affords the public a "higher degree of privacy" than standard surveillance techniques, which store the images of law-abiding citizens indefinitely.

No one is quite certain how far the use of computer technology will go in the field of criminal investigation; however, there is no doubt that, as the benefits of using technology to analyze data become more well known, police organizations will find more and better ways to utilize these databases in their investigations.

Compare sample database of 1,700 known criminals and terrorists!

PROJECT 2

Manipulating Table Data

The Challenge

So far, Mr. Traylor is pleased with the work you have accomplished in designing and building the database. Now he's interested in testing the database design to determine design edits that need to be made to accommodate different data formats. Mr. Traylor has six tasks for you. He wants you to accomplish the following:

- Format the datasheet so that you can easily view and print the data from the Employees table.
- Edit existing table data to reflect the Finance Committee's decision to raise the hourly wage of all employees at certain pay levels.
- Arrange the data so that he can view employee records alphabetically by last name, by last name according to state, and by age within a state and city.
- Post all employee addresses to the company intranet so the department managers can modify them.
- Create an Excel workbook using data from the employee's data.
- Compact the database file.

Figure 2-1 displays a data access page viewed on an intranet page.

Figure 2-1

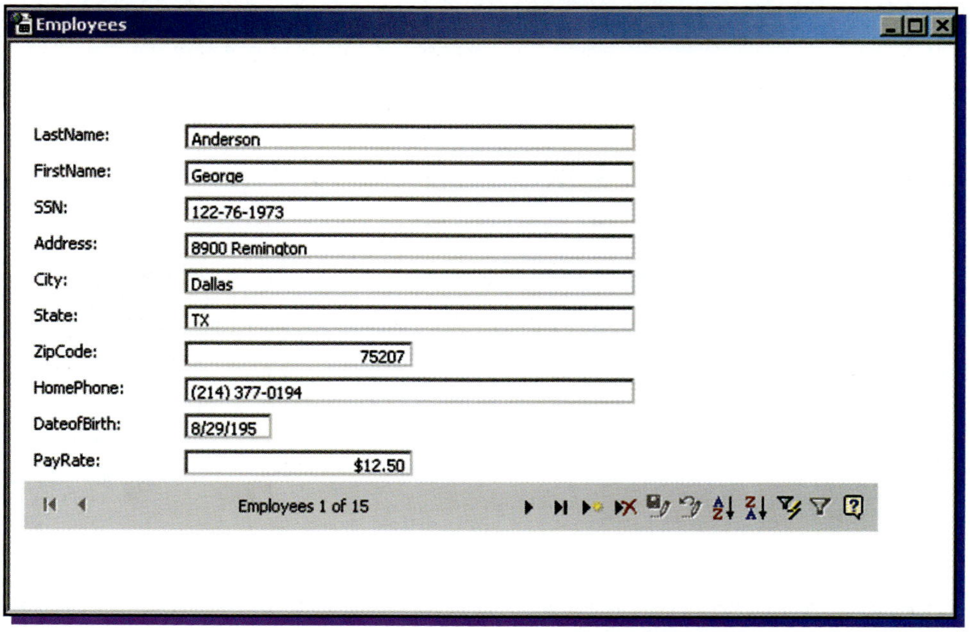

The Solution

Since you will be working with records in Table Datasheet view, you will need to know how to navigate among records using this view. Formatting the datasheet will help you to view and work with the records. You can use the Find and Replace feature to edit table records and the Sort feature to display records in a different order. To limit the records displayed in the datasheet to those from specific cities as well as the records containing specific pay rates, you'll have to learn how to filter table data. After you accomplish these basic tasks, you can create a data access page to post employee data to the corporate intranet. You'll notice as you review the file that someone has been working with the file—new records have been added and some of the field names have been changed.

Formatting and Modifying the Layout of a Datasheet

Although users typically use Access forms to interact with record data, database developers frequently use the Table Datasheet view to interact with data. Modifying the layout of the datasheet can be helpful with viewing, searching, and printing table data. You can rearrange the table columns to display data in a different order.

Task 1:
To Format and Modify the Layout of a Table Datasheet

1. Launch Access and open the *e-Selections@Work.mdb* file.

2. Click the Tables button on the database Objects bar, select the **Employees** table, click the Open button, and then maximize the Datasheet window.

Figure 2-2

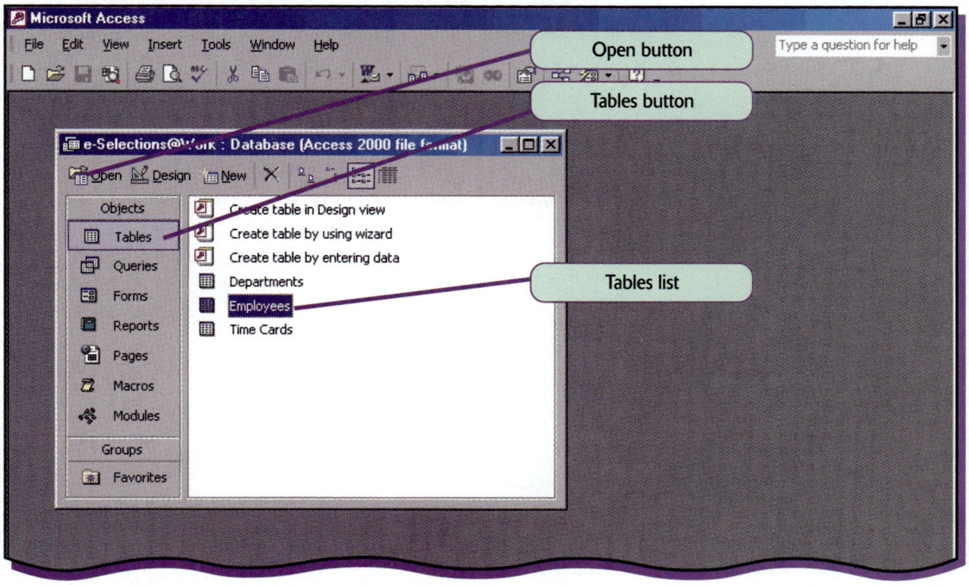

3 Position the mouse pointer on the right edge of the **Address** field selector button until the pointer changes to a two-headed arrow and double-click the border to resize the column.

4 Double-click the right border of each additional field to resize the fields.

Figure 2-3

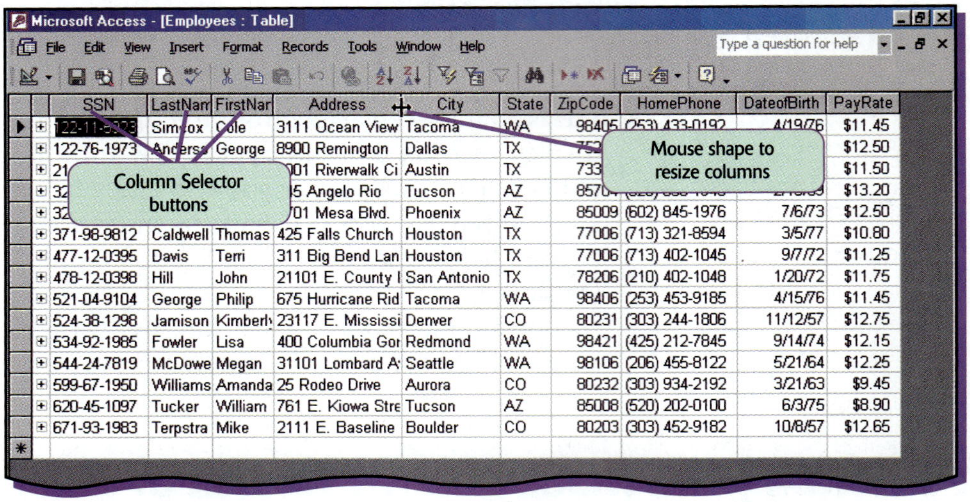

Tip To access additional columns, click the horizontal scroll bar button at the bottom of the Table window.

5 Click the **PayRate** column selector button to select the column.

6 Drag the **PayRate** column to the right of the **FirstName** column.

7 Drag the **FirstName** column to the left of the **LastName** column.

Figure 2-4

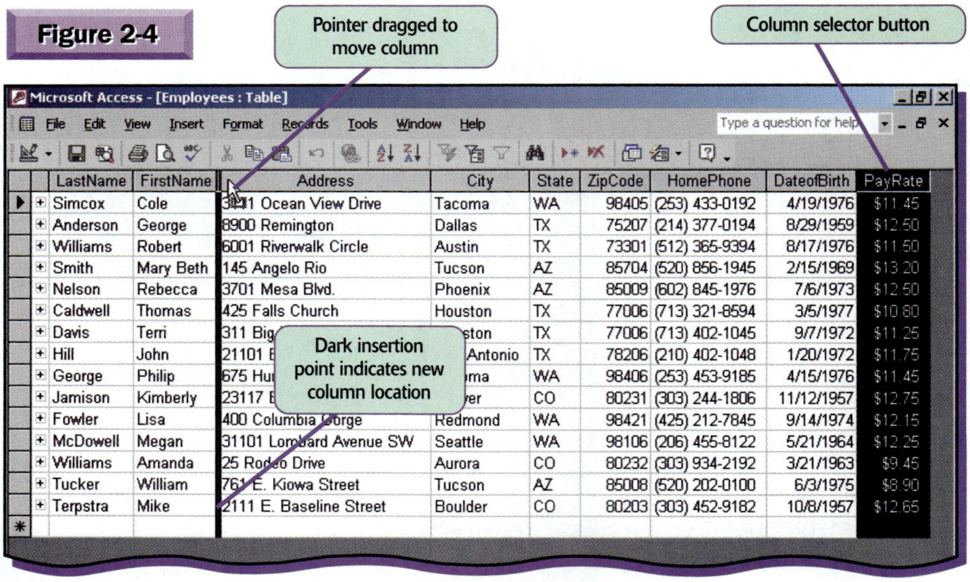

Tip When you point to a column to select it, the mouse pointer changes to a thick, down-pointing black arrow.

8 Select the **Address** column and choose **Format | Hide Columns** to remove this column from the preview screen.

9 Click the Save button to save the changes in the layout of the datasheet and click the Print Preview button to review the datasheet.

Figure 2-5

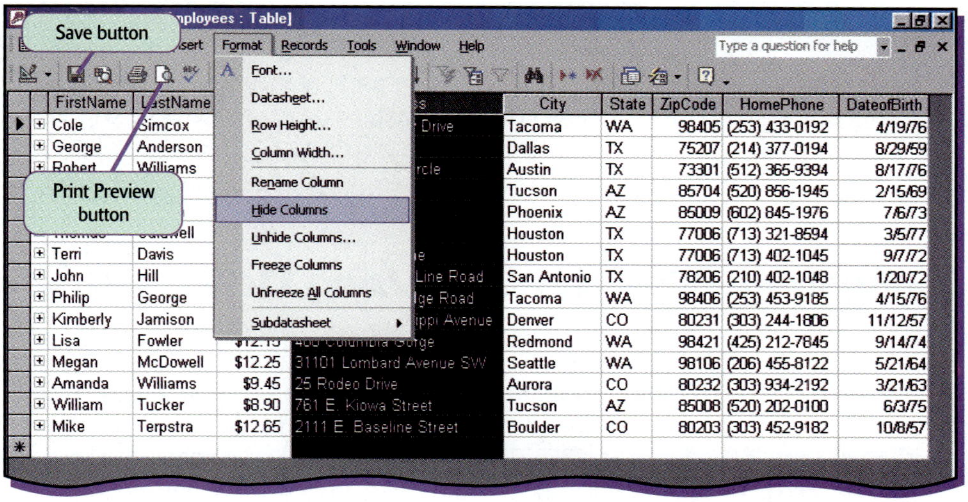

Tip

To show hidden columns, choose **Format | Unhide columns**. A dialog box containing a list of hidden columns will appear. Place a check mark in the column you want to show and click **OK**.

10 Click **Close** on the Print Preview toolbar to return to Datasheet view.

Figure 2-6

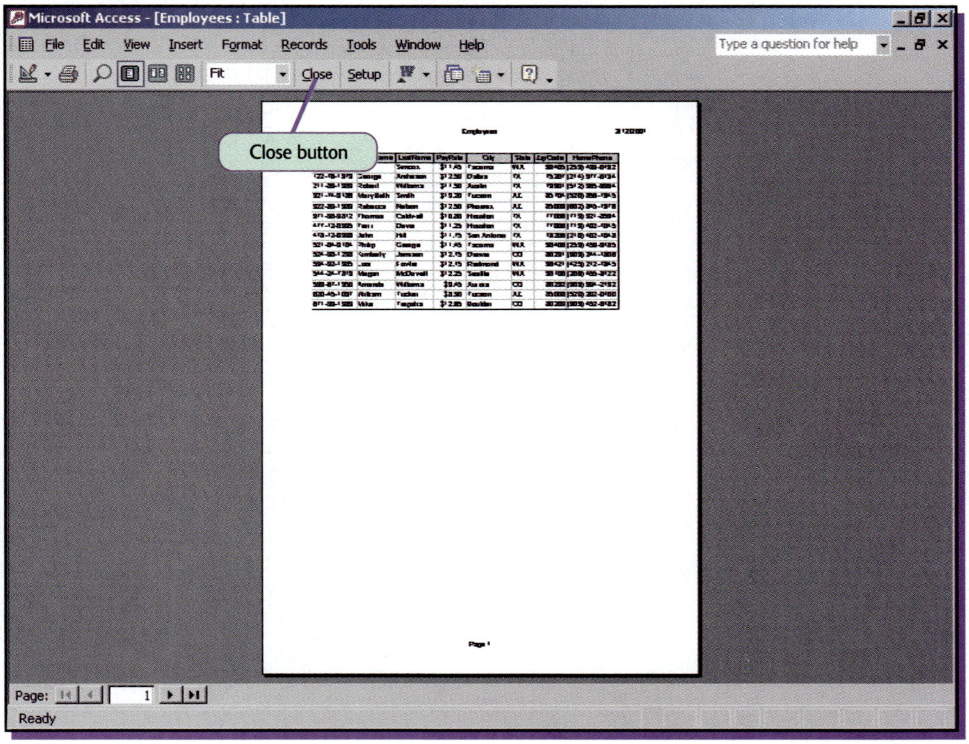

Troubleshooting

Be sure to click the Close button identified in Figure 2-6 rather than the close window button in the upper left corner of the window. Clicking the close window button closes the table datasheet while the Close button closes print preview and leaves the table datasheet open.

CHECK POINT

Access contains a wealth of different tools that you can use to format database objects. As you become more comfortable with different database objects, you'll want to explore some of these features. Simply click the **Format** menu and review the commands you see. Keep in mind that these commands may change when you select or display a different database object.

Navigating Table Records Using Datasheet View

Access contains special tools that you can use to navigate, or move among, table records. Datasheet view displays navigation buttons in the lower left corner of the table window for moving one record at a time, to the first or last record, or to a specific record. These buttons are often referred to as controls because they control the record that is active.

Tip These same navigation controls are also found on forms, reports, and data access pages.

Task 2:

To Navigate Records in Datasheet View

1 Open the **Employees** table and click the First Record control to select the first record.

2 Click the Last Record control to move to the last record in the table.

Other Ways

To navigate to specific records:

- Choose **Edit | Go To** and select the record to display.

Figure 2-7

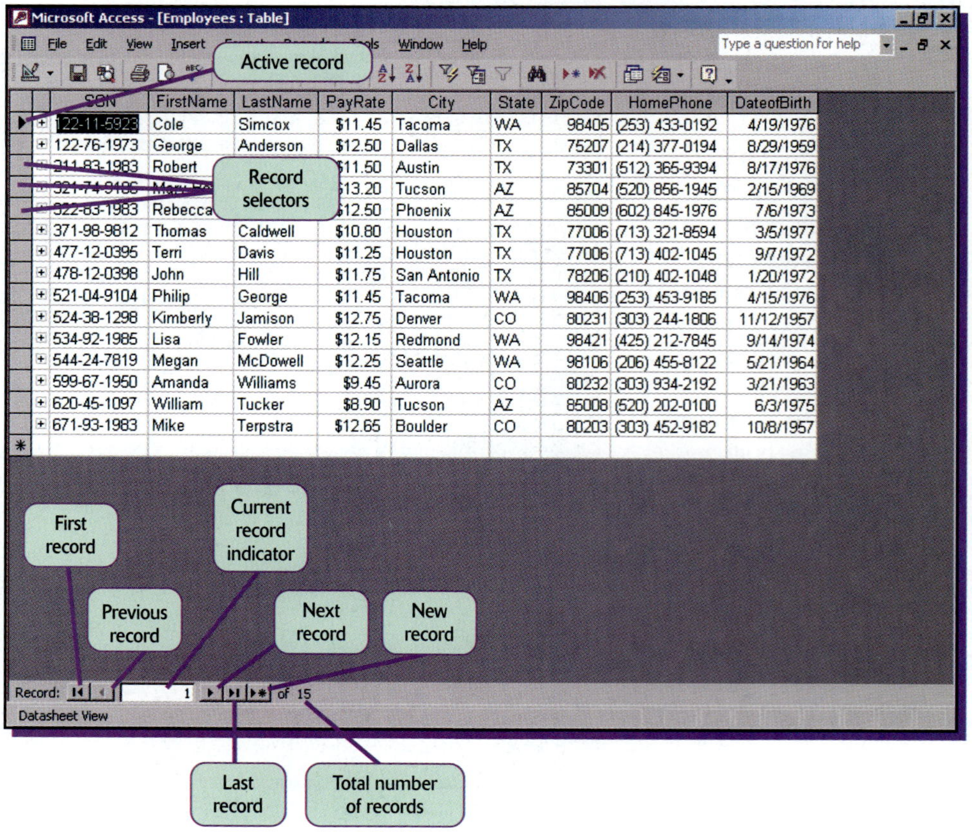

3 Double-click the current record indicator to select the value, type **8**, and press the Enter key to select the eighth record in the table.

Tip Access highlights the field that was active in the previous record when you navigate to a different record. If you click the record selector button to select all fields in a record and then navigate to another record, Access highlights the entire record.

Figure 2-8

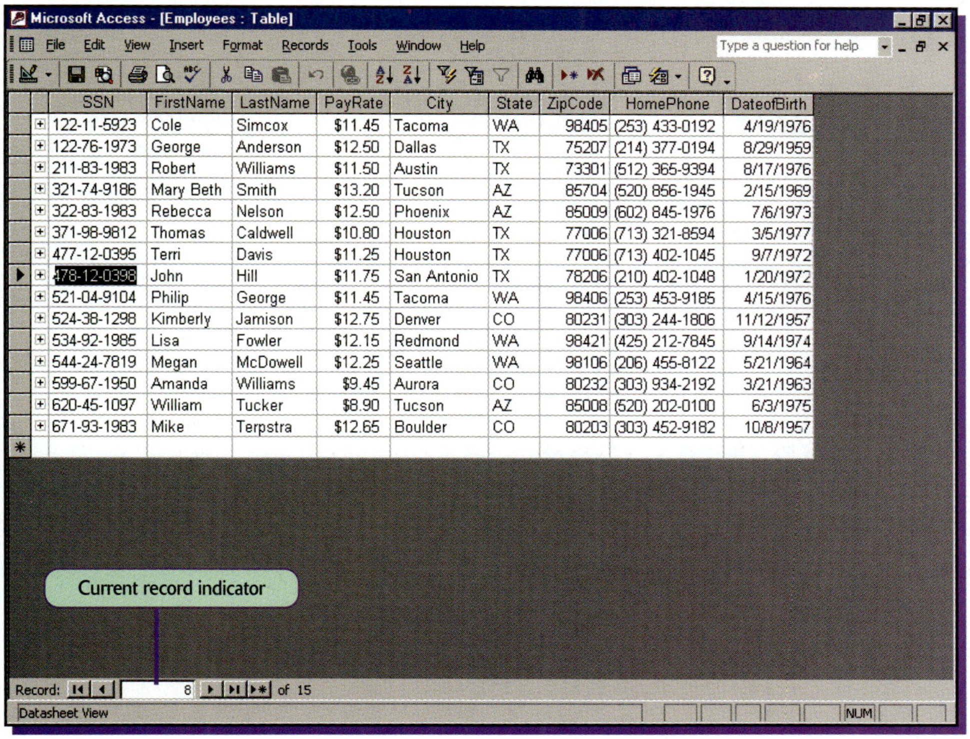

SSN	FirstName	LastName	PayRate	City	State	ZipCode	HomePhone	DateofBirth
122-11-5923	Cole	Simcox	$11.45	Tacoma	WA	98405	(253) 433-0192	4/19/1976
122-76-1973	George	Anderson	$12.50	Dallas	TX	75207	(214) 377-0194	8/29/1959
211-83-1983	Robert	Williams	$11.50	Austin	TX	73301	(512) 365-9394	8/17/1976
321-74-9186	Mary Beth	Smith	$13.20	Tucson	AZ	85704	(520) 856-1945	2/15/1969
322-83-1983	Rebecca	Nelson	$12.50	Phoenix	AZ	85009	(602) 845-1976	7/6/1973
371-98-9812	Thomas	Caldwell	$10.80	Houston	TX	77006	(713) 321-8594	3/5/1977
477-12-0395	Terri	Davis	$11.25	Houston	TX	77006	(713) 402-1045	9/7/1972
478-12-0398	John	Hill	$11.75	San Antonio	TX	78206	(210) 402-1048	1/20/1972
521-04-9104	Philip	George	$11.45	Tacoma	WA	98406	(253) 453-9185	4/15/1976
524-38-1298	Kimberly	Jamison	$12.75	Denver	CO	80231	(303) 244-1806	11/12/1957
534-92-1985	Lisa	Fowler	$12.15	Redmond	WA	98421	(425) 212-7845	9/14/1974
544-24-7819	Megan	McDowell	$12.25	Seattle	WA	98106	(206) 455-8122	5/21/1964
599-67-1950	Amanda	Williams	$9.45	Aurora	CO	80232	(303) 934-2192	3/21/1963
620-45-1097	William	Tucker	$8.90	Tucson	AZ	85008	(520) 202-0100	6/3/1975
671-93-1983	Mike	Terpstra	$12.65	Boulder	CO	80203	(303) 452-9182	10/8/1957

CHECK POINT

As you work in the Table Datasheet view, you will notice that the icon that appears in the Record Selector bar will change to display different symbols. These symbols and their purposes are described in Table 2-1.

Table 2-1 Record Selector Symbols

Symbol	Purpose
▶	Identifies the active or current record that has been saved.
✎	Identifies the record being edited or entered.
*	Identifies a new blank record.

Expanding a Subdatasheet

Along with navigating the main datasheet, you can view data from related tables by viewing the *subdatasheet*. Subdatasheets are created by Access in tables containing relationships. When Access creates a subdatasheet, a column appears on the left side of the Table Datasheet view, and a plus appears beside each record with a valid subdatasheet. Expanding a subdatasheet enables you to view and enter data in the related table. Part of navigating databases includes learning how to expand and collapse subdatasheets.

Task 3:
To Expand a Subdatasheet

1. Open the **Employees** table, if necessary, and click the Expand ⊞ indicator for the first record in the table.

2. Click the Collapse ⊟ indicator to collapse the subdatasheet so that it is no longer visible.

Figure 2-9

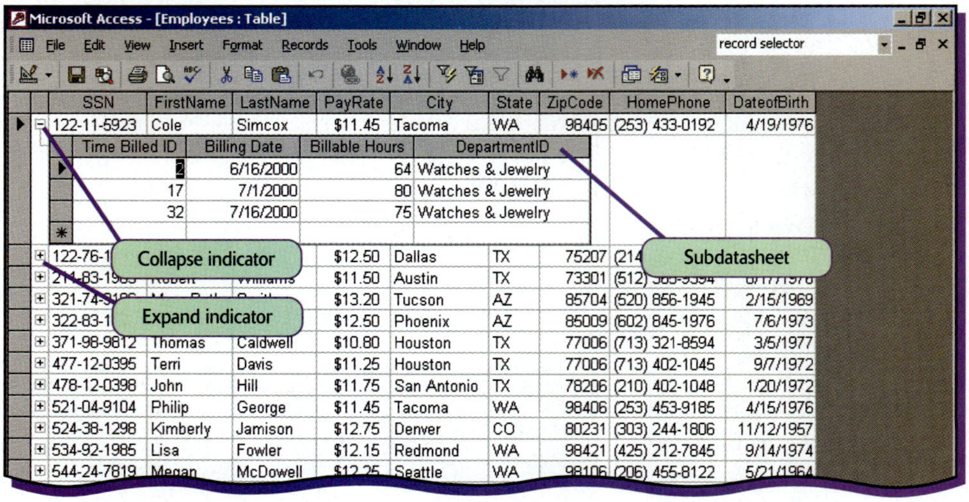

Locating and Editing Records

When database tables contain relatively few records, it is easy to locate the record you need. Many databases contain thousands of records, and finding the record you need to review or edit becomes more of a challenge. Maintaining database data as it changes over time requires that you be able to locate database data quickly and efficiently. Fortunately, Access contains search capabilities. Using the Find and Replace dialog box to search for a specific record enables you to edit and update the record quickly. You can use the feature to update the Employees table records.

CHECK POINT

Access queries can also be used to locate records. Queries offer more sophisticated tools for locating records by setting criteria and identifying records based on criteria from multiple tables. Learning simple techniques for locating records now will help prepare you for using the more advanced techniques required for creating queries.

Task 4:
To Locate and Edit a Specific Record

1. Open the **Employees** table and click the Find button.

2. Type **Smith** in the **Find What** box, select **Employees: Table** from the **Look in** drop-down list, and select **Any Part of Field** from the **Match** drop-down list.

3. Click **Find Next** to find Mary Beth Smith's record.

4. Click the **Cancel** button to close the dialog box.

5. Type **Miller** in the **LastName** field and press the Enter key to replace Smith with Miller.

Figure 2-10

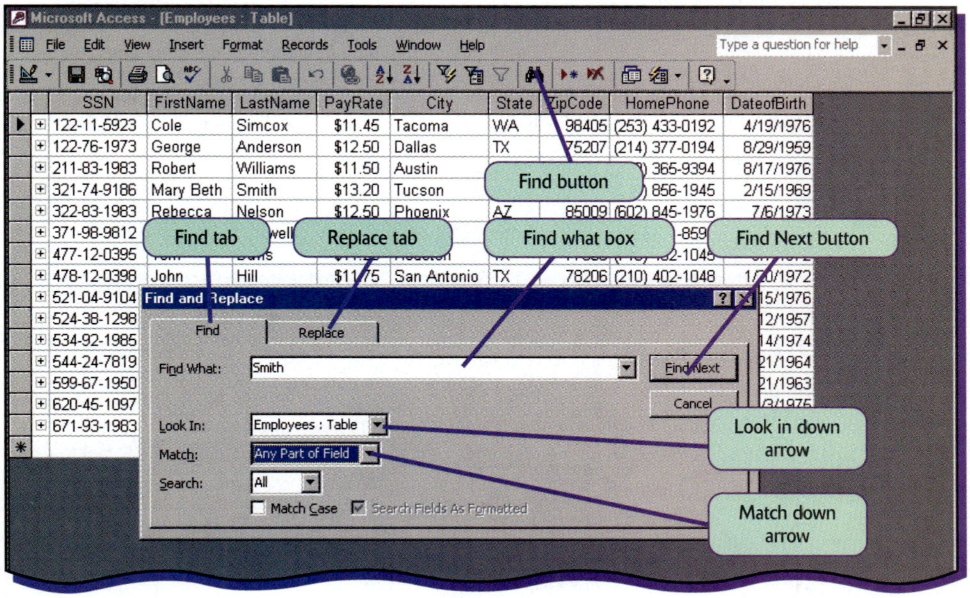

Other Ways

To display the Find dialog box:

- Press Ctrl + F.
- Choose **Edit | Find.**

Updating Multiple Records in a Table Using Replace

The Find and Replace dialog box contains two tabs—one to locate field data and another to contain the text with which you want to replace the text that Access finds. You can use the Replace page of the dialog box to replace the old hourly wages identified by Mr. Traylor with the new hourly wage resulting from the raises. All employees earning $8.90 per hour will be paid $9.25, and those earning $9.45 will now earn $9.80.

Task 5:
To Use Search and Replace to Edit Records

1 Open the **Employees** table, if necessary, and click the Find button and click the **Replace** tab of the Find and Replace dialog box.

2 Type **8.90** in the **Find What** box and **9.25** in the **Replace With** box and click the **Replace All** button to replace all instances of the previous pay rate.

3 Click **Yes** to acknowledge the warning message, click **Cancel** to close the Find and Replace dialog box, and close the table.

Figure 2-11

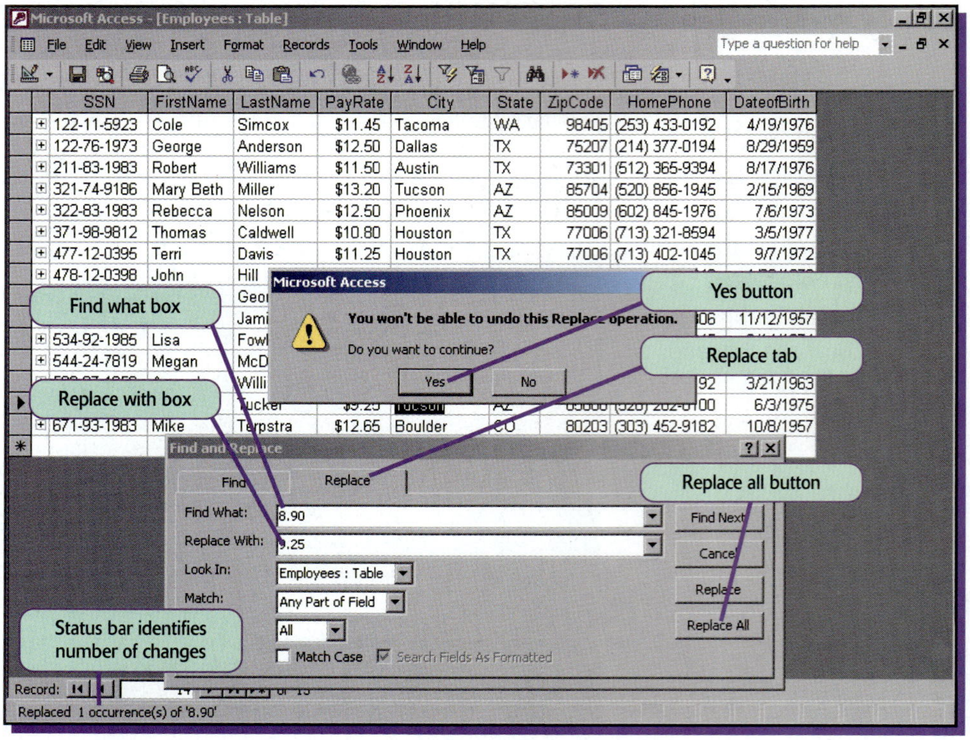

Other Ways

To display the Replace page of the Find and Replace dialog box:

- Press Ctrl + H.
- Choose **Edit | Replace.**

Replacing Data in Forms

The Find and Replace feature can also be used to locate and replace data in database forms. The same basic techniques are used to initiate the Find and Replace command regardless of which database object you use to make the edits.

Task 6:
To Locate and Edit Data in Forms

1 Click the Forms button on the Objects bar in the Database window and double-click the **Employees Data Entry** form to open it in Form view.

Figure 2-12

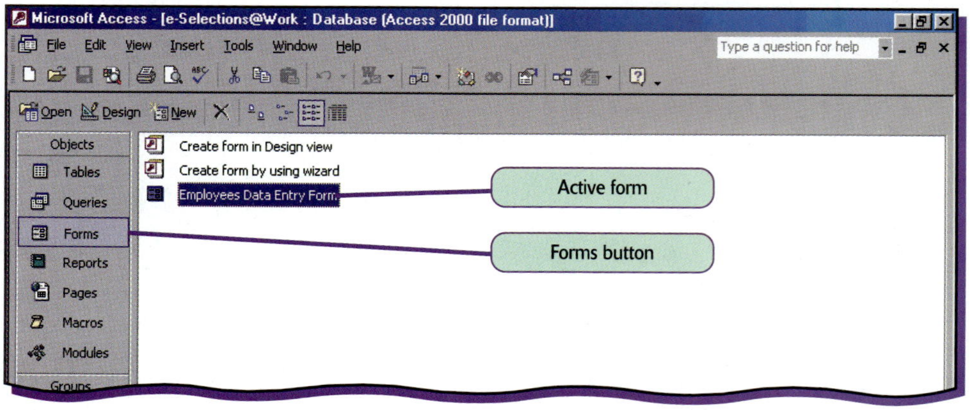

2 Click into the **PayRate** field for the first record, click the **Find** button on the Form View toolbar, and click the **Replace** tab.

3 Type **9.45** in the **Find What** box, type **9.80** in the **Replace With** box, and select **PayRate** from the **Look In** drop-down list.

4 Click **Replace All** and click **Yes** to acknowledge the warning message.

5 Click **Cancel** to close the Find and Replace dialog box and then close the form.

Figure 2-13

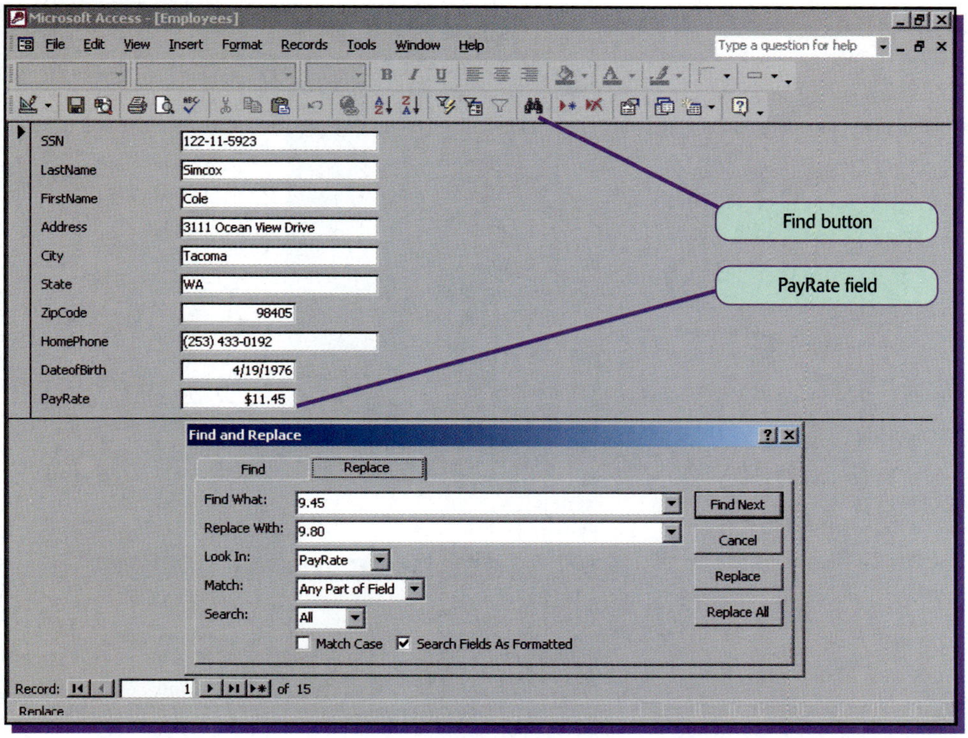

WEB TIP

Each time you request information, order items, or sign up for "free" services from a Web site, data that you provide goes into a database. This information can be used by companies to send you catalogs and unsolicited e-mail. In addition, your personal information may be discovered by someone looking for a new identify—so be careful what information you provide!

Sorting Records

The Access sort feature enables you to rearrange data contained in database tables according to the entries in a specific field. To sort records in a table, you select the field containing the data you want to sort and select a sorting order—ascending A–Z/smallest value to highest value or descending Z–A/highest value to smallest value. When multiple columns are selected, Access sorts data by the column on the left first and then by the next selected column. As a result, some rearrangement of columns may be necessary. Access saves the sort order if you save a form or datasheet after sorting and reapplies it automatically when you reopen the object.

Task 7:
To Sort Records in a Table

1 Open the **Employees** table in Datasheet view, select the **LastName** column, and click the Sort Ascending button to sort the records in ascending order by last name.

Figure 2-14

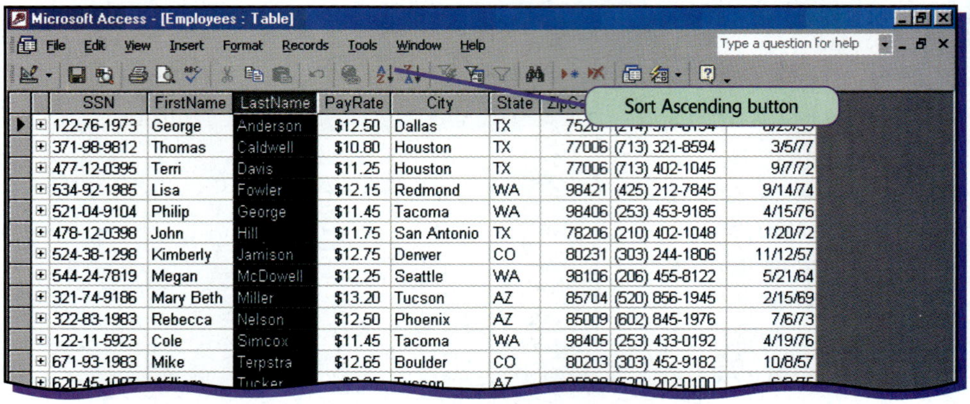

2 Move the **LastName** column to the left of the **FirstName** column, press Shift, and click the field selector buttons for both columns.

3 Click the Sort Ascending button to sort the records first by **LastName** and then by **FirstName**.

4 Click the **Save** button to save the changes of the datasheet layout and restore the datasheet window.

Figure 2-15

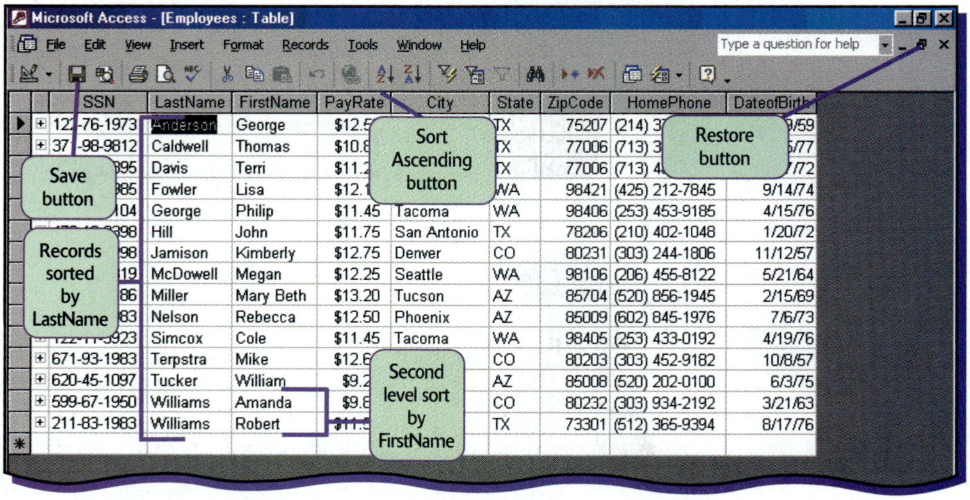

Other Ways

To sort a selected column in a specific order:

- Choose **Records** | **Sort** and select the sort order.

Viewing Table Properties

Table properties are settings for database objects that control how data is displayed when you open the object or another characteristic set for the object. Many times you can display the table properties for an object to determine why it sorts or displays data the way it does. For example, when a sort order is set, Access sets a table property that identifies the sort order in the Order By property and specifies the field or fields on which the table is currently sorted. You can use the Table Properties window to remove or change the sort specifications or delete the entry instead of returning to the Datasheet view and resorting the table.

Task 8:
To View Table Properties

1 Open the **Employees** table, if necessary, and click the Design View button to switch to Table Design view.

2 Click the Properties button on the Table Design toolbar and resize the window as necessary to view the **Order By** row.

Tip The Order By row displays information about the sort order you applied to the table.

3 Close the table and save changes, if necessary.

Figure 2-16

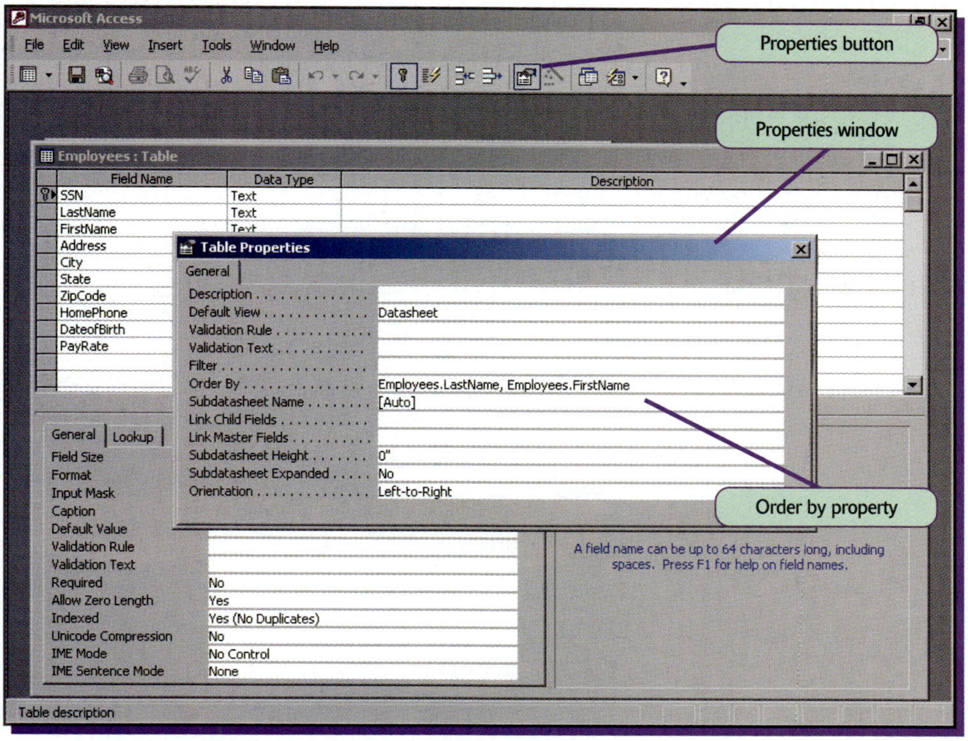

Other Ways

To display the Properties window:
- Press F4.
- Choose **View** | **Properties.**
- Right-click the table title bar and select Properties.

Filtering Records

The features you have been using locate records within a database for editing or rearrange all table records according to specific sort orders. Access contains a *filter* feature that enables you to retrieve a subset of records from a table. You can use the filter feature to locate and print the sorted list of employees for different states that Mr. Traylor requested. A filter temporarily displays table records that meet specific criteria you set in the form or Datasheet view. Access supports two methods for quickly filtering records.

- The *Filter By Selection* filter selects all records containing data that matches selected values and that appears in the same field as the selected field.
- The *Filter By Form* option enables you to specify a value in one or more form fields and select records that meet the criteria.

When you are finished viewing the filtered data, you remove the filter to restore the datasheet or form to its previous order.

Task 9:

To Filter Database Tables

1. Open the **Employees** table in Datasheet view, double-click the **State** field for George Anderson's record to select the *TX*, and click the Filter By Selection button.

Figure 2-17

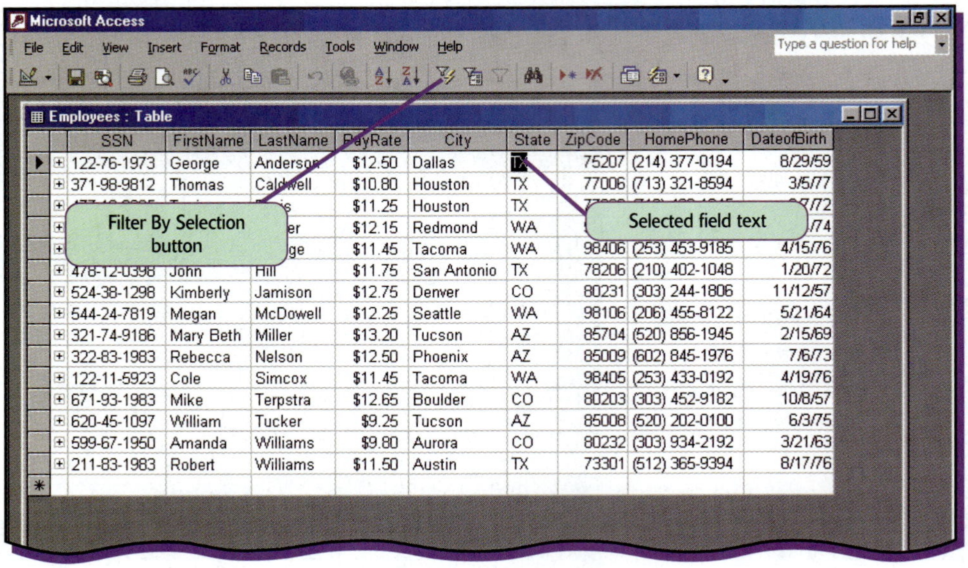

2. Click the Remove Filter button to remove the filter.

Figure 2-18

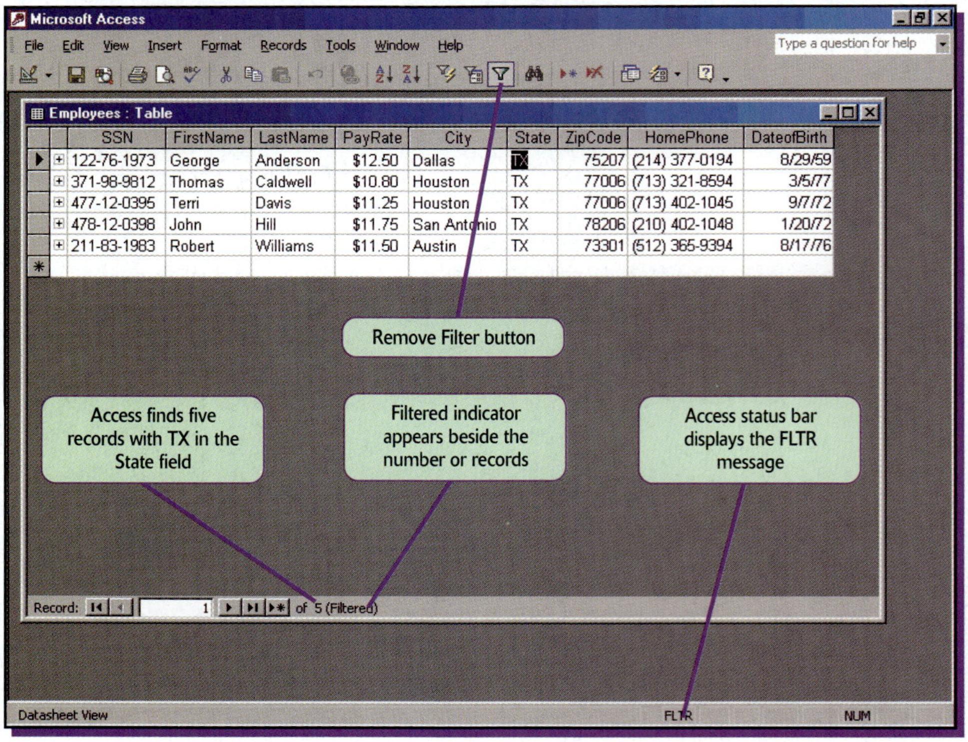

Other Ways

To Filter By Selection:

- Choose **Records | Filter | Filter By Selection.**

To Filter By Form:

- Choose **Records | Filter | Filter By Form.**

3 Click the Filter By Form button.

Figure 2-19

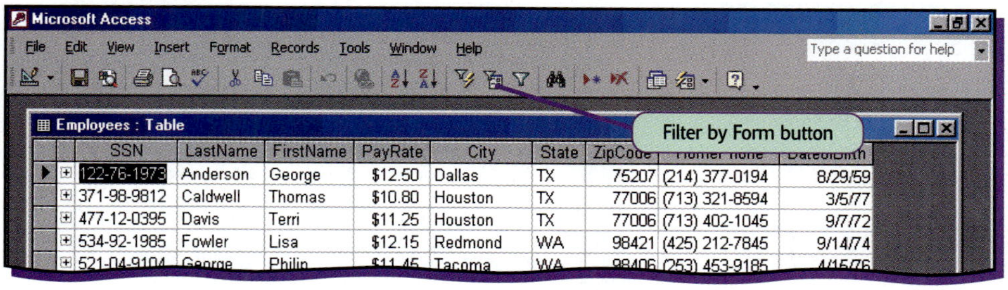

Troubleshooting Point to each filter button on the toolbar and wait for the screen tip to appear to help you determine which button is the Filter By Form button and which is the Filter By Selection button.

4 Click the **City** field, click the down arrow, select **Houston,** and click the Apply Filter button to apply the filter.

Figure 2-20

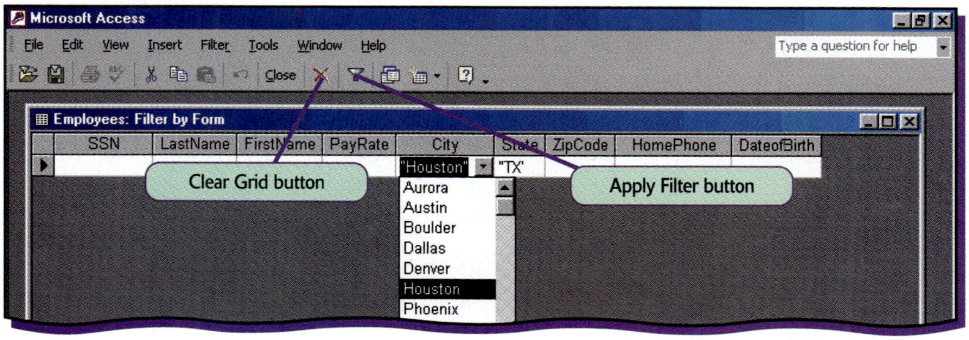

5 Click the Filter By Form button to return to the grid.

Figure 2-21

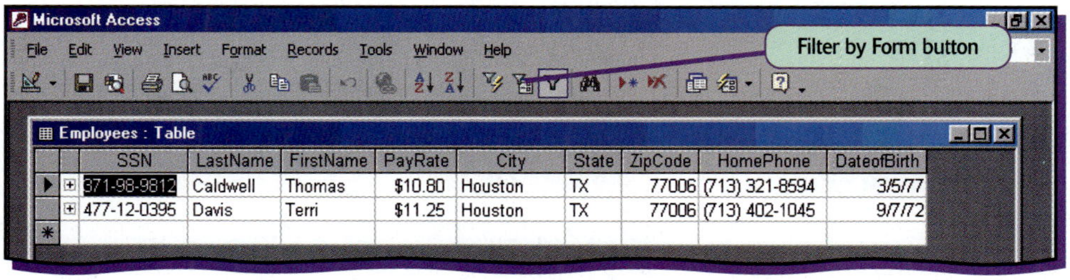

6 Click the Clear Grid button to clear the Filter By Form grid, select **TX** from the **State** field drop-down list, click the **Or** tab at the bottom of the screen, and select **WA** from the **State** field drop-down list.

7 Click the Apply Filter button.

Figure 2-22

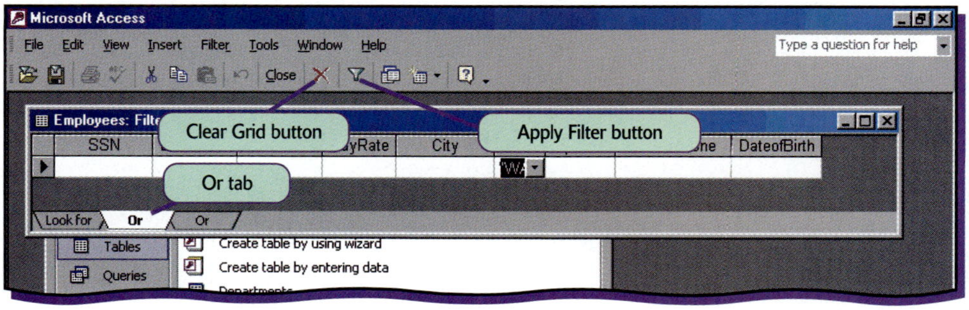

8 Position the insertion point in any row of the **DateofBirth** field and click the Sort Descending button to sort the filtered records by birth date.

9 Close the datasheet without saving the changes.

Tip Saving the changes to the datasheet stores the filter and sort specifications as part of the table design.

Figure 2-23

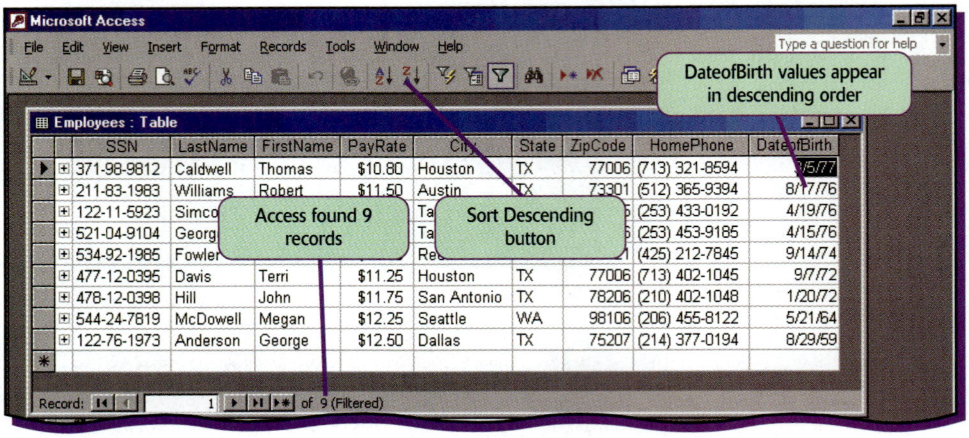

Exporting Table Data

Data stored in databases is designed to locate vital information efficiently. Data that is stored in database tables can be used to create or enhance files in other applications, such as Microsoft Excel worksheets or Microsoft Word documents. Access provides several methods for exporting data from a table or query to these other applications. You can use these techniques to create the workbook Mr. Traylor has requested.

Troubleshooting Microsoft Excel must be installed on your computer to complete this task.

Task 10: To Export Data from a Table to an Excel Workbook

1 Open the **Employees** table and use the Filter By Selection button to display only the records of employees from TX.

2 Sort the records in ascending order by **PayRate** and click the Print Preview button.

Figure 2-24

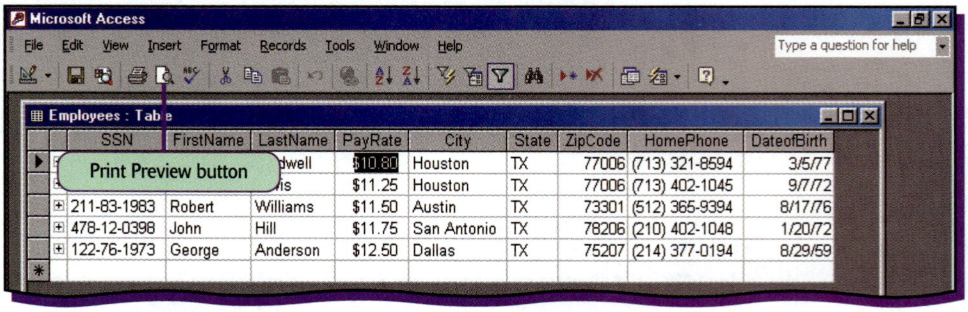

3 Click the **OfficeLinks** button down arrow and select **Analyze It with Microsoft Excel** to create a Microsoft Excel workbook with the name *Employees*.

4 Exit Microsoft Excel and return to Access.

Figure 2-25

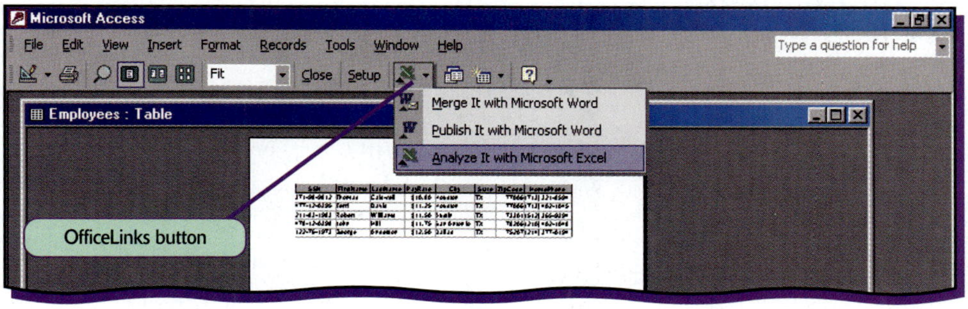

5 Click **Close** on the Print Preview toolbar to return to Datasheet view and close the table datasheet without saving changes.

Other Ways

To export records:

- Choose **File** | **Export**.

Figure 2-26

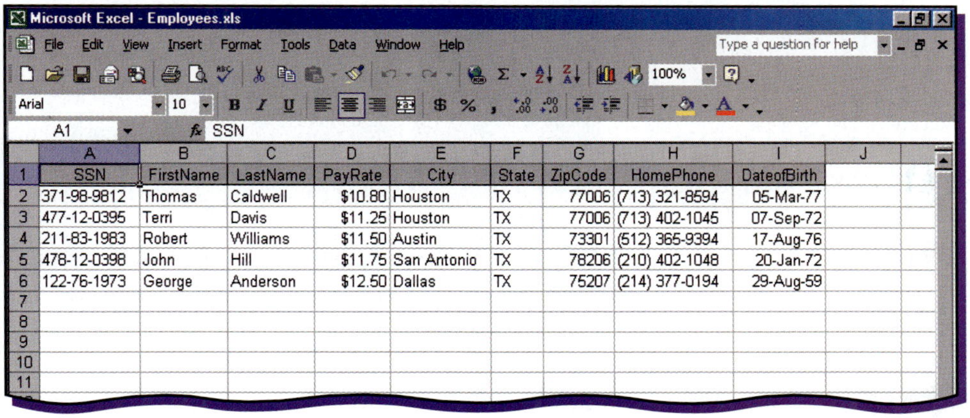

Creating a Data Access Page

Now that you have data in your database, wouldn't it be great to allow others in your company to view or update the data easily? Well, you're in luck! One of the Access database objects that you can create is the *data access page*—a Web page that you publish from Access that has a connection to a database. Using a data access page, you can create an *interactive Web page* that enables others to view, add to, edit, and manipulate the data stored in the database.

Task 11:
To Create a Data Access Page

1 Click the Pages button on the Objects bar in the Database window.

2 Click the New button on the Database toolbar, select the options shown in Figure 2-27 and click OK.

Other Ways

To display the New Data Access Page dialog box:

- Choose **Insert | Page.**

Figure 2-27

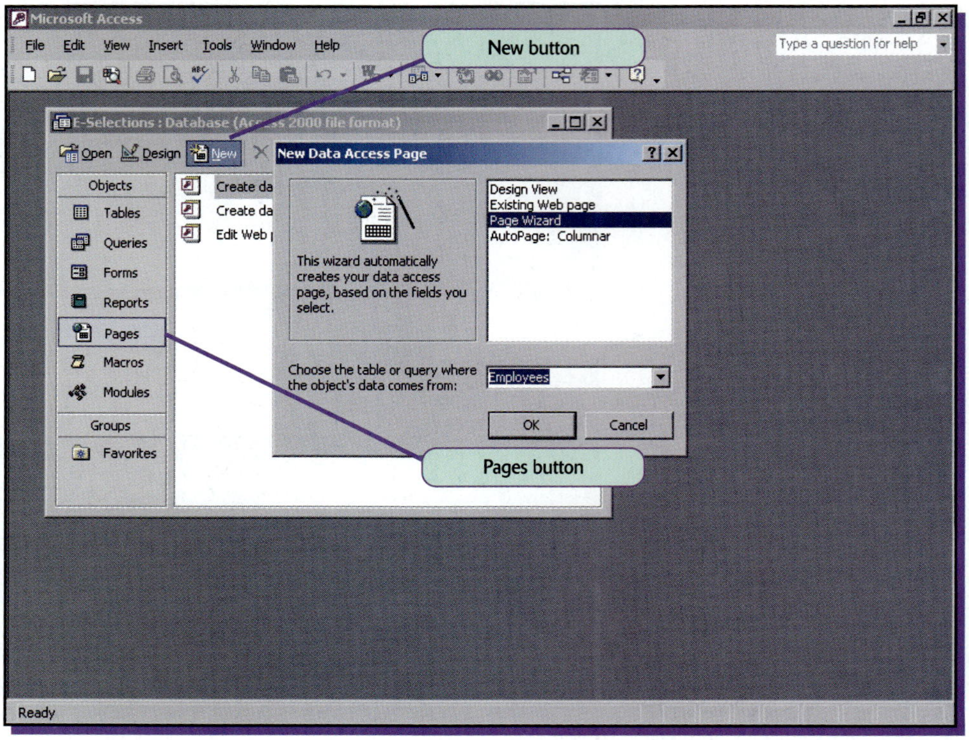

3 Click the Move All >> button to move all fields from the **Available fields** list to the **Selected fields** list and click **Next**.

Figure 2-28

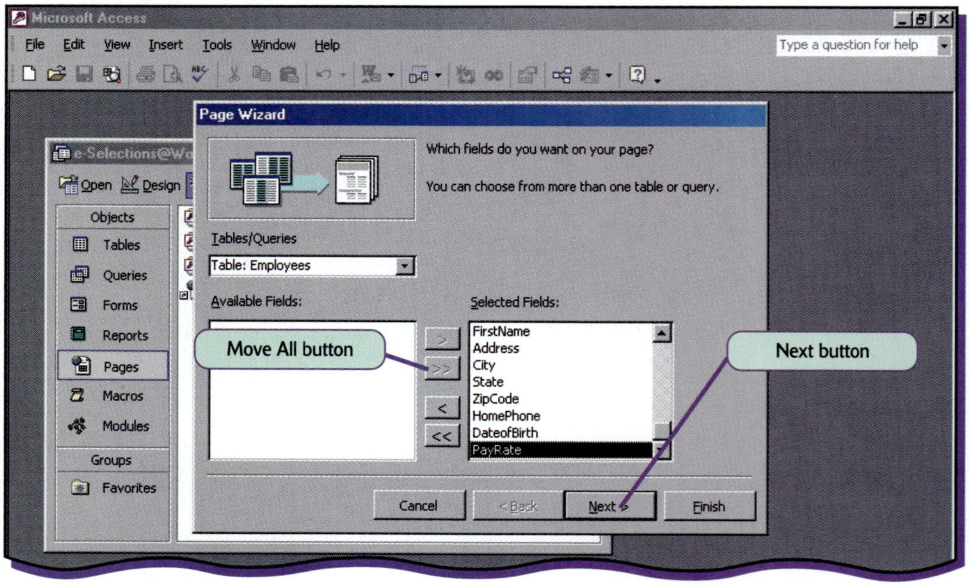

4 Click **Next** to accept the default settings for grouping levels.

Tip Grouping is an effective way of organizing table records when multiple records for one person exist. For example, if you are working with a database table that contains time sheets for several weeks, you could group the records for each employee together or group the records by pay period. The grouping field simply tells Access how to organize the data access page.

Figure 2-29

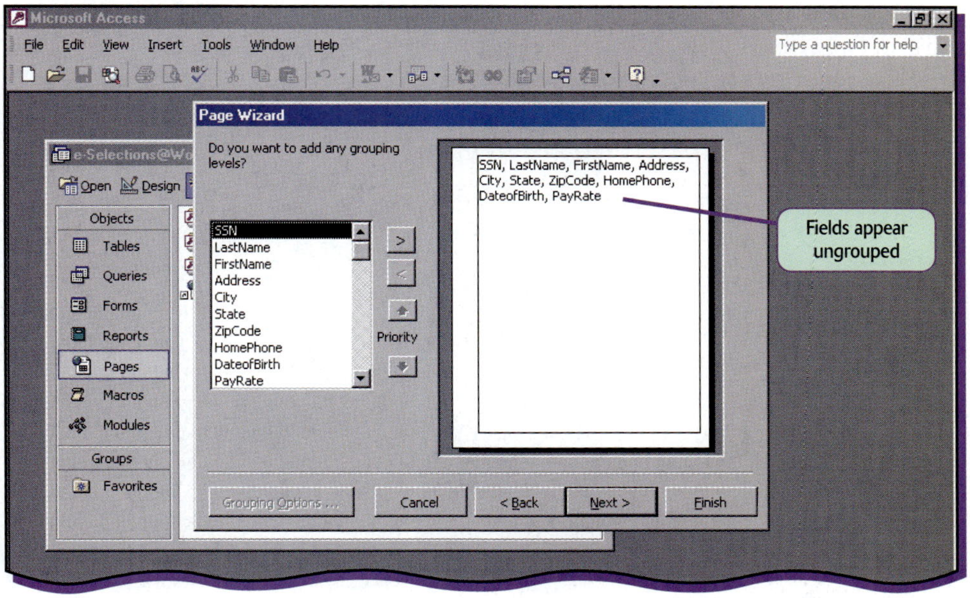

5 Select **LastName** from the **1** drop-down list, select **FirstName** from the **2** drop-down list and click **Next**.

Tip Access provides four different sort levels for each data access page you create.

Figure 2-30

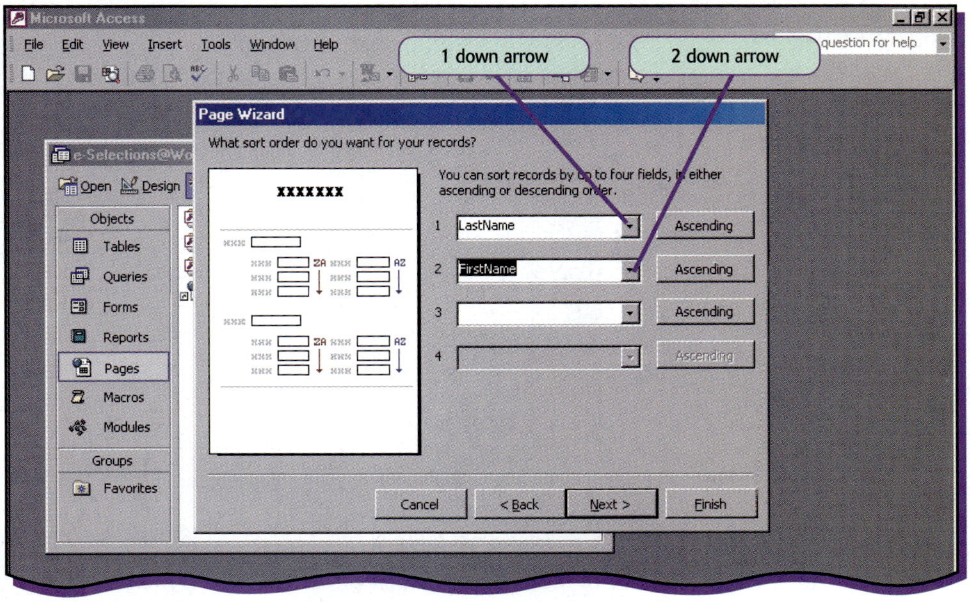

6 Review the Page Wizard options, select the **Open the page** option and click **Finish** to create the interactive data access page.

Figure 2-31

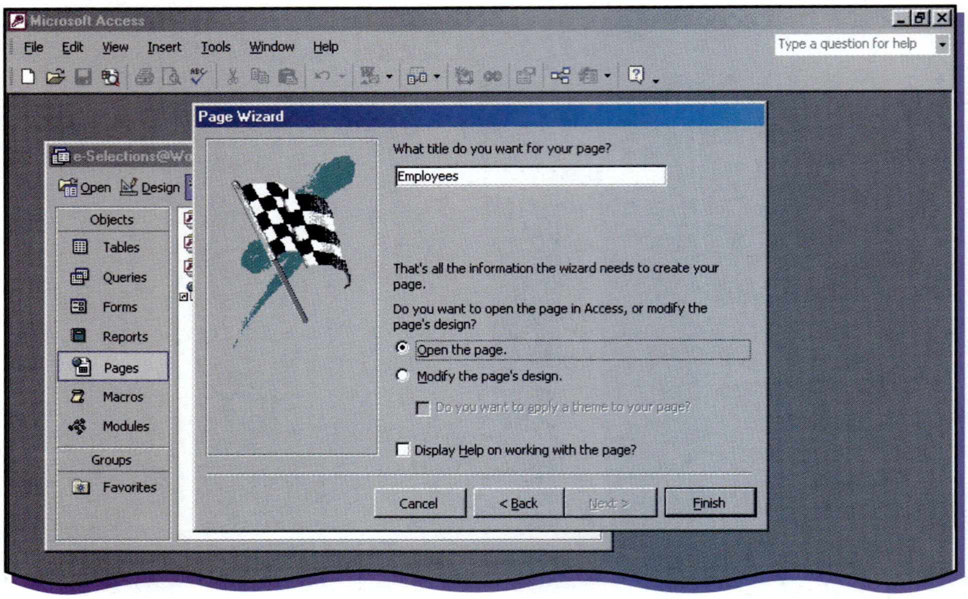

7 Click the Save button to open the **Save As Data Access Page** dialog box and save the file using the file name *Employees*.

Figure 2-32

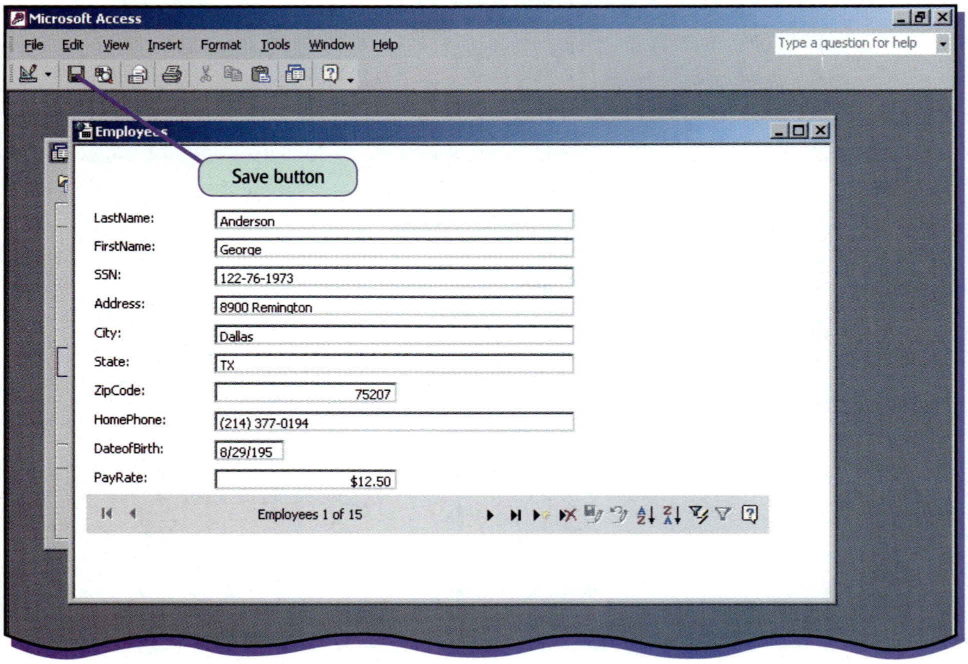

Troubleshooting A warning message may appear informing you that you have specified an absolute path that may be inaccessible by other users. As a result, the page may not be available from the network. If you were actually trying to save this page on a network File Server, you would most likely need to specify the UNC (Universal Naming Convention) path. A UNC path syntax looks something like this: \\computer name\folder name\file name.

8 Close the data access page and return to the Database window.

WEB TIP

Now that you know what a data access page is, can you locate one on the Web? Visit some sites or search for data access pages and see what you find. Then identify any special features that make the data access page unique.

Figure 2-33

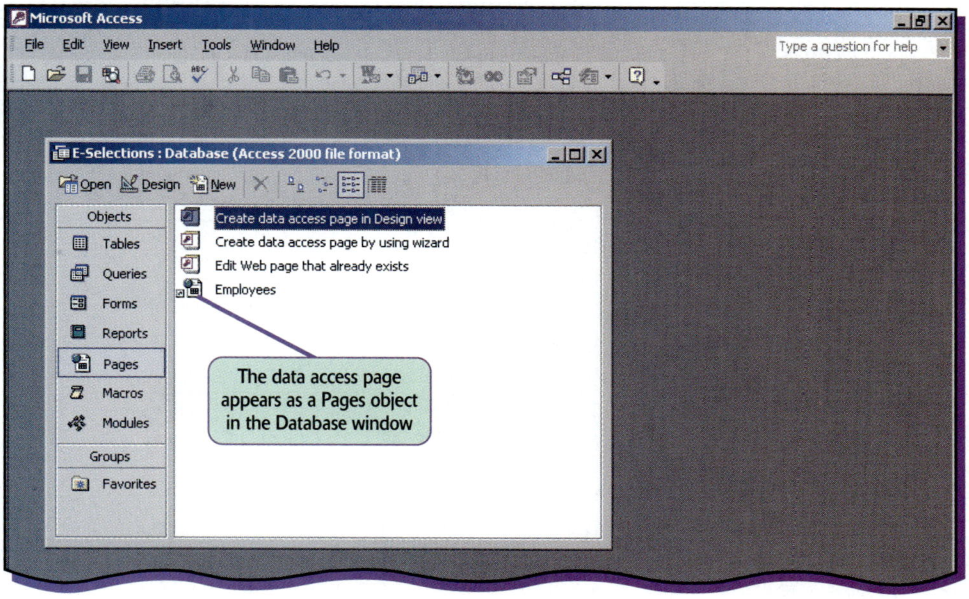

Viewing a Data Access Page Using Microsoft Internet Explorer 5.0 or Later

The data access page you just created is stored as a separate file outside the e-Selections@Work database. However, because you created the data access page from the e-Selections@Work database, Access created a link to the file. As a result, the data displayed from the data access page reflects the most current data contained in the database. You can view the data in the Microsoft Internet Explorer 5.0 browser of a computer that has access to the data access page.

Tip You must use Internet Explorer 5.0 or a later version to view the data page.

Task 12:
To Open the Data Access Page in Microsoft Internet Explorer

1. Click **Start** | **Programs** | **Internet Explorer**.

2. Press Ctrl + O, open the folder containing the data access page, and double-click the *Employees.htm* file.

Other Ways

To display the Open dialog box:
- Click the Open button on the Database toolbar.
- Choose **File** | **Open**

3. Review the data access page and then close the browser.

Figure 2-34

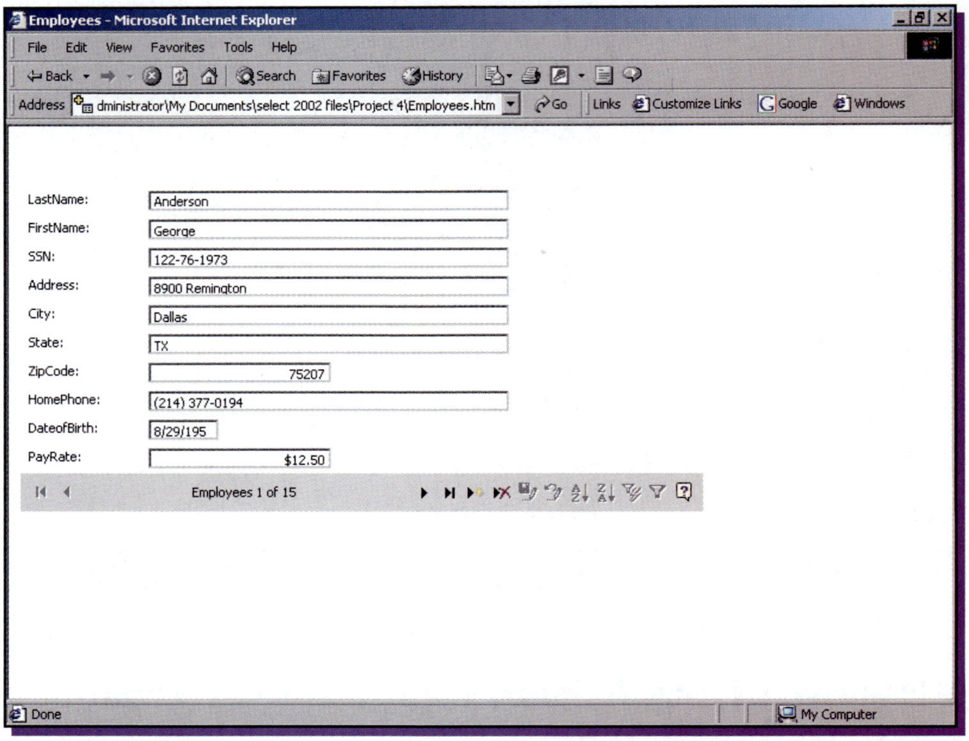

Compacting and Repairing an Access Database

To ensure optimal performance, Access contains tools that enable you to compact and repair databases as often as you believe is appropriate. If a database has a serious problem that Access recognizes, Access will attempt to repair the file the next time you open it. Even if there is no file corruption, the normal maintenance tasks of adding and deleting records and creating queries and other objects in the database may fragment and reduce database performance. You can test these tools by compacting and repairing the e-Selections@Work database file.

Task 13:
To Compact and Repair the e-Selections @Work Database File

1 Display the Database window, choose **File | Database Properties**, and click the General tab.

2 Click OK to close the dialog box.

Figure 2-35

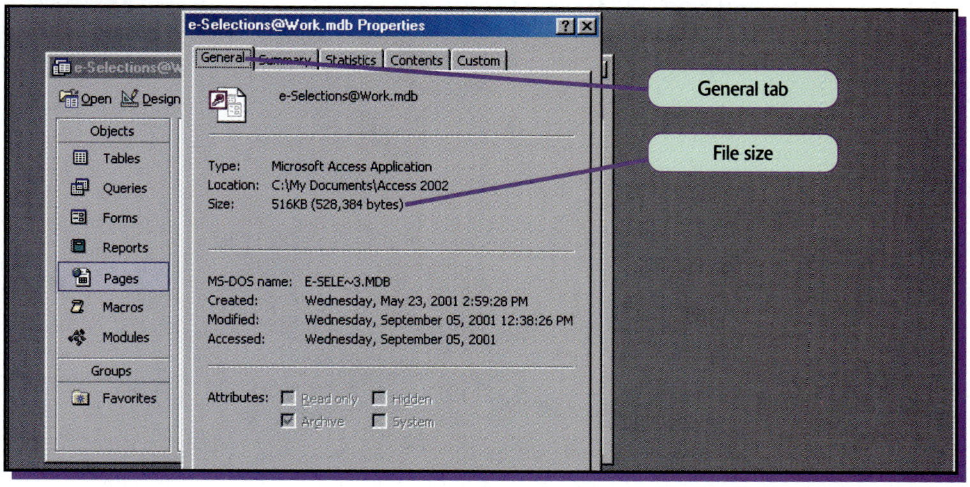

3 Choose **Tools | Database Utilities** and select **Compact and Repair Database**. The Database window will disappear for a few seconds. When it reappears, Access will have compacted and repaired your file.

Figure 2-36

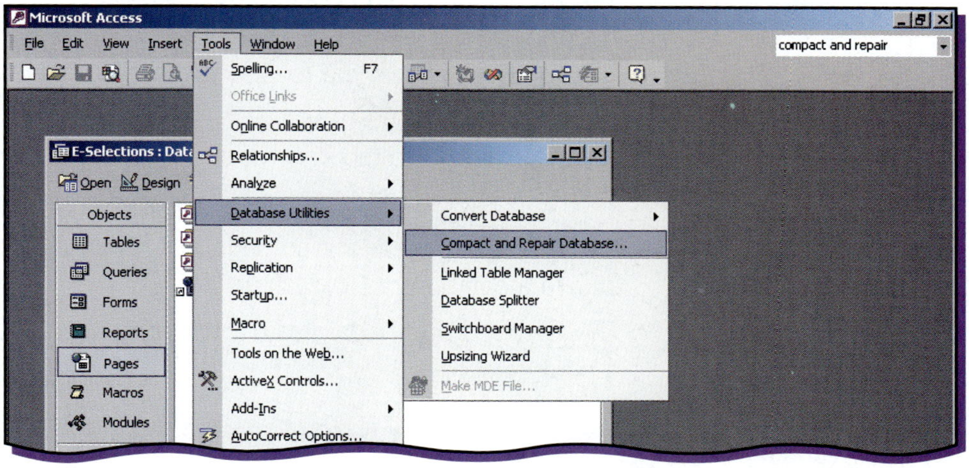

CHECK POINT

Backing Up and Restoring an Access Database

Large corporations store vast amounts of data on networks that employees can access. As a result, they have a backup routine that they perform regularly—usually at night when they are certain no one needs to access the data. If something happens to a database that is backed up by a system administrator, the data from the last backup tape can be restored to the network and little time is lost reentering data.

When individual users store data on local hard disks, floppy disks, or CDs, the chances of experiencing data corruption or loss increase dramatically. Creating a routine to regularly back up your work is a good idea. While Access does not provide a built-in backup and restore utility, you can use features that come with most Windows operating systems to copy your data to another disk or backup media. Windows Explorer is an efficient program to use and one with which many computer users are familiar. Try using it to make a copy of your database. If you never use the backup, great! If you do need it, though, you'll be glad you took the time!

SUMMARY AND EXERCISES

SUMMARY

- You can select, resize, hide, or move columns in a datasheet.
- Datasheets include controls that will allow you to navigate among the records and to add new records.
- Subdatasheets allow you to view and modify linked records in the related table.
- You can use Find and Replace to locate fields meeting specific criteria or to change the field data.
- You can sort records in a table by any one field or multiple fields.
- You can modify table properties by opening the Properties window while in Table Design view.
- Filter By Form allows you to view records in a table datasheet that meets specific criteria.
- Filter By Selection filters records according to data that you select.
- You can easily export data from a datasheet to other MS Office applications.
- A data access page is a Web page that allows users to view or modify data in a database.
- The Compact and Repair feature will compact databases and repair corrupted databases.

KEY TERMS & SKILLS

KEY TERMS

data access page (p. 2-19)
filter (p. 2-15)
Filter By Form (p. 2-15)
Filter By Selection (p. 2-15)
interactive Web page (p. 2-19)
subdatasheet (p. 2-9)
table properties (p. 2-14)

SKILLS

Compact and repair the e-Selections@Work database file (p. 2-25)
Create a data access page (p. 2-20)
Expand a subdatasheet (p. 2-10)
Export data from a table to an Excel workbook (p. 2-18)
Filter database tables (p. 2-16)
Format and modify the layout of a table datasheet (p. 2-5)
Locate and edit a specific record (p. 2-11)
Locate and edit data in forms (p. 2-12)
Navigate among records in Datasheet view (p. 2-8)
Open the data access page in Microsoft Internet Explorer (p. 2-24)
Sort records in a table (p. 2-14)
Use Search and Replace to edit records (p. 2-12)
View table properties (p. 2-15)

STUDY QUESTIONS

MULTIPLE CHOICE

1. Compacting and repairing a database should be done
   a. often to increase the performance of the database.
   b. rarely because it will degrade the performance of the database.
   c. only when a database corruption has occurred.
   d. never because Access will do it for you.

2. To use a data access page in your Web browser, you must open it with
   a. any Web browser of your choice.
   b. Microsoft Internet Explorer 5.0 or later or Netscape Navigator 5.0 or later.
   c. any version of Microsoft Internet Explorer.
   d. Microsoft Internet Explorer 5.0 or a later version.

3. The filter option that lets you select records according to multiple criteria is
   a. Filter By Selection.
   b. apply filter.
   c. Filter By Form.
   d. query by selection.

4. Which feature allows you to select a filter criterion using a drop-down list?
   a. Filter By Selection
   b. apply filter
   c. Filter By Form
   d. query by selection

5. Columns in a datasheet can be modified in all but what way?
   a. resizing
   b. hiding
   c. deleting
   d. moving

6. You can do all but what with the navigation controls on a datasheet?
   a. Go to first record.
   b. Delete first record.
   c. Go to last record.
   d. Add a new record.

7. To identify the field that you want to use to sort records,
   a. select the table.
   b. select the column.
   c. click any part of the field.
   d. both b and c

8. To create a "form" to modify and view records on a corporate intranet, you should
   a. create a new form based on a Web query.
   b. modify any form.
   c. create an HTML report.
   d. create a data access page.

SHORT ANSWER

1. What is a subdatasheet and how do you use it?
2. What is the difference between Filter By Form and Filter By Selection?
3. Why should you be careful about using the Replace All feature?
4. What is an easy method for locating records to update?
5. How do you include multiple criteria in the Filter Form method?
6. How will date values appear if a datasheet is sorted in descending order?

7. When would you want to hide a column in a datasheet?
8. What does the Compact and Repair utility do?
9. How can you export data from a datasheet to a Word table?
10. What is a data access page?

FILL IN THE BLANK

1. A(n) ____________ is a Web page that allows users to view or modify data in a database.
2. A(n) ____________ is useful to view and edit records in a related table.
3. You can use the ____________ button to view all records in a datasheet.
4. ____________ on a datasheet allow you to move from record to record.
5. A good practice to keep your database running at an optimal level is to use the ____________ feature.
6. Having a good ____________ of your database is essential if you need to restore it after a hard disk crash.
7. Filter by ____________ is a method that you can use to filter records with only one criterion.
8. Filter by ____________ is a more powerful method that allows you to filter records by specifying multiple criteria.
9. A data access page can be opened in Access or ____________.

FOR DISCUSSION

1. Explain how editing, filtering, and sorting records differ.
2. When would you use the Filter By Selection method rather than the Filter By Form method?
3. When would hiding a column be useful?
4. Why would you want to export data to a Microsoft Excel workbook or a Microsoft Word table?

GUIDED EXERCISES

1 THE HOME THEATER WARRANTY REPAIR DATABASE

The Home Theater Warranty Repair database contains information that will be used to locate warrantee information. It makes a great database for practicing your sorting and filtering techniques to determine how proficient you can become and how functional the database is. These steps will guide your practice:

1. Open the *Home Theater Warranty Repair.mdb* file and open the **Customers** table in Datasheet view.
2. Resize all of the columns to best fit.
3. Select the **LastName** field and click the Sort Ascending button.

4. Select the *S* in Sanchez's **LastName**, click the Filter By Selection button to select all customers whose last name begins with an *S*, and then click the Remove Filter button.

5. Filter the file on the **State** field to locate all records for the state of Texas, print the datasheet, and then remove the filter.

6. Click the Filter By Form button, select **Dallas** from the **City** drop-down list, click the **Or** tab, choose **Houston** from the **City** drop-down list, click the Apply Filter button, and print the datasheet.

7. Remove the filter, use the **Find and Replace** dialog box to replace all of the *206* area codes with *210*, and close the dialog box.

8. Click the Print Preview button and then select **Publish It with Microsoft Word** from the **OfficeLinks** drop-down list. Then, print the Word document and close it. Close the Print Preview window, save changes to the table, and then close the table.

Troubleshooting You must have Microsoft Word installed on your computer to complete Step 8.

2 MAKING THE HOME THEATER WARRANTY REPAIR DATABASE ACCESSIBLE

The Home Theater Warranty Repair database will be used by a number of different people as they receive calls from warranty holders. Making the database more easily accessible will increase the efficiency of using the database and will give you a chance to practice your skills creating a data access page. Follow these steps to create a data access page and to compact the database.

1. Open the *Home Theater Warranty Repair.mdb* file and click the Pages button on the database Objects bar.

2. Double-click the **Create Data Access page by using wizard** option.

3. Select the **Customers** table, move all the fields to the **Selected Fields** list, and click **Next**.

4. Click **Next** to accept the grouping defaults, add a sort by **LastName**, and click **Next**.

5. Keep the default name of the page as *Customers*, select the option to open the page, and click **Finish**.

6. Open your page in Internet Explorer 5.0.

7. Choose **Tools** | **Database Utilities** | **Compact and Repair Database**.

3 THE PROFIT-MAKING DATABASE

Now that you have some idea about the types of things you can do with databases, practicing different techniques will make you more efficient in using them and will also provide a chance to test the functionality and design of your databases. The more practice you have extracting data using the filter and sort features, the more efficient you will become. Follow these steps to filter and sort records in the Profit-Making database.

1. Open the *Profit-Making.mdb* file and then open the **Items** table in Datasheet view.
2. Resize all of the columns for the best fit and sort the items in Ascending order by the **Item** description field.
3. Increase the price of all items in the **SellingPrice** field that are selling for $25.00 to $25.25 by using the **Edit | Replace** command.
4. Filter the records so that only shirts are displayed, print the datasheet, and then remove the filter.
5. Filter the records so that only those items selling for more than $10.00 are displayed, print the datasheet, and then remove the filter.
6. Close the table when you are finished.
7. Compact and repair the database and then close it.

4 TESTING BRENT'S CUSTOMERS & ORDERS DATABASE

Practice makes perfect, as the saying goes. Brent has been busy working on his database and has added a number of new customers to the file. By testing Brent's updated database, you'll have a chance to review the functionality and design of the database along with the subdatasheets that Access has created between database tables. Follow these steps to sort records and to review subdatasheets contained in the database:

1. Open the *Brent's Customers & Orders.mdb* file and open the Customers table in Datasheet view.
2. Sort the customers in ascending order by **CompanyName**.
3. Expand the subdatasheets for customers 2 and 8, switch to Print Preview, print the datasheet with the subdatasheets, and close the Print Preview window, saving changes as you close.
4. Close the database.

ON YOUR OWN

The difficulty of these case studies varies:

⚑ *are the least difficult;* ⚑⚑ *are more difficult; and* ⚑⚑⚑ *are the most difficult.*

1 SCHOOL ASSIGNMENTS

⚑ The *Collegiate Work.mdb* file contains an Assignments table that contains information you need to take to class. Display and print the following datasheets:

- assignments for any month sorted by date due
- test assignments sorted by date due
- assignments for any class sorted by date due
- all test or quizzes sorted by class
- assignments for any week sorted by class

Make a data access page based on the Assignments table and print a copy of the page.

2 NANCY'S KNICK-KNACK NOOK

⚑ Nancy has been busy managing her shop and has discovered that she may be running short of a few items. She has also managed to find a few minutes to update her database but has not had time to print the document to take home and review. She'd like for you to prepare some documents for her so that she can evaluate her needs. Open the *Nancy's Nook.mdb* file. Using the Items table, resize the columns so that all data is displayed. Then filter and sort records to display the following information, printing each datasheet before clearing the filter:

- records for items listed in alphabetical order that cost $19.95
- records with 75 or fewer items on hand sorted by description

Create a data access page based on the Items table. Compact the database.

3 PINE VALLEY ORGANIZERS DATABASE

Open the *Pine Valley Fund Raising.mdb* file. The director wants you to show her how to filter and sort contributor and contribution information since all she needs is a few quick lists. Filter and sort records in the appropriate table to display and print:

- contributions over $50.00 sorted by contribution amount in ascending order
- contributions given in a specific month sorted by date in ascending order
- contributions given in a specific month which are greater than $50.00
- contributions sorted by date

Preview the file. Publish the datasheet from the Print Preview window to Word if Word is installed on your computer.

4 SHAPING UP

The manager of the Shaping Up Fitness Club has requested a number of printouts from the database and each of the printouts requires sorting or filtering. Because Access has assigned relationships between the tables in the database, subdatasheets appear for each record in the Classes and Members tables. You can sort and filter records in subdatasheets using the same filter techniques you use to sort and filter records in tables to complete the tasks requested by the manager. Open the *Shaping Up.mdb* file and complete the following tasks:

- Open each table and print a copy of the table with subdatasheets displayed.
- Sort records in the subdatasheets of the Classes table alphabetically and print the results.
- Filter records in the Classes table subdatasheets to display students who have been enrolled in each class for 10 hours and print the results.
- Locate those students in the Classes table using the subdatasheets who have paid more than $100.00 for any class and print the results.
- Export all records in each table to an Excel workbook. Print a copy of each workbook.

FROM THE FILES

You Will Need

- ✔ e-Selections Working.mdb
- ✔ @Home Warranty.mdb
- ✔ Show a Profit.mdb
- ✔ Tool Orders.mdb
- ✔ Collegiate Class Assignments.mdb
- ✔ Pine Valley Reachout.mdb
- ✔ The Nook's Inventory.mdb
- ✔ Conference Scheduling.mdb
- ✔ Staying in Shape.mdb

PROJECT 3

Modifying Tables and Establishing Relationships

Establishing a relationship between database tables is what gives a relational database management system (RDBMS) program such as Microsoft Access its power. Relationships enable you to share information among tables and specify rules about how records are related. Maintaining databases by adding records, removing records, and updating records is an ongoing task—a task made easier because the data is stored in database tables. As you create relationships between database tables, you will often identify changes that need to be made to the table structure—fields that need to be added or removed, fields that need to be redefined, or field properties that need to be changed. In this project, you will learn how to modify table structures, change field properties, and establish relationships between tables contained in databases.

OBJECTIVES

After completing this project, you will be able to:

- *Add a lookup field to a table using the Lookup Wizard*
- *Open the Relationships window and add tables*
- *Create relationships among database tables*
- *Print relationships*
- *Establish validation properties*
- *Create input masks*
- *Add a lookup field to a table in Design view*
- *Add records to tables using lookup lists*

e-selections Running Case

As you work toward building a database in which data is easy to enter and is entered accurately, it's important to ensure that data is entered in a consistent format to reduce the number of data entry errors. It's time for you to explore several Access features and functions to see what Access has to offer for controlling data that is entered.

Building Relationships

We all know that romantic relationships require good communication and a strong foundation if they are to last. If you think about it, you will see that these same rules apply to all of the relationships in our lives. It is easy to see how these rules can strengthen family bonds and friendships, but developing stronger relationships with your classmates and professors (or coworkers and bosses) can make your life a lot easier.

Just as you need to relate with everyone around you, the data that you work with often needs to relate to other types of data.

Communication is the key to strong relationships

We all know that marriages are not the only relationships that require good communication. If we look at a library database, we can see how communication plays a part in developing your databases.

Every record in a library's database contains at least four essential types of interrelated information: Author, Subject, Title, and Keyword. What makes the database powerful is the ability to cross-reference or, more specifically, to retrieve records based on their relationship to the search parameter.

If the data in your database does not use consistent wording and format, the communication between the records breaks down. If the communication breaks down, the search engine cannot locate the related records.

Establishing a strong foundation

Relational databases take the concept of cross-referencing a step further. When you have a large amount of interrelated data, it is often wise to break down the information into more than one table. To link your tables into a relational database, you have to establish solid connections.

When you are creating a relational database, you can bring two or more different tables together into one database. The first step is to determine the nature of the

Communication plays a part in developing your databases.

relationship involved. You can create three types of relationships with Access: one-to-one, one-to-many, and many-to-many.

- ***One-to-One.*** *A one-to-one relationship is a monogamous relationship. In other words, for any given record in the primary table there would be only one related record in the secondary. For example, a school could link one table containing every student's contact information and another containing the academic records.*
- ***One-to-Many.*** *A one-to-many relationship is used when a single record from the primary table relates to multiple records in secondary tables. In the library example, a single record in a table of cardholders can be linked to the table of books checked out. A search could determine which books have been checked out by which person.*
- ***Many-to-Many.*** *Many-to-many relationships contain a third junction table. This junction table maintains a one-to-many relationship with both of the other tables. So, a dating service could create two tables (one for the men and one for the women) of interested singles. They could then match up all the men and women that have the same likes and dislikes using the junction table.*

Luckily, it is much easier to blend your data tables than it is to blend the many different relationships in real life. Access conveniently places all of the fields from all of your tables in one place, the Relationship Window, where you can quickly create links between related fields in different tables.

"What do you mean we don't communicate? I sent you e-mail on Monday."

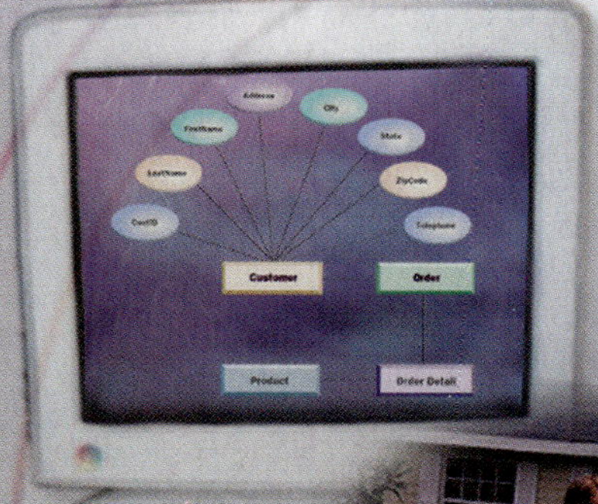

PROJECT 3

Modifying Tables and Establishing Relationships

The Challenge

Mr. Traylor has reviewed the work you have done so far on the database, and has approved the initial design. He wants to be able to pull information from both the Time Cards and Departments tables so that the department names can be included on each employee's time card statement. He would also like to have some controls set to ensure accurate data entry and would like you to modify the tables and forms so that data entry personnel can easily add new employee data as new employees are hired. Finally, he would like controls set to ensure that the data entry personnel will be able to create a time card record using only valid employee numbers and limiting billable hours to 80 hours for each pay period.

The Solution

Although it may seem that Mr. Traylor is asking you to make significant modifications to the database, you can accommodate his request with a few simple steps. By adding a lookup field to the Time Cards table, data entry personnel can select each employee's department from a list as they enter time card records, thereby ensuring that the department names are always accurate. When you add this field, Access will create a relationship between the Time Cards and Department tables. By creating a relationship between the Time Cards and the Employees tables, you will be able to pull data from all tables to create time card records for specific employees. You can then create multiple time cards for each employee, as shown in Figure 3-1, and print the relationship layout as a way of documenting the database design for future reference. Setting properties for table fields enables you to set the controls that will limit the data that is entered in each field.

Figure 3-1

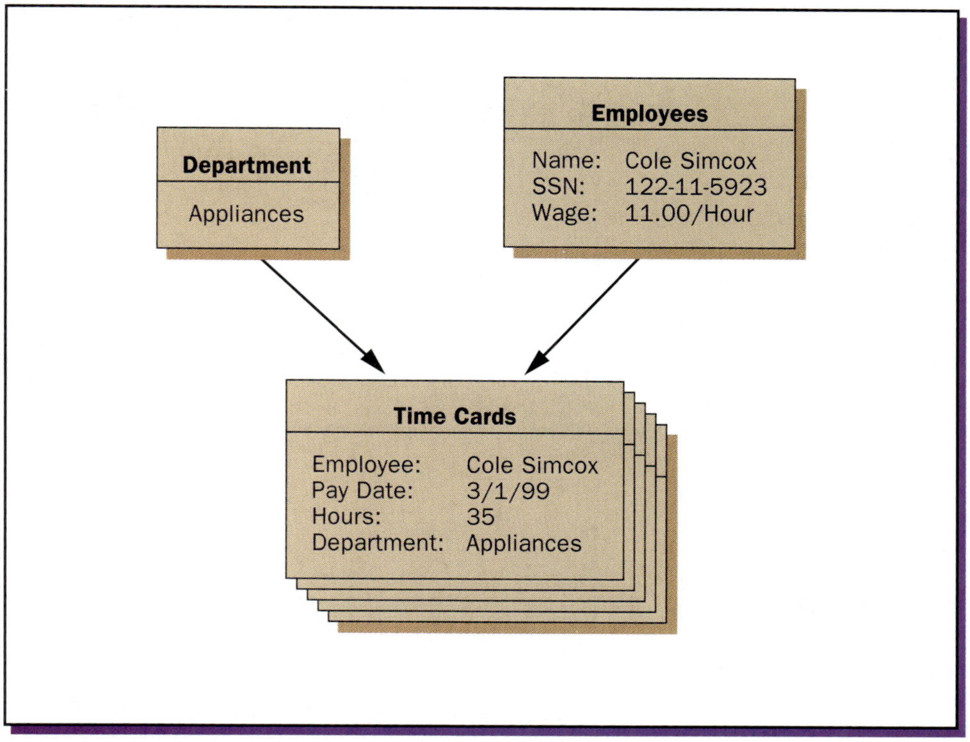

Adding a Lookup Field to the Time Cards Table

A relational database with data stored in multiple tables provides an efficient way to reduce the amount of data duplication while enabling you to access the data to create other database objects. A *lookup field* accesses values from a field in one table and displays field values in a list so that you can select the value you want to use and reduce data entry errors. By adding a lookup field to the Time Cards table, you can look up a specific department from the Departments table and associate that particular record with the selected department.

CHECK POINT

Do you remember the difference between primary keys and foreign keys?

A *foreign key* is simply a field in a one table that duplicates a field in another table that contains unique data so that the two tables can be linked. The field that contains unique data is a *primary key*. In this case, the data can be looked up because the *foreign key*—DepartmentID— in the Time Cards table corresponds with the *primary key*—DepartmentID—in the Departments table. You can use these values to look up department names using the department IDs.

Task 1:

To Add a Lookup Field to the Time Cards Table

1. Launch Access, open *e-Selections Working.mdb*, and click the Tables button in the Objects bar, if necessary.

2. Select the **Time Cards** table and click the Design button.

Figure 3-2

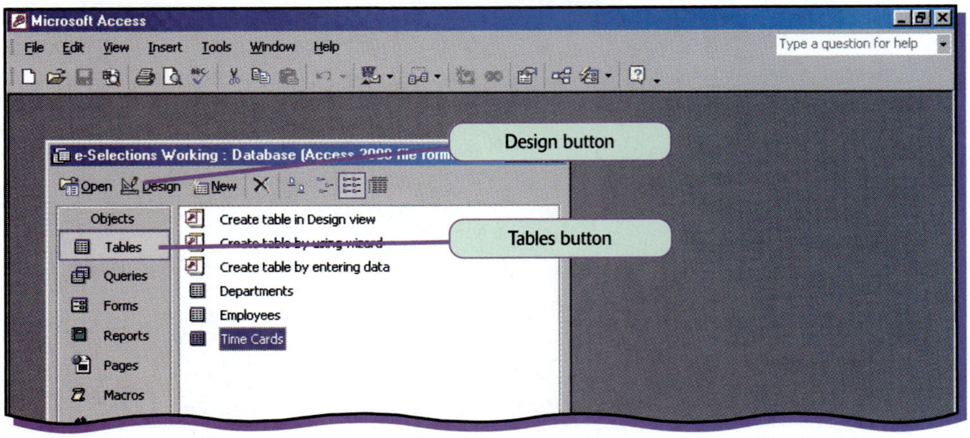

3. Position the insertion point in the row below the **HoursWorked** field and type **DepartmentID** in the **Field Name** column.

4. Press Tab and click the down arrow to display the **Data Type** list.

5. Select **Lookup Wizard**.

Figure 3-3

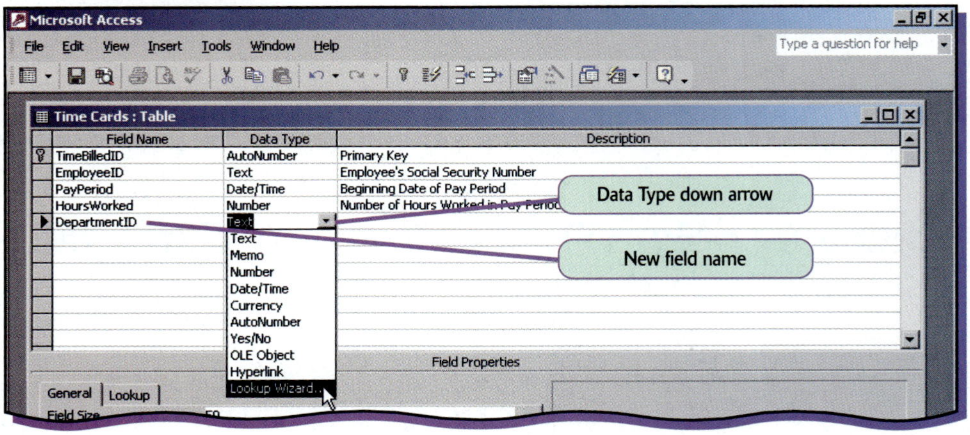

6. Click **Next** to accept the default option to look up values in a table or query.

Figure 3-4

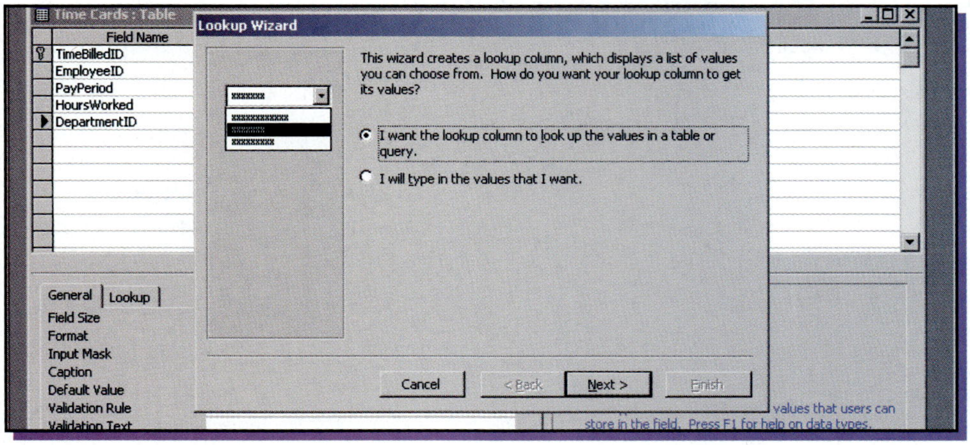

7 Select **Table: Departments** and click **Next**.

Tip By default, Tables are listed in the Wizard. To display other database objects on which you might want to base the lookup field, select the appropriate option in the View section of the dialog box.

Figure 3-5

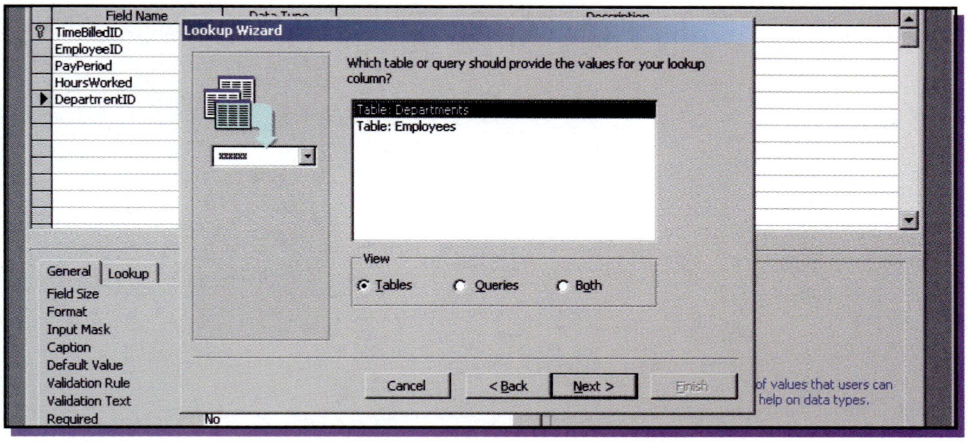

8 Select the **DepartmentName** field from the **Available Fields** list and click the Move [>] button to move it to the **Selected Fields** list.

9 Click **Next**.

Figure 3-6

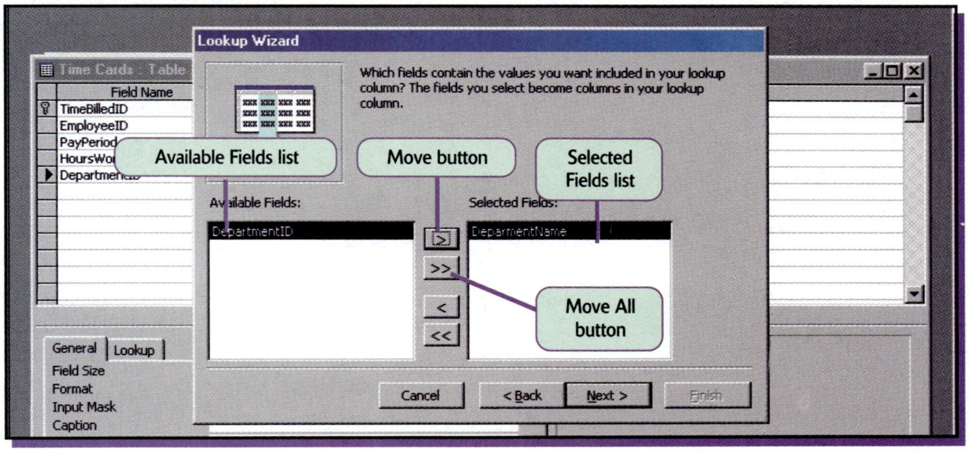

10 Double-click the right border of the **DepartmentName** field name to widen the column and then click **Next** to accept the default option to hide the key column.

11 Click **Finish** to accept the default label, **DepartmentID**. A Lookup Wizard message box asks if you want to save the table.

Figure 3-7

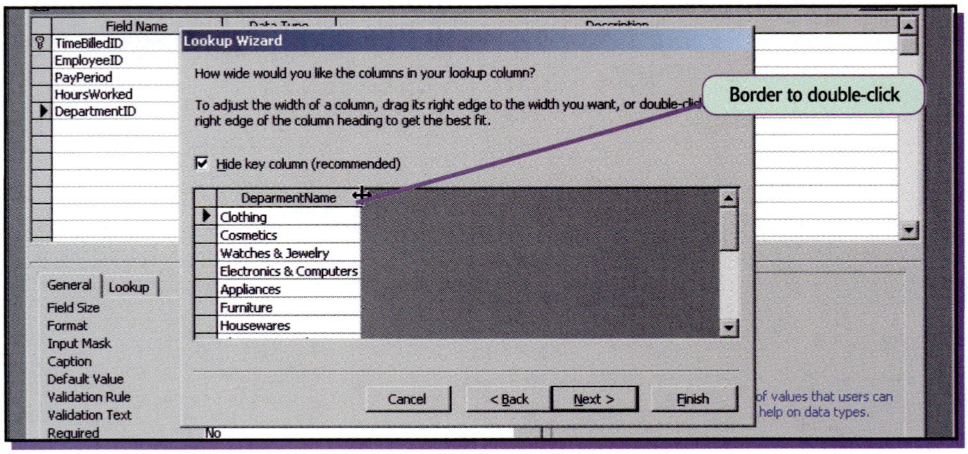

12 Click **Yes** to save changes to the table.

13 Press [Tab], type **Foreign Key** in the **Description** column, close the table, and click **Yes** to save the table again.

Figure 3-8

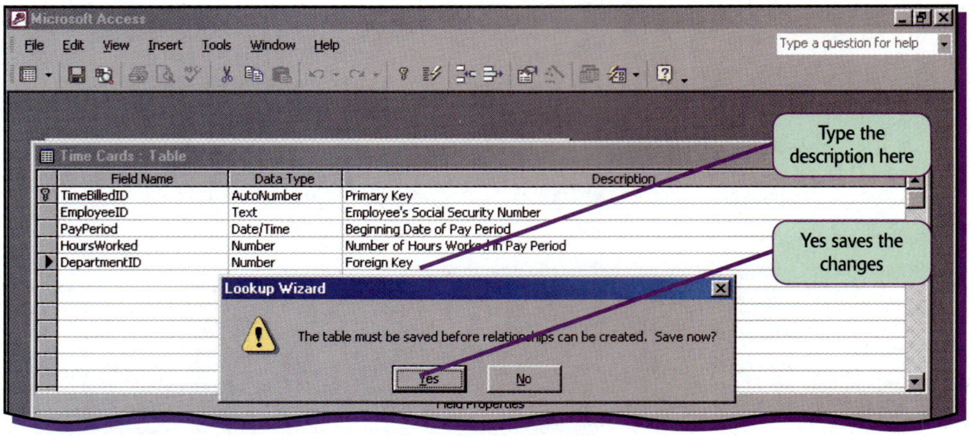

Tip

By default, the Hide Key column check box is selected. If you clear it, the primary key, DepartmentID, will be visible and Access will enter the DepartmentID number from the Departments table into the DepartmentID field in the Time Cards table. Because we want the table to show the department name rather than the ID, we want to leave the Hide Key option checked.

CHECK POINT

After adding a lookup field to a database table, you can use the lookup field to select accurate and valid values for records contained in the table. The list you see when you click the down arrow for a lookup field contains values that are easy to identify, even though Access is actually entering the value from the lookup table's primary key field.

WEB TIP

The Microsoft Web site contains information about defining lookup fields in Access database tables. To find the information, choose **Help | Office on the Web** and search for Lookup Fields.

Creating and Modifying Relationships

To be able to share data that is entered into one table with other objects in the database, relationships between the tables must exist. Access automatically creates relationships between database tables when it finds fields that appear to contain the same information. You can also create relationships manually by *joining* fields in different database tables. Table 3-1 identifies the three types of relationships that Access supports, and Figures 3-9, 3-10, and 3-11 illustrate these relationships.

Table 3-1 Access Relationship Types

Relationship Type	Description
One-to-one	Each record in Table A can have only one matching record in Table B, and each record in Table B can have only one matching record in Table A. This type of relationship is not common, however, because most of the information related in this way would normally be in one table.
One-to-many	A one-to-many relationship is the most common type of relationship. In a one-to-many relationship, a record in Table A can have many matching records in Table B, but a record in Table B can have only one matching record in Table A.
Many-to-many	In a many-to-many relationship, a record in Table A can have many matching records in Table B, and a record in Table B can have many matching records in Table C. A many-to-many relationship uses a *junction table,* so that it is really two one-to-many relationships.

One-to-One

Figure 3-9

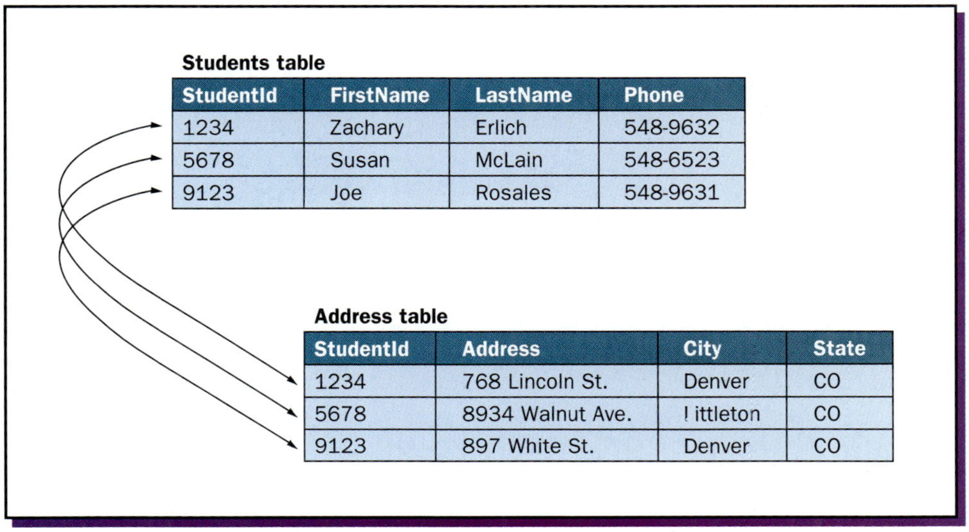

One-to-Many

Figure 3-10

Students table

StudentId	FirstName	LastName	Phone
1234	Zachary	Erlich	548-9632
5678	Susan	McLain	548-6523
9123	Joe	Rosales	548-9631

Registration table

Student ID	Class ID
1234	EDU201-01
1234	CIS102-03
5678	CIS102-03
9123	HIS400-01
9123	BIO360-02

Many-to-Many

Figure 3-11

Students table

StudentId	FirstName	LastName	Phone
1234	Zachary	Erlich	548-9632
5678	Susan	McLain	548-6523
9123	Joe	Rosales	548-9631

Registration table

Student ID	Class ID
1234	EDU201-01
1234	CIS102-03
5678	CIS102-03
9123	HIS400-01
9123	BIO360-02

Class Schedule table

ClassID	Course Name	Days
EDU201-01	Educational Psychology	MWF
CIS102-03	Computer Applications	TR
HIS400-01	American History	TR
BIO360-02	Genetics	MWF

CHECK POINT

Can you figure out what type of relationship Access created when you added a lookup field to the Time Cards table? When you added a lookup field to the Time Cards table, Access created a one-to-many relationship between the Time Cards table and the Departments table. Now each time card record can be linked to a specific department. In the following tasks, you will modify this relationship and create a new relationship between the Time Cards table and the Employees table.

Task 2:
To Open the Relationships Window and Add Tables

1. Click the Relationships button on the Database toolbar to open the Relationships window.

Figure 3-12

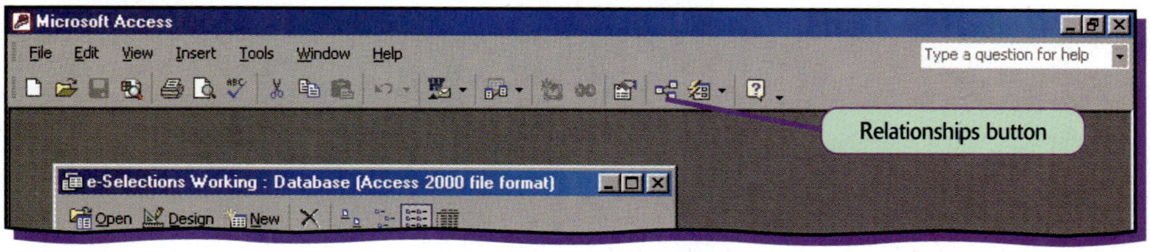

Other Ways

To display the Show Table dialog box:
- Choose **Relationships | Show Table**.

2. Click the Show Table button, select the **Employees** table from the Show Table dialog box, and click **Add**.

Troubleshooting

Drag the Show Table dialog box title bar to position it as shown in Figure 3-13. If the tables already appear in the Relationships window, skip Step 2.

Figure 3-13

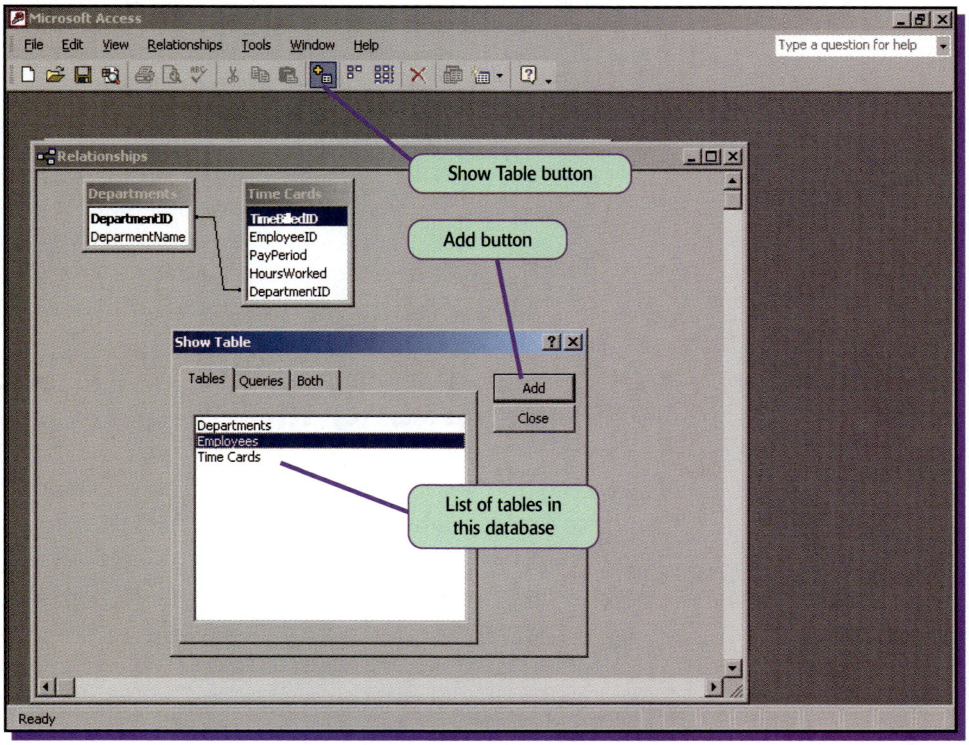

3 Click **Close** on the **Show Table** dialog box and click the **Save** button to save the relationships.

Figure 3-14

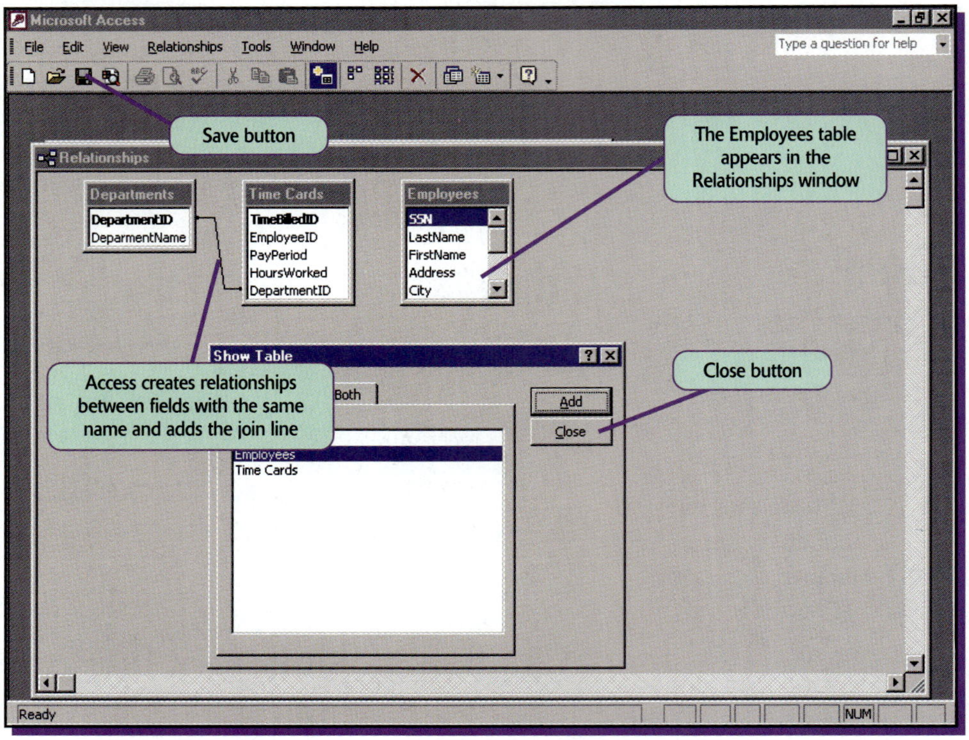

Troubleshooting It is possible to add multiple instances of a table to the Relationships window. If you inadvertently add the same table to the Relationships window more than once, click the title bar of the table you want to delete and then press the Delete key to delete it.

Tip Each table that appears in the Relationships window is formatted to contain a title bar. As a result, you can drag the table title bars to reposition tables in the Relationships window.

Creating Relationships Among Tables

Now that you have modified the table structure to reduce data entry errors and have added tables to the Relationships window, you can turn your attention to joining the fields that appear in the different tables to create relationships between the tables so that Access knows how the tables are related. By setting the relationships manually, you are, in effect, establishing rules to ensure that the references to data in one table accurately represent the appropriate data from another table. Access uses the relationships you set to maintain the *referential integrity*—the integrity of the references—between table data. In this case, Mr. Traylor wants to ensure that time cards are created only for employees listed in the Employees table. In other words, the employee must first exist in the Employees table before you can give him or her a time card record in the Time Cards table.

Task 3:
To Create Relationships Between Tables

1 Display the **Relationships** window, if necessary, click the **SSN** field name in the **Employees** table, and drag the field on the **EmployeeID** field name in the **Time Cards** table.

Figure 3-15

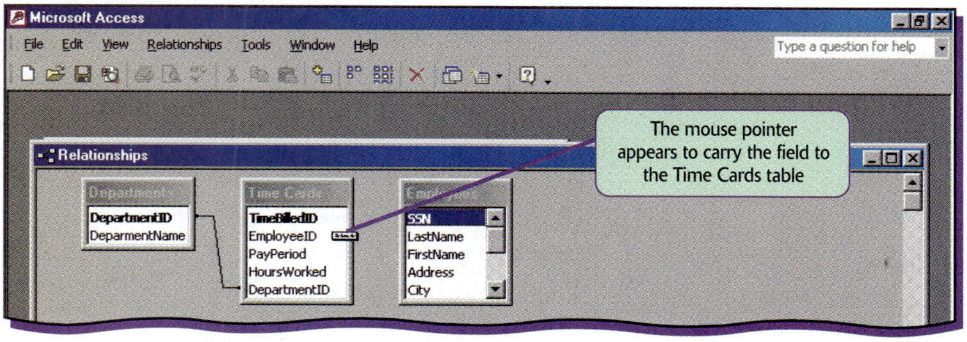

2 Select the **Enforce Referential Integrity** option.

Figure 3-16

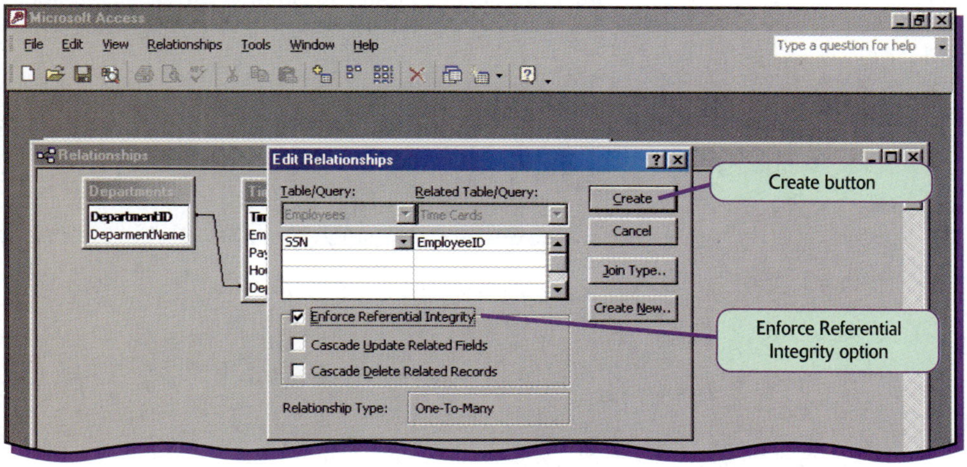

Tip The Edit Relationships dialog box opens when you are joining fields from two different tables that have different field names.

3 Click **Create** and drag a corner of each table field list to resize the list as shown in Figure 3-17.

4 Right-click on the join line between the **Time Cards** and **Departments** tables, select **Edit Relationships**, select the **Enforce Referential Integrity** option, and click **OK**. The join line now appears with the symbols indicating that referential integrity is enforced.

5 Click the Save button to save changes to the layout of the Relationships window.

Figure 3-17

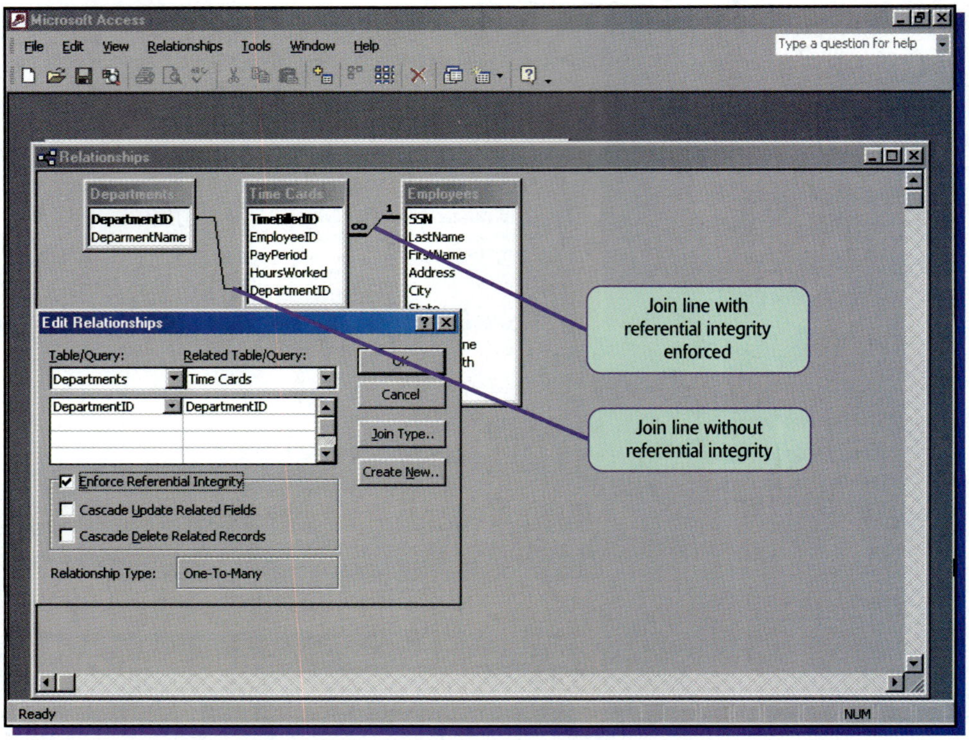

CHECK POINT

It's easy to tell when referential integrity is enforced between tables. The *1* and the infinity symbol (∞) indicate that this is a one-to-many relationship with referential integrity enforced. The relationship between the Departments and Time Cards tables is also a one-to-many relationship, but since the *1* and the ∞ symbol are not displayed, referential integrity is not currently enforced.

WEB TIP

The links you find on Web sites identify other sites that are related to the current site. Therefore, it could be said that these links form relationships between Web sites.

Printing Relationships

In Access, you can create a report that displays the relationships layout and print the report to save as part of the database structure documentation.

Task 4:
To Print the Relationships

1. Open the **Relationships** window, if necessary, and choose **File | Print Relationships**.

2. Click the Print button on the Print Preview toolbar to print the report.

3. Close the report and click **Yes** to save it.

4. Click **OK** to keep the default report name, **Relationships for e-Selections Working**, and close the **Relationships** window.

Figure 3-18

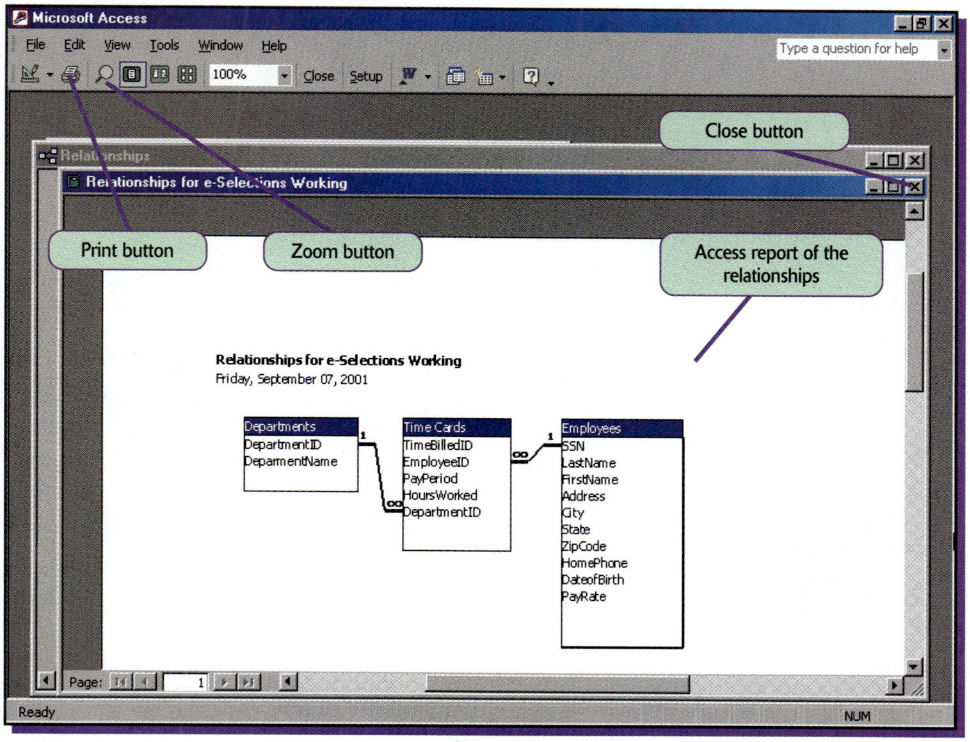

Tip Click the Zoom button to activate the Zoom feature and then click the mouse pointer on the report window to zoom in and out to see different portions of the report.

Improving Data Accuracy Using Input Masks and Validation Rules

Mr. Traylor has voiced a concern about the format of data entered into tables as well as concerns about the accuracy and format of data. By setting controls using field properties, you can reduce the risk that data entered in specific fields will appear improperly formatted, and this will also help maintain data accuracy. Access supports several property controls that will help you control data input and prompt the data entry operator for the valid data:

- An *input mask* is a field property that displays specific characters in the field with blanks to fill in.
- A *validation rule* is a field property that specifies requirements for data entered intro a record, field, or control.
- The *validation text* field property contains the text that appears to prompt the data entry operator for valid data.

Setting Validation Rules and Validation Text Properties

Validation rules are generally set to control the specific values that can be entered in a field to prevent invalid information from being entered. You can use the validation rule and validation text properties to limit entries in the HoursWorked field to 80 hours or less for each two-week payroll period.

Task 5:

To Set Validation Rule and Validation Text Properties

1. Select the **Time Cards** table in the Database window and click the Design button to open the table in Design view.

2. Click the **HoursWorked** field, press the F6 key to move to the lower pane of the Table Design window, click the **Validation Rule** box, and type **>=0 and <=80.**

3. Press Tab to move to the **Validation Text** box and type **Hours worked must be greater than or equal to zero and less than or equal to 80 hours.**

4. Click the **Save** button to update the table and close the Time Cards table.

Figure 3-19

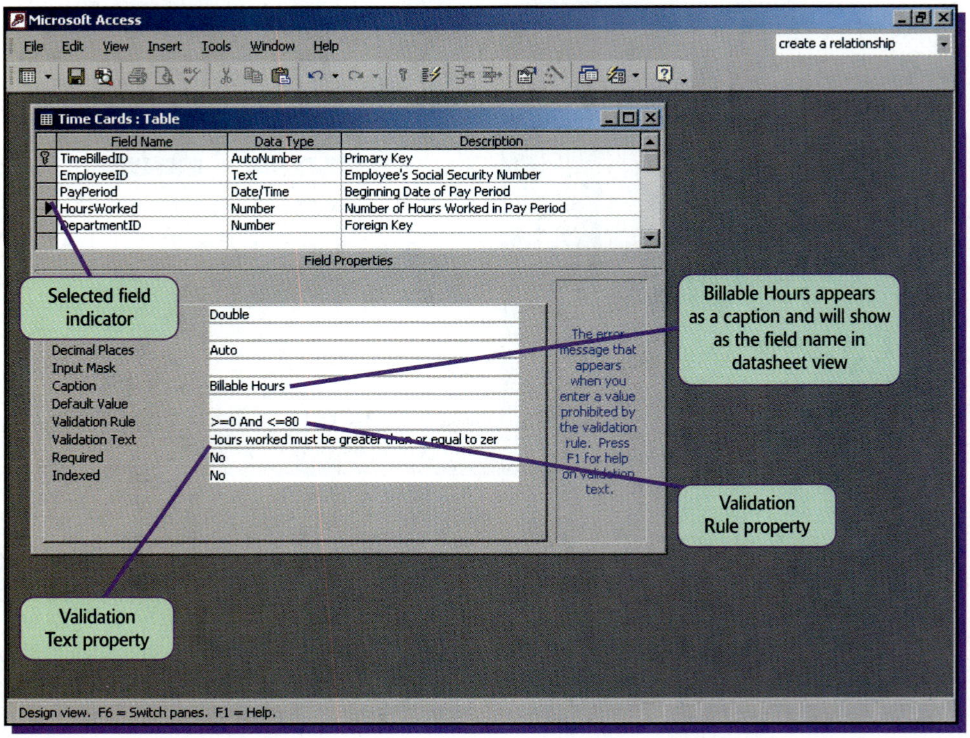

Troubleshooting When you apply a validation rule to a field that already contains data, Access displays a message box asking whether you want to verify the existing data with the new validation rule. Click **Yes**. If the existing data violates the validation rule, then Access will display another dialog box that will let you choose to delete the offending data. Click **Yes** to delete invalid data.

Setting Input Masks

The primary use for input masks is to format text values entered into specific fields to ensure that the data entered for all records is formatted the same and to limit the values entered to a specific number of characters. You can use the input mask property to control the format and number of characters contained in the Social Security Number field.

Task 6:
To Define Input Masks

1 Select the **Employees** table and click the Design button to open the table in Design view.

Figure 3-20

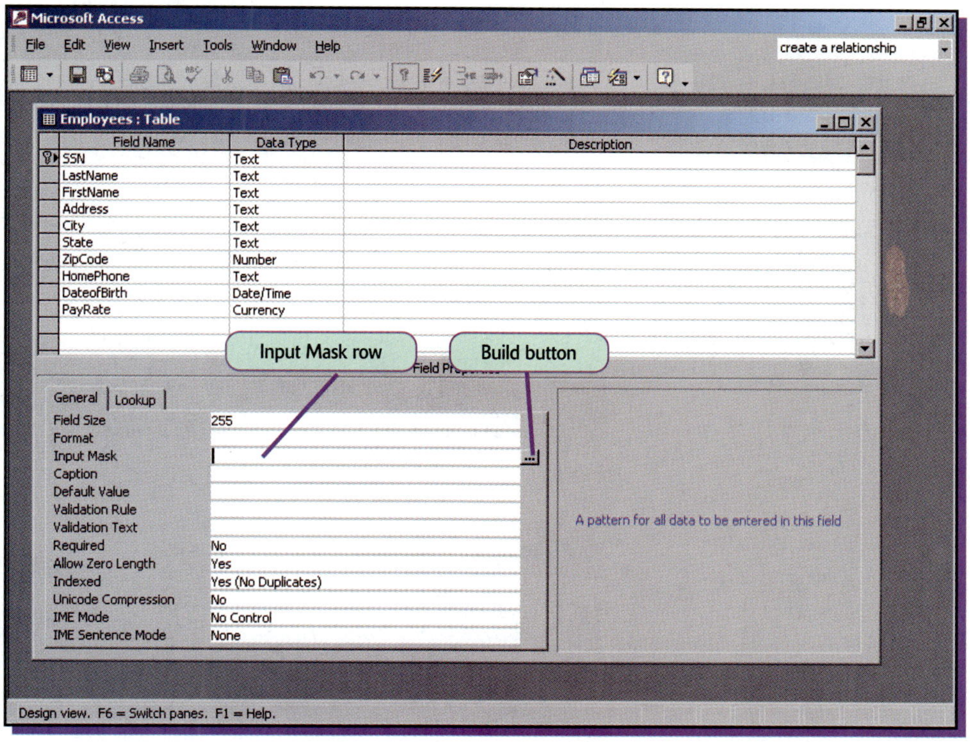

2 Click the **SSN** field, press the F6 key, and click the **Input Mask** field in the lower pane.

3 Click the Build button and select **Social Security Number** from the **Input Mask** list.

> **Troubleshooting**
> If the Input Mask Wizard is not installed, Access will ask you if you would like to install it. You may need your installation CD to install the Wizard.

4 Click **Next**. The Input Mask Wizard displays the format for the Social Security number.

Figure 3-21

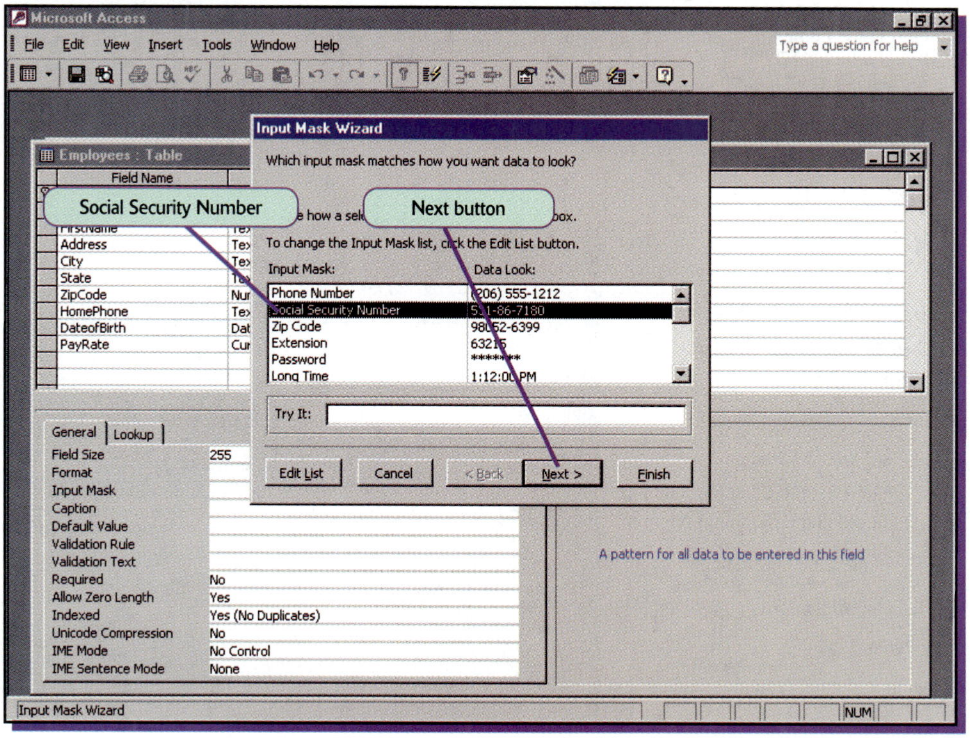

5 Click **Next** to accept the default format.

Tip Access identifies the standard structure and format for common fields. As a result, when you are uncertain what format to select, let Access make the selection for you.

Figure 3-22

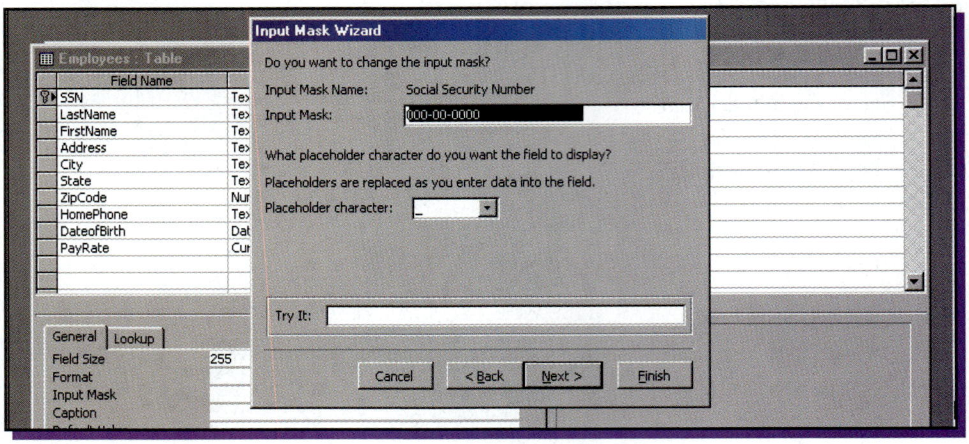

6 Select the **With the symbols in the mask, like this** option, click **Finish,** and click the Save button to save changes to the table.

Figure 3-23

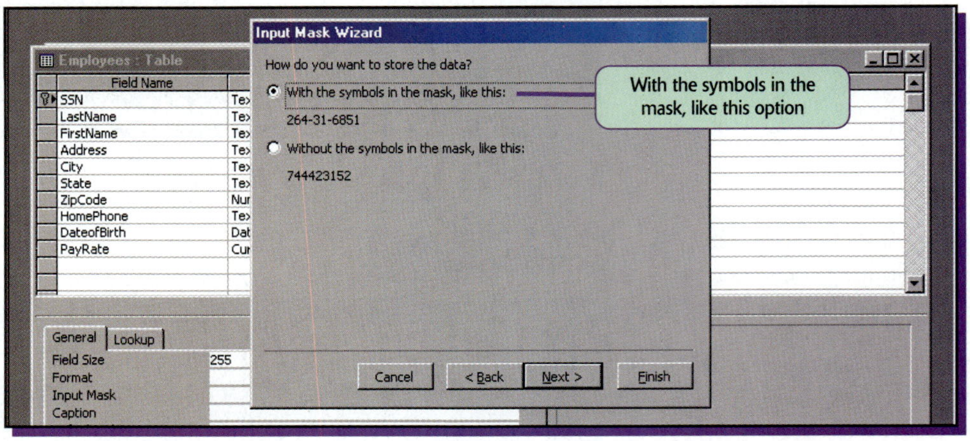

7 Select the **HomePhone** field row, click the **Input Mask** field in the lower pane, and click the **Build** button.

8 Select **Phone Number** from the **Input Mask** list and click Next.

Figure 3-24

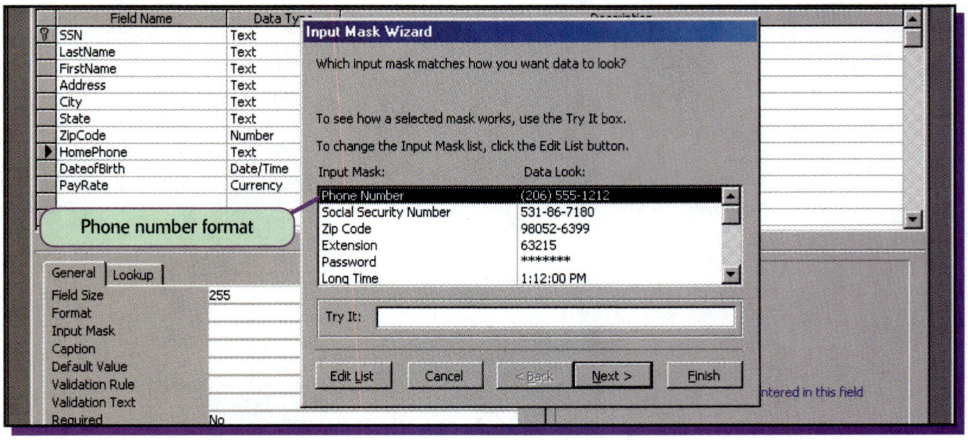

9 Click **Next**, select the **With the symbols in the mask, like this** option, and click **Finish**.

10 Click the Save button to update the table structure and close the table.

Figure 3-25

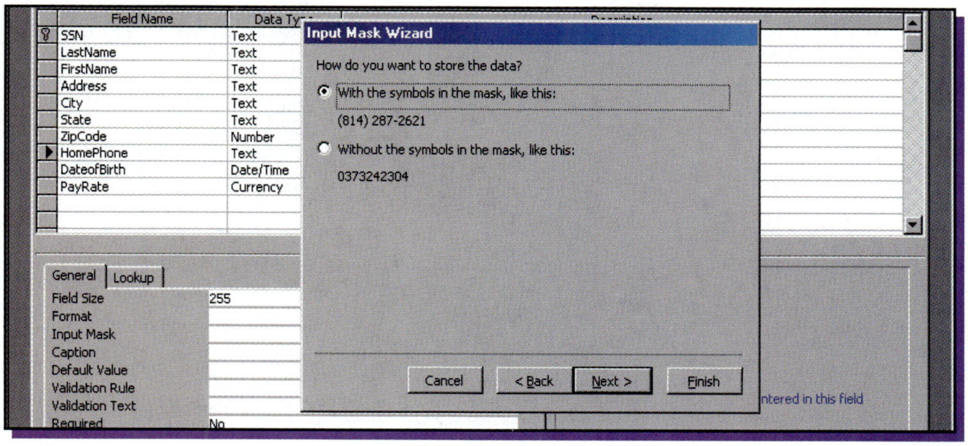

CHECK POINT

Input masks not only guide data entry format but place additional characters, such as dashes, in fields. The user can immediately identify the format for entering data and the miscellaneous characters that are entered automatically.

Adding a Lookup Field to a Table in Design View

The Lookup Wizard is an efficient way to add lookup fields to tables so that you can access values from other tables. In addition to the Table Wizard, you can set properties to create lookup fields.

Task 7:
To Define a Lookup Field Using Field Properties

1 Open the **Time Cards** table and display the **Design** view.

2 Select the **EmployeeID** field, press F6 to move to the lower pane, and click the **Lookup** tab.

3 Position the insertion point in the **Display Control** field, click the **Display Control** down arrow and select **Combo Box**.

Figure 3-26

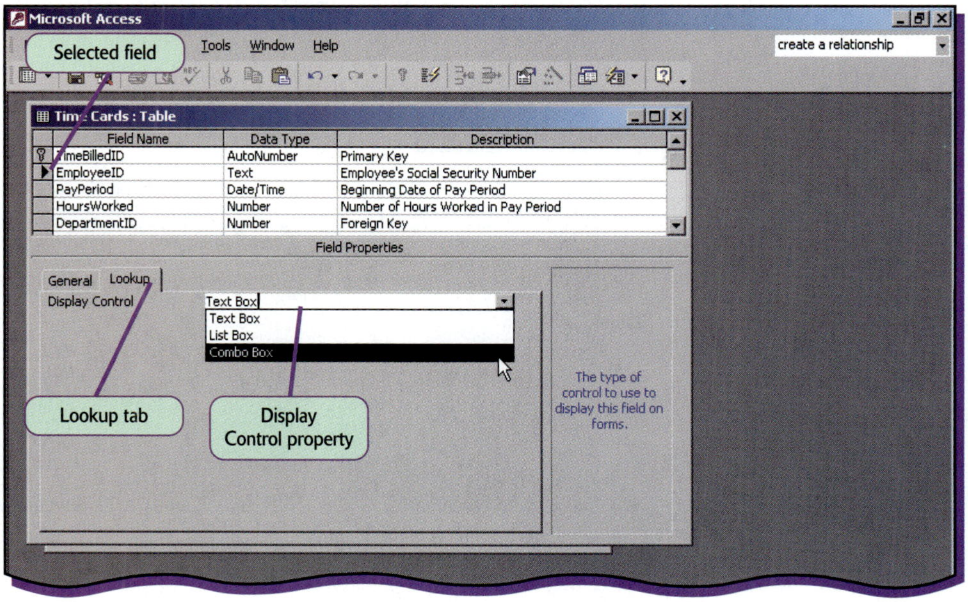

4 Click the **Row Source** field, click the down arrow to display a list of tables, select **Employees**, and type the values shown for additional properties in Figure 3-27.

5 Click the Save button to save changes to the table design and close the table.

Figure 3-27

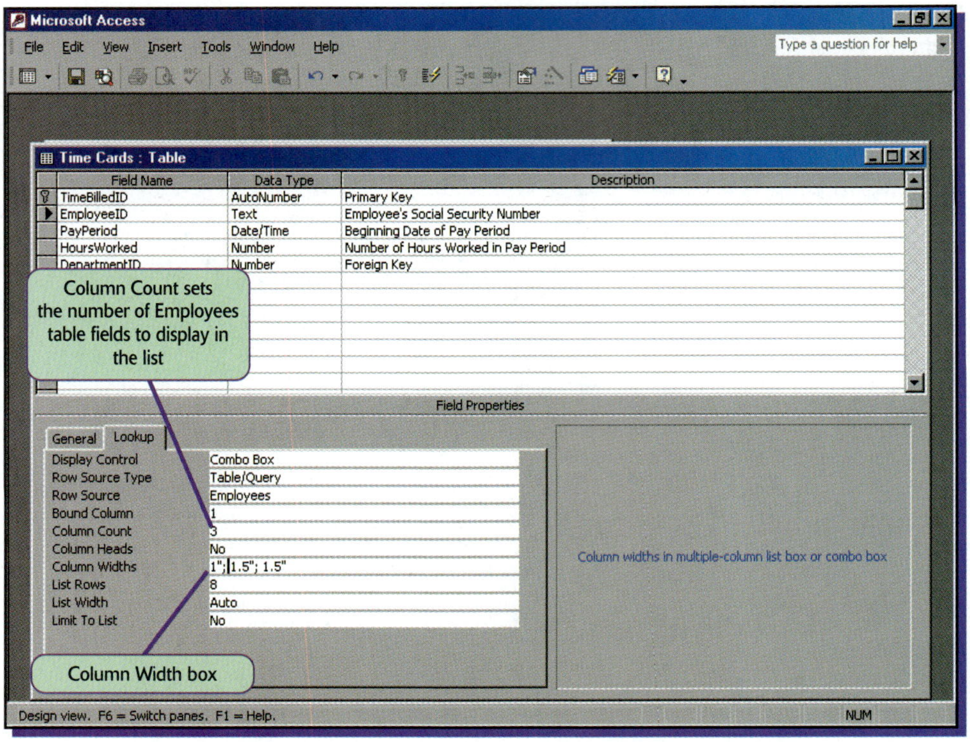

Adding Records to the Time Cards Table Using Lookup Lists

Now that you have modified the table to help validate data entered into the tables, you can start entering the records. Controls you set and lookup fields you added to the tables will make entering data in some table fields more efficient, will reduce the amount of typing required, and will ensure that the data you enter is valid. Entering records into the table will test validation rules and lookup values.

Task 8:
To Add Table Records

1 Open the **Time Cards** table, click the **Employee ID** field for the first record, click the down arrow on the right end of the field, select the first Social Security number from the list.

Figure 3-28

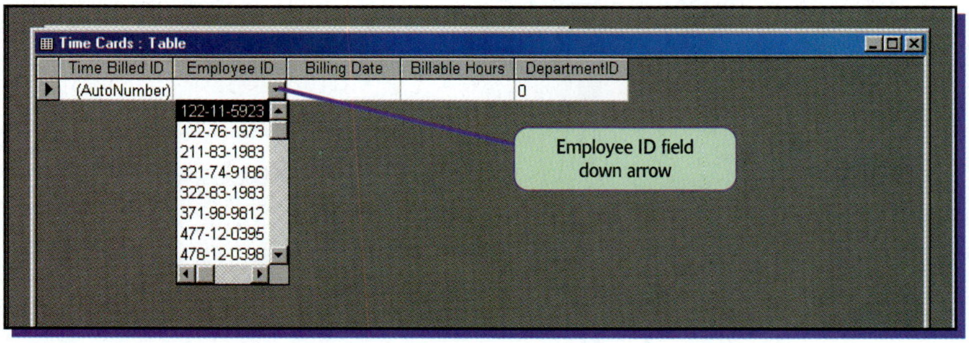

2 Press the [Tab] key to move to the next field, type **061600** in the **Billing Date** field, and press [Tab] to move to the next field.

3 Type **86** in the **Billable Hours** field and press [Tab].

Figure 3-29

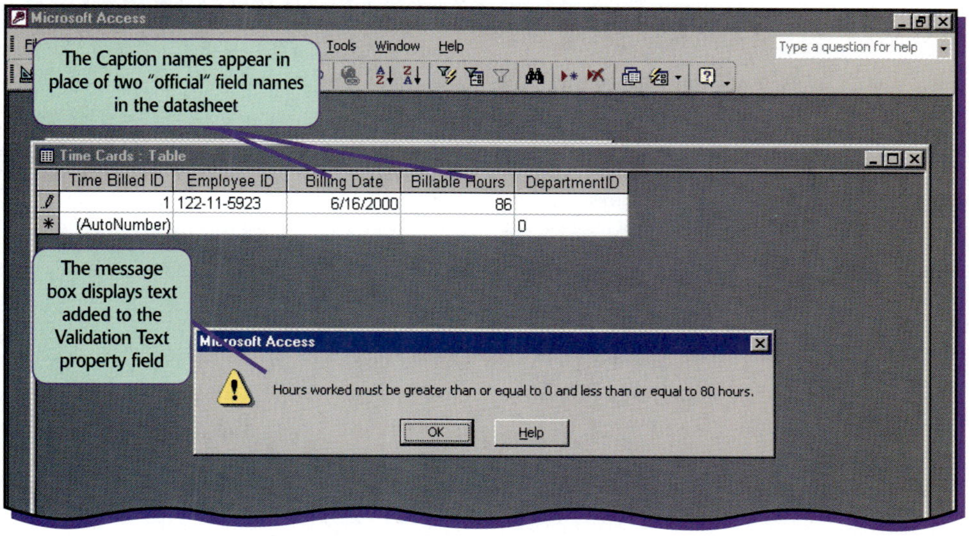

4 Click **OK**, select the invalid number, type **42**, and press [Tab].

5 Click the **DepartmentID** down arrow and select **Housewares**.

Figure 3-30

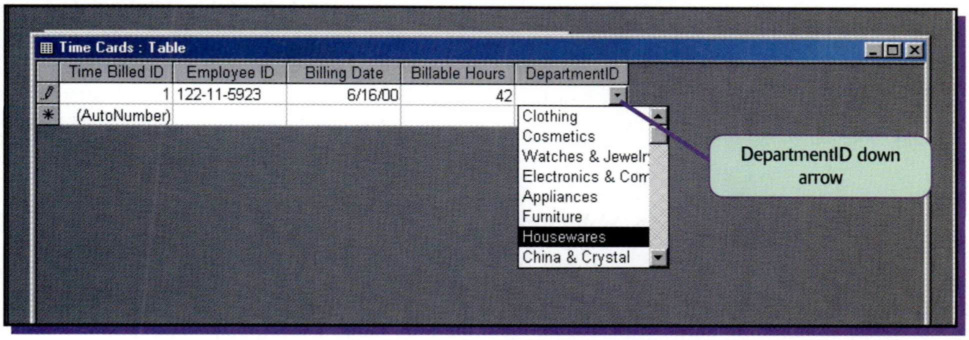

6 Press [Tab] and repeat the procedures identified in Steps 1 through 5 to complete the records shown in Figure 3-31 and close the **Time Cards** table.

Figure 3-31

Time Cards : Table

Time Billed ID	Employee ID	Billing Date	Billable Hours	DepartmentID
1	122-11-5923	6/16/2000	42	Housewares
2	322-83-1983	6/16/2000	64	Watches & Jewelry
3	371-98-9812	6/16/2000	71	Furniture
4	477-12-0395	6/16/2000	78	China & Crystal
5	534-92-1985	6/16/2000	80	Watches & Jewelry
(AutoNumber)				

SUMMARY AND EXERCISES

SUMMARY

- A lookup field will look up values from a related table or list.
- When you use the Lookup Wizard to create a lookup field, Access will create the relationship if one does not already exist.
- Access supports three types of relationships: one-to-one, one-to-many, and many-to-many.
- The most common type of relationship is a one-to-many relationship.
- In a one-to-many relationship, each record in the primary table may have many matching records in the related table.
- A many-to-many relationship uses a junction table. It is made up of two one-to-many relationships.
- You establish relationships between tables in the Relationships window.
- Referential integrity prevents orphan records from being created.
- A relationship with referential integrity displays a 1 and an infinity symbol on the join line.
- Access can create a report displaying your database relationships.
- Validation rules and input masks help to improve the accuracy of your data.

KEY TERMS & SKILLS

KEY TERMS

input mask (p. 3-15)
joining (p. 3-9)
junction table (p. 3-9)
lookup field (p. 3-5)
many-to-many relationship (p. 3-9)
one-to-many relationship (p. 3-9)
one-to-one relationship (p. 3-9)
orphan records (p. 3-22)
referential integrity (p. 3-12)
validation rule (p. 3-15)
validation text (p. 3-15)

SKILLS

Add a data validation rule (p. 3-16)
Add a lookup field to a table by modifying field properties (p. 3-19)
Add a lookup field to a table using the Lookup Wizard (p. 3-6)
Add an input mask to a field using the Input Mask Wizard (p. 3-17)
Add records to a table datasheet using lookup fields (p. 3-20)
Add tables to the Relationships window (p. 3-11)
Enforce referential integrity (p. 3-13)
Establish one-to-many relationship between two tables (p. 3-12)
Print the relationships in a database (p. 3-15)
Specify data validation text (p. 3-16)

STUDY QUESTIONS

MULTIPLE CHOICE

1. A relationship in which many records in Table B can have a matching record in Table A is what type of relationship?
   a. one-to-one
   b. one-to-many
   c. many-to-many
   d. either b or c

2. Relationships can be modified or established in
   a. Form view.
   b. Table Design view.
   c. the Relationships window.
   d. the Show Table dialog box.

3. Data Validation text
   a. limits the values that can be entered into a field.
   b. informs the user when a value is accepted by a validation rule.
   c. informs the user when a value violates the validation rule.
   d. guides the user in entering a value by displaying helpful characters.

4. A lookup field can
   a. look up a value from a list that you type.
   b. look up a value from a specified table.
   c. be created only by using the Lookup Wizard.
   d. both a and b

5. If you are using a table to look up values, a lookup field requires
   a. an AutoNumber data type.
   b. a primary and a foreign key.
   c. a relationship between tables.
   d. none of the above

6. The "many" side of a one-to-many relationship with referential integrity enforced is represented with
   a. a line.
   b. the number *1*.
   c. the word *many*.
   d. the infinity symbol.
7. Referential integrity prevents
   a. inaccurate data from being entered.
   b. orphan records.
   c. database corruption
   d. inaccurate reports from being generated.
8. You specify a validation rule and validation text in
   a. Datasheet view.
   b. the upper pane of the Table Design window.
   c. the lower pane of the Table Design window.
   d. the second screen of the Table Wizard.
9. A one-to-one relationship is not common because
   a. there must be three tables in the database.
   b. it is difficult to accomplish.
   c. the related table would need two foreign keys.
   d. most of the information related this way would normally be in one table.
10. A many-to-many relationship
   a. uses a junction table.
   b. always has referential integrity enforced.
   c. needs three foreign keys.
   d. both a and c

SHORT ANSWER

1. What sources can be used for a lookup list?
2. How many tables can be related?
3. What happens when you specify a Lookup Wizard as a data type?
4. Where do you modify relationships?
5. How do you print table relationships?
6. A many-to-many relationship uses how many tables?
7. How does an input mask help the user to enter data?
8. What happens when you violate a validation rule?
9. What field property do you modify to restrict the values that a user can enter?
10. How do you enter data into a datasheet with a lookup field?

FILL IN THE BLANK

1. A(n) ____________ allows data in one table to look up values in another.
2. A(n) ____________ appears whenever a validation rule is violated.
3. You create and modify relationships in the ____________
4. ____________ prevents orphan records.
5. A(n)____________ table is used to create a many-to-many relationship.
6. When you create a lookup field, Access will establish a ____________ if there is not one.
7. A(n) ____________ relationship is the most common type of relationship between two tables.
8. To assist users in entering a telephone number into a field, add a(n) ____________ .
9. A(n) ____________ restricts the values that a user can enter into a field.
10. In a one-to-many relationship with referential integrity enforced, a ____________ is displayed next to the "many" table.

FOR DISCUSSION

1. Explain how lookup fields utilize primary and foreign keys.
2. Why should you consider enforcing referential integrity in a relationship?
3. Why should you change the validation text property of a field if you modify the validation rule property?
4. How do relationships between tables help maintain data accuracy?
5. Why would you want to print database relationships?

GUIDED EXERCISES

1 LOOKING UP AND PUTTING IN DATA CONTROLS

The @Home Warranty database needs modification so that accurate information about repairs can be easily entered. You will create several lookup fields, an input mask, and a validation rule and text to streamline data entry. Follow these steps to complete these tasks:

1. Launch Access, open the *@Home Warranty.mdb* database, and open the **Repairs** table in Table Design view.
2. Click the **Data Type** column for the **SystemPart** field, select **Lookup Wizard** from the drop-down list, select the **I will type in the values that I want** option, and click **Next**.
3. Update the table using the values in Figure 3-32 as a guide and then click **Next**.

Figure 3-32

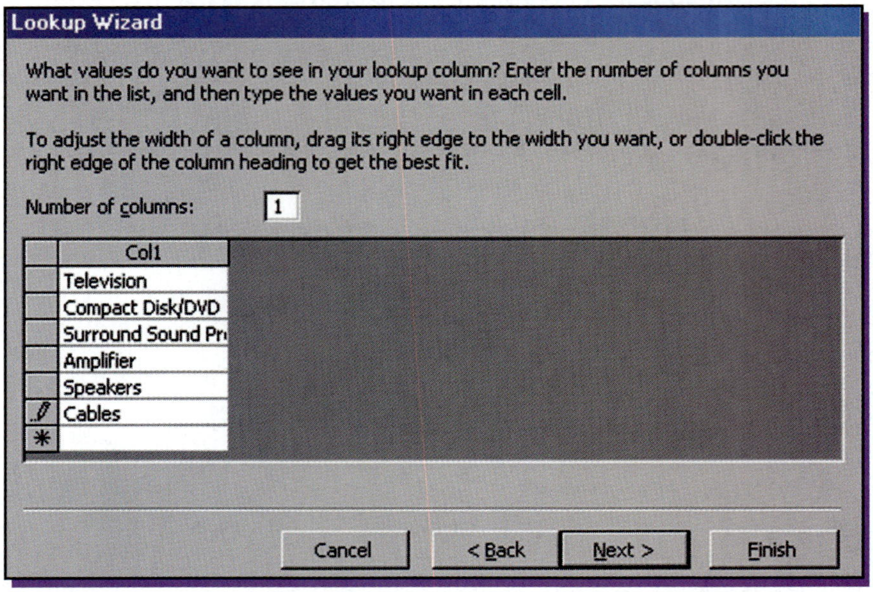

4. Keep the default label name, **SystemPart**, and click **Finish**.
5. Click the **Data Type** column for the **CustomerID** field, select **Lookup Wizard** from the drop-down list, select the **I want the lookup column to lookup the values in a table or query** option, and click **Next**.
6. Select the **Customers** table, click **Next**, move the **LastName** and **FirstName** fields to the **Selected Fields** columns, and click **Next**.
7. Resize the columns to fit the data, click **Next**, click **Finish**, and click **Yes** to save the table.
8. Click the **SerialNumber** field, click the **Validation Rule** box, and type **Like "EX?????"** to accept only values that begin with *EX* and have seven total characters.
9. Click the **Validation Text** box and type **Serial Number always begins with the letters EX.**
10. Save and close the **Repairs** table and close the database.

2 THE SHOWING A PROFIT DATABASE

Showing a profit is the aim of all businesses. The Show a Profit database needs modification so that information about departments and orders can be entered. You will create several lookup fields, an input mask, and a validation rule and text to streamline data entry. You will also modify the relationship between the Orders and Items tables. Follow these steps to complete the modifications:

1. Launch Access, open the *Show a Profit.mdb* file, and open the **Items** table in Design view.
2. Click the **Data Type** column of the **DepartmentCode** field, select **Lookup Wizard** from the drop-down list, and click **Next** to accept the default settings.
3. Select the **Departments** table, click **Next**, move the **DepartmentName** field to the **Selected Fields** list, and click **Next**.
4. Clear the **Hide Key Column** check box, click **Next**, and select **DepartmentCode** as the column that contains the value that you want to store. Then click **Next**, click **Finish**, and click **Yes** to save the table.
5. Enter the **Department Codes** shown in Figure 3-33 and close the table.

Figure 3-33

Items : Table

ItemID	Description	InStock	Cost	SellingPrice	DepartmentCode
FP10	Baseball Cap	50	$5.50	$6.75	FP
HP23	Coffee Mug	35	$3.25	$4.25	HP
IC15	T-Shirt (L)	25	$8.00	$9.75	IC
IC16	T-Shirt (M)	25	$8.00	$9.75	IC
IC17	T-Shirt (S)	25	$8.00	$9.75	IC
IC20	Polo Shirt (S)	25	$15.50	$19.95	IC
IC21	Polo Shirt (M)	25	$15.50	$19.95	IC
IC22	Polo Shirt (L)	25	$15.50	$19.95	IC
		0	$0.00	$0.00	

6. Open the **Departments** table in Design view, select the **Telephone** field, click the **Input Mask** box Build button, and use the Input Mask Wizard to create an input mask appropriate for a telephone number displayed without the symbols in the mask.

7. Enter the telephone numbers shown in Figure 3-34 and close the table.

Figure 3-34

Departments : Table

	DepartmentCod	DepartmentNam	Telephone
+	FP	Fields of Play	(888) 768-8765
+	HP	Home Page	(888) 768-9435
+	IC	Image Control	(888) 768-9888
*			

Record: 3 of 3

8. Open the **Orders** table in Design view, select the **ItemID** field, and modify the field so that it will look up **Item** descriptions from the **Items** table.

9. Create a validation rule for the **ItemsOrdered** field so that the value that is entered must be 10 or greater and create an appropriate message in the **Validation Text** field.

10. Enter the data into the **Orders** table as shown in Figure 3-35, test the validation rule by entering a value smaller than 10, and then close the table.

Figure 3-35

Orders : Table

OrderID	OrderDate	ItemsOrdered	ItemID
1	8/15/2002	10	T-Shirt (L)
2	8/15/2002	15	T-Shirt (M)
3	8/15/2002	25	Coffee Mug
4	9/1/2002	10	Polo Shirt (S)
5	9/1/2002	15	T-Shirt (M)
6	9/1/2002	10	Polo Shirt (L)
(AutoNumber)		0	

Record: 1 of 6

11 Open the **Relationships** window, add necessary tables so that all three tables (Items, Orders, and Departments) are displayed in the window, and modify the relationship between the Orders and Departments tables so that referential integrity is enforced.

12 Save the report with the default name, print the Relationships report, and then close the report, the Relationships window, and the database.

3 CREATING BRENT'S TOOL ORDERS DATABASE

Brent's Tool Orders database needs modification so that orders can be easily entered. You will create a lookup field, an input mask, and a validation rule and text to streamline data entry. You will also modify the relationship between the Customers and the Orders tables.

1 Open the Tool Orders database and display the **Orders** table in Design view.

2 Make the following modifications to the fields in the table:

- Modify the **CustomerID** field so that it will look up company names from the **Customers** table.
- Modify the **ShipMethod** field so that it will look up shipping methods from a list that includes USPS, UPS, and FedEx.
- Modify the **PayMethod** field so that it will look up payment types from a value list that includes check, Visa, MC, and cash.
- Add a validation rule for the **TotalInvoice** field so that the value must be more than zero and then add an appropriate validation text message.

3 Save the table, enter the data shown in Figure 3-36, and then close the table.

Figure 3-36

Orders : Table

OrderID	CustomerID	SalesDate	ShipMethod	TotalInvoice	AmountPaid	PayMethod
1	Tom's Tool Shack	10/6/2001	UPS	$2,500.00	$0.00	
2	The Hardware Store	10/21/2001	FedEx	$3,250.00	$3,000.00	Check
3	Expert Hardware and Lumber	10/30/2001	FedEx	$5,000.00	$5,000.00	Check
4	Tom's Tool Shack	11/6/2001	UPS	$1,500.00	$0.00	
5	Around the Corner Tools	11/8/2001	USPS	$15,000.00	$10,000.00	Visa
6	e-Tools For You	11/24/2001	UPS	$4,000.00	$0.00	
7	Pine Center Lumber	9/8/2001	UPS	$5,600.00	$5,600.00	Check
8	Acer Hardware	9/15/2001	FedEx	$7,000.00	$0.00	
9	The Hardware Store	11/8/2001	FedEx	$6,000.00	$3,000.00	
10	Pine Center Lumber	10/1/2001	UPS	$3,000.00	$0.00	
(Number)				$0.00	$0.00	

Record: 1 of 10

4. Open the **Customers** table and create appropriate input masks for the **Phone** and **ZipCode** fields.

5. Switch to Datasheet view, enter the phone numbers of your choice to the **Customers** table, and then close the table.

6. Open the **Relationships** window and modify the relationship so that referential integrity is enforced.

7. Print the Relationships report, save the report with the default name, and then close the report, the Relationships window, and the database.

ON YOUR OWN

The difficulty of these case studies varies:
are the least difficult; *are more difficult; and* *are the most difficult.*

1 UPGRADING TO COLLEGIATE ASSIGNMENTS

As the number of college assignments grows, you will want to simplify the input process to reduce the amount of time it takes to add assignments to the database. You can simplify data entry by creating relationships, formatting data using input masks, and adding lookup fields. Open the *Collegiate Class Assignments.mdb* file. Modify the ClassID field in the Assignments table so that it will look up the class name from the Classes table. Modify the Type field in the Assignments table so that it will look up the type of an assignment—Test, Quiz, Paper, or Reading—from a value list. After you have completed the modifications to the Assignments table, open the Classes table and add an input mask to the phone field and modify the relationship between the tables so that referential integrity is enforced. Print and save the relationships report. Finally, add hypothetical data that represents assignments to the assignment table.

2 NANCY'S KNICK-KNACK NOOK

Nancy has become so busy that she is looking for ways to make data entry in different tables of her database more efficient. You can help Nancy by using the skills developed in this project. Open *The Nook's Inventory.mdb* file. Create a lookup field in the Items table that will allow you to look up each supplier's name. Create appropriate input masks and validation rules and text for different fields in each table. Enter the sample data shown in Table 3-2. Then search the Internet for additional items that you can add to the Items table. Create at least five additional records using data you find. Modify the relationship between the Items and Suppliers tables so that referential integrity is enforced. Print a copy of the completed table and a copy of the relationships report.

Table 3-2

ItemID	Description	Units on Hand	Cost	Selling Price	Supplier ID	Supplier Name	Supplier Telephone
101	Large Fruit and Gourmet Basket	100	75.95	89.95	FN	Fruits and Nuts Unlimited	800-555-4444
102	The Ambassador Gift Basket	250	40.95	59.95	AW	Acme Wholesale Gifts	888-666-6547
105	Chocolate Lovers Basket	75	30.95	39.95	XC	X-tream Candies	800-873-5476
108	Holiday Celebration Basket	100	33.95	49.95	AW	Acme Wholesale Gifts	888-666-6547
109	Annie Get Your Gun Basket	125	30.95	39.95	XC	X-tream Candies	800-873-5476
200	Never Leave Home Without It Basket	75	19.95	29.95	FN	Fruits and Nuts Unlimited	800-555-4444
205	Snack Attack Basket	100	21.95	39.95	XC	X-tream Candies	800-873-5476
300	Let's Go Nuts Basket	50	19.95	29.95	FN	Fruits and Nuts Unlimited	800-555-4444
350	Just for Her Basket	100	25.95	39.95	AW	Acme Wholesale Gifts	888-666-6547
400	Bazooka Basket	125	12.95	19.95	AW	Acme Wholesale Gifts	888-666-6547

3 TRACKING REPAIRS

The home theater warranty database is getting more use. As a result, the tables can use some modification to make using them more efficient and to maintain data validity. Open the *@Home Warranty.mdb* file and modify the Customers table by completing the following:

- Adding an input mask to the Telephone Number field that formats the number with standard characters.
- Adding the Technicians table to the Relationships window and ensuring that all three tables appear in the Relationships window.
- Edit the relationship between the Customers and Repairs tables to enforce referential integrity.
- Create a relationship between the TechnicianID field in the Technicians table and the TechnicianID field in the Repairs table without enforcing referential integrity.

After you have completed the modifications, print a copy of the relationships report and save the report using the default file name. Then add the data shown in Figure 3-37 to the Repairs table and print a copy of the completed table.

Figure 3-37

Repairs : Table

	RepairID	RepairDate	SystemPart	SerialNumber	CustomerID	TechnicianID	RepairTime
	1	3/4/2002	Amplifier	EX4587	Jones	1	2
	2	3/4/2002	Speakers	EX7698	Green	4	4
	3	3/5/2002	Compact Disk/DVD	EX8112	Clinton	3	2
	4	3/5/2002	Speakers	EX8112	Clinton	3	1
▶	5	3/5/2002	Surround Sound Processor	EX3233	Crist	5	2
*						0	0

Record: 5 of 5

4 SIMPLIFYING THE PINE VALLEY REACHOUT DATABASE

Being able to identify contributor names each time you add data to the contributions table would simplify the data entry process for the Pine Valley Reachout. Open the *Pine Valley Reachout.mdb* file. Create a lookup field that will allow you to look up the contributors name in the table containing the contributions information. Specify appropriate input masks, validation rules, and validation text for the database. Modify the relationship between the two tables by enforcing referential integrity. Enter sample contribution data into the appropriate table. Print a copy of each table to which you add data.

5 BEAVER BROOK INN AND CONFERENCE CENTER FACILITY SCHEDULING DATABASE

Beaver Brook Inn and Conference Center has become so busy that those scheduling the facilities are having trouble keeping track of availability for both guest rooms and conference rooms. Open the *Conference Scheduling.mdb* file. Create appropriate lookup fields, input masks, validation rules, and text to streamline data entry. Modify the relationship(s) between the tables so that a group and room must exist before you can enter a room schedule record. Enter additional data into the tables. Then print a copy of your completed table and the relationships report.

6 STAYING IN SHAPE

Getting in shape is only half the challenge—staying in shape means maintaining what you learn during your fitness classes. As more and more people have joined the fight to keep in shape, the classes at the fitness center are filling up. In an effort to ensure that no classes will overbook and to track classes in which members are enrolled and those who have paid, you need to make some changes to the database. Open the *Staying in Shape.mdb* file. Create appropriate lookup fields, input masks, and validation rules and text to streamline data entry and to ensure that you can locate the classes for which a member is enrolled as well as the names of members enrolled in a class. Then search the Internet for fitness clubs and locate data for the Classes table. Enter the data into the Classes table and data for at least five of your friends, family members, or classmates in the Members and Registration tables. Modify table relationships so that referential integrity is enforced. Then print copies of each table and the relationship report.

Photospread credits pages 3-2 & 3-3

FROM THE FILES

You Will Need

- ✔ e-Selections Online.mdb
- ✔ Home Theater Repairs.mdb
- ✔ More Profits.mdb
- ✔ Brent's Orders.mdb
- ✔ Assignment Due Dates.mdb
- ✔ Pine Valley Donations.mdb
- ✔ Knick-Knack Nook.mdb
- ✔ Beaver Brook Facilities.mdb
- ✔ Fitness Club.mdb

PROJECT 4

Creating Queries

The goal of databases is to store data in such a way that it is easy to retrieve. Suppose you want to locate the employees who worked more than 60 hours during the last pay period or the departments that use part-time employees. You can find this information and much more by creating and saving queries. By designing and running Access queries, you are able to select and display specific fields of data from single and multiple database tables and locate specific records based on criteria you set. You can then use the data that meets the criteria to create reports and make business decisions.

e-selections Running Case

Other employees in the e-Selections Division of Selections, Inc., have been using the databases you created. They have edited data, added records, and tested the structure of each database. Now they are ready to start pulling information from the databases. It's time to learn some of the tricks and treats Access has for using databases to locate specific information and to display or print only the information requested.

OBJECTIVES

After completing this project, you will be able to:

- Create a select query based on one table
- Add fields to a select query
- View the results of a select query
- Create a select query based on multiple tables
- Add calculated fields to a query
- Define the sort order for a query
- Specify query conditions
- Save a query with a new name
- Use a function in an expression
- Create an AutoReport based on a query

Finding a Needle in a Haystack

Let's face it. The real reason we spend the time and energy required to create a database is not to store information. If that was all we wanted, a cardboard box in a warehouse could do the job. What we really want is the ability to quickly retrieve information from our records without the hassle of shuffling through files to find it.

The procedure for retrieving information from a database is called a query. In essence, you are asking the database to find the proverbial "needle in the haystack." Queries make it possible to use enormous amounts of stored information efficiently. They allow you to filter your database to find records that match multiple parameters. By saving your queries, you can also create complex reports.

Most databases use Structured Query Language (SQL) statements to form database queries. Although SQL is not a true programming language, it does provide standard format for writing queries. Fortunately, with Access, you don't have to be an SQL expert to query your database because Access provides three convenient query wizards, allowing you to structure your questions in a format that suits your needs.

Queries in Action

In 1996, IBM had the unenviable job of coordinating all the data for the Atlanta Olympics. They had to combine the databases of some 26 different organizing committees into a format that would be accessible to television networks, security, logistics coordinators, and organizers.

According to Allison Butterall, of the Toronto Development Lab and a member of the team that developed the coordinated information system for the 1996 Olympics, "...the best comparison to the information managed by the event is of running a major hotel chain (not one hotel, the whole chain), and putting on two Superbowls a day for ten days straight. Some three terabytes of data will be generated and processed during the 10-day period."

With Access, you don't have to be a SQL expert to query your database

The next time you watch the Olympics and the sports announcer tells you that the Bulgarian, who is the surprise winner of the biathalon, was born in the same small town that produced three other Nordic medallists in the 1950s, you can truly appreciate the effort that goes into producing those statistics.

We've always known that politicians use demographics and voter registration records to decide where to pitch their ideas, but now they are using the power of selected queries to send directed messages to those voters they feel they can best influence.

Many politicians are using a new system called Geo-Voter, created by Map Applications of Norwich, VT, to get the job done. Geo-Voter, is a combined database and mapping system that makes it possible to add multiple query parameters to identify the most receptive voters.

As Darryl Howard, executive director of the Oregon Republican Party, explained in an October 2000 Computerworld, "...when I can tell you that this person, in this district, is a known contributor, likely to take a yard sign for a candidate, a member of a Christian organization, he signed a couple of initiatives, he has a hunting license and he owns a four-wheel drive [vehicle], I know what issues are likely to drive [his voting decisions]."

As you can see, well-structured queries can have a major effect on the success of any database. As your database grows, you can customize your queries to increase their complexity by increasing your knowledge and understanding of SQL.

PROJECT 4

Creating Queries

The Challenge

Mr. Traylor is pleased with the work you have done on the e-Selections Online database and with the reports from others who have used the database. Now he wants to see a report that contains employee names, Social Security numbers, pay rates, and gross pay for a specific pay period. In addition, he wants a separate listing of the payroll data by department with the employees sorted by last name.

The Solution

Access has powerful database query capabilities that will help you to deliver the exact information that Mr. Traylor has requested. As you build the queries, you can create a calculated field in a query that will compute each employee's payroll data according to the specifications Mr. Traylor gave you. In addition, you can specify criteria that will return records that meet specific conditions from multiple tables. Figure 4-1 shows a report displaying a payroll for the month of July.

Figure 4-1

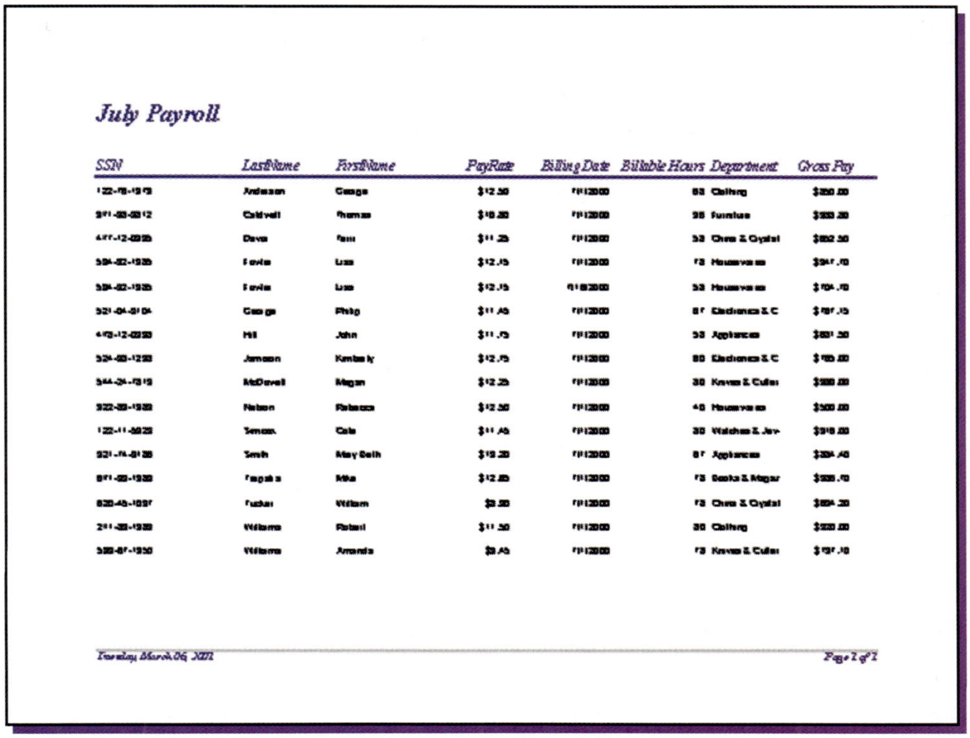

Creating Select Queries

An Access *query* is a database object that you create to view, change, and analyze data based on criteria that you set. Queries filter records in a table so that you can view records meeting the specific criteria. You can also use queries to view data from multiple database tables and to create forms and reports. Some important points about queries include the following:

- A query acts as a saved question you ask of your data, or as a subset of data from one or more tables.
- Data returned by a query remains part of the table in which it is stored rather than in the query.
- When you edit data in a query, you are actually editing the data stored in the table.
- Queries are dynamic objects that change as data in database tables changes.
- Queries will always display the most recent data in your database and enable you to filter or organize the data in different ways.

The most common type of query is a *select query*—a query that retrieves data from one or more tables and displays the results in a datasheet in which you can update the records.

Task 1:
To Create a Select Query Using the Query Wizard Based on One Table

1. Launch Access and open the *e-Selections Online.mdb* file.

2. Click the Queries button on the Objects bar and double-click the **Create query by using wizard** shortcut.

3. Select the **Table: Employees** from **Tables/Queries** drop-down list.

4. Click the **SSN** field name in the **Available Fields** list and then click the Move button to move the field to the **Selected Fields** list.

5. Move the **LastName**, **FirstName**, and **PayRate** fields to the **Selected Fields** list and click **Next**.

Figure 4-2

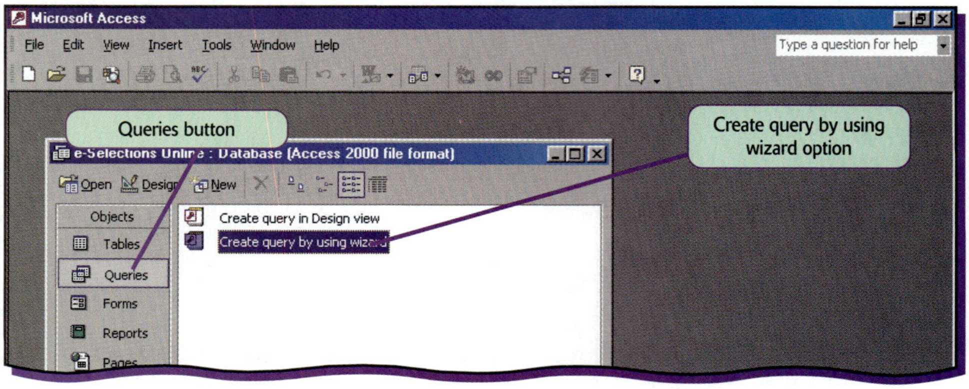

Other Ways

To display database queries:

- Choose **View** | **Database Objects** | **Queries**

Figure 4-3

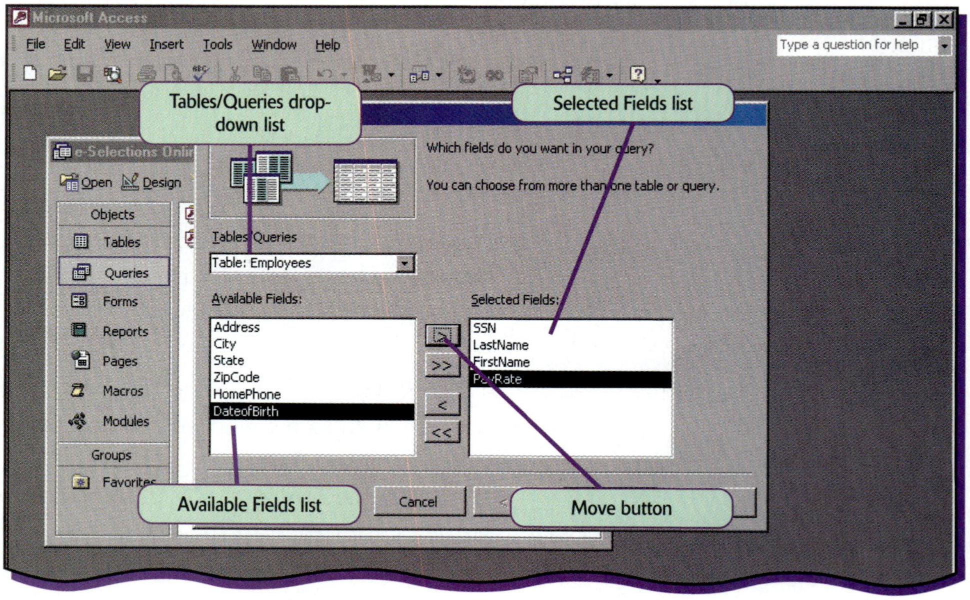

Tip

You can move fields from all database tables to the Selected Fields list as you create a query. Move the fields from one table that you want to include in the query, select another table from the Tables/Queries drop-down list, and move fields from the second table. Repeat this procedure to move fields from additional tables, if necessary.

6 Click **Next** to accept the default value for a detail query.

Tip Detail queries display all selected fields for each record. Summary queries report the total, average, minimum, or maximum values of all records for selected fields.

Figure 4-4

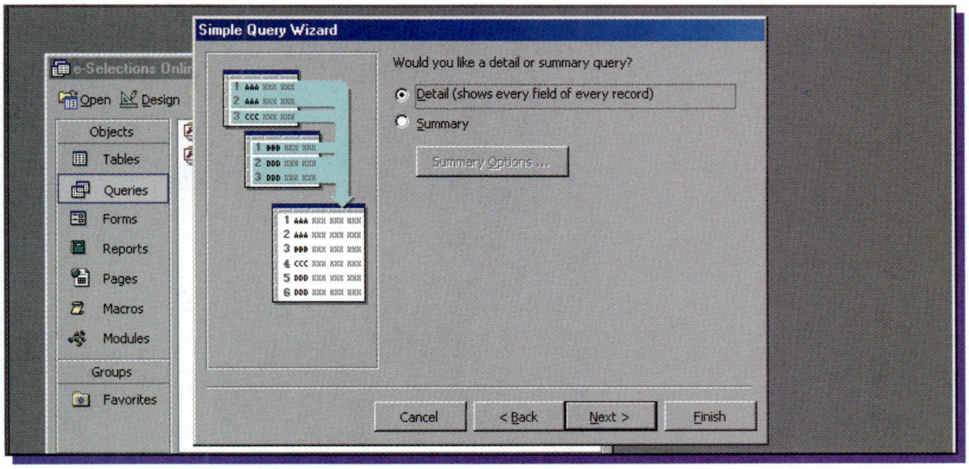

7 Change the query title to **Employee Pay Rates**.

8 Click **Finish** to open the query in Datasheet view.

Figure 4-5

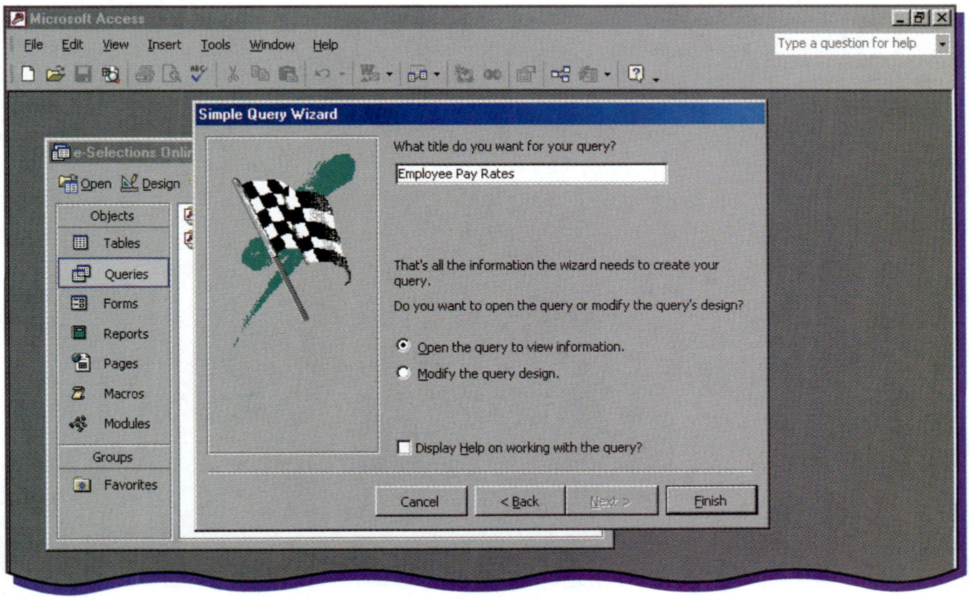

WEB TIP

Access creates a statement behind the scenes using SQL (Structured Query Language). After you create a query, you can view the SQL statement by using the SQL view. Search the World Wide Web to learn more about SQL.

9 Close the Query Datasheet window to return to the Database window.

Figure 4-6

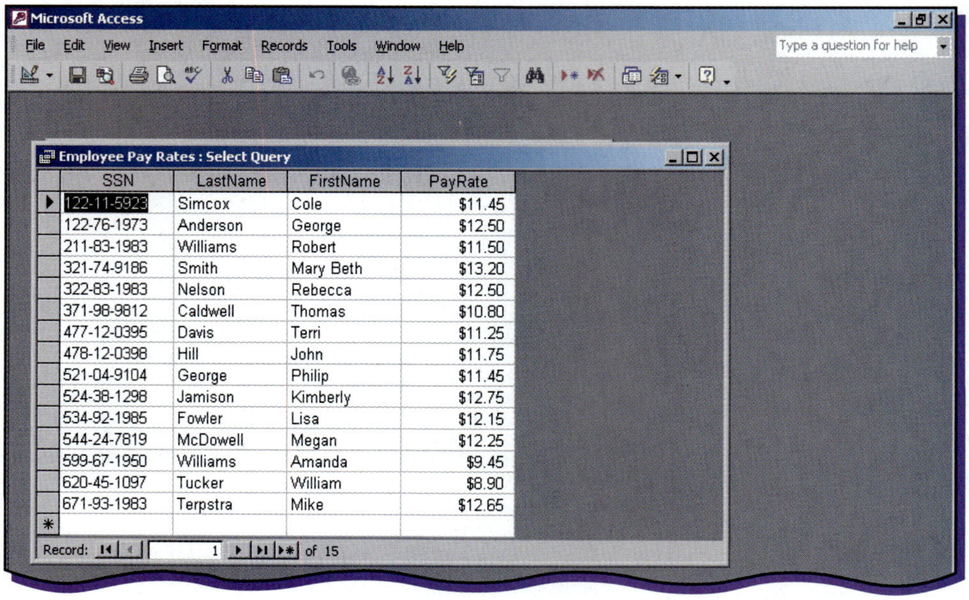

SSN	LastName	FirstName	PayRate
122-11-5923	Simcox	Cole	$11.45
122-76-1973	Anderson	George	$12.50
211-83-1983	Williams	Robert	$11.50
321-74-9186	Smith	Mary Beth	$13.20
322-83-1983	Nelson	Rebecca	$12.50
371-98-9812	Caldwell	Thomas	$10.80
477-12-0395	Davis	Terri	$11.25
478-12-0398	Hill	John	$11.75
521-04-9104	George	Philip	$11.45
524-38-1298	Jamison	Kimberly	$12.75
534-92-1985	Fowler	Lisa	$12.15
544-24-7819	McDowell	Megan	$12.25
599-67-1950	Williams	Amanda	$9.45
620-45-1097	Tucker	William	$8.90
671-93-1983	Terpstra	Mike	$12.65

Creating a Query Displaying Data from Multiple Tables

The query you created using the *Simple Query Wizard* pulls only the data from specific fields in a single table. When you completed the query, Access ran the query and displayed the information in a Datasheet view. When you have established relationships between database tables, you can display data from multiple tables in a single datasheet.

Task 2:
To Create a Query Based on Multiple Tables

1 Click the Queries button, if necessary, and then click the New button.

2 Select **Design View** in the New Query dialog box and click **OK**.

Other Ways To display the New Query dialog box:
- Choose **Insert | Query.**
- Click the New Object down arrow and select **Query.**

Figure 4-7

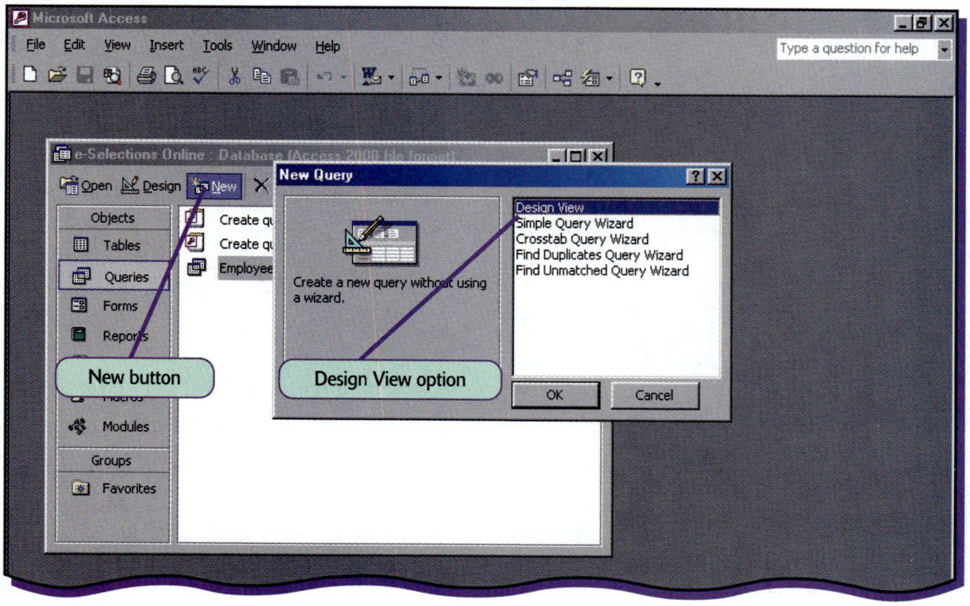

3 Press [Ctrl] and select all three tables displayed in the **Show Table** dialog box and then click **Add** to add the tables to the query.

4 Click **Close** to close the Show Table dialog box.

Tip Notice that relationship lines appear between tables added to the query grid.

Figure 4-8

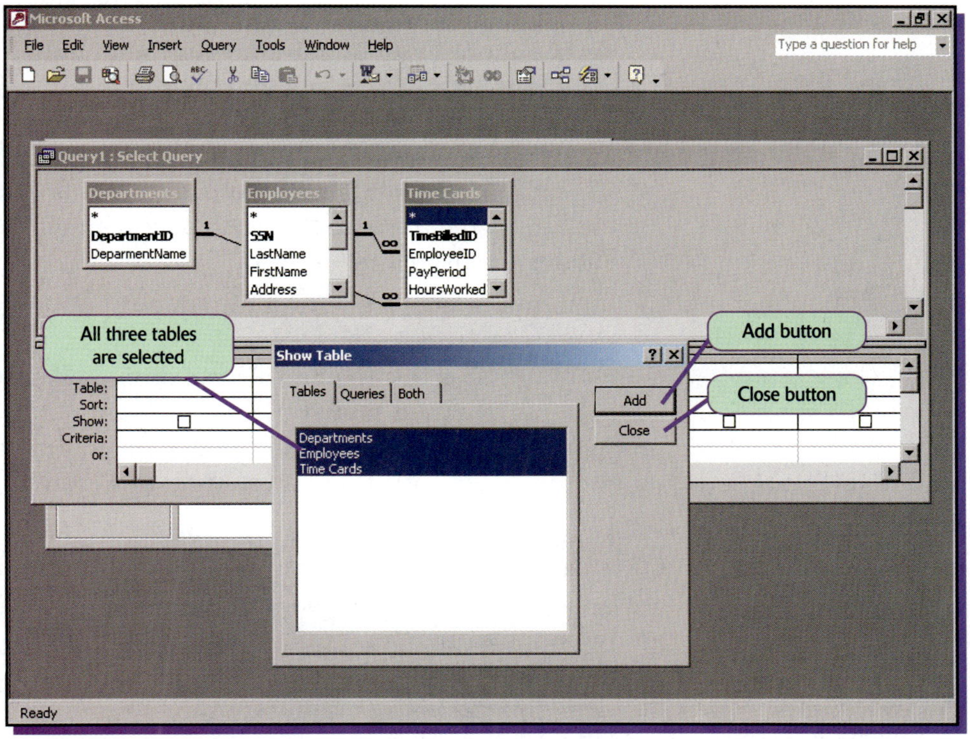

5 Click the Save button, type **Gross Pay** in the **Query Name** field, and click **OK**.

Other Ways To open the object Save As dialog box:

- Press [Ctrl] + [S].
- Choose **File | Save.**

Figure 4-9

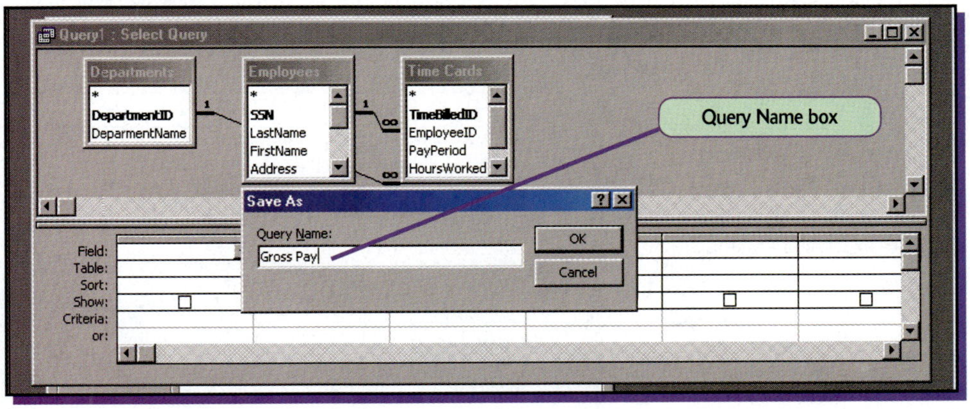

Adding Fields to a Select Query

Before a query datasheet will display any records, you must specify the fields you want to view. By selecting and adding the fields from the three tables in this database, you create what is sometimes referred to as a *select query*—a query containing selected fields you want to view. By creating a select query, you will be able to generate the payroll information that Mr. Traylor requested and display it in a single datasheet. Fields contained in a select query are added in the *query design grid*. Access provides three different methods for adding fields to a query grid:

- Dragging the field from the table field list to the appropriate column of the grid
- Selecting the field from a drop-down list of the grid column in which the field should appear
- Double-clicking the field in the table field list to place the field in the next available grid column

Task 3: Adding Fields to a Select Query

1 Open the **Gross Pay** query, if necessary; click the **SSN** field in the **Employees** table field list, and drag the field name to the first row/first column of the query design grid.

Troubleshooting

As you select fields from the field list, be sure you select the field from the list for the correct table.

Figure 4-10

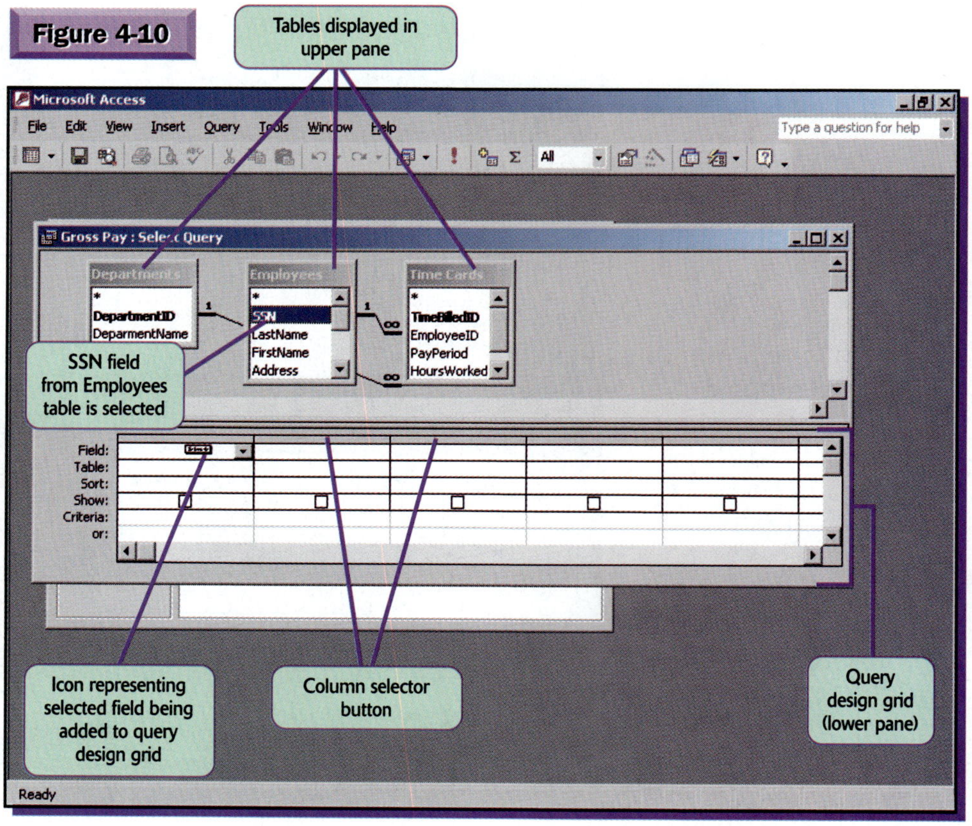

2 Release the left mouse button, press Tab to position the insertion point in the second column, click the down arrow, and select **Employees.LastName** to add the next field to the query design grid.

3 Double-click the **FirstName** field in the **Employees** table to add the field to the next available column in the query design grid

> **Tip** If you have trouble seeing all of the available fields, scroll through the table to display additional fields. You may also find that maximizing the window makes adding fields easier.

4 Add the fields shown in Table 4-1 to the query design grid using the method you prefer.

Figure 4-11

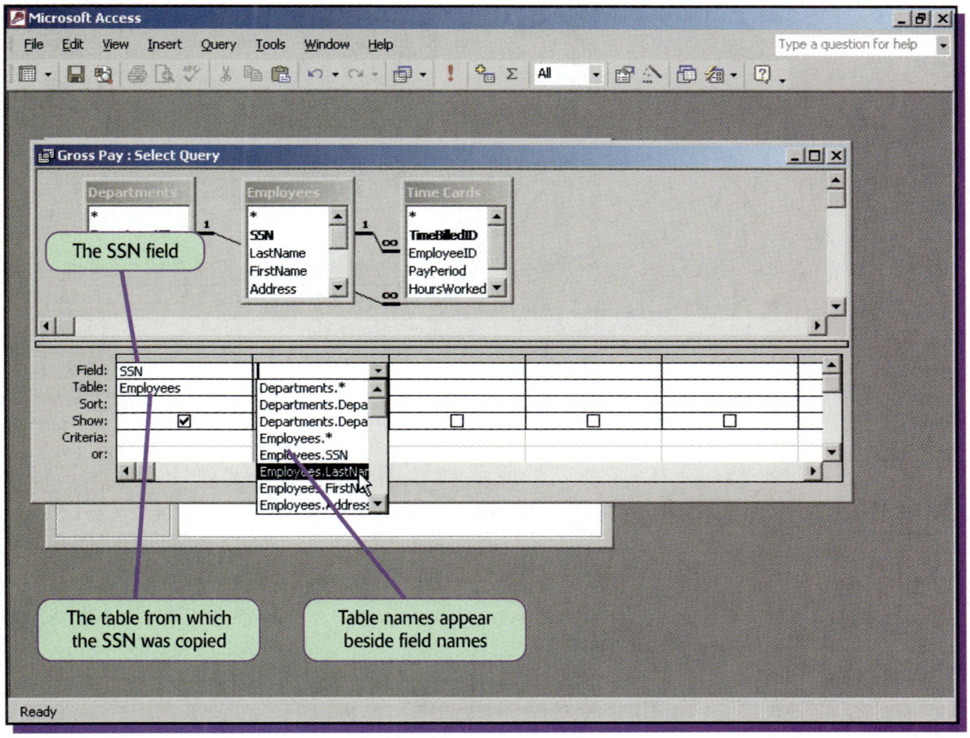

Table 4-1 Fields to Add

Field	Located in Table
PayRate	Employees
PayPeriod	Time Cards
HoursWorked	Time Cards
DepartmentID	Time Cards

> **Troubleshooting** To delete a field that you've added to the column by mistake, click the column selector button and press the Delete key. To move a column, select the column by clicking on the column selector button and drag the column to the new position. The other columns will automatically move to the right.

5 Click the Save button to save changes to the query.

Figure 4-12

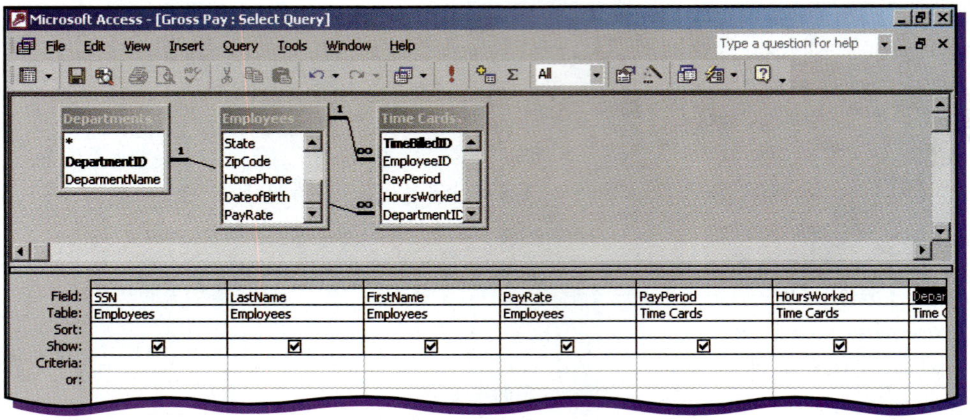

Running the Query and Viewing the Results

To see the results of your query design, you need to run the query. Only the fields you have added to the query design grid will appear in the query datasheet.

Task 4:

To View the Results of a Query

1 Open the **Gross Pay** query in Design view, if necessary, and click the Run button on the Query Design toolbar.

Other Ways To run a query:

- Choose **Query | Run**.

Figure 4-13

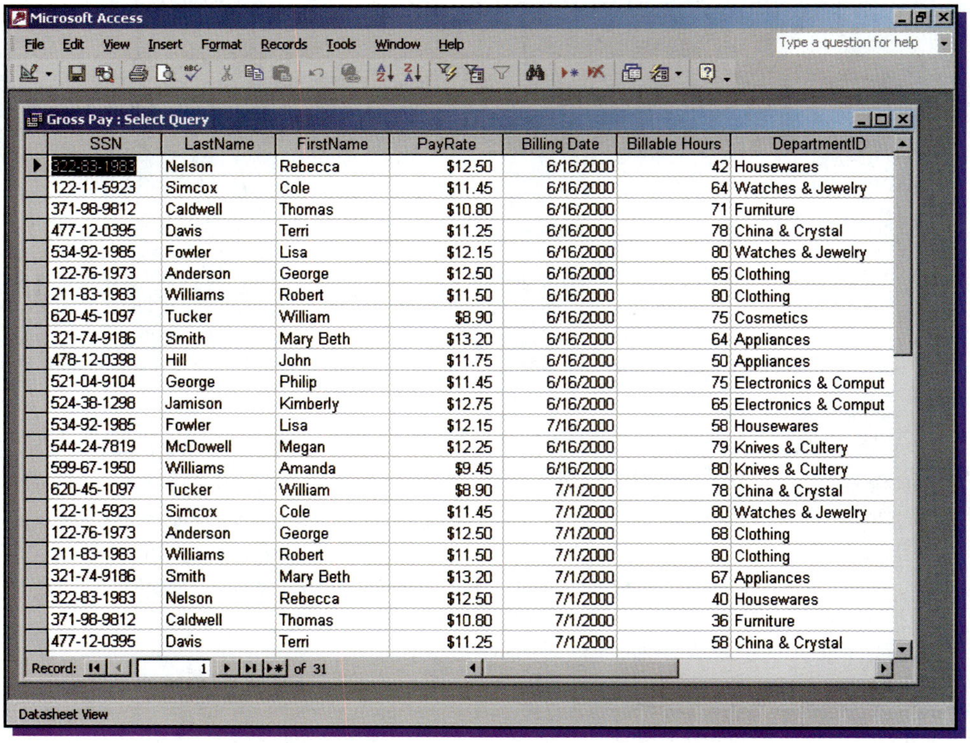

SSN	LastName	FirstName	PayRate	Billing Date	Billable Hours	DepartmentID
322-83-1983	Nelson	Rebecca	$12.50	6/16/2000	42	Housewares
122-11-5923	Simcox	Cole	$11.45	6/16/2000	64	Watches & Jewelry
371-98-9812	Caldwell	Thomas	$10.80	6/16/2000	71	Furniture
477-12-0395	Davis	Terri	$11.25	6/16/2000	78	China & Crystal
534-92-1985	Fowler	Lisa	$12.15	6/16/2000	80	Watches & Jewelry
122-76-1973	Anderson	George	$12.50	6/16/2000	65	Clothing
211-83-1983	Williams	Robert	$11.50	6/16/2000	80	Clothing
620-45-1097	Tucker	William	$8.90	6/16/2000	75	Cosmetics
321-74-9186	Smith	Mary Beth	$13.20	6/16/2000	64	Appliances
478-12-0398	Hill	John	$11.75	6/16/2000	50	Appliances
521-04-9104	George	Philip	$11.45	6/16/2000	75	Electronics & Comput
524-38-1298	Jamison	Kimberly	$12.75	6/16/2000	65	Electronics & Comput
534-92-1985	Fowler	Lisa	$12.15	7/16/2000	58	Housewares
544-24-7819	McDowell	Megan	$12.25	6/16/2000	79	Knives & Cultery
599-67-1950	Williams	Amanda	$9.45	6/16/2000	80	Knives & Cultery
620-45-1097	Tucker	William	$8.90	7/1/2000	78	China & Crystal
122-11-5923	Simcox	Cole	$11.45	7/1/2000	80	Watches & Jewelry
122-76-1973	Anderson	George	$12.50	7/1/2000	68	Clothing
211-83-1983	Williams	Robert	$11.50	7/1/2000	80	Clothing
321-74-9186	Smith	Mary Beth	$13.20	7/1/2000	67	Appliances
322-83-1983	Nelson	Rebecca	$12.50	7/1/2000	40	Housewares
371-98-9812	Caldwell	Thomas	$10.80	7/1/2000	36	Furniture
477-12-0395	Davis	Terri	$11.25	7/1/2000	58	China & Crystal

2 Point to the right edge of the **PayRate** column heading until the mouse pointer appears as a two-headed arrow and drag the pointer to size the column as shown in Figure 4-14.

3 Resize the other fields as shown in Figure 4-14.

4 Click the Save button to save the changes in the datasheet layout.

Figure 4-14

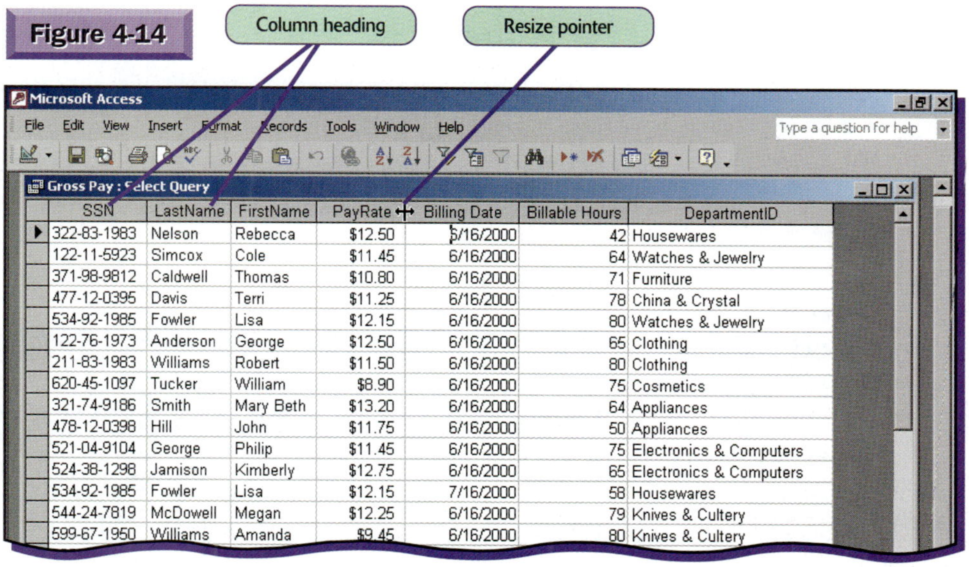

SSN	LastName	FirstName	PayRate	Billing Date	Billable Hours	DepartmentID
322-83-1983	Nelson	Rebecca	$12.50	6/16/2000	42	Housewares
122-11-5923	Simcox	Cole	$11.45	6/16/2000	64	Watches & Jewelry
371-98-9812	Caldwell	Thomas	$10.80	6/16/2000	71	Furniture
477-12-0395	Davis	Terri	$11.25	6/16/2000	78	China & Crystal
534-92-1985	Fowler	Lisa	$12.15	6/16/2000	80	Watches & Jewelry
122-76-1973	Anderson	George	$12.50	6/16/2000	65	Clothing
211-83-1983	Williams	Robert	$11.50	6/16/2000	80	Clothing
620-45-1097	Tucker	William	$8.90	6/16/2000	75	Cosmetics
321-74-9186	Smith	Mary Beth	$13.20	6/16/2000	64	Appliances
478-12-0398	Hill	John	$11.75	6/16/2000	50	Appliances
521-04-9104	George	Philip	$11.45	6/16/2000	75	Electronics & Computers
524-38-1298	Jamison	Kimberly	$12.75	6/16/2000	65	Electronics & Computers
534-92-1985	Fowler	Lisa	$12.15	7/16/2000	58	Housewares
544-24-7819	McDowell	Megan	$12.25	6/16/2000	79	Knives & Cultery
599-67-1950	Williams	Amanda	$9.45	6/16/2000	80	Knives & Cultery

CHECK POINT

The fields that are displayed in the datasheet are the ones that contain a check mark in the query design grid **Show** check box. To include a field in the grid but omit it from the datasheet, clear the **Show** check mark.

WEB TIP

Ever wondered how sportscasters could keep so much statistical information in their heads? You'll be happy to know that they use databases and queries to provide on-the-spot data while they are on the air. You'll find a number of different databases on the Web that hold sports statistics. See what you can learn about your favorite sports figure by searching the Web.

Adding a Calculated Field to the Query

None of the tables in the database contains a field that holds gross pay for each employee. Fields do appear, however, that you can use to calculate the gross pay. Access contains tools that enable you to perform calculations using multiple fields and to add the field containing the calculation as a *calculated field* to the query design grid. Calculated fields traditionally hold a combination of the following items to form an *expression* that produces a result:

- Object identifiers—tables, fields, etc.
- Arithmetic or relational operators—+, -, *, /, >, =, etc.
- Values—numbers

Access includes an *Expression Builder* that you can use to create an expression and displays the results of expressions in the query datasheet when you run the query.

CHECK POINT

Although a query datasheet displays the results of calculated fields, it is important to modify the expression to achieve the desired results of a calculated field rather than changing the contents of the calculated field.

Task 5:

To Create a Calculated Field to Compute Gross Pay

1 Click the Design View button for the **Gross Pay** query on the Query Datasheet toolbar to switch to Query Design view and click the horizontal scroll bar in the query design grid to display additional columns.

2 Right-click the Field row of the first available column to display the shortcut menu and select **Build.**

Figure 4-15

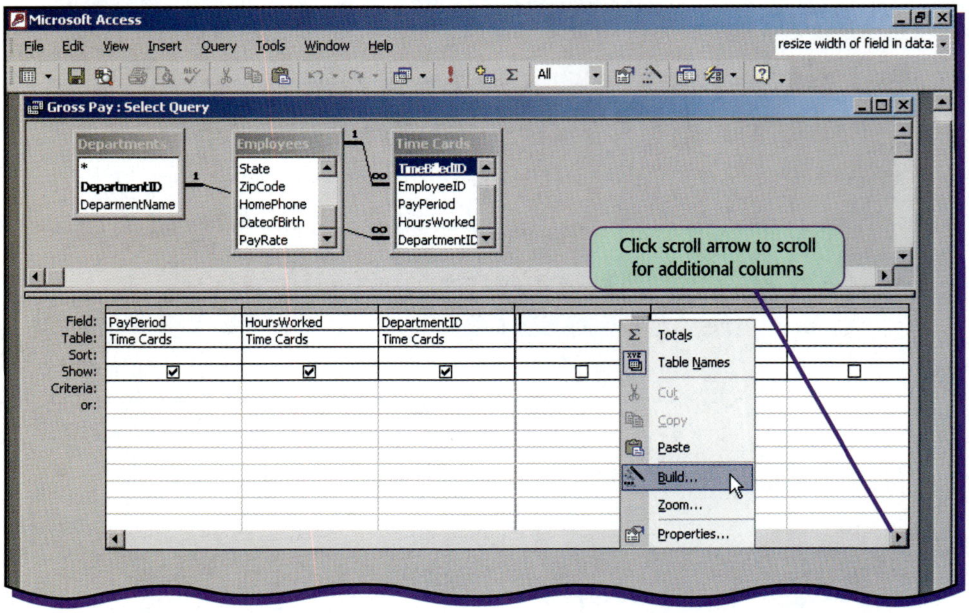

3 Click the Equal operator button to add an equal sign to the expression box.

4 Select the **Gross Pay** folder in the left bottom pane of the Expression Builder to display a list of fields in the Gross Pay query, select the **PayRate** field name, and click the **Paste** operator button.

5 Click the Multiplication operator button, click the **HoursWorked** field, and click **Paste** to complete the expression.

6 Click **OK** and click the Save button to save changes to the query.

Figure 4-16

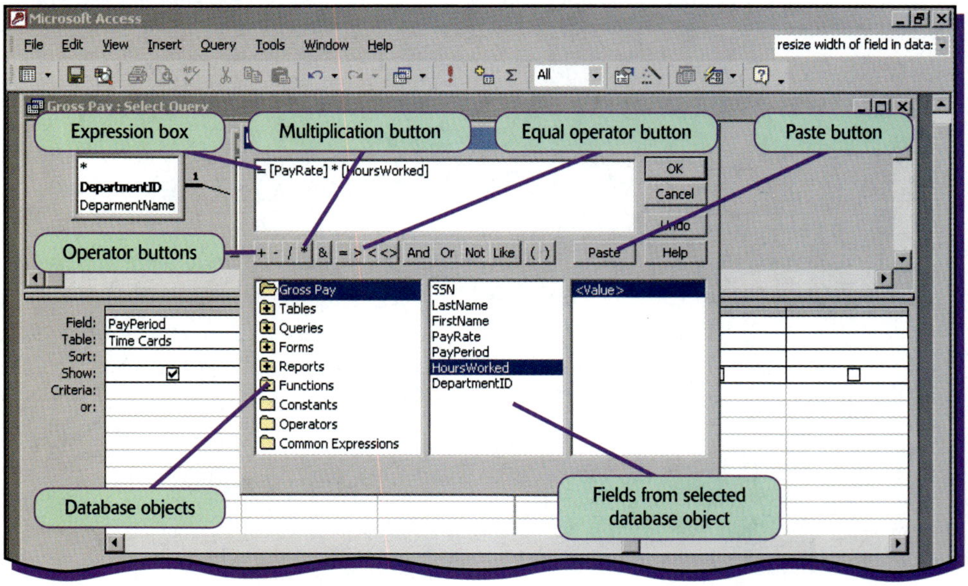

Tip You can also type an asterisk (*) to add the operator to the expression.

Troubleshooting The expression will appear truncated, since it is too wide to appear in the current column width. Make sure that the Show check box is selected so that the calculated field will be displayed in the datasheet when you run the query.

Tip Double-clicking the table's folder accesses other table fields so that you can use them in an expression.

Running and Modifying Expressions

Once you create a calculated field, you can format the field so that it will display properly. In this task, you will modify the expression so that the proper field name will be displayed, and you will format the expression with a currency format.

Task 6:

To Run a Query Containing a Calculated Field and Modify Its Format

1 Click the Run button on the Query Design toolbar and click the horizontal scroll bar to display the calculated field.

Tip When you run a query, scroll bars appear at the bottom of the datasheet window when the datasheet contains more columns than will fit in the window. Different monitor sizes and resolution settings display different numbers of columns.

Figure 4-17

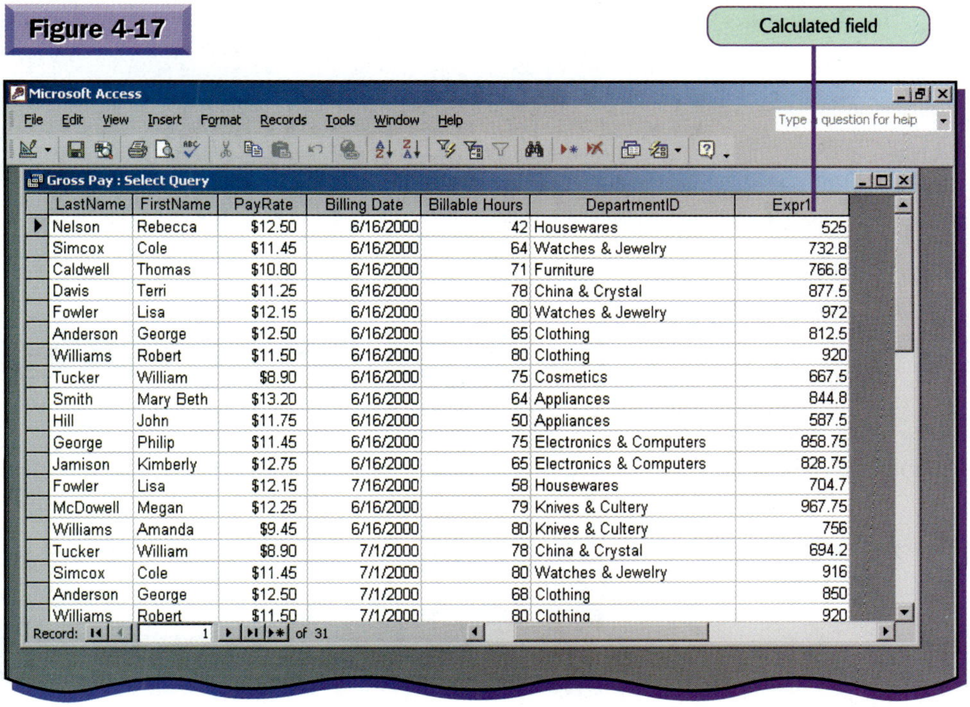

LastName	FirstName	PayRate	Billing Date	Billable Hours	DepartmentID	Expr1
Nelson	Rebecca	$12.50	6/16/2000	42	Housewares	525
Simcox	Cole	$11.45	6/16/2000	64	Watches & Jewelry	732.8
Caldwell	Thomas	$10.80	6/16/2000	71	Furniture	766.8
Davis	Terri	$11.25	6/16/2000	78	China & Crystal	877.5
Fowler	Lisa	$12.15	6/16/2000	80	Watches & Jewelry	972
Anderson	George	$12.50	6/16/2000	65	Clothing	812.5
Williams	Robert	$11.50	6/16/2000	80	Clothing	920
Tucker	William	$8.90	6/16/2000	75	Cosmetics	667.5
Smith	Mary Beth	$13.20	6/16/2000	64	Appliances	844.8
Hill	John	$11.75	6/16/2000	50	Appliances	587.5
George	Philip	$11.45	6/16/2000	75	Electronics & Computers	858.75
Jamison	Kimberly	$12.75	6/16/2000	65	Electronics & Computers	828.75
Fowler	Lisa	$12.15	7/16/2000	58	Housewares	704.7
McDowell	Megan	$12.25	6/16/2000	79	Knives & Cultery	967.75
Williams	Amanda	$9.45	6/16/2000	80	Knives & Cultery	756
Tucker	William	$8.90	7/1/2000	78	China & Crystal	694.2
Simcox	Cole	$11.45	7/1/2000	80	Watches & Jewelry	916
Anderson	George	$12.50	7/1/2000	68	Clothing	850
Williams	Robert	$11.50	7/1/2000	80	Clothing	920

2 Click the Design button on the Query Datasheet toolbar to switch to Design view and right-click the **Expr1** field.

3 Select **Zoom** from the shortcut menu to open the Zoom dialog box.

Tip Although it is not necessary to use the Zoom feature, the Zoom feature will allow you to modify your expression much more easily.

Figure 4-18

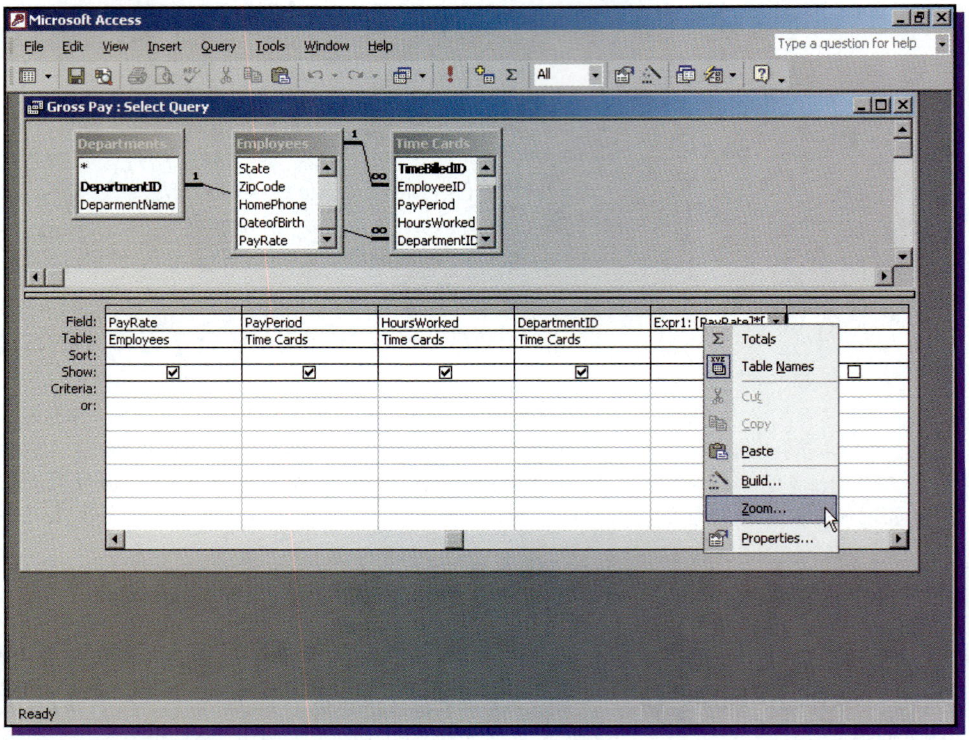

4 Select the text *Expr1*, type **GrossPay**.

Troubleshooting Be careful to leave the colon in the expression.

5 Click OK.

Figure 4-19

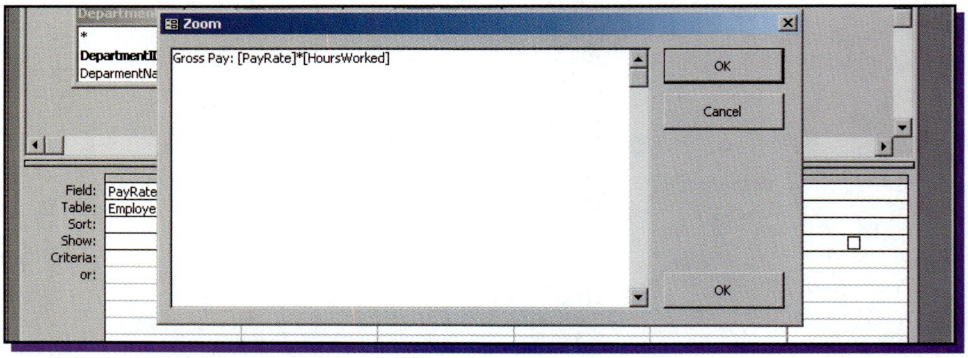

6 Click the Properties button and type **Gross Pay** in the **Caption** row.

Other Ways

To display the Properties dialog box:

- Right-click on the field name in the query grid and select **Properties**.

7 Click the **Format** row and then click the down arrow and select **Currency**.

8 Close the **Properties** window, run the query, and adjust the borders of each column to display the datasheet as shown in Figure 4-21.

9 Click the Save button to save your changes.

Figure 4-20

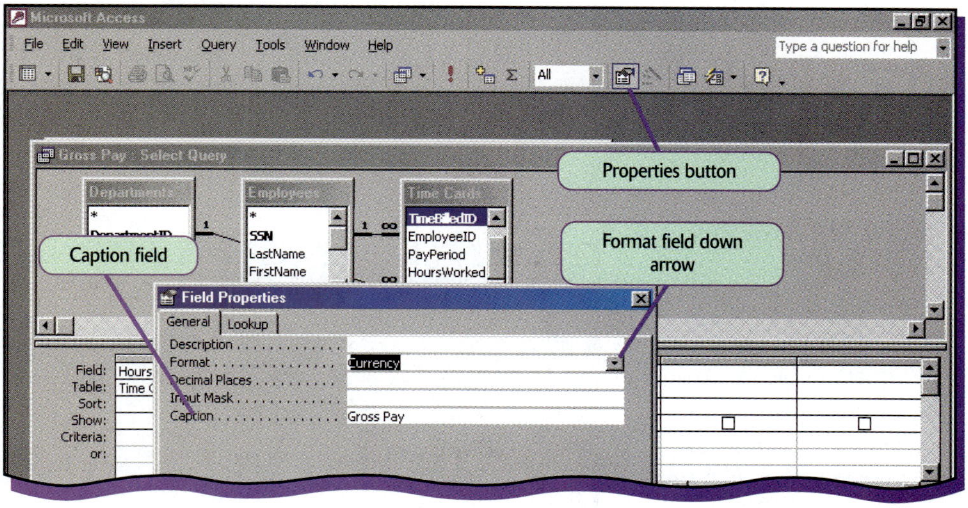

Figure 4-21

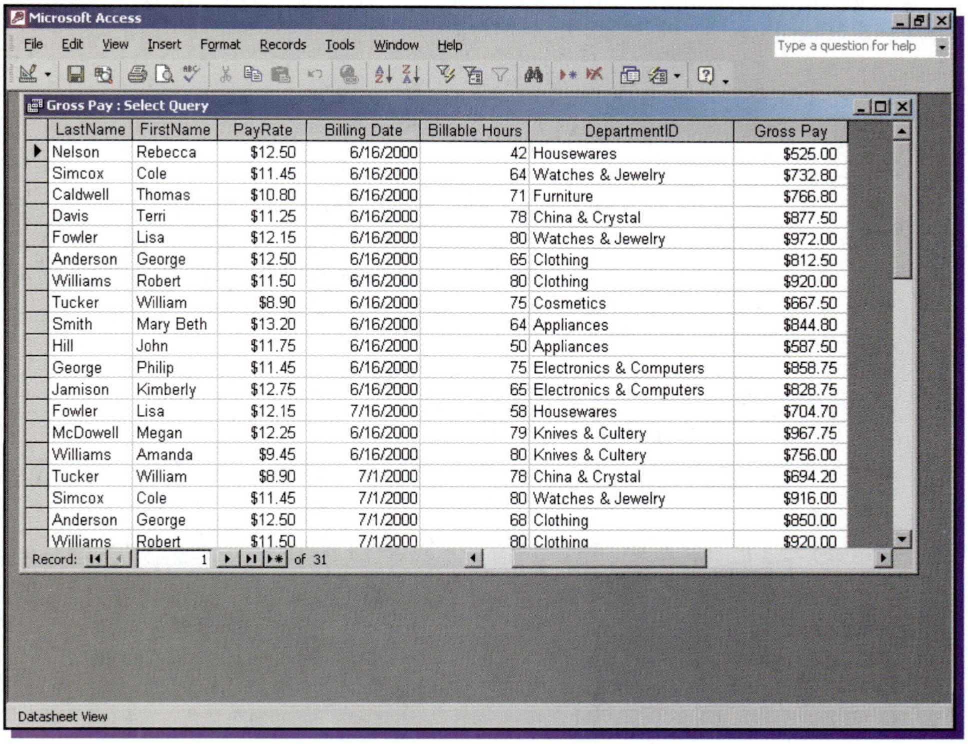

LastName	FirstName	PayRate	Billing Date	Billable Hours	DepartmentID	Gross Pay
Nelson	Rebecca	$12.50	6/16/2000	42	Housewares	$525.00
Simcox	Cole	$11.45	6/16/2000	64	Watches & Jewelry	$732.80
Caldwell	Thomas	$10.80	6/16/2000	71	Furniture	$766.80
Davis	Terri	$11.25	6/16/2000	78	China & Crystal	$877.50
Fowler	Lisa	$12.15	6/16/2000	80	Watches & Jewelry	$972.00
Anderson	George	$12.50	6/16/2000	65	Clothing	$812.50
Williams	Robert	$11.50	6/16/2000	80	Clothing	$920.00
Tucker	William	$8.90	6/16/2000	75	Cosmetics	$667.50
Smith	Mary Beth	$13.20	6/16/2000	64	Appliances	$844.80
Hill	John	$11.75	6/16/2000	50	Appliances	$587.50
George	Philip	$11.45	6/16/2000	75	Electronics & Computers	$858.75
Jamison	Kimberly	$12.75	6/16/2000	65	Electronics & Computers	$828.75
Fowler	Lisa	$12.15	7/16/2000	58	Housewares	$704.70
McDowell	Megan	$12.25	6/16/2000	79	Knives & Cultery	$967.75
Williams	Amanda	$9.45	6/16/2000	80	Knives & Cultery	$756.00
Tucker	William	$8.90	7/1/2000	78	China & Crystal	$694.20
Simcox	Cole	$11.45	7/1/2000	80	Watches & Jewelry	$916.00
Anderson	George	$12.50	7/1/2000	68	Clothing	$850.00
Williams	Robert	$11.50	7/1/2000	80	Clothing	$920.00

CHECK POINT

Fields that are based on expressions can be created in two database objects only: queries and reports. As a result, it is a good idea to include calculated fields in your initial database design for queries and reports, mark them as calculated fields, and identify the table fields you will use to create the calculations. That way you'll be sure to include all the fields you need as you build the database tables.

Defining the Sort Order for a Query

Sorting query results enables you to arrange the information in the query datasheet before printing the report so that you can locate information more efficiently. Access makes sorting the results of a query to meet specific conditions easy.

Task 7:

To Set a Query Sort Order

1 Display the **Gross Pay** query in Query Design view, position the insertion point in the **LastName** column **Sort** row, and click the down arrow.

Troubleshooting The down arrow appears in the field only when the row for the appropriate field is active.

Figure 4-22

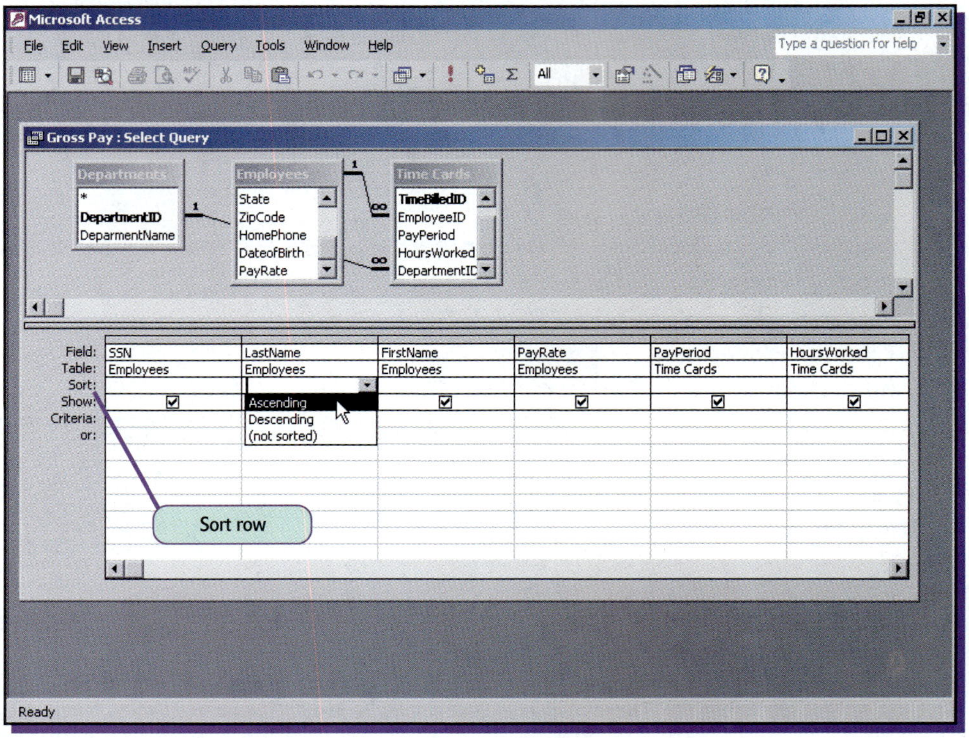

2 Select **Ascending** and click the Run button to run the query.

Tip Sorting text fields in ascending order arranges the records alphabetically. Sorting numeric fields in ascending order sorts fields from lowest to highest.

3 Click the Save button.

Figure 4-23

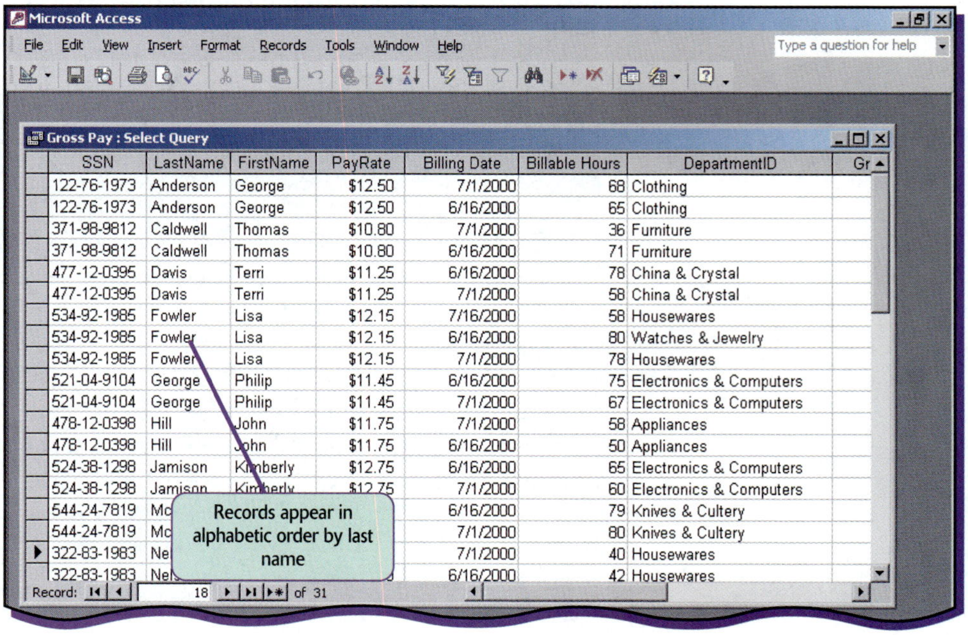

Specifying Query Conditions

Queries are powerful not only because they return records with data from fields in multiple tables but also because you can retrieve specific records based on criteria you set. You can use query *conditions*—specifications that must be met for Access to select a record—to create the list of employees sorted by department and last name for Mr. Traylor. In Access, you set conditions using the criteria field in the query design grid. Access enables you to specify simple criteria, criteria using wildcards, or multiple criteria using AND and OR conditions.

Task 8:
To Set Query Criteria

1. Display the **Gross Pay** query in Query Design view.

2. Click the **Criteria** row in the **DepartmentID** column and type 1 to set the criteria to locate records for employees in the Clothing Department.

Figure 4-24

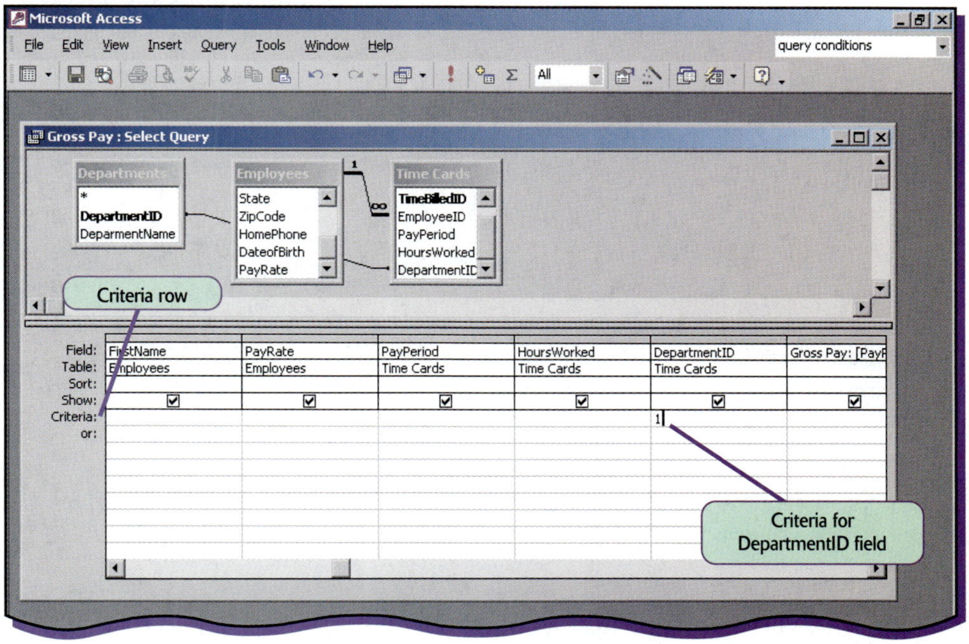

CHECK POINT

Remember, the DepartmentID field is a lookup field that uses a numeric value to locate a department name. As a result, typing the numeric value for the Clothing Department will display the department name in the datasheet. However, Access actually looks up the DepartmentID number (primary key) in the Departments table to determine the department name to display in the Time Cards table.

3. Run the query.

Figure 4-25

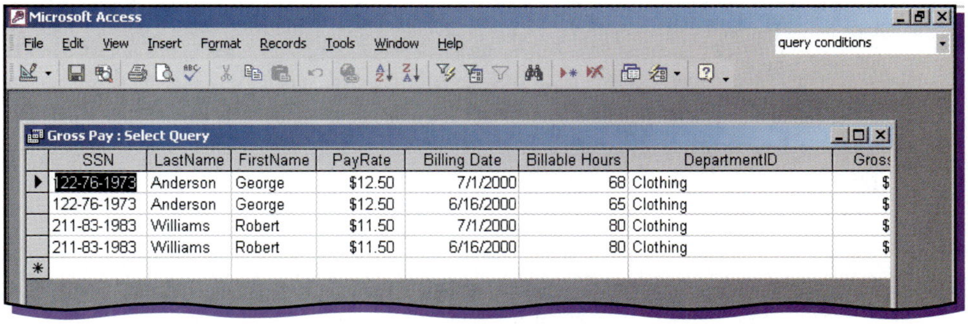

Using Wildcards to Specify Conditions

Wildcards—symbols designed to represent any character or group of characters—make it possible to locate records that contain specific text or values but may also contain additional text or numeric characters. Suppose, for example, you wanted to select records for all employees whose last name begins with *S*. You could use a wildcard in the criteria. Access recognizes two wildcards:

- The asterisk (*) is used to represent any number of characters at the position in which it is placed. For example, typing Like S* in the **LastName** field will return Cole **S***imcox* and Mary Beth **S***mith*.
- The question mark (?) is used to represent a single character at the position of the mark. For example, typing Like R?B* in the **FirstName** field will return **R***o***b***ert* Williams and **R***e***b***ecca* Nelson.

Task 9: To Use Wildcards in Criteria

1. Display the **Gross Pay** query in Query Design view and delete the *1* in the **DepartmentID** column **Criteria** row.

2. Position the insertion point in the **LastName** column **Criteria** row and type Like S*.

Tip If you type the S* without typing the word Like, Access adds the word Like for you.

Figure 4-26

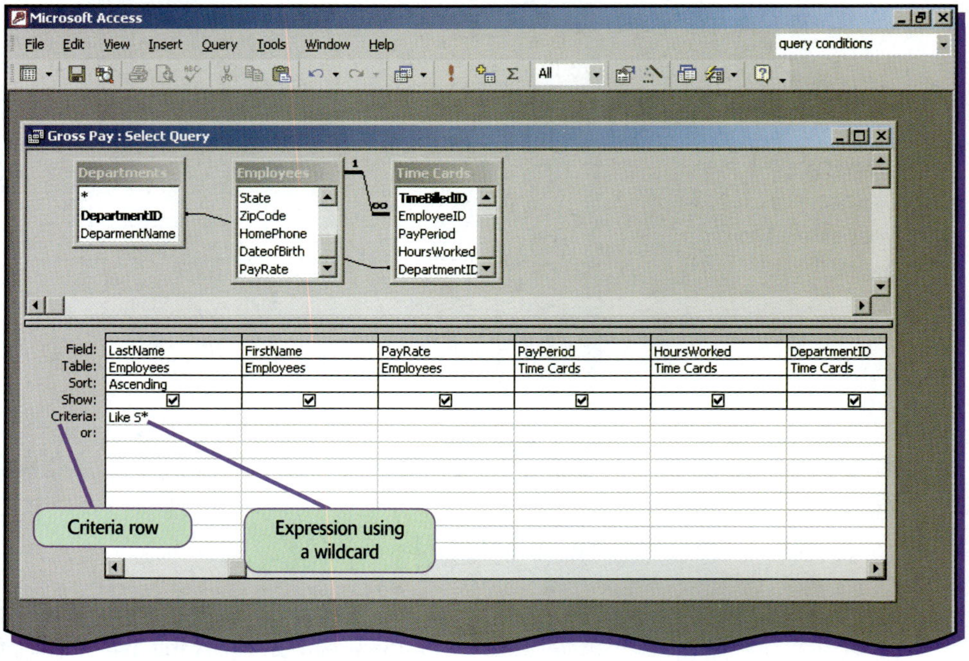

3 Run the query.

> **Tip** The position of criteria you add to different columns in the query grid control whether Access considers the criteria AND or OR criteria. Be careful as you add the criteria to place it in the correct grid row.

Figure 4-27

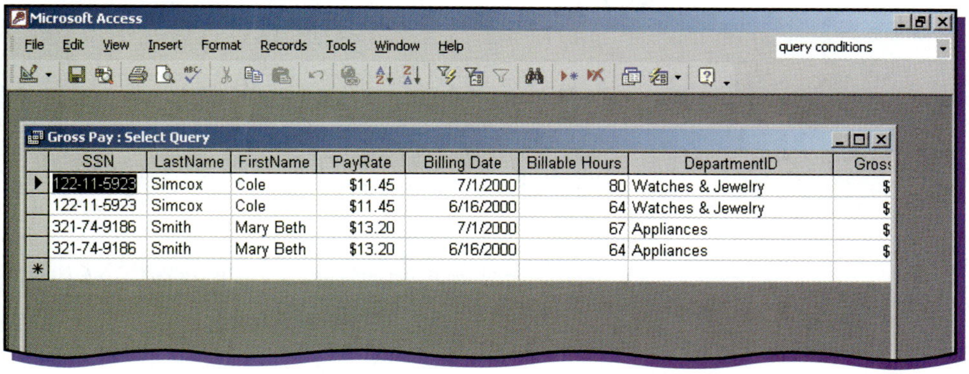

Specifying AND and OR Conditions

In some cases, you will need to select records that meet multiple criteria as well as criteria in multiple fields. Access provides two basic multiple criteria conditions that you can use to select records based on multiple fields:

- The *AND condition* is used to select records meeting all criteria set in all query design grid fields. Use the AND condition, for example, to list employees who work in the Clothing Department and earn $12 or more per hour.
- The *OR condition* is used to select records meeting one or another criteria set in the query design grid fields. For example, you would use the OR condition to create a list of employees who work in either the Clothing or Electronics & Computers departments.

Task 10:
To Set AND and OR Conditions

1 Display the **Gross Pay** query in Query Design view and clear the **Criteria** row for all fields, if necessary.

2 Position the insertion point in the **PayRate** column **Criteria** row and type >=12.

3 Move to the **DepartmentID** column **Criteria** row and type 4.

Figure 4-28

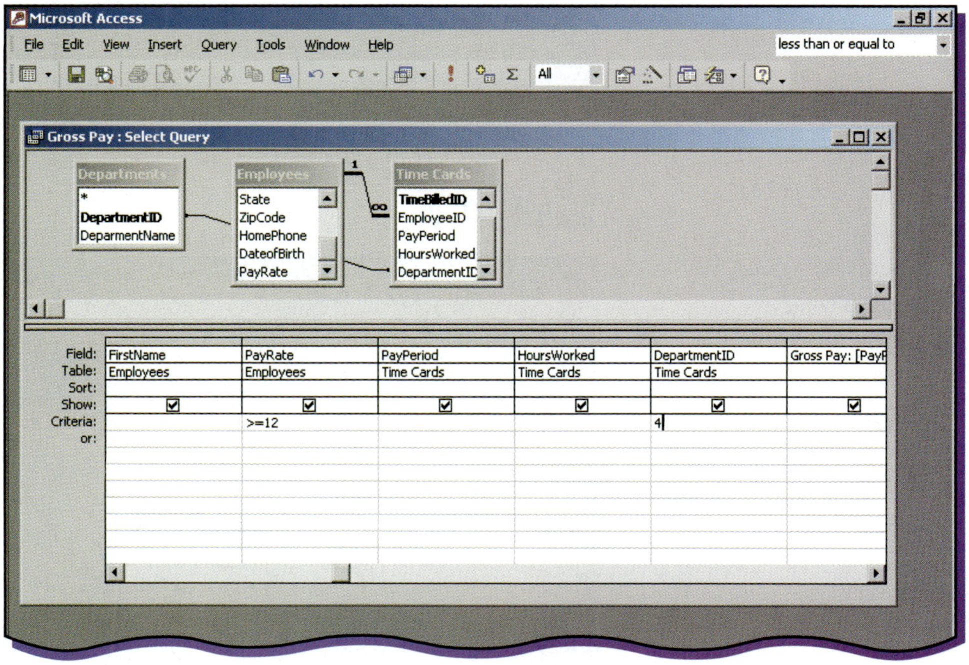

4 Run the query.

> **Tip** Access finds employees who work in department 4 AND who earn more than $12 and hour.

Figure 4-29

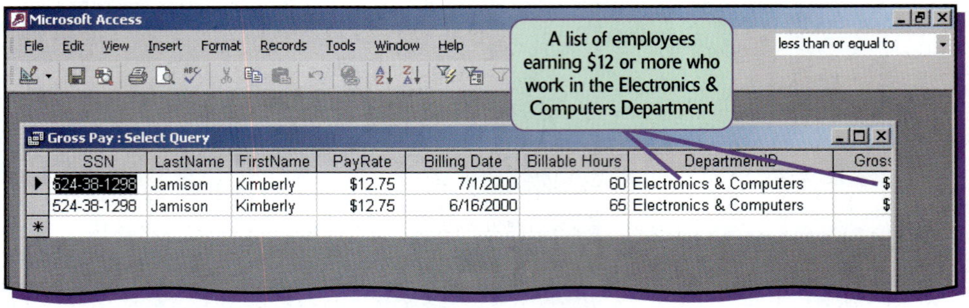

5 Return to the Query Design view and delete the criteria in the **PayRate** column.

6 Position the insertion point in the **DepartmentID** column *or* row and type 1.

> **Tip** Because you're using the *or* row for this query, you are setting an OR condition.

Figure 4-30

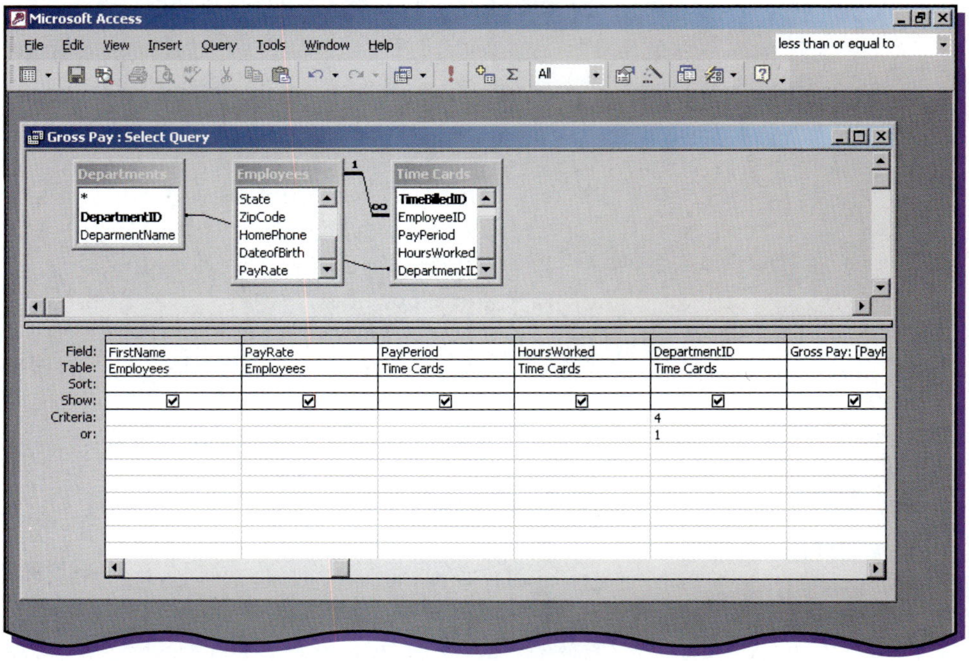

7 Run the query.

8 Close the query without saving it.

Figure 4-31

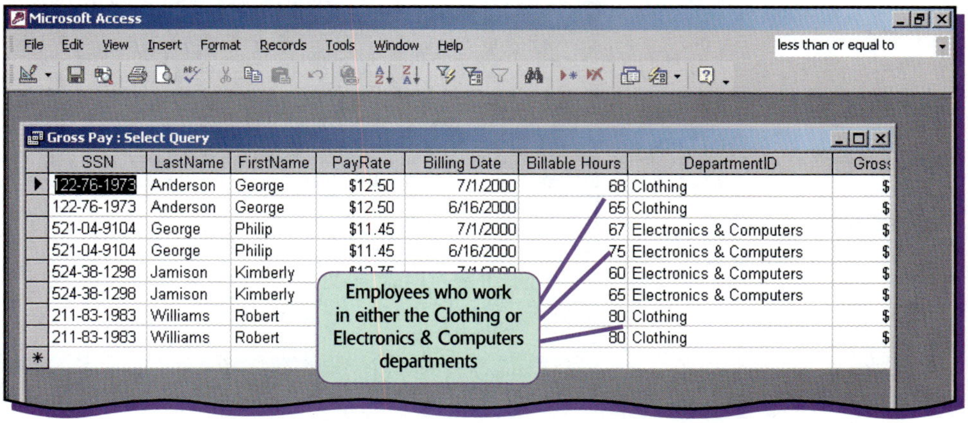

Using a Function in an Expression

Now that you have saved the query using a different file name, you have a new query that you can edit to create powerful expressions using a *function*—a predefined formula or expression that performs calculations using specific values in a specific order. By building a date function called *Month*, you can create the last list requested by Mr. Traylor.

Task 11: To Create a Query Expression Using a Function

1 Right-click the **Gross Pay** query in the database window, select **Save As**, type **July Payroll**, and click **OK**.

Figure 4-32

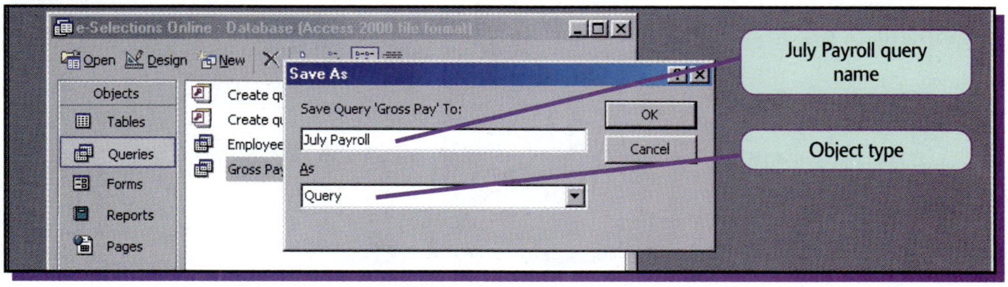

2 Select the **July Payroll** query and click the Design button.

3 Position the insertion point in the **PayPeriod** column **Criteria** row and type **Month([PayPeriod])=7**.

4 Run the query.

5 Click the Save button to save the changes in this query and close the query.

Figure 4-33

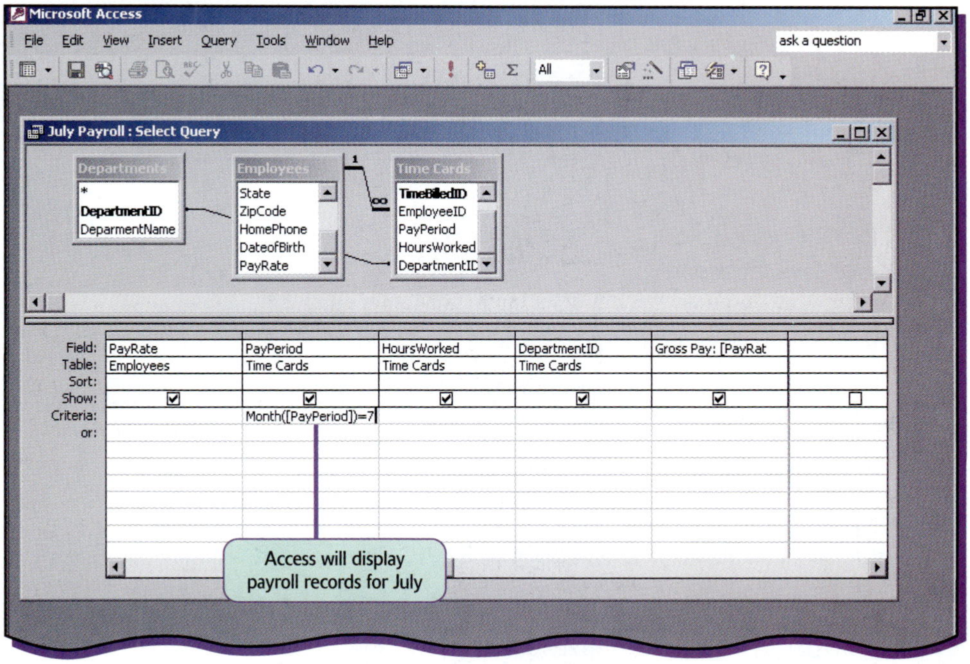

Creating an AutoReport Based on a Query

Once you have a query that sorts and selects the records you need, you can use the query to create reports and forms. You can use the July Payroll query to create an AutoReport for Mr. Traylor.

Task 12:

To Create an AutoReport from a Query

1 Display the Database window, click the Reports button, and click the New button to open the **New Report** dialog box.

2 Select **AutoReport: Tabular**, click the **Choose the table or query where the object's data comes from** down arrow, and select **July Payroll**.

3 Click **OK**.

Figure 4-34

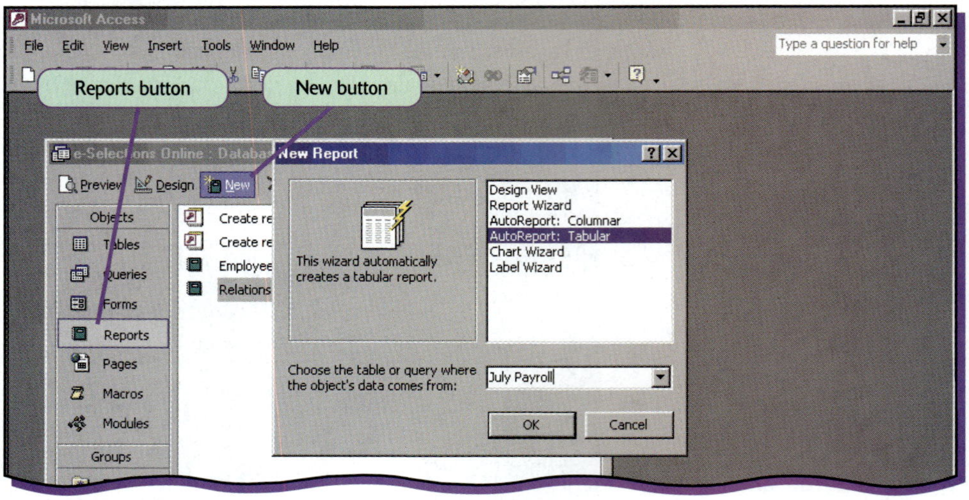

Other Ways

To create a new AutoReport from a query:

- Select the query in the Database window and choose **Insert | AutoReport**.
- Select the query in the Database window, click the New Object down arrow, and select **AutoReport**.

The AutoReport that appears using these techniques will be formatted without the tabular layout.

4 Close the report, click **Yes** to save the report, and click **OK** to accept the default name.

5 Close the *e-Selections Online* database.

Tip All query fields with checked Show boxes appear in the AutoReport. If you clear the Show box for a field in the query grid, it will not appear in the AutoReport.

Figure 4-35

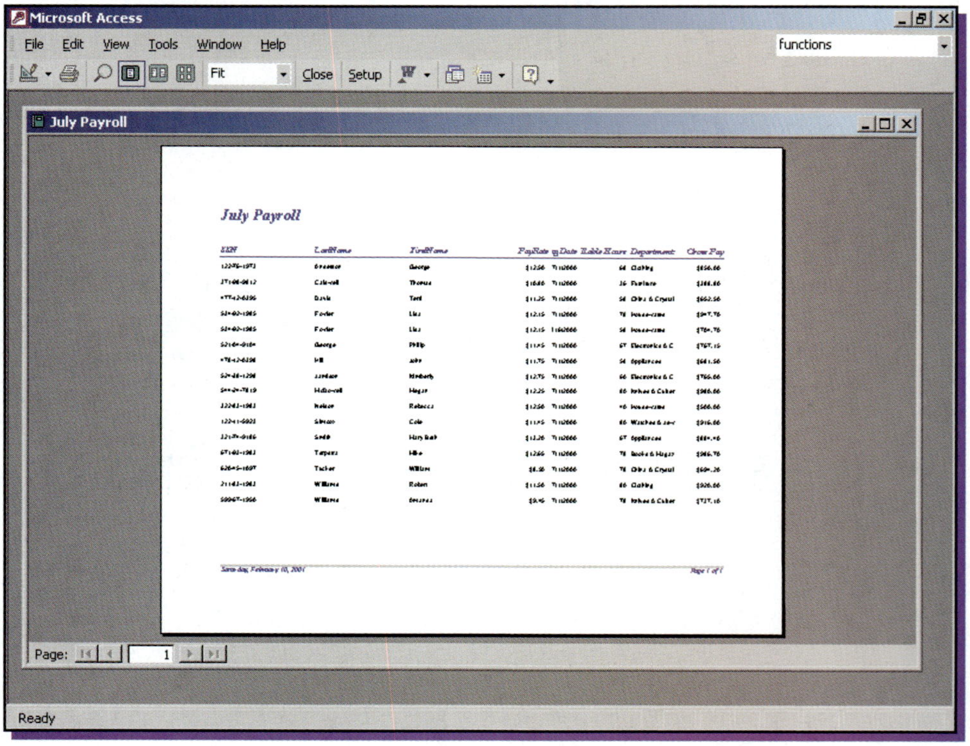

SUMMARY AND EXERCISES

SUMMARY

- A query is a database object that you create to view, change, and analyze your data in different ways.
- A select query lets you select specific records according to criteria you specify.
- Queries are often used as the record source for forms and reports.
- A query allows you to work with fields from multiple tables.
- Query results are displayed in a datasheet.
- Use the Expression Builder to create a calculated field.
- You can sort records by any field(s).
- You can retrieve specific records matching criteria by entering the criteria in the query design grid.
- Wildcards enable you to create more powerful criteria expressions.
- Records must meet *all* criteria expressions in an AND condition.
- Records can meet *any* of the criteria expression in an OR condition.

KEY TERMS & SKILLS

KEY TERMS

AND condition (p. 4-21)
calculated field (p. 4-13)
conditions (p. 4-19)
expression (p. 4-23)
Expression Builder (p. 4-13)
function (p. 4-23)
OR condition (p. 4-19)
query (p. 4-5)
query design grid (p. 4-10)
select query (p. 4-10)
Simple Query Wizard (p. 4-8)
wildcards (p. 4-20)

SKILLS

Add fields to the query design grid (p. 4-10)
Add tables to a query (p. 4-8)
Build an expression using the Expression Builder (p. 4-15)
Create an AutoReport based on a query (p. 4-24)
Create a calculated field (p. 4-14)
Create a query using Design view (p. 4-8)
Create a query using the Query Wizard (p. 4-6)
Establish a sort order in a query (p. 4-18)
Filter records by defining specific criteria (p. 4-19)
Run a query (p. 4-12)
Specify multiple criteria by creating an AND and OR condition (p. 4-21)
Use a function expression to select records (p. 4-23)
Use wildcards in an expression (p. 4-20)

STUDY QUESTIONS

MULTIPLE CHOICE

1. The query design grid appears in the
  a. Database window.
  b. query datasheet.
  c. upper pane of the Query Design window.
  d. lower pane of the Query Design window.

2. A select query allows you do all of the following *except*
  a. filter records according to specific criteria.
  b. create a calculated field.
  c. add a field to a table.
  d. edit and enter data.

3. Data returned when you run a query is stored
  a. in the query.
  b. in a form.
  c. in a module.
  d. in a table.

4. In the Query Design window, tables are displayed
  a. in the query datasheet.
  b. in the upper pane of the window.
  c. in the lower pane of the window.
  d. in the Properties window.

5. In the Query Design window, tables are added by
  a. clicking the Add Table button.
  b. choosing the Table from the drop-down list in the query design grid.
  c. clicking the Show Table button.
  d. none of the above

6. In the Query Design window, fields are added by
  a. choosing the field from the drop-down list in the query design grid.
  b. double-clicking a field displayed in a table.
  c. clicking the Add Field button.
  d. both a and b

7. What do you use to create a calculated field in a query?
  a. a formula
  b. an expression
  c. a condition
  d. a filter

8. To help you create a calculated field, you can use the
  a. Function Expresser.
  b. Function Builder.
  c. Expression Wizard.
  d. Expression Builder.

9. If you want a list of people who live in CA, IL, or PA, you need to create what kind of condition?
  a. AND
  b. OR
  c. Multiple
  d. Tri-condition

10. What characters do you use to surround a field in an expression?
  a. [ ]
  b. { }
  c. < >
  d. " "

SHORT ANSWER

1. What is the query design grid?
2. What does the upper portion of the query design grid display?
3. When you run a query, where are the results displayed?
4. What are wildcards?
5. What can a select query do?

6. What does the Expression Builder help you to do?
7. What database objects are the record sources for forms?
8. How do you sort records in a query?
9. Give an example of an AND condition.
10. Give an example of an OR condition.

FILL IN THE BLANK

1. Queries can be the source for ____________ and ____________.
2. A calculated field is created by entering a(n) ____________.
3. Queries are modified in Query ____________ view.
4. Fields are added to a query by adding them to the query design ____________.
5. ____________ allow you to create powerful criteria expressions.
6. When you run a query, the results are displayed in a(n) ____________.
7. A condition for returning records meeting two criteria simultaneously is called a(n) ____________ condition.
8. The ____________ property of a field determines whether currency data is displayed as such.
9. A query allows you to work with fields from multiple ____________.
10. A(n) ____________ uses an expression to return data in a query.

FOR DISCUSSION

1. How do you specify a sort order in a query?
2. How does the Expression Builder help you to create an expression?
3. How does an AND condition differ from an OR condition?
4. Explain why a query is the best database object to base a report upon.

GUIDED EXERCISES

1 THE HOME THEATER REPAIRS DATABASE

The Home Theater Repairs database is designed to make retrieving information about warranties more efficient. To eliminate the need to create a query for each and every repair request that comes in, you can build some initial queries and use the queries to process requests. Follow these steps to complete the queries:

1. Open the *Home Theater Repairs.mdb* file.
2. Click the Queries button on the Database Objects bar.
3. Click the New button, select **Design** view, add the **Customers** table to the query, and click **Close** to close the Show Table dialog box.
4. Add the **FirstName**, **LastName**, **City**, and **State** fields to the query design grid.

5. Type **TX** in the **State** column **Criteria** row and set **Ascending** as the sort order to the **LastName** field. Run the query.
6. Print the query and save it as *Texas Customers*.
7. Create a new query in Design view, add all three tables, and then add the following fields:

Table	Field
Technician	LastName
Repairs	RepairDate
Repairs	SystemPart
Technicians	PayRate
Repairs	RepairTime

8. Create a calculated field to determine the total cost of repair using the expression **Total Cost: [PayRate]*[RepairTime]**.
9. Sort the query on the **Total Cost** field in descending order, run the query, print it, and save the query as *Technician Cost*.
10. Select the **Technician Cost** query, choose **File | Save As**, and type **Repairs by System Part** as the name of the new query.
11. Create a new query based on the **Customers** and **Repairs** tables and add the **LastName**, **FirstName**, **State**, **RepairDate**, and **SystemPart** fields to the query design grid.
12. Select all repairs for the system part **Amplifier** by typing **Amplifier** in the Criteria row of the SystemPart field and run the query.
13. Switch back to Design view, type **Speakers** in the ***or*** row of the SystemPart field, and run the query.
14. Switch back to Design view, type **TX** in the Criteria row of the State field, and run the query.
15. Save the query as *Texas Amplifier and Speaker Repairs*, print the query, close the query, and close the database.

2 THE MORE PROFITS DATABASE

When you're a business owner, it's always great to see that you're making a profit. It's even more interesting to review information contained in your database to determine just where these profits are coming from. Follow these instructions to create several queries using the More Profits database:

1. Open the *More Profits.mdb* file.
2. Click the Queries button in the Database Objects bar.
3. Create a query using the **Items** table; place the **ItemID**, **Description**, **InStock**, **Cost**, and **SellingPrice** fields in the query grid; set an Ascending sort order on the **InStock** field; and run the query.
4. Save the query using the query name *Current Inventory*.
5. Open the Query Design view, create a calculated field using the expression **Profit: [SellingPrice]-[Cost]**, print the query, and then save and close the query.
6. Create a new query named *Orders by Department* based on all three tables (**Items**, **Orders**, and **Departments**) and add the following fields on the query design grid:

Table Name	Field
Departments	DepartmentName
Items	ItemID
Items	Description
Orders	OrderDate
Orders	ItemsOrdered
Items	Cost
Calculated field	TotalCost: [ItemsOrdered]*[Cost]

7. Save, run, and print the query.
8. Open the **Orders by Department** query, choose **File | Save As**, and name the new query *September Orders*.
9. Open the **September Orders** query, position the insertion point in the **Criteria** row of the **OrderDate** field, type **Month([OrderDate])=9**, set an Ascending sort order on the **OrderDate** field, and then save, run, and print the query.
10. Create an **AutoReport: Columnar** based on the **September Orders** query, print the report, and save it using the report name *September Orders*.
11. Close the database.

3 USING BRENT'S ORDERS DATABASE

Brent at Brent's Tools has identified a number of criteria that are used frequently to locate information. Search time will be significantly reduced by creating and saving these queries. Follow these steps to create several queries that you can use to create reports:

1. Open the *Brent's Orders.mdb* file.
2. Create a query using both tables. Place the **CustomerID** and **CompanyName** fields from the **Customers** table and the **SalesDate**, **TotalInvoice**, and **AmountPaid** fields from the **Orders** table in the query design grid. Set an Ascending sort order on the **CompanyName** field.
3. Create a calculated field using the expression **AmountOwed: [TotalInvoice]-[AmountPaid]**.
4. Save the query using the query name *Invoice Report Query*, and run and print the query.
5. Select the **Invoice Report Query**, choose **File | Save As**, and save a new query using the query name *Totals*.
6. Click the Totals Σ button on the Query Design toolbar to add a **Total** row to the grid, click the **Total** down arrow for the **TotalInvoice** field, and choose **Sum**.
7. Repeat the procedures outlined in Step 6 to total the **AmountPaid** and **AmountOwed** fields.
8. Run, print, and close the query.
9. Open the **Invoice Report Query**, choose **File | Save As**, and name the new query *Accounts Due Query*.
10. Add the **Phone** field to the next available column and type **<>0** in the **Criteria** row for the **AmountOwed** field.
11. Run, save, and print the query.
12. Close the database.

ON YOUR OWN

The difficulty of these case studies varies:
are the least difficult; *are more difficult; and* *are the most difficult.*

1 ASSIGNMENT DUE DATES

Open the *Assignment Due Dates.mdb* file. Now that you have entered class and assignment information, you can create queries to help you locate information. Create queries that meet the following specifications, naming the queries appropriately. Run and print each query.

- Class ID, class name, assignment name, assignment due date, and assignment type sorted by date due.
- All assignments for the current month.
- All tests for the semester.
- All tests and quizzes.

2 NANCY'S KNICK-KNACK NOOK

Nancy needs several specific reports generated from the *Knick-Knack Nook.mdb* file. Using the database, create queries to display the following information, saving and naming the queries appropriately:

- Inventory list with **ItemID**, **Description**, **UnitsOnHand**, **SellingPrice**, **Cost**, and **Supplier Name**.
- An order list similar to the Inventory list that contains the supplier's phone number and lists only the items of which Nancy has 50 or less on hand.
- An inventory list showing markup (**SellingPrice-Cost**) and Nancy's total income (**UnitsOnHand*SellingPrice**) if she sold her entire stock for each item.

Use the queries to create AutoReports, and save and print a copy of each report.

3 PINE VALLEY DONATIONS ARE COMING IN

The Director of the Pine Valley Organization would like to obtain several lists from the database file:

- A list of contributors and contributions sorted by last name.
- A list of contributors and contributions for a specific month.
- A list of all contributors and contributions over $100.
- A list of contributors and the total amount they have given sorted by amount. (Use a total query; see Guided Exercise 3).

Open the *Pine Valley Donations.mdb*. Create, save, and print queries that will meet the director's requirements. Use the AutoReport: Tabular format to create reports from each of these queries and print copies of each report.

4 BEAVER BROOK INN FACILITIES ARE BOOKING UP

Your supervisor would like for you to use the *Beaver Brook Facilities.mdb* database to generate several reports. Create and save queries that you can use as the data source for the required reports, create and save the reports, and print a copy of each report.

- A room list sorted by date that includes the group name, room ID, room name, and beginning and ending times.
- A list of rooms by date that includes group name, room name, number of hours the group reserved the room, hourly cost, and total cost (hourly cost*hours) for the group that will use the room.
- A list showing total cost per group that shows only group name and total cost.
- A list showing only the rooms used in the afternoon on a specific date.

5 FITNESS CLUB OVERBOOKING

Use the *Fitness Club.mdb* file to create and save queries to generate, save, and print the following reports for the Director:

- A list showing the class ID, class name, name of participant, amount owed, amount paid, and the amount due sorted by class code.
- A list of participants who have signed up for 10 or more hours in any class.
- A list of participants showing the amount paid and total amount owed for all classes.

Photospread credits pages 4-2 & 4-3

©Tony Stone: ©Mark Green; ©FPG: ©Navaswan, ©Pearson Education, ©Lorraine Castellano

FROM THE FILES

You Will Need

- ✔ BBIC.gif
- ✔ Beaver Conference Facilities.mdb
- ✔ BTC Orders.mdb
- ✔ Brent's Tools Logo.gif
- ✔ e-Selections.jpg
- ✔ e-Selections Forms.mdb
- ✔ Get in Shape Spa.mdb
- ✔ GIS.gif
- ✔ Home Theater Service Plans.mdb
- ✔ Earning a Profit.mdb
- ✔ Nancy.jpg
- ✔ KKN Inventory.mdb
- ✔ PVO Fund Raising.mdb
- ✔ PVO.gif
- ✔ College Tests & Assignments.mdb

PROJECT 5

Creating and Modifying Forms

Each Access database object is designed to meet special user needs. *Forms* simply present data contained in a database on screen in a more aesthetically pleasing layout, one record at a time. You can use forms to enter and edit data, display individual records, and navigate database records. Most forms are designed using single tables. When data from multiple tables is used in a form, you can create a query and base the form on the query. In this project, you will learn how to design, create, and modify forms that can be used to enter data. You will also learn how to add controls to simplify data entry.

OBJECTIVES

After completing this project, you will be able to:

- *Create a form using the Form Wizard*
- *Modify form controls*
- *Select, move, and delete controls on a form*
- *Add controls to a form*
- *Add a graphic to a form*
- *Modify form properties*
- *Add subforms to forms*
- *Add records using a form*

e-selections Running Case

Others at e-Selections are impressed by the work you are doing to develop the e-Selections database. As you've worked toward getting the data into appropriate tables, you've discovered a number of new features that you believe will aid others when it comes time to turn the database over to data entry personnel. One of these features is the data entry form that you created early in the database development process. It's time to look at some of the tools Access provides for enhancing and revising this form.

Databases for Emergency Management

That might seem like a tall order, but most humanitarian and emergency management organizations depend heavily on databases to coordinate their rapid deployment to areas where lives are threatened by disaster, disease, and violence. Every day that aid is delayed could mean hundreds or thousands more sick, injured, or dead.

The International Red Cross (IRC) and the Centers for Disease Control (CDC) are two organizations that assist in emergency relief efforts, often dealing with multiple emergencies at the same time. Using databases helps them to manage their resources effectively.

When large refugee migrations occur, thousands of people can become ill or die, usually within the first month. Most of these illnesses are preventable given proper healthcare and living conditions. The primary goal of the IRC in these situations is to determine the needs of the refugees and provide the necessary aid.

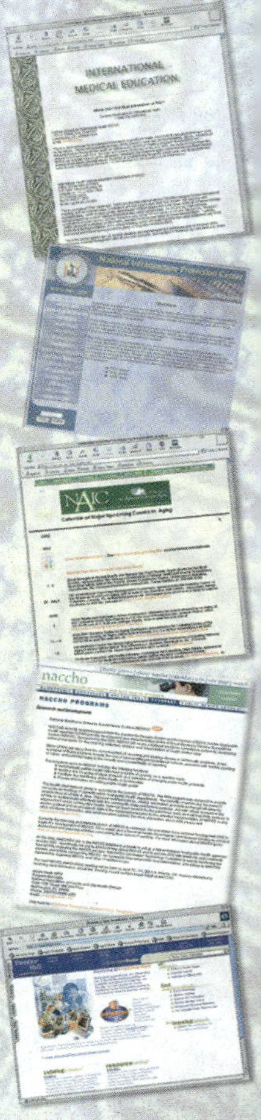

The IRC uses the Emergency Response Roster to expedite this process. This database contains the contact information, experience, and areas of expertise of current and former IRC employees, qualified candidates, and volunteers in fields such as healthcare, logistics, engineering, and administration. The IRC can query this database to find people with exact qualifications, linguistics, and availability needed for any given situation.

As of 2000, the IRC had used this program to help with deployments to over 15 different emergency situations, including East Timor and Chechnya.

In addition to the Emergency Response Roster, the IRC uses other databases. For example, in 1994, approximately 600,000 Rwandans were killed and nearly 2 million fled their country to escape war and genocide. Many international relief agencies decided to work together to find a way to reunite the many thousands of children that were separated from their families during this crisis. Their solution was to create a centralized database, and the IRC assumed the responsibility.

911

During the course of their efforts, 119,577 children were registered in the database, along with some 151,000 parents or relatives. By 1997, they had closed out all the cases in which either families were reunited or the children were found to have been registered in error. To date, only 13,878 children are still looking for their families. Although the database wasn't responsible for every reunion, it did facilitate the process.

Many organizations are changing the way they do business as the need for effective information management becomes more crucial. At one time, the CDC was responsible only for tracking and containing tropical diseases (such as malaria). Their responsibilities have now expanded to include tracking and controlling the spread of all infectious and chronic diseases, and working with health officials to prevent injuries, birth defects, and disabilities by improving the country's health standards and by educating the public.

As responsibilities have been added to their plate, they have increased the number of health surveillance and information systems to over 100. They are now in the process of coordinating all these disparate information systems under the umbrella of the Health Information Surveillance Systems Board (HISSB).

The lynchpin of the HISSB will be the National Electronic Disease Surveillance System (NEDSS). The NEDSS will integrate their many different monitoring systems into one national infrastructure, giving healthcare workers a standardized method of reporting information critical to public health. This will increase the speed with which the CDC can act to isolate and prevent the spread of dangerous diseases.

Crisis Prevention

PROJECT 5

Creating and Modifying Forms

The Challenge

Mr. Traylor wants you to design and develop a form that can be used for viewing, modifying, and entering both customer and payroll information. He would also like the company logo to appear on this form.

The Solution

Access contains a number of tools that will enable you to create a form that meets Mr. Traylor's needs. You can use the *Form Wizard* to create the basic form layout and then use the Form Design view to modify the form so that it is both easy to use and attractive. A special feature that you would like to add to the form—and one you think will impress Mr. Traylor—would enable data entry personnel to work with employee and payroll information at the same time. After you complete the form layout, you can add the e-Selections logo graphic to create the form shown in Figure 5-1.

Figure 5-1

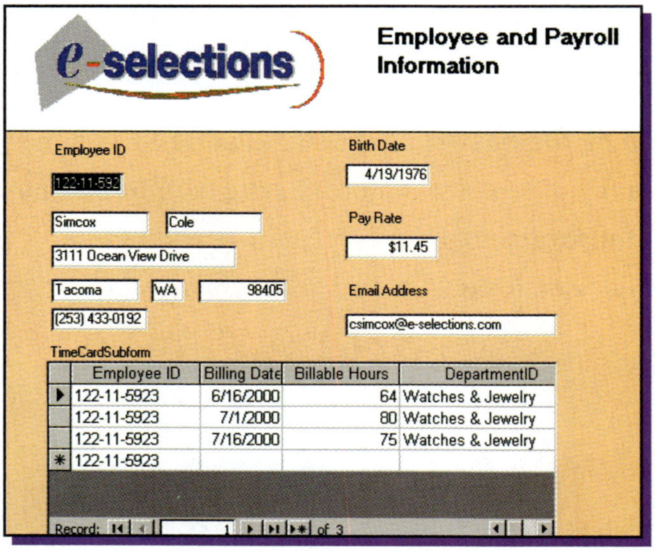

Creating Forms

By now, you may have discovered the AutoForm feature and used it to create a simple form based on fields contained in a table. Forms contain fields that appear in either a table or query—the *record source*. Access provides a variety of ways that you can create and modify forms. The easiest way to create the form Mr. Traylor requested is to create the form using the Form Wizard. Then you can modify the form in Form Design view.

Task 1:
To Create a New Form Using the Form Wizard

1. Open the *e-Selections Forms.mdb* file and click the Forms button in the Objects bar.

2. Double-click the **Create form by using wizard** option to start the Form Wizard.

3. Select **Table: Employees** from the **Tables/Queries** drop-down list, and click the Move All >> button to move all fields from the **Available Fields** list to the **Selected Fields** list. Click **Next**.

Tip To select fields from multiple tables, you can create a form based on a query. You can also move fields from one table to the Selected Fields list and then select another table from the Tables/Queries list and move fields from the it into the Selected fields list before clicking Next.

Figure 5-2

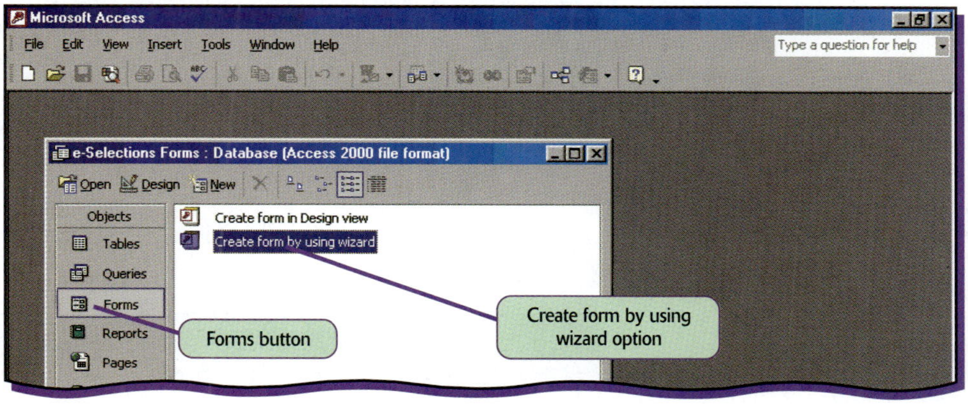

Figure 5-3

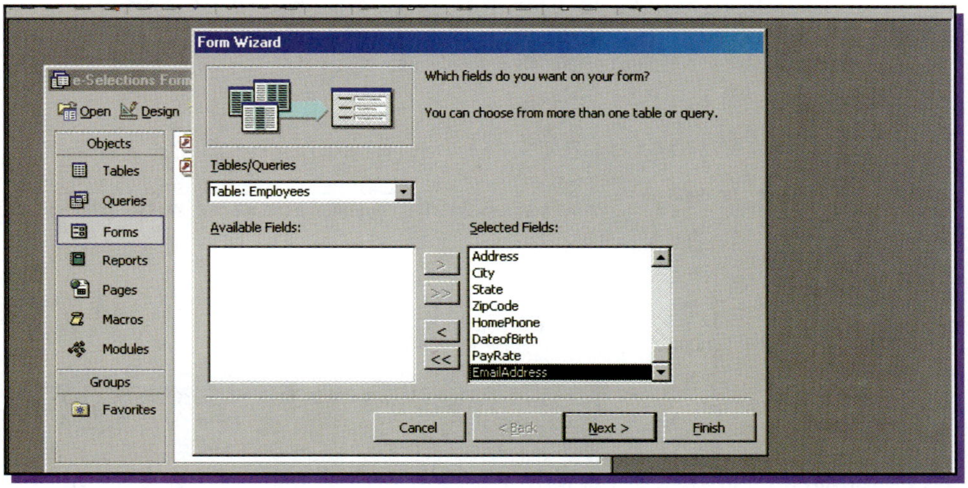

4 Select **Columnar**, and click **Next**.

Tip The Wizard pages presented vary, depending on the table or query you select and the fields they contain. The options on the Form Wizard page shown in Figure 5-4 control the overall layout of information on the form.

Figure 5-4

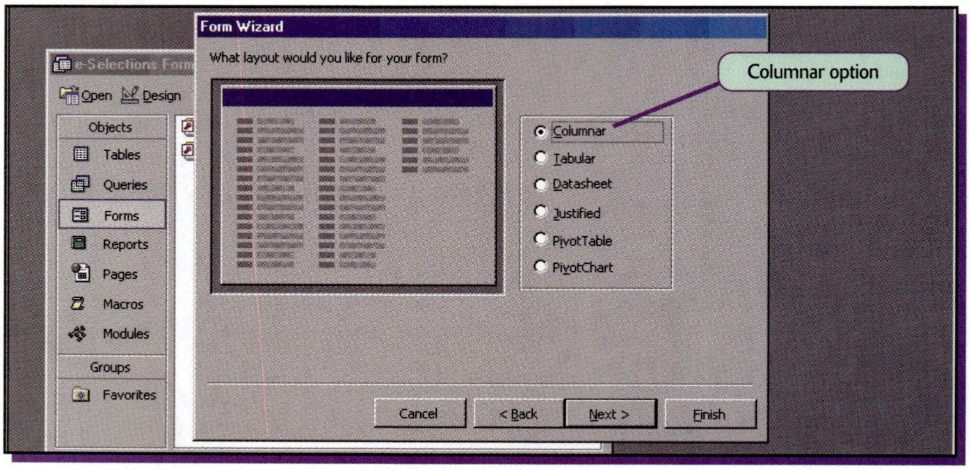

5 Select **Standard** as the style for the form, if necessary. Click **Next**.

Tip Form style sets the general appearance of the background and data entry boxes. Select different styles and view the appearance in the area on the left before clicking Next.

Figure 5-5

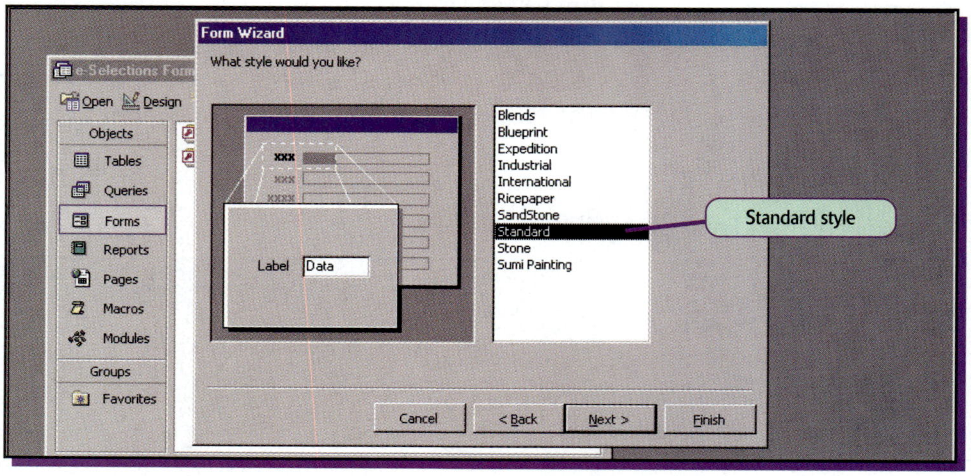

6 Type **Employees and Payroll** in the **What title do you want for your form** text box, select the **Open the form to view or enter information** option, and click **Finish**. The form opens in Form view.

Figure 5-6

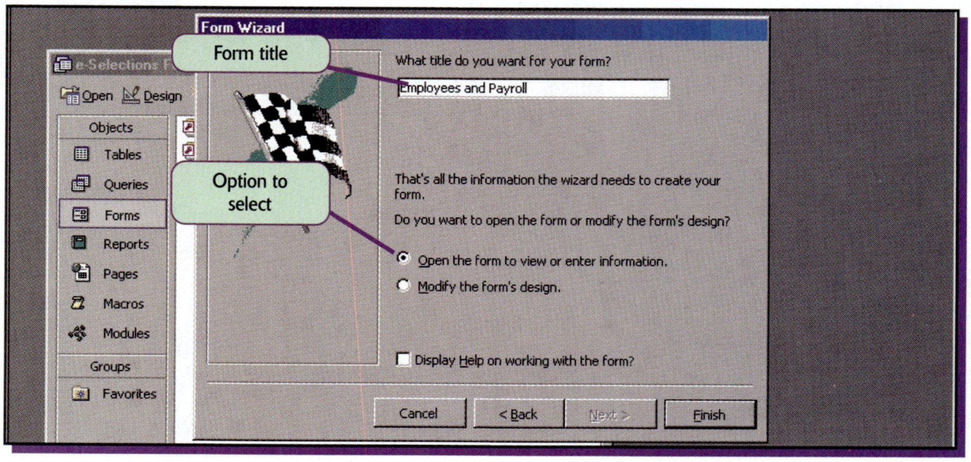

Modifying a Form's Controls

> **Tip** You'll use bound and unbound controls to design forms as well as to design reports and data access pages in Design view.

Now that you have a basic form that contains the fields you want to include for data entry, you can change field names, size the form and fields, and arrange the fields using Form Design view to create the form Mr. Traylor wants. *Controls* are objects on a form, report, or data access page that display data, perform actions, and decorate the form. Access offers three different types of controls:

- A *bound control* is tied to a field in the source object so that the field value appears in the form.
- An *unbound control* is an item on a form that is independent of ties to data source fields. Unbound controls can be lines, rectangles, or pictures that visually organize form data.
- A *calculated control* is tied to an expression or calculated field.

Each control added to a form is identified by a *control label*—text that identifies the data. You can delete the labels when appropriate, leaving just the *control text box*—the portion of the control that displays the field value.

Changing Field Names

The field names you assigned when you created the database tables were abbreviated or run together to facilitate data structures. When you turn a database over to data entry personnel to enter records, they will find these types of "friendly" names easier to use. As a result, you need to change the field names that appear on the form without disturbing the tie that the field has to table data.

Task 2:
To Modify Form Fields and Set Controls

1. Open the **Employees and Payroll** form in Form view, if necessary.

2. Click the View button on the Form View toolbar to switch to Design view and maximize the Form Design view window.

Figure 5-7

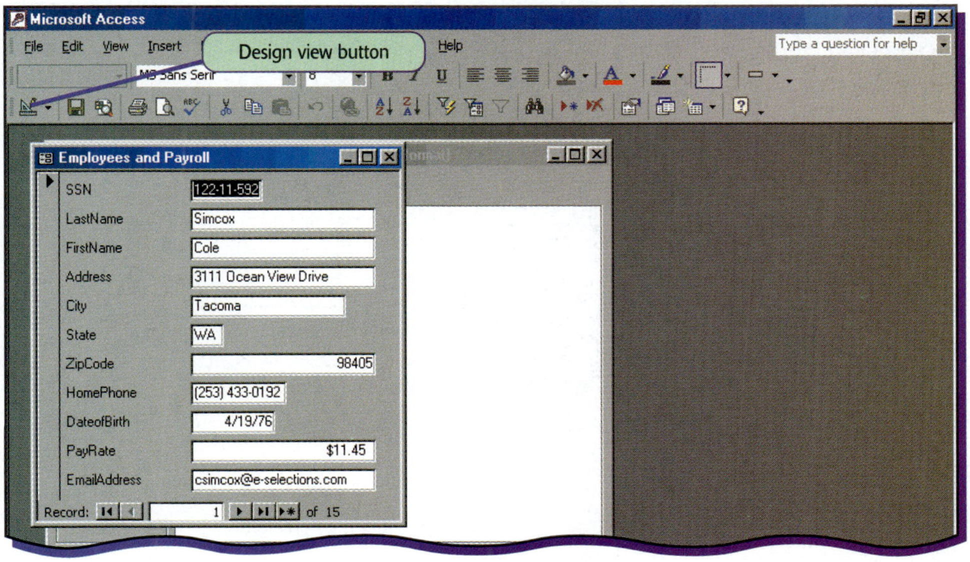

> **Other Ways**
> To display Form Design view:
> - Select the form in the Database window and choose **View | Design View.**

3 Click the **SSN** label once to select the label.

Figure 5-8

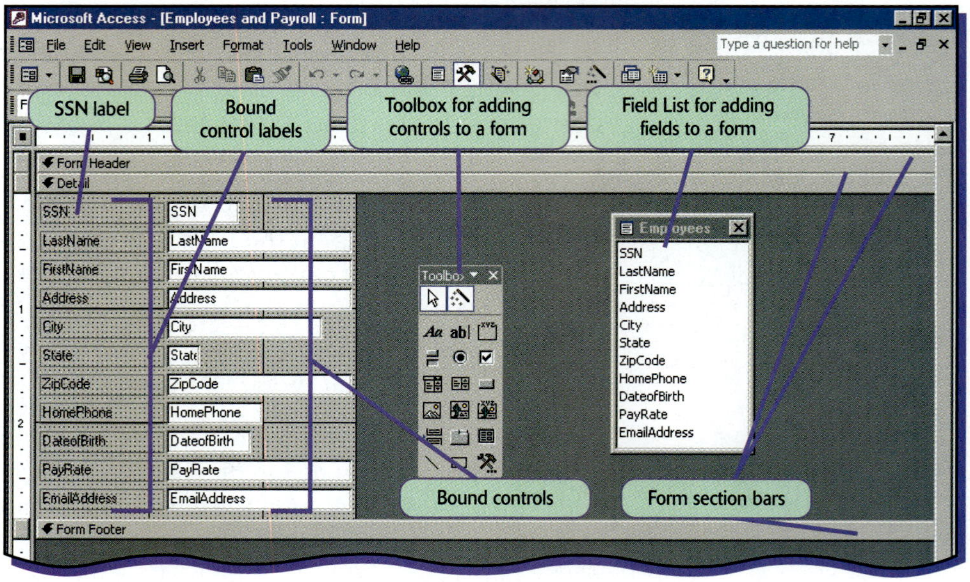

Troubleshooting The arrangement of items on your screen may be different from that shown in Figure 5-9. If you are more comfortable working with your screen arranged exactly as shown in the form, you may need to move the Toolbox by dragging its title bar and size the Toolbox by dragging a corner. To display the Field List box, choose **View | Field List.** To display the Toolbox, choose **View | Toolbox** and then size and position the box as shown.

4 Double-click the selected label to select the label text, and type **Employee ID**.

Troubleshooting
The SSN label appears in the "spotted" background while the SSN value box appears with a white background. Be sure to change the label rather than the value box.

Figure 5-9

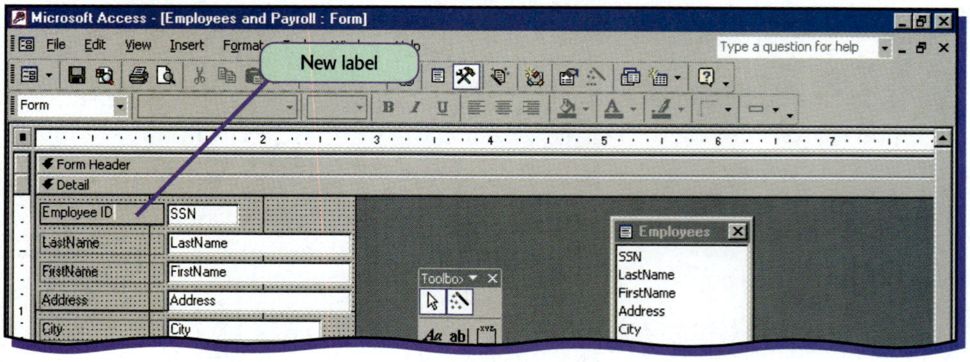

5 Select the **LastName** label, press and hold the [Shift] key, and select the **FirstName**, **Address**, **City**, **State**, **ZipCode**, and **HomePhone** labels.

Figure 5-10

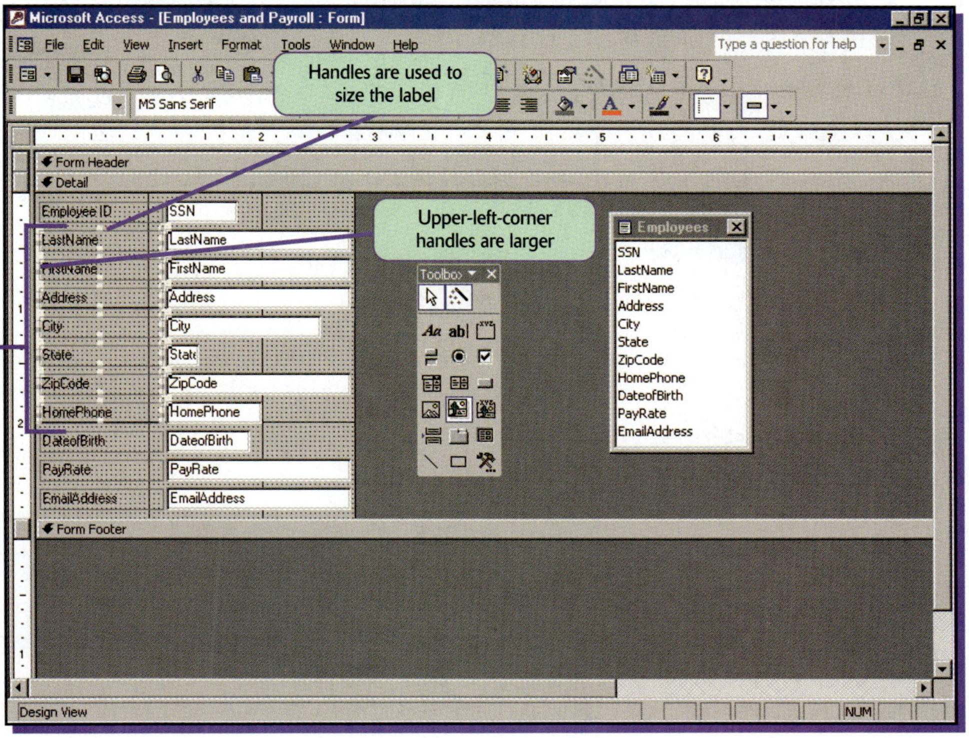

6 Press the [Delete] key to delete the fields from the form.

7 Click the **Save** button to save the changes.

Other Ways

To save an object:

- Choose **File | Save**.
- Press [Ctrl] + [S].

8 Edit additional form labels identified in Table 5-1 and save changes to the form.

Figure 5-11

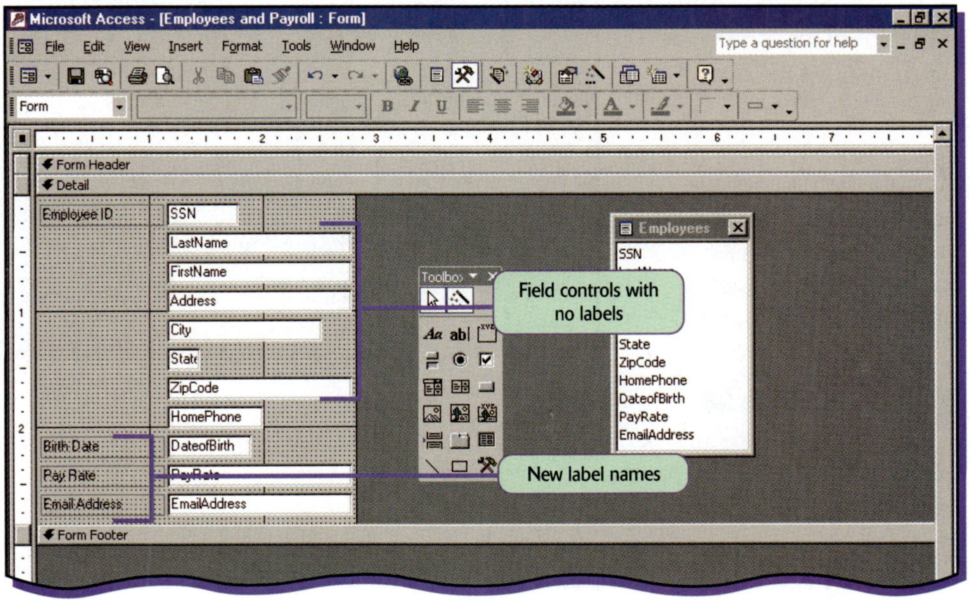

> **Tip** Many terms associated with computers appear in a variety of different formats. The abbreviation for electronic mail is one such word. You'll see it as e-mail, email, Email, e-Mail, and E-Mail.

Table 5-1

Label	Edited Label
DateofBirth	Birth Date
PayRate	Pay Rate
EmailAddress	Email Address

Modifying the Form Size

To create the form Mr. Traylor sketched out, the form sheet needs to be enlarged. Access provides tools in Form Design view for sizing the form.

Task 3:
To Modify the Form Size

1. Open the **Employees and Payroll** form in Form Design view and close the **Toolbox** and **Field List**.
2. Point to the right edge of the form until the pointer appears as a two-headed arrow and drag the right edge of the form to the 5-inch mark on the ruler.
3. Point to the edge of the form just above the **Form Footer** section bar and drag the form to the 3-inch mark on the vertical ruler.
4. Click the **Save** button to save changes to the form.

Figure 5-12

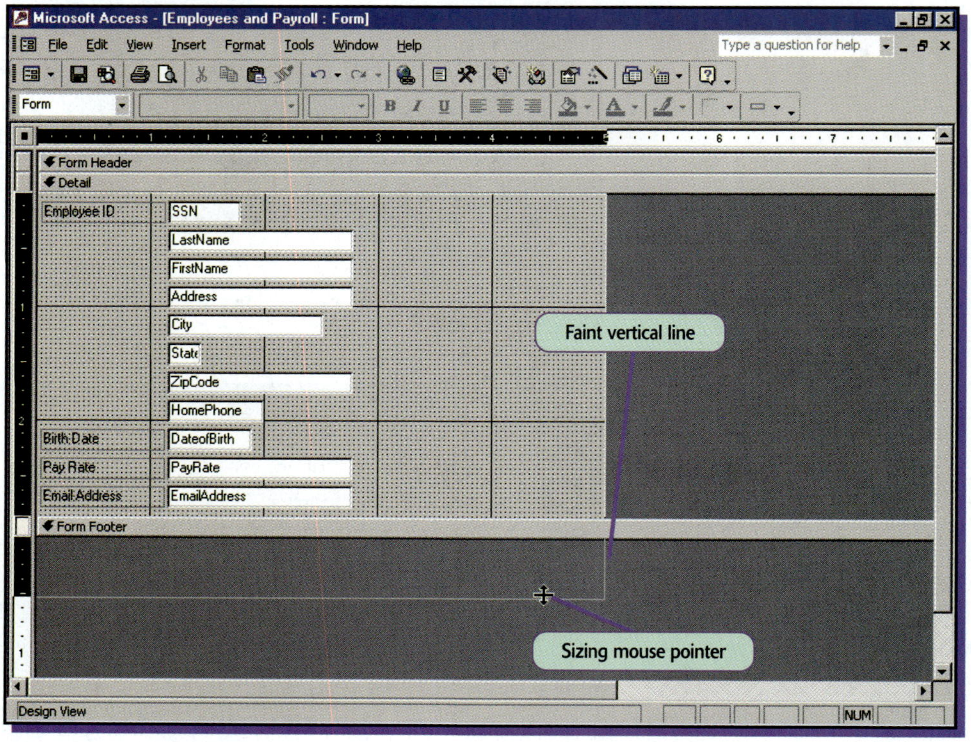

Resizing and Moving Form Controls

Now that you have more working space on the form page, you can move field controls into the proper positions. You can also change the size of the controls to accommodate the data they contain.

CHECK POINT

While some techniques used to modify forms are unique to Access, many of the techniques you use to size and move objects in other applications can be used to position and size controls and other objects on Access forms. Tips for working with controls on Access forms are identified in Table 5-2.

Table 5-2 Tips for Working with Form Controls

To	Action
Select a control	Click the control once.
Select multiple controls	Press Shift as you click each control.
Size a control box	Select the control and drag a handle.
Move a control box and label together	Select the control and drag a border away from all handles using the flat hand mouse or select the control and tap an arrow key.
Move a control independently of the label	Select the control and drag the upper-left-corner handle using the pointing hand mouse.
Edit a control label	Select the label and then double-click the text inside the label box.
Position controls more precisely	Press and hold the Alt key as you drag selected controls or press and hold the Ctrl key and tap the arrow keys to nudge the control into place.

Task 4:
To Resize and Move Controls on a Form

1. Click the **LastName** text box control and drag the right size handle to about the 2-inch mark on the rules, as shown in Figure 5-13.

2. Resize the remaining field text box controls so that they appear as shown in Figure 5-13.

Figure 5-13

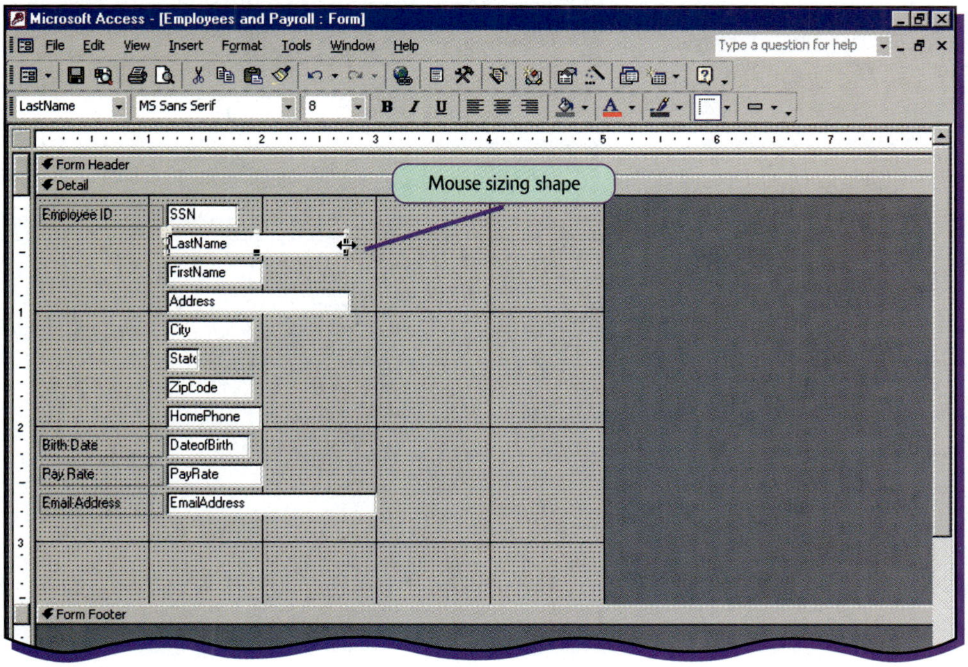

3 Click the **FirstName** text box control to select it, point to the text box control border away from a size handle until the mouse pointer appears as a flat hand, and drag the field to the right of the **LastName** field.

4 Repeat the procedures identified in Step 3 to move fields into the positions displayed in Figure 5-14.

5 Click the Save button to save the changes.

Figure 5-14

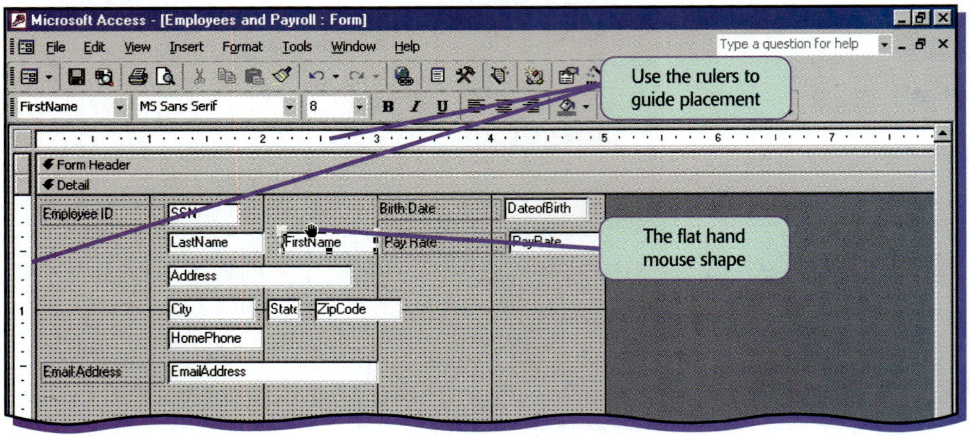

6 Point to the vertical ruler directly across from the **LastName** text box control and drag the selection line down to a position below the **Email Address** field to select all field controls in that area.

7 Drag one of the selected controls down about an inch to reposition all selected controls.

Figure 5-15

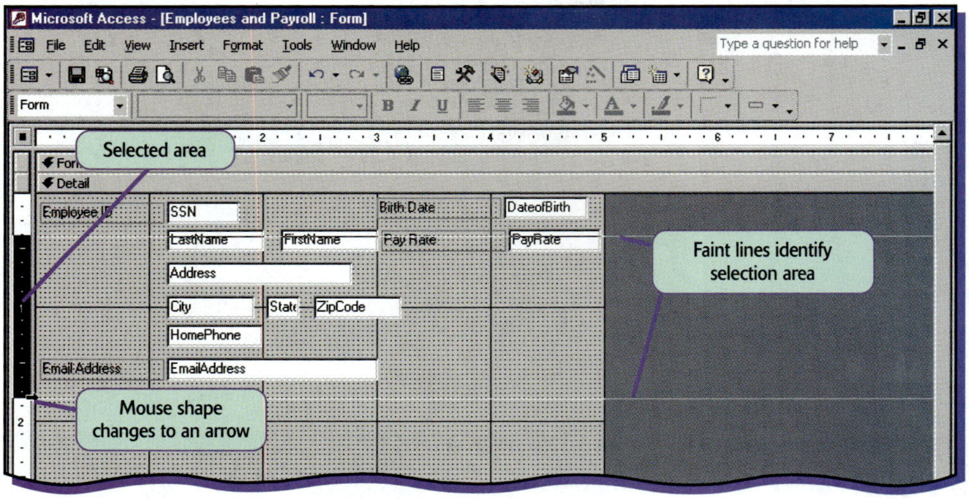

8 Click the **SSN** text box control and point to the upper-left-corner handle until the mouse pointer appears as a pointing hand.

Tip The pointing hand lets you know that dragging the control will move it independently from the control label.

Figure 5-16

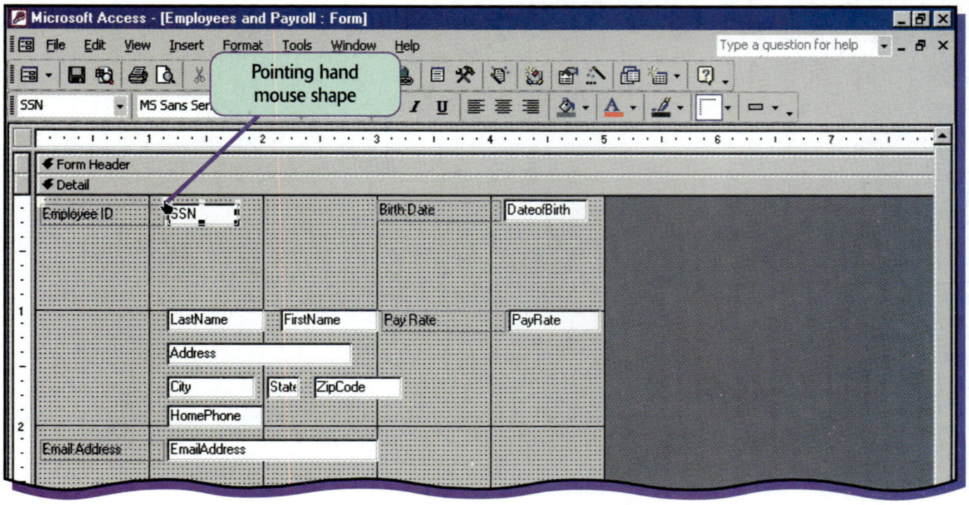

9 Drag the text box control to a position below the **Employee ID** label, and then drag the **Employee ID** label to align the left edge with the **SSN** text box control, as shown in Figure 5-17.

Figure 5-17

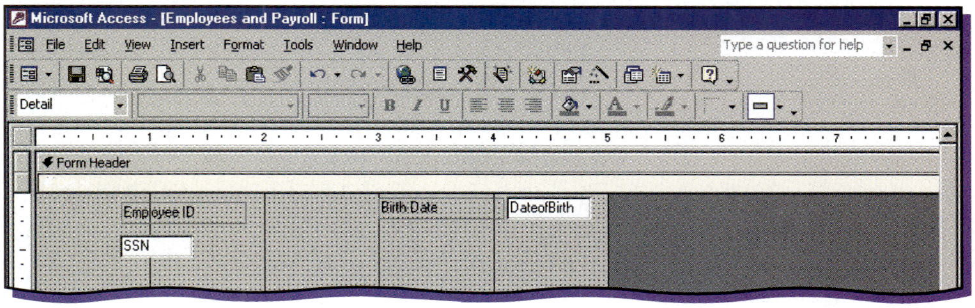

10 Repeat the procedures outlined in Step 9 to position controls as shown in Figure 5-18.

11 Click the Save button to save form changes.

Figure 5-18

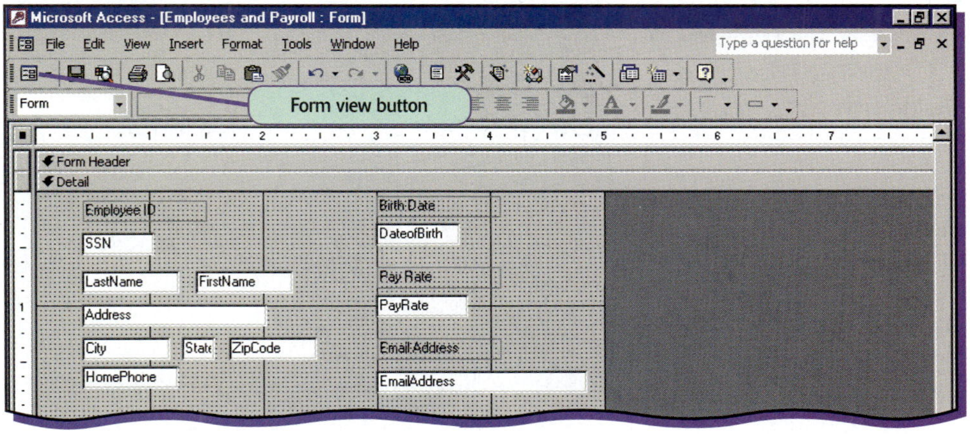

12 Click the Form View button to view the modified form.

Figure 5-19

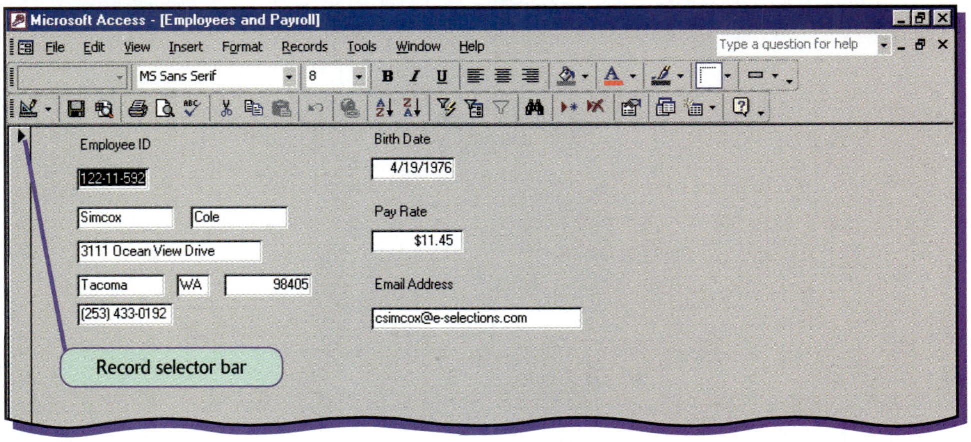

WEB TIP

You know those forms on the Internet you complete to register for workshops, order items from eBay, and send in surveys? Many were created by arranging controls just the way you have been arranging them on your forms.

Adding Unbound Controls to a Form

So far, you have sized and repositioned the bound controls that Access placed on the form from the table. Now it's time to add the labels, graphics, lines, and rectangles—the unbound controls—to give the form character. Unbound controls are independent of data sources so these controls simply enhance the form without displaying data from a table or query. Unbound labels add descriptive information to a form, and graphics, such as the company logo, project the corporate image. The *Toolbox* contains tools that you can use to add different types of controls to forms. Each tool identifies the specific type of control it creates.

Task 5:

To Add Unbound Controls to Forms

1. Open the **Employees and Payroll** form in Design view and maximize the window, if necessary.

2. Drag the **Form Header** section bar to increase the size to about 1 inch, click the Toolbox button on the **Form Design** toolbar to display the **Toolbox**, and reposition the Toolbox on screen, if necessary.

3. Click the Image button in the Toolbox.

Figure 5-20

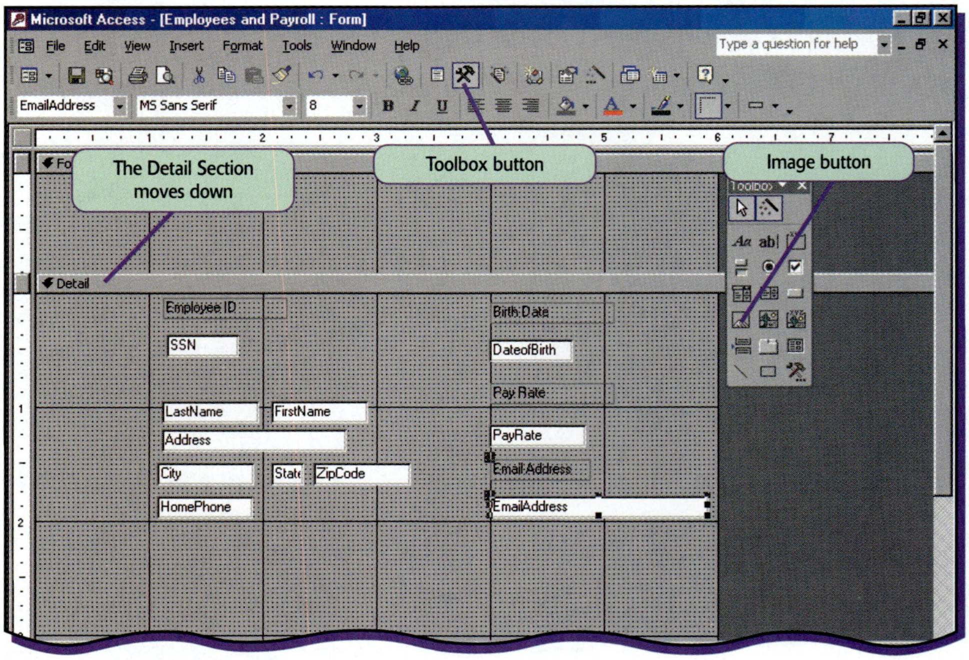

Tip Position the pointer between the Form Header bar and the Detail bar to increase the size of the Form Header.

4 Click in the upper-left corner of the **Form Header** section.

5 Select **e-Selections.jpg** and click **OK** to insert the logo.

Other Ways To insert a graphic:

- Choose **Insert | Picture | From File.**

Figure 5-21

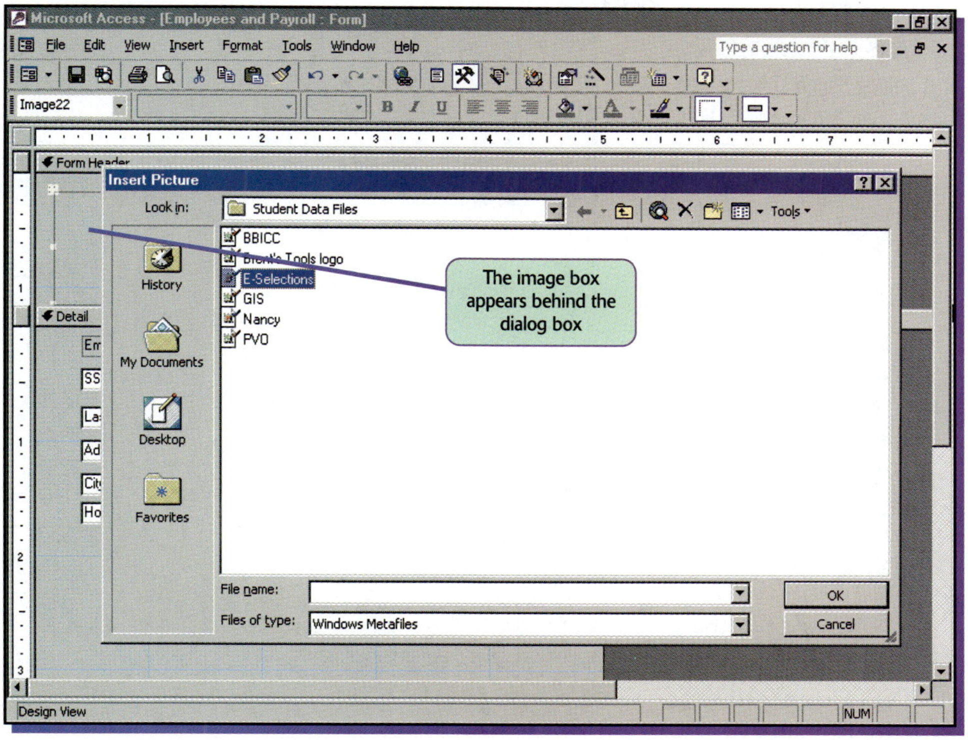

6 Size and position the logo so that it appears as shown in Figure 5-22.

Troubleshooting
Resizing the image box on the form has no affect on the size of the graphic it contains. As a result, the graphic will appear truncated—chopped off—on both sides. You will fix the graphic size by changing the image box properties.

Figure 5-22

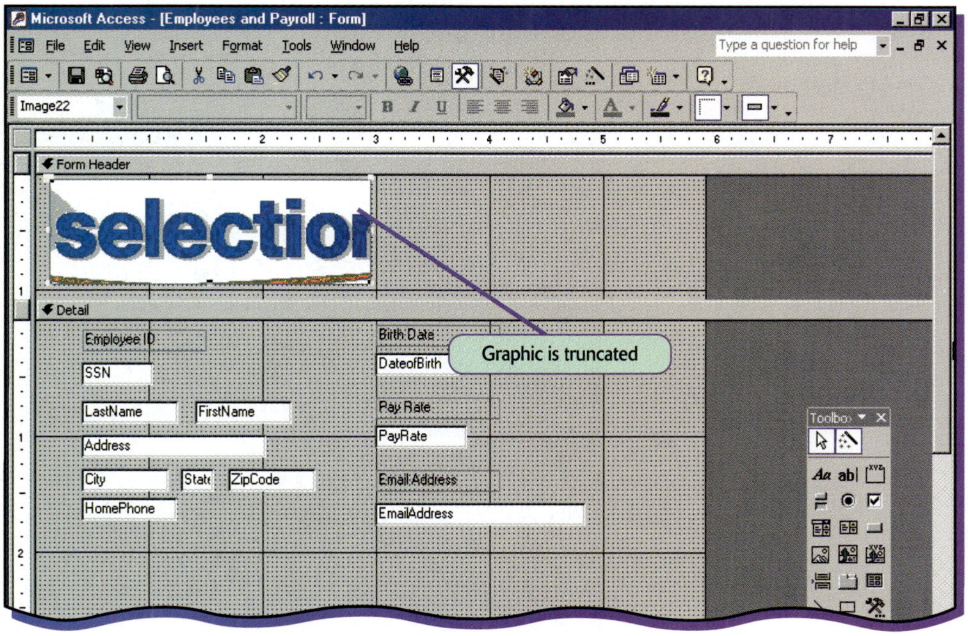

7 Select the logo, if necessary; click the Properties button to open the **Properties** dialog box; and select **Stretch** from the **Size Mode** drop-down list.

Other Ways

To open the Properties dialog box:

- Right-click the graphic and select Properties.
- Select the graphic and press F4.
- Select the graphic and choose **View | Properties.**

8 Close the **Properties** dialog box and save the changes.

9 Click the **Label tool** in the **Toolbox** and click and drag in the **Form Header** section to create the rectangle shown in Figure 5-24.

Troubleshooting

After drawing the initial box, you can change the size of the box to appear as you want it or choose Edit | Undo to try drawing the box again.

Figure 5-23

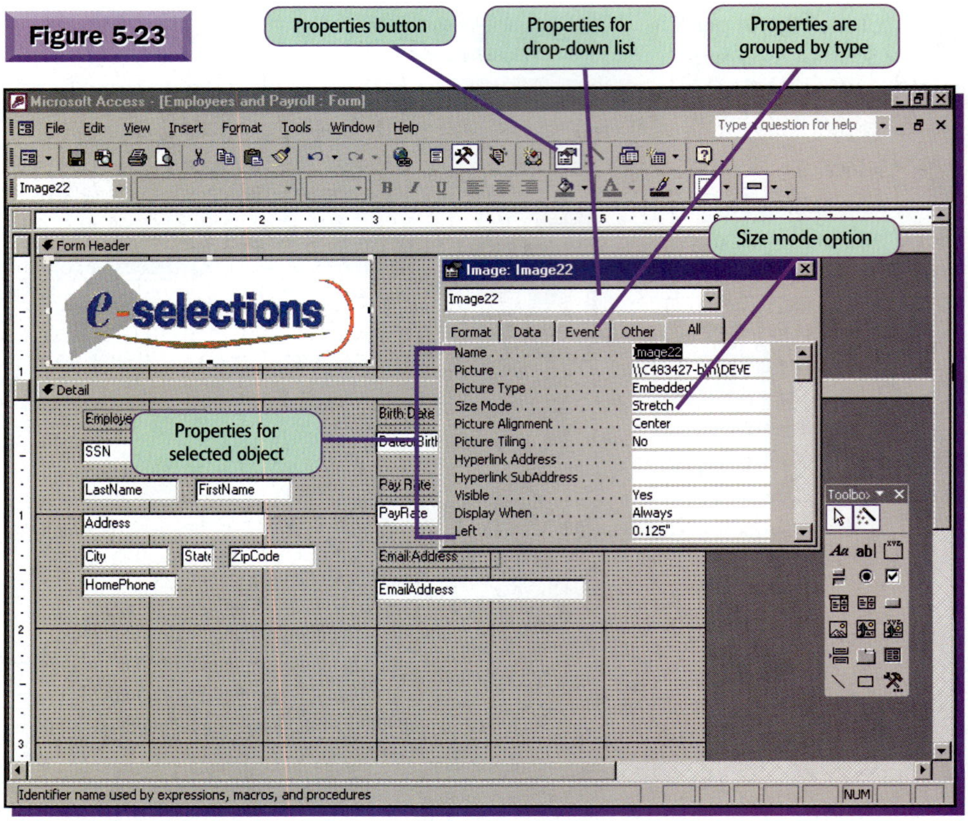

Figure 5-24

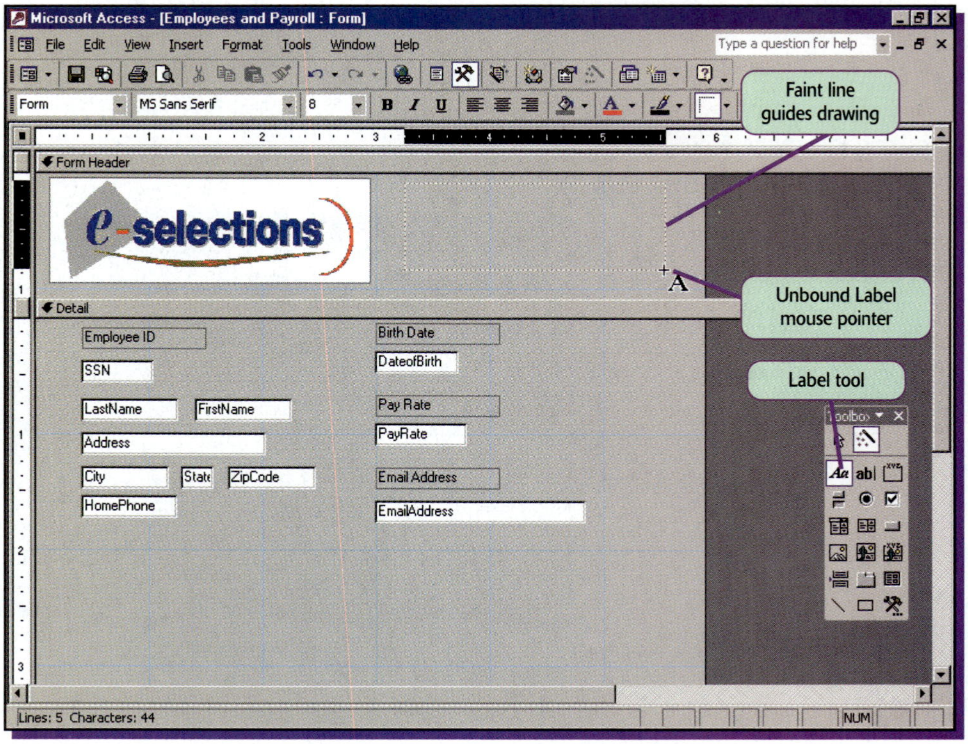

10 Type **Employee and Payroll Information**; click **Properties** on the Form Design toolbar; click the **Format** tab, if necessary; type **14** in the **Font Size** property field; and select **Bold** from the **Font Weight** property list.

Tip If the Font Size and Font Weight properties are not visible, scroll until they appear in the Properties dialog box.

11 Close the **Properties** dialog box; size the label to display all label text; adjust the size of the Form Header section back to 1 inch, if necessary; and save changes to the form.

Figure 5-25

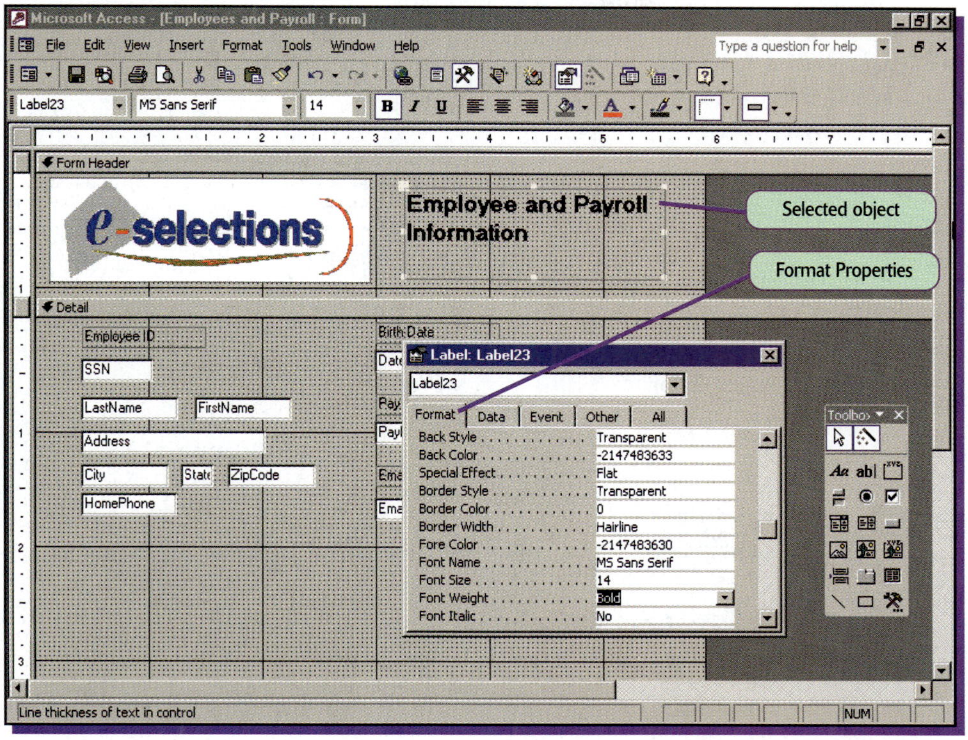

Modifying Form Sections and Form Properties

Each Access object—tables, queries, forms, reports, etc.—contain default properties that Access sets when you create the object. You can use features on the Formatting toolbar or formatting menu to format the most common elements of most objects. As you have already discovered, you can also use the Properties window to modify other properties. You can use the Properties window to modify the background colors of the *Form Header section*—the section at the top of the form that contains a title, graphic, or other items that appear at the top of each form page—and the *Detail section*—the section of the form that contains data stored in table records. When the format is set, you can remove the record selector bar from the form.

Task 6:
To Modify Form Background Colors and Remove the Record Selector Bar

1. Click the **Form Header** section bar to select the **Form Header** section.

2. Click the **Fill/Back Color** down arrow and click the color **White**.

Other Ways

To change the background color:

- Right-click the Form Header section, select **Fill/Back Color**, and select a color.

Figure 5-26

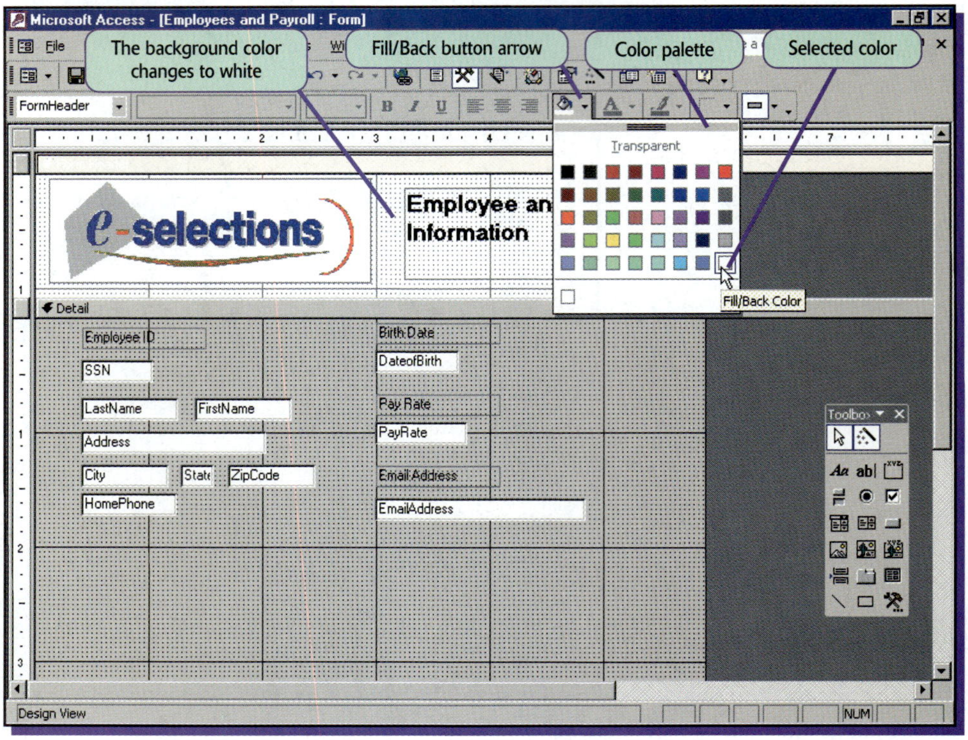

3. Select the **Detail** section bar, click the **Fill/Back Color** down arrow, and click the color **Peach** to match the color shown in Figure 5-27.

Tip

Check with your instructor to see if it's okay to experiment with your final form design. If you receive approval, dress up the form using your school colors or the colors you prefer.

Figure 5-27

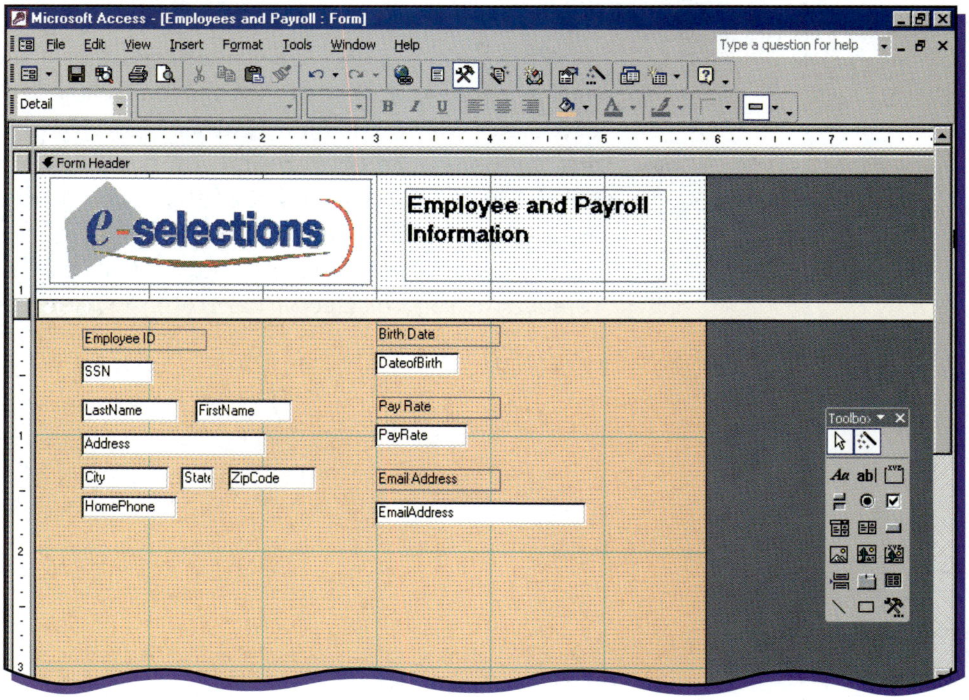

4 Click the Form View button to view the form in Form view.

Tip Options available in the Properties dialog box enable you to remove the selector bar and navigation buttons from the form.

Figure 5-28

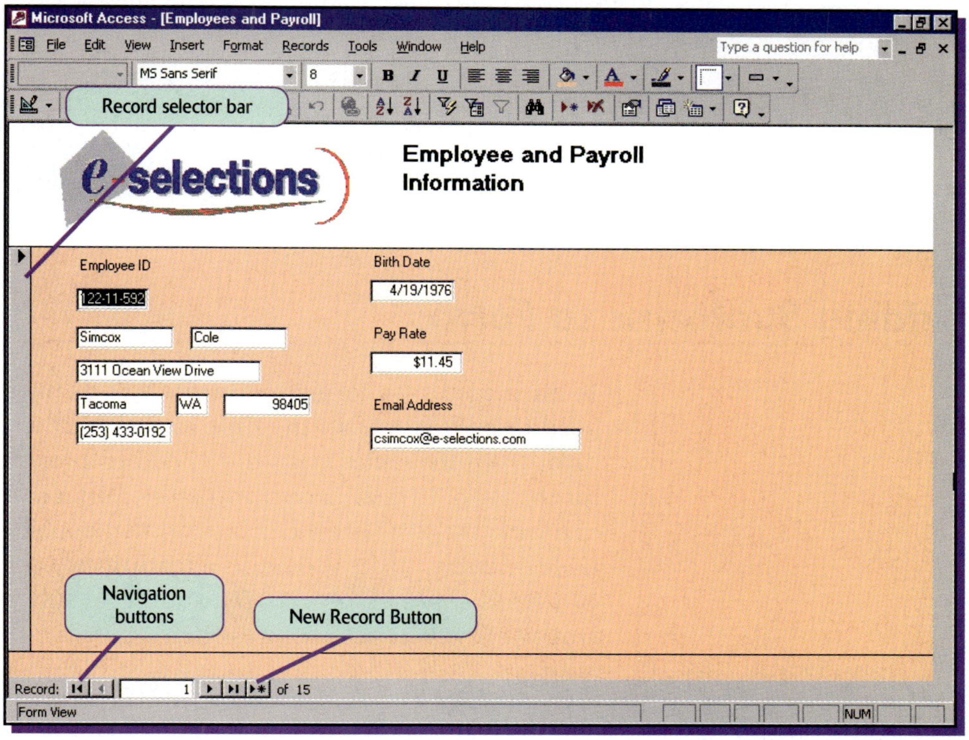

5 Click the Design View button, click the Properties button, select **Form** from the **Properties for** drop-down list, select **No** from the **Record Selectors** drop-down list, and switch to **Form** view.

6 Save changes to the form.

Figure 5-29

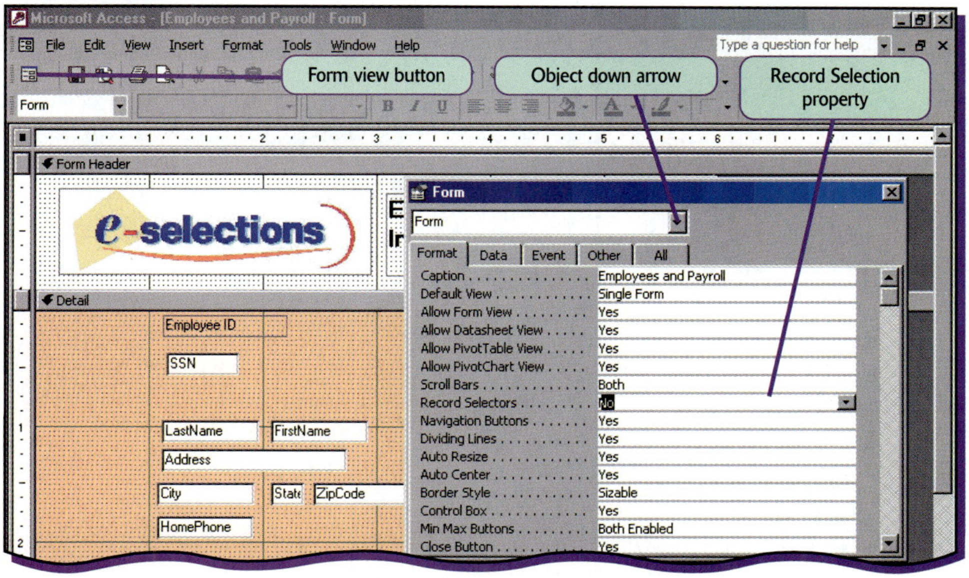

CHECK POINT

When you create a form based on a table or query, Access adds fields contained in the table or query to the form. When these controls are deleted—either intentionally or inadvertently—you can add the controls manually. The *Field List* window displays a list of all the fields contained in the table or query you used to create a form. By displaying the Field List window, you can simply drag the field you want to add to the form and then size and position it appropriately.

Adding Subforms to Forms

In most cases, the forms you create will be based on a single table. When you need to pull data from multiple tables, you'll create a query that contains the fields from the tables you want to add to a form and use the query as the basis for the form. In special circumstances, you may want to create a form based on one table or query but add a control that enables you to review data in another table or query. Access contains a feature called *subforms* to add such a control to access another object. By adding a subform to the form Mr. Traylor requested, you hope to impress him with your Access expertise.

Task 7:
To Add a Subform to a Form

1. Open the **Employees and Payroll** form in Design view and click the Toolbox button on the **Form Design** toolbar to display the Toolbox, if necessary.

2. Click the Subform/SubReport button and drag a rectangle on the form to start the **Subform Wizard**.

3. Select the **Use existing Tables and Queries** option and click Next.

Figure 5-30

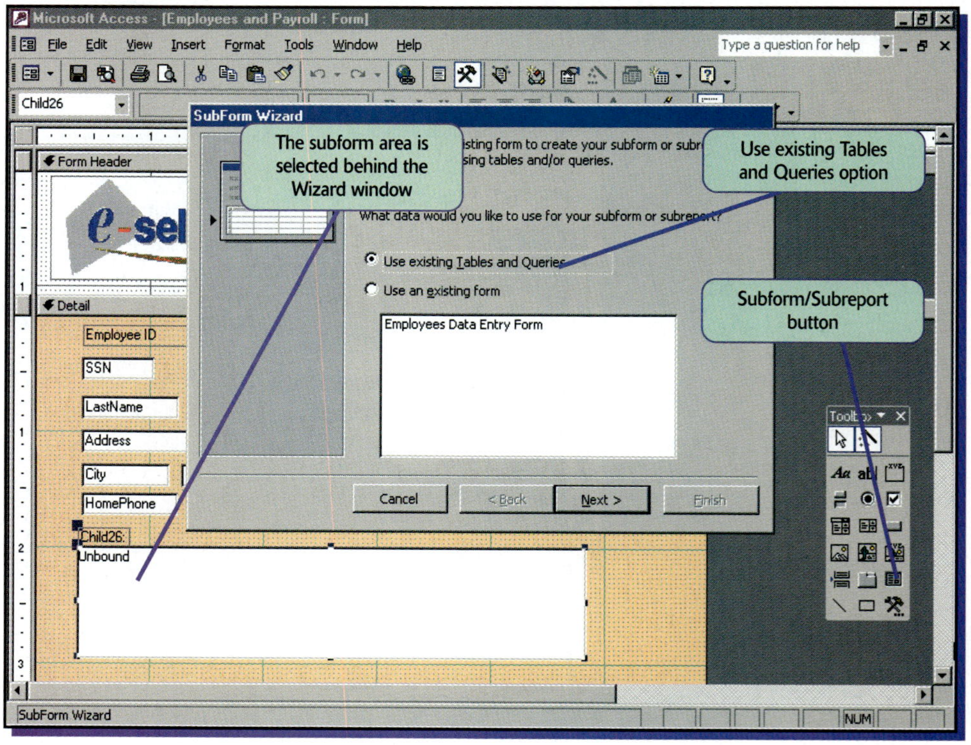

4 Click the **Tables/ Queries** down arrow, select **Table:Time Cards**, click the Move All >> button to move all fields to the **Selected Fields** list, and click Next.

Figure 5-31

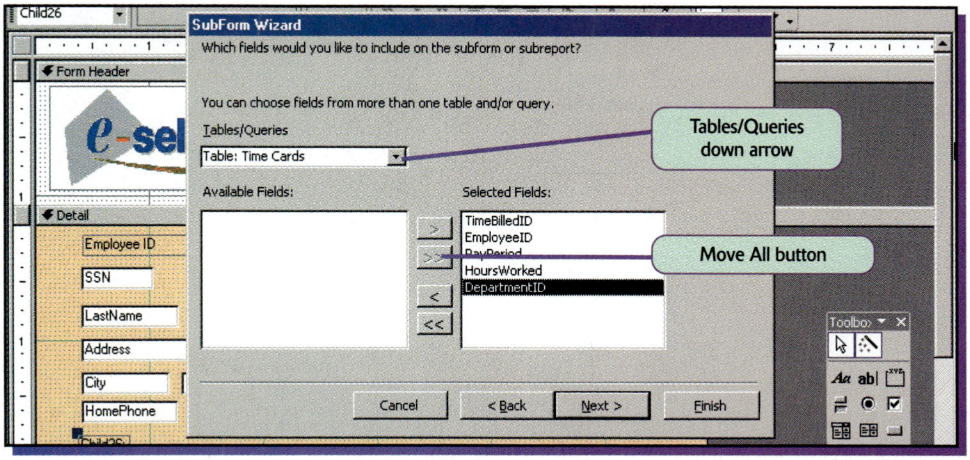

5 Select the **Show Time Cards for each record in Employees using SSN** option to link the **SSN** fields between the tables and click Next.

Tip Linking the SSN numbers from both tables ensures that the time card data for the correct employee will appear.

Figure 5-32

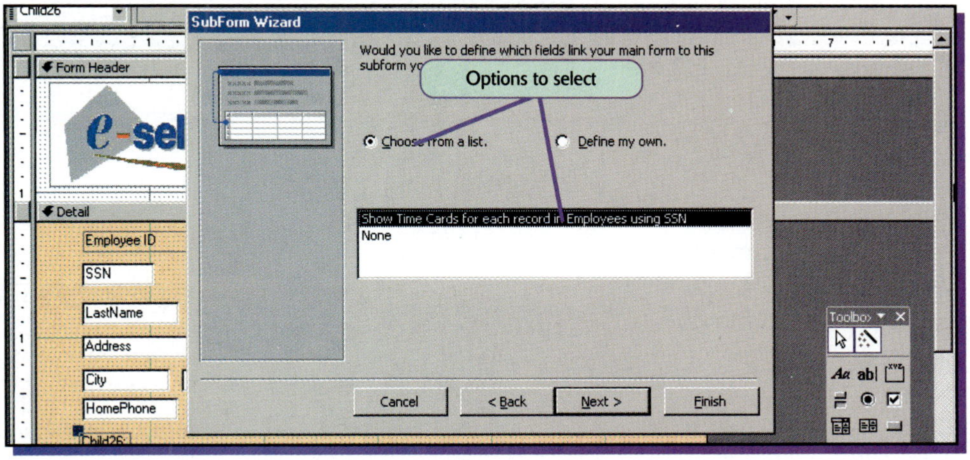

6 Type **TimeCardSubform** in the name box, click **Finish** to create the subform, and maximize the form window, if necessary.

7 Resize the subform control so that it appears as shown in Figure 5-33.

Troubleshooting

If the position of other form fields limits the size of the subform, try moving the fields on the right side of the form to the right so that you can extend the size of the subform so that all subform fields are displayed.

Figure 5-33

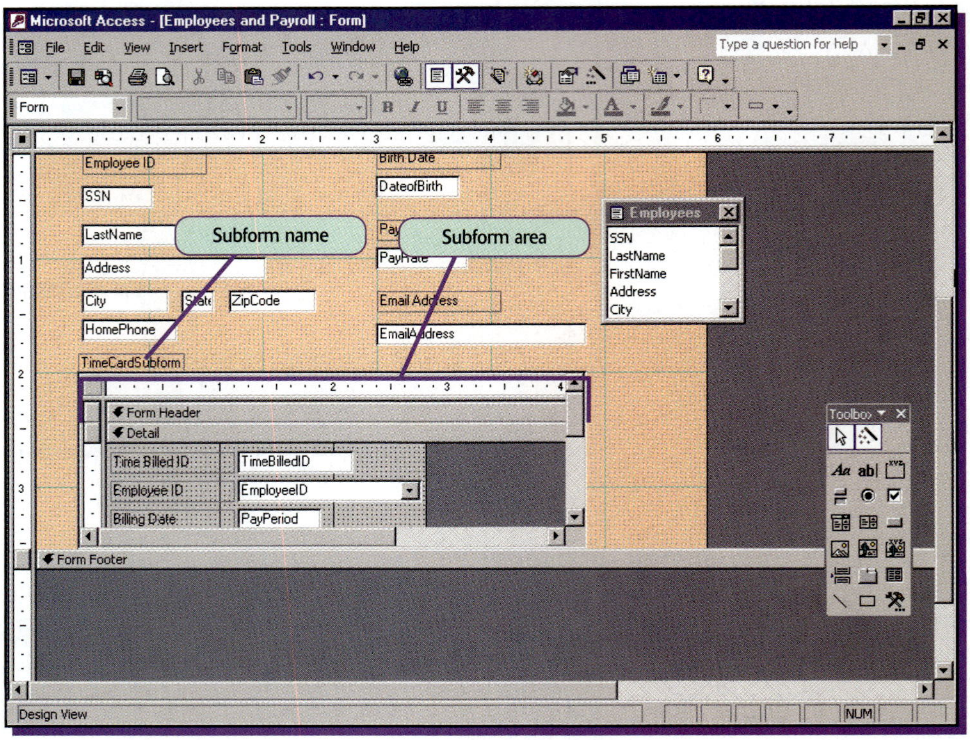

8 Switch to **Form** view, select the **Time Billed ID** column, and choose **Format | Hide Columns** to hide the TimeCardID column.

9 Switch back to **Form Design** view, drag the right side of the form to about the 5-inch mark, adjust the size of the subform table columns as well as the size of the subform control to display Time Card data appropriately, and then save changes to the form.

Figure 5-34

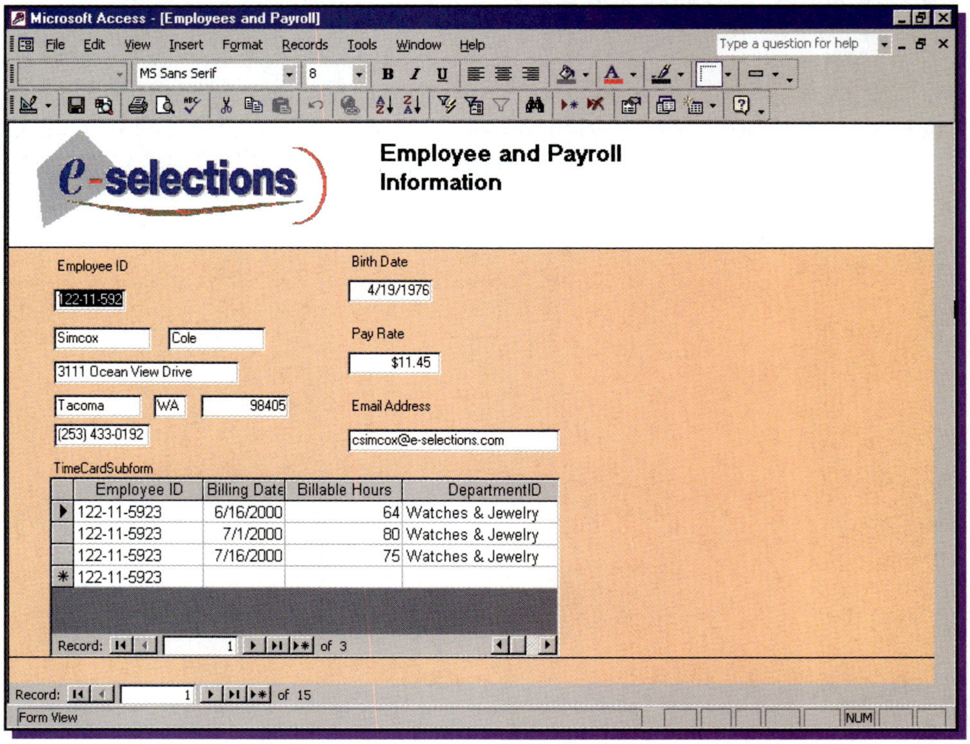

Maintaining Data Using a Form

Before closing the form, it's important to test the form by using the form as the data entry personnel will use it to enter, modify, and delete records. There are two objectives to testing the form:

- To ensure that a record is added to the Time Cards table when you add a new record to the Employee database.
- To ensure that entries made to the Time Cards table using the subform display the information in the form for the correct employee.

When you're satisfied that the form is functioning properly, you can submit the work to Mr. Traylor.

Task 8:
To Test the Employees and Payroll Form

1. Open the **Employees and Payroll** form in **Form** view, if necessary, and click the **New Record** control at the bottom of the form.

2. Type **331-84-2838** in the **Employee ID** field, press Tab, and review the subform to ensure that the number appears in the **Employee ID** column of the subform.

3. Click the **Employee ID** field of the subform, type **477-12-0395**, click the **Employee ID** down arrow, and verify that *Terri Davis* is selected.

4. Close the form, close the database, and exit Access.

Figure 5-35

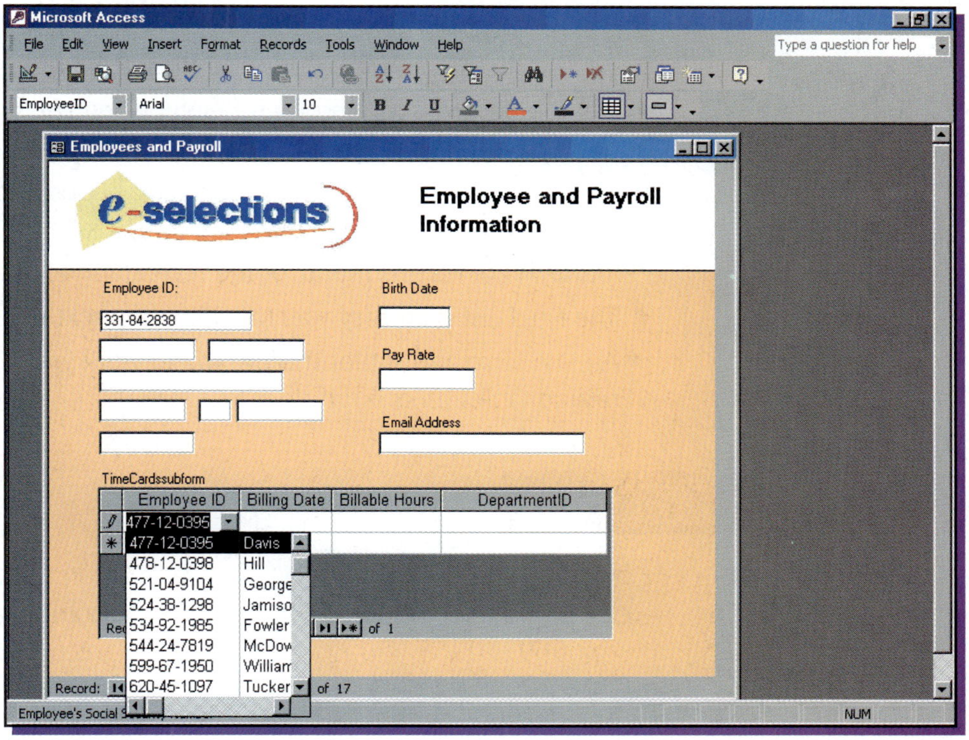

Troubleshooting When you type the new employee ID in step 2, no other information should appear on the form. However, the new ID should appear in the Employee ID field of the subform. If you then complete the information on the form, the new employee would appear in the Employees table.

SUMMARY AND EXERCISES

SUMMARY

- Forms are used to enter, edit, and view data and to navigate through your database.
- You can create a form by using the Form Wizard, one of the AutoForm choices, or in Design view.
- Controls on a form can be resized, deleted, added, or modified in various ways.
- A form can be resized by dragging the right and bottom edges.
- Selecting controls as a group is helpful when you want to move them or modify them as a group.
- The Toolbox has tools you can use to add bound and unbound controls.
- You can modify controls using the Property window, the commands found in the Format menu, or the Formatting toolbar.
- The Field List is an easy way to add bound text box controls.
- A main form and subform allow you to work with records in two related tables on one form.

KEY TERMS & SKILLS

KEY TERMS

bound control (p. 5-7)
calculated control (p. 5-7)
controls (p. 5-7)
Detail section (p. 5-17)
Field List (p. 5-20)
Form Header section (p. 5-17)
Form Wizard (p. 5-4)
forms (p. 5-5)
control label (p. 5-7)
record source (p. 5-5)
subforms (p. 5-20)
text control box (p. 5-7)
toolbox (p. 5-14)
unbound control (p. 5-7)

SKILLS

Add a label control to the Form Header section (p. 5-14)
Add a record to a table using a form (p. 5-20)
Add a subform to a main form (p. 5-20)
Add an image to a form (p. 5-14)
Create a new form using the Form Wizard (p. 5-5)
Modify a form using Form Design view (p. 5-7)
Modify form properties (p. 5-17)
Modify form section properties (p. 5-17)
Modify the caption on a label (p. 5-11)
Move a text box label independently of the text box control (p. 5-11)
Resize a form (p. 5-10)
Resize, move, and modify controls on a form (p. 5-10)
Select a control and a group of controls (p. 5-11)

STUDY QUESTIONS

MULTIPLE CHOICE

1. A control on a form or report that is based on a field in a table or query is what kind of control?
   a. calculated
   b. bound
   c. unbound
   d. label

2. Forms are used for all but what?
   a. viewing data
   b. navigating through the database
   c. selecting out data
   d. modifying data

3. To move a label independent of its text box control you drag
   a. the upper-left-corner handle.
   b. the upper-right-corner handle.
   c. the lower-left-corner handle.
   d. the lower-right-corner handle.

4. Pressing the Shift key while clicking on controls allows you to
   a. select the controls as a group.
   b. format the controls as a group.
   c. change the data source of the controls.
   d. delete the controls.

5. Dragging the pointer in the rulers allows you to
   a. change the size of the form.
   b. add a form section.
   c. modify form properties.
   d. select controls as a group.
6. To add a graphic to a form, you would use what tool?
   a. image control
   b. unbound object control
   c. rectangle
   d. subform control
7. The Field List allows you to add what type of control to a form?
   a. bound image
   b. unbound text box control
   c. bound label
   d. bound text box control
8. A subform/subreport control is usually based on what table?
   a. the table on the "one" side of the relationship
   b. the table on the "many" side of the relationship
   c. the table without any relationship
   d. both a and b
9. Label controls are used to display
   a. field data.
   b. graphics.
   c. navigational buttons.
   d. descriptive text.
10. A form displays records in
   a. Form Design view.
   b. Form view.
   c. Form Datasheet view.
   d. both b and c

SHORT ANSWER

1. What do you use to add various types of controls to a form?
2. To add a graphic to a form, what type of control do you use?
3. What would you use to add a bound text box control to a form?
4. How do you select a group of controls?
5. What is a subform?
6. What are forms used for?
7. What database objects can be used as a record source for a form?
8. What view must you be in to modify a form?
9. How do you modify form or control properties?
10. What is a label control used for?

FILL IN THE BLANK

1. You can create a form by using _____________ or _____________.
2. Forms are used to view, modify, or enter data and to _____________ through the database.
3. To resize a form you would drag the _____________ of the form.
4. You use the _____________ to add controls to a form.
5. A _____________ control does not have a data source.
6. To select a group of controls, you can press the _____________ key while clicking on each control.
7. The _____________ is an easy way to format controls and forms sections.
8. You use _____________view to modify a form.
9. Once you _____________ a form from the database, it cannot be restored using Undo.
10. Dragging in the ruler allows you to _____________controls.

FOR DISCUSSION

1. How do bound controls differ from unbound controls?
2. What are the various ways to select a group of controls?
3. Describe a situation in which you might want to display images on a form that are bound to a record source? What form section would you place this image control in?
4. How do text box controls and label controls differ?
5. What do forms allow database users to do?

GUIDED EXERCISES

1 THE HOME THEATER SERVICE PLANS DATABASE

Now that you have a custom form in the *e-Selections Forms.mdb* database, you can add custom forms to the Home Theater Service Plans database. A copy of the finished form appears in Figure 5-36.

Figure 5-36

Follow these steps to create a form based on the Customers table.

1. Open the *Home Theater Service Plans.mdb* file.
2. Use the Form Wizard to create a form based on the **Customers** table, add all fields to the form, format the form using a columnar layout with the standard style, and name the form *Customers*.
3. Switch to Form Design view, maximize the window, and drag the corners of the form to 5 inches wide by 3 inches high.
4. Delete the **FirstName**, **LastName**, **Address, City**, **State,** and **ZipCode** labels.
5. Using the skills you learned in this project, move and size controls to match those shown in Figure 5-36. Remember to drag the upper-left-hand corner of a text box control to move it independently of its label.
6. Enlarge the **Form Header** section by dragging the top edge of the **Detail** section bar down to the 1-inch mark on the vertical ruler.
7. Add the *e-Selections.jpg* file to the header section, open the **Properties** window and modify the **Size** mode property to **Stretch**, resize the image so that it is about 3 inches wide by 1 inch high, and position the image as shown in Figure 5-36.
8. Add an unbound label control to the header, type **The Home Theater Warranty Repair Database Entry Form** in the label text box, and set the label font to **Tahoma**, **14**, **Bold**.
9. Click the **Font/Fore Color** down arrow and click the **dark blue** color.
10. Format the Form Header background so that it appears white and the Form Detail background section so that it appears blue.
11. Save changes to the form, switch to Form view, and print a copy of one record.

2 SUBDIVIDING THE HOME THEATER SERVICE PLANS DATABASE

You can spiff up the basic form created for the Home Theater Service Plans database by adding a subform to access the Repairs table. When you're finished, your form will resemble the form shown in Figure 5-37.

Figure 5-37

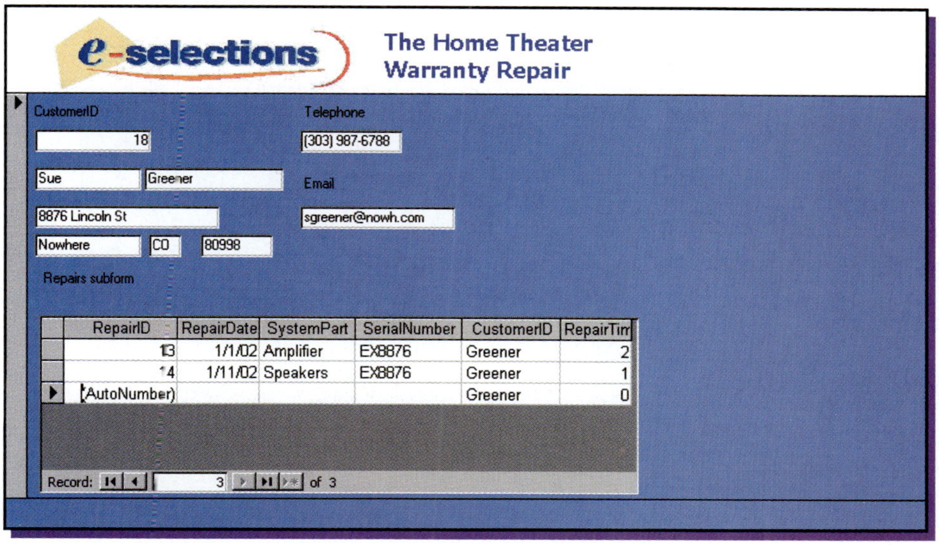

Follow these steps to add the subform to the Customers form:

1. Open the *Home Theater Service Plans.mdb* file and display the **Customers** form in Form Design view.
2. Add a subform control based on the **Repairs** table to the lower portion of the Detail section of the form, keeping the default subform name.
3. Add the **RepairID**, **RepairDate**, **SystemPart**, **SerialNumber**, **CustomerID**, and **RepairTime** fields to the subform, and link the two forms on the **CustomerID** field.
4. Size the subform and columns so that they appear as shown in Figure 5-37.
5. Add the record for *Sue Greener* and her repair records as shown in Figure 5-37.
6. Save the changes to the form, print a copy of one record using the form, close the form, compact the database, and close it.

3 THE EARNING A PROFIT DATABASE

The Earning a Profit database can benefit from a custom form that enables data entry personnel to view data from the Orders table while looking at information in the Items table. You can create the form shown in Figure 5-38 to meet their needs.

Figure 5-38

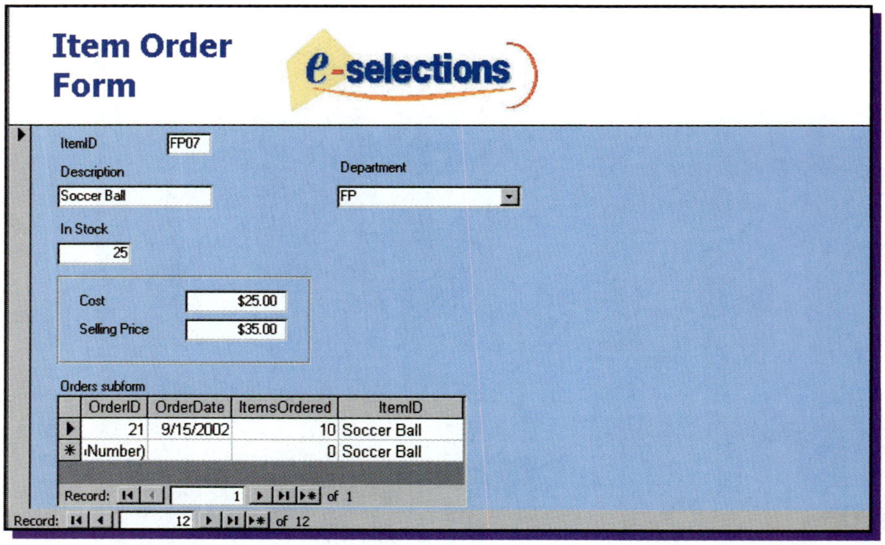

Follow these steps to create the form:

1. Open the *Earning a Profit.mdb* file.
2. Use the Form Wizard to create a form based on the **Items** table that contains all fields and displays the columnar layout and the standard style. Keep the default form name.
3. Resize the form so that it is about 5 inches wide and 3 inches high, and modify, size, and move form labels and text box controls so that they appear as shown in Figure 5-38.
4. Use the **Rectangle** tool to draw a rectangle around the **Cost** and **Selling Price** labels and text box controls.
5. Size the **Form Header** section to about 1 inch, add the *e-Selections.jpg* graphic to the Form Header section, stretch the **Size Mode** property, and size the graphic as shown in Figure 5-38.
6. Add an unbound label control containing the words *Item Entry Form*, and format the text to appear as shown in Figure 5-38.

7 Add a subform control to the form based on the **Orders** table, add all **Orders** table fields, and link the tables using the **ItemID** field. Keep the default subform name. Size and position the subform as shown in Figure 5-38.

8 Save changes to the database, print a copy of one record using the form, and then close the database.

4 CREATING BTC ORDERS DATABASE

Brent wants to make the data entry process for his customer orders more efficient for the data entry personnel. As a result, he has decided to have you create a form for the personnel to use. The form that he has suggested is shown in Figure 5-39.

Figure 5-39

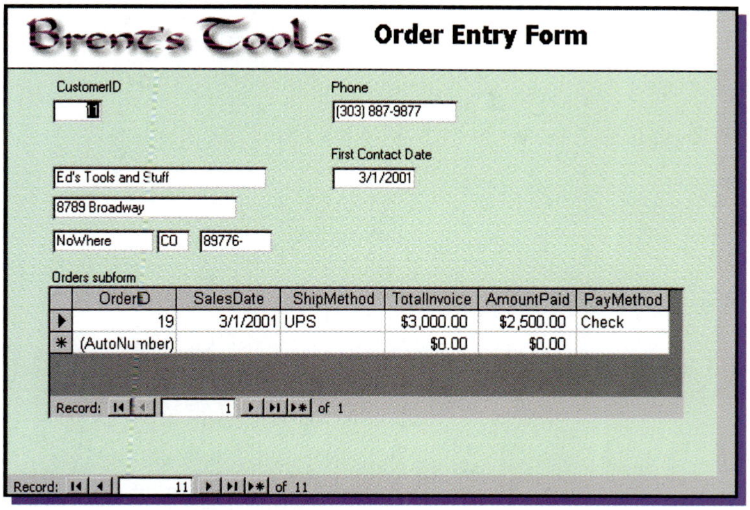

Follow these steps to create the form:

1 Open the *BTC Orders.mdb* file or your personal copy of the database, if available.

2 Use the Form Wizard to create a form based on the **Customers** table, add all fields to the form, select the columnar layout and the standard style, and accept the default form name.

3 Size the form so that it is about 5 inches wide and 3 inches high, and then modify, size, and position labels and text box controls so that they appear as shown in Figure 5-39.

4. Size the **Form Header** section to about 1 inch, add the *Brent's Tools Logo.gif* graphic to the Form Header, set the **Size Mode** property to **Stretch**, and size and position the graphic as shown in Figure 5-39.

5. Add the unbound label control to the **Form Header** section as shown in Figure 5-39, create a subform that links to the **Orders** table, and format the subform as shown in Figure 5-39.

> **Tip** Notice that the **CustomerID** field is not displayed in Figure 5-39. You must add this field to the form when you run the Subform wizard. Then, after creating the subform, switch to **Form Design** view and hide the column.

6. Remove the record selector by modifying the form **Record Selectors** property.

7. Save changes to database objects, print a copy of one record using the form, and close the database.

ON YOUR OWN

The difficulty of these case studies varies:

are the least difficult; *are more difficult; and* *are the most difficult.*

1 COLLEGE TESTS & ASSIGNMENTS

Wouldn't it be great if you could add data to your assignments database in a form that contained your school emblem? Download a copy of the emblem from the school Web site and then use the *College Tests & Assignments.mdb* file to create a form that will enable you to enter both classes and assignments. Add a copy of your school emblem to the Form Header section and then use the form to add a few records to the database. Print a copy of one record using the form.

2 NANCY'S KNICK-KNACK NOOK

Nancy needs a form that will enable her to review information for a supplier and identify the items that the supplier provides. Open the *KKN Inventory.mdb* file and create a main form based on the **Suppliers** table. Add a subform based on the **Items** table and add the *Nancy.jpg* graphic to the Form Header section. Then arrange the items on the form appropriately. Print a copy of one record using the form.

3 PINE VALLEY CONTRIBUTIONS DATABASE

Viewing the contributions along with the contributors for Pine Valley would make searching the database for information much easier. Open the *PVO Fund Raising.mdb* file. Create a form that contains a subform that can be used to enter contributors and contributions from the same form. Insert the *PVO.gif* graphic on the form and arrange the fields and other objects appropriately. Test the form by adding a few records using your form. Then create a form based on one of the queries contained in the database, arranging the data appropriately and inserting the *PVO.gif* graphic in the **Form Header** section. Print a copy of one record using each of the forms you create.

4 BEAVER CONFERENCE FACILITIES DATABASE

The Beaver Brook Inn and Conference Center has been overwhelmed with requests from different organizations to schedule conferences at the Center. Each request has been accompanied by a request for specific numbers of rooms to be reserved for each conference. Reservations personnel are finding it a challenge to determine Center and room availability as the requests come in. Creating a form with a subform will enable reservationists to schedule both group information and room assignments at the same time. Create a form in the *Beaver Conference Facilities.mdb* database that contains a subform that can be used to enter group information and to schedule rooms for each group at the same time. Test the form by adding a few fictitious records using your form. Then create a form based on at least one of the queries contained in the database and print a copy of one record using each of the new forms.

5 GET IN SHAPE SPA

With the onset of spring, the Get in Shape Spa has been inundated with new members, each trying to schedule classes and get in shape for the warm weather. As a result, the club needs a form that enables their personnel to enter information for new members and register them for classes at the same time. Create a form in the *Get in Shape Spa.mdb* file for entering, modifying, and viewing member and class registration information. Then search the Web for an appropriate graphic to add to the Form Header to dress up the form. Test the form by adding a few records using your form. Print a copy of one record using the form.

Photospread credits pages 5-2 & 5-3

©FPG: ©FPG 1995, ©VCG 1997, ©Guy Marche, 1994; ©Pearson Education, ©Lorraine Castellano

FROM THE FILES

You Will Need

- ✔ e-Selections Reports.mdb
- ✔ e-Selections.jpg
- ✔ College Assignments Report.mdb
- ✔ HTS Warranty Repair Reports.mdb
- ✔ Make A Profit Reports.mdb
- ✔ Brent's Tools Order Reports.mdb
- ✔ Brent's Tools Logo.gif
- ✔ PVO Contributions Report.mdb
- ✔ PVO.gif
- ✔ Nancy's Inventory Reports.mdb
- ✔ Nancy.jpg
- ✔ BBICC Facilities Reports.mdb
- ✔ BBIC.gif
- ✔ GIS Fitness Club Reports.mdb
- ✔ GIS.gif

PROJECT 6

Creating and Modifying Reports

Each database object is designed for specific purposes: tables hold data and records, queries provide a grid for selecting records that meet specific criteria, and forms can be used for data entry and on-screen viewing. Reports are designed to present summarized database data in printed form. Reports enable you to display information from tables and queries, summarize the data, and design the layout of report elements as you want them to appear on the printed document. If you have already explored features for designing custom forms, you'll discover that many of the design and layout techniques you used can be used to create custom reports. In this project, you will use the Report Wizard to create a report and then modify the report to sort, group, and summarize data and to add visual elements to the report.

e-selections Running Case

As you worked with designing and using different database objects, you identified a number of features that you believed would enable you to design reports that summarize data and track activity and information more efficiently. Now that you have a number of tables containing data within the database, you can turn your attention to exploring these report features more thoroughly.

OBJECTIVES

After completing this project, you will be able to:

- *Display Report Design view and identify window features*
- *Create a report using the Report Wizard*
- *Modify a report design*
- *Create a report using Report Design view*
- *Add sorting and grouping levels to a report*
- *Add a calculated control to a report*
- *Add visual elements to a report header and footer*
- *Create mailing labels*

Databases and the Web

The Internet is here to stay. So much of the information we use every day is stored and retrieved via the Web. Information sites provide such resources as dictionaries, people finders, and encyclopedias, and e-commerce sites pop up every day—selling everything imaginable.

The power of these database-driven sites is incredible. For example, Amazon maintains an inventory of millions of books, CDs, videos, DVDs, toys, games, and electronics. They use databases to maintain records on every item. They use these databases to provide customers with instant information about each item. Like Amazon.com, most e-commerce and information Web sites use databases to manage their content.

How, you ask? These sites accept the information request from a client through a Web browser, and then query the database. Helper applications can create HTML pages based on the results of that query.

Travelocity uses the power of linking multiple databases to help customers plan entire vacations. Using this one site, you can buy airline tickets, rent cars, and book hotel rooms. All of these features are made possible in one Web site because Travelocity has made arrangements that allow it to tap into the databases of many companies throughout the world.

Because of the ever-growing need for databases in e-commerce, more and more database engines are being designed with e-commerce in mind. Carl Olofson, an analyst for IDC, recently stated in an article for InfoWorld, "As users expose more functionality over the Internet for e-business purposes you will have intense demand for data that is immediately accessible online."

As the need for this type of database grows, the competition between database products grows. Consequently, database engines are getting smarter and better at managing content. They are beginning to create databases that are directly integrated with server platforms.

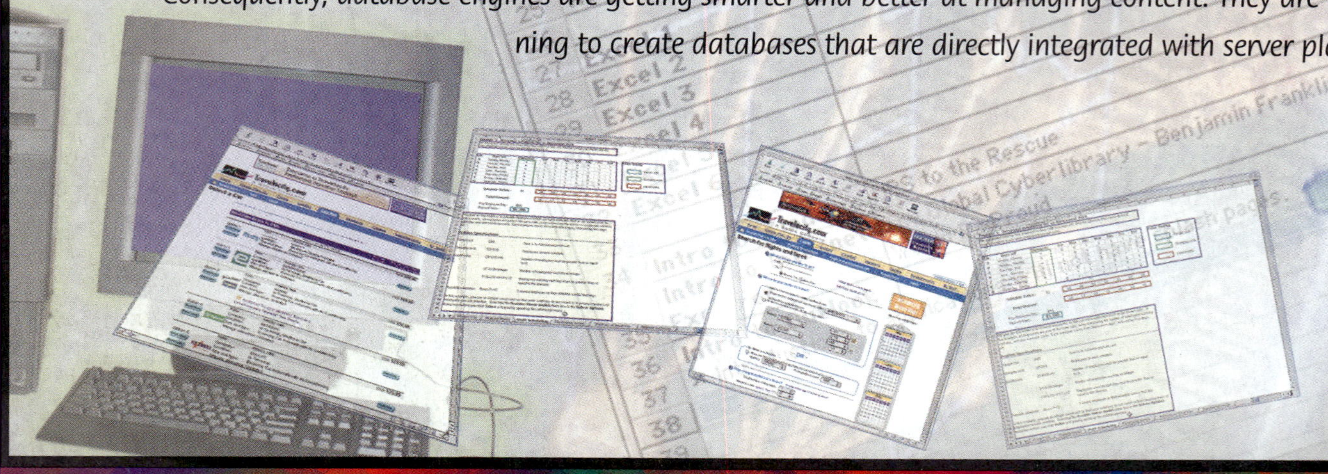

Connecting Your Data to the Web

You don't need to be an e-commerce guru to utilize this Web technology. Your information can be there, too. You can connect your Web site to your database so that your information can be accessed by one and all. Microsoft has conveniently fused Access and Internet Explorer in several ways to do this.

Did you know that you can create links within your database? Using Access, you can link to:

- ***A Web page:*** *Think how convenient it will be to access a client's home page or e-mail with just a click.*
- ***A document:*** *Creating form letters was never so easy.*
- ***Another object:*** *You can quickly jump to related information within the same database or even related information from another database.*

You can even go a step further and publish your database on your company's intranet site or even to an Internet Web site. By doing this you create a way for clients and sales staff to retrieve information about products and services or to check on the status of an order.

You can publish your data by exporting your database to the Web using one of two methods. First, you can export to an Internet Information Server (IIS) or to an Active Server Page (ASP). This method keeps your database dynamic. This means that every change will be updated instantly.

The second method is to export to a static HTML page. When you publish your database to the Web using this method, the data remains constant; you have to re-export the database to update it.

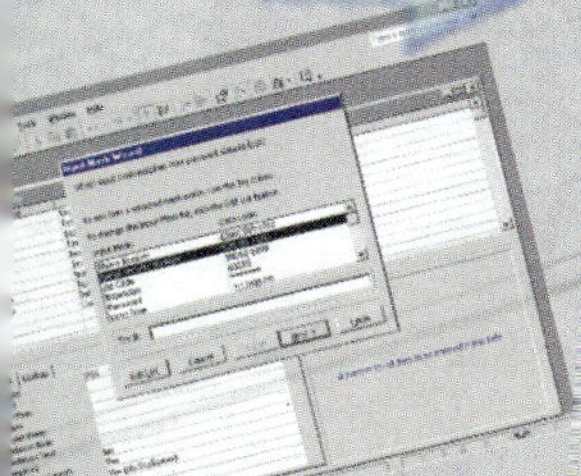

PROJECT 6

Creating and Modifying Reports

The Challenge

Mr. Traylor is very pleased with the work you have done on the Employees database, and he now wants to begin distributing printed information using the data. Mr. Traylor has requested a list of employee addresses to distribute to the Human Resources Department and a summary of each employee's earnings so far this year.

The Solution

The tasks Mr. Traylor has requested provides you with a good excuse to learn some of the skills required to design custom reports that summarize data. As you complete the tasks in this project, you will learn how to create reports using the Report Wizard and how to apply report design techniques to create the reports shown in Figure 6-1.

Figure 6-1

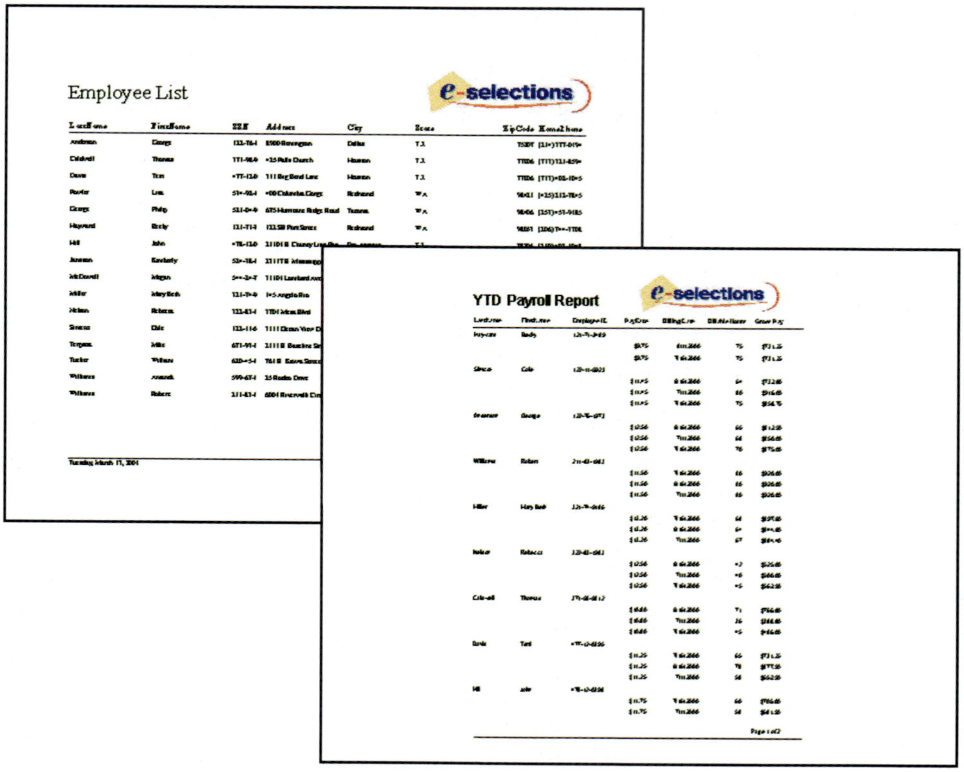

Displaying Report Design View and Identifying Window Features

Access provides a number of different techniques for creating and customizing reports. You can use the Report Wizard to create the report and then customize it using the Report Design window. Another option is to start from scratch using the Report Design window to add and position report elements—fields, data, titles, graphics, etc.—where you want them. The *Report Design window* contains a graphical workspace with the following five sections, each designed to hold different report elements:

- The *Page Header* and *Page Footer* sections contain information that will appear on every page of the report.
- The *Detail* section holds information that is bound to specific fields in the database table or query.
- The *Report Header* and *Report Footer* sections contain information that appears at either the top or bottom of a report.

Task 1:
To Display Report Design View and Identify Window Features

1. Open the *e-Selections Reports.mdb* file and click the Reports button on the Objects bar.
2. Click the **Employees List** report name to select it and then click the Design button.
3. Close the **Field List**, if necessary; arrange screen features as shown in Figure 6-2; and review the contents of each report section.
4. Close the report without saving changes.

Figure 6-2

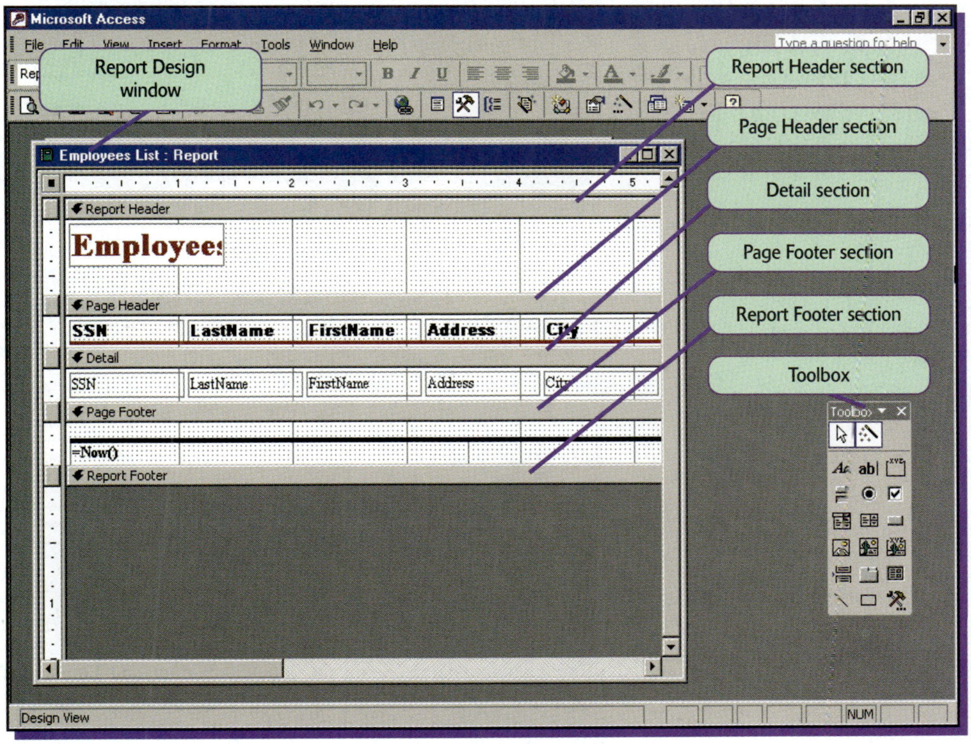

WEB TIP

Looking for other ways to report data in Microsoft Access? How about using report snapshots or static HTML pages? Search the Internet for these terms to learn more about them.

Creating a Report Using the Report Wizard

While Access provides a number of different ways to create a report, the Report Wizard walks you through the process and simplifies the process of creating your first report. After the report is complete, you can view the report and then switch to the Report Design window to make necessary modifications.

Task 2:

To Create a Report Using the Report Wizard

1. Click the Reports button on the Objects bar, if necessary, and click the New button to open the New Report dialog box.

2. Select **Report Wizard** and select **Employees** from the **Choose the table or query where the object's data comes from** list.

Figure 6-3

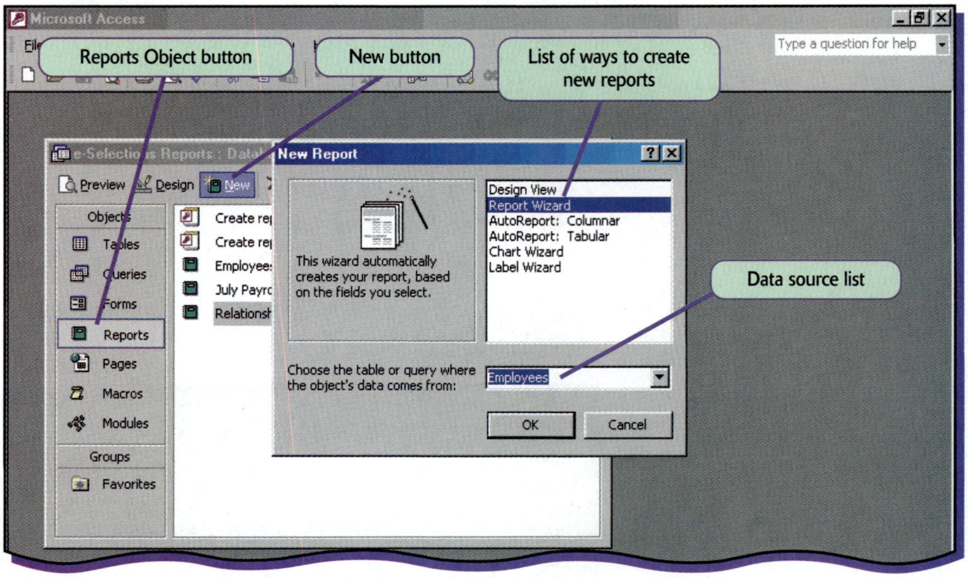

Other Ways

To display the New Report dialog box:

- Choose **Insert** | **Report**.
- Click the New Object down arrow and select **Report**.

3. Click **OK** and move the **SSN**, **LastName**, **FirstName**, **Address**, **City**, **State**, **ZipCode**, and **HomePhone** fields from the **Available Fields** list to the **Selected Fields** list.

Figure 6-4

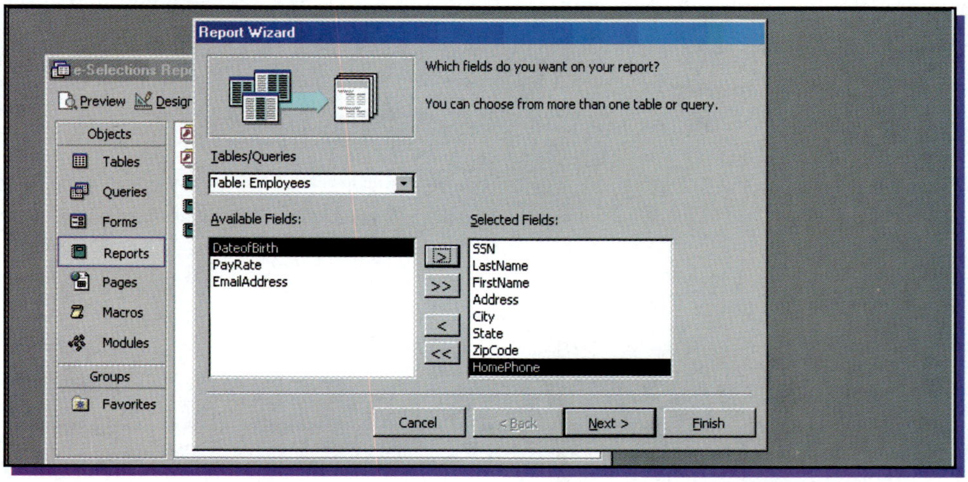

4 Click **Next** and then click **Next** again to accept the default grouping levels.

5 Click the **1** down arrow and select **LastName**, click the **2** down arrow and select **FirstName**, select the **Ascending** sort order for both fields and click Next.

Figure 6-5

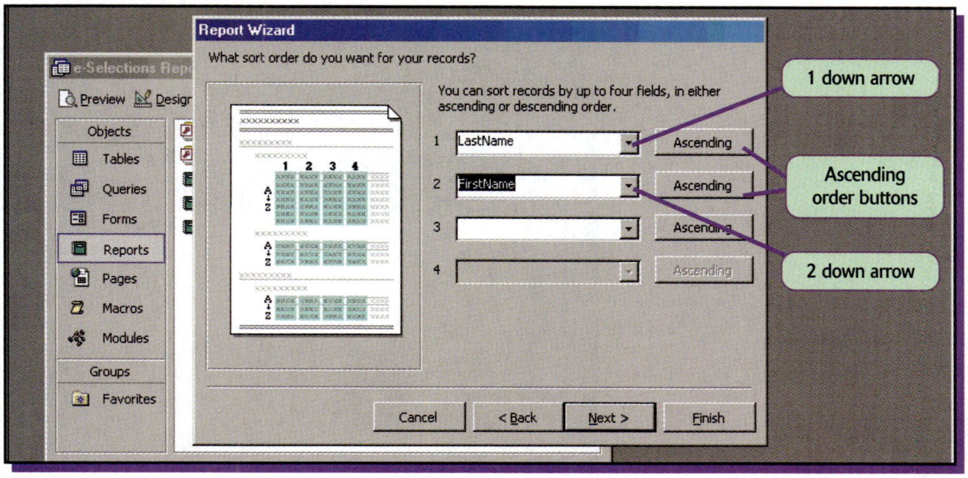

6 Select the **Columnar** layout option and the **Landscape** orientation option, and select the **Adjust the field widths so all fields fit on a page** option and click **Next**.

Tip By changing the orientation to Landscape when you have numerous columns to display, you can easily adjust the column widths to show all columns on the page.

Figure 6-6

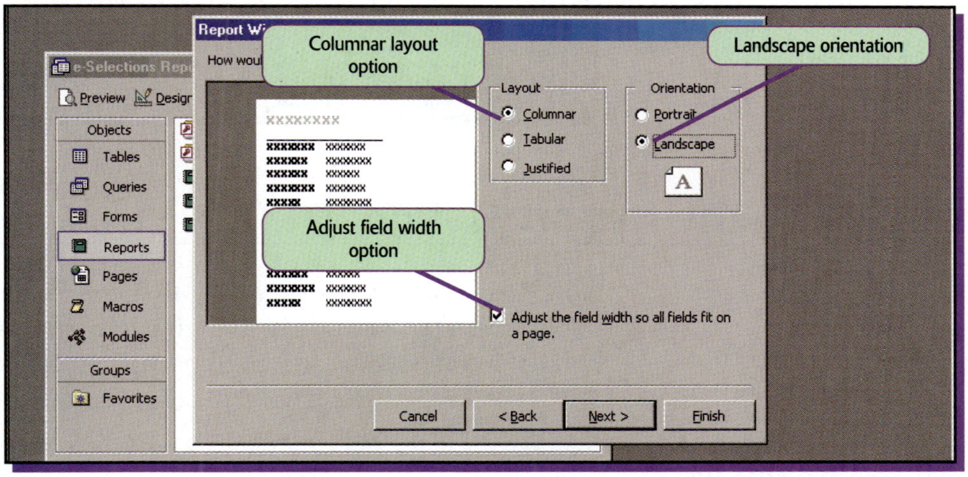

7 Select **Formal** from the styles list, and click **Next**.

Figure 6-7

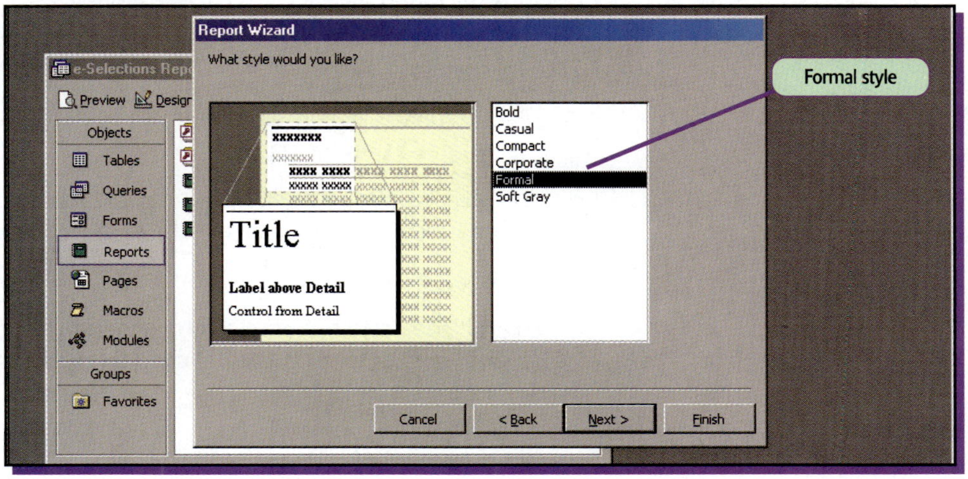

8 Click **Finish** to accept the default report name and other options on the final Wizard page.

Tip You can display a report in the Print Preview at any time by clicking the Print Preview button on the Database toolbar.

9 Close the report window.

Figure 6-8

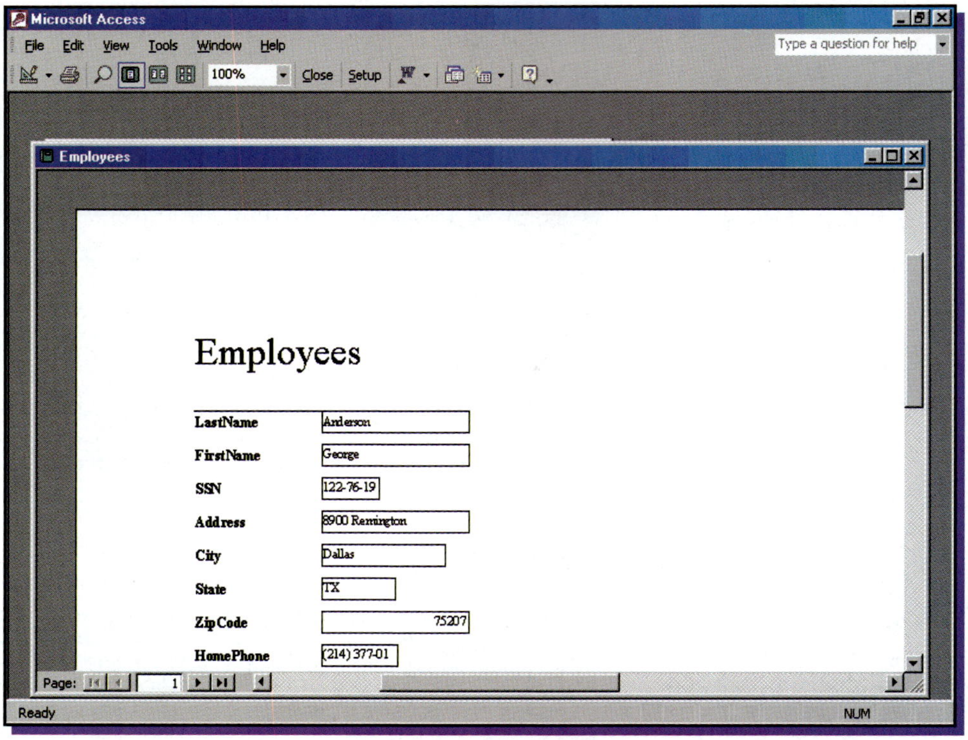

Modifying the Report Design

Now that you have a basic report that contains the fields you want to include in the report, you can customize each section of the report, change field names, size the report and fields, arrange the fields, and add graphic elements. You'll use Report Design view to customize the report layout in order to create the report Mr. Traylor wants.

CHECK POINT

As you work with fields and other information in Report Design view, you will move, size, and change report *controls*. You may recall that controls are objects on a form, report, or data access page that display data, perform actions, and decorate database objects. The three different types of controls on Access objects are the following:

- *Bound* controls—information tied to a field in a table or query so that the field value appears on the report.
- *Unbound* controls—independent items on a report page such as lines, rectangles, or pictures that visually organize report data.
- *Calculated* controls—information tied to an expression or calculated field.

A control label identifies each control added to a report. You can delete the labels when appropriate, leaving just the control text box that displays the field value.

Modifying the Report Header

When you create a report, Access automatically adds the report name to the Report Header section of the report. You can modify the text that appears in the Report Header to better reflect the contents of the report.

Task 3:
To Customize the Report Header

1. Click the Reports button on the Objects bar, if necessary; select the **Employees** report; and click the Design button.

2. Click the **Employees** label in the Report Header section to select it, double-click the label text to select it, and type **Employee List.**

Figure 6-9

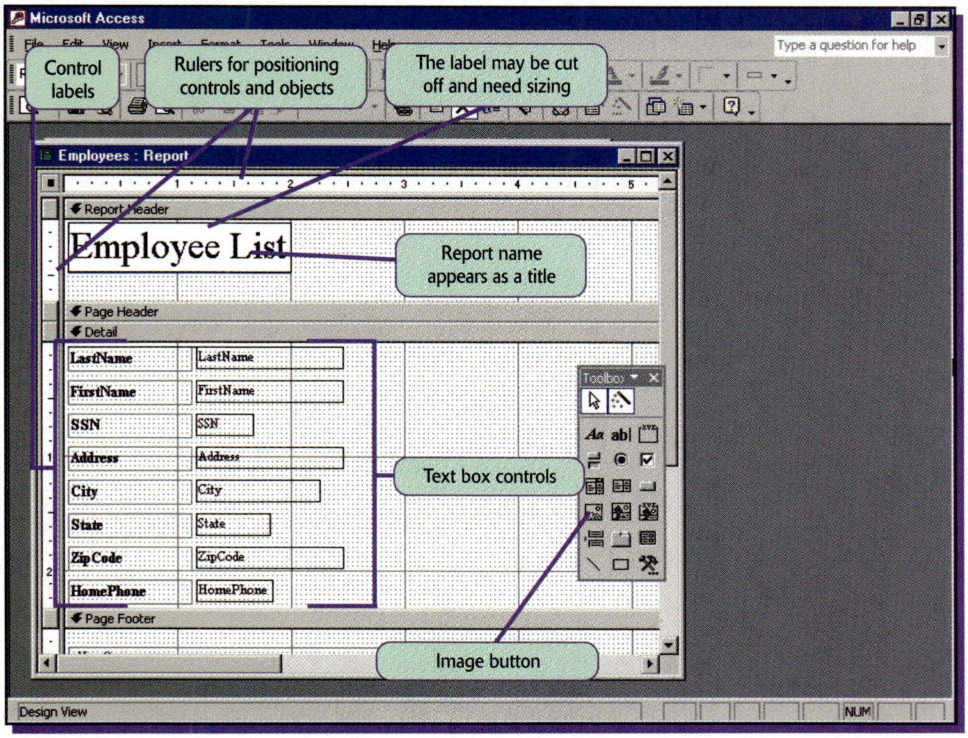

Troubleshooting If the Toolbox is hidden, click the Toolbox button to display it and close the **Employees** field list if it opens.

3 Maximize the Report Design window, if necessary; click the Image button in the Toolbox; and click the **Report Header** section of the report layout at about the 5-inch mark.

Other Ways

To insert a graphic in a report section:

- Select the section to contain the graphic and choose **Insert | Picture | From File.**

Figure 6-10

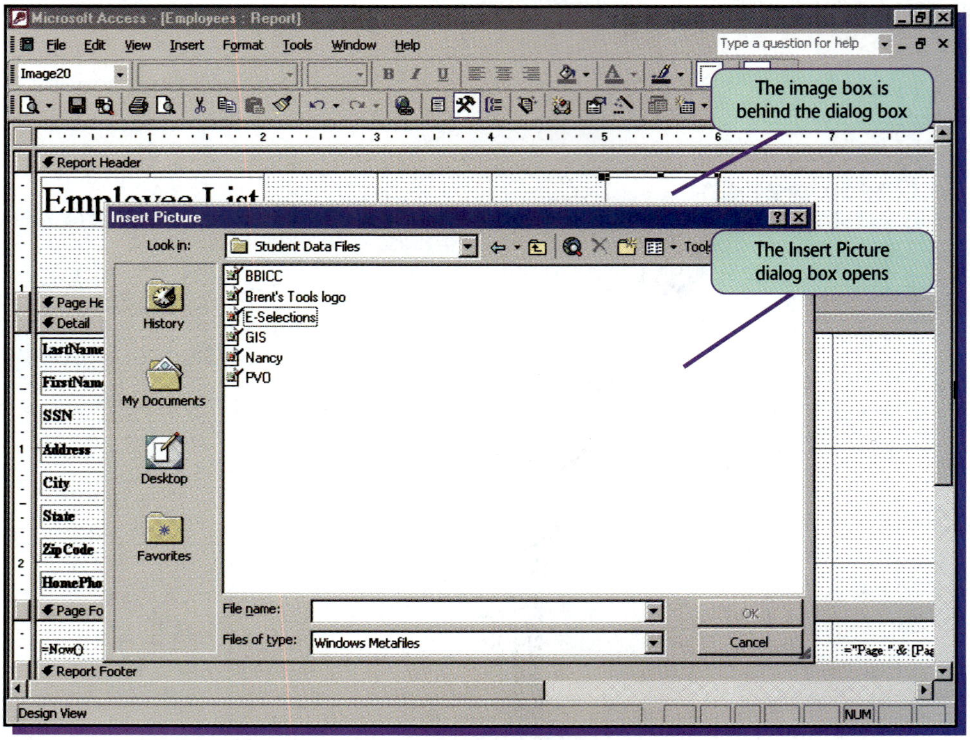

4 Select the *e-Selections.jpg* file and click **OK** to insert the logo into the Report Header section.

Troubleshooting

Depending on the setting for your computer, graphics may be hidden. To display graphics in formats other than Windows Metafile (.wmf), select the correct file format from the **Files of type** list.

5 Right-click the logo and select **Properties** from the shortcut menu.

Figure 6-11

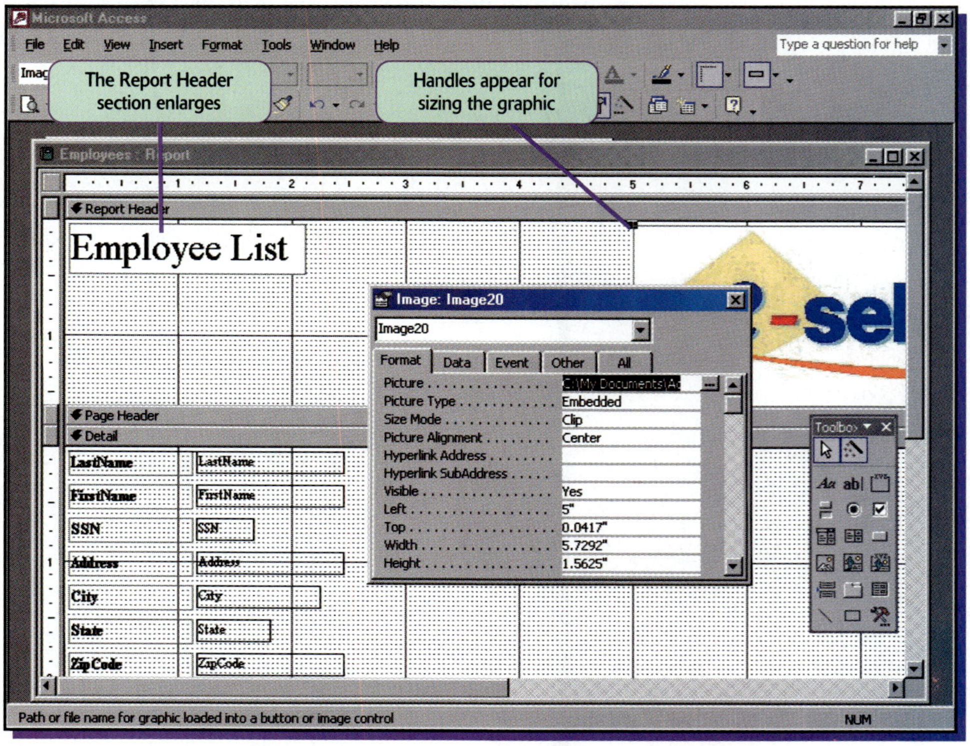

Other Ways

To open the Properties dialog box:

- Click the Properties button on the toolbar.
- Select the graphic and press F4.
- Select the graphic and choose **View | Properties.**

6 Select **Stretch** from the **Size Mode** drop-down list, change the value of the **Width** property to **3**, change the value of the **Height** property to **.75**, and then close the dialog box.

7 Drag the **Page Header** section bar up to position it just below the logo.

8 Save changes to the report and click the Print Preview button to view the report.

Tip

By now, you may already be familiar with tools on the Print Preview toolbar. For a quick review of these tools, point to each button and review the screen tip to see what tools are available.

Figure 6-12

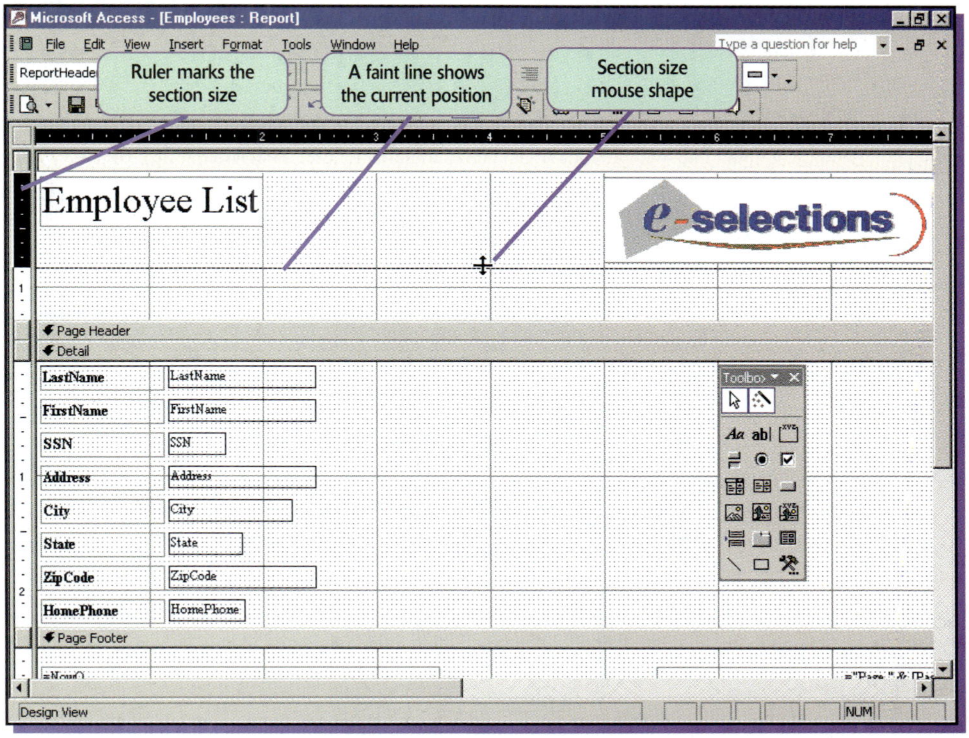

Figure 6-13

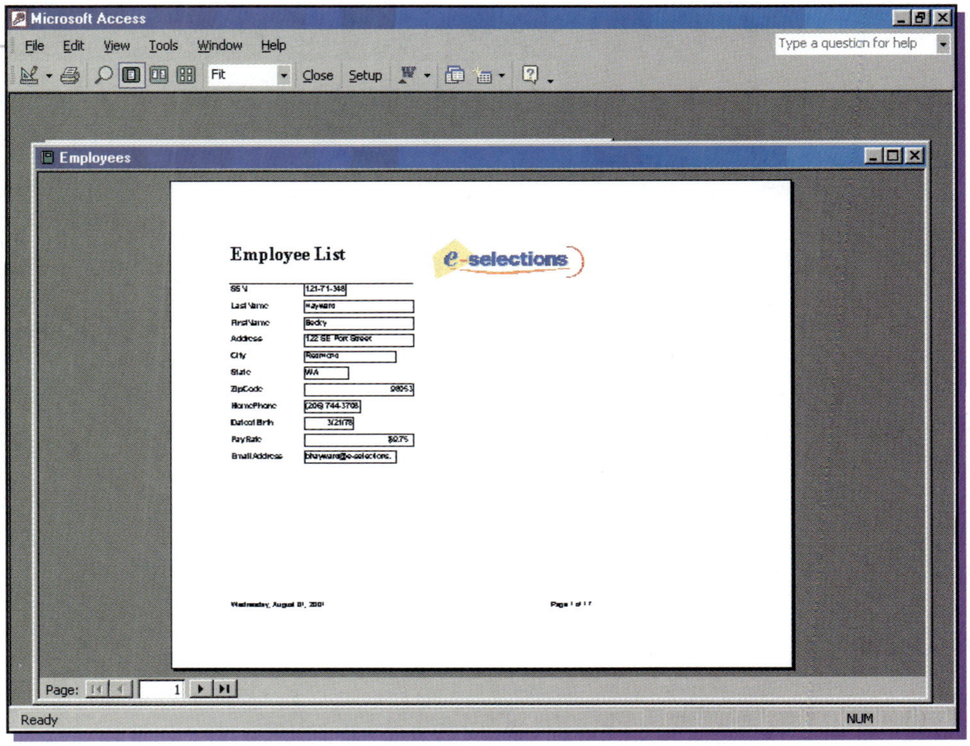

Customizing the Page Header and Detail Sections

The information you place in the Report Header section appears at the top of the first page of the report only. Titles of columns and other information important to a person reviewing a report are placed in the Page Header section so that the information is repeated at the top of each report page. Information placed in the Detail section draws data from database tables, and the Detail section expands to accommodate details for each database record. To create the report Mr. Traylor wants, you need to reposition field data and labels.

Task 4:
To Modify the Page Header and Detail Sections of a Report

1. Open the **Employees** report in Design view, if necessary.
2. Click the **FirstName** label in the Detail section to select it and press Delete to delete the label.
3. Select the **LastName** label, double-click the label text, type **Name**, select the text in the **SSN** label, and change it to **Employee ID**.

Figure 6-14

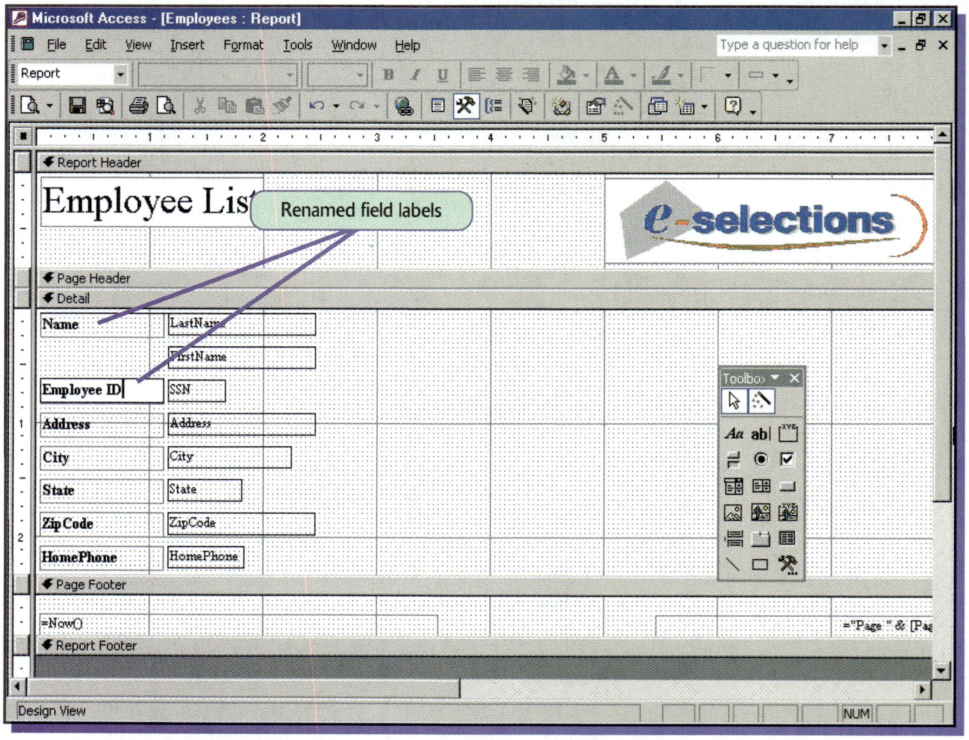

CHECK POINT

Do you remember the different ways you can copy and move text? To cut and paste information:

To cut:

- Press Ctrl + X.
- Choose **Edit | Cut**.

To paste:

- Press Ctrl + V.
- Choose **Edit | Paste**.

4 Drag the **Detail** section bar down about 1/2 inch to open space for the Page Header section.

5 Right-click the **Name** label and click Cut to remove the label.

6 Position the insertion point in the **Page Header** section and click the Paste button.

7 Repeat the procedures outlined in Step 4 to move additional field labels into the **Page Header** section, sizing and positioning them as shown in Figure 6-15.

8 Size and position the text box controls in the **Detail** section so that they appear as shown in Figure 6-16, and drag the **Page Footer** section bar to a position just below the text box controls.

9 Save changes to the report and click the Print Preview button to review the report and click OK to acknowledge any message windows that open.

10 Close the Print Preview window, make the necessary adjustments to the text box controls in the Report Design window, and save and close the report.

Figure 6-15

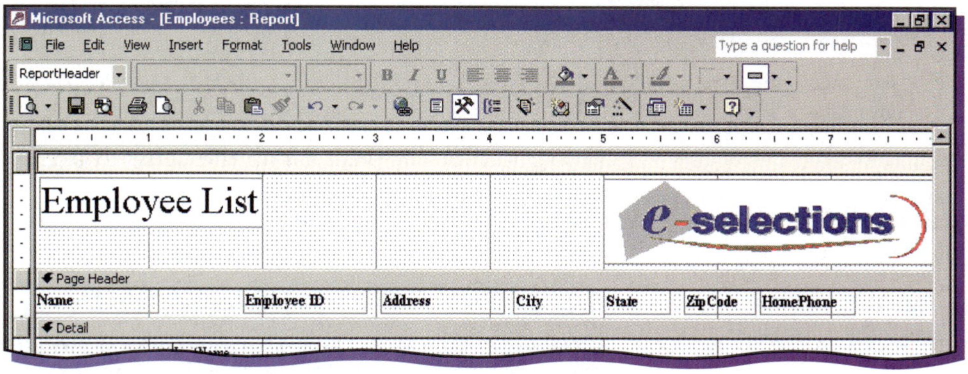

Tip As you place each label in the Page Header section, the label appears at the far left edge of the report. To move a field label or field text box control, position the mouse pointer on the control border until it appears as a flat hand and then drag the label or control into position. Select a label and drag the side handle to change the size of the label.

Figure 6-16

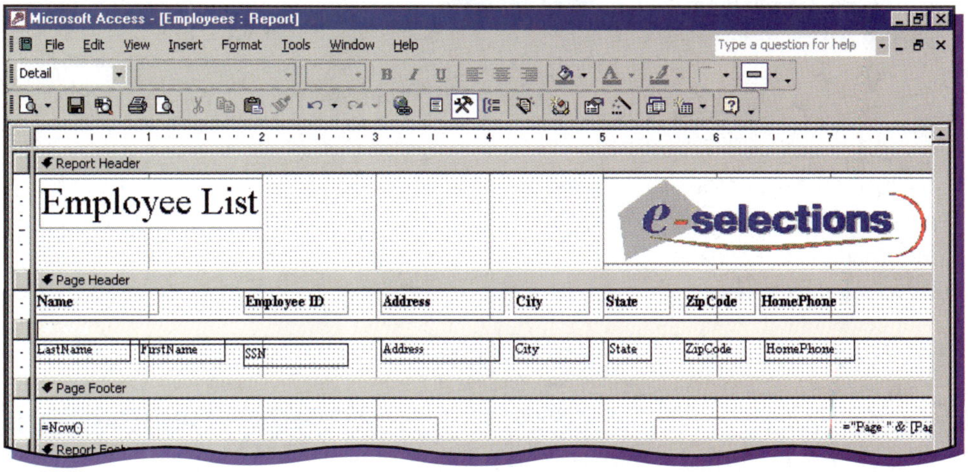

Tip As you review the report, ensure that no record data is cut off in any column and that no columns are too wide for the data they display.

Creating a Report Using Report Design View

Although the Report Wizard is an efficient way to quickly generate a new report, you can also create a report in Report Design view and build the report from scratch. Using this technique to create a report enables you to select the fields you want to add to the report and size and position them in the report as you add them or position all the controls after all are added.

Task 5:

To Create a New Report Using Design View

1. Click the Reports button on the Objects bar, if necessary, and click the New button to open the New Report dialog box.

2. Select the **Design View** option and select **Gross Pay** from the **Choose the table or query where the object's data comes from** list.

3. Click **OK**, maximize the report window, and drag the right edge of the report page to just past the 6-inch mark on the horizontal ruler to enlarge the page.

4. Drag the **SSN**, **LastName**, **FirstName**, **PayRate**, **PayPeriod**, **HoursWorked**, and **Gross Pay** fields into the Detail section, and then cut the labels and paste them in the **Page Header** section and arrange the labels and text box controls as shown in Figure 6-18.

Figure 6-17

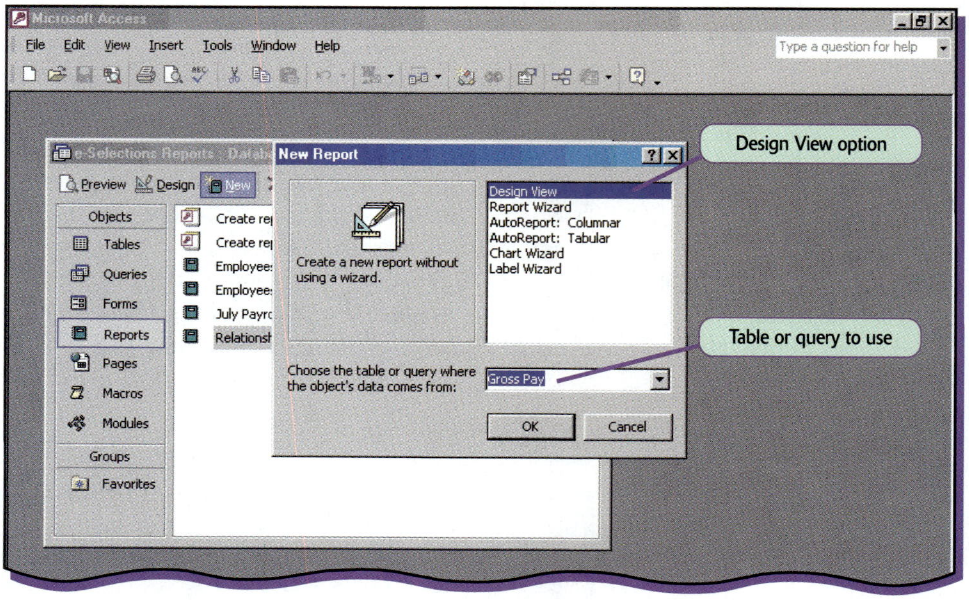

Troubleshooting Click the Field List button on the Report Design toolbar to display the field list if it is hidden.

Figure 6-18

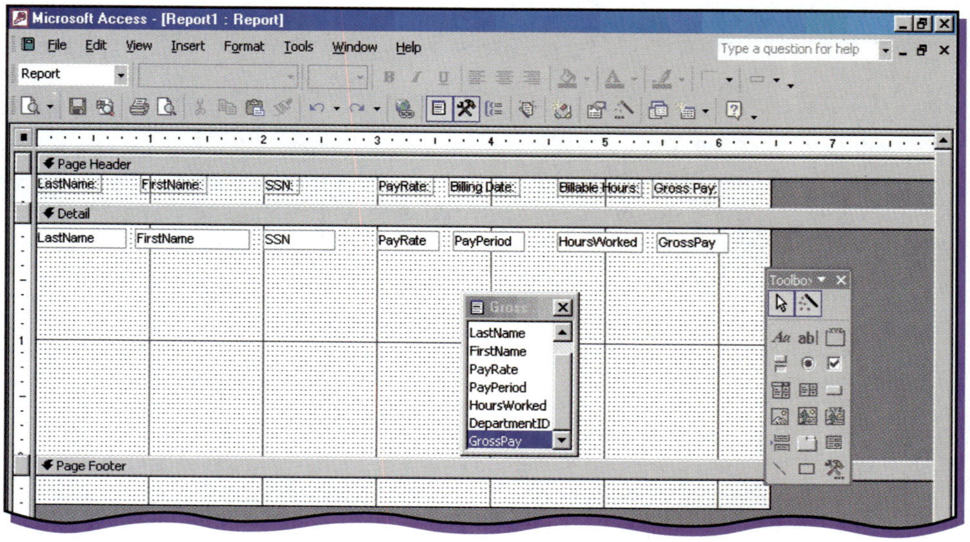

5 Change the **SSN** label caption to Employee ID and delete the colon at the end of each of the remaining labels.

6 Drag the **Page Footer** section bar up to a position just below the text box controls.

Figure 6-19

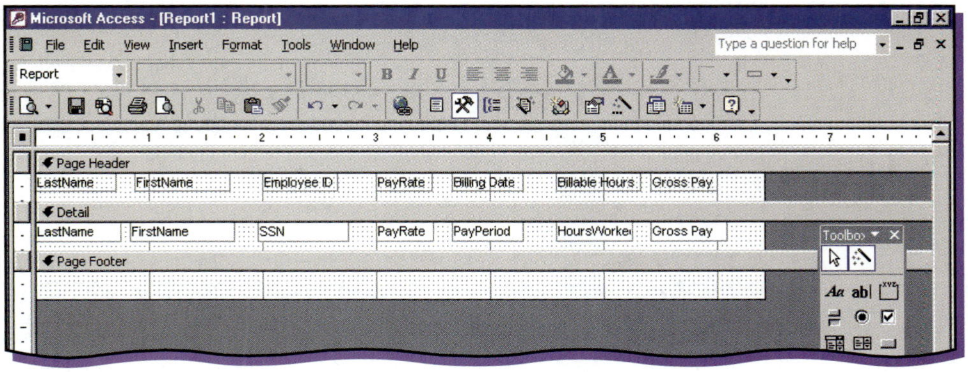

7 Click the vertical ruler in the **Page Header** section to select all of the labels and click the **Bold** button on the Formatting toolbar.

Figure 6-20

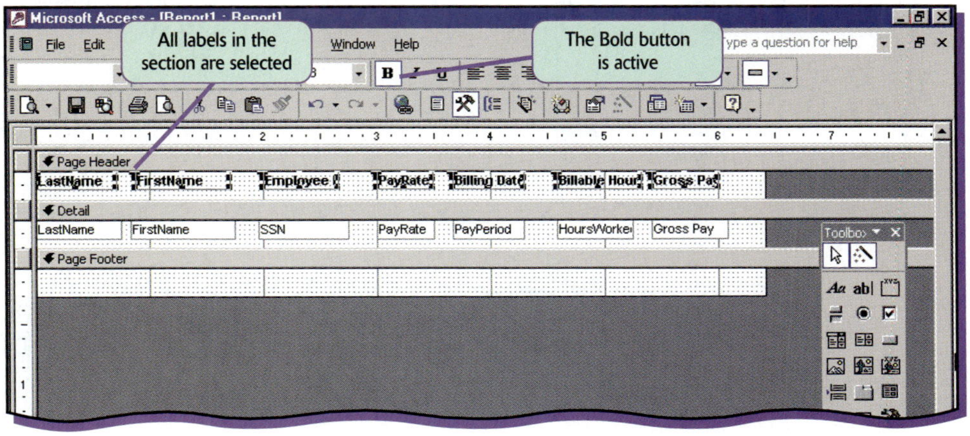

CHECK POINT

Most of the data you work with in Access is formatted in tables or queries where text enhancement is normally not required. As a result, text enhancement in these objects is limited.

Because reports provide a form of printed output for database information, many of the same formatting tools you see in other applications are available for formatting text in reports. Explore the Formatting toolbar to see what features are available. Then look at the commands on the Format menu to see how they differ from commands on the Format menu in other applications. Finally, open the Properties dialog box and review options on the Format page of the dialog box to see what unique features Access offers.

8 Save the report using the report name *Gross Pay* and click **Print Preview**.

Figure 6-21

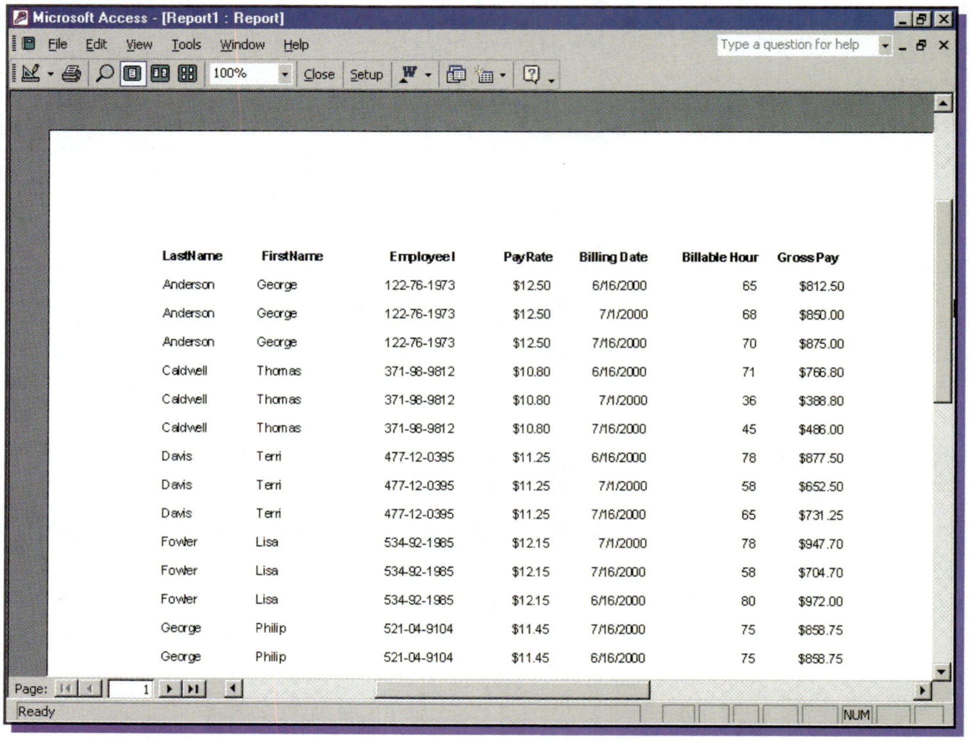

Tip To adjust the position of fields and controls, switch back to Design view and make the necessary adjustments. It may take you several tries to get the fields positioned just right.

Adding Sorting and Grouping Levels to the Report

The two reports Mr. Traylor requested are formatted and saved, but the Gross Pay report needs to be formatted to display each employee's name and Employee ID only once for each employee. By grouping all time cards for each employee into a separate section, you can modify the report to meet Mr. Traylor's specifications.

Task 6:

To Add Sorting and Grouping Levels to the Report

1 Open the **Gross Pay** report in **Report Design** view, if necessary.

2 Choose **View | Sorting and Grouping** to open the Sorting and Grouping window.

Figure 6-22

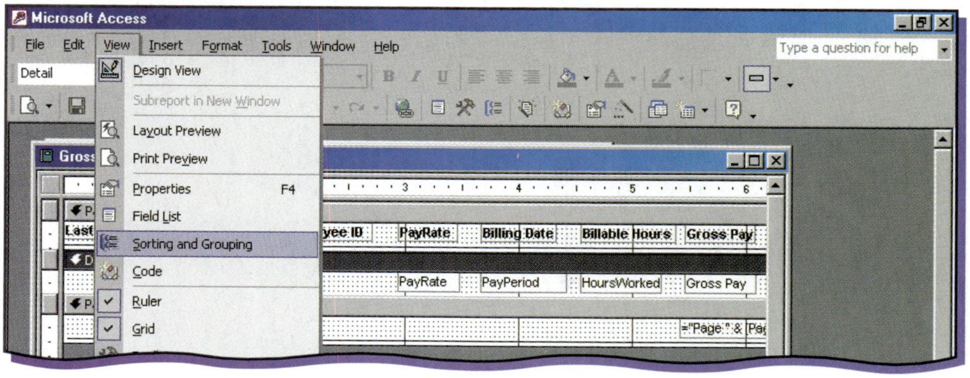

3 Click the **Field/ Expression** down arrow in the first row, select **SSN**, press F6, and select **Yes** from the **Group Header** drop-down list to add a Group Header section to the report.

WEB TIP

Do you need an answer to a tough question about a report you are trying to create? Join the Tek-Tips forums for help. Search for Tek-Tips and see if it leads you to the Access reports forum.

Figure 6-23

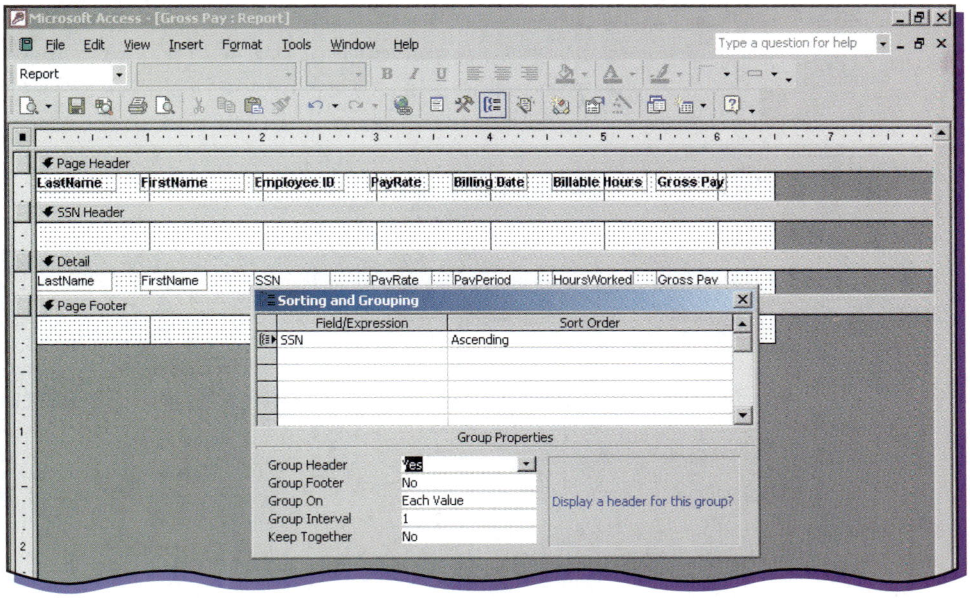

4 Press F6 and ↓, select **PayPeriod** from the **Field/Expression** drop-down list, and close the Sorting and Grouping window.

Figure 6-24

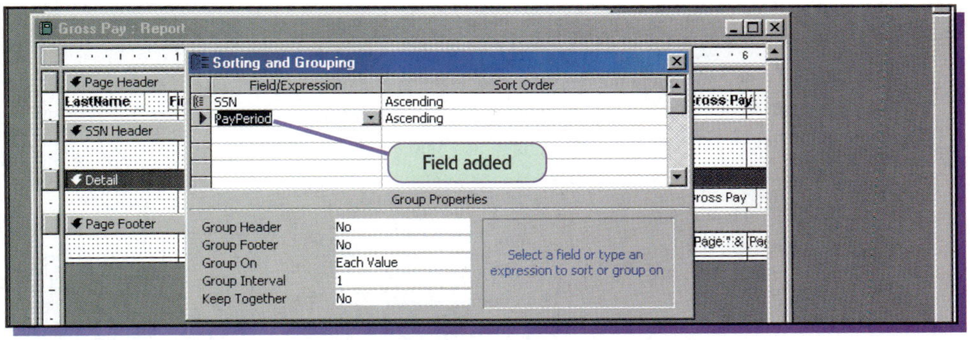

5 Drag the **SSN**, **LastName**, and **FirstName** text box controls into the **SSN Group Header** section.

6 Save changes to the report, view the report in the Preview window and close the preview.

Figure 6-25

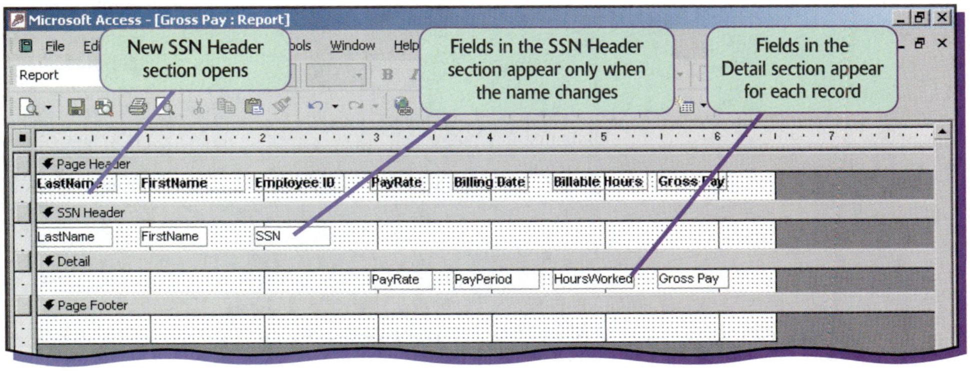

Adding a Calculated Control to the Report

The reports are almost complete. All you need to add to the Gross Pay report is the total payroll amount that Mr. Traylor wants the report to display. By creating a calculated expression and adding the control to the Report Footer area, the total will appear only at the end of the report.

Task 7:

To Add a Calculated Control to a Report Footer

1. Open the **Gross Pay** report in **Report Design** view; choose **View | Report Header/Footer** to display the **Report Header** and **Report Footer** sections; close the **Field List**, if necessary; and display the **Toolbox**.

Figure 6-26

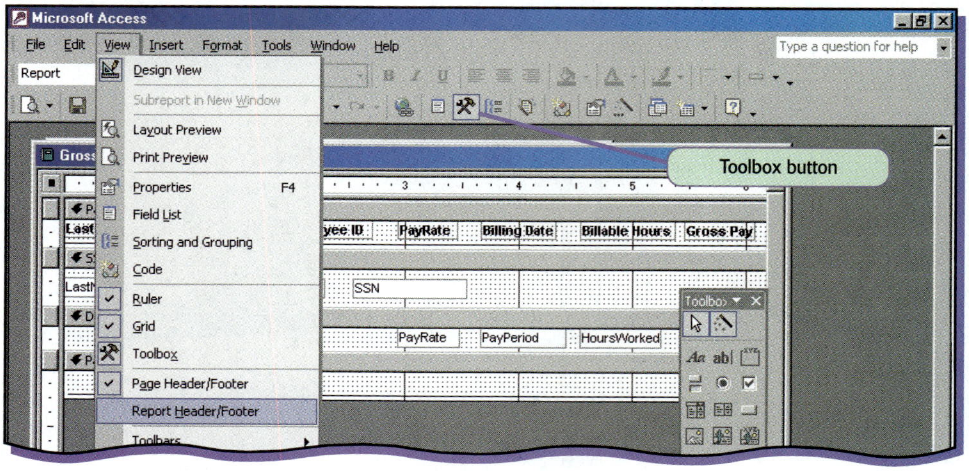

2. Click the Text Box ab| button in the **Toolbox** and draw a rectangular-shaped text box on the right side of the **Report Footer** section, immediately below the **Gross Pay** text box in the **Detail** section.

Figure 6-27

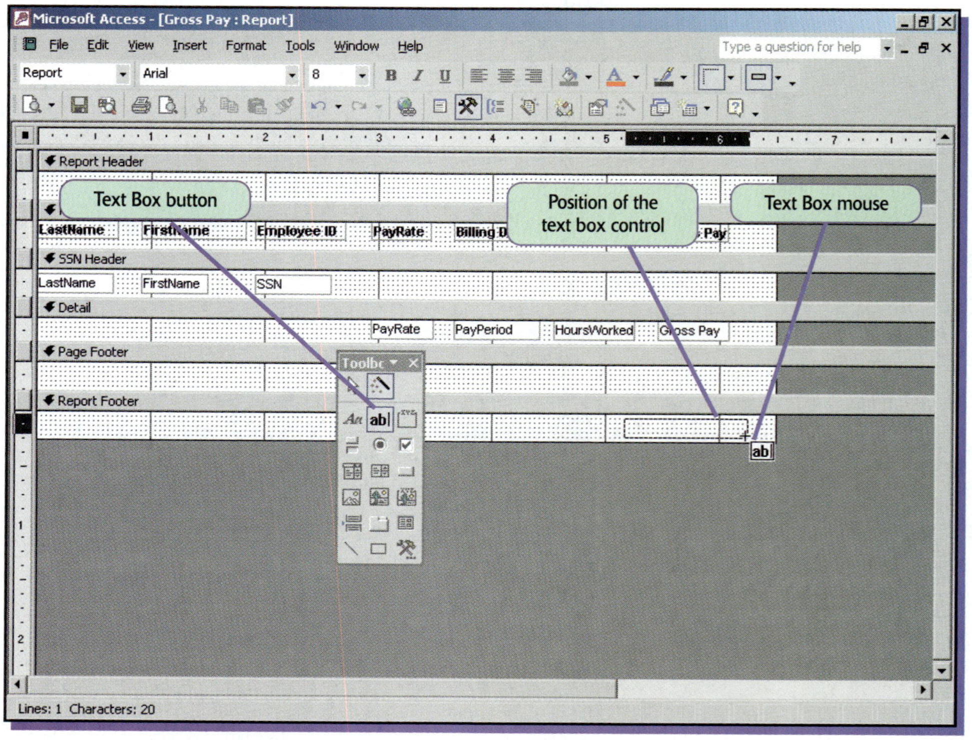

3 Select the text in the new label control and type Total:.

Figure 6-28

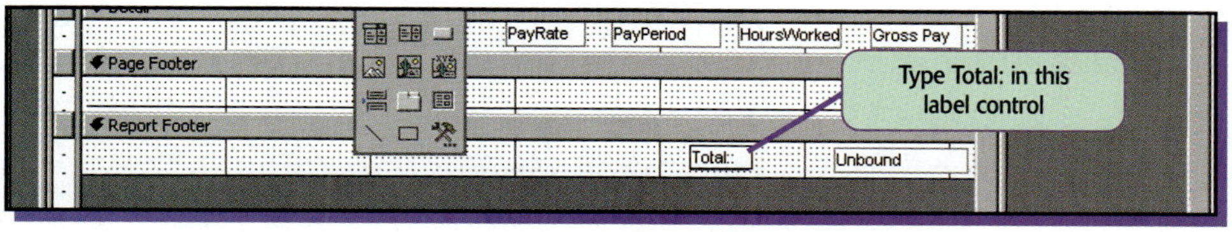

Troubleshooting

The colon following the word Total is important. Don't forget to include it.

4 Right-click the text box control, select **Properties**, and click the **Data** tab.

5 Click the **Control Source** ellipsis button to open the Expression Builder.

Figure 6-29

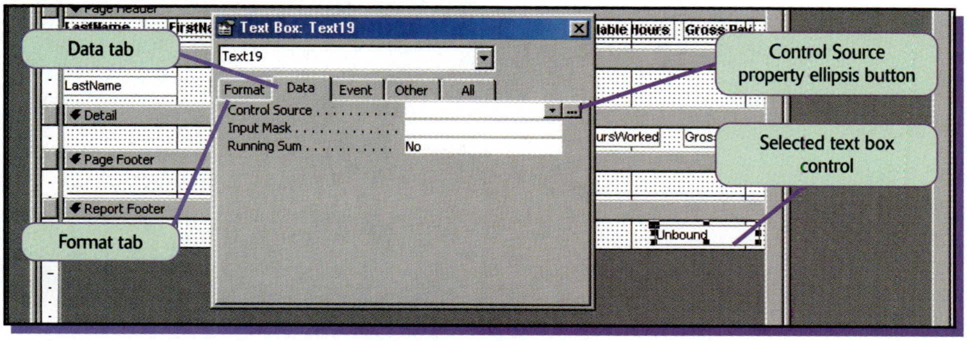

6 Type =Sum([Gross Pay]) in the **Expression Builder**, and click **OK**.

Figure 6-30

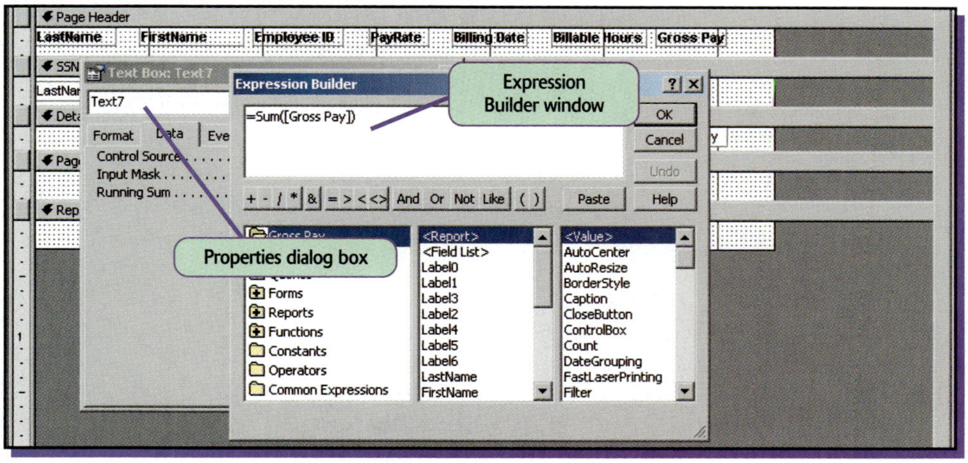

Troubleshooting

Be sure to include the standard parentheses and the square brackets exactly as shown in Step 6 when you type the expression. If you mix them up or omit one, the expression will fail to provide an accurate sum.

7 Click the **Format** tab of the Properties dialog box, click the **Format** down arrow, and select **Currency**.

8 Save and preview the report, switch back to **Report Design** view, adjust the placement and size of the text box controls as necessary, and compare your report to the one shown in Figure 6-1.

9 Save changes and close the report.

Figure 6-31

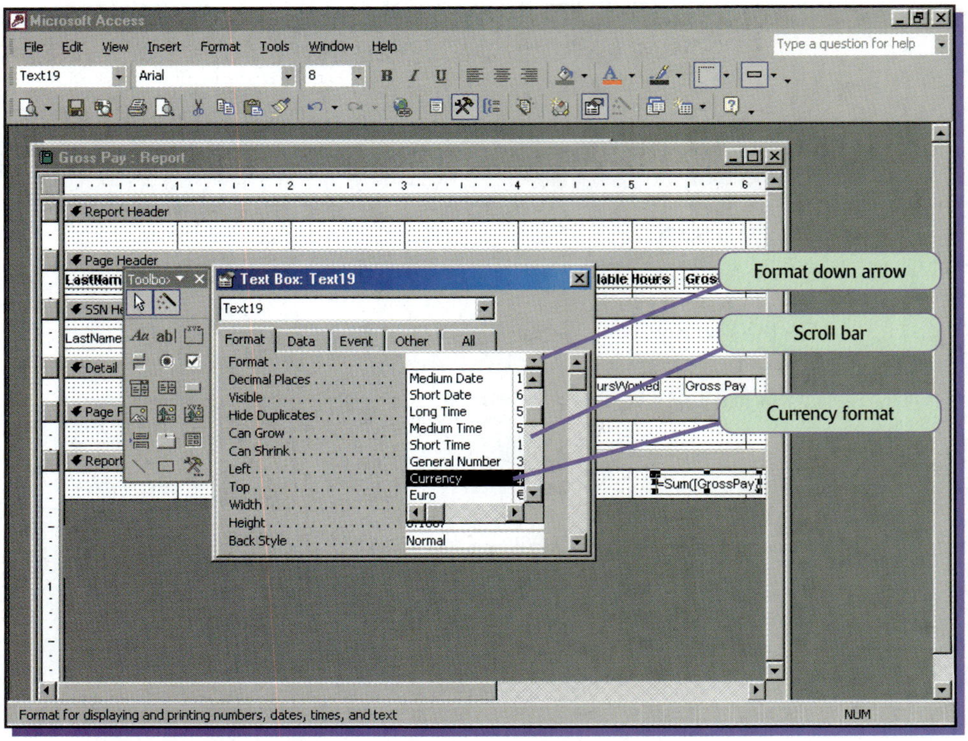

CHECK POINT

Each major section of a report can contain a header and footer. For example, the SSN group you created in Task 6 has a footer as well as a header. You simply told Access to display the group header. To display the group footer, choose **View | Sorting and Grouping**, select the SSN group in the **Field/Expression** list, and change the **Group Footer** property to **Yes**. You can then use the SSN Footer section to display summary information pertaining to each employee, such as subtotals or hours worked.

Adding Visual Elements to a Report Header and Footer

No report would be complete without a title. Titles are usually placed in the Report Header section. After you add a descriptive report title and company logo to the report, you can apply the finishing touches to complete the report.

Task 8:

To Add Visual Elements to a Report

1 Open the **Gross Pay** report in **Report Design** view and display the **Toolbox**, if necessary.

2 Click the Label button, and draw a rectangle in the **Report Header** section that extends from the left side of the report to about the 2.25-inch mark and that is about 1 inch tall.

3 Type YTD Payroll Report.

4 Click the Properties button, scroll down the **Format** properties to display the **Font Size** and **Font Weight** options, and set the properties to those shown in Figure 6-33.

Tip Most of the options shown in Figure 6-33 are the default settings. Be sure to scroll down the list of options and check those displayed in the dialog box.

Figure 6-32

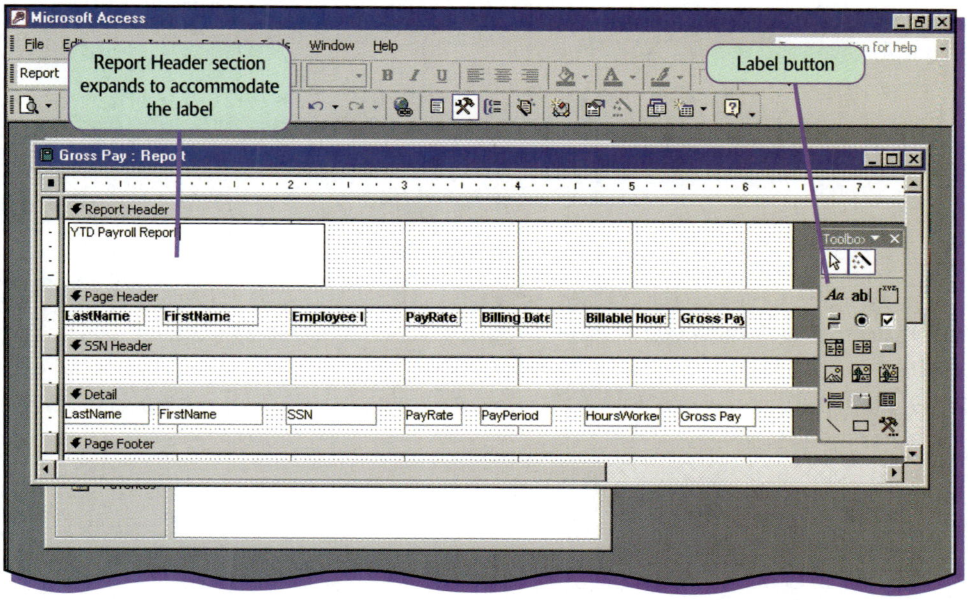

Figure 6-33

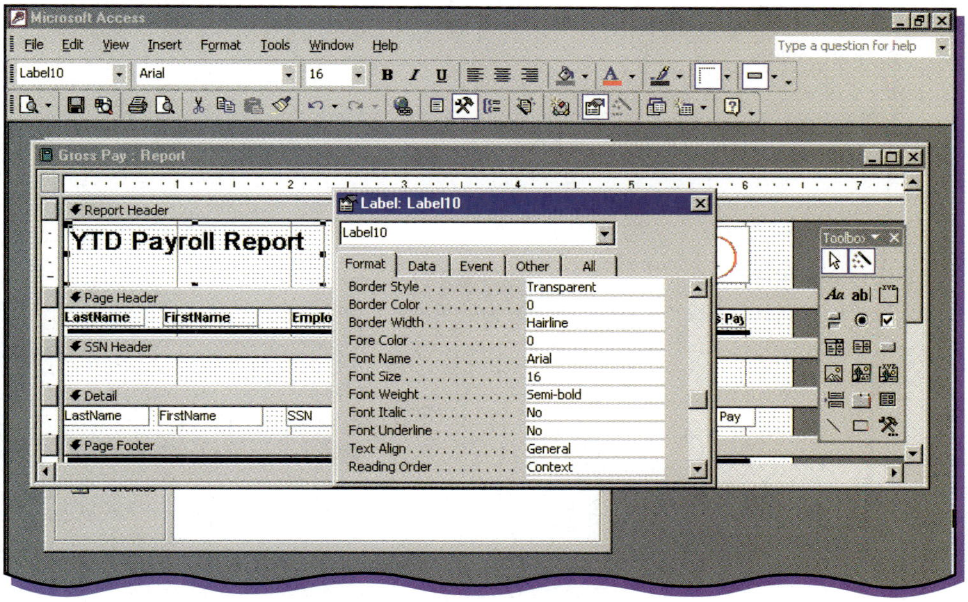

5 Close the **Properties** dialog box, click the Image button in the Toolbox, add the *e-Selections.jpg* logo to the **Report Header** section, and change the **Size Mode** property to **Stretch**.

6 Click the Line button in the Toolbox, draw a line below the labels in the **Page Header** section, and draw another line at the top of the **Page Footer** section as shown in Figure 6-34.

Tip Press Shift as you draw to create a straight line.

7 Press Shift, click the two lines to select both of them, display the **Properties** dialog box, select **3 pt** from the **Border Width** drop-down list, and close the dialog box.

8 Choose **Insert | Page Numbers** and select the settings shown in Figure 6-35.

9 Click OK, save changes to the report, close the report.

Figure 6-34

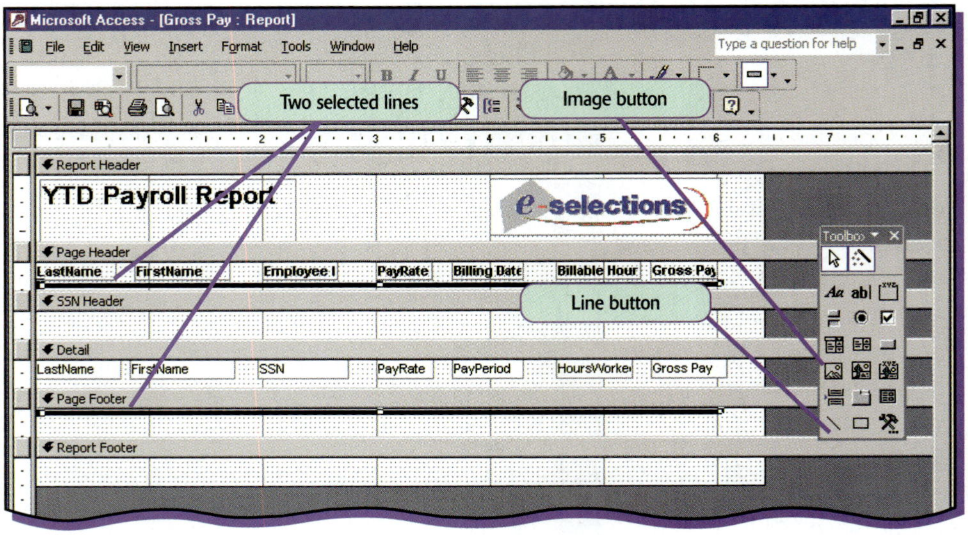

Troubleshooting Depending on your computer settings, you may need to adjust the size and position of the graphic so that it appears as shown in Figure 6-34 and then readjust the Page Header section.

Figure 6-35

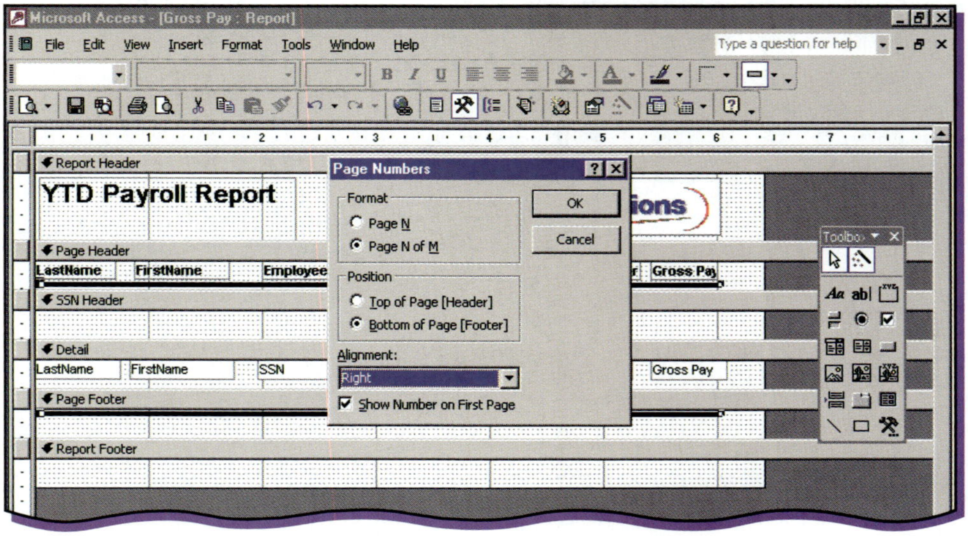

Creating Mailing Labels

Now that you know many of the special techniques for creating custom reports, you can use the techniques to create mailing labels and other types of labels using the information contained in Access database tables. Access provides a Label Wizard to walk you through.

Task 9:
To Create Labels

1 Click the **Reports** button on the **Objects bar** and click the New **New** button.

2 Select the **Label Wizard** option, select **Employees** from the **Choose the table or query where the object's data comes from** list, and click **OK**.

3 Select options shown in Figure 6-36 and click **Next**.

Figure 6-36

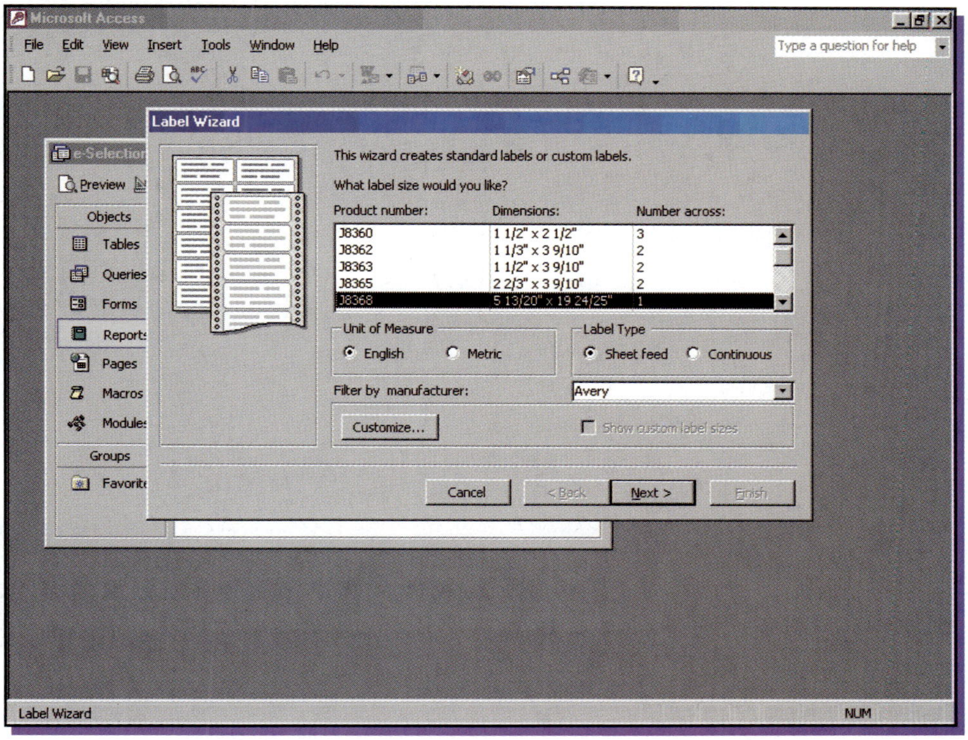

4 Select the font options of your choice and click **Next**.

Figure 6-37

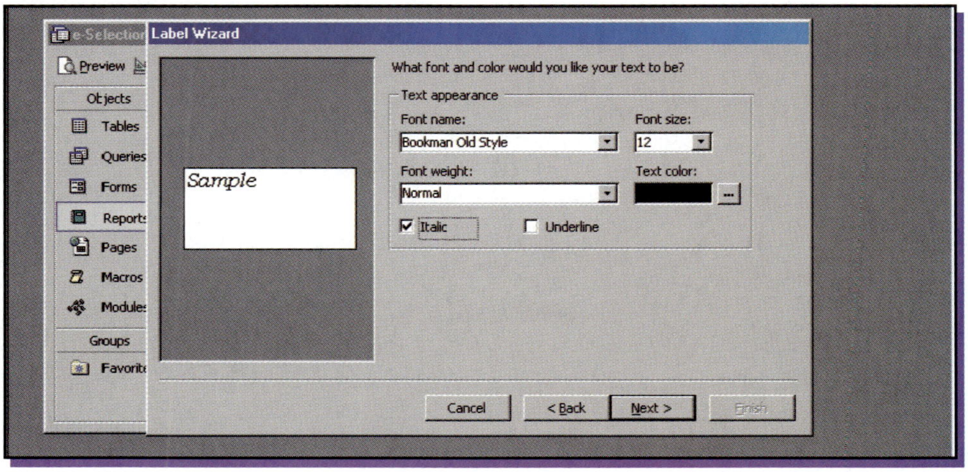

Tip Font options available on for Access reports are basically the same options available for formatting text in other applications. If you have a favorite font, select it.

5 Select **FirstName** from the **Available fields** list and click the **Add** button.

6 Press Spacebar, select **LastName** from the **Available fields** list, click the **Add** button, and press Enter.

7 Repeat the procedures outlined in Steps 5 and 6 to place the fields as shown in Figure 6-38.

8 Click **Next** twice and then click **Finish**. Review and close the report.

Figure 6-38

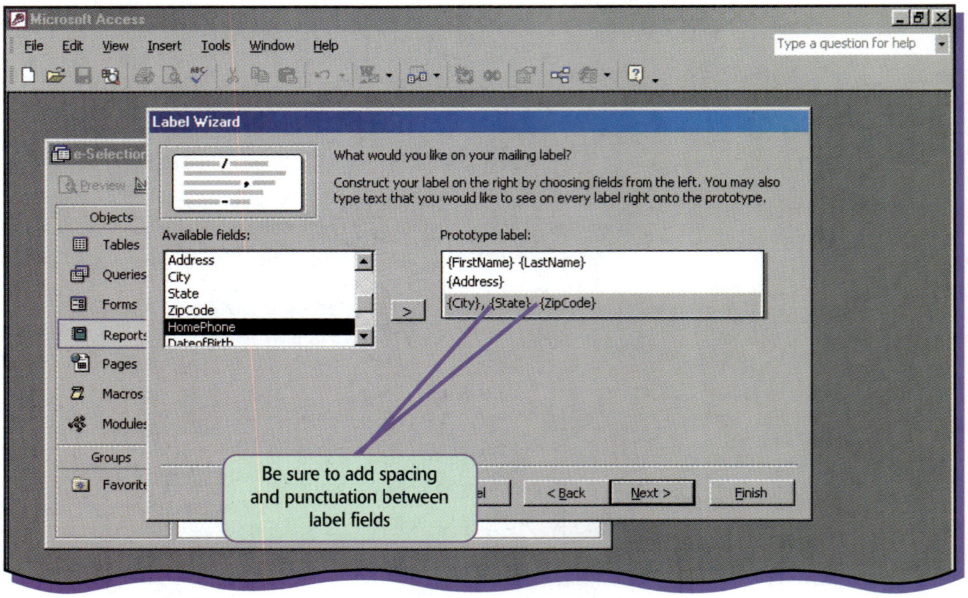

SUMMARY AND EXERCISES

SUMMARY

- Database reports are used to print information from a database.
- You can create a report by using one of the Report Wizards or by using Report Design view.
- A report contains bound and unbound controls that specify where information will appear on the report.
- Once you create a report, you can view it in the Print Preview window.
- You can modify a report by changing the properties of each control in the report.
- Calculated controls perform calculations based upon an expression.
- A report can be grouped and or sorted on up to four fields when you create a report using the Report Wizard.
- You can change the sort order of information in a report by using the Sorting and Grouping option.
- You can add group headers and footers to group information together on a report.
- You can add a graphic to a report for visual interest.

KEY TERMS & SKILLS

KEY TERMS

Detail section (p. 6-5)
Page Footer (p. 6-5)
Page Header (p. 6-5)
Report Design window (p. 6-5)
Report Footer (p. 6-5)
Report Header (p. 6-5)

SKILLS

Add a group header to a report (p. 6-16)
Add an image to a report (p. 6-21)
Add report sections to a report (p. 6-8)
Add sorting orders to a report (p. 6-16)
Create a calculated control for a report (p. 6-18)
Create a report in Design view (p. 6-14)
Create a report using the Report Wizard (p. 6-6)
Modify and reposition controls on a report (p. 6-8)

STUDY QUESTIONS

MULTIPLE CHOICE

1. Where would you place a control so that it will appear at the top of every page?
a. Report Header section
b. Page Header section
c. Detail section
d. Page Footer section

2. You can add bound text box controls easily to reports by using the
a. field list.
b. Toolbox.
c. Properties window.
d. Tools menu.

3. Controls placed in the Report Header section appear
a. at the top of every page.
b. at the top of the report.
c. at the bottom of every page.
d. at the end of the report.

4. To modify a report created by the Report Wizard, you use the
a. Print Preview view.
b. Print Layout view.
c. Report Design view.
d. a or c

5. To insert a graphic on a report, you use a(n)
a. graphic tool.
b. label tool.
c. text box tool.
d. image tool.

6. To create a calculated field, modify the
a. Data source.
b. Record source.
c. Control source.
d. Query source.

7. For the data to change at each record, a bound text box control is placed in what report section?
a. Page Header
b. Page Footer
c. Report Header
d. Detail

8. To add descriptive text to a report, use the
a. label tool.
b. text box tool.
c. image tool.
d. text tool.

9. To create a calculated control you can type the expression or you can use the
a. Calculation Wizard.
b. Expression Wizard.
c. Expression Window.
d. Expression Builder.

10. To group information together, add a
a. Page header or footer.
b. Report header or footer.
c. Group header or footer.
d. Detail header or footer.

SHORT ANSWER

1. What is the purpose of a report?
2. What methods can you use to create a report?
3. How do you add bound text box controls to a report?
4. How do you add a graphic to a report?
5. How can you group information on a report?
6. How do you move labels from the Detail section of a report to the Page Header section?
7. How do you preview your report before you print it?
8. What methods can you use to change the zoom settings when you preview your report?
9. How do you add a group header or footer to a report?
10. How do you specify a sort order for a report?

FILL IN THE BLANK

1. Calculated controls perform calculations based on a(n) ____________.
2. The ____________ contains a graphical workspace displaying the report's bound and unbound controls.
3. If your information needs to appear on the bottom of every page of the report, add a control to the ____________.
4. You can use the ____________ to quickly create a formatted report with only the fields you select.
5. A text box control that displays data is a(n) ____________ control.
6. Use the ____________ tool to add a graphic to a report.
7. To create a report using Report Design view, add various ____________ to the report.
8. The ____________ view displays all the records in a report exactly as they will be printed.
9. A label is a(n) ____________ control.
10. To group information on your report you need to add a group ____________ or ____________ .

FOR DISCUSSION

1. What two database objects can you use to create a report? When might you use one rather than the other?
2. What are some ways you might use calculated controls in a report?
3. When do you use bound versus unbound controls in a report?
4. Describe the three views associated with reports.
5. When should you consider changing the sorting and grouping options for a report?

GUIDED EXERCISES

1 THE HOME THEATER WARRANTY REPORTS DATABASE

Each month, e-Selections personnel are required to submit a report to the Board of Directors of Selections, Inc., that shows the labor costs for repairs made to home theaters. A copy of one of the reports is displayed in Figure 6-39.

Figure 6-39

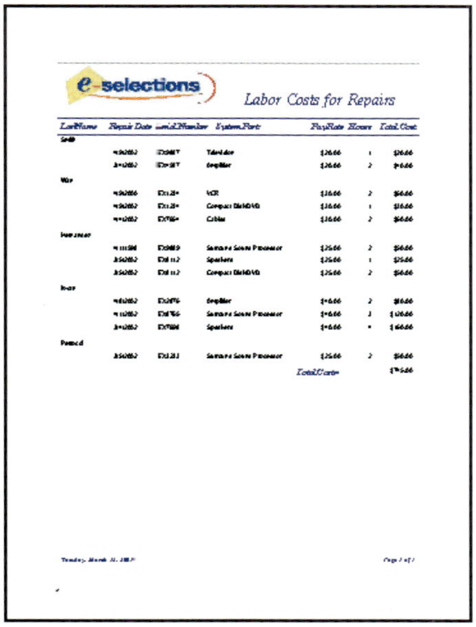

Follow these steps to create the report:

1. Open the *HTS Warranty Reports.mdb* file, click the Reports button on the Objects bar, and click the New button.
2. Select **Report Wizard**, select **Technician Cost** as the data source, and then click **OK**.
3. Move all the fields to the Selected field list and click **Next**.
4. Select the **LastName** field to add a grouping level and click **Next**.

5. Click **Next** to accept the query sort on **LastName**.
6. Select **Stepped** from the **Layout** options and **Portrait** from the **Orientation** options and then click **Next**.
7. Select the **Corporate** style and click **Next**.
8. Type Labor Costs for Repairs as the title and click **Finish**.
9. Switch to **Report Design** view, and size, rename, and arrange labels and fields so that all text is visible and the **Preview** layout resembles Figure 6-39.
10. Save changes to the report.
11. Display the Toolbox if necessary, and use the tools to add a stretched logo to the **Report Header**.
12. Move the **Page Header** bar up to resize the **Report Header** section, size the report page so that it extends to the 6-inch mark on the horizontal ruler, and move the graphic to the left side of the **Report Header** section and the label to the right side.
13. Drag the bottom edge of the **Report Footer** bar to make the **Report Footer** section larger, add an unbound text box control to the **Report Footer** section, type =Sum([Total Cost]) in the **Control Source** box, change the **Format** property to **Currency**, and close the **Property** window.
14. Change the label of the new control to read *Total Cost*.
15. Save changes to the report, print the report, and close the file.

2 THE MAKE A PROFIT REPORTS DATABASE

Making a profit is the goal of every business. Department stores are no exception, especially when they have recently initiated an online division. Department stores, however, often like to determine the earnings generated by each department so that they can determine which departments to maintain and which departments they will phase out. The report to the Board of Directors shown in Figure 6-40 is generated to reflect the earnings by each department for the new e-Selections Division.

Figure 6-40

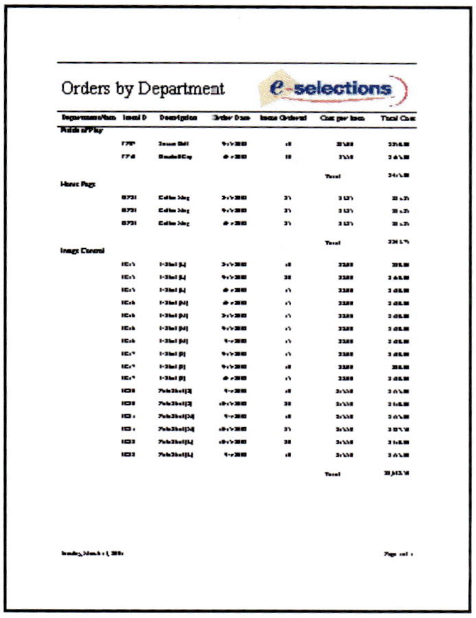

Follow these steps to create the report based on the **Orders by Department** query:

1. Open the *Make a Profit Reports.mdb* file, display the **Reports**, and create a new report using the **Report Wizard** and the **Orders by Department** query.
2. Run the wizard and select the following options:
   - Place all fields on the report.
   - Add a grouping level for the **DepartmentName** field.
   - Sort the report by the **ItemID** field.
   - Format the report with a **Portrait** orientation and a **Stepped** layout using the **Formal** style.
   - Save the report using the default report name.
3. Modify the labels and text box controls to match Figure 6-40, sizing the labels so that the full label text shows, and add a stretched *e-Selections.jpg* graphic to the Report Header section.
4. Click the Sorting and Grouping button on the Form Design toolbar, select the **DepartmentName** row, select **Yes** for the **Group Footer** row, and close the Sorting and Grouping window.
5. Add an unbound text box to the **DepartmentName** footer section, type **=Sum([Total Cost])** as the expression in the **Control Source** row, change the format property to **Currency**, and change the label to *Total*.
6. Save changes to the report, print the report, and then close it.

3 BRENT'S TOOLS ORDER REPORTS DATABASE

Brent has sent out a number of invoices for which he has not yet received payment. As a result, he has created the report shown in Figure 6-41 to determine which customers are significantly overdue with their payments.

Figure 6-41

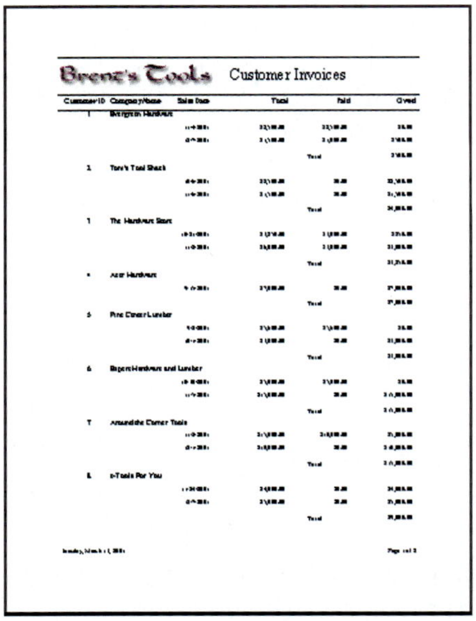

To create this report, you will use the Invoice Report query.

1. Open the *Brent's Tools Order Reports.mdb* file, display **Reports**, and create a new report using the **Report Wizard** and the **Invoice Report** query.
2. Run the wizard and select the following options:
   - Place all fields on the report and view the data by the **Customer** field.
   - Select **CustomerID** as a grouping level and display the **CustomerID in the Footer** section.
   - Sort the data by the **SalesDate** field.
   - Create a **Formal** format using **Portrait** orientation and a **Stepped** layout.
   - Title the report *Customer Invoices*.
3. Modify the labels and text box controls to look similar to those in Figure 6-41, add the stretched *Brent's Tools Logo.gif* graphic to the **Form Header** section, and size and position the graphics as shown in Figure 6-41.
4. Add a currency calculated text box control titled **Total** to the **CustomerID Footer** section and type the expression **=Sum([AmountOwed]).**
5. Save changes to the report, print the report, and close it.

ON YOUR OWN

The difficulty of these case studies varies:
▶ are the least difficult; ▶▶ are more difficult; and ▶▶▶ are the most difficult.

1 COLLEGE ASSIGNMENTS REPORT

▶ The assignments added to the College Assignments Report database tables have been entered as the assignments were made. As a result, it is often a challenge to sift through the list of assignments and locate assignments for a specific class. You can create a report that will sort and group the assignments by class. Open the *College Assignments Report.mdb* file or your personal file, if available, and create a report based on the All Assignments query. Group the assignments by class. Add a copy of your own school logo to the report and print a copy of the report.

2 NANCY'S KNICK-KNACK NOOK

▶ Tracking items by supplier is important in order to maintain adequate supplies of items at Nancy's Knick-Knack Nook. Nancy has decided that preparing a report each month that groups items according to supplier would help her determine the supplier who stocks the items she needs to order. Open the *Nancy's Inventory Reports.mdb* file and add the Supplier Name field to the Inventory List query. Then create a report based on the Inventory List query that groups items according to supplier. Add a subtotal for each supplier and Nancy's logo graphic to the report. Print the report.

3 PINE VALLEY CONTRIBUTIONS REPORT DATABASE

▶▶ Tracking the contributions of each contributor, especially when contributors make donations throughout the year, is important to Pine Valley. As a result, the organization would like to have a report that groups contribution information by contributor and prints a subtotal for each contributor. Use the *PVO Contributions Report.mdb* file to create the report based on the Contributors and Contributions query. Add an appropriate graphic to the report and print the report.

4 BEAVER BROOK INN AND CONFERENCE CENTER FACILITY REPORT DATABASE

Room schedules, meeting-room schedules, conference banquets, and other facility schedules can become quite convoluted. A number of different organizations are trying to schedule rooms at the same time for the same dates. Printing a report at the end of each day that identifies room schedules would be a great help and at the same time would provide an overview of the earnings generated by renting different rooms. Open the *BBICC Facilities Reports.mdb* file and create a query that displays the group name, date, room name, beginning and end times, and room costs from different database tables. Then use the query to create a report that groups room-schedule information by the organization renting the rooms. Include a subtotal calculation field that will calculate the total cost per group. Add the *BBIC.gif* graphic to the report and print a copy of the report.

5 GET IN SHAPE FITNESS CLUB REPORTS

The Get in Shape Fitness Club has determined that it needs to get its files in shape to determine what members still owe for classes they have taken and also to track the success of some of their classes. Open the *GIS Fitness Club Reports.mdb* file and create the necessary query upon which you can base a report that will display the participants' names, the classes for which they are registered, the number of hours, the amount they owe for each class, the amount they have paid, and the amount still due for each class. Group this information by participant and create a calculated field that will calculate the subtotal each participant still owes for all of his or her classes. Add a second calculated field that shows a grand total of the amount due to GIS for all participants. Add the *GIS.gif* logo to the report and print a copy of the report.

Photospread credits pages 6-2 & 6-3

Glossary

Access menu bar The menu bar appearing at the top of the screen when Access is launched.

Access page See data access page.

Action query A query that makes changes to many records in just one operation.

AND condition A query expression that sets different criteria in the same criteria row of the query design grid so that Access identifies only the records that meet all of the criteria in all fields.

Ascending order A sort order in which records are arranged alphabetically from A to Z or numerically from smallest to largest.

AutoForm A database form object created from the fields and information stored in a table or query.

AutoNumber field A field set to automatically enter a sequential number as each record is added to the table.

AutoReport A database report object created from the fields contained in a table or query.

Bound control A control that is tied to a field in an underlying table or query so that the values contained in the field appear on the report or form.

Calculated control A control that uses an expression as its source of data to perform a calculation.

Calculated field A field in a query that contains an expression designed to perform a calculation each time the query is run so that the results are always based on the most current data in the database.

Controls Objects on a form or report that display data, perform actions, or decorate the form or report.

ControlTip A helpful tip that pops up over controls when the mouse pointer moves over a control.

Criteria Conditions set in a query to limit the information displayed in the datasheet to those records meeting the conditions.

Currency A data type used to display money values with fixed-point values so that the values can be used in calculations.

Data Raw, unevaluated facts and figures that have not been interpreted in any meaningful way for a specific purpose.

Data access page A database object used for creating a special type of Web page for viewing and working with data stored in a Microsoft Access database or a Microsoft SQL Server database from the Internet or an intranet.

Data type The characteristic of a field or a variable that determines the kind of data it holds—text, numeric, dates, and so forth.

Data validation Controls—validation rules and input masks—set to enable Access to determine the type of data that can be entered into a database field and the format required for the data.

Database A collection of information related to a particular subject or organized for a specific purpose.

Database design process A systematic approach to designing a database that includes planning, analysis, design, implementation, and maintenance phases.

Database Management System (DBMS) A computer application used to create and maintain databases.

Database object The tables, queries, forms, pages, reports, macros, or modules that comprise an Access database.

Database window The database interface in Access that provides a listing of tables, queries, forms, reports, macros, and modules.

Datasheet view The display of a table, query, or form in which a user can see multiple records on-screen at the same time; this view makes data entry more efficient.

Date/Time A data type that contains date and time values for the years 100 through 9999.

Descending order A sort order in which records are arranged alphabetically from Z to A or numerically from largest to smallest.

Design modifications Any enhancements made to a database object.

Design view The display of a table, query, form, or report object that enables you to modify the object layout or properties.

Detail section The part of a form or report that holds the field data controls and pulls information from database tables.

Edit To change the field information contained in a record.

Expression A combination of symbols—identifiers, operators, and values—that produces a calculation or result.

Expression Builder A graphical workspace for designing expressions for a specific control object or control.

Field A single piece of information contained in a database table, represented by a column of data with a common data type and a common set of properties.

Field properties Field settings that define or control a field's characteristics, such as size, format, background color, and so forth.

Filter To select records in a table based on a predetermined condition.

Filter-By-Form A filtering technique that selects data records based on criteria entered for specific form fields.

Filter-By-Selection A filtering technique that selects data records based on data selected in a form, datasheet, or data access page.

Find To use the Find dialog box to locate one or more records displayed in a table or form.

Find and Replace To locate specific text or values and replace them with different text or values.

Form An Access database object used to display data from tables or queries in an aesthetically pleasing format.

Form view The display of data records using a form.

Groups bar A button on the Database Objects bar used to access stored collections of database objects.

Hyperlink Underlined text or graphic used to jump to a location on the Internet or on an intranet, to an object in your database or in another database, or to a document on your computer or on another computer connected by a network.

Hyperlink data type A data type in Access that displays a URL for a file resource formatted as a functioning hyperlink.

Image control A control used to display pictures in a database object, such as a form or report.

Information Data that has been analyzed, interpreted, processed, and reported to be meaningful in a given context.

Input mask A field property that displays literal display characters—hyphens, parentheses, and so forth—in the field with blanks to fill in.

Join To create an association between a field in one table or query and a field of the same data type in another table or query.

Join line The line that identifies fields in different tables or queries that are related.

Label control An unbound control used to display descriptive text—titles, captions, or brief instructions—on a form or report.

Literal expression A literal value and expression, such as >400, that express the criteria for locating records using a query or filter.

Lookup field A field that displays a list of data values found in an existing table or query, or a list containing a fixed set of values that won't change.

Macro A set of one or more actions, each performing a particular operation, that are saved so that they can be used to automate common tasks such as opening a form or printing a report.

Memo A data type used to store random entries exceeding 255 characters.

Many-to-many relationship An association between two tables in which one record in either table can relate to many records in the other table.

Module A collection of Visual Basic programming procedures stored together to customize the Access environment.

Navigate To move from one record to another in a table or form or from one database object to another in the Database window.

Null value A value that indicates missing or unknown data in a field.

Numeric (number) A data type used to hold numeric data that may be used to perform mathematical calculations.

Objects Different types of database items—tables, queries, forms, pages, reports, macros, or modules.

Objects bar A vertical toolbar that contains buttons for viewing database objects in the current database.

Object shortcut Shortcuts in the Database window for creating new objects using Design view or using a wizard.

Office Assistant The interactive Help feature that appears on-screen to offer help on the task a user is performing.

OLE (Object Linking and Embedding) A data type that links data, graphics, and other objects. This data type can be stored outside the database and provides a way of automating information sharing.

One-to-many relationship An association between two tables in which one record in a database table can have many matching records in another table, but a record in the second table can have only one matching record in the first table.

One-to-one relationship An association between two tables in which one record in either table relates to only one record in the other table.

Online help Software-specific help accessible from the computer.

OR condition A query result in which the records returned meet any of the conditions specified.

Page Footer A section at the bottom of a report that contains any information you want to appear on each page of the report.

Page Header A section at the top of a report that contains any information you want to appear at the top of each page of a report.

Primary key A field or set of fields that contains unique data for each record stored in the table.

Property An attribute of an object that defines one of the object's characteristics—size, color, or screen location—or an aspect of its behavior—enabled or visible.

Query A database object used to view, change, and analyze fields of data contained in different database tables and to provide the source of records for forms and reports.

Query datasheet A window that displays the results of a query in a row-and-column format.

Query design grid The lower pane of the query design window in which fields from different tables can be placed in order to locate and display data when the query is run.

Query Design view A display that enables you to create, edit, set criteria, and sort data from multiple tables.

Record A collection of fields related to a specific person, place, or thing—a customer's name and address, an item description, and so forth—and stored in a table row.

Record source A table or query that contains the records the form displays.

Referential integrity Rules to preserve the defined relationships between tables when records are entered or deleted.

Relational database management system (RDBMS) A database management system (DBMS) specifically designed to utilize the relational database model.

Relationships The associations that exist between fields contained in different tables within the same database.

Relationships window A window containing a graphical workspace for establishing relationships between tables.

Replace An option available in the Find dialog box to replace field values.

Report An organized format for summarizing and grouping database data to provide meaningful information in a printed format.

Report Design window A graphical workspace displaying the report's bound and unbound controls, report headers and footers, and page headers and footers.

Report Footer A report section containing the data and controls you want to appear at the end of an Access report.

Report Header A report section containing the data and controls you want to appear at the beginning of an Access report.

Run To apply query specifications so that only the records from associated tables that meet the query criteria display.

Select query A query that returns record information in a query datasheet without changing the underlying data.

Sort To organize records in ascending or descending order.

Sort criteria Criteria added to a query or report that specifies how the records will be ordered.

Subform A form added to a main form that displays related records on the "many" side of a one-to-many relationship.

Subform/subreport control An Access control used to add and display a subform on a main form or a report.

Switchboard An Access form that is displayed when the database is opened and which contains command buttons or other controls for opening the various parts of the database.

Table The primary object of a database that stores field names, field descriptions, and field data. Tables display multiple records in a row/column format similar to a spreadsheet layout.

Table Datasheet view The display of table data with multiple records on the screen in a row-and-column format.

Table Design view The view used to create or modify the structure of a table.

Table Design window A window displaying the table design grid.

Table Design Wizard An Access wizard used for creating tables.

Table structure The field names, data types, and properties defining the physical arrangement of a table.

Text A data type that includes letters, numbers, and symbols, as well as combinations of text and numbers that don't require calculations, such as phone numbers.

Text box control A bound control used primarily on a form to modify or add field data to an underlying field.

Unbound control A control on a form or report that is not bound to a specific field.

Update To change the field data contained in a record.

Update query An action query that makes global changes to a group of records in one or more tables.

Validation rule A property used to specify requirements for data entered into a record, field, or control.

Validation text A property used to specify the message to be displayed to the user when a validation rule is violated.

Wizard A step-by-step assistant that guides the user through creation and design of specific database objects.

Yes/No A data type for fields that can contain only one of two values Yes/No, True/False, or On/Off.

Index

C

D

E

G

H

I

J-K

Q

R

S

T

U

V

W-X-Y-Z